FOR
STUDENTS

Over the past four years we have spent time in classrooms across Canada, speaking to students just like you.

We've asked what you want to see in a textbook, how you learn, how many hours a week you spend online, and what you find most valuable when preparing for a test. Based on your feedback, we've developed a new hybrid learning solution—**HDEV**. Your textbook, the Chapter in Review cards, and the online resources found at **www.icanhdev.com** present a new, exciting, and fresh approach to learning. Check out the website for great tools like

- Interactive quizzing
- Interactive e-book
- Flashcards
- Games
- Audio chapter reviews
- Animated visual summaries
- Videos
- **And more!**

Purestock/Getty Images

NELSON / EDUCATION

HDEV, Canadian Edition
by Spencer A. Rathus and Shauna Longmuir

Vice President, Editorial Director:
Evelyn Veitch

Editor-in-Chief, Higher Education:
Anne Williams

Senior Acquisitions Editor:
Lenore Taylor-Atkins

Marketing Manager:
Ann Byford

Senior Developmental Editor:
Sandy Matos

Photo Researcher:
Natalie Barrington

Permissions Coordinator:
Natalie Barrington

Senior Content Production Manager:
Imoinda Romain

Content Production Manager:
Christine Gilbert

Production Service:
MPS Limited, a Macmillan Company

Copy Editor:
Mariko Obokata

Proofreader:
Barbara Storey

Indexer:
Edwin Durbin

Manufacturing Manager— Higher Education:
Joanne McNeil

Design Director
Ken Phipps

Managing Designer:
Franca Amore

Interior Design Revisions:
Peter Papayanakis

Cover Design:
Peter Papayanakis

Cover Images:
TOP: Juliet Laleye photo by Dan Gordon. MIDDLE ROW LEFT: © Shauna Longmuir. MIDDLE ROW RIGHT: Christina Kennedy/Alamy. BOTTOM LEFT: Andy Dean Photography/ Shutterstock. BOTTOM MIDDLE: Blend Images/MaXx Images. BOTTOM RIGHT: Blend Images/ Alamy. BACKGROUND IMAGES: (corkboard) Joe Belanger/Alamy Images; (sticky note and Polaroid) Gino's Premium Images/Alamy Images.

Compositor
MPS Limited, a Macmillan Company

Printer
RR Donnelley

Library and Archives Canada Cataloguing in Publication

Rathus, Spencer A.

HDEV/Spencer A. Rathus, Shauna Longmuir. — Canadian ed.

Includes bibliographical references and index.

ISBN 978-0-17-650365-9

1. Developmental psychology— Textbooks. I. Longmuir, Shauna II. Title.

BF713.R377 2011   155 C2010-907872-1

ISBN-13: 978-0-17-650365-9
ISBN-10: 0-17-650365-X

BRIEF CONTENTS

Hulton Archive/Getty Images/
© Farrell Grehan/CORBIS

© Todd Taulman/Shutterstock

Rubberball/Jupiter Images

© The Copyright Group/SuperStock

Fancy/Jupiter Images

CONTENTS

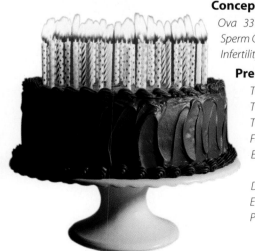

3 Birth and the Newborn Baby: In the New World 49

Darren Brode/Shutterstock

4 Infancy: Physical Development 69

Photos.com

5 Infancy: Cognitive Development 87

© Lenore Taylor-Atkins, photo by Christopher Ellison

6 Infancy: Social and Emotional Development 107

© Radius Images/Jupiterimages

StockdIsc/Photolibrary

Vadim Ponomarenko/Shutterstock

9 Middle Childhood: Physical and Cognitive Development 165

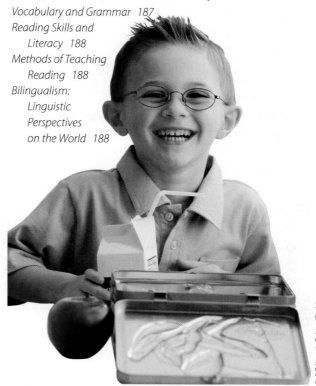

© JLP/Jose L. Pelaez/Corbis

10 Middle Childhood: Social and Emotional Development 191

Monkey Business Images/Shutterstock

F64/Digital Vision/Getty Images

© Thinkstock Images/Jupiterimages

© Breanna Webster and Chad Cole, photo by Shauna Longmuir

15 Middle Adulthood: Physical and Cognitive Development 279

ColorBlind Images/Blend Images/Jupiter Images

16 Middle Adulthood: Social and Emotional Development 297

Ronnie Kaufman/Blend Images/Jupiter Images

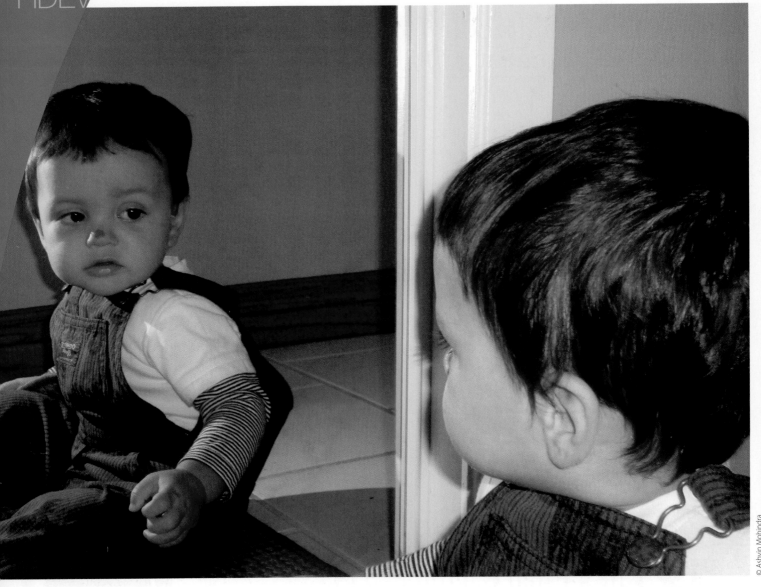

© Ashvin Mohindra

You

are unique, and things will happen to you, and because of you, that have never
happened before.

1

History, Theories, and Methods

> **D1** During the Middle Ages, children were often treated as miniature adults.
>
> **D2** Research with monkeys has helped psychologists understand the formation of attachment in humans.
>
> **D3** To learn how a person develops over a lifetime, researchers have tracked some individuals for more than 50 years.

This book has a story to tell. An important story. It is your story. It is about the remarkable journey you have already taken through childhood. It is about the unfolding of your adult life. Billions of people have made this journey before. You have much in common with them. Yet you are unique, and things will happen to you, and because of you, that have never happened before.

LO1 The Development of the Study of Development

Scientific inquiry into human development has existed for little more than a century. In ancient times and in the Middle Ages, children often were viewed as innately evil and discipline was harsh. Legally, medieval children were treated as property and servants. They could be sent to the monastery, married without consultation, or convicted of crimes. Children were nurtured until they were 7 years old, which was considered the "age of reason." Then they were expected to work alongside adults in the home and in the field.

> **D1** During the Middle Ages, children were often treated as miniature adults.
> Though more was expected of them, they weren't given more privileges.

THE STUDY OF CHILD AND ADOLESCENT DEVELOPMENT

The transition to modern thinking about children is marked by the writings of philosophers such as John Locke and Jean-Jacques Rousseau. Englishman John Locke (1632–1704) believed that the child came into the world as a

Learning Outcomes

LO1 Relate the history of the study of human development

LO2 Compare and contrast theories of human development

LO3 Enumerate key controversies in human development

LO4 Describe ways in which researchers study human development

tabula rasa—a "blank tablet" or clean slate—that was written on by experience. Locke did not believe that inborn predispositions toward good or evil played an important role in the conduct of the child. Instead, he focused on the role of the environment or of experience. Locke believed that social approval and disapproval are powerful shapers of behaviour. But Jean-Jacques Rousseau (1712–1778), a Swiss–French philosopher, argued that children are inherently good and that, if allowed to express their natural impulses, they will develop into generous and moral individuals.

During the Industrial Revolution, family life came to be defined in terms of the nuclear unit of mother, father, and children rather than the extended family. Children became more visible, fostering awareness of childhood as a special time of life. Still, children often laboured in factories from dawn to dusk through the early years of the 20th century.

In the 20th century, laws were passed to protect children from strenuous labour, to require that they attend school until a certain age, and to prevent them from getting married or being sexually exploited. Whereas children were once considered the property of parents to do with as they wished, laws now protect children from abuse by parents and other adults. Young offender courts see that children who break the law receive appropriate treatment in the criminal justice system.

Pioneers in the Study of Child Development

Various thoughts about child development emerged into a field of scientific study in the 19th and early 20th centuries. G. Stanley Hall (1844–1924) is credited with founding child development as an academic discipline. The Frenchman Alfred Binet (1857–1911), along with Theodore Simon, developed the first standardized intelligence test near the beginning of the 20th century. Binet's purpose was to identify elementary school children who were at risk of falling behind their peers in academic achievement. By the start of the 20th century, child development had emerged as a scientific field of study. Soon major theories of the developing child had begun to emerge, proposed by theorists such as Arnold Gesell, Sigmund Freud, John B. Watson, and Jean Piaget.

THE STUDY OF ADULT DEVELOPMENT

The traditional focus has been on childhood and adolescence because of the dramatic physical and cognitive changes that occur during those years. In addition to focusing on the marked decline of late adulthood, many theorists today also focus on changes that occur during young and middle adulthood.

William Perry and Gisella Labouvie-Vief, for example, have studied the development of cognitive complexity from adolescence to late adulthood. K. W Schaie and others have studied trends in various mental abilities throughout middle and late adulthood, emphasizing differences between so-called *crystallized* intellectual factors and *fluid* factors. Though young adulthood is the time of peak physical development, people perform at their best on some of the most complex intellectual tasks during midlife, and many people are most well-adjusted during late adulthood. All of these theories are integrated to form a definition of **developmental psychology**, which is the biological, psychological, and sociocultural study of development across the lifespan. Developmental psychology examines the progressive

© Banana Stock/Jupiterimages

challenges and changes that an individual encounters from cradle to grave, which are prompted by maturation and the learning process.

LO2 Theories of Development

Give me a dozen healthy infants, well-formed, and my own specified world to bring them up in, and I'll guarantee to train them to become any type of specialist I might suggest—doctor, lawyer, merchant, chief, and, yes, even beggar and thief, regardless of their talents, penchants, tendencies, abilities, vocations, and the race of their ancestors.

—Watson, 1924, p. 82.

John B. Watson, the founder of North American **behaviourism**, viewed development in terms of learning theory. He generally agreed with Locke that children's ideas, preferences, and skills are shaped by experience. There has been a long-standing nature–nurture debate in the study of children. In his theoretical approach to understanding children, Watson came down on the side of nurture—the importance of the physical and social environments—as found, for example, in parental training and approval.

Arnold Gesell expressed the opposing idea that biological **maturation** was the main principle of development: "All things considered, the inevitability and surety of maturation are the most impressive characteristics of early development. It is the hereditary ballast which conserves and stabilizes growth of each individual infant" (Gesell, 1928, p. 378). Watson was talking about the behaviour patterns that children develop, whereas Gesell was focusing mainly on physical aspects of growth and development.

Theories such as behavioural theory and maturational theory help developmentalists explain, predict, and influence the events they study. Let us consider theories that are popular among developmentalists today. They fall within broad perspectives on development.

THE PSYCHOANALYTIC PERSPECTIVE

A number of theories fall within the psychoanalytic perspective. Each owes its origin to Sigmund Freud and views children—and adults—as caught in conflict. Early in development the conflict is between the child and the world outside. The expression of basic drives, such as sex and aggression, conflict with parental expectations, social rules, moral codes, even laws. But the external limits—parental demands and social rules—are brought inside or *internalized*. Once internalization occurs, the conflict takes place between opposing *inner* forces. The child's observable behaviour, thoughts, and feelings reflect the outcomes of these hidden battles.

Let us consider Freud's theory of **psychosexual development** and Erik Erikson's theory of psychosocial development. Each is a **stage theory** that sees children as developing through distinct periods of life. Each suggests that the child's experiences during early stages affect the child's emotional and social life at the time and later on.

behaviourism Watson's view that science must study observable behaviour only and investigate relationships between stimuli and responses.

maturation the unfolding of genetically determined traits, structures, and functions.

psychosexual development the process by which libidinal energy is expressed through different erogenous zones during different stages of development.

stage theory a theory of development characterized by distinct periods of life.

Sigmund Freud's Theory of Psychosexual Development

Sigmund Freud's (1856–1939) theory of psychosexual development focused on emotional and social development and on the origins of psychological traits such as dependence, obsessive neatness, and vanity. Freud theorized three parts of the personality: *the id, ego,* and *superego*. The id is present at birth and is *unconscious*. It represents biological drives, and it demands instant gratification, as suggested

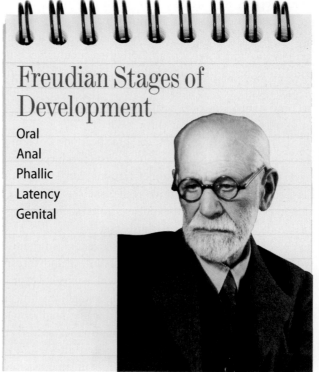

Freudian Stages of Development
Oral
Anal
Phallic
Latency
Genital

by a baby's wailing. The ego, or the conscious sense of self, begins to develop when children learn to obtain gratification consciously, without screaming or crying. The ego curbs the appetites of the id and makes plans that are in keeping with social conventions so that a person can find gratification but avoid social disapproval. The superego develops throughout infancy and early childhood. It brings inward the wishes and morals of the child's caregivers and other members of the community. This theory has become a favourite cartoon technique. Often a popular character is conflicted by what is desired (id) and what is the "right" thing to do (superego). The character (ego) is left to make the decision and deal with the consequences.

According to Freud, psychosexual development has five stages: *oral, anal, phallic, latency,* and *genital.* If a child receives too little or too much gratification during a stage, the child can become *fixated* in that stage. For example, during the first year of life, which Freud termed the *oral stage,* "oral" activities such as sucking and biting bring pleasure and gratification. If the child is weaned early or breast-fed too long, the child may become fixated on oral activities such as nail biting or smoking, or even show a "biting wit."

In the second, or *anal,* stage, gratification is obtained through control and elimination of waste products. Excessively strict or permissive toilet training can lead to the development of anal-retentive traits, such as perfectionism and neatness, or anal-expulsive traits, such as sloppiness and carelessness. In the third stage, the *phallic stage,* parent–child conflict may develop over masturbation, which many parents treat with punishment and threats. According to Freud's psychoanalytical perspective, it is normal for children to develop strong sexual attachments to the parent of the opposite sex during the phallic stage and to begin to view the parent of the same sex as a rival.

By age 5 or 6, Freud believed, children enter a *latency stage* during which sexual feelings remain unconscious, children turn to schoolwork, and they typically prefer playmates of their own sex. The final stage of psychosexual development, the *genital stage,* begins with the biological changes that usher in adolescence. Adolescents generally desire sexual gratification through intercourse with a partner. Freud believed that oral or anal stimulation, masturbation, and male–male or female–female sexual activity are immature forms of sexual conduct that reflect fixations at early stages of development.

Evaluation   Freud's views about the anal stage have influenced child-care workers to recommend that toilet training not be started too early or handled punitively. His emphasis on the emotional needs of children has influenced educators to be more sensitive to the possible emotional reasons behind a child's misbehaviour. Freud's work has also been criticized. For one thing, Freud developed his theory on the basis of contacts with adult patients (mostly women) (Schultz & Schultz, 2008), rather than observing children directly. Freud may also have inadvertently guided patients into expressing ideas that confirmed his views. Although Freud's theory forms the basis of many psychological theories, many suggest that his ideas need to be placed within a more modern context that recognizes the role of relationships and the desire to achieve.

Erik Erikson's Theory of Psychosocial Development

Erik Erikson (1902–1994) modified Freud's theory and extended it through the adult years. Erikson's theory,

Erik Erikson was married to his Canadian wife, Joan, for 64 years.

like Freud's, focuses on the development of the emotional life and psychological traits, but Erikson focuses on social relationships rather than unconscious motivations, such as sexuality or aggressive instincts. Erikson emphasized the desire to achieve and to help others. Therefore, Erikson speaks of **psychosocial development** rather than of *psychosexual development*. Furthermore, Erikson places greater emphasis on the ego, or the sense of self. Erikson (1963) extended Freud's five stages to eight to include the concerns of adulthood. Rather than label his stages after parts of the body, Erikson labelled them after the **life crisis** that people might encounter during that stage (see Table 1.1).

Erikson proposed that social relationships and physical maturation give each stage its character. For example, the parent–child relationship and the infant's dependence and helplessness are responsible for the nature of the earliest stages of development. Early experiences affect future developments.

Erikson's views, like Freud's, have influenced child rearing, early childhood education, and child therapy. For example, Erikson's views about an adolescent **identity crisis** have entered the popular culture and have affected the way many parents and teachers deal with teenagers. Some schools help students master the crisis by means of life-adjustment courses and study units on self-understanding in social studies and literature classes.

Evaluation Erikson's views are appealing because they emphasize the importance of human consciousness and choice and portray us as prosocial and helpful, whereas Freud portrayed us as selfish and needing to be compelled to comply with social rules. Some empirical findings support the Eriksonian view that positive outcomes of early life crises help put us on the path to positive development (Hoegh & Bourgeois, 2002).

psychosocial development Erikson's theory, which emphasizes the importance of social relationships and conscious choice throughout eight stages of development.

life crisis an internal conflict that attends each stage of psychosocial development.

identity crisis according to Erikson, a period of inner conflict during which one examines one's values and makes decisions about one's life roles.

TABLE 1.1
The Eight Stages of Psychosocial Development in Erikson's Theory

PSYCHOSOCIAL STAGE	AGE	CHALLENGE
Basic trust vs. mistrust	Birth to 1 year	To develop a sense that the world is safe, a "good place"
Autonomy vs. shame and doubt	1 to 3 years	To realize that one is an independent person who can make decisions
Initiative vs. guilt	3 to 6 years	To develop the ability to try new things and to handle failure
Industry vs. inferiority	6 years to adolescence	To learn basic skills and to work with others
Identity vs. identity confusion	Adolescence	To develop a lasting, integrated sense of self
Intimacy vs. isolation	Young adulthood	To commit to another in a loving relationship
Generativity vs. stagnation	Middle adulthood	To contribute to younger people, through child rearing, child care, or other productive work
Integrity vs. despair	Late life	To view one's life as satisfactory and worth living

From Kail/Cavanaugh. *Human Development*, 2e. © 2009 Nelson Education Ltd. Reproduced by permission. www.cengage.com/permissions

© Richard Ransier/Corbis

THE LEARNING PERSPECTIVE: BEHAVIOURAL AND SOCIAL COGNITIVE THEORIES

Behaviourism

John B. Watson argued that a scientific approach to development must focus on the observable behaviour only and not on unobservable activities, such as thoughts, fantasies, and other mental images.

Classical conditioning is a simple form of learning in which an originally neutral stimulus comes to bring forth, or elicit, the response usually brought forth by a second stimulus as a result of being paired repeatedly with the second stimulus.

The opening of a can does not initially elicit a response from a dog. But once the dog learns to associate the opening of a can with being fed, then anytime the dog hears that familiar sound, it will run toward the opening can from

B. F. Skinner

anywhere in the house. The can might contain dog food or a can of beans but, either way, the dog will associate the sound of it being opened with the act of being fed.

Behaviourists argue that much emotional learning is acquired through classical conditioning. In **operant conditioning** (a different kind of conditioning), children learn to do something because of its effects. B. F. Skinner introduced the key concept of **reinforcement**. Reinforcers are stimuli that increase the frequency of the behaviour they follow. Most children learn to adjust their behaviour to conform to social codes and rules to earn reinforcers such as the attention and approval of their parents and teachers. Other children, ironically, may learn to misbehave because misbehaviour also draws attention. Any stimulus that increases the frequency of the responses preceding it serves as a reinforcer. Skinner distinguished between positive and negative reinforcers. **Positive reinforcers** increase the frequency of behaviours when they are *applied*. Food and approval usually serve as positive reinforcers. **Negative reinforcers** increase the frequency of behaviours when they are *removed*. Fear acts as a negative reinforcer in that its removal increases the frequency of the behaviours preceding it. Figure 1.1 on the following page compares positive and negative reinforcers.

Extinction results from repeated performance of operant behaviour without reinforcement. After a number of trials, the operant behaviour is no longer shown. Children's temper tantrums and crying at bedtime can often be extinguished by parents' remaining out of the bedroom after the children have been put to bed. **Punishments** are aversive events that suppress or *decrease* the frequency of the behaviour they follow. (Figure 1.2 on page 10 compares negative reinforcers with punishments.) Many learning theorists agree that punishment should be used sparingly in child rearing and is most appropriate when mild and prompt, such as the case with time outs. Punishment on its own does not suggest alternative behaviour and can lead to anger and resentment. Inappropriate behaviour will not be consistently suppressed unless punishment is guaranteed.

Research suggests that when teachers praise and attend to appropriate behaviour and ignore misbehaviour, studying and classroom behaviour improve while disruptive and aggressive behaviours decrease (McIlvane & Dube, 2003; Takahashi & Sugiyama, 2003). By ignoring misbehaviour or by using *time out* from positive reinforcement, we can avoid reinforcing children for misbehaviour. When using time out, children who behave disruptively are placed in drab, restrictive environments for a specified time period, such as 10 minutes.

Operant conditioning is used every day in the *socialization* of young children. Parents and peers influence children to acquire gender-appropriate behaviours through the elaborate use of rewards and punishments. Thus, boys may ignore boys who play with dolls and housekeeping toys but will show interest in playing with boys who use transportation toys.

Albert Bandura

Social Cognitive Theory

Behaviourists tend to limit their view of learning to conditioning. **Social cognitive theorists** such as Canadian-born Albert Bandura (1986, 2006a, 2006b) have shown that much learning also occurs by observing other people, reading, and viewing characters in the media. People may need practice to refine their skills, but they can acquire the basic know-how through observation and modelling.

Observational learning occurs when children observe how parents cook, clean, or repair a broken appliance. It takes place when adults watch supervisors sketch out sales strategies on a blackboard or hear them speak a foreign language. In social cognitive theory, the people after whom we pattern our own behaviour are termed *models*.

Evaluation of Learning Theories

Learning theories allow us to explain, predict, and influence many aspects of behaviour. Many of the teaching approaches used in educational TV shows are based on learning theory.

THE COGNITIVE PERSPECTIVE

Cognitive theorists focus on people's mental processes. They investigate the ways in which children perceive and mentally represent the world and how they develop thinking, logic, and problem-solving ability. One cognitive perspective is **cognitive-developmental theory**, advanced by Swiss biologist

FIGURE 1.1
Positive versus Negative Reinforcers

All reinforcers *increase* the frequency of behaviour. In these examples, teacher approval functions as a positive reinforcer when students study harder because of it. Teacher *disapproval* functions as a negative reinforcer when its *removal* increases the frequency of studying.

Procedure	Behaviour	Consequence	Change in behaviour
Use of positive reinforcement	Behaviour (studying)	Positive reinforcer (teacher approval) is presented when student studies	Frequency of behaviour increases (student studies more)
Use of negative reinforcement	Behaviour (studying)	Negative reinforcer (teacher disapproval) is removed when student studies	Frequency of behaviour increases (student studies more)

HDEV *Go to www.icanhdev.com to access an interactive version of this figure.*

scheme an action pattern or mental structure that is involved in the acquisition and organization of knowledge.

adaptation the interaction between the organism and the environment, consisting of assimilation and accommodation.

assimilation the incorporation of new events or knowledge into existing schemes

accommodation the modification of existing schemes to permit the incorporation of new events or knowledge.

Jean Piaget (1896–1980) and further developed by many theorists. Another is information-processing theory.

Cognitive-Developmental Theory

During adolescence, Jean Piaget studied philosophy, logic, and mathematics, but years later he took his Ph.D. in biology. In 1920, he obtained a job at the Binet Institute in Paris, where research on intelligence tests was being conducted. Through his studies, Piaget realized that when children answered questions incorrectly, their wrong answers still often reflected consistent—although illogical—mental processes. Piaget regarded children as natural physicists who actively intend to learn about and take intellectual charge of their worlds. In the Piagetian view, children who squish their food and laugh enthusiastically are often acting as budding scientists. They are

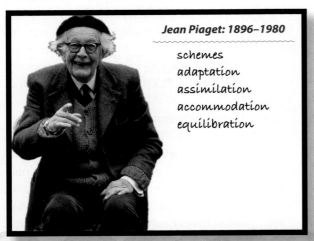
© Farrell Grehan/Corbis

Piaget's early training as a biologist led him to view children as mentally assimilating and accommodating aspects of their environment.

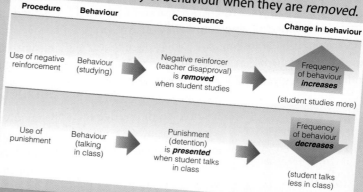

FIGURE 1.2
Negative Reinforcers versus Punishments

Both negative reinforcers and punishments tend to be aversive stimuli. Reinforcers, however, *increase* the frequency of behaviour. Punishments *decrease* the frequency of behaviour. Negative reinforcers increase the frequency of behaviour when they are *removed*.

Procedure	Behaviour	Consequence	Change in behaviour
Use of negative reinforcement	Behaviour (studying)	Negative reinforcer (teacher disapproval) is **removed** when student studies	Frequency of behaviour **increases** (student studies more)
Use of punishment	Behaviour (talking in class)	Punishment (detention) is **presented** when student talks in class	Frequency of behaviour **decreases** (student talks less in class)

HDEV Go to www.icanhdev.com to access an interactive version of this figure.

studying both the texture and consistency of their food, as well as their parents' response.

Piaget used concepts such as *schemes, adaptation, assimilation, accommodation,* and *equilibration* to describe and explain cognitive development. Piaget defines the **scheme** as a pattern of action or mental structure that is involved in acquiring or organizing knowledge. For example, newborn babies might be said to have a sucking scheme (others call this a *reflex*), responding to things put in their mouths as "things I can suck" versus "things I can't suck."

Adaptation refers to the interaction between the organism and the environment. According to Piaget, all organisms adapt to their environment. Adaptation consists of assimilation and accommodation, which occur throughout life. Cognitive **assimilation** refers to the process by which someone responds to new objects or events according to existing schemes or ways of organizing knowledge. Two-year-olds who refer to horses as "doggies" can be said to be assimilating horses into the dog scheme. Sometimes a novel object or event cannot be made to fit into an existing scheme. In that case, the scheme may be changed or a new scheme may be created to incorporate the new event. This process is called **accommodation**. Consider the sucking reflex. Infants accommodate by rejecting objects that are too large, that taste bad, or that are of the wrong texture or temperature.

Piaget theorized that when children can assimilate new events to existing schemes, they are in a state of cognitive harmony, or equilibrium. When something that does not fit happens along, their state of equilibrium is disturbed and they may try to accommodate. The process of restoring equilibrium is termed **equilibration**. Piaget believed that the attempt to restore equilibrium lies at the heart of the natural curiosity of the child.

Piaget's Stages of Cognitive Development

Piaget (1963) hypothesized that children's cognitive processes develop in an orderly sequence, or series, of stages. Piaget identified four major stages of cognitive development: *sensorimotor, preoperational, concrete operational,* and *formal operational.* These stages are discussed in subsequent chapters.

Because Piaget's theory focuses on cognitive development, its applications are primarily in educational settings and provide the foundation for curriculum decisions made throughout the public school system in Canada. Teachers following Piaget's views actively engage the child in solving problems. They gear instruction to the child's developmental level and offer activities that challenge the child to advance to the next level.

Piaget's theory ends with formal operational thought. Lifespan theorists such as William Perry note that college students' views on what they know and how they get to know what they know become more complex as they are exposed to the complexities of college thought.

Evaluation Many researchers, using a variety of methods, find that Piaget may have underestimated the ages when children are capable of doing certain things. It also appears that many cognitive skills may develop gradually and not in distinct stages. Nevertheless, Piaget has provided a strong theoretical foundation for researchers concerned with sequences in cognitive development.

> **equilibration** the creation of an equilibrium, or balance, between assimilation and accommodation.

Information-Processing Theory

Another face of the cognitive perspective is information processing (Flavell et al., 2002; Siegler & Alabali, 2005). Many psychologists speak of people as having working, or short-term, memory and a more permanent long-term memory (storage). If information has been placed in long-term memory, it must be retrieved before we can work on it. Retrieving information from our own long-term memories requires certain cues, without which the information may be lost.

Thus, many cognitive psychologists focus on information processing in people—the processes by which people encode (input) information, store it (in long-term memory), retrieve it (place it in short-term memory), and manipulate it to solve problems. Our strategies for solving problems are sometimes referred to as our "mental programs" or "software." In this computer metaphor, our brains are the "hardware" that runs our mental programs. Our brains—containing billions of brain cells called *neurons*—become our most "personal" computers. When psychologists who study information processing contemplate cognitive development, they are likely to talk in terms of the *size* of the person's short-term memory and the *number of programs* she or he can run simultaneously.

The most obvious applications of information processing occur in teaching. For example, information-processing models alert instructors to the sequence of steps by which individuals acquire information, commit it to memory, and retrieve it to solve problems. By understanding this sequence, instructors can provide experiences that give students practice with each stage. Understanding information-processing theory can assist you in establishing more productive study habits.

We now see that the brain is a sort of biological computer. Let us next see what other aspects of biology can be connected with development.

> "Information processing in people is the process by which people encode (input) information, store it (in long-term memory), retrieve it (place it in short-term memory), and manipulate it to solve problems."

silver-john/Shutterstock

Two questions that research seeks to answer are: Do human behaviour and development **involve instincts?** If so, how powerful are instincts **in people?**

THE BIOLOGICAL PERSPECTIVE

ethology the study of behaviours that are specific to a species.

fixed action pattern (FAP) a stereotyped pattern of behaviour that is evoked by a "releasing stimulus"; an instinct.

ecology the branch of biology that deals with the relationships between living organisms and their environment.

ecological systems theory the view that explains child development in terms of the reciprocal influences between children and environmental settings.

microsystem the immediate settings with which the child interacts, such as the home, the school, and peers.

mesosystem the interlocking settings that influence the child, such as the interaction of the school and the larger community.

exosystem community institutions and settings that indirectly influence the child, such as the school board and the parents' workplaces.

The biological perspective directly relates to physical development: to gains in height and weight; development of the brain; and developments connected with hormones, reproduction, and heredity. Here we consider one biologically oriented theory of development, *ethology*.

Ethology: "Doing What Comes Naturally"

Ethology was heavily influenced by the 19th-century work of Charles Darwin and by the work of 20th-century ethologists Konrad Lorenz and Niko Tinbergen (Washburn, 2007). Ethology is concerned with instinctive, or inborn, behaviour patterns.

The nervous systems of most, and perhaps all, animals are "prewired" to respond to some situations in specific ways. For example, birds raised in isolation from other birds build nests during the mating season even if they have never seen a nest or have never seen another bird building a nest. Nest-building could not have been learned. Birds raised in isolation also sing the songs typical of their species. These behaviours are "built in," or instinctive. They are also referred to as inborn **fixed action patterns (FAPs).**

During prenatal development, genes and sex hormones are responsible for the physical development of female and male sex organs. Most theorists also believe that in many species, including humans, sex hormones can "masculinize" or "feminize" the embryonic brain by creating tendencies to behave in stereotypical masculine or feminine ways. Testosterone, the male sex hormone, seems to be connected with feelings of self-confidence, high activity levels, and—the negative side—aggressiveness (Archer, 2006; Davis et al., 2005; Geary, 2006).

Evaluation Research into the ethological perspective suggests that instinct may play a role in human behaviour. Two questions that research seeks to answer are: Do human behaviour and development involve instincts? If so, how powerful are instincts in people?

THE ECOLOGICAL PERSPECTIVE

Ecology is the branch of biology that deals with the relationships between living organisms and their environment. The **ecological systems theory** of development addresses aspects of psychological, social, and emotional development as well as aspects of biological development. Development is explained in terms of the interaction between people and the settings in which they live (Bronfenbrenner & Morris, 2006).

According to Urie Bronfenbrenner (1917–2005), for example, we need to focus on the two-way interactions between the child and the parents, not just maturational forces (nature) or child-rearing practices (nurture). Bronfenbrenner (Bronfenbrenner & Morris, 2006) suggested that we can view the setting or contexts of human development as consisting of multiple systems, each embedded within the next larger context. From narrowest to widest, these systems are the microsystem, the mesosystem, the exosystem, the macrosystem, and the chronosystem (see Figure 1.3).

The **microsystem** involves the interactions of the child and other people in the immediate setting, such as the home, the school, or the peer group. Initially, the microsystem is small, involving care-giving interactions with the parents or others, usually at home. As children get older, they do more, with more people, in more places.

The **mesosystem** involves the interactions of the various settings within the microsystem. For instance, the home and the school interact during parent–teacher conferences. The school and the larger community interact when children go on field trips. The ecological systems approach addresses the joint effect of two or more settings on the child.

The **exosystem** involves the institutions in which the child does not directly participate but which exert

FIGURE 1.3
The Contexts of Human Development

According to ecological systems theory, the systems within which children develop are embedded within larger systems. Children and these systems reciprocally influence each other.

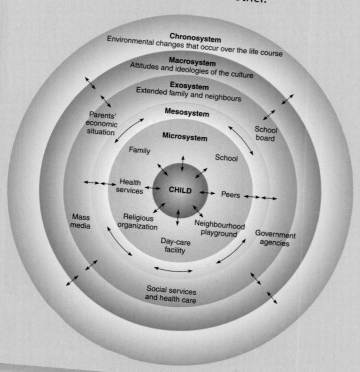

about a year after the event, and then children begin to recover. The breakup has more of an effect on boys than on girls. The ecological approach broadens the strategies for intervention in issues such as prevention of teenage pregnancy, child abuse, youth in conflict with the law, and substance abuse (Kaminski & Stormshak, 2007).

THE SOCIOCULTURAL PERSPECTIVE

The sociocultural perspective teaches that people are social beings who are affected by the cultures in which they live. Developmentalists use the term *sociocultural* in a couple of different ways. One refers quite specifically to the *sociocultural theory* of Russian psychologist Lev Semenovich Vygotsky (1896–1934). The other addresses the effect of human diversity on people, including such factors as ethnicity and gender.

Vygotsky's Sociocultural Theory

Whereas genetics is concerned with the biological transmission of traits from generation to generation, Vygotsky's (1978) theory is concerned with the transmission of information and cognitive skills from generation to generation. The transmission of skills involves teaching and learning, but Vygotsky does not view learning in terms of conditioning. Rather, he focuses on how the child's social interaction with adults, largely in the home, organizes a child's learning experiences in such a way that the child can obtain cognitive skills—such as computation or reading skills—and use them to acquire information. Like Piaget, Vygotsky sees the child's functioning as adaptive (Kanevsky & Geake, 2004), and the

Lev Semenovich Vygotsky

an indirect influence on the child. For example, the school board is part of the child's exosystem because board members put together programs for the child's education, determine what textbooks will be adopted, and so forth. In similar fashion, the parents' workplaces and economic situations determine the hours during which they will be available to the child, and so on (Kaminski & Stormshak, 2007). As a result, children may misbehave at home and in school.

The **macrosystem** involves the interaction of children with the beliefs, values, expectations, and lifestyles of their cultural settings. Cross-cultural studies examine children's interactions with their macrosystem. Macrosystems exist within a particular culture. In Canada, the dual-earner family, the low-income single-parent household, and the family with father as sole breadwinner describe three different macrosystems. Each has its lifestyle, set of values, and expectations (Bronfenbrenner & Morris, 2006; Silbereisen, 2006).

The **chronosystem** considers the changes that occur over time. For example, the effects of divorce peak

Archives of the History of American Psychology, The Center for the History of Psychology - The University of Akron/© catnap72/iStockphoto

child adapts to his or her social and cultural interactions.

Key concepts in Vygotsky's theory include the *zone of proximal development* and *scaffolding*. The **zone of proximal development (ZPD)** refers to a range of tasks that a child can carry out with the help of someone who is more skilled, as in an apprenticeship. When learning with other people, children internalize—or bring inward—the conversations and explanations that help them gain the necessary skills (Ash, 2004; Umek et al., 2005; Vygotsky, 1962).

A *scaffold* is a temporary skeletal structure that enables workers to fabricate a building or other more permanent structure. In Vygotsky's theory, teachers and parents provide children with problem-solving methods that serve as cognitive **scaffolding** while the child gains the ability to function independently. For example, children may be offered scaffolding that enables them to use their fingers or their toes to do simple calculations. Eventually, the scaffolding is removed and the cognitive structures stand alone.

The Sociocultural Perspective and Human Diversity

The sociocultural perspective asserts that we cannot understand individuals without awareness of the rich-

According to Vygotsky's theory, teachers and parents provide children with problem-solving methods that serve as cognitive scaffolding.

ness of their diversity (Fouad & Arredondo, 2007). For example, people differ in their ethnicity, gender, and socioeconomic status.

People's ethnic groups involve their cultural heritage, their race, their language, and their common history. Figure 1.4, from the website of Citizenship and Immigration Canada (2008), highlights more than 200 multicultural groupings that populate our country. Canadian society is built upon the acceptance and promotion of multiculturalism. Diversity within the Canadian population must not be taken for granted but should be fostered and developed.

Studying diversity is necessary so that students have appropriate educational experiences. To teach students and guide their learning, educators need to understand children's family values and cultural expectations. Issues that affect people from various ethnic groups include bilingualism, ethnic differences in intelligence test scores, the prevalence of suicide among members of different backgrounds, and patterns of child rearing among parents of various groups, such as same-sex unions.

Gender is another aspect of human diversity. Gender is the psychological state of being male or being female, as influenced by cultural concepts of gender-appropriate behaviour. Expectations of females and males are often polarized by cultural expectations. That is, gender differences may be exaggerated, as in the case of intellectual abilities. Males may differ from females in some respects, but history has created more burdens for women than men. Historically, females have been discouraged from careers in the sciences, politics, and business. Women today are making inroads into academic and vocational spheres that were traditionally male preserves—such as medicine, law, engineering, and the military. It is worth noting that females were not considered qualified for education until relatively recent times. But even today, women are prevented from obtaining an education in many parts of the world.

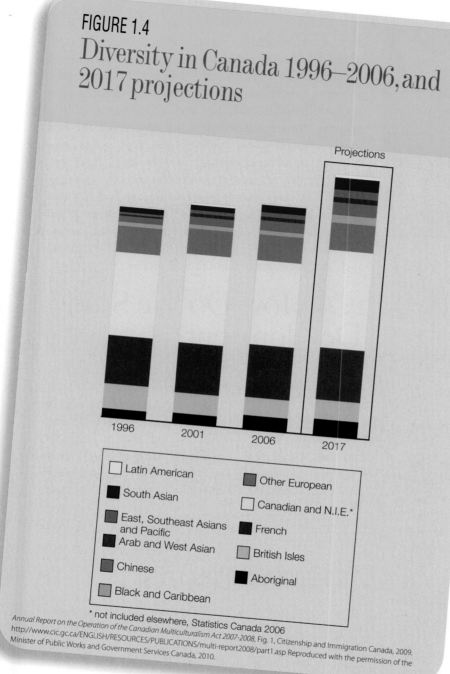

FIGURE 1.4
Diversity in Canada 1996–2006, and 2017 projections

Projections

1996   2001   2006   2017

- ☐ Latin American
- ■ South Asian
- ▨ East, Southeast Asians and Pacific
- ■ Arab and West Asian
- ▨ Chinese
- ☐ Black and Caribbean
- ▨ Other European
- ☐ Canadian and N.I.E.*
- ■ French
- ▨ British Isles
- ■ Aboriginal

* not included elsewhere, Statistics Canada 2006

Annual Report on the Operation of the Canadian Multiculturalism Act 2007-2008, Fig. 1, Citizenship and Immigration Canada, 2009. http://www.cic.gc.ca/ENGLISH/RESOURCES/PUBLICATIONS/multi-report2008/part1.asp Reproduced with the permission of the Minister of Public Works and Government Services Canada, 2010.

nature the processes within an organism that guide it to develop according to its genetic code.

nurture environmental factors that influence development.

(heredity) and of **nurture** (environmental influences). What aspects of behaviour originate in our genes and are biologically programmed to unfold as time goes on, as long as minimal nutrition and social experience are provided? What aspects of behaviour can be traced largely to such environmental influences as nutrition and learning?

Scientists seek the natural causes of development in children's genetic heritage, the functioning of the nervous system, and in maturation. Scientists seek the environmental causes of development in children's nutrition, cultural and family backgrounds, and opportunities to learn about the world, including cognitive stimulation during early childhood and formal education.

Most researchers agree that both nature and nurture play important roles in nearly every area of development. Consider the significant health threat that cardiovascular disease presents to Canadians. A person may be genetically predisposed (nature) to this disease, but lifestyle choices (nurture) will also strongly affect this person's health outcome. Modern theorists rarely view nature and nurture as mutually exclusive.

LO3 Debates in Development

the discussion of theories of development reveals that developmentalists can see things in very different ways. Let us consider how they react to three of the most important debates in the field.

NATURE AND NURTURE

Researchers are continually trying to sort out the extent to which human behaviour is the result of **nature**

CONTINUITY AND DISCONTINUITY

Some developmentalists view human development as a continuous process in which the effects of learning mount gradually, with no sudden major qualitative changes. In contrast, other theorists believe that a number of rapid qualitative changes usher in new stages of development. Maturational theorists point out that the environment, even when enriched, profits us little until we are ready, or mature enough, to develop in a certain way. For example, newborn babies will not imitate their parents' speech, even when parents speak clearly and deliberately. Similarly, aided practice in "walking" during the first few

Girls usually spurt in growth before boys do, as these graduating grade eights are very much aware.

© Shauna Longmuir

empirical based on observation and experimentation.

months after birth will not significantly accelerate the emergence of independent walking. Developmentally, they are not yet ready for these activities.

Stage theorists such as Sigmund Freud and Jean Piaget saw development as discontinuous. They saw biological changes as providing the potential for psychological changes. Freud focused on the ways in which biological developments might provide the basis for personality development. Piaget believed maturation of the nervous system allowed cognitive development.

Certain aspects of physical development do occur in stages. For example, from the age of 2 years to the onset of puberty, children gradually grow larger. Then the adolescent growth spurt occurs as rushes of hormones cause rapid biological changes in structure and function (as in the development of the sex organs) and in size. Psychologists disagree on whether developments in cognition occur in stages.

ACTIVE AND PASSIVE ROLES

Historical views of children as willful and unruly suggest that people have generally seen children as active, even if mischievous (at best) or evil (at worst). John Locke introduced a view of children as passive beings (blank tablets); experience "wrote" features of personality and moral virtue on them.

At one extreme, educators who view children as passive may assume that instructors must motivate children to learn. Such educators are likely to provide a rigorous traditional curriculum with a powerful system of rewards and punishments to promote absorption of the subject matter. At the other extreme, educators who view children as active may assume that children have a natural love of learning. Such educators are likely to argue for open education and encourage children to explore and pursue their unique likes and talents, focusing on a love of learning for learning's sake.

These debates are theoretical. Scientists value theory for its ability to tie together observations and suggest new areas of investigation, but they also follow an **empirical** approach. That is, to find evidence for or against various theoretical positions, they engage in research methods, such as those described in the next section.

LO4 How Do We Study Development?

What are the effects of maternal use of aspirin and alcohol on the fetus? What are the effects of parental divorce on children? What are the effects of early retirement? We may have expressed opinions on such questions at one time or another, but scientists insist that such questions be answered by research. Strong arguments or reference to authority figures are not evidence. Scientific evidence is obtained only by gathering sound information and conducting research.

GATHERING INFORMATION

Researchers use various methods to gather information. For example, they may ask teachers or parents to report on the behaviour of children, use interviews or questionnaires with adults, or study statistics compiled by the government or the United Nations. They also directly observe children in the laboratory, the playground, or the classroom. Let us discuss two ways of gathering information: the naturalistic-observation method and the case-study method.

Naturalistic Observation

Naturalistic-observation studies are conducted in "the field," that is, in the natural, or real-life, settings in which the activities being studied occur. For example, in field studies, investigators observe the natural behaviour of children in settings such as homes, playgrounds, and classrooms. Because researchers do not want their presence to interfere with children's normal behaviour, they may try to "blend into the woodwork" by sitting quietly in the back of a classroom or by observing the class through a one-way mirror.

Naturalistic-observation studies have been done with children of different cultures. For example, researchers have observed the motor behaviour of Native American Hopi children who are strapped to cradle boards during their first year. You can read more about this study in Chapter 4.

The Case Study

The **case study** is a carefully drawn account of the behaviour of an individual. Parents who keep diaries of their children's activities are involved in informal case studies. Case studies themselves often use a number of different kinds of information. In addition to direct observation, case studies may include questionnaires, **standardized tests**, and interviews. Information gleaned from public records may be included. Scientists who use the case-study method try to record all relevant factors in a person's behaviour, and they are cautious in drawing conclusions about what leads to what.

CORRELATION: PUTTING THINGS TOGETHER

Researchers use the correlational method to determine whether one behaviour or trait being studied is related to, or correlated with, another. Consider intelligence and achievement. These variables are assigned numbers such as intelligence test scores and grade point averages. Then the numbers or scores are mathematically related and expressed as a **correlation coefficient**—a number that varies between +1.00 and −1.00.

In general, the higher people score on intelligence tests, the more likely they are to have better academic performance (or income). The scores attained on intelligence tests are **positively correlated** (about +0.60 to +0.70) with overall academic achievement (and income). A **negative correlation** exists between adolescents' grades and delinquent acts. That is, the higher an adolescent's grades, the less likely he or she is to engage in criminal behaviour. Figure 1.5 illustrates positive and negative correlations.

Limitations of Correlational Information

Correlational information can reveal relationships between variables, but does not show cause and effect. It may seem logical to assume that exposure to violent media makes people more aggressive, but it may also be that more aggressive people *choose* violent media. This research bias is termed a *selection factor*.

Similarly, studies report that children (especially boys) in divorced families tend

case study a carefully drawn biography of the life of an individual.

standardized test a test that compares an individual's score to the scores of a group of similar individuals.

correlation coefficient a number ranging from +1.00 to −1.00 that expresses the direction (positive or negative) and strength of the relationship between two variables.

positive correlation a relationship between two variables in which one variable increases as the other increases.

negative correlation a relationship between two variables in which one variable increases as the other decreases.

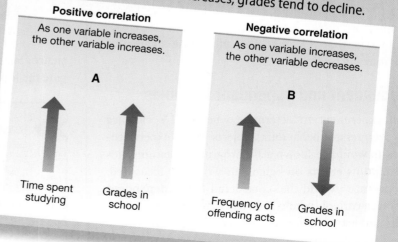

FIGURE 1.5
Examples of Positive and Negative Correlations

When two variables are correlated positively, one increases as the other increases. For example, a positive correlation exists between the amount of time spent studying and grades, as shown in Part A. When two variables are correlated negatively, one increases as the other decreases. For example, a negative correlation exists between the frequency of a child's offending acts and his or her grades, as shown in Part B. As offending behaviour increases, grades tend to decline.

Positive correlation
As one variable increases, the other variable increases.

A

Time spent studying   Grades in school

Negative correlation
As one variable increases, the other variable decreases.

B

Frequency of offending acts   Grades in school

experiment a method of scientific investigation that seeks to discover cause-and-effect relationships by introducing independent variables and observing their effects on dependent variables.

hypothesis a proposition to be tested.

independent variable a condition in a scientific study that is manipulated so that its effects can be observed.

dependent variable a measure of an assumed effect of an independent variable.

experimental group a group made up of subjects who receive a treatment in an experiment.

control group a group made up of subjects in an experiment who do not receive the treatment but for whom all other conditions are comparable to those of subjects in the experimental group.

THE EXPERIMENT: TRYING THINGS OUT

The experiment is the preferred method for investigating questions of cause and effect. In the **experiment**, a group of subjects receives a treatment and another group does not. The subjects are then observed to determine whether the treatment changes their behaviour. Experiments are usually undertaken to test a **hypothesis**. For example, a researcher might hypothesize that TV violence will cause aggressive behaviour in children.

© Lilyana Vynogradova/iStockphoto

Independent and Dependent Variables

In an experiment to determine whether TV violence causes aggressive behaviour, subjects in the experimental group would be shown a TV program containing violence, and its effects on behaviour would be measured. TV violence would be considered an **independent variable**, a variable whose presence is manipulated by the experimenters so that its effects can be determined. The

to show more behavioural problems than children in intact families (Greene et al., 2006; Lansford et al., 2006). These studies, however, do not show that divorce causes these adjustment problems. It could be that the factors that led to divorce—such as parental conflict—also led to adjustment problems among the children (Hetherington, 2006). To investigate cause and effect, researchers turn to the experimental method.

measured result—in this case, the child's behaviour—is called a **dependent variable**. Its presence or level presumably depends on the independent variable.

Experimental and Control Groups

Experiments use experimental and control groups. Subjects in the **experimental group** receive the treatment, whereas subjects in the **control group** do not. All other conditions are held constant for both groups. Thus, we can have confidence that experimental outcomes reflect the treatments and not chance factors.

Random Assignment

Subjects should be assigned to experimental or control groups on a chance or random basis. We could not conclude much from an experiment on the effects of TV violence if the children were allowed to choose whether they would be in a group that watched TV violence or in a group that did not. A *selection factor* rather than the treatment might then be responsible for the results of the experiment.

Ethical and practical considerations also prevent researchers from doing experiments on the effects of many life circumstances, such as divorce or different patterns of child rearing. We cannot randomly assign some families to divorce or conflict and assign other families to "bliss." Nor can we randomly assign parents to rearing their children in an authoritarian or permissive manner. In some areas of investigation, we must settle for correlational evidence.

When experiments cannot ethically be performed on humans, researchers sometimes carry them out with animals and try to generalize the findings to humans. No researcher would separate human infants from their parents to study the effects of isolation on development, yet experimenters have deprived monkeys of early social experience. Such research has helped psychologists investigate the formation of parent–child bonds of attachment.

> **D2** Research with monkeys has helped psychologists understand the formation of attachment in humans.
> Scientists cannot ethically research the formation of attachments on humans, so they conduct tests on animals that are genetically similar to people and then extrapolate their findings.

LONGITUDINAL RESEARCH: STUDYING DEVELOPMENT OVER TIME

The processes of development occur over time, and researchers have devised different strategies for comparing children of one age with children or adults of other ages. In **longitudinal research**, the same people are observed repeatedly over time, and changes in development, such as gains in height or changes in mental abilities, are recorded. In **cross-sectional research**, children of different ages are observed and compared. It is assumed that when a large number of children are chosen at random, the differences found in the older age groups are a reflection of how the younger children will develop, given time.

Longitudinal Studies

The National Longitudinal Survey of Children and Youth (NLSCY) began in Canada in 1994. The NLSCY collects information on the factors that influence children's social, emotional, and behavioural development and studies the impact of these factors on children's development over time. Also gathered are data concerning Canadian children's social environment (family, friends, schools, and communities) (Statistics Canada, 2008b).

> **D3** To learn how a person develops over a lifetime, researchers have tracked some individuals for more than 50 years, as seen in Lewis Terman's Genetic Studies of Genius. These studies, which began in the 1920s, tracked the professional achievements of male subjects with high IQs. These studies allow long-term vision; however, they are also costly and require an extensive time commitment.

Most longitudinal studies span months or a few years, not decades. For example, briefer longitudinal studies have found that the children of divorced parents undergo the most severe adjustment problems within a few months of the divorce. By 2 or 3 years afterward, many children regain their equilibrium, as indicated by improved academic performance and social behaviour (Hetherington et al., 1992).

Longitudinal studies have drawbacks. For example, it can be difficult to enlist volunteers to participate in a study that will last a lifetime. Many subjects fall out of touch as the years pass; others die. The researchers must be patient or arrange to enlist future generations of researchers.

Cross-Sectional Studies

Because of the drawbacks of longitudinal studies, most research that compares children of different ages is cross-sectional. In other words, most investigators gather data on what the "typical" 6-month-old is doing by finding children who are 6 months old today. When they expand their research to the behaviour of typical 12-month-olds, they seek another group of children, and so on.

A major challenge to cross-sectional research is the **cohort effect**. A cohort is a group of people born at about the same time. As a result, they experience cultural and other events unique to their age group. In other words, children and adults of different ages are not likely to have shared similar cultural backgrounds. People who are 80 years old today, for example, grew up without TV. Today's children are growing up taking iPods and the Internet for granted.

Children of past generations also grew up with different expectations about gender roles and appropriate social behaviour.

In longitudinal studies, we know that we have the same individuals as they have developed over 5, 25, even 50 years or more. In cross-sectional research, we can only hope that they will be comparable.

Cross-Sequential Research

Cross-sequential research combines the longitudinal and cross-sectional methods so that many of their individual drawbacks are overcome. In the cross-sequential

longitudinal research the study of developmental processes by taking repeated measures of the same group of participants at various stages of development.

cross-sectional research the study of developmental processes by taking measures of participants of different age groups at the same time.

cohort effect similarities in behaviour among a group of peers that stem from the fact that group members are approximately of the same age.

cross-sequential research an approach that combines the longitudinal and cross-sectional methods by following individuals of different ages for abbreviated periods of time.

© Polina Lobanova/Shutterstock

time lag the study of developmental processes by taking measures of participants of the same age group at different times.

study, the full span of the ideal longitudinal study is broken up into convenient segments (see Figure 1.6). Assume that we wish to follow the attitudes of children toward gender roles from the age of 4 through the age of 12. The typical longitudinal study would take 8 years. We can, however, divide this 8-year span in half by attaining two samples of children (a cross-section) instead of one: 4-year-olds and 8-year-olds. We would then interview, test, and observe each group at the beginning of the study (2010) and 4 years later (2014).

An obvious advantage to this collapsed method is that the study is completed in 4 years rather than 8 years. Still, the testing and retesting of samples provides some of the continuity of the longitudinal study. By observing both samples at the age of 8 (a **time-lag** comparison), we can also determine whether they are, in fact, comparable or whether the 4-year difference in their birth date is associated with a cohort effect.

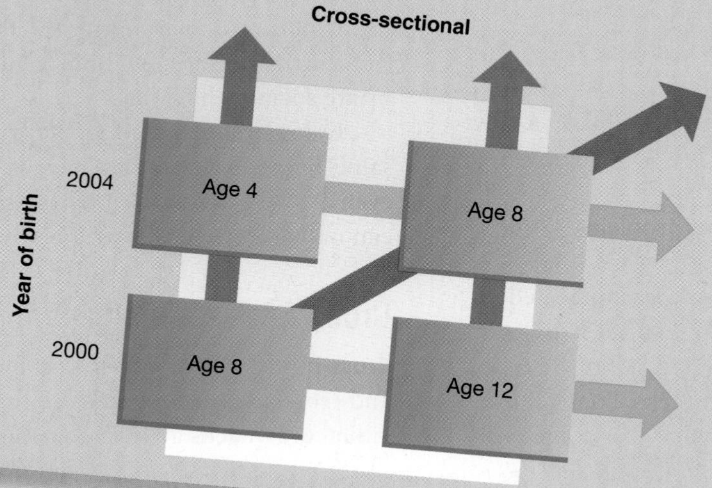

ETHICAL CONSIDERATIONS

The Canadian Psychological Association (2000) has designed an extensive 32-page Code of Ethics for psychologists conducting research in Canada. This document often makes the completion of research more difficult but ultimately safeguards the welfare of Canadians.

Some of the governing principles of the document include the following:

1. Respect for the Individual, including standards such as informed consent, confidentiality, and protection for vulnerable persons (including children, seniors and those with intellectual disabilities);

2. Responsible Care, such as risk/benefit analysis and minimizing harm;

3. Integrity in Relationships, including honesty, lack of bias, and complete disclosure;

4. Responsibility to Society, including the pursuit of beneficial research for the development of society.

This strict and detailed code of ethics reflects the responsibility and integrity that must govern all psychological research conducted in Canada. The code promotes the dignity of the individual, fosters human welfare, and maintains scientific integrity.

FIGURE 1.6
Example of Cross-Sequential Research

Cross-sequential research combines three methods: cross-sectional, longitudinal, and time lag. The child's age at the time of testing appears in the boxes. Vertical columns represent cross-sectional comparisons. Horizontal rows represent longitudinal comparisons. Diagonals represent time-lag comparisons.

Cross-sectional

Year of birth		
2004	Age 4	Age 8
2000	Age 8	Age 12

71% The percentage of students who go online to study for a class.

LOG IN!

HDEV was designed for students just like you—busy people who want choices, flexibility, and multiple learning options.

HDEV delivers concise, electronic resources such as discipline-specific activities, flashcards, test yourself questions, and more!

At **www.icanhdev.com**, you'll find electronic resources such as **printable interactive flashcards, downloadable study aids, games, quizzes, and interactive practice** to test your knowledge of key concepts. These resources will help supplement your understanding of core **lifespan development** concepts in a format that fits your busy lifestyle.

"I really like how you use students' opinions on how to study and made a website that encompasses everything we find useful. Seeing this website makes me excited to study!"

—Abby Boston, Fanshawe College

Visit **www.icanhdev.com** to find the resources you need today!

The structures

we inherit make our behaviour possible and place limits on it.

2

Heredity and Prenatal Development

LO1 The Influence of Heredity on Development

heredity makes possible all things human. The structures we inherit make our behaviour possible and place limits on it. The field of biology that studies heredity is called **genetics**.

Genetic influences are fundamental in the transmission of physical traits, such as height, hair texture, and eye colour. Genetics also appears to play a role in psychological traits such as intelligence, activity level, sociability, shyness, anxiety, empathy, effectiveness as a parent, happiness, and even interest in arts and crafts (Johnson & Krueger, 2006; Knafo & Plomin, 2006; Leonardo & Hen, 2006). Genetic factors are also involved in psychological problems such as schizophrenia, depression, and dependence on nicotine, alcohol, and other substances (Farmer et al., 2007; Hill et al., 2007; Metzger et al., 2007).

CHROMOSOMES AND GENES

Traits are transmitted by chromosomes and genes. **Chromosomes** are rod-shaped structures found in cells. Typical human cells contain 46 chromosomes organized into

genetics the branch of biology that studies heredity.

chromosomes rod-shaped structures composed of genes that are found within the nuclei of cells.

Learning Outcomes

LO1 Describe the influences of heredity on development

LO2 Describe the influences of the environment on development

LO3 Explain what happens in the process of conception

LO4 Recount the major events of prenatal development

gene the basic unit of heredity. Genes are composed of deoxyribonucleic acid (DNA).

polygenic resulting from many (poly) genes.

deoxyribonucleic acid (DNA) genetic material that takes the form of a double helix composed of phosphates, sugars, and bases.

mitosis the form of cell division in which each chromosome splits lengthwise to double in number. Half of each chromosome combines with chemicals to retake its original form and then moves to the new cell.

mutation a sudden, or accidental, variation in a heritable characteristic that affects the composition of genes.

meiosis the form of cell division in which each pair of chromosomes splits so that one member of each pair moves to the new cell. As a result, each new cell has 23 chromosomes.

23 pairs. Each chromosome contains thousands of segments called genes. **Genes** are the biochemical materials that regulate the development of traits. Some traits, such as blood type, appear to be transmitted by a single pair of genes, one of which is derived from each parent. Other traits are **polygenic**, that is, determined by many (poly) pairs of genes.

Our heredity is governed by 20,000 to 25,000 genes (International Human Genome Sequencing Consortium, 2006). Genes are segments of strands of **deoxyribonucleic acid (DNA)**. DNA takes the form of a double spiral, or helix, similar to a twisting ladder (see Figure 2.1). The "rungs" of the ladder consist of one of two pairs of bases, either adenine with thymine (A with T) or cytosine with guanine (C with G). The sequence of the rungs is the genetic code that will cause the developing organism to grow arms or wings, skin or scales.

MITOSIS AND MEIOSIS

We begin life as a single cell, or zygote, that divides repeatedly. There are two types of cell division: *mitosis* and *meiosis*. In **mitosis**, strands of DNA break apart, or "unzip" (see Figure 2.2). The double helix then duplicates. The DNA forms two camps on either side of the cell, and then the cell divides. Each incomplete rung combines with the appropriate "partner" (i.e., G and C, A and T) to form a new complete ladder. The two resulting identical copies of the DNA strand separate when the cell divides; each becomes a member of a newly formed cell. As a result, the genetic code is identical in new cells unless **mutations** occur through radiation or other environmental influences. Mutations also occur by chance, but not often.

Sperm and ova ("egg cells") are produced through **meiosis**, or *reduction division*. In meiosis, the 46 chromosomes within the cell nucleus first line up into 23 pairs. The DNA ladders then unzip, leaving unpaired halves of chromosomes. When the cell divides, one member

FIGURE 2.1
The Double Helix of DNA

DNA takes the form of a double spiral, or helix.

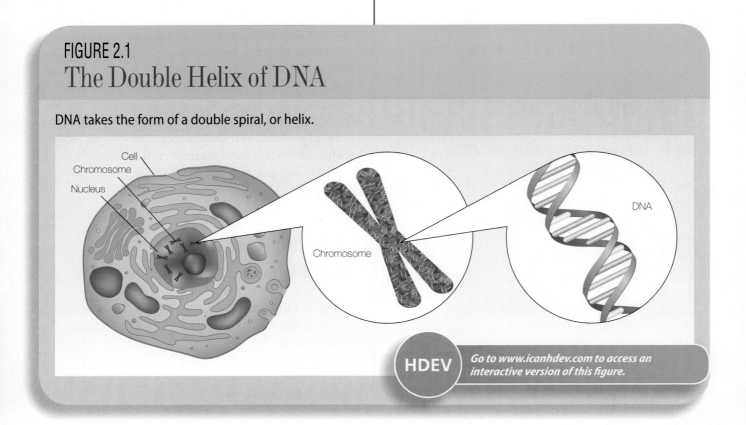

Cell
Chromosome
Nucleus
Chromosome
DNA

HDEV *Go to www.icanhdev.com to access an interactive version of this figure.*

FIGURE 2.2
Mitosis

(a) A segment of a strand of DNA before mitosis. (b) During mitosis, chromosomal strands of DNA "unzip." (c) The double helix is rebuilt in the cell as each incomplete "rung" combines with appropriate molecules.

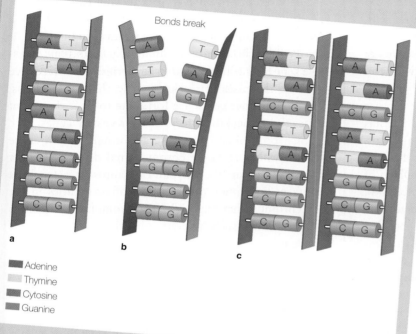

Bonds break

a   b   c

- Adenine
- Thymine
- Cytosine
- Guanine

autosome a pair of chromosomes (with the exception of sex chromosomes).

sex chromosome a chromosome in the shape of a Y (male) or X (female) that determines the sex of the child.

monozygotic (MZ) twins twins that derive from a single zygote that has split into two; identical twins. Each MZ twin carries the same genetic code.

of each pair goes to each newly formed cell. Each new cell nucleus contains only 23 chromosomes, not 46.

When a sperm cell fertilizes an ovum, we receive 23 chromosomes from our father's sperm cell and 23 from our mother's ovum, and the combined chromosomes form 23 pairs (see Figure 2.3). Twenty-two of the pairs are **autosomes**—pairs that look alike and possess genetic information concerning the same set of traits. The 23rd pair are **sex chromosomes**, which look different from other chromosomes and determine our sex. We all receive an X sex chromosome (so called because of its X shape) from our mothers. The father supplies either a Y or an X sex chromosome. If we receive another X sex chromosome from our fathers, we develop into females, and if a Y (named after its Y shape), males.

D1 Your father determined whether you are female or male.
Males supply either an X or Y chromosome, which determines the sex of the baby. Imagine how shocked King Henry VIII would be if he were a student in this class. Many women were isolated in medieval times for "their" inability to produce a male heir.

IDENTICAL AND FRATERNAL TWINS

Now and then, a zygote divides into two cells that separate so that each develops into an individual with the same genetic makeup. These individuals are identical twins, or **monozygotic (MZ) twins**. In very rare cases, the eggs do not completely

FIGURE 2.3
The 23 Pairs of Human Chromosomes

People normally have 23 pairs of chromosomes. Females have two X chromosomes, whereas males have an X and a Y sex chromosome.

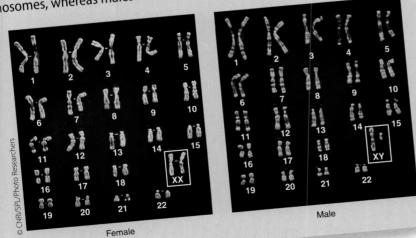

Female

Male

dizygotic (DZ) twins twins that derive from two separate zygotes; fraternal twins with different genetic codes.

ovulation the releasing of an ovum from an ovary.

allele a member of a pair of genes.

homozygous having two identical alleles.

heterozygous having two different alleles.

dominant trait a trait that is expressed.

recessive trait a trait that is not expressed when the gene or genes involved have been paired with dominant genes.

carrier a person who carries and transmits characteristics but does not exhibit them.

separate on the 13th day after conception, and conjoined twins are the result, as was the case for Tatiana and Krista, born in British Columbia in March 2007. If a woman produces two ova in the same month, which are each fertilized by different sperm cells, they develop into fraternal twins, or **dizygotic (DZ) twins**. DZ twins run in families. If a woman is a twin, if her mother was a twin, or if she has previously borne twins, the chances rise that she will bear twins (Office of National Statistics, 2006).

As women reach the end of their childbearing years, **ovulation** becomes less regular, resulting in a number of months when more than one ovum is released. Thus, the chances of twins increase with parental age (National Guideline Clearinghouse, 2007). Adding to this likelihood is the social reality in Canada that women are postponing parenting later than their mothers and grandmothers. Of the mothers who gave birth in 2005, 48.9 percent were 30 years of age or older, more than double the percentage in 1974 (Human Resources and Development Canada, 2010a). Fertility drugs also enhance the chances of multiple births by causing more than one ovum to ripen and be released during a woman's cycle (National Guideline Clearinghouse, 2007).

DOMINANT AND RECESSIVE TRAITS

Traits are determined by pairs of genes. Each member of a pair of genes is termed an **allele**. When both of the alleles for a trait, such as hair colour, are the same, the person is said to be **homozygous** for that trait. When the alleles for a trait differ, the person is **heterozygous** for that trait. Some traits result from an "averaging" of the genetic instructions carried by the parents. When the effects of both alleles are shown, the trait is said to have incomplete dominance or codominance. When a *dominant* allele is paired with a *recessive* allele, the trait determined by the dominant allele appears in the offspring. For example, the offspring from the crossing of brown eyes with blue eyes have brown eyes, suggesting that brown eyes are a **dominant trait** and blue eyes are a **recessive trait**.

If one parent carried genes for only brown eyes and if the other parent carried genes for only blue eyes, the children would invariably have brown eyes. But brown-eyed parents can also carry recessive genes for blue eyes, as shown in Figure 2.4. If the recessive gene from one parent combines with the recessive gene from the other parent, the recessive trait will be shown. As suggested by Figure 2.4, approximately 25 percent of the children of brown-eyed parents who carry recessive blue eye colour will have blue eyes. Table 2.1 shows a number of dominant and recessive traits in humans.

People who bear one dominant gene and one recessive gene for a trait are said to be **carriers** of the recessive gene. In the cases of recessive genes that cause illness, carriers of those genes are fortunate to have dominant genes that cancel the effects of the recessive genes.

Chromosomal or genetic abnormalities can cause health problems. Some chromosomal disorders reflect abnormalities in the 22 pairs of autosomes (such as Down's syndrome); others reflect abnormalities in the sex chromosomes (e.g., XYY syndrome). Some genetic abnormalities, such as cystic fibrosis, are caused by a single pair of genes; others are caused by combinations of genes. Diabetes mellitus, epilepsy, and peptic ulcers

FIGURE 2.4
Transmission of Dominant and Recessive Traits

These two brown-eyed parents each carry a gene for blue eyes. Their children have an equal opportunity of receiving genes for brown eyes and blue eyes.

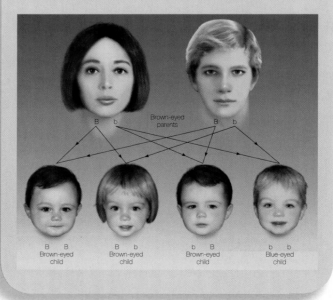

TABLE 2.1
Examples of Dominant and Recessive Traits

DOMINANT TRAIT	RECESSIVE TRAIT
Dark hair	Blond hair
Dark hair	Red hair
Curly hair	Straight hair
Normal colour vision	Red-green colour blindness
Normal vision	Myopia (nearsightedness)
Farsightedness	Normal vision
Normal pigmentation	Deficiency of pigmentation in skin, hair, and retina (albinism)
Normal sensitivity to touch	Extremely fragile skin
Normal hearing	Some forms of deafness
Dimples	Lack of dimpling
Type A blood	Type O blood
Type B blood	Type O blood
Tolerance of lactose	Lactose intolerance

multifactorial problems problems that stem from the interaction of heredity and environmental factors.

Down's syndrome a chromosomal abnormality characterized by mental retardation and caused by an extra chromosome in the 21st pair.

sex-linked chromosomal abnormalities abnormalities that are transmitted from generation to generation and carried by a sex chromosome.

(Virji-Babul et al., 2006) and usually die from cardiovascular problems by middle age, although modern medicine has extended life appreciably.

Sex-Linked Chromosomal Abnormalities

Numerous disorders stem from an abnormal number of sex chromosomes and are therefore called **sex-linked chromosomal abnormalities**. Most individuals with an abnormal

are **multifactorial problems**; they reflect both a genetic predisposition and environmental contributors.

CHROMOSOMAL ABNORMALITIES

People normally have 46 chromosomes. Children with more or fewer chromosomes usually experience health problems or behavioural abnormalities. The risk of chromosomal abnormalities rises with the age of the parents (American Fertility Association, 2007).

Down's Syndrome

Down's syndrome is usually caused by an extra chromosome on the 21st pair, resulting in 47 chromosomes. The probability of having a child with Down's syndrome increases with the age of the parents. People with Down's syndrome have characteristic features that include a rounded face; a protruding tongue; a broad, flat nose; and a sloping fold of skin over the inner corners of the eyes (see Figure 2.5). They show deficits in cognitive development (Rondal & Ling, 2006) and motor development

FIGURE 2.5
Down's Syndrome

Development and adjustment of individuals with Down's syndrome are greatly enhanced through family and community encouragement.

© Mika/zefa/CORBIS

number of sex chromosomes are infertile. Beyond that common finding, these individuals experience many differences, some of them associated with "maleness" or "femaleness" (Wodrich, 2006).

Approximately 1 male in 700 to 1,000 has an extra Y chromosome. The Y chromosome is associated with "maleness," and the extra Y sex chromosome apparently heightens male secondary sex characteristics. For example, XYY males tend to be taller than average and develop heavier beards. For these reasons, males with XYY sex chromosomal structure were once called "supermales." However, XYY "supermales" tend to have more problems than XY males. For example, they are often mildly delayed in language development.

Approximately 1 male in 500 has **Klinefelter syndrome,** which is caused by an extra X sex chromosome (an XXY sex chromosomal pattern). XXY males produce less of the male sex hormone **testosterone** than normal males. As a result, male primary and secondary sex characteristics—such as the testes, deepening of the voice, musculature, and the male pattern of body hair—do not develop properly. XXY males usually have enlarged breasts (gynecomastia) and are usually mildly mentally retarded, particularly in language skills (van Rijn et al., 2006). XXY males are typically treated with testosterone replacement therapy, which can foster growth of sex characteristics and elevate the mood, but they remain infertile.

Approximately 1 girl in 2,500 has a single X sex chromosome and as a result develops **Turner syndrome.** The external genitals of such girls are normal, but their ovaries are poorly developed, and they produce little **estrogen.** Girls with this problem are shorter than average and infertile. Researchers have connected a specific pattern of cognitive deficits with low estrogen levels: problems

in visual–spatial skills, mathematics, and nonverbal memory (Hart et al., 2006).

Approximately 1 girl in 1,000 has an XXX sex chromosomal structure, *Triple X syndrome.* Such girls are normal in appearance but tend to show lower-than-average language skills and poorer memory for recent events. Development of external sexual organs appears normal enough, although these girls experience an increased incidence of infertility (Wodrich, 2006).

GENETIC ABNORMALITIES

A number of disorders have been attributed to genes.

Phenylketonuria

The enzyme disorder **phenylketonuria (PKU)** is transmitted by a recessive gene. The Canadian PKU and Allied Disorders (2010) estimates that 1 in 12,000 newborns in North America have PKU, approximately 300 newborns per year. Children with PKU cannot metabolize an amino acid called phenylalanine, which builds up in their bodies and impairs the functioning of the central nervous system, resulting in mental retardation, psychological disorders, and physical problems. There is no cure for PKU, but children in Canada are screened for PKU when they are born. Those testing positive can be placed on diets low in phenylalanine within three to six weeks of birth and develop normally (Brazier & Rowlands, 2006).

Huntington Disease

Huntington disease (HD) is a fatal, progressive degenerative disorder and a dominant trait. According to the Huntington Society of Canada (n.d.), one in every

genetic abnormalities

Phenylketonuria
Huntington Disease
Sickle-Cell Anemia
Tay-Sachs Disease
Cystic Fibrosis
Hemophilia
Muscular Dystrophy

© Uyen Le/iStockphoto

10,000 Canadians has HD, but one in every 1,000 is touched by HD, whether by being at risk, or by being a caregiver, family member, or friend. Physical symptoms include uncontrollable muscle movements (Jacobs et al., 2006). Psychological symptoms include loss of intellectual functioning and personality change (Robins Wahlin et al., 2007). Because the onset of HD is delayed until middle adulthood, many individuals with the defect have borne children only to discover years later that they and possibly half their offspring will inevitably develop it. Medicines can help deal with some symptoms.

Sickle-Cell Anemia

Sickle-cell anemia is caused by a recessive gene. Sickle-cell anemia is most common among African North Americans. In Canada, many refer to sickle-cell anemia as the "neglected disease" because Health Canada does not keep statistics on the disease (CBC News, 2003). Nearly 1 African North American in 10 is a carrier. In sickle-cell anemia, red blood cells take on the shape of a sickle and clump together, obstructing small blood vessels and decreasing the oxygen supply. The reduced oxygen supply can impair cognitive skills and academic performance (Hogan et al., 2005; Ogunfowora et al., 2005). Episodes of acute pain are also common, as are complications such as blindness and failure of the heart, kidney, and liver, which can be fatal.

Tay-Sachs Disease

Tay-Sachs disease is also caused by a recessive gene. It causes the central nervous system to degenerate, resulting in death. The disorder is commonly found among children in Jewish families of Eastern European background, where 1 person in 30 carries the recessive gene. A disproportionate rate of Tay-Sachs disease has also been found in French-Canadian communities, leading doctors to recommend Tay-Sachs testing for French Canadians who either have a family history of the disease or live in a population with a high incidence of the disease (WebMD, 2010). Children with the disorder progressively lose control over their muscles, experience sensory losses, develop mental retardation, become paralyzed, and usually die by about the age of 5.

Cystic Fibrosis

Cystic fibrosis, also caused by a recessive gene, is the most common fatal hereditary disease among Canadian children and young adults, according to the Canadian Cystic Fibrosis Foundation (2010). Approximately 1 in every 3,500 children in Canada is born with this disease. Children with the disease suffer from excessive production of thick mucus that clogs the pancreas and lungs. Mucus and protein build up in the digestive tract, resulting in extreme difficulty digesting food and absorbing adequate nutrients. Most victims die of respiratory infections in their 20s. Lung transplantation can enable individuals with end-stage lung disease to regain their health, but Canada has a limited number of organ donors. The Canadian Cystic Fibrosis Foundation supports organ donor awareness and encourages Canadians to discuss organ donation with their loved ones.

> **sickle-cell anemia** a genetic disorder that decreases the blood's capacity to carry oxygen.
>
> **Tay-Sachs disease** a fatal genetic neurological disorder that causes degeneration and premature death.
>
> **cystic fibrosis** a fatal genetic disorder in which mucus obstructs the lungs and pancreas.
>
> **hemophilia** a genetic disorder in which blood does not clot properly.
>
> **sex-linked genetic abnormalities** abnormalities resulting from genes that are found on the X sex chromosome. They are more likely to be shown by male offspring (who do not have an opposing gene from a second X chromosome) than by female offspring.

Sex-Linked Genetic Abnormalities

Some genetic defects, such as **hemophilia**, are carried on only the X sex chromosome. For this reason, they are referred to as **sex-linked genetic abnormalities**. These

© Photo 12/The Image Works

Queen Victoria was a carrier of hemophilia and transmitted the blood disorder to many of her children, who in turn carried it into a number of the ruling houses of Europe. For this reason, hemophilia has been dubbed the "royal disease."

muscular dystrophy a chronic disease characterized by a progressive wasting away of the muscles.

prenatal before birth.

amniocentesis a procedure for drawing and examining fetal cells sloughed off into amniotic fluid to determine the presence of various disorders.

defects also involve recessive genes. Females, who have two X sex chromosomes, are less likely than males to show sex-linked disorders because the genes that cause the disorder would have to be present on both of a female's sex chromosomes for the disorder to be expressed. Sex-linked diseases are more likely to afflict sons of female carriers because males have only one X sex chromosome, which they inherit from their mothers.

One form of **muscular dystrophy**, Duchenne muscular dystrophy, is sex-linked. Muscular dystrophy is characterized by a weakening of the muscles, which can lead to wasting away, inability to walk, and sometimes death. Other sex-linked abnormalities include diabetes, colour blindness, and some types of night blindness. In Canada, 8 percent of the male Caucasian population and 1 percent of the female Caucasian population experience colour blindness. The occurrence of this sex-linked genetic abnormality is much less common among First Nations people and people of Asian and African descent (Body and Health Canada, 2010).

GENETIC COUNSELLING AND PRENATAL TESTING

It is possible to detect genetic abnormalities that are responsible for many diseases. Genetic counsellors compile information about a couple's genetic heritage to explore whether their children might develop genetic abnormalities. Couples who face a high risk of passing genetic defects to their children sometimes elect to adopt or to not have children rather than conceive their own. In addition, **prenatal** testing can indicate whether the embryo or fetus is carrying genetic abnormalities.

Amniocentesis

Amniocentesis is usually performed on the mother at 14–16 weeks after conception, although many physicians now perform the procedure earlier ("early amniocentesis"). In this method, the health professional uses a syringe (needle) to withdraw fluid from the amniotic sac (see Figure 2.6). The fluid contains cells that are sloughed off by the fetus. The cells are separated from the amniotic fluid, grown in a culture, and then examined microscopically for genetic and chromosomal abnormalities.

FIGURE 2.6
Amniocentesis

Amniocentesis allows prenatal identification of certain genetic and chromosomal disorders by examining genetic material sloughed off by the fetus into amniotic fluid.

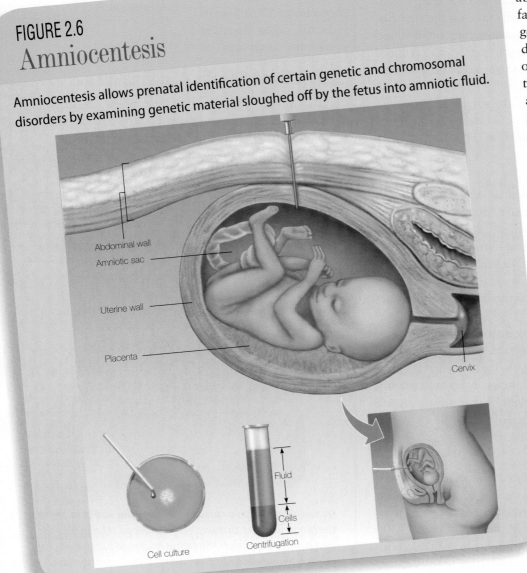

Abdominal wall
Amniotic sac
Uterine wall
Placenta
Cervix
Fluid
Cells
Cell culture
Centrifugation

Amniocentesis has become routine among Canadian women who become pregnant past the age of 35 because the chances of Down's syndrome and other chromosomal abnormalities increase dramatically as women approach or pass the age of 40. In Canada, the risk of fetal loss because of an amniocentesis procedure is one half of one percentage of all pregnancies (Wilson et al., 2007). Amniocentesis is not conducted simply to learn the sex of the child, which can be determined earlier through an ultrasound.

Chorionic Villus Sampling

Chorionic villus sampling (CVS) is similar to amniocentesis but is carried out between the 9th and 12th week of pregnancy. A small syringe is inserted through the vagina into the **uterus** and sucks out some threadlike projections (villi) from the outer membrane that envelops the amniotic sac and fetus. Results are available within days. CVS has not been used as frequently as amniocentesis because CVS carries a slightly greater risk of spontaneous abortion. More recent studies suggest that both amniocentesis and CVS increase the risk of miscarriage and that the risks might not be equal (Alfirevic et al., 2003; Philip et al., 2004).

Ultrasound

Health professionals also use sound waves that are too high in frequency to be heard by the human ear— ultrasound—to obtain information about the fetus. Ultrasound waves are reflected by the fetus, and a computer uses the information to generate a picture of the fetus. The picture is termed a **sonogram** (see Figure 2.7).

Ultrasound is used to guide the syringe in amniocentesis and CVS by determining the position of the fetus. Ultrasound is also used to locate fetal structures when intrauterine transfusions are necessary for the survival of a fetus with Rh disease. Ultrasound also is used to track the growth of the fetus, to determine fetal age and sex, and to detect multiple pregnancies and structural abnormalities.

chorionic villus sampling (CVS) a method for the prenatal detection of genetic abnormalities that samples the membrane enveloping the amniotic sac and fetus.

uterus the hollow organ within females in which the embryo and fetus develop.

ultrasound sound waves too high in pitch to be sensed by the human ear.

sonogram a procedure for using ultrasonic sound waves to create a picture of an embryo or fetus.

alpha-fetoprotein (AFP) assay a blood test that assesses the mother's blood level of alpha-fetoprotein, a substance that is linked with fetal neural tube defects.

genotype the genetic form or constitution of a person as determined by heredity.

Blood Tests

Parental blood tests can reveal the presence of genetic disorders such as sickle-cell anemia, Tay-Sachs disease, and cystic fibrosis. The **alpha-fetoprotein (AFP) assay** is used to detect neural tube defects such as spina bifida and certain chromosomal abnormalities. Neural tube defects cause an elevation in the AFP level in the mother's blood. Elevated AFP levels also are associated with increased risk of fetal death. Because the mother's blood is tested, the fetus is not at risk.

LO2 Heredity and the Environment

In addition to inheritance, the development of our traits is also influenced by nutrition, learning, exercise, and—unfortunately—accident and illness. A potential Shakespeare who is reared in poverty and never taught to read or write will not create a *Hamlet*. Our traits and behaviours represent the interaction of heredity and environment. The sets of traits that we inherit from our parents are referred to as our **genotypes**. The actual

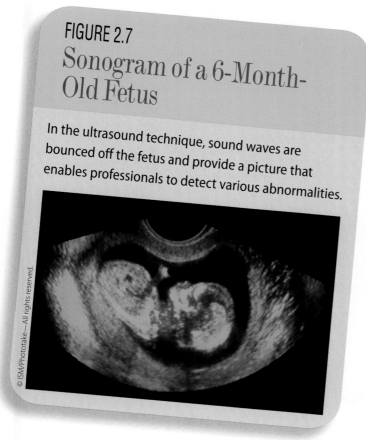

FIGURE 2.7
Sonogram of a 6-Month-Old Fetus

In the ultrasound technique, sound waves are bounced off the fetus and provide a picture that enables professionals to detect various abnormalities.

phenotype the actual form or constitution of a person as determined by heredity and environmental factors.

autism a developmental disorder characterized by failure to relate to others, communication problems, intolerance of change, and ritualistic behaviour.

conception the union of a sperm cell and an ovum that occurs when the chromosomes of each of these cells combine to form 23 new pairs.

sets of traits that we exhibit are called our **phenotypes**. Our phenotypes reflect both genetic and environmental influences.

Researchers have developed a number of strategies to help sort out the effects of heredity and the environment on development.

(Plomin, 2002). Heredity even affects their preference for coffee or tea (Luciano et al., 2005). MZ twins resemble one another more strongly than DZ twins in intelligence and personality traits (Hur, 2005; Johnson et al., 2004; McCrae et al., 2000). MZ twins are also more likely to share psychological disorders such as **autism**, depression, schizophrenia, and vulnerability to alcoholism (Belmonte & Carper, 2006; Plomin, 2002; Ronald et al., 2006).

But one might ask whether MZ twins resemble each other so closely partly because they are often treated so similarly? One way to answer this question is to find and compare MZ twins who were reared apart. Except for the uterine environment, similarities between MZ twins reared apart would appear to be a result of heredity. In the Minnesota Study of Twins Reared Apart (T. J. Bouchard et al., 1990; DiLalla et al., 1999; Lykken, 2006), researchers have been measuring the physiological and psychological characteristics of 56 sets of MZ adult twins who were separated in infancy and reared in different homes. The MZ twins reared apart are about as similar as MZ twins reared together on measures of intelligence, personality, temperament, occupational and leisure-time interests, and social attitudes. These traits would thus appear to have a genetic underpinning.

> A potential Shakespeare who is reared in poverty and never taught to read or write will not create a *Hamlet*.

KINSHIP STUDIES

Researchers study the distribution of a trait or behaviour among relatives who differ in degree of genetic closeness. The more closely people are related, the more genes they have in common. Parents and children have a 50 percent overlap in their genetic endowments, and so do siblings (brothers and sisters). Aunts and uncles have a 25 percent overlap with nieces and nephews, as do grandparents with grandchildren. First cousins share 12.5 percent of their genetic endowment. If genes are implicated in a trait, people who are more closely related are more likely to share it.

TWIN STUDIES: LOOKING IN THE GENETIC MIRROR

Monozygotic (MZ) twins share 100 percent of their genes, whereas dizygotic (DZ) twins have a 50 percent overlap, just as other siblings do. If MZ twins show greater similarity on some trait or behaviour than DZ twins do, a genetic basis for the trait or behaviour is indicated.

MZ twins resemble each other more closely than DZ twins on a number of physical and psychological traits, even when the MZ twins are reared apart and the DZ twins are reared together (Bouchard & Loehlin, 2001). MZ twins are more likely to look alike and to be similar in height

ADOPTION STUDIES

Adoption studies in which children are separated from their natural parents at an early age and reared by adoptive parents provide special opportunities for sorting out nature and nurture. When children who are reared by adoptive parents are nonetheless more similar to their natural parents in a trait, a powerful argument is made for a genetic role in the appearance of that trait.

Traits are determined by pairs of genes. One member of each pair comes from each parent in the process called conception.

LO3 Conception: Against All Odds

Conception is the union of an ovum and a sperm cell. Conception, from one perspective, is the beginning of a new human life. From another perspective, though, conception is also the end of a fantastic voyage in

which one of several hundred thousand ova produced by the woman unites with one of hundreds of million sperm produced by the man in the average ejaculate.

OVA

At birth, women already have all the ova they will ever have: some 400,000. The ova, however, are immature in form. The ovaries also produce the female hormones estrogen and progesterone. At puberty, in response to hormonal command, some ova begin to mature. Each month, an egg (occasionally more than one) is released from its ovarian follicle about midway through the menstrual cycle and enters a nearby fallopian tube. It might take 3 to 4 days for an egg to be propelled by small, hairlike structures called cilia and, perhaps, by contractions in the wall of the tube (perhaps resulting in cramping), along the several centimetres (a few inches) of the fallopian tube to the uterus. Unlike sperm, eggs do not propel themselves.

If the egg is not fertilized, it is discharged through the uterus and the vagina along with the **endometrium**

that had formed to support an embryo, in the menstrual flow. During a woman's reproductive years, about 400 ova (that is, 1 in 1,000) will ripen and be released.

Ova are much larger than sperm but also are a single cell. The chicken egg and the 15-cm (6-in.) ostrich egg are each just one cell as well, although the sperm of these birds are microscopic. Human ova are barely visible to the eye, but their bulk is still thousands of times larger than that of sperm cells.

SPERM CELLS

Sperm cells develop through several stages. They each begin with 46 chromosomes, but after meiosis, each sperm has 23 chromosomes, half with X sex chromosomes and half with Y. Each sperm cell is about 1/200 cm (1/500 in.) long, one of the smallest types of cells in the body. Sperm with Y sex chromosomes appear to swim faster than sperm with X sex chromosomes. This difference contributes to the conception of 120 to 150 boys for every 100 girls. Male fetuses suffer a higher rate of **spontaneous abortion** than females, however, often during the first month of pregnancy and likely before the mother is aware that she is pregnant. At birth, boys outnumber girls by a ratio of only 106 to 100. Boys also have a higher incidence of infant mortality, which further equalizes the numbers of girls and boys.

The 150 million or so sperm in the ejaculate may seem to be a wasteful investment because only one sperm can fertilize an ovum, but only 1 in 1,000 sperm will ever approach an ovum. Millions of sperm deposited in the vagina flow out of the woman's body because of gravity. Normal vaginal acidity kills many more sperm. Many surviving sperm then have to swim against the current of fluid coming from the cervix (see Figure 2.8 on the next page).

Sperm that survive these initial obstacles may reach the fallopian tubes 60 to 90 minutes after ejaculation. About half the sperm enter the tube without the egg. Perhaps 2,000 enter the correct tube. Fewer still manage to swim the final 5 cm (2 in.) against the currents generated by the cilia that line the tube. It is *not* true that sperm travel about at random inside the woman's reproductive tract. Sperm cells are apparently "egged on" (pardon the pun) by a change in calcium ions that occurs when an ovum is released (Angier, 2007). You are one sperm cell of approximately 50 million per ejaculation (Kennard, 2010). You should feel very special. You won the race.

FIGURE 2.8
Female Reproductive Organs

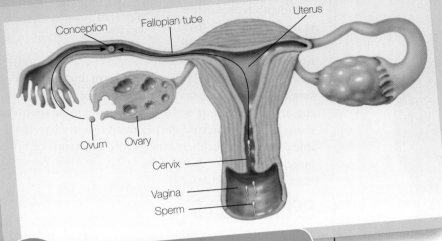

Conception

Fallopian tube

Uterus

Ovum

Ovary

Cervix

Vagina

Sperm

HDEV Go to www.icanhdev.com to access an interactive version of this figure.

> **D2** Approximately 120 to 150 boys are conceived for every 100 girls.
> Sperm with Y chromosomes swim faster, resulting in the conception of more boys than girls.

Of all the sperm swarming around the egg, only one enters (see Figure 2.9). Ova are surrounded by a gelatinous layer that must be penetrated if fertilization is to occur. Many of the sperm that have completed their journey to the ovum secrete an enzyme that briefly thins the layer, but it enables only one sperm to penetrate. Once a sperm cell has entered, the layer thickens, locking other sperm out.

The chromosomes from the sperm cell line up across from the corresponding chromosomes in the egg cell. They form 23 new pairs with a unique set of genetic instructions.

> **D3** Sperm do *not* travel about at random inside the woman's reproductive tract.
> The direction that sperm travel is guided by a change in calcium ions that occurs when an ovum is released.

INFERTILITY AND OTHER WAYS OF BECOMING PARENTS

Approximately one in six Canadian couples will have difficulties conceiving a child. Beverly Hanck, the executive director of the Infertility Awareness Association of Canada, recommends that couples begin planning their families in their 20s because a woman's reproduction begins to decline in her mid- to late 20s (The Health Journal, 2010). The social reality in Canada, however, is that the mean age of women giving birth rose from 27 in 1980 to 29.2 in 2005 (Human Resources and Skills Development Canada, 2010). Canadian women are waiting longer to begin families, and this decision could collide with human biology. Infertility was once viewed as a problem of the woman, but it turns out that the problem lies with the man in about 40 percent of cases.

FIGURE 2.9
Human Sperm Swarming Around an Ovum in a Fallopian Tube

Fertilization normally occurs in a fallopian tube. Thousands of sperm may wind up in the vicinity of an ovum, but only one fertilizes it.

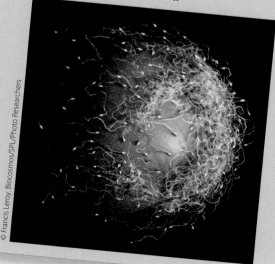

© Francis Leroy, Biocosmos/SPL/Photo Researchers

Causes of Infertility

A low sperm count—or lack of sperm—is the most common infertility problem in men. Men's fertility problems have a variety of causes: genetic factors, environmental poisons, diabetes, sexually transmitted infections (STIs), overheating of the testes (which is sometimes experienced by athletes, such as long-distance runners), pressure (as from using narrow bicycle seats), aging, and certain prescription and illicit drugs (Hatcher et al., 2007). Sometimes the sperm count is adequate, but other factors such as prostate or hormonal problems deform sperm or deprive them of their **motility**. Motility can also be impaired by the scar tissue from infections, such as STIs.

The most common problem in women is irregular ovulation or lack of ovulation. This problem can have many causes, including irregularities among the hormones that govern ovulation, stress, and malnutrition. So-called fertility drugs (e.g., *clomiphene* and *pergonal*) are made up of hormones that cause women to ovulate. These drugs may cause multiple births by stimulating more than one ovum to ripen during a month (Legro et al., 2007).

Infections may scar the fallopian tubes and other organs, impeding the passage of sperm or ova. Such infections include **pelvic inflammatory disease (PID)**. PID can result from bacterial or viral infections, including the STIs gonorrhea and chlamydia. Health Canada is particularly concerned that women aged 15 to 19 have chlamydia infections at a rate nine times the national average, which could significantly affect these women when, later in life, they wish to start families (Bissell & McKay, 2005). Antibiotics are usually helpful in treating bacterial infections, but infertility may be irreversible.

> Women aged 15 to 19 have chlamydia infections (which can result in infertility if left untreated) at a rate nine times the national average.

Endometriosis can obstruct the fallopian tubes, where conception normally takes place. Endometriosis has become fairly common among women who delay childbearing. Each month, tissue develops to line the uterus in case the woman conceives. This tissue—the endometrium—is then sloughed off during menstruation. But for women who have endometriosis, some of this tissue backs up into the abdomen through the fallopian tubes. It then collects in the abdomen, where it can cause abdominal pain and reduce the chances of conception. Physicians may treat endometriosis with hormones that temporarily prevent menstruation or through surgery.

Let us consider methods used to help infertile couples bear children.

Artificial Insemination

Men with low sperm counts can collect multiple ejaculations, which are then quick-frozen. The sperm can then be injected into the woman's uterus at the time of ovulation. This method is one **artificial insemination** procedure. Sperm from men with low sperm motility can also be injected into their partners' uteruses so that the sperm can begin their journey closer to the fallopian tubes. When a man has no sperm or an extremely low sperm count, his partner can be artificially inseminated with the sperm of a donor who may or may not resemble the man in physical traits. Some women who want a baby but do not have a partner also use artificial insemination.

In Vitro Fertilization

So called "test-tube babies" are not actually grown in a test tube but are conceived through **in vitro fertilization (IVF)**, a method of conception in which ripened ova are removed surgically from the mother and placed in a laboratory dish. The father's sperm are also placed in the dish. One or more ova are fertilized and then injected into the mother's uterus to become implanted.

motility self-propulsion.

pelvic inflammatory disease (PID) an infection of the abdominal region that may have various causes and that may impair fertility.

endometriosis inflammation of endometrial tissue sloughed off into the abdominal cavity rather than out of the body during menstruation; the condition is characterized by abdominal pain and sometimes infertility.

artificial insemination injection of sperm into the uterus to fertilize an ovum.

in vitro fertilization (IVF) fertilization of an ovum in a laboratory dish.

Dawid Zagorski/Shutterstock

donor IVF the transfer of a donor's ovum, fertilized in a laboratory dish, to the uterus of another woman.

germinal stage the period of development between conception and the implantation of the embryo.

blastocyst a stage within the germinal period of prenatal development in which the zygote has the form of a sphere of cells surrounding a cavity of fluid.

IVF may be used when the fallopian tubes are blocked, because the ova need not travel through them. If the father's sperm are low in motility, they are sometimes injected directly into the ovum. A variation known as **donor IVF** can be used when the intended mother does not produce ova. An ovum from another woman is fertilized and injected into the uterus of the mother-to-be.

Because only a minority of attempts lead to births, it can take several attempts to achieve a pregnancy. Several embryos may be injected into the uterus at once, heightening the odds. IVF remains costly, which excludes many Canadians from exploring this option. In 2010, Quebec became the first jurisdiction in North America to offer subsidized IVF treatments (CBC News, 2010). IVF is a routine procedure but has a significant failure rate and its success is not guaranteed.

Surrogate Mothers

Surrogate mothers bring babies to term for women who are infertile. Surrogate mothers may be artificially inseminated by the partners of infertile women, in which case the baby carries the genes of the father. But sometimes—as with 60-year-old singer-songwriter James Taylor and his 54-year-old wife—ova are surgically extracted from the biological mother, fertilized in vitro by the biological father, and then implanted in another woman's uterus, where the baby is brought to term.

Adoption

Adoption is another way for people to obtain children. Despite occasional conflicts that pit adoptive parents against biological parents who change their minds about giving up their children, most adoptions result in the formation of loving new families. Many Canadians find it easier, or more desirable, to adopt infants from other countries or with special needs.

Selecting the Sex of Your Child

Today, a reliable method is available for selecting the sex of a child prior to implantation: preimplantation genetic diagnosis (PGD). PGD was developed to detect genetic disorders, but it also reveals the sex of the embryo. In PGD, ova are fertilized in vitro. After a few days of cell division, a cell is extracted from each, and its sex chromosomal structure is examined microscopically to learn of its sex. Embryos of the desired sex are implanted in the woman's uterus, where one or more can grow to term. However, successful implantation cannot be guaranteed. In 2004, sex selection was made illegal in Canada, though it is available in other countries. This issue raises interesting ethical concerns, such as those raised at the end of this chapter.

LO4 Prenatal Development

the most rapid and dramatic human developments are literally "out of sight" and take place in the uterus. Within 9 months, a fetus develops from a nearly microscopic cell to a neonate about 50 cm (20 in.) long. Its weight increases a billionfold.

We can date pregnancy from the onset of the last menstrual period before conception, which makes the normal gestation period 280 days. We can also date pregnancy from the assumed date of fertilization, which normally occurs 2 weeks after the beginning of the woman's last menstrual cycle. With this accounting method, the gestation period is 266 days.

Prenatal development is divided into three periods: the germinal stage (approximately the first 2 weeks), the embryonic stage (the third through the eighth weeks), and the fetal stage (the third month until birth).

THE GERMINAL STAGE: WANDERINGS

Within 36 hours after conception, the zygote divides into two cells. It then divides repeatedly as it undergoes its 3- to 4-day journey to the uterus. Within another 36 hours, it has become approximately 32 cells. The mass of dividing cells wanders about the uterus for another 3 to 4 days before it begins to implant in the uterine wall. Implantation takes another week or so. The period from conception to implantation is called the **germinal stage** (see Figure 2.10).

A few days into the germinal stage, the dividing cell mass takes the form of a fluid-filled ball of cells called a **blastocyst**. In the blastocyst, cells begin to separate into groups that will eventually become different structures. The inner part of the blastocyst has two distinct layers that form

FIGURE 2.10
The Ovarian Cycle, Conception, and the Early Days of the Germinal Stage

Division of the zygote creates the hollow sphere of cells termed the blastocyst, which becomes implanted in the uterine wall.

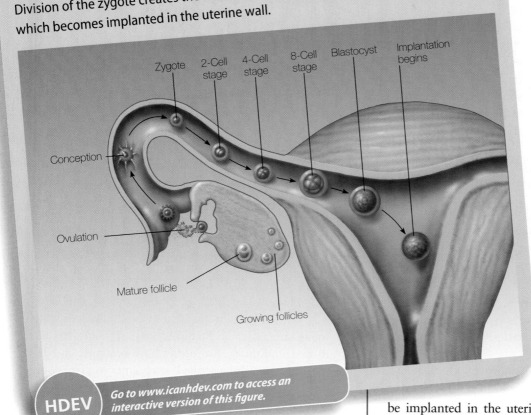

Zygote 2-Cell stage 4-Cell stage 8-Cell stage Blastocyst Implantation begins

Conception

Ovulation

Mature follicle

Growing follicles

HDEV *Go to www.icanhdev.com to access an interactive version of this figure.*

embryonic disk the platelike inner part of the blastocyst that differentiates into the ectoderm, mesoderm, and endoderm of the embryo.

trophoblast the outer part of the blastocyst from which the amniotic sac, placenta, and umbilical cord develop.

umbilical cord a tube that connects the fetus to the placenta.

placenta an organ connected to the uterine wall and to the fetus by the umbilical cord. The placenta serves as a relay station between mother and fetus for the exchange of nutrients and wastes.

embryonic stage the stage of prenatal development that lasts from implantation through the eighth week of pregnancy; it is characterized by the development of the major organ systems.

cephalocaudal from head to tail.

proximodistal from the inner part (or axis) of the body outward.

a thickened mass of cells called the **embryonic disk**. These cells will become the embryo and eventually the fetus.

The outer part of the blastocyst, or **trophoblast**, at first consists of a single layer of cells, but it rapidly differentiates into four membranes that will protect and nourish the embryo. One membrane produces blood cells until the embryo's liver develops and takes over this function. Then it disappears. Another membrane develops into the **umbilical cord** and the blood vessels of the **placenta**. A third develops into the amniotic sac, and the fourth becomes the chorion, which will line the placenta.

The cluster of cells that will become the embryo and then the fetus is at first nourished only by the yolk of the egg cell. A blastocyst gains mass only when it receives nourishment from outside. For that to happen, it must

D4 Newly fertilized egg cells survive without any nourishment from the mother for more than a week.
And because of that, they make no gains in mass.

be implanted in the uterine wall. Implantation may be accompanied by bleeding, which is usually normal, but bleeding can also be a sign of miscarriage. Most women who experience implantation bleeding, however, do not miscarry, but have normal pregnancies. Miscarriage usually stems from abnormalities in the developmental process. Nearly one-third of pregnancies end in miscarriage, with most miscarriages occurring in the first 3 months (Miscarriage, 2007).

THE EMBRYONIC STAGE

The **embryonic stage** begins with implantation and covers the first 2 months, during which the major organ systems differentiate. Development follows **cephalocaudal** (Latin for "head to tail") and **proximodistal** (Latin for "near to far") trends. Growth of the head takes precedence over growth of the lower parts of the body (see Figure 2.11 on page 38). You can also think of the body as containing a central axis that coincides with the spinal cord. The growth of the organ systems near the spine occurs earlier than growth of the extremities. Relatively early maturation of the brain

ectoderm the outermost cell layer of the newly formed embryo from which the skin and nervous system develop.

neural tube a hollowed-out area in the blastocyst from which the nervous system develops.

endoderm the inner layer of the embryo from which the lungs and digestive system develop.

mesoderm the central layer of the embryo from which the bones and muscles develop.

androgens male sex hormones.

amniotic sac the sac containing the fetus.

amniotic fluid fluid within the amniotic sac that suspends and protects the fetus.

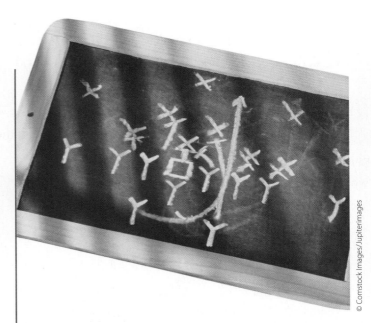

and organs that lie near the spine allows them to play key roles in further development.

During the embryonic stage, the outer layer of cells of the embryonic disk, or **ectoderm**, develops into the nervous system, sensory organs, nails, hair, teeth, and outer layer of skin. At approximately 21 days, two ridges appear in the embryo and fold to compose the **neural tube**, from which the nervous system will develop. The inner layer, or **endoderm**, forms the digestive and respiratory systems, the liver, and the pancreas. A bit later, the mesoderm, a middle layer of cells, becomes differentiated. The **mesoderm** develops into the excretory, reproductive, and circulatory systems, the muscles, the skeleton, and the inner layer of the skin.

During the third week after conception, the head and blood vessels begin to form. Your heart started beating when you were only 0.6 cm (¼ in.) long and weighed just a few grams (a fraction of an ounce). The major organ systems develop during the first 2 months. Arm buds and leg buds begin to appear toward the end of the first month. Eyes, ears, nose, and mouth begin to take shape. By this time, the nervous system, including the brain, has also begun to develop. During the second month, the cells in the nervous system begins to "fire"; that is, they send messages among themselves. Most likely, it is random cell firing, and the "content" of such "messages" is anybody's guess. By the end of the second month, the embryo is looking quite human. The head has the lovely, round shape of your own, and the facial features have become quite distinct. All this detail is inscribed on an embryo that is only about 2.5 cm (1 in.) long and weighs about 10 g (1/30 oz.). The embryo's kidneys are filtering acid from the blood, and its liver is producing red blood cells.

Sexual Differentiation

By 5 to 6 weeks, the embryo is only 0.6 to 1.2 cm (¼ to ½ in.) long. At this stage of development, both the internal and the external genitals resemble primitive female structures. By about the seventh week, the genetic code (XY or XX) begins to assert itself, causing sex organs to differentiate. Genetic activity on the Y sex chromosome causes the testes to begin to differentiate. The ovaries begin to differentiate if the Y chromosome is *absent*. By about 4 months after conception, males and females show distinct external genital structures. Once the testes have developed in the embryo, they begin to produce male sex hormones, or **androgens**, the most important of which is testosterone. Female embryos and fetuses produce small amounts of androgens, but they are usually not enough to cause sexual differentiation along male lines.

The Amniotic Sac

The embryo and fetus develop within a protective **amniotic sac** in the uterus. This sac is surrounded by a clear membrane and contains **amniotic fluid**. The fluid

FIGURE 2.11
A Human Embryo at 7 Weeks

The head is oversized in relation to the rest of the body.

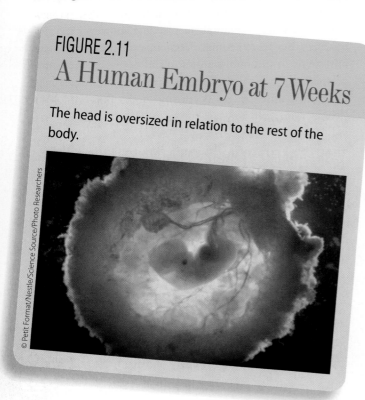

serves as a kind of natural air bag, allowing the embryo and fetus to move around without injury. It also helps maintain an even temperature.

The placenta is a mass of tissue that permits the embryo (and, later on, the fetus) to exchange nutrients and wastes with the mother. The placenta is unique in origin. It grows from material supplied by both the mother and the embryo. The fetus is connected to the placenta by the umbilical cord. The mother is connected to the placenta by blood vessels in the uterine wall.

The Placenta: A Filtration System

Mother and embryo have separate circulatory systems. The pancake-shaped placenta contains a membrane that acts as a filter that permits oxygen and nutrients to reach the embryo from the mother, and permits carbon dioxide and waste products to pass to the mother from the embryo. The mother then eliminates them through her lungs and kidneys. Some harmful substances can also sneak through the placenta, including various "germs," such as the ones that cause syphilis and German measles, but HIV (the virus that causes AIDS) is more likely to be transmitted through childbirth. Some drugs—aspirin, narcotics, alcohol, tranquilizers, and others—cross the placenta and affect the fetus.

The placenta also secretes hormones that preserve the pregnancy, prepare the breasts for nursing, and stimulate the uterine contractions that prompt childbirth. Ultimately, the placenta passes from the birth canal after the baby; for this reason, it is also called the afterbirth.

THE FETAL STAGE

The **fetal stage** lasts from the beginning of the third month until birth. The fetus begins to turn and respond to external stimulation at about the ninth or tenth week. By the end of the first trimester, the major organ systems have been formed. The fingers and toes are fully formed. The eyes and the sex of the fetus can be clearly seen.

The second trimester is characterized by further maturation of fetal organ systems and dramatic gains in size. The brain continues to mature, contributing to the fetus's ability to regulate its own basic body functions. The fetus advances from 28 g (1 oz.) to 0.9 kg (2 lb.) in weight and grows four to five times in length, from about 7.5 cm (3 in.) to 35.5 cm (14 in.). By the end of the second trimester, the fetus opens and shuts its eyes, sucks its thumb, alternates between wakefulness and sleep, and perceives light and sounds.

During the third trimester, the organ systems mature further. The fetus gains about 2.5 kg (5.5 lb.) and doubles in length. During the seventh month, the fetus normally turns upside down in the uterus so that delivery will be head first. By the end of the seventh month, the fetus will have almost doubled in weight, gaining another 0.8 kg (1 lb. 12 oz.), and will have increased another 5 cm (2 in.) in length. If born now, chances of survival are nearly 90 percent. If born at the end of the eighth month, the odds are overwhelmingly in favor of survival. Newborn boys average about 3.4 kg (7.5 lb.) and newborn girls about 3.2 kg (7 lb.).

Fetal Perception

By the 13th week of pregnancy, the fetus responds to sound waves. Sontag and Richards (1938) rang a bell near the mother's abdomen, and the fetus responded with movements similar to those of the startle reflex shown after birth. During the third trimester, fetuses respond to sounds of different frequencies through a variety of movements and changes in heart rate, suggesting that they can discriminate pitch (Lecanuet et al., 2000).

An experiment by Anthony DeCasper and William Fifer (1980) is even more intriguing. In this study, women read the Dr. Seuss book *The Cat in the Hat* out loud twice daily during the final month and a half of pregnancy. After birth, their babies were given special pacifiers. Sucking on these pacifiers in one way would activate recordings of their mothers reading *The Cat in the Hat*, and sucking on them in another way would activate their mothers' readings of a book which was written in very different rhythms. The newborns "chose" to hear *The Cat in the Hat*. Fetal learning may be one basis for the development of attachment to the mother (Krueger et al., 2004; Lecanuet, et al., 2005).

> **fetal stage** the stage of development that lasts from the beginning of the ninth week of pregnancy through birth; it is characterized by gains in size and weight and by maturation of the organ systems.

> **D5** Fetuses suck their thumbs, sometimes for hours on end.
> Fetuses express a right- or left-handed preference in vitro, which raises an interesting argument that genetics plays a role in handedness since nurture has not yet been introduced.

© Vince Bucci/Getty Images

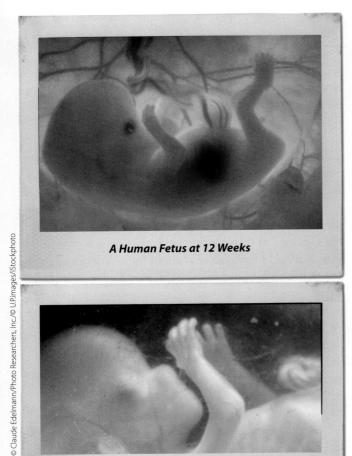

A Human Fetus at 12 Weeks

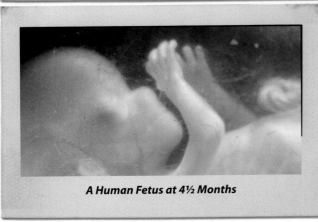

A Human Fetus at 4½ Months

stillbirth the birth of a dead fetus.

teratogens environmental influences or agents that can damage the embryo or fetus.

FETAL MOVEMENTS

The mother usually feels the first fetal movements in the middle of the fourth month (Adolph & Berger, 2005). By 29 to 30 weeks, the fetus moves its limbs so vigorously that the mother may complain of being kicked. The fetus also turns somersaults, which are clearly felt by the mother. The umbilical cord will not break or become dangerously wrapped around the fetus, no matter how many acrobatic feats the fetus performs. As the fetus grows, it becomes cramped in the uterus, and movement is constricted, so that the fetus becomes markedly less active during the ninth month of pregnancy.

ENVIRONMENTAL INFLUENCES ON PRENATAL DEVELOPMENT

The developing fetus is subject to many environmental hazards. Scientific advances have made us keenly aware of the types of things that can go wrong and what we can do to prevent these problems.

Nutrition

It is a common misconception that fetuses "take what they need" from their mothers. However, maternal malnutrition has been linked to low birth weight, prematurity, retardation of brain development, cognitive deficiencies, behavioural problems, and even cardiovascular disease (Giussani, 2006; Guerrini et al., 2007; Morton, 2006). The effects of fetal malnutrition are sometimes overcome by a supportive, care-giving environment. Experiments with children who suffered from fetal malnutrition show that enriched day-care programs enhance intellectual and social skills by 5 years of age (Ramey et al., 1999). Supplementing the diets of pregnant women who might otherwise be deficient in their intake of calories and protein also shows modest positive effects on the motor development of infants (Morton, 2006). On the other hand, maternal obesity is linked with a higher risk of **stillbirth** (Fernandez-Twinn & Ozanne, 2006) and neural tube defects. Over the course of pregnancy, women who do not restrict their diet normally will gain 11.3–15.8 kg (25–35 lb.). Overweight women may gain less, and slender women may gain more. Regular weight gains of about 0.2 kg (½ lb.) per week during the first half of pregnancy and 0.5 kg (1 lb.) per week thereafter are desirable (Christian et al., 2003; Hynes et al., 2002).

Maternal malnutrition has been linked to low birth weight, prematurity, retardation of brain development, cognitive deficiencies, behavioural problems, and even cardiovascular disease.

Teratogens and Health Problems of the Mother

Teratogens are environmental agents that can harm the embryo or fetus. They include drugs taken by the mother, such as thalidomide and alcohol, and substances that the mother's body produces, such as Rh-positive antibodies. Another class of teratogens is heavy metals, such as lead and mercury, which are toxic to the embryo. Hormones are healthful in countless ways—for example, they help maintain pregnancy—but excessive quantities are harmful to the embryo. Exposure to radiation can harm the embryo. Disease-causing organisms—also called pathogens—such as bacteria and viruses are also teratogens.

Critical Periods of Vulnerability

Exposure to particular teratogens is most harmful during **critical periods** that correspond to the times when organs are developing. For example, the heart develops rapidly in the third to fifth weeks after conception. As you can see in Figure 2.12, the heart is most vulnerable to certain teratogens at this time. The arms and legs, which develop later, are most vulnerable in the fourth through eighth weeks. Because the major organ systems differentiate during the embryonic stage, the embryo is generally more vulnerable to teratogens than the fetus. Even so, many teratogens are harmful throughout the entire course of prenatal development.

Let us consider the effects of various health problems of the mother. We begin with sexually transmitted infections (STIs).

Sexually Transmitted Infections

The **syphilis** bacterium can cause miscarriage, stillbirth, or **congenital** syphilis. Routine blood tests early in pregnancy can diagnose syphilis. The syphilis bacterium is vulnerable to antibiotics. The fetus will probably not contract syphilis if an infected mother is treated with antibiotics before the fourth month of pregnancy (Centers for Disease Control

critical period in this usage, a period during which an embryo is particularly vulnerable to a certain teratogen.

syphilis a sexually transmitted infection that, in advanced stages, can attack major organ systems.

congenital present at birth; resulting from the prenatal environment.

FIGURE 2.12
Critical Periods in Prenatal Development

Specific teratogens are most harmful during certain periods of prenatal development.

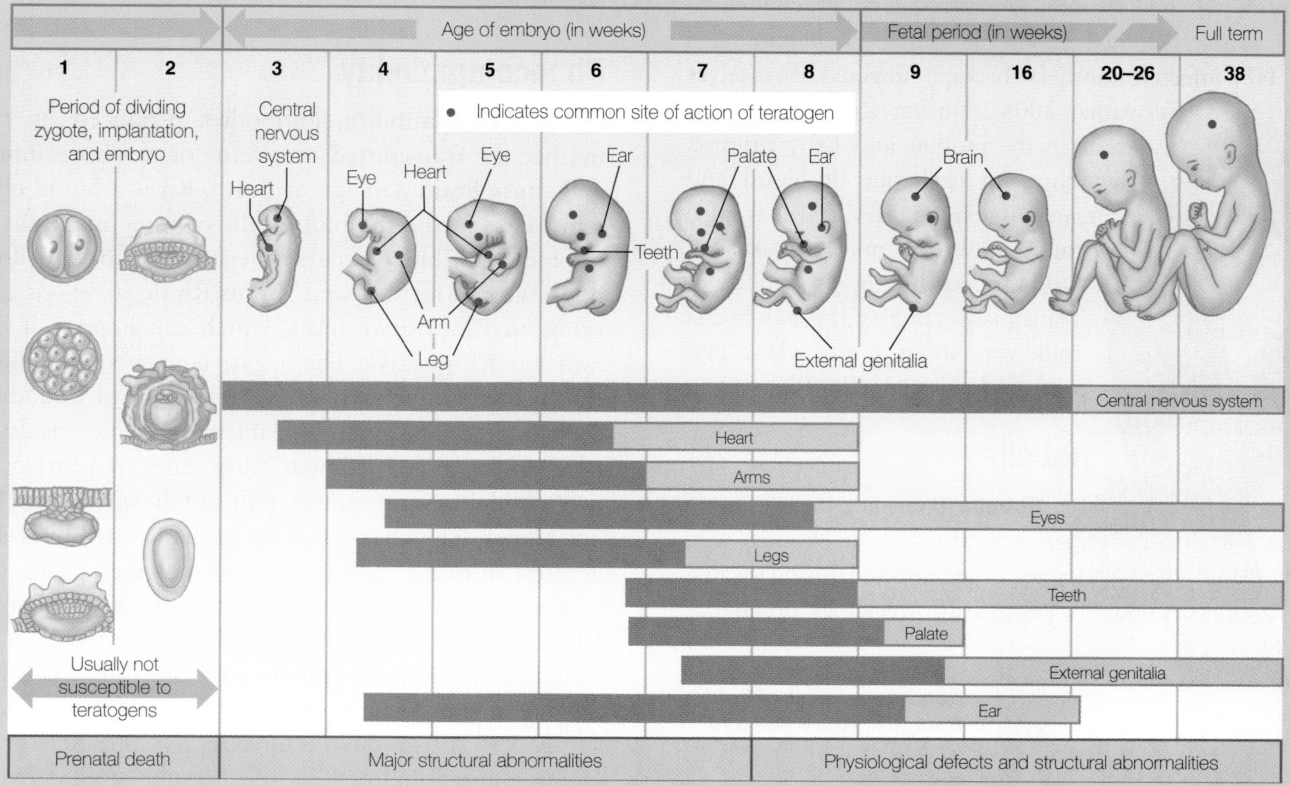

and Prevention, 2006). If the mother is not treated, the baby may be infected in utero and develop congenital syphilis. About 12 percent of those infected die.

HIV/AIDS (human immunodeficiency virus/acquired immunodeficiency syndrome) disables the body's immune system and leaves victims prey to a variety of fatal illnesses, including respiratory disorders and cancer. HIV/AIDS is lethal unless treated with a "cocktail" of antiviral drugs. Even then, the drugs do not work for everyone, and the eventual outcome remains in doubt (Rathus et al., 2008).

HIV can be transmitted by sexual relations, blood transfusions, sharing hypodermic needles while shooting up drugs, childbirth, and breast feeding. About one-fourth of babies born to HIV-infected mothers become infected themselves (Coovadia, 2004). During childbirth, blood vessels in the mother and baby rupture, enabling an exchange of blood and transmission of HIV. HIV is also found in breast milk. An African study found that the probability of transmission of HIV through breast milk was about 1 in 6 (16.2 percent) (Nduati et al., 2000).

Rubella

Rubella (German measles) is a viral infection. Women who are infected during the first 20 weeks of pregnancy

About one-fourth of babies born to mothers infected with HIV become infected themselves.

stand at least a 20 percent chance of bearing children with birth defects such as deafness, mental retardation, heart disease, or eye problems, including blindness (Food and Drug Administration, 2004; Reef et al., 2004).

Many adult women had rubella as children and became immune in this way. Women who are not immune are best vaccinated before they become pregnant if the pregnancy is planned. A mother can be inoculated during pregnancy, if necessary. Inoculation has led to a dramatic decline in the number of North American children born with defects caused by rubella, from approximately 2,000 cases in 1964–1965 to 21 cases in 2001 (Food and Drug Administration, 2004; Reef et al., 2004).

Toxemia

Toxemia is a life-threatening disease characterized by high blood pressure that may afflict women late in the second or early in the third trimester. Women with toxemia often have **premature** or undersized babies. Toxemia is also a cause of pregnancy-related maternal deaths (Rumbold et al., 2006). Toxemia appears to be linked to malnutrition, but the causes are unclear. Women who do not receive prenatal care are much more likely to die from toxemia than those who receive prenatal care (Scott, 2006). Universal health care in Canada is a protection for both mother and the developing baby so long as the services are accessed.

Rh Incompatibility

In **Rh incompatibility**, antibodies produced by the mother are transmitted to a fetus or newborn infant and cause brain damage or death. Rh is a blood protein found in the red blood cells of some individuals. Rh incompatibility occurs when a woman who does not have this factor—and is thus Rh negative—is carrying an Rh-positive fetus, which can happen if the father is Rh positive. The negative–positive combination occurs in approximately 10 percent of Canadian couples and becomes a problem in some resulting pregnancies. Rh incompatibility does not affect a first child because women will not have formed Rh antibodies. The chances of an exchange of blood are greatest during childbirth. If an exchange occurs, the mother produces Rh-positive antibodies to the baby's Rh-positive blood. These antibodies can enter the fetal bloodstream during subsequent deliveries, causing anemia, mental deficiency, or death.

If an Rh-negative mother is injected with Rh immunoglobulin within 72 hours after delivery of an Rh-positive baby, she will not develop the antibodies. This series of injections is provided to affected

Canadian mothers after the delivery of their first child and during subsequent pregnancies.

DRUGS TAKEN BY THE PARENTS

Rh antibodies can be lethal to children, but many other substances can have harmful effects. Even commonly used medications, such as aspirin, can be harmful to the fetus. If a woman is pregnant or thinks she may be, she should consult her obstetrician before taking any drugs, not just prescription medications. A physician usually can recommend a safe and effective substitute for a drug that could potentially harm a developing fetus.

Thalidomide

Thalidomide was marketed in the 1960s as a treatment for insomnia and nausea and provides a dramatic example of critical periods of vulnerability to various teratogens. A fetus's extremities undergo rapid development during the second month of pregnancy (see Figure 2.12). Thalidomide taken during this period almost invariably causes birth defects, such as missing or stunted limbs.

Hormones

Women at risk for miscarriages have been prescribed hormones to help maintain their pregnancies. **Progestin** is chemically similar to male sex hormones and can masculinize the external sex organs of female embryos. **DES** (short for diethylstilbestrol), a powerful estrogen, often prescribed during the 1940s and 1950s to help prevent miscarriage, has been shown to have caused cervical and testicular cancer in some of the offspring. Among daughters of DES users, about 1 in 1,000 will develop cancer in the reproductive tract (Centers for Disease Control and Prevention, 2005).

Vitamins

Although pregnant women are often prescribed multivitamins to maintain their own health and to promote the development of their fetuses, high doses of vitamins A and D have been associated with central nervous system damage, small head size, and heart defects (National Institutes of Health, 2002).

Heroin and Methadone

Maternal addiction to heroin or methadone is linked to low birth weight, prematurity, and toxemia. Narcotics such as heroin and methadone readily cross the placental membrane, and the fetuses of women who use them regularly can become addicted (Lejeune et al., 2006). Addicted newborns may be given the narcotic

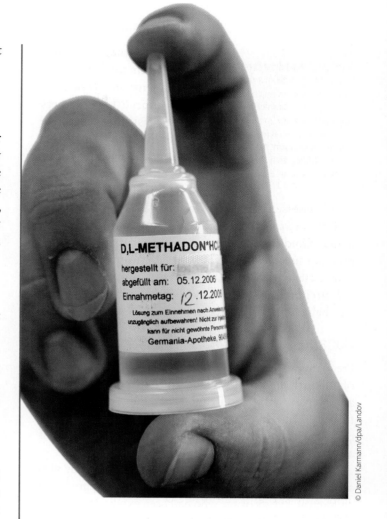

© Daniel Karmann/dpa/Landov

or a substitute shortly after birth so that they will not suffer serious withdrawal symptoms. The drug is then withdrawn gradually. Addicted newborns may also have behavioural effects, such as delays in motor and language development at the age of 12 months (Bunikowski et al., 1998).

thalidomide a sedative used in the 1960s that has been linked to birth defects, especially deformed or absent limbs.

progestin a hormone used to maintain pregnancy that can cause masculinization of the fetus.

DES diethylstilbestrol, an estrogen that has been linked to cancer in the reproductive organs of children of women who used the hormone when pregnant.

Marijuana (Cannabis)

Smoking marijuana during pregnancy apparently poses a number of risks for the fetus, including slower growth (Hurd et al., 2005) and low birth weight (Visscher et al., 2003). The babies of women who regularly used marijuana show increased tremors and startling, suggesting immature development of the nervous system (Huestis et al., 2002).

Research into the cognitive effects of maternal prenatal use of marijuana shows mixed results.

fetal alcohol spectrum disorder (FASD) a cluster of symptoms shown by children of women who drank heavily during pregnancy, including characteristic facial features and mental retardation. A spectrum disorder indicates a range of linked conditions.

Some studies suggest that there may be no impairment (Fried & Smith, 2001). Others suggest that cognitive skills, including learning and memory, may be impaired (Huizink & Mulder, 2006). One study assessed the behaviour of 10-year-olds who had been exposed prenatally to maternal use of marijuana (Goldschmidt et al., 2000), and suggested that prenatal use of marijuana was significantly related to increased hyperactivity, impulsivity, problems in paying attention, and increased delinquency and aggressive behaviour.

Cocaine

Pregnant women who abuse cocaine increase the risk of stillbirth, low birth weight, and birth defects. Infants are often excitable and irritable, or lethargic; sleep is disturbed (Schuetze et al., 2006). There are suggestions of delays in cognitive development even at 12 months of age (Singer et al., 2005).

Children who are exposed to cocaine prenatally also show problems at later ages. One study compared 189 children at 4 years of age who had been exposed to cocaine in utero with 185 4-year-olds who had no exposure (Lewis et al., 2004). The children exposed to cocaine had much lower receptive and expressive language abilities.

Alcohol

Because alcohol passes through the placenta, when a pregnant woman drinks alcohol, she poses risks for the embryo and fetus. Heavy drinking can be lethal and is also associated with deficiencies and deformities in growth. Some children of heavy drinkers develop **fetal alcohol spectrum disorder (FASD)** (Connor et al., 2006; see Figure 2.13). Babies with FASD are often smaller than normal, and so are their brains. They have distinct facial features: widely spaced eyes, an underdeveloped upper jaw, a flattened nose. Psychological characteristics appear to reflect dysfunction of the brain (Guerrini et al., 2007).

The facial deformities of FASD diminish as the child moves into adolescence, and most children

FIGURE 2.13
Fetal Alcohol Spectrum Disorder (FASD)

The children of many mothers who drank alcohol during pregnancy exhibit FASD. This spectrum disorder is characterized by a range of developmental lags and possible facial features such as an underdeveloped upper jaw, a flattened nose, and widely spaced eyes.

© George Steinmetz

catch up in height and weight, but the intellectual, academic, and behavioural deficits of FASD persist to varying degrees (Guerrini et al., 2007). Maladaptive behaviours such as poor judgment, distractibility, and difficulty perceiving social cues are common (Schonfeld et al., 2005). Although some health professionals allowed pregnant women a glass of wine with dinner in the past, research suggests that even moderate drinkers place their offspring at increased risk (Newburn-Cook et al., 2002). The First Nations and Inuit Health Committee proactively promote the idea, to all Canadian women, that since it is not known what a safe amount of alcohol to consume is, it's best to have none. FASD is an abnormality that is completely preventable.

Caffeine

Many pregnant women consume caffeine in the form of coffee, tea, soft drinks, chocolate, and nonprescription drugs.

Wolfe Larry/Shutterstock

Research findings on caffeine's effects on the developing fetus have been inconsistent (Signorello & McLaughlin, 2004). Some studies report no adverse findings, but other studies do (Weng et al., 2008).

Cigarettes

Cigarette smoke contains many ingredients, including the stimulant nicotine, the gas carbon monoxide, and hydrocarbons ("tars"), which are carcinogens. Nicotine and the carbon monoxide pass through the placenta and reach the fetus. Nicotine stimulates the fetus, but its long-term effects are uncertain. Carbon monoxide decreases the amount of oxygen available to the fetus. Oxygen deprivation is connected with impaired motor development, academic delays, learning disabilities, mental retardation, and hyperactivity (Secker-Walker & Vacek, 2003). Second-hand smoke and even third-hand smoke (smoke residue found after smoking has occurred) are also topics of interest in prenatal research.

Pregnant women who smoke are likely to deliver smaller babies than nonsmokers (Bernstein et al., 2005). Their babies are also more likely to be stillborn or to die soon after birth (Cnattingius, 2004). Babies of fathers who smoke have higher rates of birth defects, infant mortality, lower birth weights, and cardiovascular problems (Goel et al., 2004).

ENVIRONMENTAL HAZARDS

Mothers know when they are ingesting drugs, but they may unknowingly take in other harmful substances from the environment. These substances are environmental hazards to which we are all exposed, and we refer to them collectively as pollution.

Prenatal exposure to heavy metals such as lead, mercury, and zinc threatens to delay mental development at 1 and 2 years of age (Heindel & Lawler, 2006). Polychlorinated biphenyls (PCBs), used in many industrial products, accumulate in fish that feed in polluted waters. Newborns whose mothers consumed PCB-contaminated fish from Lake Michigan were smaller and showed poorer motor functioning and memory defects (Jacobson et al., 1992).

Experiments with mice show that fetal exposure to radiation in high doses can damage the eyes, central nervous system, and skeleton (e.g., Hossain et al., 2005). Pregnant women are advised to avoid unnecessary exposure to X-rays. (Ultrasound, which is not an X-ray, has not been shown to harm the fetus.) Even a house cat can pose a life-threatening risk to a fetus if the mother is exposed (through litter boxes or gardening) to cat feces infected with the tiny parasite that causes toxoplasmosis. Exposure to this parasite can result in severe birth defects or even death for the fetus (Kidshealth, 2010).

PARENTS' AGES

What about the parents' ages? Sperm production slows in old age but remains throughout men's life span, though older fathers are more likely to produce abnormal sperm. The mother's age also matters. From a biological vantage point, the 20s may be the ideal age for women to bear children. The offspring of teenage mothers have a higher incidence of infant mortality and are more likely to have a low birth weight (Phipps et al., 2002; Save the Children, 2004b). Girls who become pregnant in their early teens may place a burden on bodies that may not have adequately matured to facilitate pregnancy and childbirth (Berg et al., 2003).

Women's fertility declines gradually until the mid-30s, after which it declines more rapidly. Women who wait until their 30s or 40s to have children also increase the likelihood of having stillborn or preterm babies (Berg et al., 2003). With adequate prenatal care, however, the risk of bearing a premature or unhealthy baby still is relatively small, even for older first-time mothers (Berg et al., 2003).

Whatever the age of the mother, the events of childbirth provide some of the most memorable moments in the lives of parents. In Chapter 3, we continue our voyage with the process of birth and the characteristics of the newborn child.

Medical Discovery versus Bioethics

In 1996, the cloning of Dolly the Sheep (or the Dolly Lamba, as she is often called) prompted Canada and the world to examine how far they were willing to stretch the boundaries of medical discovery and ethics. The Canadian government enacted legislation in March of 2004 banning human and stem cell cloning, rent-a-womb contracts, the sale of human eggs and sperm, and the creation of people with animal DNA. This legislation was designed to keep children safe and to ensure research into new reproductive technology is ethically sound (CBC News, 2009).

Canadians had to decide where to draw the line

Scenario One: In April 2007, a Quebec woman froze some of her eggs so that her 7-year-old daughter, who has a genetic disorder that causes infertility, can use them in the future.

Scenario Two: In April 2007, England approved the right of a couple to have doctors select embryos free from a gene that carries a greater risk of breast cancer. The presence of this gene does not necessarily mean the cancer will develop. The embryos free of the gene would be implanted, and the embryos with the gene would be aborted.

Scenario Three: In February 2009, 60-year-old Ranjit Hayer gave birth to twin boys in Calgary after undergoing in vitro fertilization procedures in India, after decades of trying the old-fashioned way.

Where do you as an individual draw the line?

AP Photo/Paul Clements/CP Images

Jim Barber/Shutterstock

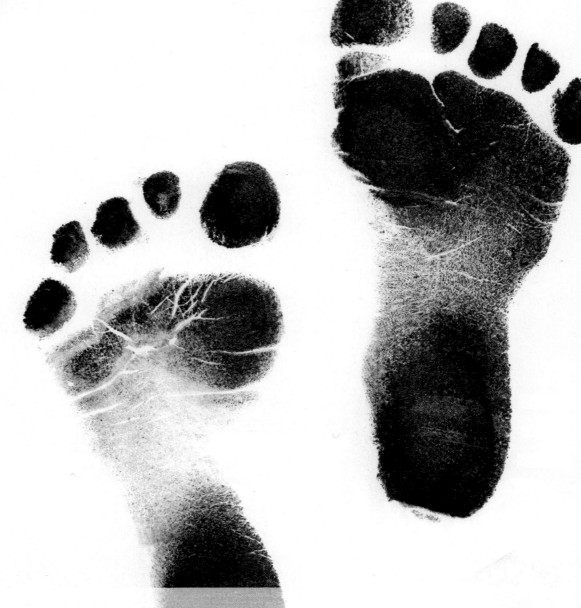

Nearly all

mothers struggle through the last weeks of pregnancy and worry about the
mechanics of delivery.

3

Birth and the Newborn Baby: In the New World

DID YOU KNOW?

D1 ▸ Slapping babies on the bottom to stimulate breathing is an outdated Hollywood image.

D2 ▸ Women who give birth according to the Lamaze method report experiencing less pain.

D3 ▸ In Canada, nearly 1 of every 5 births is by cesarean section.

D4 ▸ It is normal to feel depressed following childbirth.

D5 ▸ Parents do not require early contact with their newborn child for adequate bonding to occur.

Learning Outcomes

LO1 Identify the stages of childbirth

LO2 Examine different methods of childbirth

LO3 Discuss potential problems with childbirth

LO4 Describe the postpartum period

LO5 Examine the characteristics of a neonate

During the last few weeks before she gave birth, Michele explained: "I couldn't get my mind off the pregnancy—what it was going to be like when I finally delivered Lisa. I'd had the amniocentesis, so I knew it was a girl. I'd had the ultrasounds, so all her fingers and toes had been counted, but I was still hoping and praying that everything would turn out all right. To be honest, I was also worried about the delivery. I had always been an A student, and I guess I wanted to earn an A in childbirth as well. Matt was understanding, and he was even helpful, but, you know, it wasn't him."

Nearly all mothers struggle through the last weeks of pregnancy and worry about the mechanics of delivery. Childbirth is a natural function, of course, but so many mothers have gone to classes to learn how to do what comes naturally! They worry about whether they'll get to the hospital or birthing centre on time ("Is there gas in the car?" "Is it snowing?"). They worry about whether the baby will start breathing on its own properly. They may wonder if they'll do it on their own or need a C-section. They may also worry about whether it will hurt, and how much, and when they should ask for anesthetics, and, well—how to earn that A.

Close to full **term**, Michele and other women are sort of front-loaded and feel bent out of shape, and guess what? They are. The weight of the fetus may also be causing backaches. Will they deliver the baby, or will the baby—by being born—deliver them from discomfort? "Hanging in and having Lisa was a wonderful experience," Michele said in the end. "I think Matt should have had it."

> **term** a set period of time such as the typical period between the conception and birth of a baby.

Countdown ...

Early in the last month of pregnancy, the head of the fetus settles in the pelvis. This process is called dropping or lightening. Because lightening decreases pressure on the diaphragm, the mother may, in fact, feel lighter.

The first uterine contractions are called **Braxton-Hicks contractions**, or false labour contractions. They are relatively painless and may be experienced as early as the sixth month of pregnancy. They increase in frequency as the pregnancy progresses and may serve to tone the muscles that will be used in delivery. True labour contractions are more painful and regular, and are usually intensified by walking.

A day or so before labour begins, increased pelvic pressure from the fetus may rupture blood vessels in the birth canal so that blood appears in vaginal secretions. Mucous that had plugged the cervix and protected the uterus from infection becomes dislodged. About 1 woman in 10 has a rush of warm liquid from the vagina at this time. This liquid is amniotic

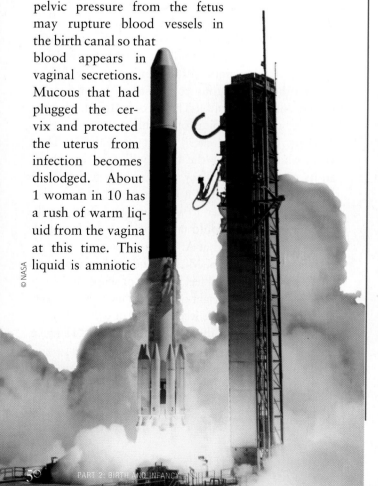

© NASA

Braxton-Hicks contractions the first, usually painless, contractions of childbirth.

prostaglandins hormones that stimulate uterine contractions.

oxytocin a hormone that stimulates labour contractions.

efface to become thin.

dilate to widen.

episiotomy a surgical incision between the birth canal and anus that widens the vaginal opening.

fluid, and its discharge means that the amniotic sac has burst. The sac usually does not burst until the end of the first stage of childbirth, as described later. Other signs that labour is beginning include indigestion, diarrhea, an ache in the small of the back, and cramps.

The fetus may actually signal the mother when it is "ready" to be born by secreting hormones that stimulate the placenta and uterus to secrete **prostaglandins** (Snegovskikh et al., 2006). Prostaglandins not only cause the cramping women may feel before or during menstruation, they also excite the muscles of the uterus to engage in labour contractions. As labour progresses, the pituitary gland releases the hormone **oxytocin**, which stimulates contractions powerful enough to expel the baby.

LO1 The Stages of Childbirth

regular uterine contractions signal the beginning of childbirth. Childbirth occurs in three stages. In the first stage, uterine contractions **efface** and **dilate** the cervix, which needs to widen to about 10 cm (4 in.) to allow the baby to pass. Dilation of the cervix causes most of the pain of childbirth.

The first stage is the longest stage. Among women undergoing their first deliveries, this stage may last from a few hours to more than a day. Subsequent pregnancies take less time. The first contractions are not usually all that painful and are spaced 10 to 20 minutes apart. They may last from 20 to 40 seconds each. As the process continues, the contractions become more powerful, frequent, and regular. Women are usually advised to go to the hospital or birthing centre when the contractions are 4 to 5 minutes apart. Until the end of the first stage of labour, the mother is usually in a labour room.

If the woman is to be "prepped"—that is, if her pubic hair is to be shaved—it takes place now. The prep is intended to lower the chances of infection during delivery and to facilitate the performance of an **episiotomy**. A woman may be given an enema to prevent an involuntary bowel movement during labour. But many women find prepping and enemas degrading and seek obstetricians who do not perform them routinely.

During the first stage of childbirth, fetal monitoring may be used. One kind of monitor is an electronic device strapped around the woman's abdomen that measures both the fetal heart rate and the mother's contractions. An abnormal heart rate alerts the medical staff to possible fetal distress so that appropriate steps can be taken, such as speeding up the delivery. When the cervix is nearly fully dilated, the head of the fetus begins to move into the vagina. This process is called **transition**. During transition, which lasts about 30 minutes or less, contractions are usually frequent and strong.

The second stage of childbirth begins when the baby appears at the opening of the vagina (now called the "birth canal"; see Figure 3.1). The second stage is briefer than the first, possibly lasting minutes or a few hours and ending with the birth of the baby. The woman may be taken to a delivery room for the second stage.

The contractions of the second stage stretch the skin surrounding the birth canal farther and propel the baby along. The baby's head is said to have crowned when it begins to emerge from the birth canal. Once crowning has occurred, the baby normally emerges completely within minutes.

The physician, nurse, or midwife may perform an episiotomy once crowning takes place. The purpose of the episiotomy is to prevent random tearing when the area between the birth canal and the anus becomes severely stretched. Women are unlikely to feel the incision of the episiotomy because the pressure of the crowning head tends to numb the region between the vagina and the anus. The episiotomy, like prepping and the enema, is controversial and is not practiced in Europe. The incision may cause itching and discomfort as it heals. In 1992, half of all women who had vaginal deliveries in Canada had an episiotomy. This rate fell to 24 percent in 2005 (Spears, 2005). According to research conducted at the Ottawa Hospital Research Institute, an episiotomy provides no advantage other than speeding up the delivery.

To clear any obstructions from the passageway for breathing, mucus is suctioned from the baby's mouth when the head emerges from the birth canal. When the baby is breathing adequately on its own, the umbilical cord is clamped and severed (Figure 3.2). Mother and infant are now separate beings. The stump of the umbilical cord will dry and fall off on its own in about 7 to 10 days.

transition movement of the head of the fetus into the birth canal.

FIGURE 3.1
Stages of Childbirth

In the first stage, uterine contractions efface and dilate the cervix. The second stage begins with movement of the baby into the birth canal and ends with birth of the baby. During the third stage, the placenta separates from the uterine wall and is expelled through the birth canal.

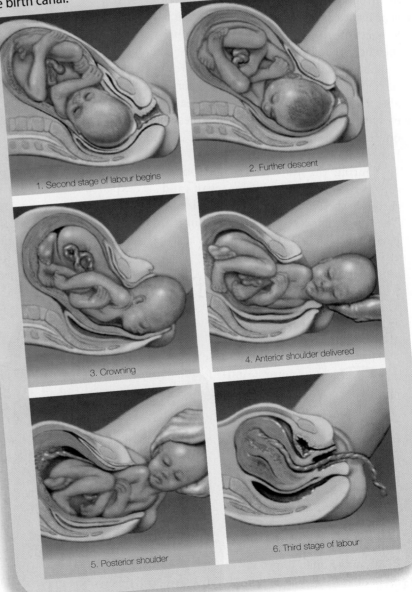

1. Second stage of labour begins

2. Further descent

3. Crowning

4. Anterior shoulder delivered

5. Posterior shoulder

6. Third stage of labour

midwife an individual who helps women in childbirth.

anesthetics agents that lessen pain.

Now the baby is often whisked away by a nurse, who will perform various procedures, including footprinting the baby, supplying an ID bracelet, putting antibiotic ointment or drops of silver nitrate into the baby's eyes to prevent bacterial infections, and giving the baby a vitamin K injection to help its blood clot properly if it bleeds (newborn babies do not manufacture vitamin K). In Canada, one drop of blood is taken from newborns to screen for more than 50 obscure disorders and anomalies (such as PKU) that may be treatable if detected early (CBC News, 2007b). While these procedures go on, the mother is in the third stage of labour, which can last from minutes to hours.

During the third stage of labour, the placenta separates from the uterine wall and is expelled through the birth canal. Some bleeding is normal. The obstetrician sews the episiotomy, if one has been performed.

LO2 Methods of Childbirth

Childbirth was once a more intimate procedure that usually took place in the woman's home and involved her, perhaps a **midwife**, and family. This pattern is followed in many less developed nations today, but of the 330,000 babies born in Canada in 2006, only about 10 percent were delivered by a midwife

FIGURE 3.2
A Clamped and Severed Umbilical Cord

The stump of the cord dries and falls off in about 10 days.

© Owen Franken/Getty Images

(Babycenter, 2010). Using a midwife is a growing trend in Canada, particularly within the Aboriginal population. Most contemporary Canadian childbirths take place in hospitals, where physicians use sophisticated instruments and anesthetics to protect mother and child from complications and discomfort. Modern medicine has saved lives, but childbearing has also become more impersonal. Some argue that modern methods wrest control from women over their own bodies.

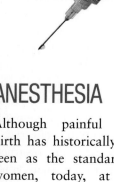

© Shannon Matteson/Shutterstock

ANESTHESIA

Although painful childbirth has historically been seen as the standard for women, today, at least some anesthesia is used in most Canadian deliveries. Two types of **anesthetics** are used to lessen the pain

© Brand X Pictures/Jupiterimages

associated with childbirth. **General anesthesia** achieves its anesthetic effect by putting the woman to sleep by means of an injected barbiturate or through tranquilizers, oral barbiturates, and narcotics. These drugs reduce anxiety and the perception of pain without causing sleep. General anesthesia reduces the responsiveness of the baby shortly after birth when parents are eager to interact with their new arrival, but there is little evidence that it has long-term negative effects (Caton et al., 2002).

Regional or **local anesthetics** are analgesics that deaden pain without putting the mother to sleep. The mother's external genitals are numbed by local injection. With an epidural block and the spinal block, anesthesia is injected into the spinal canal or spinal cord, temporarily numbing the body below the waist. Local anesthesia has minor depressive effects on neonates shortly after birth, but the effects have not been shown to linger (Caton et al., 2002; Eltzschig et al., 2003).

In so-called **natural childbirth**, a woman uses no anesthesia. Instead, she is educated about the biological aspects of reproduction and delivery, encouraged to maintain physical fitness, and taught relaxation and breathing exercises.

PREPARED CHILDBIRTH

In the **Lamaze method**, or prepared childbirth, women engage in breathing and relaxation exercises that reduce fear and pain and distract them from discomfort. The mother-to-be attends Lamaze classes with a "coach"—most often, her partner—who will aid her in the delivery room by doing things such as massaging her, timing the contractions, offering social support, and coaching her in patterns of breathing and relaxation. Women using the Lamaze method often report less pain and ask for less medication (Meldrum, 2003).

 D2 Women who give birth according to the Lamaze method report experiencing less pain.
Women using the Lamaze method often report less pain and ask for less medication, but this could have more to do with psychological preparation than a reduction in actual pain.

DOULAS

Social support during labour can be provided by individuals other than a woman's partner, such as a mother, sibling, friend, or another experienced but nonprofessional female companion, such as a doula (Guzikowski, 2006). Women who have doulas present during birth appear to have shorter labours than women without doulas (Campbell et al., 2006).

CESAREAN SECTION

In a **cesarean section** (C-section), the physician delivers the baby by abdominal surgery. The physician cuts through the mother's abdomen and uterus and physically removes the baby. The incisions are then sewn.

Physicians prefer C-sections to vaginal delivery when they believe that normal delivery may threaten the mother or child or may be more difficult than desired. Nearly 1 of every 5 births (20 percent) in Canada are currently by C-section (Pittman, 2010, September 1).

D3 In Canada, nearly 1 of every 5 births is by cesarean section.
This is true. This trend of opting for a cesarean section is increasingly being considered by young couples in Canada today.

C-sections are also performed when the physician wants to prevent the circulatory systems of the mother and baby from mixing, as might occur when (normal) bleeding occurs during vaginal delivery. C-sections in such cases help prevent transmission of the viruses that cause genital herpes and AIDS.

L○3 Birth Problems

 lthough most deliveries are unremarkable from a medical standpoint, perhaps every delivery is most remarkable from the parents' point of view. Still, a number of problems can and do occur.

general anesthesia elimination of pain by putting a person to sleep.

local anesthetic reduction of pain in an area of the body.

natural childbirth childbirth without anesthesia.

Lamaze method a childbirth method in which women are educated about childbirth, breathe in patterns that reduce pain during birth, and have a coach present.

cesarean section delivery of a baby by abdominal surgery.

anoxia absence of oxygen.

hypoxia less oxygen than required.

breech (bottom-first) presentation buttocks-first childbirth.

preterm born prior to 37 weeks of gestation.

small for dates descriptive of neonates who are small for their age.

lanugo fine, downy hair on premature babies.

vernix oily white substance on the skin of premature babies.

OXYGEN DEPRIVATION

Researchers use two terms to discuss oxygen deprivation: anoxia and hypoxia. **Anoxia** derives from roots meaning "without oxygen." **Hypoxia** derives from roots meaning "under" and "oxygen," the point again being that the baby does not receive enough oxygen in utero to develop properly. Prenatal oxygen deprivation can impair the development of the fetus's central nervous system, leading to cognitive problems, especially in memory and spatial relations, motor problems and psychological disorders (Golan & Huleihel, 2006; Hogan et al., 2006). Prolonged cutoff of the baby's oxygen supply during delivery can also cause psychological and physical health problems, such as early-onset schizophrenia and cerebral palsy (Rees et al., 2006).

Oxygen deprivation can be caused by maternal disorders such as diabetes, by immaturity of the baby's respiratory system, and by accidents, some of which involve pressure against the umbilical cord during birth. Passage through the birth canal is tight, and the umbilical cord is usually squeezed during the process. If the squeezing is temporary, the effect is like holding one's breath for a moment and no problems are likely to ensue. But if constriction of the umbilical cord is prolonged, problems can result. Prolonged constriction is more likely during a **breech (bottom-first) presentation**, which occurs when the baby's body may press the umbilical cord against the birth canal.

PRETERM AND LOW-BIRTH-WEIGHT INFANTS

A baby is considered premature or **preterm** when birth occurs at or before 37 weeks of gestation compared with the normal 40 weeks. A baby is considered to have a low birth weight when it weighs less than about 2.5 kg (5.5 lb.). When a baby is low in birth weight, even though it is born at full term, it is referred to as being **small for dates**. Mothers who smoke, abuse drugs, or are malnourished place their babies at risk of being small for dates. Small-for-dates babies tend to remain shorter and

lighter than their age-mates and show slight delays in learning and problems in attention when compared with their age-mates (O'Keeffe et al., 2003). Preterm babies are more likely than small-for-dates babies to achieve normal heights and weights. Prematurity is more common in the case of multiple births—even twins (Kogan et al., 2000).

Risks Associated with Prematurity and Low Birth Weight

Neonates weighing between 1.475 kg (3.25 lb.) and 2.5 kg (5.5 lb.) pounds are 7 times more likely to die than infants of normal birth weight, whereas those weighing less than 1.5 kg (3.3 lb.) are nearly 100 times as likely to die (Nadeau et al., 2003). By and large, the lower a child's birth weight, the more poorly he or she fares on measures of neurological development and cognitive functioning throughout the school years (Dorling et al., 2006; Nadeau et al., 2003; Wocadlo & Rieger; 2006).

There are also risks for motor development. One study compared 96 very low birth weight (VLBW) children with normal-term children at 6, 9, 12, and 18 months, correcting for age according to the expected date of delivery (Jeng et al., 2000). The median age at which the full-term infants began to walk was 12 months, compared with 14 months for the VLBW infants. By 18 months of age, all full-term infants were walking, compared with 89 percent of the VLBW infants. The outcomes for low-birth-weight children are variable. Studies seem to indicate that the severity of disabilities corresponds to the deficiency of birth weight (Walther et al., 2000).

Signs of Prematurity

Preterm babies are relatively thin because they have not yet formed the layer of fat that gives full-term children their round, robust appearance. They often have fine, downy hair, referred to as **lanugo**, and an oily white substance on the skin known as **vernix**. If the babies are born 6 weeks or more before term, their nipples will not

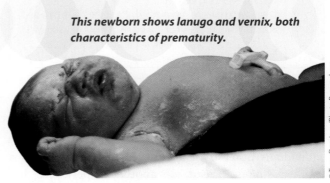

This newborn shows lanugo and vernix, both characteristics of prematurity.

© Tracy Dominey/Photo Researchers

have emerged. The testicles of boys born this early will not yet have descended into the scrotum.

Preterm babies have immature muscles, so their sucking and breathing reflexes are weak. In addition, the walls of the tiny air sacs in their lungs may tend to stick together because the babies do not yet secrete substances that lubricate the walls of the sacs. As a result, babies born more than a month before full term may breathe irregularly or may suddenly stop breathing, evidence of **respiratory distress syndrome**. Preterm infants with respiratory stress syndrome show poorer development in cognitive, language, and motor skills over the first 2 years of development than full-term infants. Injecting pregnant women at risk for delivering preterm babies with corticosteroids increases the babies' chances of survival (Crowther et al., 2006).

Strides have been made in helping low-birth-weight children survive, but children who survive often have below-average verbal ability and academic achievement and various motor and perceptual impairments (Saigal et al., 2006).

Treatment of Preterm Babies

Because of their physical frailty, preterm infants usually remain in the hospital and are placed in **incubators**, which maintain a temperature-controlled environment and afford some protection from disease. The babies may be given oxygen, although excessive oxygen can cause permanent eye injury.

Parents and Preterm Neonates

Parents often do not treat preterm neonates as well as they treat full-term neonates. For one thing, preterm infants usually do not have the robust, appealing appearance of many full-term babies. Their cries are more high pitched and grating, and they are more irritable (Bugental & Happaney, 2004; Eckerman et al., 1999). The demands of caring for preterm babies can be depressing to mothers (Davis et al., 2003; Drewett et al., 2004). Mothers of preterm babies frequently report that they feel alienated from their babies and harbour feelings of failure, guilt, and low self-esteem (Bugental & Happaney, 2004). Fear of hurting preterm babies can further discourage parents from handling them, but encouraging mothers to massage their preterm infants can help them cope with this fear (Feijó et al., 2006). Once they come home from the hospital, preterm infants remain more passive and less sociable than full-term infants (Larroque et al., 2005; McGrath et al., 2005). Preterm infants fare better when they have responsive and caring parents.

respiratory distress syndrome weak and irregular breathing, typical of preterm babies.

incubator a heated, protective container for premature infants.

Maternal and Infant Mortality around the World

Modern medicine has made vast strides in decreasing the rates of maternal and infant mortality, but the advances are not equally spread throughout the world. Save the Children, a nonprofit relief and development organization, tracks the likelihood that a woman will die in childbirth and that an infant will die during its first year. The likelihood of maternal and infant mortality is connected with factors such as the percentage of births that are attended by trained people, the literacy rate of adult women (which is one measure of the level of education of women), and the participation of women in national government (which is one measure of the extent to which a society empowers women). In Canada the infant mortality rate in 2007 was 5.1 per 1,000 babies born (Statistics Canada, 2010a). Factors contributing to this lower number are our system of universal health care, our high literacy rate (99 percent), and strong female leadership within the country. In contrast, in Afghanistan, 1 woman in 6 will die as a result of pregnancy, and 165 children of 1,000 will die during their first year. In Afghan society, the literacy rate for women is only 21 percent. There is little, if any, professional assistance during childbirth (12 percent), and women have virtually no role in government.

Intervention Programs

Preterm infants benefit from early stimulation just as full-term babies do—being cuddled, rocked, talked to, and sung to; being exposed to recordings of their mothers' voices; having mobiles in view; and having live and recorded music in their environment (Arnon et al., 2006; Lai et al., 2006). Other forms of stimulation include massage (Field et al., 2006) and "kangaroo care" (Lai et al., 2006), in which the baby spends time each day lying skin to skin and chest to chest with a parent. By and large, stimulated preterm infants tend to gain weight more rapidly, show fewer respiratory problems, and make greater advances in motor, intellectual, and neurological development than control infants (Caulfield, 2000; Dombrowski et al., 2000) (see Figure 3.3).

FIGURE 3.3
Stimulating a Preterm Infant

Preterm infants usually benefit from stimulation.

© Louie Psihoyos/Getty Images

Unicef Report: Leaving No Child Behind

In the last 20 years, the world has reduced the infant mortality rate by 30 percent. If we can achieve this change in some of the poorest nations in the world, why are infant mortality rates for some indigenous children much higher than they are for other Canadian children (see Figure 3.4)? In 2009, UNICEF asked, why are Indigenous children generally not as healthy as other Canadian children (UNICEF Canada, 2009)?

In the past, Canadians attributed their health to biological and medical causes. Then we began to also factor in the effects of lifestyle choices. Now we know that it's much more complicated than that. Health depends on a web of economic, social, political, and environmental factors. The figure on the right shows some of the factors affecting the health of indigenous children:

Prenatal care and infant mortality rates are the starting point of a child's health. We have the knowledge, technology, and information to make changes. The UNICEF document states the priority of leaving no child behind. We are leaving some Canadian children behind, and this must change.

© UNICEF Canada/2008/Sri Utami (reproduced with the permission of UNICEF Canada).

- poverty
- lack of education
- substandard housing
- poor nutrition
- lack of access to health care and social services
- a legacy of family,

community, and cultural breakdown left by residential school policies

FloridaStock/Shutterstock

LO4 The Postpartum Period

the **postpartum period** refers to the weeks following delivery, but there is no specific limit. The "parting" from the baby is frequently a happy experience. The family's long wait is over. Concerns about pregnancy and labour are over, fingers and toes have been counted, and despite some local discomfort, the mother finds her "load" to be lightened, most literally. According to the Canadian Paediatric Society (Province of British Columbia, 2010), about 80 percent of new mothers can expect to experience periods of tearfulness, sadness, and irritability that the association refers to as the "baby blues."

MATERNAL DEPRESSION

Problems related to maternal depression include the "baby blues" and more serious mood disorders ("postpartum-onset mood episodes"), which occasionally include "psychotic features" (American Psychiatric Association, 2000). Postpartum mood problems are so common that they are statistically normal (Gavin et al., 2005). Researchers believe that they are often due to hormonal changes that follow delivery (Kohl, 2004). They last about 10 days and are generally not severe enough to impair the mother's functioning.

Perhaps as many as 13 percent of Canadian mothers will encounter the more serious mood disorder frequently referred to as **postpartum depression (PPD)**, which begins about a month after delivery and may linger for weeks or months. PPD is characterized by serious sadness, feelings of hopelessness, helplessness, and worthlessness, difficulty concentrating, mood swings, and major changes in appetite (usually loss of appetite) and sleep patterns (frequently insomnia). Some women show obsessive concern with the well-being of their babies.

FIGURE 3.4
United Nations Statistics on the Health of Canadian Children

1 : 9
The number of Canadian children on average living in poverty

1 : 4:
The number of children in First Nations communities living in poverty

5:
Infant deaths per 1,000 infants born in Canada

16:
Infant deaths per 1,000 infants born in Nunavut (where 85% of the population is Inuit)

3 out of 177:
Canada's ranking in the Human Development Index (HDI), a widely used United Nations standard that measures a country's achievements in three basic aspects of human development: health, knowledge, and decent standard of living

68 out of 177:
The HDI ranking of Canada's First Nations communities

85
The percentage of all children in Canada who accessed a doctor in 2000–01

63:
The percentage of First Nations children on selected reserves who accessed a doctor in 2000–01

21:
The percentage of non-Aboriginal children in census metropolitan areas living in low-income families

45:
The percentage of Inuit children in census metropolitan areas living in low-income families

2 to 3×
The multiple by which First Nations, Inuit, and Metis children are worse off than other Canadian children. They are less likely to see a doctor. As teens, they are more likely to become parents, and they are more likely to commit suicide.

Source: Adapted from *Canadian Supplement to The State of The World's Children 2009: Aboriginal Children's Health: Leaving No Child Behind*, UNICEF

Many researchers suggest that PPD is caused by a sudden drop in estrogen (Kohl, 2004). The focus is on physiological factors because of the major changes in body chemistry during and after pregnancy

postpartum period the period immediately following childbirth.

postpartum depression (PPD) serious maternal depression following delivery; characterized by sadness, apathy, and feelings of worthlessness.

bonding formation of parent–infant attachment.

and because women around the world seem to experience similar disturbances in mood, even when their life experiences and support systems are radically different from those found here in Canada. (Cohen et al., 2006).

Mothers who experience psychotic features may have a break with reality that leads to delusional thoughts about their infant that place the infant at risk of injury or death. Some women experience delusions that their infant is possessed by the devil. Some women have "command hallucinations" and experience an external command to kill their infant.

Margaret Trudeau, controversial wife of late Prime Minister Pierre Trudeau, has waged a lonely battle against depression and bipolar disorder, which first became an issue after the birth of her son Sacha. She now shares her personal story with Canadians, and the world, in the hope of helping others.

The Canadian Press Images/Mario Beauregard

Women who experience PPD usually profit from social support and counselling, even if it does little more than explain that many women encounter PPD and it usually eases and ends as time goes on. Drugs that increase estrogen levels or act as antidepressants may help.

D4 It is normal to feel depressed following childbirth.
Postpartum mood problems are so common that they are statistically normal (Gavin et al., 2005).

BONDING

Bonding—that is, the formation of bonds of attachment between parents and their children—is essential to the survival and well-being of children. Since the publication of controversial research by Marshall Klaus and John Kennell in the 1970s, many have wondered whether extended parent–infant contact is required during the first hours postpartum in order to foster parent–infant bonding (Klaus & Kennell, 1978). In their study, one group of mothers was randomly assigned to standard hospital procedure in which their babies were whisked away to the nursery shortly after birth. Throughout the remainder of the hospital stay, the babies visited their mothers during feeding. The other group of mothers spent 5 hours a day with their infants during the hospital stay. The hospital staff encouraged and reassured the group of mothers who had extended contact. Follow-ups over 2 years found that mothers with extended contact were more likely than control mothers to cuddle their babies, soothe them when they cried, and interact with them. Critics note that the Klaus and Kennell studies did not separate the benefits of extended contact from benefits attributable to parents' knowledge that they were in a special group and from the extra attention of the hospital staff. Despite these criticisms of the study, encouraging extended contact between mothers and their infants is considered to be important for bonding and has become standard practice in Canadian maternity wards today.

Parent–child bonding has been shown to be a complex process involving desire to have the child; parent–child familiarity with one another's sounds, odours, and tastes; and caring. On the other hand, serious maternal depression can delay bonding with newborns (Klier, 2006),

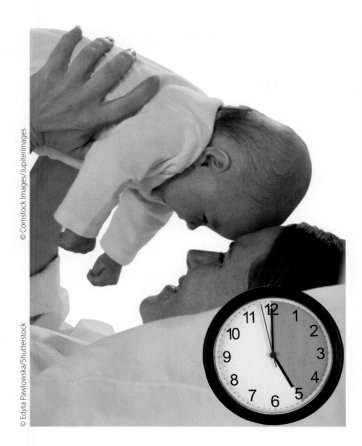

and a history of rejection by parents can interfere with women's bonding with their own children (Leerkes & Crockenberg, 2006).

Despite the Klaus and Kennell studies, which made a brief splash in the 1970s, parents do not require early contact with their newborn children for adequate bonding to occur. Many parents, for instance, adopt children at advanced ages and bond closely with them.

 **D5** Parents do not require early contact with their newborn child for adequate bonding to occur.
For instance, many parents adopt children at an advanced age and still bond well with them.

LO5 Characteristics of Neonates

many neonates come into the world seeing things a bit fuzzy, but even though they are utterly dependent on others, they are probably more aware of their surroundings than you had imagined. Neonates also make rapid adaptations to the world around them.

ASSESSING THE HEALTH OF NEONATES

The neonate's overall level of health is usually evaluated at birth according to the **Apgar scale** (Table 3.1). Apgar scores are based on five signs of health: appearance, pulse, grimace, activity level, and respiratory effort. The neonate can receive a score of 0, 1, or 2 on each sign. The total Apgar score can therefore vary from 0 to 10. A score of 7 or above usually indicates that the baby is not in danger. A score below 4 suggests that the baby is in critical condition and requires medical attention. By 1 minute after birth, most normal babies attain scores of 8 to 10 (Clayton & Crosby, 2006).

The **Brazelton Neonatal Behavioural Assessment Scale** measures neonates' reflexes and other behaviour patterns. This test screens neonates for behavioural and neurological problems by assessing four areas of behaviour: motor behaviour, response to stress, adaptive behaviour, and control over physiological state.

REFLEXES

Reflexes are unlearned, automatic responses that are elicited by certain types of stimulation. They occur without thinking. Of these reflexes, most are exhibited by neonates very shortly after birth, disappear within a few months, and—if the behaviours still serve a purpose—are replaced by corresponding voluntary actions.

Pediatricians learn about a neonate's neural functioning by testing its reflexes. The absence or weakness of a reflex may indicate immaturity (as in prematurity), slowed responsiveness (which can result from anesthetics used during childbirth), brain injury, or retardation.

TABLE 3.1
The Apgar Scale

POINTS	0	1	2
Appearance: Colour	Blue, pale	Body pink, extremities blue	Entirely pink
Pulse: Heart Rate	Absent (not detectable)	Slow—below 100 beats/minute	Rapid—100–140 beats/minute
Grimace: Reflex Irritability	No response	Grimace	Crying, coughing, sneezing
Activity level: Muscle tone	Completely flaccid, limp	Weak, inactive	Flexed arms and legs; resists extension
Respiratory effort: Breathing	Absent (infant is apneic)	Shallow, irregular, slow	Regular breathing; lusty crying

© Brand X Pictures/Jupiterimages

rooting reflex turning the mouth and head toward stroking of the cheek or the corner of the mouth.

Moro reflex arching the back, flinging out the arms and legs, and drawing them back to the chest in response to a sudden change in position.

The rooting and sucking reflexes are basic to survival. In the **rooting reflex**, the baby turns the head and mouth toward a stimulus that strokes the cheek, chin, or corner of the mouth. The rooting reflex facilitates finding the mother's nipple in preparation for sucking. Babies will suck almost any object that touches their lips. The sucking reflex grows stronger during the first days after birth and can be lost if not stimulated, which can lead to difficulty feeding and result in malnourishment. As the months go on, reflexive sucking becomes replaced by voluntary sucking.

In the startle or **Moro reflex** (the startle response), the back arches and the legs and arms are flung out and then brought back toward the chest, with the arms in a hugging motion. The Moro reflex occurs when a baby's position is suddenly changed or when support for the head and neck is suddenly lost. It can also be elicited by loud noises or sudden movements. The Moro reflex is usually lost within 6 to 7 months after birth. Absence of the Moro reflex can indicate immaturity or brain damage.

The Rooting Reflex

© Dan Bryant

During the first few weeks following birth, babies show an increasing tendency to reflexively grasp fingers or other objects pressed against the palms of their hands. In this **grasping reflex**, or palmar reflex, they use four fingers only (the thumbs are not included). Absence of the grasping reflex may indicate depressed activity of the nervous system, which can stem from use of anesthetics during childbirth. The grasping reflex is usually lost within 3 to 4 months of age, and babies generally show voluntary grasping within 5 to 6 months.

Within 1 or 2 days after birth, babies show a reflex that mimics walking. When held under the arms and tilted forward so that the feet press against a solid surface, a baby will show a **stepping reflex** in which the feet advance one after the other. A full-term baby "walks" heel to toe, whereas a preterm infant is more likely to remain on tiptoe. The stepping reflex usually disappears by about 3 or 4 months of age.

In the **Babinski reflex**, the neonate fans or spreads the toes in response to stroking of the underside of the foot from heel to toes. The Babinski reflex normally disappears toward the end of the first year, to be replaced by curling downward of the toes.

The **tonic-neck reflex** is observed when the baby is lying on its back and turns its head to one side. The arm and leg on that side extend, while the limbs on the opposite side flex. This reflex is believed to aid the baby in the rolling process later, on when greater mobility is apparent.

Some reflexes, such as breathing regularly and blinking the eye in response to a puff of air, remain with us for life. Others, such as the sucking and grasping reflexes, are gradually replaced after a number of months by voluntary sucking and grasping. Still others, such as the Moro and Babinski reflexes, disappear, indicating that the nervous system is maturing on schedule.

SENSORY CAPABILITIES

In 1890, William James, a founder of modern psychology, wrote that the neonate must sense the world "as one great blooming, buzzing confusion." The neonate emerges from being literally suspended in a quiet and pleasant temperature-controlled environment to being—again, in James's words— "assailed by eyes, ears, nose, skin, and entrails at once." We now describe the sensory capabilities of neonates, and we see that James, for all his eloquence, exaggerated their disorganization.

grasping reflex grasping objects that touch the palms.

stepping reflex taking steps when held under the arms and leaned forward so the feet press the ground.

Babinski reflex fanning the toes when the soles of the feet are stroked.

tonic-neck reflex turning the head to one side, extending the arm and leg on that side, and flexing the limbs on the opposite side.

© Design Pics/Leah Warkentin

> Neonates prefer their mothers' voices to those of other women, but they do not show similar preferences for the **voices of their fathers.**

visual accommodation automatic adjustments of the lenses to focus on objects.

convergence inward movement of the eyes to focus on an object that is drawing nearer.

amplitude loudness (of sound waves).

pitch highness or lowness (of a sound), as determined by the frequency of sound waves.

Vision

Neonates can see, but they are nearsighted. They can best see objects that are about 18 to 23 cm (7 to 9 in.) from their eyes (Kellman & Arterberry, 2006). They also do not have the peripheral vision of older children (Candy et al., 1998). Neonates can visually detect movement, and many neonates can visually follow, or track, movement the first day after birth. In fact, they appear to prefer (i.e., they spend more time looking at) moving objects to stationary objects (Kellman & Arterberry, 2006).

Visual accommodation refers to the self-adjustments made by the eye's lens to bring objects into focus. Neonates show little or no visual accommodation; rather, they see as through a fixed-focus camera. Objects placed about 18 to 23 cm (7 to 9 in.) away are in clearest focus for most neonates, but visual accommodation improves dramatically during a baby's first 2 months (Kellman & Arterberry, 2006).

Neonates do not have the muscle control to converge their eyes on an object that is close to them. For this reason, one eye may be staring off to the side while the other fixates on an object straight ahead. **Convergence** does not occur until 7 or 8 weeks of age for nearby objects (Kellman & Arterberry, 2006).

The degree to which neonates perceive colour remains an open question. By 4 months, however, infants can see most of, if not all, the colours of the visible spectrum (Franklin et al., 2005).

Even at birth, babies do not just passively respond to visual stimuli. Babies placed in absolute darkness open their eyes wide and search around (Kellman & Arterberry, 2006).

Hearing

Fetuses respond to sound months before they are born. Although myelination of the auditory pathways is not complete before birth, fetuses' middle and inner ears normally reach their mature shapes and sizes before birth. Normal neonates hear well unless their middle ears are clogged with amniotic fluid (Priner et al., 2003). Most neonates turn their heads toward unusual sounds, such as the shaking of a rattle.

Neonates have the capacity to respond to sounds of different **amplitude** and **pitch**. They are more likely to respond to high-pitched sounds than to low-pitched sounds (Trehub & Hannon, 2006). By contrast, speaking or singing to infants softly, in a relatively low-pitched voice, can have a soothing effect (Volkova et al., 2006).

The sense of hearing may play a role in the formation of affectional bonds between neonates and mothers that goes well beyond the soothing potential of the mothers' voices. Neonates prefer their mothers' voices to those of other women, but they do not show similar preferences for the voices of their fathers (DeCasper & Prescott, 1984; Freeman et al., 1993). This preference may reflect the sheer amount of prenatal exposure to sounds produced by their mothers.

Neonates are particularly responsive to the sounds and rhythms of speech, although they do not show preferences for specific languages. Neonates

The Moro Reflex   **The Grasping Reflex**   **The Stepping Reflex**   **The Tonic-Neck Reflex**

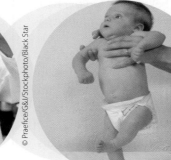

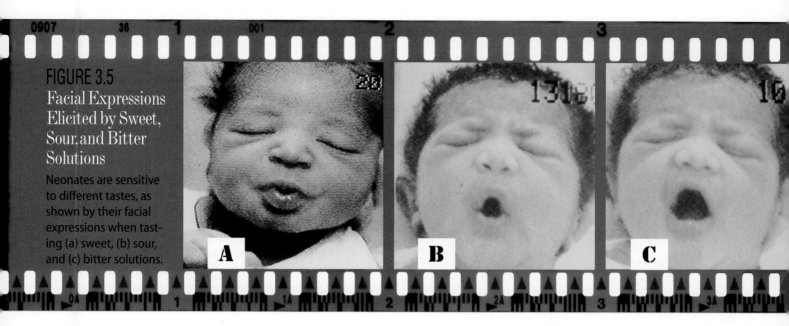

FIGURE 3.5

Facial Expressions Elicited by Sweet, Sour, and Bitter Solutions

Neonates are sensitive to different tastes, as shown by their facial expressions when tasting (a) sweet, (b) sour, and (c) bitter solutions.

A

B

C

© Nicholas Belton/iStockphoto.com/Courtesy of Rosenstein, D. S. and Oster, H. (1988)

can discriminate different speech sounds (Dehaene-Lambertz et al., 2004), and they can discriminate new sounds of speech from those they have heard before (Brody et al., 1984).

Smell: The Nose Knows—Early

Neonates can discriminate distinct odours, such as those of onions and licorice. They show more rapid breathing patterns and increased bodily movement in response to powerful odours. They also turn away from unpleasant odours, such as ammonia and vinegar, as early as the first day after birth (Werner & Bernstein, 2001). The nasal preferences of neonates are similar to those of older children and adults (Werner & Bernstein, 2001).

The sense of smell, like hearing, may provide a vehicle for mother–infant recognition and attachment (Macfarlane, 1975, 1977). Neonates may be sensitive to the smell of milk because, when held by the mother, they tend to turn toward her nipple before they have had a chance to see or touch it. In one experiment, Macfarlane placed nursing pads above and to the sides of neonates' heads. One pad had absorbed milk from the mother, the other was clean. Neonates less than 1 week old spent more time turning to look at their mothers' pads than at the new pads.

Breast-fed 15-day-old infants also prefer their mother's underarm odour to odours produced by other milk-producing women and by other women. Bottle-fed infants do not show this preference (Cernoch & Porter, 1985; Porter et al., 1992). Smell may contribute to the early development of recognition and attachment.

Taste

Neonates are sensitive to different tastes, and their preferences, as suggested by their facial expressions in response to various fluids, are like those of adults (Werner & Bernstein, 2001). Neonates swallow without showing any facial expression suggestive of a positive or negative response when distilled water is placed on their tongues. Sweet solutions are met with smiles, licking, and eager sucking, as in Figure 3.5a (Rosenstein & Oster, 1988). Neonates discriminate among solutions with salty, sour, and bitter tastes, as suggested by reactions in the lower part of the face (Rosenstein & Oster, 1988). Sour fluids (Figure 3.5b) elicit pursing of the lips, nose wrinkling, and eye blinking. Bitter solutions (Figure 3.5c) stimulate spitting, gagging, and sticking out the tongue.

Sweet solutions have a calming effect on neonates (Blass & Camp, 2003). One study found that sweeter solutions increase the heart rate, suggesting heightened arousal, but also slow down the rate of sucking (Crook & Lipsitt, 1976). Researchers interpret this finding to suggest an effort to savour the sweeter solution, to make the flavour last.

Touch

The sense of touch is an extremely important avenue of learning and communication for babies. Not only do the skin senses provide information about the external world, but the sensations of skin against skin also appear to provide feelings of comfort and security that may be major factors in the formation of bonds of attachment between infants and their caregivers. Baby

© Blend Images/Jupiterimages

massage has become an increasingly popular method of promoting a relationship between baby and caregiver.

LEARNING: REALLY EARLY CHILDHOOD "EDUCATION"

The limited sensory capabilities of neonates suggest that they may not learn as rapidly as older children do. After all, we must sense clearly those things we are to learn about. Neonates do, however, seem capable of conditioning.

Classical Conditioning of Neonates

In classical conditioning of neonates, involuntary responses are conditioned to new stimuli. In a typical study (Lipsitt, 2002), neonates were taught to blink in response to a tone, much like the dog in Chapter 1 learns to respond to the opening of a can of dog food. Blinking (the unconditioned response) was elicited by a puff of air directed toward the infant's eye (the unconditioned stimulus). A tone was sounded (the conditioned stimulus) as the puff of air was delivered. After repeated pairings, sounding the tone caused the neonate to blink (the conditioned response). This response indicates that neonates are equipped to learn that events peculiar to their own environments (touches or other conditioned stimuli) may mean that a meal is at hand. The conditioned stimuli are culture specific; the capacity to learn is universal.

Operant Conditioning of Neonates

Operant conditioning, like classical conditioning, can take place in neonates. A prime example of operant conditioning is the experiment from Chapter 2 in which neonates learned to suck on a pacifier in such a way as to activate a recording of their mothers reading *The Cat in the Hat* (DeCasper & Fifer, 1980; DeCasper & Spence, 1991).

SLEEPING AND WAKING

As adults, we spend about one-third of our time sleeping. Neonates greatly outdo us, spending two-thirds of their time, or about 16 hours per day, in sleep. And, in one of life's basic challenges to parents, neonates do not sleep their 16 hours consecutively.

A number of different states of sleep and wakefulness have been identified in neonates and infants, as shown in Table 3.2 (Cornwell & Feigenbaum, 2006; Salzarulo & Ficca, 2002; Wulff & Siegmund, 2001). Although individual babies differ in the amount of time they spend in each of these states, sleep clearly predominates over wakefulness in the early days and weeks of life.

Different infants require different amounts of sleep and follow different patterns of sleep, but virtually all infants distribute their sleeping throughout the day and night through a series of naps. The typical infant has about six cycles of waking and sleeping in a 24-hour period. The longest nap typically approaches 4½ hours, and the neonate is usually awake for a little more than 1 hour during each cycle.

TABLE 3.2
States of Sleep and Wakefulness in Infancy

STATE	COMMENTS
Quiet sleep (non-REM)	Regular breathing, eyes closed, no movement
Active sleep (REM)	Irregular breathing, eyes closed, rapid eye movement, muscle twitches
Drowsiness	Regular or irregular breathing, eyes open or closed, little movement
Alert inactivity	Regular breathing, eyes open, looking around, little body movement
Alert activity	Irregular breathing, eyes open, active body movement
Crying	Irregular breathing, eyes open or closed, thrashing of arms and legs, crying

FIGURE 3.6

REM Sleep and Non-REM Sleep

The percentage of time spent in REM sleep declines as people age.

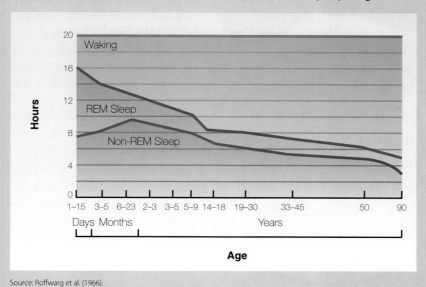

Source: Roffwarg et al. (1966).

rapid-eye-movement (REM) sleep a sleep period when dreams are likely, as suggested by rapid eye movements.

non-rapid-eye-movement (non-REM) sleep a sleep period when dreams are unlikely.

After a month or so, the infant has fewer but longer sleep periods and will usually take longer naps during the night. By the ages of about 6 months to 1 year, many infants begin to sleep through the night. Some infants start sleeping through the night even earlier (Salzarulo & Ficca, 2002). A number of infants begin to sleep through the night for a week or so and then revert to their wakeful ways again for a while.

REM and Non-REM Sleep

Sleep can be divided into **rapid-eye-movement (REM) sleep** and **non-rapid-eye-movement (non-REM) sleep** (see Figure 3.6). REM sleep is characterized by rapid eye movements that can be observed beneath closed lids. About 80 percent of adults who are roused during REM sleep report that they have been dreaming. Is the same true of neonates?

Note from Figure 3.6 that neonates spend about half their time sleeping in REM sleep. As they develop, the percentage of sleeping time spent in REM sleep declines. By 6 months or so, REM sleep accounts for only about 30 percent of the baby's sleep. By 2 to 3 years, REM sleep drops off to about 20–25 percent (Salzarulo & Ficca, 2002). As we develop, we experience a dramatic falling-off in the total number of hours spent in sleep (Salzarulo & Ficca, 2002).

What is the function of REM sleep in neonates? Research with humans and other animals, including kittens and rat pups, suggests that the brain requires a certain amount of stimulation for the creation of proteins that are involved in the development of neurons and synapses (Dang-Vu et al., 2006). Perhaps neonates create this stimulation by means of REM sleep, which most closely parallels the waking state in terms of brain waves. Preterm babies spend an even greater proportion of their time in REM sleep, perhaps because they need relatively more stimulation of the brain.

Crying

No discussion of the sleeping and waking states of the neonate would be complete without mentioning crying, a comment that parents will view as an understatement. The main reason babies cry seems to be simple enough. Studies suggest a one-word answer: pain (Gormally et al., 2001; Zeifman, 2004). Whether crying is healthful remains an open question, but some crying among babies seems to be universal.

Before parenthood, many people wonder whether they will be able to recognize the meaning of their babies' cries, but it

© Dorling Kindersley/Getty Images

pacifier a device such as an artificial nipple or teething ring that soothes babies when sucked.

sudden infant death syndrome (SIDS) the death, while sleeping, of apparently healthy babies who stop breathing.

usually does not take them long. Parents typically learn to distinguish cries that signify hunger, anger, and pain. The pitch of an infant's cries appears to provide information (Zeifman, 2004). Adults perceive high-pitched crying to be more urgent, distressing, and sick sounding than low-pitched crying (Zeifman, 2004). A sudden, loud, insistent cry associated with flexing and kicking of the legs may indicate colic, that is, pain resulting from gas or other sources of distress in the digestive tract. Crying from colic can be severe and persistent; it may last for hours (Barr et al., 2005). Much to the relief of parents, colic tends to disappear by the third to sixth month, as a baby's digestive system matures.

Certain high-pitched cries, when prolonged, may signify health problems. The cries of chronically distressed infants differ from those of nondistressed infants in both rhythm and pitch. Patterns of crying may be indicative of chromosomal abnormalities, infections, fetal malnutrition, and exposure to narcotics (Zeifman, 2004).

Peaks of crying appear to be concentrated in the late afternoon and early evening (McGlaughlin & Grayson, 2001). Although some cries may seem extreme and random at first, they tend to settle into a recognizable pattern. Infants seem to produce about the same number of crying bouts during the first 9 months or so, but the duration of the bouts lessens during this period (van IJzendoorn & Hubbard, 2000). The response of the caregiver influences crying. It turns out that the more frequently mothers ignore their infants' crying bouts in the first 9 weeks, the less frequently their infants cry in the following 9-week period (IJzendoorn & Hubbard, 2000). This finding should certainly not be interpreted to mean that infant crying is best ignored. At least at first, crying communicates pain and hunger, and these are conditions that it is advisable to correct. Persistent crying can strain the mother–infant relationship (Reijneveld et al., 2004).

> More Canadian children die from sudden infant death syndrome (SIDS) than die from cancer, heart disease, pneumonia, child abuse, AIDS, cystic fibrosis, and muscular dystrophy combined.

Soothing

Sucking seems to be a built-in tranquilizer. Sucking on a **pacifier** decreases crying and agitated movement in hungry neonates (Field, 1999). Therefore, the soothing function of sucking need not be learned through experience.

Parents soothe infants by picking them up, patting them, caressing and rocking them, swaddling them, and speaking to them in a low voice. Parents then usually try to find the specific cause of the distress by offering a bottle or pacifier or checking the diaper. Parents learn by trial and error what types of embraces and movements are likely to soothe infants, and infants learn quickly that crying is followed by being picked up or other interventions. Whether it is possible to spoil a crying baby remains a hotly debated question.

SUDDEN INFANT DEATH SYNDROME (SIDS)

It is true that more children die from **sudden infant death syndrome (SIDS)** than die from cancer, heart disease, pneumonia, child abuse, AIDS, cystic fibrosis, and muscular dystrophy combined (Lipsitt, 2003). The awareness campaign "Back to Sleep" was initiated in 1994; however, despite a 50 percent decrease in incidence, three babies succumb to SIDS each week in Canada (The Canadian Foundation for the Study of Infant Deaths, 2005). SIDS—also known as crib death—is a disorder of infancy that apparently strikes while a baby is sleeping. In the typical case, a baby goes to sleep, apparently in perfect health, and is found dead. There is typically no sign that the baby struggled or was in pain.

The incidence of SIDS has been declining, but many infants in Canada still die each year of SIDS. It is the most common cause of death during the first year, and most of these deaths occur between 2 and 5 months of age (Paterson et al., 2006). New parents frequently live in dread of SIDS and check a sleeping baby regularly to see if they are still breathing. It is not abnormal for

Shaken Baby Syndrome is an impulsive act of an often exhausted or frustrated caregiver. SBS cases happen in all cultural and socioeconomic groups.

SIDS is more common among the following (Hunt & Hauck, 2006; Paterson et al., 2006):

- Babies aged 2–4 months
- Babies who are put to sleep on their stomachs or their sides
- Premature and low-birth-weight infants
- Male babies
- Babies in families of lower socio-economic status
- African North American babies
- Babies of teenage mothers
- Babies whose mothers smoked during or after pregnancy or whose mothers used narcotics during pregnancy

*It is important to note that these are risk factors and not causes of SIDS

© Radius Images/Jupiterimages

babies occasionally to suspend breathing for a moment which heightens caregiver anxiety.

What should *you* do about SIDS? Bear in mind that the prevention of SIDS begins during pregnancy. Smoking and using other drugs during pregnancy increase the risk of SIDS. Obtain adequate nutrition and health care during pregnancy. Place your baby to sleep on its back. Keep current with research data on SIDS by checking with your pediatrician and by exploring websites such as those of the Centers for Disease Control and Prevention (http://www.cdc.gov/) and the SIDS Network (http://www.sids-network.org/). Perhaps within a few years we will have a screening test for SIDS and a method for preventing or controlling it.

SHAKEN BABY SYNDROME (SBS)

Shaken Baby Syndrome (SBS) and Abusive Head Trauma (AHT) are terms used to describe the injuries sustained by an infant or young child who is roughly shaken. In a Canadian study of 364 victims of SBS and AHT who were admitted to hospital (King et al., 2003), 81 percent of the children survived but suffered neurological deficit, visual impairment, and ongoing care issues; the other 19 percent died. The authors concluded that any estimate of the number of SBS cases was likely just the "tip of the iceberg," as the incidence of SBS and AHT is likely significantly underestimated due to misdiagnoses and underreporting.

We all need to realize that shaking a baby *can happen to anyone*. SBS is an impulsive act of an often exhausted or frustrated caregiver. SBS happens in all cultural and socioeconomic groups. If you know someone who has a baby, and you are able to help out, offer your assistance. If you have a baby and you need support, ask. For more information, visit www.shakenbaby.ca, a website maintained by the Alberta SBS Prevention Campaign (2010).

Shaken Baby Syndrome: Take a Break—Don't Shake

photos.com

Monkey Business Images/Shutterstock/ Courtesy of Alberta Health Services

Three key sequences

of physical development are cephalocaudal development, proximodistal development, and differentiation.

4

Infancy: Physical Development

What a fascinating creature the newborn is: tiny, delicate, apparently oblivious to its surroundings, yet perfectly formed and fully capable of letting its caregivers know when it is hungry, thirsty, or uncomfortable. And what a fascinating creature is this same child 2 years later: running, playing, talking, hugging, and kissing.

It is hard to believe that only 2 short years—the years of infancy—bring about so many changes. It seems that nearly every day brings a new accomplishment. But as we will see, not all infants share equally in the explosion of positive developments. Therefore, we will also enumerate some developmental problems and what can be done about them.

Learning Outcomes

LO1 Describe trends in the physical development of the infant

LO2 Describe the physical development of the brain and the nervous system

LO3 Describe the key events in the motor development of the infant

LO4 Describe patterns of sensory and perceptual development in infancy

LO1 Physical Growth and Development

during the first 2 years, children make enormous strides in physical growth and development. In this section, we explore sequences of physical development, changes in height and weight, and nutrition. As we see next, development is "head first."

SEQUENCES OF PHYSICAL DEVELOPMENT

Three key sequences of physical development are cephalocaudal development, proximodistal development, and differentiation.

Cephalocaudal Development

Development proceeds from the upper part of the head to the lower parts of the body (tip to toe). When we consider the central role of the brain, which is contained within the skull, the cephalocaudal sequence appears quite logical. The brain regulates essential functions, such as heartbeat. Through the secretion of hormones, the brain also regulates the growth and development of the body and influences basic drives, such as hunger and thirst.

The head develops more rapidly than the rest of the body during the embryonic stage. By 8 weeks after conception, the head constitutes half the entire length of the embryo. The brain develops more rapidly than the spinal cord. Arm buds form before leg buds. Most newborn babies have a strong, well-defined sucking reflex, although their legs are spindly and their limbs move back and forth only in diffuse excitement or agitation. Infants can hold up their heads before they gain control over their arms, their torsos, and, finally, their legs. They can sit up before they can crawl and walk.

The lower parts of the body, because they get off to a later start, must do more growing to reach adult size. The head doubles in length between birth and maturity, but the torso, arms, and legs increase in length by three, four, and five times, respectively.

> The head doubles in length between birth and maturity, but the torso, arms, and legs increase in length by three, four, and five times, respectively.

> **D1** The head of the newborn child doubles in length by adulthood, but the legs increase in length by about five times.
> The torso increases by about three times and the arms by four.

Proximodistal Development

Growth and development also proceed from the trunk outward (from the centre out), from the body's central axis toward the periphery. The proximodistal principle, too, makes sense. The brain and spinal cord follow a central axis down through the body, and it is essential that the nerves be in place before the infant can gain control over the arms and legs. Consider also that the life functions of the newborn baby—heartbeat, respiration, digestion, and elimination of wastes—are all carried out by organ systems close to the central axis. These functions must be in operation or ready to operate when the child is born.

In terms of motor development, infants gain control over their trunks and their shoulders before they can control their arms, hands, and fingers. Similarly, infants gain control over their hips and upper legs before they can direct their lower legs, feet, and toes.

Differentiation

As children mature, their physical reactions become less global and more specific. The tendency of behaviour to become more specific and distinct is called **differentiation**. If a neonate's finger is pricked or burned, he or she may withdraw the finger but also thrash about, cry, and show general signs of distress. Toddlers may also cry, show distress, and withdraw the finger, but they are less likely to thrash about wildly. Thus, the response to pain has become more specific. An older child or adult is also likely to withdraw the finger, but less likely to wail (sometimes) and show general distress.

GROWTH PATTERNS IN HEIGHT AND WEIGHT

The most dramatic gains in height and weight occur during prenatal development. Within a span of 9 months, children develop from a zygote about 0.015 cm (1/175th of an inch) long to a neonate about 50 cm (20 in.) in length. Weight increases by billions.

During the first year after birth, gains in height and weight are also dramatic, although not by the standards of prenatal gains. Infants usually double their birth weight in about 5 months and triple it by the first birthday (Kuczmarski et al., 2000). Their height increases by about 50 percent in the first year, so that a child whose length at birth was 50 cm (20 in.) is likely to be about 75 cm (30 in.) tall at 12 months.

> **D2** Infants, on average, triple their birth weight within a year.
> Infants usually double their birth weight in about 5 months and triple it by the first birthday if development is proceeding according to the norm.

Growth in infancy has long been viewed as a slow and steady process. Growth charts in pediatricians' offices resemble the smooth, continuous curves shown in Figure 4.1, but research suggests that infants actually grow in spurts. About 90–95 percent of the time, they are not growing at all. One study measured the height of infants throughout their first 21 months (Lampl et al., 1992). The researchers found that the infants would remain the same size for 2 to 63 days and then would shoot up in height by 0.5 to 2.5 cm (1/5 to 1 in.) in less than 24 hours.

Infants grow another 10 to 15 cm (4 to 6 in.) during the second year and gain another 1.8 to 3.2 kg (4 to 7 lb.). Boys generally reach half their adult height by their second birthday. Girls, however, mature more quickly than boys and are likely to reach half their adult height at the age of 18 months (Tanner, 1989). The growth rates of taller-than-average infants, as a group, tend to slow down. Those of shorter-than-average infants, as a group, tend to speed up. Tall infants, as a group, achieve a taller adult height than the adult height achieved by short infants, but in most cases not by as much as seemed likely during infancy.

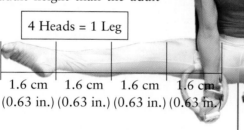

1 Head

4 Heads = 1 Leg

3 Heads = 1 Arm

1.6 cm (0.63 in.)   1.6 cm (0.63 in.)   1.6 cm (0.63 in.)   1.6 cm (0.63 in.)

1.6 cm (0.63 in.)

Changes in Body Proportions

Development proceeds in a cephalocaudal manner. A few weeks after conception, an embryo is almost all head. At the beginning of the fetal stage, the head is about half the length of the unborn child. In the neonate, it is about one-fourth the length of the body. The head gradually diminishes in proportion to the rest of the body, even though it doubles in size by adulthood.

Typically, an adult's arms are nearly three times the length of the head. The legs are about four times as long. Among neonates, the arms and legs are about equal in length. Each is only about one and a half times the length of the head. By the first birthday, the neck has begun to lengthen, as have the arms and legs. The arms grow more rapidly than the legs at first; by the second birthday, the arms are actually longer than the legs, but soon the legs catch up with and surpass the arms in length.

Failure to Thrive

Haley is 4 months old. Her mother, as she puts it, is breast-feeding Haley "all the time" because she is not gaining weight. Not gaining weight for a while is normal, but Haley is also irritable and feeds fitfully, sometimes refusing the breast entirely. Her pediatrician is evaluating her for a syndrome called **failure to thrive (FTT)**.

FTT is a serious disorder that impairs growth in infancy and early childhood (Simonelli et al., 2005). Yet FTT is sometimes an unclear diagnosis. Historically, researchers have spoken of biologically based (or "organic") FTT versus nonbiologically based ("nonorganic") FTT. The idea is that in organic FTT an underlying health problem accounts for FTT. Nonorganic FTT (NOFTT) apparently has psychological roots, social roots, or both. In either case, the infant does not make normal gains in weight and size (Simonelli et al., 2005).

Regardless of the cause or causes, feeding problems are central. As in Haley's case, infants are more likely to be described as variable eaters and less often as hungry (Wright & Birks, 2000). FTT is linked not only to slow physical growth but also to cognitive, behavioural, and emotional problems (Simonelli et al., 2005). At the age of 8½, children who had been diagnosed with FTT in infancy were smaller, less cognitively advanced, and more emotionally disturbed than normal children (Dykman et al., 2001).

Catch-Up Growth

A child's growth can be slowed from its genetically predetermined course by many environmental factors, including illness and malnutrition. If the problem is alleviated, the child's rate of growth frequently accelerates to approximate its normal course (van IJzendoorn & Juffer, 2006).

failure to thrive (FTT) a disorder of infancy and early childhood characterized by variable eating and inadequate gains in weight.

FIGURE 4.1

Growth Curves for Weight and Height (Length) from Birth to Age 18 Months for Boys and Girls

The curves indicate the percentiles for weight and length at different ages. Lines labelled 95 show the height and weight of children who are taller and heavier than 95 percent of children of a particular age. Lines marked 50 indicate the height and weight of the average child of a given age.

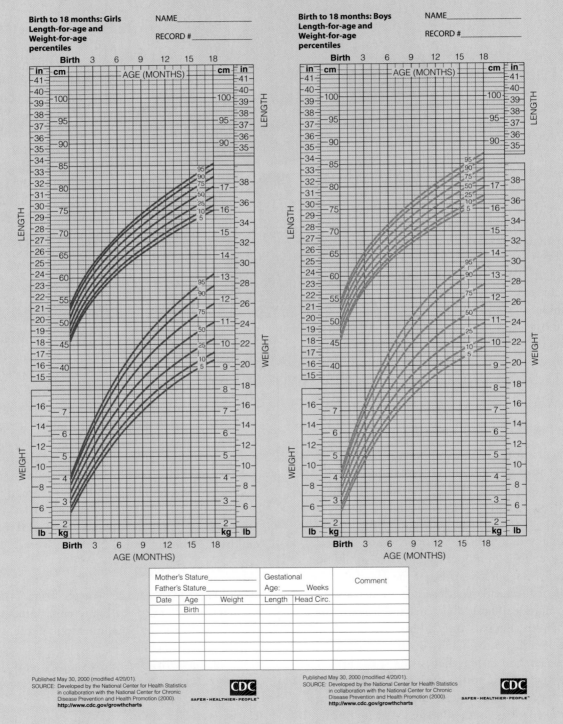

The tendency to return to one's genetically determined pattern of growth is referred to as **canalization**. Once Haley's parents receive counselling and once Haley's FTT is overcome, Haley will put on weight rapidly and catch up to the norms for her age.

NUTRITION: FUELLING DEVELOPMENT

The nutritional status of most children in Canada is good compared with that of children in developing countries (Arija et al., 2006). However, infants and young children from low-income families are more likely than other children to display signs of poor nutrition, such as anemia and FTT (National Center for Children in Poverty, 2004).

From birth, infants should be fed either breast milk or an iron-fortified infant formula. The Canadian Paediatric Society recommends exclusive breast feeding for the first six months of life for healthy, term infants. Breast milk is the optimal food for infants, and breast feeding may continue for up to two years and beyond for mothers who are socially comfortable with this practice. (Boland, 2009). The introduction of solid foods is not recommended until about 4 to 6 months of age. Infants typically begin a solid-food diet by eating iron-enriched cereal, followed by strained fruits, vegetables, meats, poultry, and fish. Whole cow's milk is normally delayed until the infant is 9 to 12 months old. Finger foods such as teething biscuits are introduced in the latter part of the first year.

Here are some useful guidelines for infant nutrition (Infant and Toddler Nutrition, 2007):

- Build up to a variety of foods. Introduce new foods one at a time. The infant may be allergic to a new food, and introducing foods one at a time helps isolate its possible effects.
- Pay attention to the infant's appetite to help avoid overfeeding or underfeeding.
- Generally avoid items with added sugar and salt.
- Encourage eating of high-iron foods; infants need more iron, pound for pound, than adults do.

Canadians live in a very diet-conscious society. Low-fat, high-fibre diets with a focus on sugar substitutes are not healthy for infants.

BREAST FEEDING VERSUS BOTTLE FEEDING

In many developing nations, mothers have to breast-feed. Even in developed nations, where formula is readily available, breast milk is considered by most health professionals to be the "medical gold standard" (Knaak, 2005). An 8 percent global increase in exclusive breast feeding to 6 months is estimated to have reduced infant mortality by 1,000,000, decreased fertility by 600,000, and saved countries billions of dollars in unneeded breast milk substitutes (UNICEF, 2010). Perhaps for this reason, popular magazines tend to carry more articles on breast feeding than on bottle feeding (Frerichs et al., 2006).

> **canalization** the tendency of growth rates to return to normal after undergoing environmentally induced change.

Over the past few decades, breast feeding has become more popular, largely because of increased knowledge of its health benefits (Sloan et al., 2006). Today, most Canadian mothers—more than 85 percent—breast-feed their children for at least a while, but only 47 percent breast-feed for 6 months or more (Millar & Mclean, 2005).

Many women bottle-feed because they return to work after childbirth and breast feeding becomes logistically complicated. Caregivers give their children bottles during the day. Some mothers pump their milk and bottle it for use when they are away. Some parents bottle-feed because it permits both parents to share in feeding. Although breast feeding is a bonding experience for the mother and the child, it is also a stressful relationship, requiring support for it to continue.

There are numerous advantages to breast milk, according to Health Canada (2007a):

- Breast feeding is associated with better neural and behavioural organization in the infant.
- Breast milk contains the mother's antibodies and reduces the infant's incidence of infection.
- Breast milk enhances cognitive development.
- Breast-fed infants are less likely to develop allergic responses and diarrhea.
- Breast-fed infants are less likely to die of SIDS.

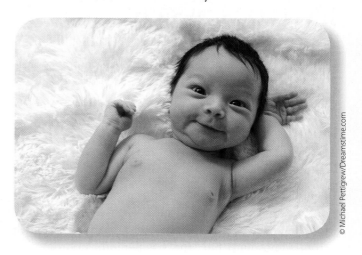

© Michael Pettigrew/Dreamstime.com

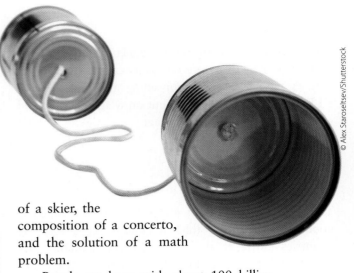

© Alex Staroseltsev/Shutterstock

nerves bundles of axons from many neurons.

neurons cells in the nervous system that transmit messages.

dendrites rootlike parts of neurons that receive impulses from other neurons.

axon a long, thin part of a neuron that transmits impulses to other neurons through branching structures called axon terminals.

neurotransmitter a chemical that transmits a neural impulse across a synapse from one neuron to another.

myelin sheath a fatty, whitish substance that encases and insulates axons.

myelination the coating of axons with myelin.

Breast feeding also has health benefits for the mother: It reduces the risk of early breast cancer and ovarian cancer, and it builds the strength of bones, which can reduce the likelihood of the hip fractures that result from osteoporosis following menopause. Breast feeding also helps shrink the uterus after delivery and hastens post-birth weight loss.

There are downsides to breast feeding. For example, breast milk is one of the bodily fluids that transmit HIV. As many as one-third of the world's infants who have HIV/AIDS were infected in this manner (UNAIDS, 2006). Alcohol, many drugs, and environmental hazards such as polychlorinated biphenyls (PCBs) can also be transmitted through breast milk. Moreover, for breast milk to contain the necessary nutrients, the mother must be adequately nourished herself. The mother also encounters the physical demands of producing and expelling milk, a tendency for soreness in the breasts, and the emotional demands of being continually available to meet the infant's feeding needs.

LO2 Development of the Brain and Nervous System

t he nervous system is a system of **nerves** involved in heartbeat, visual–motor coordination, thought and language, and so on.

DEVELOPMENT OF NEURONS

The basic units of the nervous system are cells called **neurons**. Neurons receive and transmit messages from one part of the body to another. The messages account for phenomena such as reflexes, the perception of an itch from a mosquito bite, the visual–motor coordination

of a skier, the composition of a concerto, and the solution of a math problem.

People are born with about 100 billion neurons, most of which are in the brain. Neurons vary according to their functions and locations in the body. Some neurons in the brain are only a fraction of a centimetre in length, whereas neurons in the leg can grow more than a couple of metres (several feet) long. Each neuron possesses a cell body, dendrites, and an axon (see Figure 4.2). **Dendrites** are short fibres that extend from the cell body and receive incoming messages from up to 1,000 adjoining transmitting neurons. The **axon** extends trunklike from the cell body and accounts for much of the difference in length in neurons. An axon can be up to a couple of metres (several feet) in length if it is carrying messages from the toes upward. Messages are released from axon terminals in the form of chemicals called **neurotransmitters**. These messages are received by the dendrites of adjoining neurons, muscles, or glands. As the child matures, axons lengthen, and dendrites and axon terminals proliferate.

> People are born with about 100 billion neurons, most of which are in the brain.

Myelin

Many neurons are tightly wrapped with white, fatty **myelin sheaths** that give them the appearance of a string of white sausages. The high fat content of the myelin sheath insulates the neuron from electrically charged atoms in the fluids that encase the nervous system. In this way, leakage of the electric current being carried along the axon is minimized, and messages are conducted more efficiently.

The term **myelination** refers to the process by which axons are coated with myelin. Myelination is not complete at birth, but rather is part of the maturation process that leads to the abilities to crawl and walk during the first year after birth. Myelination of the brain's prefrontal matter continues into the second decade of life and is connected with advances in working memory and language ability (Aslin & Schlaggar, 2006; Pujol et al., 2006). Breakdown of myelin is believed to be associated with Alzheimer's disease, a source of cognitive decline that begins later in life.

FIGURE 4.2
Anatomy of a Neuron

"Messages" enter neurons through dendrites, are transmitted along the axon, and sent through axon terminals to muscles, glands, and other neurons. Neurons develop by proliferation of dendrites and axon terminals and through myelination.

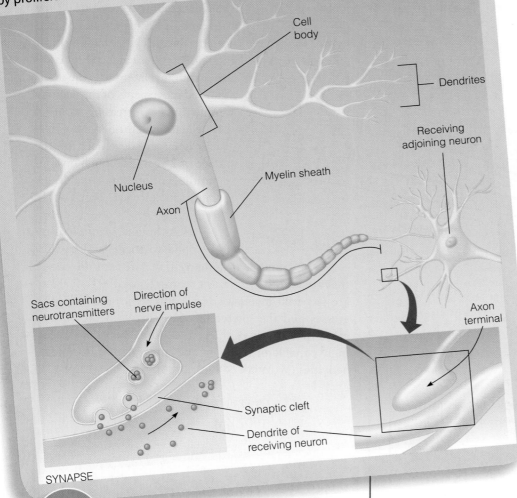

SYNAPSE

HDEV Go to www.icanhdev.com to access an interactive version of this figure.

multiple sclerosis a disorder in which hard fibrous tissue replaces myelin, impeding neural transmission.

medulla an area of the hindbrain involved in heartbeat and respiration.

cerebellum the part of the hindbrain involved in coordination and balance.

cerebrum the part of the brain responsible for learning, thought, memory, and language.

D3 A child's brain reaches half its adult weight by the age of 1 year.
By the first birthday, a child's brain usually triples in weight, reaching roughly 70 percent of its adult weight.

growth, an infant's brain reaches a good deal more than half its adult weight by the first birthday. It triples in weight, reaching nearly 70 percent of its adult weight (see Figure 4.3). Let's look at the brain, as shown in Figure 4.4, and discuss the development of the structures within.

In the disease **multiple sclerosis**, myelin is replaced by hard, fibrous tissue that disrupts the timing of neural transmission, interfering with muscle control (Stankoff et al., 2006). Phenylketonuria (PKU) causes mental retardation by inhibiting the formation of myelin in the brain (Sirrs et al., 2007).

DEVELOPMENT OF THE BRAIN

The brain of the neonate weighs a little less than half a kilogram (less than 1 lb.), or nearly one-fourth its adult weight. In keeping with the principles of cephalocaudal

Structures of the Brain

Many nerves that connect the spinal cord to higher levels of the brain pass through the **medulla**. The medulla is vital in the control of basic functions, such as heartbeat and respiration. The medulla is part of an area called the brain stem. Above the medulla lies the **cerebellum**. The cerebellum helps the child maintain balance, control motor behaviour, and coordinate eye movements with bodily sensations.

The **cerebrum** is the crowning glory of the brain. It makes possible the breadth and depth of human learning, thought, memory, and language. The surface of the cerebrum consists of two hemispheres that become increasingly wrinkled as the child develops, coming to show ridges and valleys called fissures. This surface is the cerebral cortex. The cerebral cortex is only 0.3 cm (1/8 in.) thick, yet it is the seat of thought and reason.

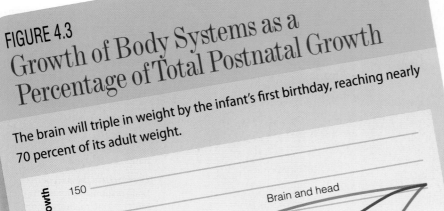

FIGURE 4.3
Growth of Body Systems as a Percentage of Total Postnatal Growth

The brain will triple in weight by the infant's first birthday, reaching nearly 70 percent of its adult weight.

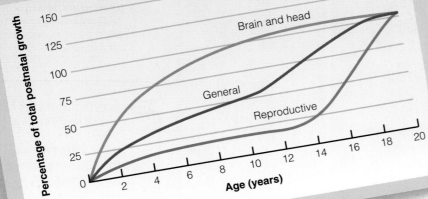

It is here that we receive sensory information from the world outside and command muscles to move.

D4 The cerebral cortex—the outer layer of the brain that is vital to human thought and reasoning—is only 0.3 cm (1/8 in.) thick.
Yet it houses the thought and the reason of the individual.

Growth Spurts of the Brain

The first major growth spurt of the brain occurs during the fourth and fifth months of prenatal development, when neurons proliferate. A second growth spurt in the brain occurs between the 25th week of prenatal development and the end of the second year after birth. Whereas the first growth spurt of the brain is due to the formation of neurons, the second growth spurt is due primarily to the proliferation of dendrites and axon terminals (see Figure 4.5).

Brain Development in Infancy

There is a link between what infants can do and myelination. At birth, the parts of the brain involved in heartbeat and respiration, sleeping and arousal, and reflex activity are fairly well myelinated and functional. Myelination of motor pathways allows neonates to show stereotyped reflexes, but otherwise neonates' physical activity tends to be random and ill-organized. Myelin develops rapidly along the major motor pathways from the cerebral cortex during the last month of pregnancy and continues after birth. The development of intentional physical activity coincides with myelination as the unorganized movements of the neonate come under increasing control. Myelination of the nerves to muscles is largely developed by the age of 2 years, although myelination continues to some degree into adolescence (Wozniak & Lim, 2006).

Although neonates respond to touch and can see and hear quite well, the areas of the cortex that are involved in vision, hearing, and the skin senses are less well myelinated at birth. As myelination progresses and the interconnections between the various areas of the cortex thicken, children become increasingly capable of complex and integrated sensorimotor activities (Wozniak & Lim, 2006).

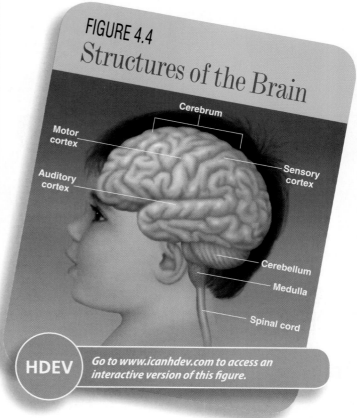

FIGURE 4.4
Structures of the Brain

HDEV *Go to www.icanhdev.com to access an interactive version of this figure.*

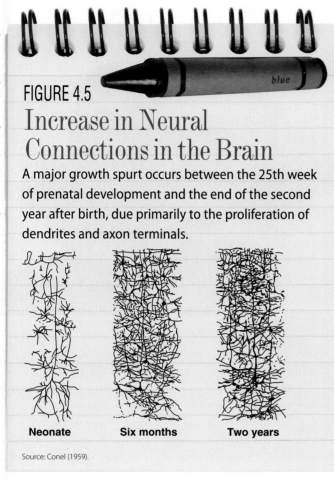

FIGURE 4.5

Increase in Neural Connections in the Brain

A major growth spurt occurs between the 25th week of prenatal development and the end of the second year after birth, due primarily to the proliferation of dendrites and axon terminals.

Neonate   **Six months**   **Two years**

Source: Conel (1959).

Myelination of the neurons involved in the sense of hearing begins at about the sixth month of pregnancy. Myelination of these pathways is developing rapidly at term and continues until about the age of 4 years. The neurons involved in vision begin to myelinate only shortly before full term, but then they complete the process of myelination rapidly. Within 5 to 6 months after birth, vision has become the dominant sense.

NATURE AND NURTURE IN BRAIN DEVELOPMENT

Development of the areas of the brain that control sensation and movement begins as a result of maturation, but sensory stimulation and physical activity during early infancy also spur the development of these areas(Güntürkün, 2006; Posner & Rothbart, 2007).

Research with animals shows how sensory

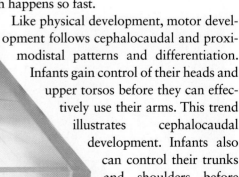

stimulation sparks growth of the cortex. Researchers have given rats "amusement parks" with toys such as ladders, platforms, and boxes to demonstrate the effects of enriched environments. In these studies, rats exposed to the more complex environments develop heavier brains than control animals. The weight differences in part reflect more synapses per neuron (Briones et al., 2004). On the other hand, animals reared in darkness show shrinkage of the visual cortex, impaired vision, and impaired visual–motor coordination (Klintsova & Greenough, 1999). If they don't use it, they lose it.

The brain is also affected by experience. Infants actually have more connections among neurons than adults do. Connections that are activated by experience survive; the others do not (Tsuneishi & Casaer, 2000; Weinberg, 2004) and are pruned over time.

The great adaptability of the brain appears to be a double-edged sword. Adaptability allows us to develop different patterns of neural connections to meet the demands of different environments, but lack of stimulation—especially during critical early periods of development—can impair adaptability.

LO3 Motor Development

m otor development involves the activity of muscles, leading to changes in posture, movement, and coordination of movement with the infant's developing sensory apparatus. Motor development provides some of the most fascinating changes in infants, because so much happens so fast.

Like physical development, motor development follows cephalocaudal and proximodistal patterns and differentiation. Infants gain control of their heads and upper torsos before they can effectively use their arms. This trend illustrates cephalocaudal development. Infants also can control their trunks and shoulders before they can use their hands and fingers, demonstrating the proximodistal trend.

LIFTING AND HOLDING THE TORSO AND HEAD

Neonates can move their heads slightly to the side. They can thus avoid suffocation if they are lying face down and their noses or mouths are obstructed by bedding. At about 1 month, infants can raise their heads. By about 2 months, they can also lift their chests while lying on their stomachs.

When neonates are held, their heads must be supported. But by 3 to 6 months of age, infants generally manage to hold their heads quite well, so supporting the head is no longer necessary. Unfortunately, infants who can normally support their heads cannot do so when they are lifted or moved about in a jerky manner; infants who are handled carelessly can thus develop neck injuries and in extreme cases, Shaken Baby Syndrome (see section SBS on page 67).

CONTROL OF THE HANDS: GETTING A GRIP

The development of hand skills is an example of proximodistal development. Infants will track slowly moving objects with their eyes shortly after birth, but they will not reach for them. Voluntary reaching and grasping require visual–motor coordination. By about 3 months, infants will make clumsy swipes at objects. Between 4 and 6 months, infants become more successful at grasping objects (Piek, 2006; Santos et al., 2000). However, they may not know how to let go and may hold an object indefinitely, until their attention is diverted and the hand

opens accidentally. Four to 6 months is a good age for giving children rattles, large plastic spoons, mobiles, and other brightly coloured hanging toys that can be grasped but are harmless when they wind up in the mouth.

Grasping is reflexive at first. Voluntary holding replaces reflexive grasping by 3 to 4 months. Infants first use an **ulnar grasp**, holding objects clumsily between their fingers and their palm. By 4 to 6 months, they can transfer objects back and forth between hands. The oppositional thumb comes into play at about 9 to 12 months, enabling infants to pick up tiny objects in a **pincer grasp**. By about 11 months, infants can hold objects in each hand and inspect them in turn.

Another aspect of visual–motor coordination is stacking blocks. On average, children can stack two blocks at 15 months, three blocks at 18 months, and five blocks at 24 months (Wentworth et al., 2000).

Pincer Grasp

Crawling

Walking

FIGURE 4.6
Motor Development in Infancy

Motor development proceeds in an orderly sequence, but there is considerable variation in the timing of marker events.

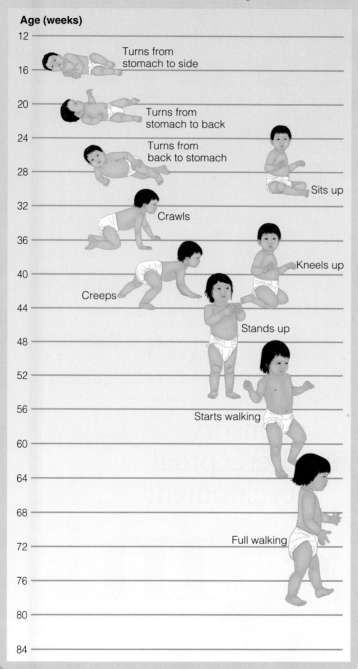

Age (weeks)

- Turns from stomach to side
- Turns from stomach to back
- Turns from back to stomach
- Sits up
- Crawls
- Kneels up
- Creeps
- Stands up
- Starts walking
- Full walking

LOCOMOTION

Locomotion is movement from one place to another. Children gain the capacity to move their bodies through a sequence of activities that includes rolling over, sitting up, crawling, creeping, walking, and running (see Figure 4.6). There is much variation in the ages at which infants first engage in these activities. Although the sequence mostly remains the same, some children will skip a step. For example, an infant may creep without ever having crawled.

Most infants can roll over, from back to stomach and from stomach to back, by about the age of 6 months. By about 7 months, infants usually begin to sit up by themselves. At about 8 to 9 months, most infants begin to crawl, a motor activity in which they lie on their bellies and use their arms to pull themselves along. Creeping, in which infants move themselves along on their hands and knees, usually appears a month or so after crawling.

Standing overlaps with crawling and creeping. Most infants can remain in a standing position by holding on to something at the age of 8 or 9 months. At this age, they may also be able to walk a bit with support. About 2 months later, they can pull themselves to a standing position by holding on to the sides of their cribs or other objects and can stand briefly without holding on. By 12 to 15 months or so, they walk by themselves, earning them the name **toddler**.

Toddlers soon run about, supporting their relatively heavy heads and torsos by spreading their legs in a bowlegged fashion. Because they are top-heavy and inexperienced, they fall frequently. Many toddlers are skillful at navigating slopes (Adolph & Berger, 2005). They walk down shallow slopes but prudently choose to slide or crawl down steep ones. Walking lends children new freedom. It allows them to get about rapidly and to grasp objects that were formerly out of reach. Give toddlers a large ball to toss and run after; it is an inexpensive and most enjoyable toy.

As children mature, their muscle strength, bone density, and balance and coordination improve (Metcalfe et al., 2005). By the age of 2 years, they can climb steps one at a time, placing both feet on each step. They can run well, walk backward, kick a large ball, and jump several inches.

Both maturation (nature) and experience (nurture) are involved in motor development Certain voluntary motor activities are not possible until the brain has matured in terms of myelination and the differentiation of the motor areas of the cortex. Although the neonate shows stepping and swimming reflexes, these behaviours are controlled by more primitive parts of the brain. They disappear when

locomotion movement from one place to another.

toddler a child who walks with short, uncertain steps.

D5 Native American Hopi infants spend the first year of life strapped to a board, yet they begin to walk at about the same time as children who are reared in other cultures. When released from the cradle board, Hopi infants learn to move around very quickly, and operate like most other children by their second year.

cortical development inhibits some functions of the lower parts of the brain; and, when they reappear, they differ in quality.

Infants also need some opportunity to experiment before they can engage in milestones such as sitting up and walking. Even so, many of these advances can apparently be attributed to maturation. In classic research, Wayne Dennis and Marsena Dennis (1940) reported on the motor development of Native American Hopi children who spent their first year strapped to a cradle board. Although denied a full year of experience in locomotion, the Hopi infants gained the capacity to walk early in their second year, about when other children do.

Can training accelerate the appearance of motor skills? In a classic study with identical twins, Arnold Gesell (1929) gave one twin extensive training in hand coordination, block building, and stair climbing from early infancy. The other twin was allowed to develop on his own. At first, the trained twin had better skills, but as time passed, the untrained twin became just as skilled. The development of motor skills can be accelerated by training (Adolph & Berger, 2005; Zelazo, 1998), but the long-lasting effect seems slight.

Although being strapped to a cradle board did not permanently prevent the motor development of Hopi infants, Wayne Dennis (1960) reported that infants in an Iranian orphanage, who were exposed to extreme social and physical deprivation, were significantly slowed in their motor development. They grew apathetic, and all aspects of development suffered. By contrast, however, the motor development of similar infants in a Lebanese orphanage accelerated dramatically in response to such minimal intervention as being propped up in their cribs and being given a few colourful toys (Sayegh & Dennis, 1965).

Nature provides the limits—the "reaction range"—for the expression of inherited traits. Nurture determines whether the child will develop skills that reach the upper limits of the range. Even such a fundamental skill as locomotion is determined by a complex interplay of maturational and environmental factors (Adolph & Berger, 2005). There may be little purpose in trying to train children to enhance motor skills before they are ready. Once they are ready, however, teaching and practice do make a difference. One does not become an Olympic athlete without "good genes," but one also usually does not become an Olympic athlete without solid training.

LO4 Sensory and Perceptual Development

many things that are obvious to us are not so obvious to infants. You may know that a coffee cup is the same whether you see it from above or from the side, but make no such assumptions about the infant's knowledge. You may know that an infant's mother is the same size whether she is standing next to the infant or approaching from two blocks away, but do not assume that the infant agrees with you.

DEVELOPMENT OF VISION

Development of vision involves development of visual acuity or sharpness, development of peripheral vision (seeing things at the sides while looking ahead), visual preferences, depth perception, and perceptual constancies, such as knowing that an object remains the same object even though it may look different when seen from a different angle.

Development of Visual Acuity and Peripheral Vision

Newborns are extremely nearsighted, with vision beginning at about 20/600. The most dramatic gains in visual acuity are made between birth and 6 months of age, with acuity reaching about 20/50 (Haith, 1990; Skoczenski, 2002). By 3 to 5 years, visual acuity generally approximates adult levels (20/20 in the best cases).

Neonates also have poor peripheral vision (Cavallini et al., 2002; Skoczenski, 2002). Adults can perceive objects that are nearly 90 degrees off to the side (i.e., directly to the left or right), although objects at these extremes are unclear. Neonates cannot perceive visual stimuli that are off to the side by an angle of more than 30 degrees, but their peripheral vision expands to an angle of about 45 degrees by the age of 7 weeks. By 6 months, their peripheral vision is about equal to that of an adult.

Let us now consider the development of visual perception. We will see that infants frequently prefer the strange to the familiar and will avoid going off the deep end—sometimes.

Visual Preferences

Neonates look at stripes longer than at blobs. This finding has been used in much of the research on visual acuity. Classic research found that by the age of 8 to 12 weeks, most infants also show distinct preferences for curved lines over straight ones (Fantz et al., 1975).

Robert Fantz (1961) also wondered whether something intrinsically interesting about the human face drew the attention of infants. To investigate this question, he showed 2-month-old infants the six disks in Figure 4.7. One disk contained human features, another newsprint, and still another a bull's-eye.

> By the age of 8 to 12 weeks, most infants show distinct preferences for curved lines over straight ones.

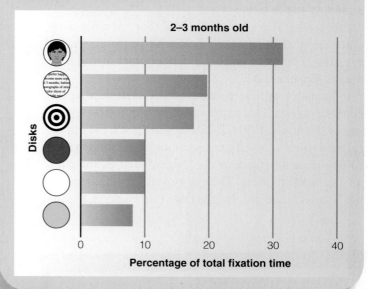

FIGURE 4.7
Preferences for Visual Stimuli in 2-Month-Olds

Infants appear to prefer complex to simple visual stimuli. By the time they are 2 months old, they also tend to show preference for the human face.

2–3 months old

Disks

Percentage of total fixation time

The remaining three disks were featureless but coloured red, white, and yellow. In this study, the infants fixated significantly longer on the human face.

Some studies suggest that the infants in Fantz's (1961) study may have preferred the human face because it had a complex, intriguing pattern of dots (eyes) within an outline, not because it was a face. But de Haan and Groen (2006) assert that "reading" faces (interpreting facial expressions) is important to infants because they do not understand verbal information as communicated through language.

Researchers therefore continue to ask whether humans come into the world "prewired" to prefer human stimuli to other stimuli that are just as complex, and—if so—what it is about human stimuli that draws attention. Some researchers—unlike de Haan and Groen—argue that neonates do not "prefer" faces because they are faces per se but because of the structure of their immature visual systems (Simion et al., 2001). A supportive study of 34 neonates found that the longer fixations on facelike stimuli resulted from a larger number of brief fixations (looks) rather than from a few prolonged fixations (Cassia et al., 2001). The infants' gaze, then, was sort of bouncing around from feature to feature rather than "staring" at the face in general. The researchers interpreted the finding to show that the stimulus properties of the visual object are more important than the fact that it represents a human face. Even so, of course, the "immature visual system" would be providing some "prewired" basis for attending to the face.

Learning also plays some role. For example, neonates can discriminate their mother's face from a stranger's after 8 hours of mother–infant contact spread over 4 days (Bushnell, 2001).

Neonates appear to direct their attention to the edges of objects. This pattern persists for the first several weeks (Bronson, 1991). When they are given the opportunity to look at human faces, 1-month-old infants tend to pay most attention to the "edges," that is, the chin, an ear, or the hairline. The eye movements of 2-month-old infants move in from the edge (see Figure 4.8). The

infants focus particularly on the eyes, although they also inspect other features such as the mouth and nose (Nelson & Ludemann, 1989).

Some researchers (e.g., Haith, 1979) explain infants' tendencies to scan from the edges of objects inward by noting that for the first several weeks, infants seem to be concerned with *where* things are. Their attention is captured by movement and sharp contrasts in brightness and shape, such as those found where the edges of objects stand out against their backgrounds. But by about 2 months, infants tend to focus on the *what* of things, scanning systematically within the boundaries of objects (Bronson, 1990, 1997).

Development of Depth Perception

Infants generally respond to cues for depth by the time they are able to crawl (6 to 8 months of age or so), and most have the good sense to avoid "going off the deep end," that is, crawling off ledges and tabletops into open space (Campos et al., 1978).

In a classic study on depth perception, Gibson and Walk (1960) placed infants of various ages on a fabric-covered runway that ran across the centre of a clever device called a *visual cliff* (see Figure 4.9). The visual cliff is a sheet of Plexiglas that covers a cloth with a checkerboard pattern. On one side, the cloth is placed immediately beneath the Plexiglas; on the other, it is dropped about 1.2 m (4 ft.). In the Gibson and Walk study, 8 out of 10 infants who had begun to crawl refused to venture onto the seemingly unsupported surface, even when their mothers beckoned encouragingly from the other side.

Psychologists can assess infants' emotional responses to the visual cliff long before infants can crawl. For example, Campos and his colleagues (1970) found that 1-month-old infants showed no change in heart rate when placed face down on the "cliff." They apparently did not perceive the depth of the cliff. At 2 months, infants showed decreases in heart rate when so placed, which psychologists interpret as a sign of interest. But the heart rates of 9-month-olds accelerated on the cliff, which is interpreted as a fear response. The study appears to suggest that infants profit from some experience crawling about (and, perhaps, accumulating some bumps) before they develop fear of heights. The 9-month-olds but not the 2-month-olds had had such experience. Other studies support the view that infants usually do not develop fear of heights until they can move around (Sorce et al., 2000; Witherington et al., 2005).

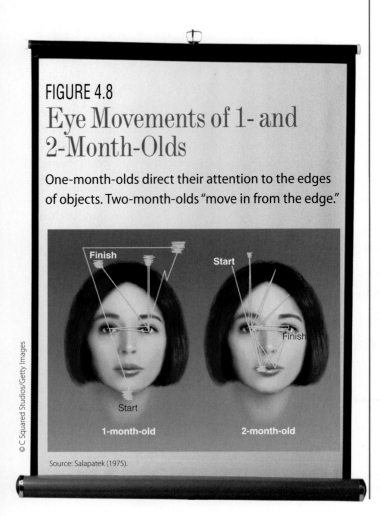

FIGURE 4.8
Eye Movements of 1- and 2-Month-Olds

One-month-olds direct their attention to the edges of objects. Two-month-olds "move in from the edge."

Finish

Start

Finish

Start

1-month-old

2-month-old

Source: Salapatek (1975).

© C Squared Studios/Getty Images

FIGURE 4.9

The Visual Cliff

This young explorer has the good sense not to crawl out onto an apparently unsupported surface, even when mother beckons from the other side.

© Mark Richards / PhotoEdit

Development of Perceptual Constancies

It may not surprise you that a 1-m (3-ft.) stick is the same length whether it is 2 m (6 ft.) or 6 m (18 ft.) away or that a door across the room is a rectangle whether closed or ajar. Awareness of these facts depends not on sensation alone but on the development of perceptual constancies. **Perceptual constancy** is the tendency to perceive an object to be the same, even though the sensations produced by the object may differ under various conditions.

Consider again the example of the metre stick. When it is 2 m (6 ft.) away, its image, as focused on the retina, has a certain "retinal size." From 6 m (18 ft.) away, the metre stick ruler is only one-third as long in terms of retinal size, but we perceive it as being the same size because of size constancy. *Size constancy* is the tendency to perceive the same objects as being of the same size even though their retinal sizes vary as a function of their distance. From 6 m (18 ft.) away, a 1-m stick (yardstick) casts an image equal in retinal size to the 30-cm (12-in.) ruler at 2 m (6 ft.), but—if recognized as a 1-m stick (yardstick)—it is perceived as longer, again because of size constancy.

Bower (1974) conditioned 2½- to 3-month-old infants to turn their heads to the left when shown a 12-inch (30-cm) cube from a distance of 3 feet (1 m). He then presented them with three experimental stimuli: (1) a 12-inch (30-cm) cube 9 feet (3 m) away, whose retinal size was smaller than that of the original cube; (2) a 36-inch (90-cm) cube 3 feet (1 m) away, whose retinal size was larger than that of the original cube; and (3) a 36-inch (90-cm) cube 9 feet (3 m) away, whose retinal size was the same as that of the original cube. The infants turned their heads most frequently in response to the first experimental cube, although its retinal image was only one-third the length of that to which they had been conditioned, suggesting that they had achieved size constancy. Later studies have confirmed Bower's finding that size constancy is present in early infancy. Some research suggests that even neonates possess rudimentary size constancy (Slater, 2000; Slater et al., 1990).

Shape constancy is the tendency to perceive an object as having the same shape even though, when perceived from another angle, the shape projected onto the retina may change dramatically. When the top of a cup or a glass is seen from above, the visual sensations are in the shape of a circle. When seen from a slight angle, the sensations are elliptical. However, because of our familiarity with the object, we still perceive the rim of the cup or glass as being a circle. In the first few months after birth, infants see the features of their caregivers, bottles, cribs, and toys from all different angles so that by the time they are 4 or 5 months old, a broad grasp of shape constancy seems to be established, at least under certain conditions (Slater, 2000).

> **perceptual constancy**
> perceiving objects as maintaining their identity although sensations from them change as their positions change.

DEVELOPMENT OF HEARING

Neonates can crudely orient their heads in the direction of a sound (Saffran et al., 2006). By 18 months of age, the accuracy of sound-localizing ability approaches that of adults. Sensitivity to sounds increases in the first few months of life (Saffran et al., 2006). As infants mature, the range of the pitch of the sounds they can sense gradually expands to include the adult's range of 20 to 20,000 cycles per second. The ability to detect differences in the pitch and loudness of sounds improves considerably throughout the preschool years. Auditory acuity also improves gradually over the first several years (Saffran et al., 2006), although infants' hearing can be so acute that many parents complain their napping infants will awaken at the slightest sound. This is especially true if parents have been overprotective in attempting to keep their rooms as silent as possible. Infants who are normally exposed to a backdrop of moderate noise levels

© Michelle D. Milliman/Shutterstock

Infants also learn at an early age to ignore small, meaningless variations in the sounds of their native language, for instance those caused by accents or head colds, as early as 6 months of age (Kuhl et al., 2006). Kuhl and her colleagues (1997) presented American and Swedish infants with pairs of sounds in either their own language or the other language. The infants were trained to look over their shoulder when they heard a difference in the sounds and to ignore sound pairs that seemed to be the same. The infants routinely ignored variations in sounds that were part of their language, because they apparently perceived them as the same sound. But the infants noticed slight variations in the sounds of the other language. Another study demonstrated the same ability in infants as young as 2 months (Marean et al., 1992).

DEVELOPMENT OF COORDINATION OF THE SENSES

Young infants can recognize that objects experienced by one sense (e.g., vision) are the same as those experienced

habituation becoming used to a stimulus and therefore paying less attention to it.

become habituated to them and are not likely to awaken unless there is a sudden, sharp noise.

By the age of 1 month, infants perceive differences between speech sounds that are highly similar. In a classic study relying on the **habituation** method, infants of this age could activate a recording of "bah" by sucking on a nipple (Eimas et al., 1971). As time went on, habituation occurred, as shown by decreased sucking so as to hear the "bah" sound. Then the researchers switched from "bah" to "pah." If the sounds had seemed the same to the infants, their lethargic sucking patterns would have continued, but they immediately sucked harder, suggesting that they perceived the difference. Other researchers have found that within another month or two, infants reliably discriminate three-syllable words such as *marana* and *malana* (Kuhl et al., 2006).

Infants can discriminate the sounds of their parent's voices by 3½ months of age. In classic research, infants of this age were oriented toward their parents as they reclined in infant seats. The experimenters (Spelke & Owsley, 1979) played recordings of the mother's or father's voice while the parents themselves remained inactive. The infants reliably looked at the parent whose voice was being played.

Young infants are capable of perceiving most of the speech sounds present in the world's languages. But after exposure to one's native language, infants gradually lose the capacity to discriminate those sounds that are not found in the native language (Werker et al., 2007), as shown in Figure 4.10 (Werker, 1989).

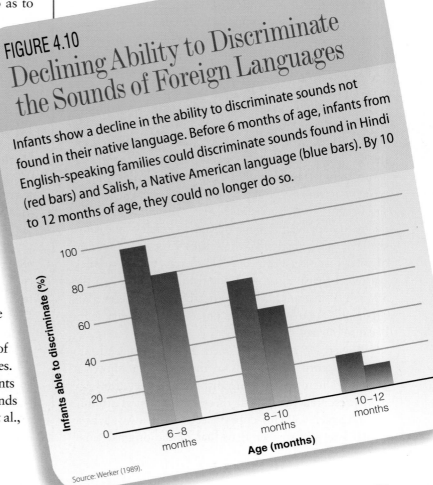

FIGURE 4.10
Declining Ability to Discriminate the Sounds of Foreign Languages

Infants show a decline in the ability to discriminate sounds not found in their native language. Before 6 months of age, infants from English-speaking families could discriminate sounds found in Hindi (red bars) and Salish, a Native American language (blue bars). By 10 to 12 months of age, they could no longer do so.

Source: Werker (1989).

through another sense (e.g., touch). This ability has been demonstrated in infants as young as 1 month of age (Bushnell, 1993). One experiment demonstrating such understanding in 5-month-olds showed that infants of this age tend to look longer at novel rather than familiar sources of stimulation. Féron and her colleagues (2006) first allowed 5-month-old infants to handle groups of either two or three objects, presented one by one, to their right hand. The infants were then shown visual displays of either two or three objects. The infants looked longer at the group of objects that differed from the one they had handled, showing a transfer of information from the sense of touch to the sense of vision.

THE ACTIVE–PASSIVE CONTROVERSY IN PERCEPTUAL DEVELOPMENT

Newborn children may have more sophisticated sensory capabilities than you expected. Still, their ways of perceiving the world are largely mechanical, or passive. Neonates seem to be generally at the mercy of external stimuli. When a bright light strikes, they attend to it. If the light moves slowly across the plane of their vision, they track it.

As time passes, broad changes occur in the perceptual processes of children, and the child's role in perception appears to become decidedly more active. Developmental psychologist Eleanor Gibson (1969, 1991) noted a number of these changes:

1. Intentional action (scanning and exploration) replaces "capture" (automatic responses to stimulation).
2. Systematic search replaces unsystematic search.
3. Attention becomes selective regardless of environmental confusion.
4. Irrelevant information becomes ignored (such as the noise of cars in the street or the playing of a radio in another room when the child is focused on playing).

In short, children develop from passive, mechanical reactors to the world about them into active, purposeful seekers and organizers of sensory information.

NATURE AND NURTURE IN PERCEPTUAL DEVELOPMENT

The nature–nurture issue is found in perceptual development, as in other areas of development.

Evidence for the Role of Nature

Compelling evidence supports the idea that inborn sensory capacities play a crucial role in perceptual development. Neonates arrive in the world with a good number of perceptual skills. They can see nearby objects quite well, and their hearing is usually fine. They are born with tendencies to track moving objects, to systematically scan the horizon, and to prefer certain kinds of stimuli. Preferences for different kinds of visual stimuli appear to unfold on schedule as the first months wear on. Sensory changes, as with motor changes, appear to be linked to maturation of the nervous system.

Evidence for the Role of Nurture

Evidence that experience plays a crucial role in perceptual development is also compelling. Children and lower animals have critical periods in their perceptual development. Failure to receive adequate sensory stimulation during these periods can result in permanent sensory deficits (Greenough et al., 2002). For example, newborn kittens raised with a patch over one eye wind up with few or no cells in the visual area of the cerebral cortex that would normally be stimulated by light that enters that eye. In effect, that eye becomes blind, even though sensory receptors in the eye itself may fire in response to light. On the other hand, if the eye of an adult cat is patched for the same amount of time, the animal will not lose vision. The critical period will have passed. Similarly, if health problems require that a child's eye must be patched for an extensive period of time during the first year, the child's visual acuity in that eye may be impaired.

Today most developmentalists would agree that nature and nurture interact to shape perceptual development. In the next chapter, we see how nature and nurture influence the development of thought and language in infants.

Photos.com

Cognitive development

focuses on the development of children's ways of perceiving and mentally representing the world.

5

Infancy: Cognitive Development

DID YOU KNOW?

D1 For 2-month-old infants, "out of sight" is "out of mind."

D2 A 1-hour-old infant may imitate an adult who sticks out his or her tongue.

D3 Psychologists can begin to measure intelligence in infancy.

D4 Infant crying is not a primitive form of language.

D5 You can advance children's development of pronunciation by correcting their errors.

D6 Children are "prewired" to listen to language in such a way that they come to understand rules of grammar.

Laurent . . . resumes his experiments of the day before. He grabs in succession a celluloid swan, a box, etc., stretches out his arm and lets them fall. He distinctly varies the position of the fall. Sometimes he stretches out his arm vertically, sometimes he holds it obliquely, in front of or behind his eyes, etc. When the object falls in a new position, he lets it fall two or three times more on the same place, as though to study the spatial relation; then he modifies the situation.

Is this description one of a scientist at work? In a way, it is. Although Swiss psychologist Jean Piaget (1963 [1936]) was describing his 11-month-old son, Laurent, children of this age frequently act like scientists, performing what Piaget called "experiments in order to see."

Learning Outcomes

LO1 Examine Jean Piaget's studies of cognitive development

LO2 Discuss the information-processing approach

LO3 Identify individual differences in intelligence among infants

LO4 Examine language development in children

LO1 Cognitive Development: Jean Piaget

Cognitive development focuses on the development of children's ways of perceiving and mentally representing the world. Piaget labelled children's concepts of the world *schemes*. He hypothesized that children try to use *assimilation* to absorb new events into existing schemes. When assimilation does not allow the child to make sense of novel events, children try to modify existing schemes through *accommodation*.

Piaget (1963 [1936]) hypothesized that cognitive processes develop in an orderly sequence of stages.

primary circular reactions the repetition of actions that first occurred by chance and that focus on the infant's own body.

Some children may advance more quickly than others, but the sequence remains constant (Flavell et al., 2002; Siegler & Alibali, 2005). Piaget identified four stages of cognitive development: sensorimotor, preoperational, concrete operational, and formal operational. In this chapter, we discuss the sensorimotor stage.

THE SENSORIMOTOR STAGE

Piaget's sensorimotor stage refers to the first 2 years of cognitive development, a time during which infants progress from responding to events with reflexes, or ready-made schemes, to goal-oriented behaviour. Piaget divided the sensorimotor stage into six substages. In each substage, earlier forms of behaviour are repeated, varied, and coordinated.

Simple Reflexes

The first substage covers the first month after birth. It is dominated by the assimilation of sources of stimulation into inborn reflexes such as grasping or visual tracking. At birth, reflexes seem stereotypical and inflexible. But even within the first few hours, neonates begin to modify reflexes as a result of experience. For example, infants will adapt patterns of sucking to the shape of the nipple and the rate of flow of fluid. During the first month or so, however, infants apparently make no connection between stimulation perceived through different sensory modalities. They make no effort to grasp objects that they visually track.

Primary Circular Reactions

The second substage, primary circular reactions, lasts from about 1 to 4 months of age and is characterized by the beginnings of the ability to coordinate various sensorimotor schemes. Infants tend to repeat stimulating actions that first occurred by chance. They may lift their arm repeatedly to bring it into view. **Primary circular reactions** focus on the infant's own body rather than on the external environment. Piaget noticed the following primary circular reaction in his son Laurent:

> *At 2 months 4 days, Laurent by chance discovers his right index finger and looks at it briefly. At 2 months 11 days, he inspects for a moment his open right hand, perceived by chance. At 2 months 17 days, he follows its spontaneous movement for a moment, then examines it several times while it searches for his nose or rubs his eye.*
> —Piaget (1963 [1936], pp. 96–97)

Thus, Laurent, early in the third month, visually tracks the behaviour of his hands, but his visual observations do not affect their movement. In terms of assimilation and accommodation, the child is attempting to assimilate the motor scheme (moving the hand) into the sensory scheme (looking at it). But the schemes do not automatically fit. Several days of apparent trial and error pass, during which the infant

© Brand X Pictures/Jupiterimages

At birth, neonates assimilate objects into reflexive responses.

© Picture Partners/Alamy

Infants repeat actions that involve their bodies (primary circular reactions).

© Picture Partners/Alamy

Patterns of activity are repeated because of their effect on the environment (secondary circular reactions).

© Matt Brasier/Masterfile

seems to be trying to make accommodations so that they will fit. By the third month, infants may examine objects repeatedly and intensely. It seems that the infant is no longer simply looking and seeing but is now "looking in order to see."

Because Laurent (and other infants) will repeat actions that allow them to see, cognitive-developmental psychologists consider sensorimotor coordination self-reinforcing. Laurent is acting on his hands to keep them in his field of vision. Piaget considers the desire to prolong stimulation to be as "basic" as the drives of hunger or thirst.

Secondary Circular Reactions

The third substage lasts from about 4 to 8 months and is characterized by **secondary circular reactions**, in which patterns of activity are repeated because of their effect on the environment. In the second substage (primary circular reactions), infants are focused on their own bodies, as in the example given with Laurent. In the third substage (secondary circular reactions), the focus shifts to objects and environmental events. Infants may now learn to pull strings in order to make a plastic face appear or to shake an object in order to hear it rattle.

Coordination of Secondary Schemes

In the fourth substage, infants no longer act simply to prolong interesting occurrences. Now they can coordinate schemes to attain specific goals. Infants begin to show intentional, goal-directed behaviour in which they differentiate between the means of achieving a goal and the goal or end itself. For example, they may lift a piece of cloth to reach a toy that they had seen a parent place under the cloth earlier. In this example, the scheme of picking up the cloth (the means) is coordinated with

the scheme of reaching for the toy (the goal or end). This example indicates that the infant has mentally represented the toy placed under the cloth.

During the fourth substage, infants also gain the capacity to imitate gestures and sounds that they had previously ignored. The imitation of a facial gesture implies that infants have mentally represented their own faces and can tell what parts of their faces they are moving through feedback from facial muscles.

Tertiary Circular Reactions

In the fifth substage, which lasts from about 12 to 18 months of age, Piaget looked on the behaviour of infants as characteristic of budding scientists. Infants now engage in **tertiary circular reactions**, or purposeful adaptations of established schemes to specific situations. Behaviour takes on a new experimental quality, and infants may vary their actions dozens of times in a deliberate trial-and-error fashion to learn how things work.

Piaget reported an example of tertiary circular reactions by his daughter Jacqueline. The episode was an experiment in which Piaget placed a stick outside Jacqueline's playpen, which had wooden bars (Piaget, 1963 [1936]). At first, Jacqueline grasped the stick and tried to pull it sideways into the playpen. The stick was too long and could not fit through the bars. After days of overt trial and error, however, Jacqueline discovered that she could bring the stick between the bars by turning it upright. In the sixth substage, described next, infants apparently engage in mental trial and error before displaying the correct overt response.

Infants coordinate their behaviour to attain specific goals (coordinating secondary schemes).

Infants use trial-and-error to learn how things work (tertiary circular reactions).

The Bayley scales measure an infant's mental and motor development. (More on pp. 93–95)

Invention of New Means through Mental Combinations

The sixth substage lasts from about 18 to 24 months of age. It serves as a transition between sensorimotor development and the development of symbolic thought. External exploration is replaced by mental exploration. At about 18 months, children may also use imitation to symbolize or stand for a plan of action.

Piaget presented his other children, Lucienne and Laurent, with the playpen and stick problem at the age of 18 months old. Rather than engage in overt trial and error, the 18-month-old children sat and studied the situation for a few moments. Then they grasped the stick, turned it upright, and brought it into the playpen with little overt effort. Lucienne and Laurent apparently mentally represented the stick and the bars of the playpen and perceived that the stick would not fit through as it was. They must then have rotated the mental image of the stick until they perceived a position that would allow the stick to pass between the bars.

> **D1** For 2-month-old infants, "out of sight" is "out of mind." Infants delight at playing peek-a-boo because once you disappear from view they don't realize you still exist!

DEVELOPMENT OF OBJECT PERMANENCE

The appearance of **object permanence** is an important aspect of sensorimotor development. Object permanence is the recognition that an object or person continues to exist when out of sight. For example, your textbook continues to exist when you leave it in the library after studying for the big test, and an infant's mother continues to exist even when she is in another room. The development of object permanence is tied into the development of infants' working memory and reasoning ability (Aguiar & Baillargeon, 2002; Saiki & Miyatsuji, 2007).

Neonates show no tendency to respond to objects that are not within their immediate sensory grasp. By the age of 2 months, infants may show some surprise if an object (such as a toy duck) is placed behind a screen and then taken away so that when the screen is lifted, it is absent. However, they make no effort to search for the missing object (see Figure 5.1). Through the first 6 months or so, when the screen is placed between the object and the infant, the infant behaves as though the

object is no longer there. It is true that "out of sight" is "out of mind" for 2-month-old infants. Apparently, they do not yet reliably mentally represent objects they see.

Some interesting advances occur in the development of the object concept by about the sixth month (Piaget's substage 3). For example, an infant at this age will tend to look for an object that has been dropped, behaviour that suggests some form of object permanence. By this age, we have reason to believe that the infant perceives a mental representation (image) of an object, such as a favourite toy, in response to sensory impressions of part of the object. This perception is shown by the infant's reaching for an object that is partly hidden.

By 8 to 12 months of age (Piaget's substage 4), infants will seek to retrieve objects that have been completely hidden. But in observing his own children, Piaget (1963 [1936]) noted an interesting error known as the A-not-B error. Piaget repeatedly hid a toy behind a screen (A), and each time, his infant removed the screen and retrieved the toy. Then, as the infant watched, Piaget hid the toy behind another screen (B) in a different place. Still, the infant tried to recover the toy by pushing aside the first screen (A). It is as though the child had learned that a certain motor activity would reinstate the missing toy. The child's concept of the object did not, at this age, extend to recognition that objects usually remain in the place where they have been most recently mentally represented.

Under certain conditions, 9- to 10-month-old infants do not show the A-not-B error (Bremner & Bryant, 2001; Marcovitch & Zelazo, 2006). If infants are allowed to search for the object immediately after seeing it hidden, the error often does not occur. But if they are forced to wait 5 or more seconds before looking, they are likely to commit the A-not-B error (Wellman et al., 1986).

EVALUATION OF PIAGET'S THEORY

Piaget's theory remains a comprehensive model of infant cognition. Many of his observations of his own infants have been confirmed by others. The pattern and sequence of events he described have been observed among North American, European, African, and Asian infants (Werner, 1988). Still, research has raised questions about the validity of many of Piaget's claims (Siegler & Alibali, 2005).

First, most researchers now agree that cognitive development is not as tied to discrete stages as Piaget suggested (Krojgaard, 2005; Siegler & Alibali, 2005). Although later developments seem to build on earlier ones, the process appears to be more gradual than discontinuous.

Second, Piaget emphasized the role of maturation, almost to the point of excluding adult and peer influences on cognitive development. However, these interpersonal influences have been shown to play important roles in cognitive development (Kuhn, 2007; Maratsos, 2007).

Third, Piaget appears to have underestimated infants' competence (Siegler & Alibali, 2005). For example, infants display object permanence earlier than he believed (Wang et al., 2005). Also consider studies on **deferred imitation** (imitation of an action that may have occurred hours, days, or even weeks earlier). The presence of deferred imitation suggests that children have mentally represented behaviour patterns. Piaget believed that deferred imitation appears at about 18 months, but others have found that infants show deferred imitation as early as 9 months. In Meltzoff's (1988) study,

deferred imitation the imitation of people and events that occurred in the past.

FIGURE 5.1
Development of Object Permanence

To the infant who is in the early part of the sensorimotor stage, out of sight is truly out of mind. Once a sheet of paper is placed between the infant and the toy monkey (top two photos), the infant loses all interest in the toy. From evidence of this sort, Piaget concluded that the toy is not mentally represented. The bottom series of photos shows a child in a later part of the sensorimotor stage. This child does mentally represent objects and pushes through a towel to reach an object that has been screened from sight.

© Doug Goodman/Photo Researchers, Inc.

© George S. Zimbel 2010

Rovee-Collier studies

9-month-old infants watched an adult perform behaviours such as pushing a button to produce a beep. When given a chance to play with the same objects a day later, many infants imitated the actions they had witnessed.

LO2 Information Processing

the information-processing approach to cognitive development focuses on how children manipulate or process information coming in from the environment or already stored in the mind. Infants' tools for processing information include their memory and imitation.

INFANTS' MEMORY

Many of the cognitive capabilities of infants—recognizing the faces of familiar people, developing object permanence, and, in fact, learning in any form—depend on one critical aspect of cognitive development: their memory (Daman-Wasserman et al., 2006; Hayne & Fagen, 2003). Even neonates demonstrate memory for stimuli to which they have been exposed previously. For example, neonates adjust their rate of sucking to hear a recording of their mother reading a story she had read aloud during the last weeks of pregnancy, as discussed in Chapter 2 (DeCasper & Fifer, 1980; DeCasper & Spence, 1991).

Memory improves dramatically between 2 and 6 months of age and then again by 12 months (Pelphrey et al., 2004; Rose et al., 2001). The improvement may indicate that older infants are more capable than younger ones

at encoding (i.e., storing) information, retrieving information already stored, or both (Hayne & Fagen, 2003).

A fascinating series of studies by Carolyn Rovee-Collier and her colleagues (Rovee-Collier, 1993) illustrates some of these developmental changes in infant memory. As shown in the image here, one end of a ribbon was tied to a brightly coloured mobile suspended above the infant's crib. The other end was tied to the infant's ankle, so that when the infant kicked, the mobile moved. Infants quickly learned to increase their rate of kicking. To measure memory, the infant's ankle was again fastened to the mobile after a period of 1 or more days had elapsed. In one study, 2-month-olds remembered how to make the mobile move after delays of up to 3 days, and 3-month-olds remembered for more than a week (Greco et al., 1986).

Infant memory can be improved if infants receive a reminder before they are given the memory test (Bearce et al., 2006). In one study that used a reminder ("priming"), infants were shown the moving mobile on the day before the memory test, but they were not allowed to activate it. Under these conditions, 3-month-olds remembered how to move the mobile after a 28-day delay (Rovee-Collier, 1993).

IMITATION: INFANT SEE, INFANT DO?

Imitation is the basis for much of human learning. Deferred imitation—that is, the imitation of actions after a time delay—occurs as early as 6 months of age (Barr et al., 2005; Campanella & Rovee-Collier, 2005). To help them remember the imitated act, infants are usually permitted to practise it when they learn it. But in one study, 12-month-old infants were prevented from practising the behaviour they imitated. Yet they were able to demonstrate it 4 weeks later, suggesting that they had mentally represented the act (Klein & Meltzoff, 1999).

But infants can imitate certain actions at a much earlier age. Neonates only 0.7 to 71 hours old have been found to imitate adults who open their mouths or stick out their tongues (Meltzoff & Prinz, 2002; Rizzolatti et al., 2002; see Figure 5.2).

Before you become too impressed with this early imitative ability of neonates, you should know that some studies have not found imitation in early infancy (Abravanel & DeYong, 1991). One key factor may be the infants' age. The studies that find imitation generally have been done with very young infants—up to 2 weeks old—whereas the studies that do not find imitation have tended to use older infants. Therefore, the imitation of neonates is likely to be reflexive. Thus, imitation might disappear when reflexes are "dropping out" and re-emerge when it has a firmer cognitive footing.

A. N. Meltzoff and M. K. Moore, "Imitation of facial and manual gestures by human neonates." *Science*, 1977, 198, 75–78

FIGURE 5.2
Imitation in Infants

These 2- to 3-week-old infants are imitating the facial gestures of an adult experimenter. How are we to interpret these findings? Can we say that the infants "knew" what the experimenter was doing and "chose" to imitate the behaviour, or is there another explanation?

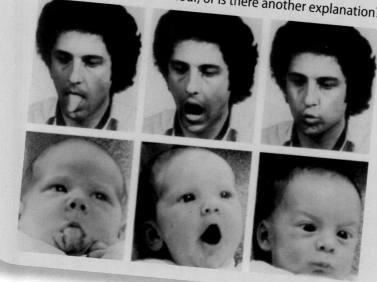

Why might newborns possess some sort of imitation reflex? Answers lie in the realm of speculation. One possibility is that such a built-in response would contribute to the formation of caregiver–infant bonding and the survival of the newborn (Meltzoff & Prinz, 2002). Some theorists speculate that the imitation reflex is made possible by *mirror neurons* that are found in human brains. Such neurons are maintained by evolutionary forces because they enhance the probability of survival as a result of caregiving (Oztop et al., 2006; Rizzolatti et al., 2002).

> **D2** A 1-hour-old infant may imitate an adult who sticks out his or her tongue.
> True, but that imitation may be reflexive rather than an action of choice.

LO3 Individual Differences in Intelligence among Infants

Cognitive development does not proceed in the same way or at the same pace for all infants (Newman et al., 2006; Rose et al., 2001, 2005). Efforts to understand the development of infant differences in cognitive development have relied on so-called scales of infant development or infant intelligence.

Measuring cognition or intelligence in infants is quite different from measuring it in adults. Infants cannot, of course, be assessed by asking them to explain the meanings of words, the similarity between concepts, or the rationales for social rules. One of the most important tests of intellectual development among infants—the Bayley Scales of Infant Development, constructed in 1933 by psychologist Nancy Bayley and revised since—contains very different kinds of items.

The Bayley test currently consists of 178 mental-scale items and 111 motor-scale items. The mental scale assesses verbal communication, perceptual skills, learning and memory, and problem-solving skills. The motor scale assesses gross motor skills, such as standing, walking, and climbing, and fine motor skills, as shown by the ability to manipulate the hands and fingers. A behaviour rating scale based on examiner observation of the child during the test is also used. The behaviour rating scale assesses attention span, goal directedness, persistence, and aspects of social and emotional development. Table 5.1 contains sample items from the mental and motor scales and shows the ages at which 50 percent of the infants taking the test passed the items.

Even though psychologists can begin to measure intelligence in infancy, they use items that differ from the kinds of items used with older children and adults. It remains unclear how well results obtained in infancy predict intellectual functioning at later ages.

© Gelpi/Shutterstock

TESTING INFANTS: WHY AND WITH WHAT?

As you can imagine, it is no easy matter to test an infant. The items must be administered on a one-to-one basis by a patient tester, and it can be difficult to judge whether the infant is showing the targeted response. Why, then, do we test infants?

One reason is to screen infants for handicaps. A tester may be able to detect early signs of sensory or neurological problems, as suggested by development of visual–motor coordination. In addition to the Bayley scales, a number of tests have been developed to screen infants for such difficulties, including the Brazelton Neonatal Behavioural Assessment Scale (see Chapter 3) and the Denver Developmental Screening Test.

INSTABILITY OF INTELLIGENCE SCORES ATTAINED IN INFANCY

Researchers have also tried to use infant scales to predict development, but this effort has been less than

TABLE 5.1
Items from the Bayley Scales of Infant Development (BSID–II)

AGE	MENTAL-SCALE ITEMS	MOTOR-SCALE ITEMS
1 month	The infant quiets when picked up.	The infant makes a postural adjustment when put to examiner's shoulder.
2 months	When examiner presents two objects (bell and rattle) above the infant in a crib, the infant glances back and forth from one to the other.	The infant holds his or her head steady when being carried about in a vertical position.
5 months	The infant is observed to transfer an object from one hand to the other during play.	When seated at a feeding-type table and presented with a sugar pill that is out of reach, the infant attempts to pick it up.
8 months	When an object (toy) in plain view of the infant (i.e., on a table) is covered by a cup, the infant removes the cup to retrieve the object.	The infant raises herself or himself into a sitting position.
12 months	The infant imitates words that are spoken by the examiner.	When requested by the examiner, the infant stands up from a position in which she or he had been lying on her or his back on the floor.
14–16 months	The infant builds a tower with two cubes (blocks) after the examiner demonstrates the behaviour.	The infant walks alone with good coordination.

successful. One study found that scores obtained during the first year of life correlated moderately at best with scores obtained a year later (Harris et al., 2005). Certain items on the Bayley scales appear to predict related intellectual skills later in childhood. For example, Bayley items measuring infant motor skills predict subsequent fine motor and visual–spatial skills at 6 to 8 years of age (Siegel, 1992). Bayley language items also predict language skills at the same age (Siegel, 1992).

One study found that the Bayley scales and socioeconomic status were able to predict cognitive development among low-birth-weight children from 18 months to 4 years of age (Dezoete et al., 2003). But overall scores on the Bayley and other infant scales apparently do not reliably predict school grades or IQ scores among schoolchildren (Colombo, 1993). Perhaps the sensorimotor test items used during infancy are not strongly related to the verbal and symbolic items used to assess intelligence at later ages.

The overall conclusion seems to be that the Bayley scales can identify gross lags in development and relative strengths and weaknesses. However, they are only moderate predictors of intelligence scores even one year later, and are still poorer predictors of scores taken beyond longer stretches of time.

USE OF VISUAL RECOGNITION MEMORY

In a continuing effort to find aspects of intelligence and cognition that might remain consistent from infancy through later childhood, a number of researchers have recently focused on visual recognition memory (Courage et al., 2004). **Visual recognition memory** is the ability to discriminate previously seen objects from novel objects. This procedure is based on *habituation*.

Let us consider longitudinal studies of this type. Susan Rose and her colleagues (Rose et al., 1992)

showed 7-month-old infants pictures of two identical faces. After 20 seconds, the pictures were replaced with one picture of a new face and a second picture of the familiar face. The amount of time the infants spent looking at each face in the second set of pictures was recorded. Some infants spent more time looking at the new face than at the older face, suggesting that they had better memory for visual stimulation. The children were given standard IQ tests yearly from ages 1 through 6. It was found that the children with greater visual recognition memory later attained higher IQ scores.

Rose and her colleagues (2001) also showed that, from age to age, individual differences in capacity for visual recognition memory are stable. This finding is important because intelligence—the quality that many researchers seek to predict from visual recognition memory—is also theorized to be a reasonably stable trait. Similarly, items on intelligence tests are age graded; that is, older children perform better than younger children, even as developing intelligence remains constant. So, too, with visual recognition memory. Capacity for visual recognition memory increases over the first year after birth (Rose et al., 2001).

A number of other studies have examined the relationship between either infant visual recognition memory or preference for novel stimulation (which is a related measure) and later IQ scores. In general, they show good predictive validity for broad cognitive abilities throughout childhood, including measures of intelligence and language ability (Heiman et al., 2006; S. A. Rose et al., 2004).

In sum, scales of infant development may provide useful data as screening devices, as research instruments, or simply as a way to describe the things that infants do and do not do, but their predictive power as intelligence tests has been disappointing. Tests of visual recognition hold better promise as predictors of intelligence at older ages.

Now let us turn our attention to a fascinating aspect of cognitive development, the development of language.

LO4 Language Development

a children develop language skills, they often begin speaking about the things more closely connected with their environments and their needs. Children enjoy playing with language. In physical development,

visual recognition memory the kind of memory shown in an infant's ability to discriminate previously seen objects from novel objects.

Infant intelligence scores are unstable; that is, a score in infancy cannot be considered to have accurate predictive power for scores obtained later in life.

© Bruce T. Brown/Getty Images

prelinguistic vocalizations made by the infant before the use of language.

cooing prelinguistic vowel-like sounds that reflect feelings of positive excitement.

babbling the child's first vocalizations that have the sounds of speech.

echolalia the automatic repetition of sounds or words.

intonation the use of pitches of varying levels to help communicate meaning.

receptive vocabulary the number of words one understands.

expressive vocabulary the number of words one can use in the production of language.

the most dramatic developments come early—fast and furious—long before the child is born. Language does not come quite as early, and its development may not seem quite so fast and furious. Nevertheless, during the years of infancy, most children develop from creatures without language to little people who understand nearly all the things that are said to them and who relentlessly sputter words and simple sentences for all the world to hear.

EARLY VOCALIZATIONS

Children develop language according to an invariant sequence of steps, or stages, as outlined in Table 5.2. We begin with the **prelinguistic** vocalizations. True words are symbols of objects and events. Prelinguistic vocalizations, such as cooing and babbling, do not represent objects or events, so infant crying is not a primitive form of language.

Newborn children, as parents are well aware, have an unlearned but highly effective form of verbal expression: crying and more crying. Crying is about the only sound that infants make during the first month. During the second month, infants begin **cooing**. Infants use their tongues when they coo. For this reason, coos are more articulated than cries. Coos are often vowel-like and may resemble extended "oohs" and "ahs." Cooing appears linked to feelings of pleasure or positive excitement. Infants tend not to coo when they are hungry, tired, or in pain.

Cries and coos are innate but can be modified by experience (Volterra et al., 2004). When parents respond

> Most children develop from creatures without language to little people who understand nearly all the things that are said to them.

positively to cooing by talking to their infants, smiling at them, and imitating them, cooing increases. Early parent–child "conversations," in which parents respond to coos and then pause as the infant coos, may foster infant awareness of taking turns as a way of verbally relating to other people.

By about 8 months of age, cooing decreases markedly. Somewhere between 6 and 9 months, children begin to babble. **Babbling** is the first vocalizing that sounds like human speech. When babbling, infants frequently combine consonants and vowels, as in *ba, ga*, and, sometimes, the much valued *dada* (Stoel-Gammon, 2002). At first, *dada* is purely coincidental (sorry, you dads), despite the family's jubilation over hearing it.

In verbal interactions between infants and adults, the adults frequently repeat the syllables produced by their infants. They are likely to say "dadada" or "bababa" instead of simply "da" or "ba." Such redundancy apparently helps infants discriminate these sounds from others and further encourages them to imitate their parents (Elkind, 2007; Tamis-LeMonda et al., 2006).

After infants have been babbling for a few months, parents often believe that their children are having conversations with themselves. At 10 to 12 months, infants tend to repeat syllables, showing what linguists refer to as **echolalia**. Parents overhear them going on and on, repeating consonant–vowel combinations ("ah-bah-bah-bah-bah"), pausing, and then switching to other combinations.

Toward the end of the first year, infants are also using patterns of rising and falling **intonation** that resemble the sounds of adult speech. It may sound as though the infant is trying to speak the parents' language. Parents may think that their children are babbling in English or in whatever language is spoken in the home.

DEVELOPMENT OF VOCABULARY

Vocabulary development refers to the child's learning the meanings of words. In general, children's **receptive vocabulary** development outpaces their **expressive vocabulary** development (Lickliter, 2001; Ouellette, 2006). In other words, at any given time, they can understand more words than they can use. One study, for example, found that 12-month-olds could speak an average of 13 words but could comprehend the meaning of 84 (Tamis-LeMonda et al., 2006). Infants usually understand much of what others are saying well before they themselves utter any words at all. Their ability to segment speech sounds into meaningful

D4 Infant crying is not a primitive form of language.
Cries do not represent objects or events, so they are not considered language.

TABLE 5.2
Milestones in Language Development in Infancy

APPROXIMATE AGE	VOCALIZATION AND LANGUAGE
Birth	• Cries.
12 weeks	• Cries less. • Smiles when talked to and nodded at. • Engages in squealing and gurgling sounds (cooing). • Sustains cooing for 15–20 seconds.
16 weeks	• Responds to human sounds more definitely. • Turns head, searching for the speaker. • Chuckles occasionally.
20 weeks	• Cooing becomes interspersed with consonant-like sounds. • Vocalizations differ from the sounds of mature language.
6 months	• Cooing changes to single-syllable babbling. • Neither vowels nor consonants have fixed pattern of recurrence. • Common utterances sound somewhat like *ma, mu, da,* or *di.*
8 months	• Continuous repetition (reduplication) enters into babbling. • Patterns of intonation become distinct. • Utterances can signal emphasis and emotion.
10 months	• Vocalizations mixed with sound play, such as gurgling and bubble blowing. • Makes effort to imitate sounds made by older people with mixed success.
12 months	• Identical sound sequences replicated more often. • Words (e.g., *mamma* or *dadda*) emerge. • Many words and requests understood (e.g., "Show me your eyes").
18 months	• Repertoire of 3–50 words. • Explosive vocabulary growth. • Babbling consists of several syllables with intricate intonation. • Little effort to communicate information. • Little joining of words into spontaneous two-word utterances. • Understands nearly everything spoken.
24 months	• Vocabulary more than 50 words, naming everything in the environment. • Spontaneous creation of two-word sentences. • Clear efforts to communicate.

Source: Table items adapted from Lenneberg (1967, pp. 128–130).
Note: Ages are approximations. Slower development does not necessarily indicate language problems. Albert Einstein did not talk until the age of 3.

units—or words—before 12 months is a good predictor of their vocabulary at 24 months (Newman et al., 2006).

The Child's First Words

Ah, that long-awaited first word! What a milestone! Sad to say, many parents miss it. They are not quite sure when their infants utter their first word, often because the first word is not pronounced clearly or because pronunciation varies from usage to usage.

A child's first word typically is spoken between the ages of 11 and 13 months, but a range of 8 to 18 months is considered normal (Hoff, 2006; Tamis-LeMonda et al., 2006). First words tend to be brief, consisting of one or two syllables. Each syllable is likely to consist of a consonant followed by a vowel. Vocabulary acquisition is slow at first. It may take children 3 or 4 months to achieve a vocabulary of 10 to 30 words after the first word is spoken (de Villiers & de Villiers, 1999).

By about 18 months of age, children may be producing up to 50 words. Many of them are quite familiar, such as *no, cookie, mama, hi*, and *eat*. Others, such as *all gone* and *bye-bye*, may not be found in the dictionary, but they function as words. That is, they are used consistently to symbolize the same meaning.

More than half (65 percent) of children's first words make up "general nominals" and "specific nominals" (Hoff, 2006; Nelson, 1973). General nominals are similar to nouns in that they include the names of classes of objects (*car, ball*), animals (*doggy, cat*), and people (*boy, girl*), but they also include both personal and relative pronouns (*she, that*). Specific nominals are proper nouns, such as *Daddy* and *Rover*. Words expressing movement are frequently found in early speech.

At about 18 to 22 months of age, there is a rapid burst in vocabulary (Tamis-LeMonda et al., 2006). The child's vocabulary may increase from 50 to more than 300 words in only a few months. This vocabulary spurt could also be called a naming explosion because almost 75 percent of the words added during this time are nouns. The rapid pace of vocabulary growth continues through the preschool years, with children acquiring an average of nine new words per day (Hoff, 2006).

Referential and Expressive Styles in Language Development

Some children prefer a referential approach in their language development, whereas others take a more expressive approach (Hoff, 2006; Nelson, 1981). Children who show the **referential language style** use language primarily to label objects in their environments. Children who use an **expressive language style** use language primarily as a means for engaging in social interactions. Children with an expressive style use more pronouns and many words involved in social routines, such as *stop, more*, and *all gone*. More children use an expressive style than a referential style (Tamis-LeMonda et al., 2006), but most use a combination of the styles.

Overextension

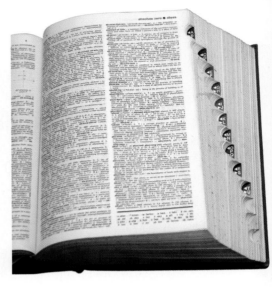

Young children try to talk about more objects than they have words for. To accomplish their linguistic feats, children often extend the meaning of one word to refer to things and actions for which they do not have words (McDonough, 2002). This process is called **overextension**. Eve Clark (1973, 1975) studied diaries of infants' language development and found that overextensions are generally based on perceived similarities in function or form between the original object or action and the new one. She provides the example of the word *mooi*, which one child originally used to designate the moon. The child then overextended *mooi* to designate all round objects, including the letter *o* and cookies and cakes. Overextensions gradually pull back

Language development in young children is enhanced when caregivers engage the infant "in conversation."

to their proper references as the child's vocabulary and ability to classify objects develop (McDonough, 2002).

DEVELOPMENT OF SENTENCES

The infant's first sentences are typically one-word utterances, but they express complete ideas and therefore can be thought of as sentences. Roger Brown (1973) called brief expressions that have the meanings of sentences **telegraphic speech**. Adults who write telegrams use principles of syntax to cut out all the unnecessary words. "Home Tuesday" might stand for "I expect to be home on Tuesday." Similarly, only the essential words are used in children's telegraphic speech—in particular, nouns, verbs, and some modifiers.

Mean Length of Utterance

The **mean length of utterance (MLU)** is the average number of **morphemes** that communicators use in their sentences (Pancsofar & Vernon-Feagans, 2006; Saaristo-Helin et al., 2006). Morphemes are the smallest units of meaning in a language. A morpheme may be a whole word or part of a word, such as a prefix or suffix. For example, the word *walked* consists of two morphemes: the verb *walk* and the suffix *ed*, which changes the verb to the past tense. In Figure 5.3, we see the relationship between chronological age and MLU for three children tracked by Roger Brown (1973, 1977): Lin, Victor, and Sarah.

The patterns of growth in MLU are similar for each child, showing swift upward movement, broken by intermittent and brief regressions. Figure 5.3 also shows us something about individual differences. Lin was precocious compared with Victor and Sarah, extending her MLU at much earlier ages. But as suggested earlier, the receptive language of all three children would have exceeded their expressive language at any given time. Also, Lin's earlier extension of MLU does

not guarantee that she will show more complex expressive language than Victor and Sarah at maturity.

Let us now consider the features of two types of telegraphic speech: the holophrase and two-word utterances.

Holophrases

Holophrases are single words that are used to express complex meanings. For example, Mama may be used by the child to signify meanings as varied as "There

telegraphic speech type of speech in which only the essential words are used.

mean length of utterance (MLU) the average number of morphemes used in an utterance.

morpheme the smallest unit of meaning in a language.

holophrase a single word that is used to express complex meanings.

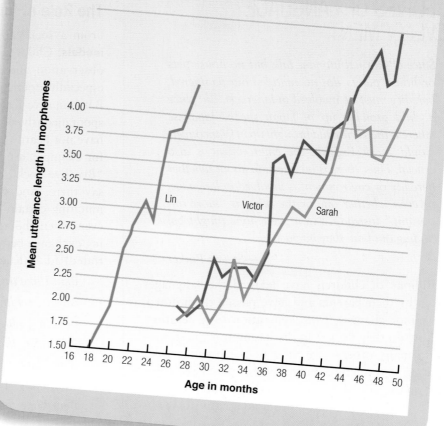

FIGURE 5.3
Mean Length of Utterance for Three Children

The mean length of utterance (MLU) increases rapidly once speech begins.

goes Mama," "Come here, Mama," and "You are Mama." Most children readily teach their parents what they intend by augmenting their holophrases with gestures, intonations, and reinforcers. That is, they act delighted when parents do as requested and howl when they do not (Tamis-LeMonda et al., 2006).

Two-Word Sentences

When the child's vocabulary consists of 50 to 100 words (usually somewhere between 18 and 24 months of age), telegraphic two-word sentences begin to appear (Tamis-LeMonda et al., 2006). In the sentence "That ball," the words *is* and *a* are implied.

Two-word sentences, although brief and telegraphic, show understanding of **syntax** (Slobin, 2001). The child will say "Sit chair," not "Chair sit," to tell a parent to sit in a chair. The child will say "My shoe," not "Shoe my," to show possession. "Mommy go" means Mommy is leaving, whereas "Go Mommy" expresses the wish for Mommy to go away.

THEORIES OF LANGUAGE DEVELOPMENT

Since all normal humans talk but no house pets or house plants do, no matter how pampered, heredity must be involved in language. But since a child growing up in Japan speaks Japanese whereas the same child brought up in [Vancouver] would speak English, the environment is also crucial. Thus, there is no question about whether heredity or environment is involved in language, or even whether one or the other is "more important." Instead, . . . our best hope [might be] finding out how they interact.

—*Steven Pinker*

Billions of children have learned the languages spoken by their parents and have passed them down, with minor changes, from generation to generation. But how do they do so? In discussing this question— and so many others—we refer to the possible roles of nature and nurture. Learning theorists have come down on the side of nurture, and those who point to a basic role for nature are said to hold a nativist view.

VIEWS THAT EMPHASIZE NURTURE

Learning plays an obvious role in language development. Children who are reared in English-speaking homes learn English, not Japanese or Russian. Learning theorists usually explain language development in terms of imitation and reinforcement.

The Role of Imitation

From a social cognitive perspective, parents serve as **models**. Children learn language, at least in part, by observation and imitation. Many vocabulary words, especially nouns and verbs, are learned by imitation. But imitative learning does not explain why children spontaneously utter phrases and sentences that they have not heard (Tamis-LeMonda et al., 2006). Parents, for example, are unlikely to model utterances such as "Bye bye sock" and "All gone Daddy" but children say them. And children sometimes steadfastly avoid imitating certain language forms suggested by adults, even when the adults are insistent. Note the following exchange between 2-year-old Ben and a (very frustrated) adult (Kuczaj, 1982, p. 48):

Ben: I like these candy. I like they.

Adult: You like them?

Ben: Yes, I like they.

Adult: Say them.

Ben: Them.

Adult: Say "I like them."

Ben: I like them.

Adult: Good.

Ben: I'm good. These candy good too.

Adult: Are they good?

Ben: Yes. I like they. You like they?

Ben is not resisting the adult because of obstinacy. He does repeat "I like them" when asked to do so. But when given the opportunity afterward to construct the object *them*, he reverts to using the subjective form *they*. Ben is likely at this period in his development to use his (erroneous) understanding of syntax spontaneously to actively produce his own language, rather than just imitate a model.

The Role of Reinforcement

B. F. Skinner (1957) allowed that prelinguistic vocalizations such as cooing and babbling may be inborn. But parents reinforce children for babbling that approximates the form of real words, such as *da*, which, in English, resembles *dog* or *daddy*. Children, in fact, do increase their babbling when it results in adults smiling at them, stroking them, and talking back to them. As the first year progresses, children babble the sounds of the language spoken at home with increasing frequency; foreign sounds tend to drop out. The behaviourist explains this pattern of changing frequencies in terms of reinforcement of the sounds of the adults' language and **extinction** of foreign sounds. Another (nonbehavioural) explanation is that children actively attend to the sounds in their linguistic environments and are intrinsically motivated to utter them.

From Skinner's perspective, children acquire their early vocabularies through **shaping**. That is, parents require that children's utterances be progressively closer to actual words before they are reinforced. In support of Skinner's position, research has shown that reinforcement accelerates the growth of vocabulary in children (August et al., 2005; Kroeger & Nelson, 2006).

But recall Ben's refusal to be shaped into correct syntax. If the reinforcement explanation of language development were sufficient, parents' reinforcement would facilitate children's learning of syntax and pronunciation. However, parents are more likely to reinforce their children for the accuracy, or "truth value," of their utterances than for their grammatical correctness (Brown, 1973). The child who points down and says "The grass

© Morgan Lane Photography/Shutterstock

is purple" is not likely to be reinforced, despite correct syntax. But the enthusiastic child who shows her empty plate and blurts out "I eated it all up" is likely to be reinforced, despite the grammatical incorrectness of "eated."

Selective reinforcement of children's pronunciation can also backfire. Children whose parents reward proper pronunciation but correct poor pronunciation develop vocabulary more slowly than children whose parents are more tolerant about pronunciation (Nelson, 1973).

Learning theory also cannot account for the invariant sequences of language development and for children's spurts in acquisition. The types of questions used, passive versus active sentences and so on, all emerge in the same order.

On the other hand, aspects of the child's language environment do influence the development of language. Studies show that language growth in young children is enhanced when adults (Tamis-LeMonda et al., 2006):

- Use a simplified form of speech known as "Motherese."
- Use questions that engage the child in conversation.
- Respond to the child's expressive language efforts in a way that is "attuned"; for example, adults relate their speech to the child's utterance by saying "Yes, your doll is pretty" in response to the child's statement "My doll."
- Join the child in paying attention to a particular activity or toy.
- Gesture to help the child understand what they are saying.
- Describe aspects of the environment occupying the infant's current focus of attention.

> **extinction** decrease in frequency of a response due to absence of reinforcement.
>
> **shaping** gradual building of complex behaviour through reinforcement of successive approximations to the target behaviour.

> **D5** You can advance children's development of pronunciation by correcting their errors.
> Maybe, but their vocabulary will not develop as rapidly if you focus on pronunciation.

psycholinguistic theory the view that language learning involves an interaction between environmental influences and an inborn tendency to acquire language.

language acquisition device (LAD) neural "prewiring" that eases the child's learning of grammar.

surface structure the superficial grammatical construction of a sentence.

deep structure the underlying meaning of a sentence.

aphasia a disruption in the ability to understand or produce language.

Broca's aphasia an aphasia caused by damage to Broca's area and characterized by difficulty speaking.

Wernicke's aphasia an aphasia caused by damage to Wernicke's area and characterized by impaired comprehension of speech and difficulty producing the right word.

- Read to the child.
- Talk to the child a great deal.

VIEWS THAT EMPHASIZE NATURE

The nativist view of language development holds that inborn factors cause children to attend to and acquire language in certain ways. From this perspective, children bring an inborn tendency in the form of neurological "prewiring" to language learning. According to Steven Pinker and Ray Jackendoff (2005), the structures that enable humans to perceive and produce language evolved in bits and pieces. Those individuals who possessed these "bits" and "pieces" were more likely to reach maturity and transmit their genes from generation to generation because communication ability increased their chances of survival.

Psycholinguistic Theory

According to **psycholinguistic theory**, language acquisition involves an interaction between environmental influences—such as exposure to parental speech and reinforcement—and an inborn tendency to acquire language. Noam Chomsky (1988, 1990) labelled this innate tendency a **language acquisition device (LAD)**. Evidence for an inborn tendency is found in the universality of human language abilities; in the regularity of the early production of sounds, even among deaf children; and in the invariant sequences of language development among all languages (Bloom, 1998; Volterra et al., 2004).

The inborn tendency primes the nervous system to learn grammar. On the surface, languages differ much in vocabulary and grammar. Chomsky labels these elements the **surface structure** of language. However, Chomsky believes that the LAD serves children all over the world because languages share a "universal grammar"—an underlying **deep structure** or set of rules for

Jose Luis Pelaez Inc/Blend Images/Getty Images

transforming ideas into sentences. From Chomsky's perspective, children are genetically prewired to attend to language and deduce the rules for constructing sentences from ideas. That is, it appears that children are prewired to listen to language in such a way that they come to understand rules of grammar.

> **D6** Children are "prewired" to listen to language in such a way that they come to understand rules of grammar.
> Brain development suggests a biological component to language acquisition.

Brain Structures Involved in Language

Many parts of the brain are involved in language development; however, some of the key biological structures that may provide the basis for the functions of the LAD are based in the left hemisphere of the cerebral cortex for nearly all right-handed people and for two out of three left-handed people (Pinker, 1994). In the left hemisphere, the two areas most involved in speech are Broca's area and Wernicke's area. Damage to either area is likely to cause an **aphasia**—a disruption in the ability to understand or produce language.

Broca's area is located near the section of the motor cortex that controls the muscles of the tongue and throat and other areas of the face that are used in speech. When Broca's area is damaged, people speak laboriously in a pattern termed **Broca's aphasia**. But they can readily understand speech. Wernicke's area lies near the auditory cortex and is connected to Broca's area by nerves. People with damage to Wernicke's area may show **Wernicke's aphasia**, in which they speak freely and with proper syntax but have trouble understanding speech and finding the words to express themselves.

A part of the brain called the angular gyrus lies between the visual cortex and Wernicke's area. The angular gyrus "translates" visual information, such as written words, into auditory information (sounds) and sends it on to Wernicke's area. Problems in the angular gyrus can

"Motherese"

Adults influence the language development of infants through the use of baby talk or "Motherese," known more technically as child-directed speech or infant-directed speech. But "Motherese" is a limiting term, because grandparents, fathers, siblings, and older children also use Motherese when talking to infants (Kidd & Bavin, 2007; Snedeker et al., 2007). In fact, one study found that women often talk to their pets in Motherese (Prato-Previde et al., 2006). Motherese occurs in languages as different as Arabic, English, Comanche, Italian, French, German, Xhosa (an African language), Japanese, and Mandarin Chinese (Nonaka, 2004; Trainor & Desjardins, 2002).

The short, simple sentences and high pitch used in Motherese are more likely to produce a response from the child and enhance vocabulary development than complex sentences and those spoken in a lower pitch. Children who hear their utterances repeated and recast seem to learn from the adults who are speaking to them (Tamis-LeMonda et al., 2001; Trevarthen, 2003). In sum, Motherese may help foster children's language development.

Motherese has several characteristics:

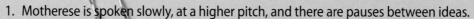

1. Motherese is spoken slowly, at a higher pitch, and there are pauses between ideas.
2. Sentences are brief.
3. Sentences are simple in grammar.
4. Key words are put at the ends of sentences and are spoken in a higher and louder voice.
5. The diminutive morpheme *y* is frequently added to nouns. *Dad* becomes *Daddy* and *horse* becomes *horsey*.
6. Adults repeat sentences several times using minor variations, as in "Show me your nose." "Where is your nose?"
7. Motherese includes reduplication. *Yummy* becomes *yummy-yummy*. *Daddy* may alternate with *Da-da*.
8. Vocabulary is concrete, referring, when possible, to objects in the immediate environment. Stuffed lions may be referred to as "kitties."
9. Objects may be overdescribed by being given compound labels. Rabbits may become "bunny rabbits," and cats may become "kitty cats."
10. Parents speak for the children, as in, "We want to take our nap now, don't we?"

sensitive period the period from about 18 months to puberty when the brain is especially capable of learning language.

cause problems in reading because it is difficult for the reader to segment words into sounds (Pugh et al., 2000).

The Sensitive Period

Language learning is most efficient during **sensitive periods**, which begin at about 18 to 24 months and last until puberty (Clancy & Finlay, 2001; Uylings, 2006).

Evidence for a sensitive period is found in recovery from brain injuries in some people. Injuries to the hemisphere that controls language (usually the left hemisphere) can impair or destroy the ability to speak (Werker & Tees, 2005). But before puberty, children suffering left-hemisphere injuries frequently recover a good deal of speaking ability due to brain plasticity. In young children, left-hemisphere damage may encourage the development of language functions in the right hemisphere. But adaptation ability wanes in adolescence, when brain tissue has reached adult levels of differentiation (Snow, 2006).

The Genie Project

The best way to determine whether people are capable of acquiring language once they have passed puberty would be to run an experiment in which one or more children were reared in such severe isolation that they were not exposed to language until puberty. Of course, such an experiment could not be conducted for ethical reasons. However, human circumstance sometimes presents such an opportunity, such as the disturbing case history of Genie, which offers insights into whether children have a sensitive period for language development (Fromkin et al., 2004; LaPointe, 2005).

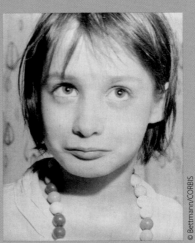

© Bettmann/CORBIS

The PBS *Nova* documentary "Secret of the Wild Child" (Garmon, 1997) explores Genie's tragic life. Genie's father locked her in a small room at the age of 20 months and kept her confined until she was 13 years old. Her social contacts during this period were limited to her mother, who entered the room only to feed Genie, and to her father, who beat her. When Genie was rescued, she weighed only about 27 kg (60 lb.), did not speak, had not been toilet trained, and could barely stand. She was observed scientifically in the *Genie Project* and thereafter her language development followed the normal sequence of much younger children in a number of ways.

Five years after her liberation, however, Genie's language remained largely telegraphic. She still showed significant problems with syntax, such as failing to reverse subjects and verbs to phrase questions. Genie's language development provides support for *the sensitive-period hypothesis,* although her language problems might also be partly attributed to her years of malnutrition and abuse. Her efforts to acquire English after puberty were laborious, and the results were substandard compared even with the language of many 2- and 3-year-olds. She never did acquire the linguistic or social skills of an adult, perhaps as a result of synaptic pruning. The synapses that could have facilitated this learning may simply have disappeared through lack of use.

In sum, the development of language in infancy represents the interaction of environmental and biological factors. Children bring a built-in readiness to the task of language acquisition, whereas houseplants and other organisms do not. Children must also have the opportunity to hear spoken language and to interact verbally with others. In the next chapter, we see how interaction with others affects social development.

71% The percentage of students who go online to study for a class.

© Anderson Ross/Getty Images

GET ONLINE

The easy-to-navigate website for **HDEV** offers guidance on key topics in **lifespan development** in a variety of engaging formats. You have the opportunity to refine and check your understanding via interactive quizzes and flashcards. Summaries provide inspiration for your own further exploration. And, in order to make **HDEV** an even better learning tool, we invite you to speak up about your experience with **HDEV** by completing a survey form and sending us your comments.

Get online and discover the following resources:
- Flashcards
- Interactive Quizzing
- Games
- Discipline-specific activities

"I think this book is awesome for students of all ages. It is a much simpler way to study."

—Yasmine Al-Hashimi, Fanshawe College

Visit **www.icanhdev.com** to find the resources you need today!

Babies are born

with behaviours—crying, smiling, clinging—that stimulate caregiving from adults.

6

Infancy: Social and Emotional Development

DID YOU KNOW?

D1 Autistic children often grow up to be independent, productive, happy, and successful professionals.

D2 Children placed in day care are more aggressive than children who are cared for in the home.

D3 Fear of strangers is normal among infants.

D4 Children are born with varying temperaments that are believed to have a significant genetic component.

D5 Girls prefer dolls and toy animals, and boys prefer toy trucks and sports equipment very early in life.

By 12 months of age, children are master social puppeteers. They demand attention consistently and on their terms. "Mommy, Mommy" or "Daddy, Daddy" can interrupt daily chores or rare moments of solitude and is expertly choreographed to demand your attention immediately. "I want you to pick up me" is a hard request to resist. Do you grab them into your arms for a cuddle or ignore their efforts in an attempt to discourage their constant efforts to get at you? Do you ignore them and let them cry it out or enjoy the affection they are offering regardless of the inconvenient timing? **Attachment**, you see, is a two-way street.

> **attachment** an affectional bond characterized by seeking closeness with another and distress upon separation.

Learning Outcomes

LO1 Describe the development of attachment in infancy and theoretical views of how it occurs

LO2 Discuss the effects of social deprivation, abuse and neglect, and autism spectrum disorders on attachment

LO3 Discuss the effects of day care

LO4 Describe the emotional development of the infant

LO5 Describe the personality development of the infant, focusing on the self-concept, temperament, and sex differences

LO1 Attachment: Bonds That Endure

attachment is what most people refer to as affection or love. Canadian-born Mary Ainsworth (1989), a preeminent researcher on attachment, defines attachment as an enduring emotional bond between one animal or person and another. John Bowlby adds that attachment is essential to the survival of the infant (Bowlby, 1988). He notes that babies are born with behaviours—crying, smiling, clinging—that encourage caregiving from adults.

Infants try to maintain contact with caregivers to whom they are attached. They engage in eye contact,

separation anxiety fear of separation from a target of attachment.

secure attachment a type of attachment characterized by mild distress at leave-takings and being readily soothed by reunion.

avoidant attachment a type of insecure attachment characterized by apparent indifference to leave-takings by and reunions with an attachment figure.

ambivalent/resistant attachment a type of insecure attachment characterized by severe distress at leave-takings by and ambivalent behaviour at reunions.

disorganized–disoriented attachment a type of insecure attachment characterized by dazed and contradictory behaviours toward an attachment figure.

secure attachment or insecure attachment. Most North American children are securely attached (Belsky, 2006a; McCartney et al., 2004).

Ainsworth developed the *strange-situation method* as a way of measuring the development of attachment (see Figure 6.1). In this method, an infant is exposed to a series of separations and reunions with a caregiver (usually the mother) and a stranger who is working with the researchers. In the test, secure infants mildly protest their mother's departure, seek interaction upon reunion, and are readily comforted by her.

There are two major types of insecurity, or "insecure attachment": **avoidant attachment** and **ambivalent/resistant attachment**. Infants who show avoidant attachment are the least distressed by their mothers'

pull and tug at them, and ask to be picked up. When they cannot maintain contact, they show **separation anxiety**—thrash about, fuss, cry, screech, or whine.

PATTERNS OF ATTACHMENT

Ainsworth and her colleagues (1978) identified various patterns of attachment. Broadly, infants show

departure. They play without fuss when alone and ignore their mothers upon reunion. Ambivalent/resistant babies are the most emotional. They show severe signs of distress when their mothers leave and show ambivalence upon reunion by alternately clinging to their mothers and pushing them away. Additional categories of insecure attachment have been proposed, including **disorganized–disoriented attachment**. Babies showing this pattern seem dazed, confused, or disoriented. They may show contradictory behaviours, such as moving toward the mother while looking away from her.

Not surprisingly, secure infants and toddlers are happier, more sociable, and more cooperative with caregivers. At ages 5 and 6, they get along better with peers and are better adjusted in school than insecure children

FIGURE 6.1
The Strange Situation

These historic photos show a 12-month-old child in the Strange Situation. In (a), the child plays with toys, glancing occasionally at mother. In (b), the stranger approaches with a toy. While the child is distracted, mother leaves the room. In (c), mother returns after a brief absence. The child crawls to her quickly and clings to her when picked up. In (d), the child cries when mother again leaves the room.

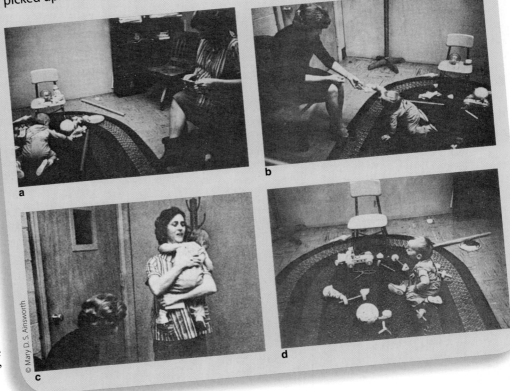

© Mary D. S. Ainsworth

© Inspirestock/Jupiterimages

(Belsky, 2006a; McCartney et al., 2004; Spieker et al., 2003). Insecure attachment at the age of 1 year predicts psychological disorders at the age of 17 (Sroufe, 1998; Steele, 2005).

ESTABLISHING ATTACHMENT

Attachment is related to the quality of infant care (Belsky, 2006a; Coleman, 2003). The parents of secure infants are more affectionate, cooperative, and predictable than parents of insecure infants. They respond more sensitively to their infants' smiles and cries (Harel & Scher, 2003).

A Japanese study found evidence for the "intergenerational transmission of attachment" (Kazui et al., 2000). The children of secure mothers showed the most secure patterns of attachment themselves (Cicchetti et al., 2006). Siblings tend to develop similar attachment relationships with their mother (van IJzendoorn et al., 2000). Siblings of the same sex are also more likely than girl–boy pairs to form similar attachment relationships with their mother.

Security is also connected with the infant's temperament (Belsky, 2006a; Kerns et al., 2007). The mothers of "difficult" children are less responsive to them and report feeling more distant from them (Morrell & Steele, 2003; Stams et al., 2002).

Involvement of Fathers

How involved is the average father with his children? The brief answer, in developed nations, is more so than in the past (Grossmann et al., 2002). But mothers engage in more interactions with their infants. Most fathers are more likely to play with their children than to feed or clean them (Laflamme et al., 2002). Fathers more often than mothers engage in rough-and-tumble play, whereas mothers are more likely to play games involving toys, and patty-cake and peek-a-boo (Laflamme et al., 2002).

How strongly, then, do infants become attached to their fathers? The more affectionate the interaction between father and infant is, the stronger the attachment (R. A. Thompson et al., 2003).

STABILITY OF ATTACHMENT

Patterns of attachment tend to persist when care-giving conditions remain constant (Ammaniti et al., 2005; Karavasilis et al., 2003). Byron Egeland and Alan Sroufe (1981) followed infants who were severely neglected and others who received high-quality care from 12 to 18 months of age. Attachment patterns remained stable (secure) for infants receiving fine care. But many

Mary Ainsworth

© Robert S. Marvin / © catnap72/iStockphoto

insecure, neglected infants became securely attached over the 6-month period, either because of a relationship with a supportive

indiscriminate attachment the display of attachment behaviours toward any person.

family member or because home life grew less tense. Children can also become less securely attached to caregivers when home life deteriorates (Belsky, 2006a). Children adopted at various ages can become securely attached to adoptive parents (Veríssimo & Salvaterra, 2006). Early attachment patterns tend to endure into middle childhood, adolescence, and even adulthood (Ammaniti et al., 2005; Karavasilis et al., 2003).

STAGES OF ATTACHMENT

Cross-cultural studies have led to a theory of stages of attachment. In one study, Ainsworth tracked the behaviour of Ugandan infants. Over a 9-month period, she noted their efforts to maintain contact with the mother, their protests when separated, and their use of the mother as a base for exploring the environment. At first, the Ugandan infants showed **indiscriminate attachment**—no particular preferences for a familiar caregiver. Specific attachment to the mother, as evidenced by separation anxiety and other behaviour, began to develop at about 4 months of age and grew intense by about 7 months. Fear of strangers developed 1 or 2 months later.

In another study, shown in Figure 6.2, Scottish infants showed indiscriminate attachment during the first 6 months or so after birth (Schaffer & Emerson, 1964). Then, indiscriminate attachment waned. Specific attachments to the mother and other familiar

initial-preattachment phase the first phase in development of attachment, characterized by indiscriminate attachment.

attachment-in-the-making phase the second phase in development of attachment, characterized by preference for familiar figures.

clear-cut-attachment phase the third phase in development of attachment, characterized by intensified dependence on the primary caregiver.

caregivers intensified, as demonstrated by the appearance of separation anxiety, and remained at high levels through the age of 18 months. Fear of strangers occurred a month or so after the intensity of specific attachments began to mushroom. In both this and the Ugandan study, fear of strangers followed separation anxiety and the development of specific attachments by weeks.

From such studies, Ainsworth and her colleagues (1978) identified the following three phases of attachment:

1. The **initial-preattachment phase** lasts from birth to about 3 months and is characterized by indiscriminate attachment.

2. The **attachment-in-the-making phase** occurs at about 3 or 4 months and is characterized by preference for familiar figures.

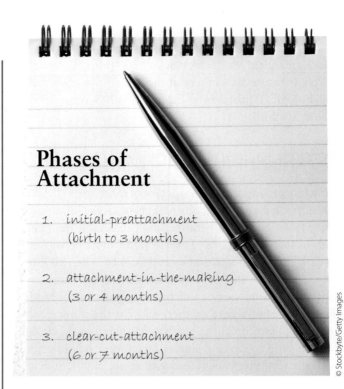

Phases of Attachment

1. initial-preattachment (birth to 3 months)

2. attachment-in-the-making (3 or 4 months)

3. clear-cut-attachment (6 or 7 months)

© Stockbyte/Getty Images

3. The **clear-cut-attachment phase** occurs at about 6 or 7 months and is characterized by intensified dependence on the primary caregiver, usually the mother.

But most infants have more than one adult caregiver and are likely to form multiple attachments: to the father, day-care providers, grandparents, and other caregivers, as well as the mother.

THEORIES OF ATTACHMENT

There are several theories of the development of attachment.

Cognitive View of Attachment

The cognitive view suggests that an infant must develop the concept of object permanence before specific attachment becomes possible. If caregivers are to be missed when absent, the infant must perceive that they continue to exist. We have seen that infants tend to develop specific attachments at about the age of 6 to 7 months. Basic object permanence concerning objects develops somewhat earlier (see Chapter 5).

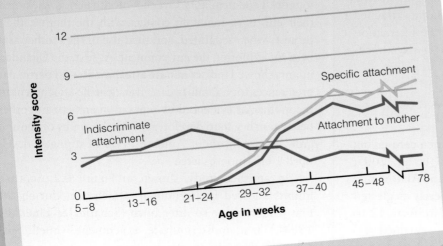

FIGURE 6.2
Development of Attachment

During the first 6 months, infants tend to show indiscriminate attachment, which then wanes as specific attachments intensify.

Specific attachment

Indiscriminate attachment

Attachment to mother

Intensity score

12
9
6
3
0

5–8   13–16   21–24   29–32   37–40   45–48   78

Age in weeks

Behavioural View of Attachment

Early in the twentieth century, behaviourists argued that attachment behaviours are conditioned. Caregivers feed their infants and tend to their other physiological needs. Thus, infants associate their caregivers with gratification and learn to approach them to meet their needs. From this perspective, a caregiver becomes a conditioned reinforcer.

Psychoanalytic Views of Attachment

According to psychoanalytic theorists, the caregiver, usually the mother, becomes not just a "reinforcer" but also a love object who forms the basis for all later attachments. Sigmund Freud emphasized the importance of oral activities, such as eating, in the first year. Freud believed that the infant becomes emotionally attached to the mother during this time because she is the primary satisfier of the infant's needs for food and sucking.

Erik Erikson believed that the first year is critical for developing a sense of trust in the mother, which fosters attachment. The mother's general sensitivity to the child's needs, not just the need for food, fosters the development of trust and attachment.

Caregiver as a Source of Contact Comfort

Harry and Margaret Harlow conducted classic experiments to demonstrate that feeding is not critical to the attachment process, as Freud suggested (Harlow & Harlow, 1966). In one infamous study, the Harlows placed rhesus monkey infants in cages with two surrogate mothers (see Figure 6.3). One "mother" was made from wire mesh, from which a baby bottle was extended. The other surrogate mother was made of soft, cuddly terry cloth. Infant monkeys spent most of their time clinging to the cloth mother, even though she did not offer food. The Harlows concluded that monkeys—and perhaps humans—have a need for **contact comfort** that is as basic as the need for food.

Ethological View of Attachment

Ethologists note that for many animals, attachment is an inborn or instinctive response to a specific stimulus. Some researchers theorize that a baby's cry stimulates

contact comfort the pleasure derived from physical contact with another.

ethologist a scientist who studies the behaviour patterns characteristic of various species.

FIGURE 6.3
Contact Comfort

Although this rhesus monkey infant is fed by the "wire-mesh mother," it spends most of its time clinging to a soft, cuddly "terry-cloth mother."

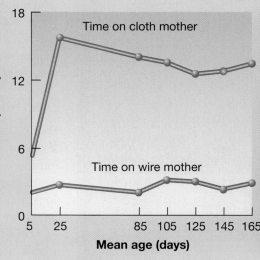

social smile a smile that occurs in response to a human voice or face.

critical period a period during which imprinting can occur.

imprinting the process by which waterfowl become attached to the first moving object they follow.

caregiving in women. By 2 to 3 months of age, the human face begins to elicit a **social smile** in infants, helping to ensure survival by eliciting affection (Ainsworth & Bowlby, 1991; Bowlby, 1988). In circular fashion, the mother's social response to her infant's face can reliably produce infant smiling by 8 months of age (Jones & Hong, 2005). The pattern contributes to a mutual attachment, or the *social dance*.

In many nonhumans, attachment occurs during a **critical period** of life. Waterfowl become attached during this period to the first moving object they encounter. Because the image of the moving object seems to become "imprinted" on the young animal, the process is termed **imprinting**.

Ethologist Konrad Lorenz (1962, 1981) became well known when pictures of his "family" of goslings (baby geese) were made public. Lorenz acquired his "following" by being present when the goslings hatched and allowing them to follow him. The critical period for geese and ducks begins when they first engage in locomotion and ends when they develop fear of strangers. The goslings followed Lorenz persistently, ran to him when frightened, honked with distress at his departure, and

tried to overcome barriers placed between them. If you substitute crying for honking, it sounds quite human.

Ethology, Ainsworth, and Bowlby

Let us return to Ainsworth and Bowlby (1991). They wrote that "the distinguishing characteristic of the theory of attachment that we have jointly developed is that it is an ethological approach." They address several distinctions for humans, noting that caregiving in humans is largely learned and not inborn. Ainsworth and Bowlby also note that the critical period for attachment in humans—if one exists—extends to months or years (Ainsworth & Bowlby, 1991; Verissimo & Salvaterra, 2006). Caregiving itself and infant responsiveness, such as smiling, also promote attachment.

LO2 When Attachment Fails

What happens when children are reared with little or no contact with caregivers? When parents neglect or abuse their children? In the case of autism spectrum disorders?

SOCIAL DEPRIVATION

Studies of children reared in institutions where they receive little social stimulation from caregivers are limited in that they are correlational. In other words, family factors that led to the children's placement in institutions may also have contributed to their developmental problems. Ethical considerations prevent us from conducting experiments in which we randomly assign children to social deprivation. However, experiments of this kind have been undertaken with rhesus monkeys, and the results are consistent with those of the correlational studies of children.

Experiments with Monkeys

The Harlows and their colleagues conducted studies of rhesus monkeys that were "reared by" wire-mesh and terry-cloth surrogate mothers. In later studies, rhesus monkeys were reared without even this questionable "social" support—without seeing any other animal, monkey or human (Harlow et al., 1971).

The Harlows found that rhesus infants reared in this most solitary confinement later avoided other monkeys. Instead, they cowered in the

Konrad Lorenz with his "family" of goslings. This type of attachment is known as imprinting.

presence of others. Nor did they try to fend off attacks by other monkeys. Rather, they sat in the corner, clutching themselves and rocking back and forth. The isolated females who later bore children ignored or abused them.

Can the damage from social deprivation be overcome? When monkeys deprived for 6 months or more are placed with younger, 3- to 4-month-old females for a couple of hours a day, the younger monkeys attempt to interact with their deprived elders. Many of the deprived monkeys begin to play with the youngsters after a few weeks, and many eventually expand their social contacts to older monkeys (Suomi et al., 1972). Socially withdrawn 4- and 5-year-old children similarly make gains in their social and emotional development when provided with younger playmates (Furman et al., 1979). One must be cautious when drawing connections between animal studies and the human population, but the correlations are undeniable.

Studies with Children

Institutionalized children whose material needs are met but who receive little social stimulation from caregivers encounter problems in all areas of development (Ganesh & Magdalin, 2007; Rutter, 2006). René A. Spitz (1965) found that many institutionalized children show withdrawal and depression. In one institution, infants were maintained in separate cubicles for most of their first year to ward off infectious diseases (Provence & Lipton, 1962). Adults tended to them only to feed them and change their diapers. As a rule, baby bottles were propped up in their cribs. Attendants rarely responded to their cries; they were rarely played with or spoken to. By the age of 4 months, the infants showed little interest in adults. A few months later, some of them sat withdrawn in their cribs and rocked back and forth, almost like the Harlows' monkeys. None were speaking at 12 months.

Why do children whose material needs are met show such dramatic deficiencies? The answer may depend, in part, on the age of the child. Research by Leon Yarrow and his colleagues (Yarrow et al., 1971; Yarrow & Goodwin, 1973) suggests that deficiencies in sensory stimulation and social interaction may cause more problems than lack of love in infants who are too young to have developed specific attachments. But once infants have developed specific attachments, separation from their primary caregivers can lead to problems.

The Capacity to Recover from Social Deprivation

Infants also have powerful capacities to recover from deprivation. One study showed how many children may be able to recover fully from 13 or 14 months of

deprivation (Kagan & Klein, 1973). The natives in an isolated Guatemalan village believe that fresh air and sunshine will sicken children. Children are thus kept in windowless huts until they can walk and are played with infrequently. During their isolation, the infants behave apathetically. They are physically and socially retarded when they start to walk. But by 11 years of age they are as alert and active as Canadian children of the same age.

A classic longitudinal study of orphanage children also offers evidence of the ability of children to recover from social deprivation (Skeels, 1966). In this study, a group of 19-month-old apparently retarded children were placed in the care of older institutionalized girls. The girls spent a great deal of time playing with and nurturing them. Four years after being placed with the girls, the "retarded" children made dramatic gains in IQ scores, whereas children remaining in the orphanage showed declines in IQ.

CHILD ABUSE AND NEGLECT

According to the Canadian Incidence Study of Reported Child Abuse and Neglect (Trocmé et al., 2005) (a follow-up report is currently being completed), in 2003, Canadian jurisdictions (except for Quebec) had an incidence rate of 21.71 cases of substantiated maltreatment per 1,000 children. Keep in mind that no reliable method exists for tracking unreported incidents of child abuse, which experts believe is a significant number. Of the substantiated cases, approximately 29 percent involved neglect, 28 percent involved exposure to domestic violence, 24 percent involved physical abuse, 15 percent involved emotional maltreatment, and 4 percent of the cases involved sexual abuse. Although girls comprised 49 percent of victims, they were the largest proportion of victims in cases of sexual abuse (63 percent) and emotional maltreatment (54 percent). Boys were more often victims in cases of physical abuse (54 percent), neglect (52 percent), and exposure to domestic violence (52 percent). Indigenous populations were isolated in this study due to their overrepresentation in

© Indexstock Imagery/Jupiterimages Photolibrary

the foster care system. Fifteen percent of the cases involved children of indigenous heritage even though they represent only about 4 percent of the Canadian population.

Effects of Child Abuse

Abused children show a high incidence of personal and social problems and psychological disorders (Letourneau et al., 2004). In general, abused children are less securely attached to their parents. They are less intimate with peers and more aggressive, angry, and noncompliant than other children (Joshi et al., 2006). They also have lower self-esteem and perform more poorly in school (Shonk & Cicchetti, 2001). Abused children are at greater risk for delinquency, risky sexual behaviour, and substance abuse (Haapasalo & Moilanen, 2004). When they reach adulthood, they are more likely to act aggressively toward their partners (Malinosky-Rummell & Hansen, 1993).

Causes of Child Abuse

Various factors contribute to child abuse, including stress, a history of child abuse in at least one parent's family of origin, lack of adequate coping and child-rearing skills, unrealistic expectations of children, and substance abuse (Maluccio & Ainsworth, 2003; Merrill et al., 2004). Stress has many sources, including divorce, loss of a job, moving, and birth of a new family member (Joshi et al., 2006).

Ironically, infants who are already in pain of some kind and difficult to soothe are more likely to be abused (Frodi, 1985). Abusive parents may find the cries of their infants particularly aversive, so infants' crying may precipitate abuse (Schuetze et al., 2003). Children who are disobedient, inappropriate, or unresponsive are also at greater risk (Bugental & Happaney, 2004).

What to Do

Canadian laws require that any person who suspects child abuse must report it to Children's Aid (Trocmé et al., 2005). It is not the responsibility of the reporter to collect any information. Parents having difficulty controlling aggressive impulses toward their children are also encouraged to call for support.

Numerous techniques have been developed to help prevent child abuse. One approach focuses on strengthening parenting skills among the general population (Joshi et al., 2006), while providing information about abuse and providing support for families. Another approach targets groups at high risk for abuse, such as poor, single teen mothers (Joshi et al., 2006). In some programs, home visitors help new parents develop skills in caregiving and home management (Duggan et al., 2004).

AUTISM SPECTRUM DISORDERS

Autism spectrum disorders (ASDs) are characterized by impairment in communication skills and social interaction, and by repetitive,

Abused children are at greater risk for delinquency, risky sexual behaviour, and substance abuse.

stereotyped behaviour (see Table 6.1). ASDs tend to become evident by the age of 3 and sometimes before the end of the first year. The term *spectrum* refers to a continuum of severity. Diagnoses of ASDs share common characteristics, but the conditions of ASDs cover a wide range, with many individual differences. Autism is the major type of ASD but, according to the Autism Society of Canada (2009), other forms include the following:

- *Asperger's disorder* (20 in 10,000 Canadians). Characterized by social deficits and stereotyped behaviour but without the significant cognitive or language delays associated with autism.

- *Rett's disorder* (1 in 10,000 female births). Characterized by a range of physical, behavioural, motor, and cognitive abnormalities that begin after a few months of normal development and are found almost exclusively in females.

- *Childhood disintegrative disorder* (0.2 in 10,000 Canadians). Abnormal functioning and loss of previously acquired skills that begins after about 2 years of apparently normal development.

TABLE 6.1
Characteristics of Autism Spectrum Disorders (ASDs)

KEY INDICATORS

Does not babble, point, or make meaningful gestures by 1 year of age

Does not speak one word by 16 months

Does not combine two words by 2 years

Does not respond to name

Loses language or social skills

OTHER INDICATORS

Poor eye contact

Doesn't seem to know how to play with toys

Excessively lines up toys or other objects

Is attached to one particular toy or object

Doesn't smile

At times seems to be hearing impaired

Source: Adapted from Strock (2004).

Autism

Autism is four to five times more common among boys than girls (Autism Society of Canada, 2009). Autistic children show limited interest in social interaction and may avoid eye contact. Attachment to others is weak or absent.

Other features of autism include communication problems, difficulty adapting to change, and ritualistic or stereotypical behaviour (Georgiades et al., 2007) (see Table 6.1). Some autistic individuals may bang their heads, slap their faces, bite their hands, or pull out their hair. Parents of autistic children often say they were "good babies," which usually means they made few demands. But as autistic children develop, they tend to shun traditional forms of affectionate contacts such as hugging, cuddling, and kissing.

Speech development is often delayed, with little babbling and few communicative gestures during the first year. Autistic children may show **mutism**, **echolalia**, and pronoun reversal, referring to themselves as "you" or "he." About half use language by middle childhood, but their speech is unusual.

The Autism Society of Canada warns that we need to distinguish between clinical descriptions and our knowledge of people who live with ASDs. Many terms are seen as labels that have limiting effects, often "medicalizing" people to the point that, despite their unique skills, abilities, and values, they become forgotten by communities or eclipsed by their "disorder."

Causes of Autism

Contrary to what some theorists say, research evidence shows no correlation between the development of autism and deficiencies in child rearing (Mackic-Magyar & McCracken, 2004).

Various lines of evidence suggest a key role for biological factors in autism. For example, very low birth

autism a disorder characterized by extreme aloneness, communication problems, preservation of sameness, and ritualistic behaviour.

mutism refusal to speak.

echolalia automatic repetition of sounds or words.

© Robin Nelson/PhotoEdit

Autism is a spectrum disorder. Many individuals with autism are able to thrive in a supportive environment.

weight and advanced maternal age may heighten the risk of autism (Maimburg & Væth, 2006). A role for genetic mechanisms is suggested by kinship studies (Constantino et al., 2006; Gutknecht, 2001). The concordance (agreement) rates for autism are about 60 percent among pairs of identical (MZ) twins, who fully share the same genes, compared with about 10 percent for pairs of fraternal (DZ) twins, whose genetic codes overlap by half (Plomin et al., 1994).

Biological factors focus on neurological involvement. Many children with autism have abnormal brain wave patterns or seizures (Canitano, 2007; Roulet-Perez, & Deonna; 2006). Other researchers have found that the brains of children with autism have abnormal sensitivities to neurotransmitters such as serotonin, dopamine, acetylcholine, and norepinephrine (Bauman et al., 2006). Other researchers note unusual activity in the motor region of the cerebral cortex (R. Mueller et al., 2001) and less activity in some other areas of the brain (Lam et al., 2006; Penn, 2006).

Treatment of Autism

Treatment for autism is mainly based on principles of learning, although investigation of biological approaches is also under way (Strock, 2004). Behaviour modification has been used to increase the child's ability to attend to others, to play with other children, and to discourage self-mutilation. Brief bursts of mild, harmless electric shock rapidly eliminate self-mutilation

> Autistic individuals should be valued for their differences and not viewed as persons who should be changed.

(Lovaas, 1977). The use of electric shock raises serious moral, ethical, and legal concerns, but O. Ivar Lovaas has countered that failure to eliminate self-injurious behaviour places the child at yet greater risk.

Because children with autism show behavioural deficits, behaviour modification is used to help them develop new behaviours. Though autistic children often experience difficulty relating to people, many can be taught to accept people as reinforcers, rather than objects, by pairing praise with food treats (Drasgow et al., 2001). Praise can then be used to encourage speech and social play.

The most effective treatment programs focus on individualized instruction (Rapin, 1997). In a classic study conducted by Lovaas (Lovaas et al., 1989), autistic children received more than 40 hours of one-to-one behaviour modification a week for at least 2 years. Significant intellectual and educational gains were reported for 9 of the 19 children (47 percent) in the program. Less intensive educational programs have yielded some positive results with autistic toddlers (Stahmer et al., 2004).

Biological approaches for the treatment of autism are being studied. Drugs that enhance serotonin activity (selective serotonin reuptake inhibitors, or SSRIs) can apparently help prevent self-injury, aggressive outbursts, depression, anxiety, and repetitive behaviour (Kwok, 2003). Drugs that are usually used to treat schizophrenia—so-called "major tranquilizers"—are helpful with stereotyped behaviour, hyperactivity, and self-injury, but not with cognitive and language problems (Kwok, 2003; McClellan & Werry, 2003).

Autistic behaviour generally continues into adulthood to one degree or another. Many autistic people go on to be productive, happy, and successful individuals.

D1 Autistic children often grow up to be independent, productive, happy, and successful professionals.
We must resist the stereotypes and consider the individual.

LO3 Day Care

Have you seen the bumper sticker that suggests we should choose our children's day care wisely because our children will grow up and one day choose our retirement home?

Most parents, including mothers with infants, are in the workforce (Carey, 2007a). About 54 percent of Canadian children aged 6 months to 5 years attend some type of nonparental child care (Bushnik, 2006).

Many parents wonder whether day care will affect their children's attachment to them. Some studies have found that infants who are in full-time day care are more likely than other children to show insecure attachment (Brandtjen & Verny, 2001). Some researchers conclude that a mother who works full time puts her infant at risk for developing emotional insecurity. Others note that infants whose mothers work may simply become less distressed by her departure and less likely to seek her out when she returns as time goes on, thus providing the appearance of being less attached. Most infants in both groups are securely attached (Timmerman, 2006).

Some studies report that infants with day-care experience are more peer oriented and play at higher developmental levels than do home-reared infants. Children in high-quality day care are more likely to share their toys. They are more independent, self-confident, outgoing, and affectionate as well as more helpful and cooperative with peers and adults (Lamb & Ahnert, 2006; Pierce & Vandell, 2006). Participation in day care is also linked with better academic performance in elementary school (Belsky, 2006b).

A study funded by the National Institute on Child Health and Human Development (NICHD) agrees that "high-quality" day care can result in scores on tests of cognitive skills that rival or exceed those of the children reared in the home by their mothers (Belsky et al., 2007). The quality of the day care was defined in terms

© PhotoObjects.net/Jupiterimages

About 54 percent of Canadian children aged 6 months to 5 years attend some type of nonparental child care.

of the richness of the learning environment (availability of toys, books, and other materials), the ratio of caregivers to children (high quality meant more caregivers), the amount of individual attention received by the child, and the extent to which caregivers talked to the children and asked them questions.

However, the researchers also found that children placed in day care may be less cooperative and more aggressive toward peers and adults than children who are reared in the home. The more time spent away from their mothers, the more likely these children were to be rated as defiant, aggressive, and disobedient when they attended kindergarten.

D2 Children placed in day care are more aggressive than children who are cared for in the home.
True, but children in day care are not abnormally aggressive and are reported to be more peer oriented and to play at higher developmental levels than home-raised infants.

Teacher ratings found that children who had attended day care were significantly more likely than children cared for in the home to interrupt in class and to tease or bully other children (Belsky et al., 2007). The degree of disturbance generally remained "within normal limits." *The quality of the day-care centre made no difference.* Children from high-quality day-care centres were also more likely to be disruptive than children cared for in the home. Moreover, the behavioural difference persisted through grade six.

Now let us note some limitations of the NICHD study. Although the differences in disruptive behaviour between children in full-time day care and those cared for in the home are statistically significant—meaning that they are unlikely to be due to chance—they are small. The study implies that day care *causes* the disruptive behaviour of concern later on, but there was no control group (Harris, 2007). Children are *not* assigned at random

to day care or care in the home. Therefore, it may be that children placed in day care have caregivers who are most stressed by work through their children's primary school years (Taylor, 2007). Also, do we know that the so-called disruptive children become less productive and less successful adults (Kulp, 2007)? Perhaps they actually become "assertive and entrepreneurial," especially since their cognitive skills and other social skills are intact.

In any case, reality intrudes. Millions of parents do not have the option of deciding whether to place their children in day care; their only choice is where. And some parents, given their financial and geographic circumstances, do not even have that choice.

LO4 Emotional Development

an emotion is a state of feeling with physiological, situational, and cognitive components. Physiologically, when emotions are strong, our hearts may beat more rapidly and our muscles may tense. Situationally, we may feel anger when frustrated or pleasure or relief when we are being held by a loved one. Cognitively, anger may be triggered by the idea that someone is purposefully withholding something we need.

It is unclear how many emotions babies have, and they cannot tell us what they are feeling. We can only observe how they behave, including changes in their facial expressions (Oster, 2005). Facial expressions appear to be universal in that they are recognized in different cultures around the world, so they are considered a reliable index of emotion.

Researchers have long debated whether newborns are born with specific emotions (Soussignan & Schaal, 2005). They have asked whether the newborn baby's crying is nothing more than a reflex in response to discomfort. It seems clear enough that as infants develop through the first year, their cognitive appraisal of events, including their interaction

with their caregivers, becomes a key part of their emotional life and their emotional expression (Camras et al., 2007; Soussignan & Schaal, 2005).

Infants' initial emotional expressions appear to comprise two basic states of emotional arousal: a positive attraction to pleasant stimulation, such as the caregiver's voice or being held, and withdrawal from aversive stimulation, such as a sudden loud noise. By the age of 2 to 3 months, social smiling has replaced reflexive smiling. Social smiling is usually highly endearing to caregivers. At 3 to 5 months, infants laugh at active stimuli, such as repetitively touching their bellies or playing "Ah, boop!"

In sum, researchers agree that infants show only a few emotions during the first few months. They agree that emotional development is linked to cognitive development and social experience. They do not necessarily agree on exactly when specific emotions are first shown or whether discrete emotions are present at birth (Camras et al., 2007).

> Infants' initial emotional expressions appear to comprise two basic states of emotional arousal: a positive attraction to pleasant stimulation and withdrawal from aversive stimulation.

EMOTIONAL DEVELOPMENT AND PATTERNS OF ATTACHMENT

Emotional development has been linked with various histories of attachment. In a longitudinal study of 112 children at ages 9, 14, 22, and 33 months, Kochanska (2001) studied the development of fear, anger, and joy by using laboratory situations designed to evoke these emotions. Patterns of attachment were assessed using the strange-situation method. Differences in emotional development could first be related to attachment at the age of 14 months. Resistant children were most fearful and they frequently responded with distress even in episodes designed to evoke joy. When they were assessed repeatedly over time, it became apparent that securely attached children were becoming significantly less angry. By contrast, the negative emotions of insecurely attached children rose: Avoidant children grew more fearful, and resistant children became less joyful. At 33 months of age, securely attached children were less likely to show fear and anger, even when they were exposed to situations designed to elicit these emotions.

© Ryan Gerber

FEAR OF STRANGERS

We live in an increasingly transient world where many adult children find themselves living across the country, or at least in a different province, from their parents. It is a proud moment to introduce your child to your parents for the first time. The new grandparents expectantly shower their grandchild with joy and affection, only to be met by screams that rival any carefully scripted horror movie. What have they done wrong? They simply existed within sight of their grandchild, who is going through the cognitive stage of stranger anxiety.

Fear of strangers—also called *stranger anxiety*—is normal. Most infants develop it. Stranger anxiety appears at about 6 to 9 months of age. By 4 or 5 months of age, infants may compare the faces of strangers and their mothers, looking back and forth. Older infants show distress by crying, whimpering, gazing fearfully, and crawling away. Fear of strangers often peaks at 9–12 months, just in time for that first picture with Santa Claus, and declines in the second year.

Children with fear of strangers show less anxiety when their mothers are present (Thompson & Limber, 1990). Children also are less fearful when they are in familiar surroundings, such as their homes, rather than in new and unfamiliar environments (Sroufe et al., 1974).

> **D3** Fear of strangers is normal among infants.
> Most infants develop some form of stranger anxiety around 6 to 9 months of age. This behaviour is not an indicator of an insecure attachment.

SOCIAL REFERENCING: WHAT SHOULD I DO NOW?

Social referencing is the seeking out of another person's perception of a situation to help us form our own view of it

(Hertenstein & Campos, 2004). Leslie Carver and Brenda Vaccaro (2007) suggest that social referencing requires three components: (1) looking at another, usually older individual in a novel, ambiguous situation; (2) associating that individual's emotional response with the unfamiliar situation; and (3) regulating their own emotional response in accord with the response of the older individual.

Infants also display social referencing, as early as 6 months of age. They use caregivers' facial expressions or tone of voice as clues on how to respond (Hertenstein & Campos, 2004). In one study, 8-month-old infants were friendlier to a stranger when their mothers exhibited a friendly facial expression in the stranger's presence than when she looked worried (Boccia & Campos, 1989). Parents quickly learn that smiling when their child has a gentle fall will help to diffuse the situation. A parent may need to suppress a personal fear of spiders and play with them to keep a child free from that same fear.

> **social referencing** using another person's reaction to a situation to form one's own response.
>
> **emotional regulation** techniques for controlling one's emotional states.

EMOTIONAL REGULATION: KEEPING ON AN EVEN KEEL

Emotional regulation refers to the ways in which young children control their own emotions. Even infants display certain behaviours to control unpleasant emotional states. They may look away from a disturbing event or suck their thumbs (Rothbart & Sheese, 2007). Caregivers help infants learn to regulate their emotions. A two-way communication system develops in which the

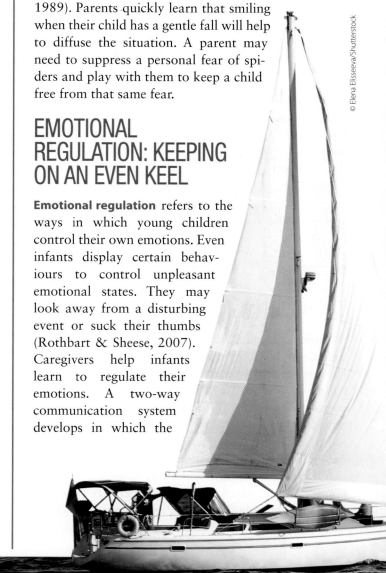

infant signals the caregiver that help is needed and the caregiver responds. Claire Kopp (1989, p. 347) provides an example of such a system:

> A 13-month-old, playing with a large plastic bottle, attempted to unscrew the cover, but could not. Fretting for a short time, she initiated eye contact with her mother and held out the jar. As her mother took it to unscrew the cover, the infant ceased fretting.

Research evidence suggests that the children of secure mothers are not only likely to be securely attached themselves but also are likely to regulate their own emotions in a positive manner (Grolnick et al., 2006; Thompson & Meyer, 2007). A German longitudinal study (Zimmermann et al., 2001) related emotional regulation in adolescence with patterns of attachment during infancy, as assessed using the strange-situation method. Forty-one adolescents, aged 16 and 17, were placed in complex problem-solving situations with friends. Those adolescents who were secure as infants were more capable of regulating their emotions to interact cooperatively with their friends.

LO5 Personality Development

i n this section, we look at the emergence of the self-concept. We then turn to a discussion of temperament. Finally, we consider sex differences in behaviour.

THE SELF-CONCEPT

At birth, we may find the world to be a confusing blur of sights, sounds, and inner sensations—yet the "we" may be missing, at least for a while. When we first see our hands, we do not yet realize that the hands "belong" to us and that we are separate and distinct from the world outside.

The self-concept appears to emerge gradually during infancy. At some point, infants understand that the hands they are moving in and out of sight are "their" hands. At some point, they understand that their own bodies extend only so far and then external objects and the bodies of others begin.

Development of the Self-Concept

Psychologists have devised ingenious methods to assess the development of the self-concept among infants. One of these is the mirror technique, which involves the use of a mirror and a dot of lipstick. Before the experiment begins, the researcher observes the infant for baseline data on how frequently the infant touches his or her nose. Then the mother places a red lipstick dot on the infant's nose, and the infant is placed before a mirror. Not until about the age of 18 months do infants begin to touch their own noses when looking in the mirror (Campbell et al., 2000; Keller et al., 2005).

Nose touching suggests that children recognize themselves and that they perceive that the red dot is an abnormality. Most 2-year-olds can point to pictures of themselves, and they begin to use "I" or their own name spontaneously (Smiley & Johnson, 2006).

Self-awareness affects the infant's social and emotional development (Foley, 2006). Knowledge of the self permits the infant and child to develop notions of sharing and cooperation. In one study, 2-year-olds with a better developed sense of self were more likely to cooperate with other children (Brownell & Carriger, 1990).

Self-awareness also facilitates the development of "self-conscious" emotions such as embarrassment, envy, empathy, pride, guilt, and shame (Foley, 2006). In one study, Deborah Stipek and her colleagues (1992) found that children older than 21 months often seek their mother's attention and approval when they have successfully completed a task, whereas younger toddlers do not.

Psychoanalytic Views of the Self-Concept

Margaret Mahler, a psychoanalyst, has proposed that development of self-concept comes about through

At about 18 months children recognize themselves in the mirror and see the red dot as an abnormality.

a process of **separation–individuation**, which lasts from about 5 months until 3 years of age (Mahler et al., 1975). Separation involves the child's growing perception that her mother is separate from herself. Individuation refers to the child's increasing sense of independence and autonomy.

One of the ways toddlers demonstrate growing autonomy, much to the dismay of caregivers, is by refusing to comply with caregivers' requests. "No!" becomes a universal reply to many parental interactions. Studies of toddlers and preschoolers between the ages of 1½ and 5 years have found that as children grow older, they adopt more skillful ways of expressing resistance to caregivers' requests (Smith et al., 2004; Stifter & Wiggins, 2004). For example, young toddlers are more likely to ignore a caregiver's request or defy it. Older toddlers and preschoolers are more likely to make excuses or negotiate.

TEMPERAMENT: EASY, DIFFICULT, OR SLOW TO WARM UP?

Each child has a characteristic **temperament**, a stable way of reacting and adapting to the world that is present early in life (Wachs, 2006). Many researchers believe that temperament involves a strong genetic component (Goldsmith et al., 2003; Wachs, 2006). The child's temperament includes many aspects of behaviour, including activity level, smiling and laughter, regularity in eating and sleep habits, approach or withdrawal, adaptability to new situations, intensity of responsiveness, general cheerfulness or unpleasantness, distractibility or persistence, and soothability (Gartstein et al., 2003; Thomas & Chess, 1989).

Types of Temperament

Thomas and Chess (1989) found that from the first days of life, many of the children in their study (65 percent) could be classified into one of three types of temperament: "easy" (40 percent of their sample), "difficult" (10 percent), and "slow to warm up" (15 percent). Some of the differences among these three types of children are shown in Table 6.2. The easy child has regular sleep and feeding schedules, approaches new situations (such as a new food or a new school) with enthusiasm and adapts to them easily, and is generally cheerful. Some children are more inconsistent and show a mixture of temperament traits.

The difficult child, on the other hand, has irregular sleep and feeding schedules, is slow to accept new people and situations, takes a long time to adjust to new routines, and responds to frustrations with tantrums and crying. The slow-to-warm-up child falls between the other two.

Stability of Temperament

Though not all children are born with the same temperament, as Thomas and Chess found, at least moderate consistency is shown in the development of temperament from infancy onward (Wachs, 2006). The infant

separation–individuation the process of becoming separate from and independent of the mother.

temperament individual difference in style of reaction that is present early in life.

TABLE 6.2
Types of Temperament

TEMPERAMENT CATEGORY	EASY	DIFFICULT	SLOW TO WARM UP
Regularity of biological functioning	Regular	Irregular	Somewhat irregular
Response to new stimuli	Positive approach	Negative withdrawal	Negative withdrawal
Adaptability to new situations	Adapts readily	Adapts slowly or not at all	Adapts slowly
Intensity of reaction	Mild or moderate	Intense	Mild
Quality of mood	Positive	Negative	Initially negative; gradually more positive

Sources: Chess & Thomas (1991) and Thomas & Chess (1989).

college with honours. She has occasional outbursts, but that's her boyfriend's problem. And they love her on the job. She's a hard worker and the most creative thing they've ever seen.

The environment also affects the development of temperament. An initial biological predisposition to a certain temperament may be strengthened or weakened by the parents' reaction to the child. Parents may react to a difficult child by imposing rigid care-giving schedules, which in turn can cause the child to become even more difficult (Schoppe-Sullivan et al., 2007). This example illustrates a poor fit between the child's behaviour style and the parents' response.

On the other hand, parents may modify a child's initial temperament in a more positive direction to achieve a **goodness of fit** between child and parent. Realization that their youngster's behaviour does not mean that the child is weak or deliberately disobedient, or that they are bad parents, helps parents modify their attitudes and behaviour toward the child, whose behaviour may then improve (Bird et al., 2006; Schoppe-Sullivan et al., 2007).

goodness of fit agreement between the parents' expectations of a child and the child's temperament.

who is highly active and cries in novel situations often becomes a fearful toddler. Difficult children in general are at greater risk for developing psychological disorders and adjustment problems later in life (Pauli-Pott et al., 2003; Rothbart et al., 2004). A longitudinal study tracked the progress of infants with a difficult temperament from 1½ through 12 years of age (Guerin et al., 1997). A difficult temperament correlated with parental reports of behavioural problems from ages 3 to 12, and teachers' reports of problems with attention span and aggression.

D4 Children are born with varying temperaments that are believed to have a significant genetic component. Though not all children are born with the same temperament, at least moderate consistency is shown in the development of temperament from infancy onward.

Goodness of Fit: The Role of the Environment

Our daughter was a difficult infant, but we weathered the storm. At the age of 15, she was climbing out the second-storey bedroom window at 2 a.m. to be with friends. When we discovered it, she sarcastically asked if we disapproved. "Yes," we said. "Use the front door; you're less likely to get hurt." She graduated

SEX DIFFERENCES

All cultures distinguish between females and males and have expectations about how they ought to behave. For this reason, a child's sex is a key factor in society's efforts to shape its personality and behaviour.

Behaviour of Infant Girls and Boys

Girls tend to advance more rapidly in their motor development in infancy: They sit, crawl, and walk earlier than boys (Matlin, 2008). Although a few studies have found that infant boys are more active and irritable than girls, others have not (Matlin, 2008). Girls and boys are similar in their social behaviours. They are equally likely to smile at people's faces, for example, and they do not differ in their dependency on adults (Maccoby & Jacklin, 1974). Girls and boys do begin to differ early in their preference for certain toys and play activities. By 12 to 18 months of age, girls prefer to play with dolls, doll furniture, dishes, and toy animals; boys prefer transportation toys (trucks, cars, airplanes, and the like), tools, and sports equipment as early as 9 to 18 month of age (Campbell et al., 2000; Serbin et al., 2001). Sex differences that show up later, such as differences in spatial relations skills, are not necessarily evident in infancy (Örnkloo & von Hofsten, 2007). By 24 months, both girls and boys appear to be aware of which behaviours are considered appropriate or inappropriate for their sex, according to cultural stereotypes (Hill & Flom, 2007). Thus it appears girls and boys may show a preference for gender stereotypical toys before they have been socialized and possibly before they understand their own sex.

> **D5** Girls prefer dolls and toy animals, and boys prefer toy trucks and sports equipment very early in life.
> It appears girls and boys may show a preference for gender stereotypical toys before they have been socialized and possibly before they understand their own sex.

Adults' Behaviour toward Infants

Adults interact differently with girls and boys. Researchers have presented adults with an unfamiliar infant who is dressed in boy's clothes and has a boy's name or an infant who is dressed in girl's clothing and has a girl's name. (In reality, it is the same baby who simply is given different names and clothing.) When adults believe they are playing with a girl, they are more likely to offer "her" a doll; when they think the child is a boy, they are more likely to offer a football or a hammer. "Boys" also

> ## Parents tend to provide baby girls and boys with different bedroom decorations and toys sometimes before they are even born.

are encouraged to engage in more physical activity than "girls" (Worell & Goodheart, 2006).

Parents, especially fathers, are more likely to encourage rough-and-tumble play in sons than daughters (Eccles et al., 2000; Fagot et al., 2000). On the other hand, parents talk more to infant daughters than infant sons. They smile more at daughters and are more emotionally expressive toward them (Powlishta et al., 2001).

Infant girls are likely to be decked out in a pink or yellow dress and embellished with ruffles and lace, whereas infant boys wear blue or red (Eccles et al., 2000; Powlishta et al., 2001). Parents tend to provide baby girls and boys with different bedroom decorations and toys sometimes even before they are born. Examination of the contents of rooms of children from 5 months to 6 years of age found that boys' rooms were often decorated with animal themes and with blue bedding and curtains. Girls' rooms featured flowers, lace, ruffles, and pastels. Girls owned more dolls; boys had more vehicles, military toys, and sports equipment.

Parents react favourably when their infant daughters play with "girls' toys" and their sons play with "boys' toys." In spite of best efforts not to stereotype their children, adults, especially fathers, show more negative reactions when girls play with boys' toys and boys play with girls' toys (Martin et al., 2002; Worell & Goodheart, 2006). Parents thus try to shape their children's behaviour during infancy and lay the foundation for development in early childhood.

During the preschool years,

physical and motor development proceeds, literally, by leaps and bounds.

7

Early Childhood: Physical and Cognitive Development

DID YOU KNOW?

D1 A disproportionately high percentage of math whizzes are left-handed.

D2 Some diseases are normal.

D3 Toilet training takes place for most Canadian children between the ages of 2 and 3.

D4 Children pursuing a relationship with an invisible friend may show many developmental advantages.

D5 Two-year-olds tend to assume that their parents are aware of everything that is happening to them, even when their parents are not present.

D6 "Because Mommy wants me to" may be a perfectly good explanation, for a 3-year-old.

The years from 2 to 6 are referred to as early childhood or the preschool years, even though many Canadian children can begin school as early as 3 years of age. During early childhood, physical growth is slower than in infancy. Children become taller and leaner, and, by the end of early childhood, they look more like adults than infants. As their motor skills develop, children become stronger, faster, and better coordinated.

Language improves enormously, and children begin to carry on conversations with others. As cognitive skills develop, a new world of make believe, or "pretend" play, emerges. Most preschoolers are curious and eager to learn. Increased physical and cognitive capabilities enable children to emerge from total dependence on caregivers to become part of the broader world outside the family.

Learning Outcomes

LO1 Describe trends in physical development in early childhood

LO2 Describe motor development in early childhood

LO3 Describe nutritional needs in early childhood

LO4 Describe trends in health and illness in early childhood

LO5 Describe sleep patterns in early childhood

LO6 Discuss elimination disorders

LO7 Describe Piaget's preoperational stage

LO8 Discuss influences on cognitive development in early childhood

LO9 Explain how "theory of mind" affects cognitive development

LO10 Describe memory development in early childhood

LO11 Describe language development in early childhood

LO1 Growth Patterns

during the preschool years, physical and motor development proceeds, literally, by leaps and bounds.

HEIGHT AND WEIGHT

Following the dramatic gains in height in a child's first 2 years, the growth rate slows during the

corpus callosum the thick bundle of nerve fibres that connects the left and right hemispheres of the brain.

plasticity the tendency of new parts of the brain to take up the functions of injured parts.

preschool years (Kuczmarski et al., 2000). Girls and boys tend to gain about 5 to 8 cm (2 to 3 in.) 2 to 3 inches in height per year, and weight gains remain fairly even at about 2 to 3 kg (4 to 6 lb.) 4 to 6 pounds per year (see Figure 7.1). Children become increasingly slender as they gain in height and shed some "baby fat." Boys as a group become slightly taller and heavier than girls (see Figure 7.1). Noticeable variations in growth occur from child to child.

DEVELOPMENT OF THE BRAIN

The brain develops more quickly than any other organ in early childhood and needs to be supported by proper nutrition. At 2 years of age, the brain already has attained 75 percent of its adult weight. By the age of 5, the brain has reached 90 percent of its adult weight, even though the body weight of the 5-year-old is barely one-third of what it will be as an adult (Tanner, 1989).

The increase in brain size is due in part to the continuing myelination of nerve fibres. Completion of myelination of the neural pathways that link the cerebellum to the cerebral cortex facilitates development of fine motor skills, balance, and coordination (Nelson & Luciana, 2001; Paus et al., 1999).

Brain Development and Visual Skills

Brain development also improves processing of visual information (Yamada et al., 2000), facilitating learning to read. The parts of the brain that enable the child to sustain attention and screen out distractions (reticular formation) become increasingly myelinated between the ages of about 4 and 7 (Nelson &

Luciana, 2001), enabling most children to focus on schoolwork. The speed of processing visual information improves throughout childhood, reaching adult levels at the onset of adolescence (Chou et al., 2006; Paus et al., 1999).

Right Brain, Left Brain?

We often hear people described as being "right-brained" or "left-brained." The notion is that the hemispheres of the brain are involved in different kinds of intellectual and emotional activities. Research does suggest that in right-handed individuals, the left hemisphere is relatively more involved in intellectual undertakings that require logical analysis and problem-solving language, and computation (Grindrod & Baum, 2005; O'Shea & Corballis, 2005). The other hemisphere (the right hemisphere) is usually superior in visual–spatial functions (such as piecing puzzles together), aesthetic and emotional responses, and understanding metaphors.

But it is not true that some children are left-brained and others are right-brained. The functions of the left and right hemispheres overlap, and the hemispheres respond simultaneously when we focus on one thing or another. They are aided in "cooperation" by the myelination of the **corpus callosum**, a thick bundle of nerve fibres that connects the hemispheres (Kinsbourne, 2003). This process is largely complete by the age of 8, enabling the integration of logical and emotional functioning.

Plasticity of the Brain

Many parts of the brain have specialized functions, allowing our behaviour to be more complex. But it also means that injuries to certain parts of the brain can result in loss of these functions. However, the brain also shows **plasticity**, or the ability to compensate for injuries to particular areas. Plasticity is greatest at about 1 to 2 years of age and then gradually declines (Kolb & Gibb, 2007; Nelson et al., 2006). When we as adults suffer damage to the areas of the brain that

© Tom Merton/Getty Images

FIGURE 7.1

Growth Curves for Height and Weight, Ages 2 to 6 Years

The numbers on the curves indicate the percentiles for height and weight at different ages. The growth rate slows down during early childhood. As in infancy, boys are only slightly taller and heavier than girls.

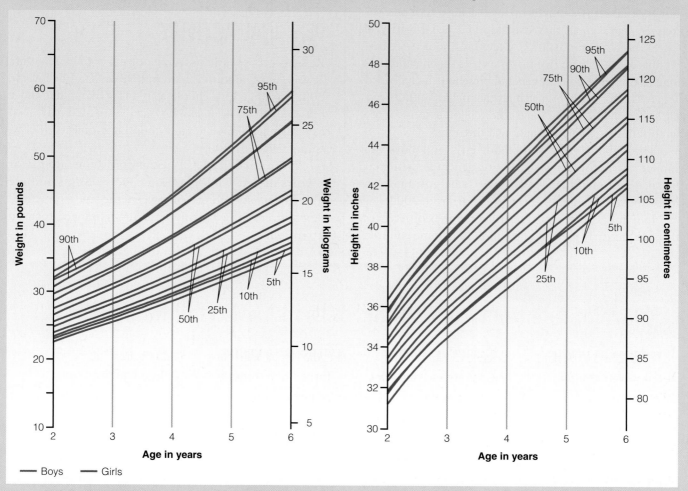

— Boys   — Girls

Developed by the National Center for Health Statistics in collaboration with the National Center for Chronic Disease Prevention and Health Promotion (2000). http://www.cdc.gov/growthcharts

control language, we may lose the ability to speak or understand language. However, other areas of the brain may assume these functions in preschoolers who suffer such damage. As a result, they may regain the ability to speak or comprehend language (Nelson et al., 2006). Neurological factors that enable plasticity include the growth of new dendrites ("sprouting") and the redundancy of neural connections (Nelson et al., 2006; Szaflarski et al., 2006).

LO2 Motor Development

he preschool years witness an explosion of motor skills, as children's nervous systems mature and their movements become more precise and coordinated.

GROSS MOTOR SKILLS

Gross motor skills involve the large muscles used in locomotion (see Table 7.1). At about the age of 3, children can balance on one foot. By age 3 or 4, they can walk up stairs as adults do, by placing a foot on each step. By age 4 or 5, they can skip and pedal a tricycle (McDevitt & Ormrod, 2002). Older preschoolers are better able to coordinate two tasks, such as singing and running at the same time. In general, preschoolers appear to acquire motor skills by teaching themselves and observing other children. Imitating other children seems more important than adult instruction at this age.

Throughout early childhood, girls and boys are similar in motor skills. Girls are generally better at balance and precision. Boys show some advantage in throwing and kicking (McDevitt & Ormrod, 2002).

Individual differences are larger than sex differences throughout early and middle childhood. Some children are genetically predisposed to developing better coordination or more strength. Motivation and practice also are important. Motor experiences in infancy may affect the development of motor skills in early childhood. For example, children with early crawling experience perform better than those who do not on tests of motor skills (McEwan et al., 1991).

PHYSICAL ACTIVITY

Preschoolers spend an average of more than 25 hours a week in large-muscle activity (D. W. Campbell et al., 2002). Younger preschoolers are more likely than older preschoolers to engage in physically oriented play, such as grasping, banging, and mouthing objects (D. W. Campbell et al., 2002).

Motor activity level begins to decline after 2 or 3 years of age. Children become less restless and are able to sit still longer. Between the ages of 2 and 4, children show an increase in sustained, focused attention.

TABLE 7.1
Development of Gross Motor Skills in Early Childhood

2 YEARS (24–35 MONTHS)	3 YEARS (36–47 MONTHS)	4 YEARS (48–59 MONTHS)	5 YEARS (60–71 MONTHS)
• Runs well straight ahead	• Goes around obstacles while running	• Turns sharp corners while running	• Runs lightly on toes
• Walks up stairs, two feet to a step	• Walks up stairs, one foot to a step	• Walks down stairs, one foot to a step	• Jumps a distance of 1 metre (3 ft.)
• Kicks a large ball	• Kicks a large ball easily	• Jumps from a height of 30 cm (12 in.)	• Catches a small ball, using hands only
• Jumps a distance of 10 to 35 cm (4 to 14 in.)	• Jumps from the bottom step	• Throws a ball overhand	• Hops 2 to 3 m (2 to 3 yd.) forward on each foot
• Throws a small ball without falling	• Catches a bounced ball, using torso and arms to form a basket	• Turns sharp corners while pushing and pulling toys	• Stands on one foot for 8 to 10 seconds
• Pushes and pulls large toys	• Goes around obstacles while pushing and pulling toys	• Hops on one foot, four to six hops	• Climbs actively and skillfully
• Hops on one foot, two or more hops	• Hops on one foot, up to three hops	• Stands on one foot for 3 to 8 seconds	• Skips on alternate feet
• Tries to stand on one foot	• Stands on one foot	• Climbs ladders	• Rides a bicycle with training wheels
• Climbs on furniture to look out of window	• Climbs on playground equipment	• Skips on one foot	
		• Rides a tricycle well	

Note: The ages are averages; there are individual variations.

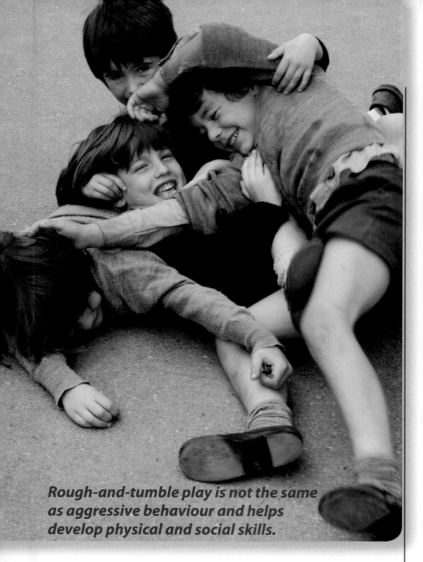

Rough-and-tumble play is not the same as aggressive behaviour and helps develop physical and social skills.

Rough-and-Tumble Play

Rough-and-tumble play consists of running, chasing, fleeing, wrestling, hitting with an open hand, laughing, and making faces. Rough-and-tumble play is not the same as aggressive behaviour, which involves hitting with a fist, pushing, taking, grabbing, and angry looks. Rough-and-tumble play helps develop physical and social skills (Fry, 2005; Smith, 2005).

Individual Differences in Activity Level

Physically active parents are likely to have physically active children. In a study of 4- to 7-year-olds, children of active mothers were twice as likely to be active as children of inactive mothers (Monroe et al., 1991). Children of active fathers were 3½ times as likely to be active.

Several reasons may explain this relationship. First, active parents may serve as role models for activity. Second, sharing of activities by family members may have an influence. Active parents may also encourage their child's participation in physical activity. Twin studies also suggest a genetic tendency for activity level (Saudino & Eaton, 1993; Stevenson, 1992).

fine motor skills skills employing the small muscles used in manipulation, such as those in the fingers.

FINE MOTOR SKILLS

Fine motor skills develop gradually and later than gross motor skills. Fine motor skills involve the small muscles used in manipulation and coordination. Control over the wrists and fingers enables children to hold a pencil properly, dress themselves, and stack blocks (see Table 7.2). Preschoolers can labour endlessly in attempting to tie their shoelaces and get their jackets zipped.

CHILDREN'S DRAWINGS

The development of drawing is linked to the development of motor and cognitive skills. Children first begin to scribble during the second year of life. Initially, they seem to make marks for the sheer joy of it (Eisner, 1990). Rhoda Kellogg (1959, 1970) found a meaningful pattern in the scribbles. She identified 20 basic scribbles that she considered the building blocks of art (see Figure 7.2).

Children progress through four stages from making scribbles to drawing pictures: the *placement, shape, design,* and *pictorial* stages. Two-year-olds scribble in various locations on the page (e.g., in the middle of the page or near one of the borders). By age 3, children are starting to draw basic shapes: circles, squares, triangles, crosses, X's, and odd shapes. As soon as they can draw shapes, children begin to combine them in the design stage. Between ages 4 and 5, children reach the pictorial stage, in which designs begin to resemble recognizable objects.

Children's early drawings tend to be symbolic of broad categories rather than specific. A child might draw the same simple building whether asked to draw a school or a house (Tallandini & Valentini, 1991). Children between ages 3 and 5 usually do not set out to draw a particular thing. They are more likely to see what they have drawn, then name it. As motor and cognitive skills develop beyond the age of 5, children become able to draw an object they have in mind (Matthews, 1990). They also improve at copying figures (Karapetsas & Kantas, 1991; Pemberton, 1990).

TABLE 7.2
Development of Fine Motor Skills in Early Childhood

2 YEARS (24–35 MONTHS)	3 YEARS (36–47 MONTHS)	4 YEARS (48–59 MONTHS)	5 YEARS (60–71 MONTHS)
• Builds tower of 6 cubes • Copies vertical and horizontal lines • Imitates folding of paper • Prints on easel with a brush • Places simple shapes in correct holes	• Builds tower of 9 cubes • Copies circle and cross • Copies letters • Holds crayons with fingers, not fist • Strings 4 beads using a large needle	• Builds tower of 10 or more cubes • Copies square • Prints simple words • Imitates folding paper three times • Uses pencil with correct hand grip • Strings 10 beads	• Builds 3 steps from 6 blocks, using a model • Copies triangle and star • Prints first name and numbers • Imitates folding a piece of square paper into a triangle • Traces around a diamond drawn on paper • Laces shoes

Note: The ages are averages; there are individual variations.

HANDEDNESS

Handedness emerges during infancy. By the age of 2 to 3 months, a rattle placed in an infant's hand is held longer with the dominant hand (Fitzgerald et al., 1991). By 4 months of age, most infants show a clear-cut right-hand preference in exploring objects (Streri, 2002). Preference for grasping with one hand or the other increases markedly between 7 and 11 months (Hinojosa et al., 2003). Handedness becomes more strongly established during early childhood (McManus et al., 1988). Most people are right-handed, although studies vary as to how many are left-handed.

The origins of handedness apparently have a genetic component (Geschwind, 2000; McManus, 2003). If both of your parents are right-handed, your chances of being right-handed are about 92 percent. If both of your parents are left-handed, your chances of being left-handed are about 50 percent (Annett, 1999; Clode, 2006). An environmental component also comes into play if children are discouraged from using their left hand.

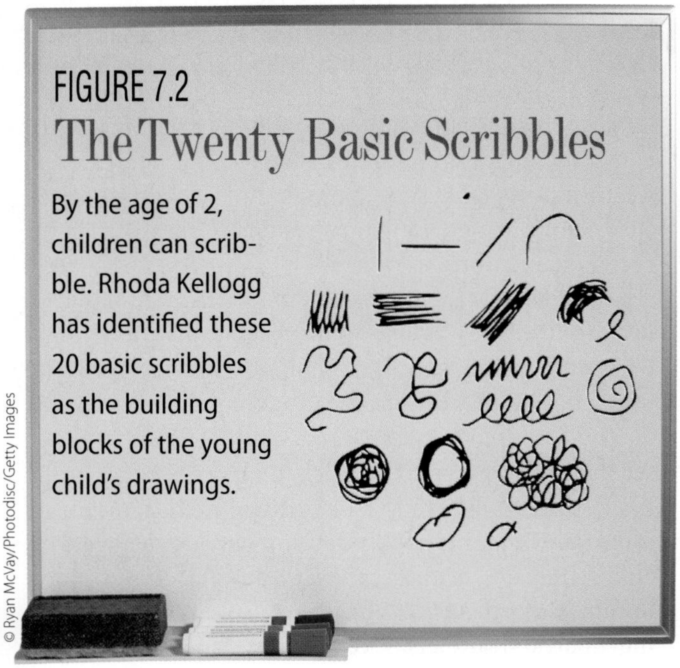

Left-Handedness

Being a "lefty" was once seen as a deficiency but today the 14 percent of the population that are left-handed are usually quite proud of their uniqueness. Being left-handed may matter because it appears to be related to language problems, such as dyslexia and stuttering, and with health problems, such as high blood pressure and epilepsy (Andreou et al., 2002; Bryden et al.,

FIGURE 7.2
The Twenty Basic Scribbles

By the age of 2, children can scribble. Rhoda Kellogg has identified these 20 basic scribbles as the building blocks of the young child's drawings.

Source: Kellogg (1970).

FIGURE 7.3
Canada Food Guide for a Toddler

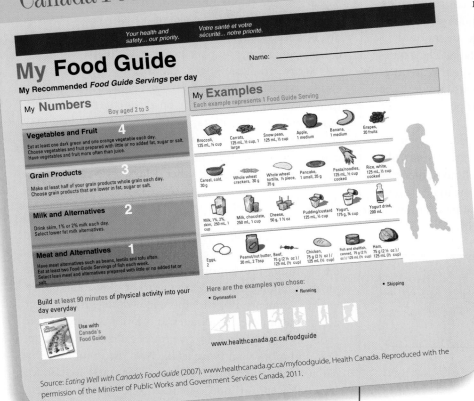

Source: *Eating Well with Canada's Food Guide* (2007), www.healthcanada.gc.ca/myfoodguide, Health Canada. Reproduced with the permission of the Minister of Public Works and Government Services Canada, 2011.

2005). Left-handedness is also apparently related to psychological disorders, including schizophrenia and depression (Annett & Moran, 2006; Dollfus et al., 2005).

Even so, being left-handed has its advantages. A disproportionately high percentage of math whizzes are left-handed, as found on the math portion of the SAT among 12- and 13-year-olds (O'Boyle & Benbow, 1990). Twenty percent of the highest-scoring group was left-handed, while only 10 percent of the general population is left-handed.

Left-handedness (and ambidexterity, the use of both hands with similar or equal dexterity) also has

> **D1** A disproportionately high percentage of math whizzes are left-handed.
>
> Twenty percent of the highest-scoring group on the math SATs was left-handed, while only 10 percent of the general population is left-handed.

been associated with success in athletic activities such as handball, fencing, boxing, basketball, and baseball (Coren, 1992; Dane & Erzurumluoglu, 2003). Higher frequencies of left-handedness are found among musicians, architects, and artists (Natsopoulos et al., 1992). Some left-handed people may try to convince you that their handedness makes them better looking but no research supports this claim.

LO3 Nutrition

health Canada recommends that a healthy diet for children should focus on a certain number of food guide servings rather than focusing on calorie intake (Health Canada, 2007b) (see Figure 7.3). During the second and third years, a child's appetite typically varies, but because the child is growing more slowly than in infancy, he or she needs fewer calories. Children who eat little at one meal may compensate by eating more at another (Cooke et al., 2003).

Many children eat too much sugar and salt, which can be harmful to their health. Preferences for these types of food increase with repeated exposure. Parents serve as role models in the development of food preferences (Hannon et al., 2003).

LO4 Health and Illness

almost all children get ill now and then. Some seem to be ill every other week. Most illnesses are minor, and children seem to eventually outgrow many of them. Fortunately, we can prevent or cure many others.

MINOR ILLNESSES

Minor illnesses refer to respiratory infections, such as colds, and to gastrointestinal upsets, such as nausea, vomiting, and diarrhea. These diseases are normal in that most children come down with them. They typically last a few days or less and are not life threatening. Although diarrheal illness in Canada is usually mild, it is a leading killer of children in developing countries (UNICEF, 2006).

Canadian children will get lots of colds, some as many as 8 to 10 each year before they are 2 years old (Canadian Paediatric Society, 2010). Childhood illnesses can lead to the creation of antibodies that may prevent children from coming down with the same illnesses in adulthood, when they can do more harm.

> **D2** Some diseases are normal.
> Minor illnesses are generally normal, insofar as most children get them and may actually be healthier in adulthood as a result of the immunities they acquire.

MAJOR ILLNESSES

Advances in immunization along with the development of antibiotics and other medications have dramatically reduced the incidence and effects of serious childhood diseases. Because most preschoolers and schoolchildren have been inoculated against major childhood illnesses such as rubella (German measles), measles, tetanus, mumps, whooping cough, diphtheria, and polio, these diseases no longer pose the threat they once did.

More than 80 percent of kids aged 11 to 17 surveyed by the University of Alberta had one or more risk factors for chronic diseases (Sinnema, 2009). These illnesses include such major disorders as arthritis, diabetes, heart disease, and lung disease.

Although many major childhood diseases have been largely eradicated in Canada and other industrialized nations, they remain fearsome killers of children in developing countries. Around the world, 8 million to 9 million children die each year from only six diseases: pneumonia, diarrhea, measles, tetanus, whooping cough, and tuberculosis (UNICEF, 2006). Air pollution from the combustion of fossil fuels used for heating and cooking causes many respiratory infections, which are responsible for nearly one death in five among children who are younger than 5 years of age (UNICEF, 2006). Diarrhea kills nearly 2 million children under the age of 5 each year. Diarrheal diseases are mostly related to unsafe drinking water, inadequate sanitation, and poor hygiene (UNICEF, 2006).

Many youngsters are exposed to lead in early childhood, often by eating chips of lead paint from their homes or by breathing in dust from the paint. Infants fed formula made with tap water are at risk of lead poisoning, because water pipes sometimes contain lead. Lead causes neurological damage and may result in lowered cognitive functioning and other delays.

ACCIDENTS

Accidents cause more deaths in early childhood than the next six most frequent causes combined (National Center for Injury Prevention and Control, 2007). The single most common cause of death in early childhood is motor vehicle accidents. Boys are more likely than girls to incur accidental injuries at all ages and in all socioeconomic groups. Poor children are five times as likely to die from fires and more than twice as likely to die in motor vehicle accidents than other children (National Center for Injury Prevention and Control, 2007). The high accident rate of low-income children may result partly from living in dangerous housing and neighbourhoods.

LO5 Sleep

Preschoolers do not need as much sleep as infants. Most preschoolers sleep 10 to 11 hours in a 24-hour period (National Sleep Foundation, 2007). A common pattern includes sleeping 9 to 10 hours at night and having a nap of 1 to 2 hours. Many children resist going to bed or going to sleep (Christophersen & Mortweet, 2003). Getting to sleep late can be a problem, because preschoolers tend not to make up fully for lost sleep (Kohyama et al., 2002). Many young children take a so-called "transitional object"—

such as a favoured blanket or a stuffed animal—to bed with them (Morelli et al., 1992).

SLEEP DISORDERS

In this section, we focus on the sleep disorders of sleep terrors, nightmares, and sleep walking.

Sleep Terrors and Nightmares

Sleep terrors are more severe than the anxiety dreams we refer to as nightmares. Sleep terrors usually occur during deep sleep. Nightmares take place during lighter, rapid-eye-movement (REM) sleep, when about 80 percent of normal dreams occur.

Sleep terrors usually begin in childhood or early adolescence and are outgrown by late adolescence. They are sometimes associated with stress, as caused by moving to a new neighbourhood, beginning school, adjusting to parental divorce, or being in a war zone. Children with sleep terrors may wake suddenly with a surge in heart and respiration rates, talk incoherently, and thrash about. Children may then fall back into more restful sleep. The incidence of sleep terrors wanes as children develop.

Children who have frequent nightmares or sleep terrors may come to fear going to sleep. They may show distress at bedtime, refuse to get into their pajamas, and insist that the lights be kept on. As a result, they can develop insomnia. Children with frequent nightmares or sleep terrors need caregivers' understanding and affection. They also profit from a regular routine in which they are expected to get to sleep at the same time each night (Christophersen & Mortweet, 2003).

Sleep Walking

Sleep walking, or **somnambulism**, is more common among children than adults. As with sleep terrors, sleep walking tends to occur during deep sleep (Stores & Wiggs, 2001). Onset is usually between the ages of 3 and 8.

When children sleepwalk they may rearrange toys, go to the bathroom, or walk to the refrigerator to get a glass of milk. Then they return to their rooms and go back to bed. Many myths surround sleep walking, such as the suggestion that sleepwalkers' eyes are closed, that they will avoid harm, and that they will become violently agitated if awakened during an episode. All these notions are false.

Sleep walking in children is assumed to reflect immaturity of the nervous system. As with sleep terrors, the incidence of sleep walking drops as children develop. It may help to discuss a child's persistent sleep terrors or sleep walking with a health professional.

> **sleep terrors** frightening dreamlike experiences that occur during the deepest stage of non-REM sleep, shortly after the child has gone to sleep.
>
> **somnambulism** sleep walking.
>
> **enuresis** failure to control the bladder (urination) once the normal age for control has been reached.

LO6 Elimination Disorders

during toilet training, a child's maturation plays a crucial role. During the first year, only an exceptional child can be toilet trained. Most Canadian children are toilet trained between the ages of 2 and 3 (Bracht, 2007). They may have nighttime "accidents" for another year or so. Children who do not become toilet trained within reasonable time frames may be diagnosed with enuresis, encopresis, or both.

> **D3** Toilet training takes place for most Canadian children between the ages of 2 and 3.
>
> It is important to allow the child to set the pace for toilet training. The average age can vary significantly, and nighttime accidents can be expected to occur for an additional year after daytime training has been achieved.

ENURESIS

Enuresis is failure to control the bladder (urination) once the "normal" age for achieving bladder control has been reached.

© Shauna Longmuir

bed-wetting failure to control the bladder during the night.

encopresis failure to control the bowels once the normal age for bowel control has been reached. Also called soiling.

preoperational stage the second stage in Piaget's scheme, characterized by inflexible and irreversible mental manipulation of symbols.

symbolic play play in which children make believe that objects and toys are other than what they are. Also called pretend play.

A nighttime "accident" is termed **bed-wetting**. Nighttime control is more difficult to achieve than daytime control. At night, children must first wake up when their bladders are full. At 5 years of age, 15 percent of Canadian children wet the bed. By 8 years, only 6–8 percent wet the bed (Canadian Paediatric Society, 2007), with the problem about twice as common among boys. Bed-wetting tends to occur during the deepest stage of sleep, the stage when sleep terrors and sleep walking may also occur.

It is believed that enuresis might have organic causes, most likely immaturity of the motor cortex of the brain (von Gontard et al., 2006). Just as children outgrow sleep terrors and sleep walking, they tend to outgrow bed-wetting (Mellon & Houts, 2006). Scientists have discovered a gene for bed wetting. If one parent wet the bed as a child, the child has a 25 percent risk of bed wetting. If both parents wet the bed as children, this likelihood increases to about 65 percent (Canadian Paediatric Society, 2007)

ENCOPRESIS

Soiling, or **encopresis**, is lack of control over the bowels. Soiling, like enuresis, is more common among boys. About 1–2 percent of children at the ages of 7 and 8 have continuing problems controlling their bowels (Mellon, 2006; von Gontard, 2006). Soiling, in contrast to enuresis, is more likely to occur during the day. Thus, encopresis can be embarrassing to the child, especially when it occurs at school.

Encopresis stems from both physical causes, such as chronic constipation, and psychological factors (Mellon, 2006; von Gontard, 2006). Soiling may follow harsh punishment of toileting accidents, especially in children who are already anxious or experiencing stress. Punishment may cause the child to tense up on the toilet, whereas moving one's bowels requires relaxation of the anal sphincter muscles.

Soiling, punishment, and anxiety can become a vicious cycle.

LO7 Jean Piaget's Preoperational Stage

according to Piaget, the **preoperational stage** of cognitive development lasts from about age 2 to age 7. Be warned: Any resemblance between the logic of a preschooler and your own may be purely coincidental. At this stage, young children's logic is at best "under construction."

SYMBOLIC THOUGHT

Preoperational thought is characterized by the use of symbols to represent objects and relationships among them. Perhaps the most important kind of symbolic activity of young children is language, but children's early use of language leaves something to be desired in the realm of logic. According to Piaget, preschoolers' drawings are symbols of objects, people, and events in children's lives. Symbolism is also expressed as symbolic or pretend play.

SYMBOLIC OR PRETEND PLAY

Children's **symbolic play**—the "let's pretend" type of play—may seem immature to busy adults meeting the realistic demands of the business world, but it requires cognitive sophistication (Feldman, & Masalha, 2007; Keen et al., 2007).

Piaget (1962 [1946]) wrote that pretend play usually begins in the second year, when the child begins to symbolize objects. The ability to engage in pretend play is based on the use and recollection of symbols, that is, on mental representations of things children have experienced or heard about.

Children first engage in pretend play at about 12 or 13 months. They make believe that they are performing familiar activities, such as sleeping or feeding themselves. By 15 to 20 months, they can shift their focus from themselves to others. A child may pretend to feed her doll. By 30 months, she or he can make believe that the other object takes an active role. The child may pretend that the doll is feeding itself (Paavola et al., 2006).

(Gleason, 2002). They have more real friends, show greater ability to concentrate, and are more advanced in language development (Taylor, 1999).

egocentrism putting oneself at the centre of things such that one is unable to perceive the world from another person's point of view.

D4 Children pursuing a relationship with an invisible friend show many developmental advantages.
Children with imaginary friends are less aggressive, more cooperative, and show greater language development and concentration.

EGOCENTRISM: IT'S ALL ABOUT ME

Sometimes the attitude "It's all about me" is a sign of early childhood, not of selfishness. One consequence of one-dimensional thinking is **egocentrism**. Egocentrism, in Piaget's use of the term, means that preoperational children do not understand that other people may have different perspectives on the world. Two-year-olds may, in fact, assume that their parents are aware of everything that is happening to them, even when their parents are not present. When children want to hide from you, they will cover their eyes, thinking that if they can't see anything, neither can you.

Piaget used the "three-mountains test" (see Figure 7.4) to learn whether egocentrism prevents young children from taking the viewpoints of others. In this demonstration, the child sits at a table before a model of three mountains. One has a house on it, and another has a cross at the summit.

The quality of preschoolers' pretend play has implications for subsequent development. For example, preschoolers who engage in violent pretend play are less empathic, less likely to help other children, and more likely to engage in antisocial behaviour later on (Dunn & Hughes, 2001). The quality of pretend play is connected with preschoolers' academic performance later on, their creativity, and their social skills (Russ, 2006; Stagnitti et al., 2000).

Imaginary friends are an example of pretend play. As many as 65 percent of preschoolers have imaginary friends; they are most common among firstborn and only children (Gleason et al., 2003). Having an imaginary playmate does not mean that the child has problems with real relationships (Gleason, 2004; Hoff, 2005). In fact, children with imaginary friends are less aggressive, more cooperative, and more creative than children without them

Piaget then placed a doll elsewhere on the table and asked the child what the doll sees. The language abilities of very young children do not permit them to provide verbal descriptions of what can be seen from where the doll is situated, so they can answer in one of two ways. They can either select a photograph taken from the proper vantage point, or they can construct

precausal a type of thought in which natural cause-and-effect relationships are attributed to will and other preoperational concepts.

transductive reasoning reasoning from the specific to the specific.

animism the attribution of life and intentionality to inanimate objects.

artificialism the belief that environmental features were made by people.

D5 Two-year-olds tend to assume that their parents are aware of everything that is happening to them, even when their parents are not present.
This attitude is a product of early childhood one-dimensional thinking and egocentrism.

CAUSALITY: WHY? BECAUSE.

Preoperational children's responses to questions such as "Why does the sun shine?" show other facets of egocentrism. At the age of 2 or so, they may answer that they do not know, or they may change the subject. Three-year-olds may report themselves as doing things because they want to do them or "Because Mommy wants me to." In egocentric fashion, this explanation of behaviour is extended to inanimate objects. The sun may be thought of as shining because it wants to shine or someone wants it to shine.

D6 "Because Mommy wants me to" may be a perfectly good explanation, for a 3-year-old.
This line of reasoning is also a reflection of early childhood egocentrism. Unfortunately, this response is not frequently heard in the teenage years.

Piaget labels this structuring of cause and effect **precausal**. Unless preoperational children know the natural causes of an event, their reasons are likely to have an egocentric flavour and not be based on science. Consider the question, "Why does it get dark outside?" The preoperational child usually does not have knowledge of Earth's rotation and is likely to answer something like, "So I can go to sleep."

In **transductive reasoning**, children reason by going from one specific isolated event to another. For example,

another model of the mountains as they would be seen by the doll. The results of a classic experiment with the three-mountains test suggest that 5- and 6-year-olds usually select photos or build models that correspond to their own viewpoints (Laurendeau & Pinard, 1970).

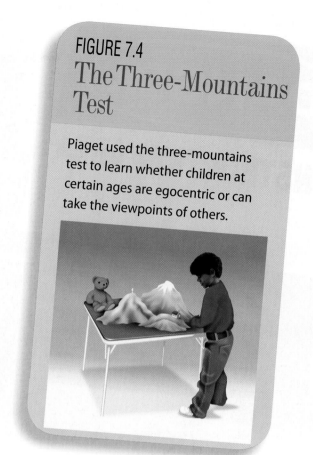

FIGURE 7.4
The Three-Mountains Test

Piaget used the three-mountains test to learn whether children at certain ages are egocentric or can take the viewpoints of others.

a 3-year-old may argue that she should go to sleep *because* it is dark outside. That is, separate events, darkness and going to sleep, are thought of as having cause-and-effect relationships.

Preoperational children also show **animism** and **artificialism** in their attributions of causality. In animistic thinking, they attribute life and intentions to inanimate objects, such as the sun and the moon. ("Why is the moon gone during the day?" "It is afraid of the sun.") Artificialism assumes that environmental features such as rain and thunder have been designed and made by people.

© Jitloac/Shutterstock

CONFUSION OF MENTAL AND PHYSICAL EVENTS

What would you do if someone asked you to pretend you were a boogaloo? Chances are, you might inquire what a boogaloo is and how it behaves. So might a 5-year-old child. But a 3-year-old might not think that

© Jitloac/Shutterstock

such information is necessary (Gottfried et al., 2003).

According to Piaget, the preoperational child has difficulty making distinctions between mental and physical events. Children between the ages of 2 and 4 show confusion between symbols and the things they represent. Egocentrism contributes to the assumption that their thoughts exactly reflect external reality. They do not recognize that words are arbitrary and that people can use different words to refer to things. In *Play, Dreams, and Imitation in Childhood,* Piaget (1962[1946]) asked a 4-year-old child, "Could you call this table a cup and that cup a table?" "No," the child responded. "Why not?" "Because," explained the child, "you can't drink out of a table!" Another example of the preoperational child's confusion of the mental and the physical is the tendency of many 4-year-olds to believe that dreams are real (Meyer & Shore, 2001).

FOCUS ON ONE DIMENSION AT A TIME

To gain further insight into preoperational thinking, consider these two problems. First, imagine that you pour water from a low, wide glass into a tall, thin glass, as in Figure 7.5(b). Now, does the tall, thin glass contain more than, less than, or the same amount of water as in the low, wide glass? We won't keep you in suspense. If you said the same amount, you were correct.

Next, if you flatten a ball of clay into a pancake, do you wind up with more, less, or the same amount of clay? If you said the same amount, you are correct once more.

To arrive at the correct answers to these questions, you must understand the law of **conservation**. The law of conservation holds that properties of substances such as volume, mass, and number remain the same—or are conserved—even if you change their shape or arrangement.

Now, preoperational children tend to focus on only one aspect of a problem at a time, a characteristic of thought that Piaget called *centration*. Conservation requires the ability to focus on two aspects of a situation at once, such as height and width. A preoperational child focuses or centres on only one dimension at a time. First, the child is shown two squat glasses of water and agrees that they have the same amount of water. Then, as he watches, water is poured from one squat glass into a tall, thin glass. Asked which glass has more water, he points to the tall glass. Why? When he looks at the glasses, he is swayed by the fact that the thinner glass is taller.

The preoperational child's failure to show conservation also comes about because of *irreversibility*. In the case of the water, the child does not realize that pouring water from the wide glass to the tall glass can be reversed,

conservation in cognitive psychology, the principle that properties of substances such as weight and mass remain the same (are conserved) when superficial characteristics such as their shapes or arrangement are changed.

FIGURE 7.5
Conservation

(a) The boy in this illustration agreed that the amount of water in two identical containers is equal. (b) He then watched as water from one container was poured into a tall, thin container. (c) When asked whether the amounts of water in the two containers are now the same, he says no.

restoring things to their original condition.

After you have tried the experiment with the water, try this experiment on conservation of number. Make two rows with four pennies in each. As the 3-year-old child watches, move the pennies in the second row to about 2.5 cm (1 in.) apart, as in Figure 7.6. Then ask the child which row has more pennies. What do you think the child will say? Why?

Class Inclusion

Class inclusion, as we are using it here, means including new objects or categories in broader mental classes or categories. Class inclusion also requires children to focus on two aspects of a situation at once. In one of Piaget's class-inclusion tasks, the child is shown several pictures from two subclasses of a larger class, for example, four cats and six dogs. She is asked whether there are more dogs or more animals. What do you think she will say? Preoperational children typically answer that there are more dogs than animals (Piaget, 1963 [1936]).

Why do preoperational children make this error? According to Piaget, they cannot think about the two subclasses and the larger class at the same time. Therefore, they cannot easily compare them. Children view dogs as dogs, or as animals, but find it difficult to see them as both dogs and animals at once (Branco & Lourenço, 2004).

LO8 Factors in Cognitive Development

two factors that influence cognitive development in early childhood are Vygotsky's concepts of scaffolding and the zone of proximal development. Others include the home environment, preschool education, and television.

SCAFFOLDING AND THE ZONE OF PROXIMAL DEVELOPMENT

Parental responsiveness and interaction with children are key ingredients in children's cognitive development. One component of this interaction is **scaffolding** (see page 14). Cognitive scaffolding refers to temporary support provided by a parent or teacher to learning children. The guidance provided by adults decreases as children become capable of carrying out the task on their own (Lengua et al., 2007; Sylva et al., 2007).

A related concept is Vygotsky's **zone of proximal development (ZPD)**. The zone refers to the gap between what children are capable of doing now and what they could do with help from others. Adults or older children can best guide children through this zone by gearing their assistance to children's

FIGURE 7.6
Conservation of Number

In this demonstration, we begin with two rows of pennies that are spread out equally, as shown in the left-hand part of the drawing. Then one row of pennies is spread out more, as shown in the drawing on the right-hand side. We then ask the child, "Do the two rows still have the same number of pennies?" Do you think that a preoperational child will conserve the number of pennies or focus on the length of the longer row in arriving at an answer?

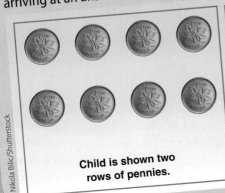

Child is shown two rows of pennies.

Experimenter moves pennies in one row.

Nikola Bilic/Shutterstock

TABLE 7.3
Scales of the HOME Inventory

SCALE	SAMPLE ITEMS
Parental emotional and verbal responsiveness	• The parent spontaneously vocalizes to the child during the visit. • The parent responds to the child's vocalizations with vocal or other verbal responses.
Avoidance of restriction and punishment	• The parent does not shout at the child. • The parent does not interfere with the child's actions or restrict the child's movements more than three times during the visit.
Organization of the physical environment	• The child's play environment seems to be safe and free from hazards.
Provision of appropriate play materials	• The child has a push toy or a pull toy. • The child has one or more toys or pieces of equipment that promote muscle activity. • The family provides appropriate equipment to foster learning.
Parental involvement with child	• The parent structures the child's play periods. • The parent tends to keep the child within her or his visual range and looks at the child frequently.
Opportunities for variety in daily stimulation	• The child gets out of the house at least four times a week. • The parent reads stories to the child at least three times a week.

capabilities (Lantolf & Thorne, 2007; Wennergren & Rönnerman, 2006). These researchers argue that the key forms of children's cognitive activities develop through interaction with older, more experienced individuals who teach and guide them. In a related study, K. Alison Clarke-Stewart and Robert Beck (1999) had 31 5-year-olds observe a videotaped film segment with their mothers, talk about it with their mothers, and then retell the story to an experimenter. Children whose mothers focused the children's attention on the tape, asked their children to talk about it, and discussed the feelings of the characters told better stories than children whose mothers did not use such scaffolding strategies and children in a control group who did not discuss the story at all.

THE "HOME" ENVIRONMENT

Bettye Caldwell and her colleagues (e.g., Bradley, Caldwell, & Corwyn, 2003) developed a measure for evaluating children's home environments labelled, appropriately enough, HOME, an acronym for Home Observation for the Measurement of the Environment. With this method, researchers directly observe parent–child interaction in the home. The HOME inventory contains six subscales, as shown in Table 7.3. The HOME inventory items are better predictors of young children's later IQ scores than social class, mother's IQ, or infant IQ scores (Bradley, 2006). Longitudinal research also shows that the home environment is connected with occupational success as an adult (Huesmann et al., 2006).

EFFECTS OF EARLY CHILDHOOD EDUCATION

Research suggests that preschool education enables children to get an early start on achievement in school. Children reared in poverty generally perform less well on standardized intelligence tests than children of higher socioeconomic status, and they are at greater risk for school failure (Stipek & Hakuta, 2007; Whitehouse, 2006). As a result, preschool programs were begun in the 1960s to enhance their cognitive development and readiness for elementary school. Canada has one of the earliest educational starts in the world, with children able to enter the school system as early as 3 years 8 months. Children in these programs typically are exposed to

© Polarworld

theory of mind a commonsense understanding of how the mind works.

letters and words, numbers, books, exercises in drawing, pegs and pegboards, puzzles, and toy animals and dolls—materials and activities that middle-class children usually take for granted.

The Aboriginal Head Start on Reserve program encourages the development of locally controlled projects in First Nation communities that strive to instill in children a sense of pride and a desire to learn, enhance parenting skills that contribute to the healthy development of children, improve family relationships, foster emotional and social development, and increase confidence (Health Canada, 2009). Studies of Head Start and other intervention programs show that environmental enrichment can enhance the cognitive development of economically disadvantaged children (Stipek & Hakuta, 2007; P. Wilson, 2004).

TELEVISION

The National Longitudinal Survey of Children and Youth (NLSCY) reported from data collected in 2004–05 that

John Lamparski/WireImage/Getty Images

27 percent of children aged 2 to 3 years, and 22 percent of children aged 4 to 6, are watching more than 2 hours of TV per day (Active Healthy Kids Canada, 2010). The good news is that some programs, such as *Sesame Street,* have mild to positive effects on preschoolers' cognitive development (Calvert & Kotler, 2003). The goal of *Sesame Street* is to promote the intellectual growth of preschoolers, particularly those of lower socioeconomic status. Large-scale evaluations of the effects of the program have concluded that regular viewing increases children's learning of numbers, letters, and cognitive skills such as sorting and classification (Fisch, 2004).

LO9 Theory of Mind

adults appear to have a commonsense understanding of how the mind works—that is, a **theory of mind**. We understand that we can gain knowledge through our senses or through hearsay. We know the distinction between actual and mental events and between how things appear and how they really are. We can infer the perceptions, thoughts, and feelings of others. We understand that mental states affect behaviour.

Piaget might have predicted that preoperational children are too egocentric and too focused on misleading external appearances to have a theory of mind, but research has shown that even preschoolers can accurately predict and explain human action and emotion in terms of mental states (Wellman et al., 2006).

FALSE BELIEFS: WHERE ARE THOSE CRAYONS?

False belief is a concept that involves children's ability to separate their beliefs from those of another person who has false knowledge of a situation. It is illustrated in a study of 3-year-olds by Louis Moses and John Flavell (1990). The children were shown a videotape in which a girl named Cathy found some crayons in a bag. When Cathy left the room briefly, a clown entered the room. The clown removed the crayons from the bag, hid them in a drawer, and put rocks in the bag instead. When Cathy returned, the children were asked whether Cathy thought there would be rocks or crayons in the bag. Most of the 3-year-olds incorrectly answered "rocks," demonstrating their difficulty in understanding that the other person's belief would be different from their own. But by the age of 4 to 5 years, children do not have trouble with this concept and correctly answer "crayons" (Flavell, 1993).

ORIGINS OF KNOWLEDGE

Another aspect of theory of mind is how we acquire knowledge. By age 3, most children begin to realize that people gain knowledge about something by looking at it (Pratt & Bryant, 1990). By age 4, children understand that particular senses provide information about only certain qualities of an object; for example, we come to know an object's colour through our eyes, but we learn about its weight by feeling it (O'Neill & Chong, 2001). In a study by Daniela O'Neill and Alison Gopnik (1991), 3-, 4-, and 5-year-olds learned about the contents of a toy tunnel in three different ways: They saw the contents, were told about them, or felt them. The children were then asked to state what was in the tunnel and how they knew. Although 4- and 5-year-olds had no trouble identifying the sources of their knowledge, the 3-year-olds did. For example, after feeling but not seeing a ball in the tunnel, a number of 3-year-olds told the experimenter that they could tell it was a blue ball. The children did not realize they could not learn the ball's colour by feeling it.

THE APPEARANCE–REALITY DISTINCTION

Children must acquire an understanding of the difference between, on the one hand, real events, and on the other hand, mental events, fantasies, and misleading appearances (Bialystock & Senman, 2004; Flavell et al., 2002). This understanding is known as the **appearance–reality distinction**.

Piaget's view was that children do not differentiate reality from appearances or mental events until the age of 7 or 8. In a study by Marjorie Taylor and Barbara Hort (1990), children age 3 to 5 were shown objects that had misleading appearances, such as an eraser that looked like a cookie. The children initially reported that the eraser looked like a cookie. However, once they learned that it was actually an eraser, they tended to report that it looked like an eraser. Apparently, the children could not mentally represent the eraser as both being an eraser and looking like a cookie.

Three-year-olds also apparently cannot understand changes in their mental states. In one study (Gopnik & Slaughter, 1991), 3-year-olds were shown a crayon box with candles inside. Before it was opened, they consistently said they thought crayons were inside. When asked what they had thought was in the box before it was opened, the children now said "candles."

Romilly Lockyer/Stone/Getty Images

LO10 Development of Memory

Children, like adults, often remember what they want to remember (Ghetti & Alexander, 2004; Sales et al., 2003). By the age of 4 years, children can remember events that occurred at least 1½ years earlier (Fivush & Hammond, 1990). Katherine Nelson (1990, 1993) interviewed children aged 2 to 5 to study their memory for recurring events in their lives, such as having dinner, playing with friends, and going to birthday parties. She found that 3-year-olds can present coherent, orderly accounts of familiar events. Furthermore, young children seem to form **scripts**, which are abstract, generalized accounts of these repeated events. For example, in describing what happens during a birthday party, a child might say, "You play games, open presents, and eat cake" (Fivush, 2002). However, an unusual experience, such as a hurricane, may be remembered in detail for years (Fivush et al., 2004).

---

appearance–reality distinction the difference between real events on the one hand and mental events, fantasies, and misleading appearances on the other hand.

scripts abstract, generalized accounts of familiar repeated events.

Even though children as young as 1 and 2 years of age can remember events, these memories seldom last into adulthood. This memory of specific events—known as **autobiographical memory** or *episodic memory*—is facilitated by children talking about them with others (Nelson & Fivush, 2004).

FACTORS INFLUENCING MEMORY

Factors that affect memory include what the child is asked to remember, the interest level of the child, the availability of retrieval cues or reminders, and what memory measure we are using. First, children find it easier to remember events that follow a fixed and logical order than events that do not follow a fixed order. For instance, 3- and 5-year-olds have a better memory for the activities involved in making pretend cookies out of Play-Doh (you put the ingredients in the bowl, then mix the ingredients, then roll out the dough, and so on) than they do for the activities involved in sand play, which can occur in any order (Fivush et al., 1992). Furthermore, children typically show better recognition and recall for the toys that interest them the most. Research consistently shows that (most) preschool boys are more interested in playing with toys such as cars and weapons, whereas (most) preschool girls are more interested in playing with dolls, dishes, and teddy bears. Later, the children typically show better recognition and recall for the toys that interest them the most (Martin & Ruble, 2004).

Although young children can remember a great deal, they depend more than older children do on cues provided by adults to help them retrieve their memories. Elaborating on the child's experiences and asking questions that encourage the child to contribute information to the narrative generally help children remember an episode (Nelson & Fivush, 2004).

A child's memory can often be measured or assessed by asking them to say what they remember. But verbal reports, especially from preschoolers, appear to underestimate children's memory (Mandler, 1990). In one longitudinal study, children's memory for certain events was tested at age 2½ and again at age 4. Most of the information recalled at age 4 had not been mentioned at age 2½, indicating that when they were younger, the children remembered more than they reported (Fivush & Hammond, 1990). One study found that when young children were allowed to use dolls to reenact an event, their recall was better than when they gave a verbal report (Goodman et al., 1990).

MEMORY STRATEGIES: REMEMBERING TO REMEMBER

Adults and older children use strategies to help them remember things. One strategy is mental repetition, or **rehearsal**. If you are trying to remember a new friend's phone number, for example, you might repeat it several times. Another strategy is to organize things to be remembered into categories. Most preschoolers do not engage in rehearsal until about 5 years of age (Labrell & Ubersfeld, 2004). They also rarely group objects into related categories to help them remember. By about age 5, many children have learned to verbalize information silently to themselves by counting mentally, for example, rather than aloud.

Having preschoolers sort objects into categories enhances memory (Howe, 2006; Lange & Pierce, 1992). Even 3- and 4-year-olds will use rehearsal and labelling if they are asked to try to remember something.

LO11 Language Development: Why "Daddy Goed Away"

hildren's language skills mushroom during the preschool years. By the fourth year, children are asking adults and each other questions, taking turns talking, and engaging in lengthy conversations.

DEVELOPMENT OF VOCABULARY

The development of vocabulary proceeds at an extraordinary pace. Preschoolers learn an average of nine new words per day (Tamis-LaMonda et al., 2006). But how can that be possible when each new word has so many potential meanings? Consider the following example.

> Although young children can remember a great deal, they depend more than older children do on cues provided by adults to help them retrieve their memories.

A toddler observes a small, black dog running through the park. His older sister points to the animal and says, "Doggy." The word *doggy* could mean this particular dog, or all dogs, or all animals. It could refer to one part of the dog (e.g., its tail) or to its behaviour (running, barking) or to its characteristics (small, black) (Waxman & Lidz, 2006). Does the child consider all these possibilities before determining what doggy actually means?

Word learning, in fact, does not occur gradually but is better characterized as a **fast-mapping** process in which the child quickly attaches a new word to its appropriate concept (Homer & Nelson, 2005; Waxman & Lidz, 2006). Children apparently have early cognitive biases or constraints that lead them to prefer certain meanings over others (Waxman & Lidz, 2006).

Children also assume that words refer to whole objects and not to their component parts or their characteristics, such as colour, size, or texture (Bloom, 2002). This bias is called the **whole-object assumption**. Therefore, the young child would assume that the word *doggy* refers to the dog rather than to its tail, its colour, or its barking.

Children also seem to assume that objects have only one label. Therefore, novel terms must refer to unfamiliar objects and not to familiar objects that already have labels. This concept is the **contrast assumption**, which is also known as the mutual exclusivity assumption (Bloom, 2002; Waxman & Lidz, 2006). Suppose that a child is shown two objects, one of which has a known label ("doggy") and one of which is unknown. Let us further suppose that an adult now says, "Look at the lemur." If the child assumes that "doggy" and "lemur" each can refer to only one object, the child would correctly figure out that "lemur" refers to the other object and is not just another name for "doggy" (Homer & Nelson, 2005; Waxman & Lidz, 2006).

DEVELOPMENT OF GRAMMAR

There is a "grammar explosion" during the third year (Tamis-LeMonda et al., 2006). Children's sentence structure expands to include the words missing in telegraphic speech. Children usually add to their vocabulary an impressive array of articles (*a, an, the*), conjunctions (*and, but, or*), possessive adjectives (*your, her*), pronouns (*she, him, one*), and prepositions (*in, on, over, around, under, through*). Usually between the ages of 3 and 4, children show knowledge of rules for combining phrases and clauses into complex sentences, as in "You goed and Mommy goed, too."

Overregularization

The apparent basis of one of the more intriguing language developments—**overregularization**—is that children acquire grammatical rules as they learn language. At young ages they tend to apply these rules rather strictly, even in cases that call for exceptions (Jacobson & Schwartz, 2005; Stemberger, 2004). Consider the formation of the past tense and plurals in English. We add *d* or *ed* to regular verbs and *s* to regular nouns. Thus, *walk* becomes *walked* and *doggy* becomes *doggies*. But then there are irregular verbs and irregular nouns. For example, *sit* becomes *sat* and *go* becomes *went*. *Sheep* remains *sheep* (plural) and *child* becomes *children*.

As children become aware of the syntactic rules for forming the past tense and plurals in English, they often misapply them to irregular words. As a result, they tend to make charming errors (Stemberger, 2004). Some 3- to 5-year-olds are more likely to say "Mommy sitted down" than "Mommy sat down" or talk about the "sheeps" they "seed" on the farm and about all the "childs" they ran into at the playground.

Grammar Explosion

© Walter Lockwood/Corbis

fast mapping a process of quickly determining a word's meaning, which facilitates children's vocabulary development.

whole-object assumption the assumption that words refer to whole objects and not to their component parts or characteristics.

contrast assumption the assumption that objects have only one label.

overregularization the application of regular grammatical rules for forming inflections to irregular verbs and nouns.

Some parents recognize that their children at first were forming the past tense of irregular verbs correctly but that they then began to make errors. Some of these parents become concerned that their children are "slipping" in their language development and attempt to correct them. However, overregularization reflects accurate knowledge of grammar, not faulty language development. In another year or two, *mouses* will be boringly transformed into *mice*, and Mommy will no longer have sitted down. Parents might as well enjoy overregularization while they can.

MOUSES OR MICE?

Asking Questions

Children's first questions are telegraphic and characterized by a rising pitch (which signifies a question mark in English) at the end. Depending on the context, "More milky?" can be translated into "May I have more milk?", "Would you like more milk?", or "Is there more milk?" It is usually toward the latter part of the third year that the *wh* questions appear. Consistent with the child's general cognitive development, certain *wh* questions (*what, who,* and *where*) appear earlier than others (*why, when, which,* and *how*) (Tamis-LeMonda et al., 2006). *Why* is usually too philosophical for a 2-year-old, and *how* is too involved. Two-year-olds are also likely to be now-oriented, so *when* is of less than immediate concern. By the fourth year, most children are spontaneously producing *why, when,* and *how* questions. These *wh* words are initially tacked on to the beginnings of sentences. "Where Mommy go?" can stand for "Where is Mommy going?", "Where did Mommy go?", or "Where will Mommy go?", and its meaning must be derived from context. Later on, the child will add the auxiliary verbs *is, did,* and *will* to indicate whether the question concerns the present, past, or future.

Passive Sentences

Passive sentences, such as "The food is eaten by the dog," are difficult for 2- and 3-year-olds to understand, and so young preschoolers almost never produce them. In a study of children's comprehension (Strohner & Nelson, 1974), 2- to 5-year-olds used puppets and toys to act out sentences that were read to them. Two- and 3-year-olds made errors in acting out passive sentences (e.g., "The car was hit by the truck") 70 percent of the time. Older children had less difficulty interpreting the meanings of passive sentences correctly. However, most children usually do not produce passive sentences spontaneously even at the ages of 5 and 6.

PRAGMATICS

Pragmatics refers to the practical aspects of communication. Children show pragmatism when they adjust their speech to fit the social situation (Nelson, 2006). For example, children show greater formality in their choice of words and syntax when they are role-playing high-status figures, such as teachers or physicians, in their games. They say "please" more often when making requests of high-status people, or when they use Motherese in talking to an infant.

Preschoolers tend to be egocentric; therefore, a 2-year-old telling another child "Gimme my book," without specifying which book, may assume that the other child knows what she herself knows. Once children can perceive the world through the eyes of others, they advance in their abilities to make themselves understood. Now the child recognizes that the other child will require a description of the book or of its location to carry out the request.

LANGUAGE AND COGNITION

Language and cognitive development are interwoven (Homer & Nelson, 2005; Waxman & Lidz, 2006). For example, the child gradually gains the capacity to

© Andy Sands/naturepl.com

discriminate between animals on the basis of distinct features, such as size, patterns of movement, and the sounds they make. At the same time, the child also is acquiring words that represent broader categories, such as mammal and animal.

But which comes first? Does the child first develop concepts and then acquire the language to describe them, or does the child's increasing language ability lead to the development of new concepts?

Does Cognitive Development Precede Language Development?

Piaget (1976) believed that cognitive development precedes language development. He argued that children must understand concepts before they use words to describe them. From Piaget's perspective, children learn words to describe classes or categories that they have already created (Nelson, 2005). Children can learn the word *kitty* because they have perceived the characteristics that distinguish cats from other things.

Some studies support the notion that cognitive concepts may precede language. For example, the vocabulary explosion that occurs at about 18 months of age is related to the child's ability to group a set of objects into two categories, such as "dolls" and "cars" (Gopnik & Meltzoff, 1992). Other research suggests that young children need to experience an action themselves or by observation to learn the meaning of a verb (Pulverman et al., 2006).

Does Language Development Precede Cognitive Development?

Although many theorists argue that cognitive development precedes language development, others reverse the causal relationship and claim that children create cognitive classes to understand things that are labelled by words (Clark, 1983). When children hear the word *dog*, they try to understand it by searching for characteristics that separate dogs from other things.

> **inner speech** Vygotsky's concept of the ultimate binding of language and thought. Inner speech originates in vocalizations that may regulate the child's behaviour and become internalized by age 6 or 7.

The Interactionist View: Outer Speech and Inner Speech

Today, most developmentalists find something of value in each of these cognitive views (Waxman & Lidz, 2006). In the early stages of language development, concepts often precede words, and many of the infant's words describe classes that have already developed. But later, language influences thought.

Vygotsky believed that during most of the first year, vocalizations and thought are separate. But during the second year, thought and speech combine forces. Children discover that objects have labels. Learning labels becomes more self-directed. Children ask what new words mean. Learning new words fosters creation of new categories, and new categories become filled with labels for new things.

Vygotsky's concept of **inner speech** is a key feature of his position. At first children's thoughts are spoken aloud. You can hear the 3-year-old instructing herself as she plays with toys. At this age, her vocalizations serve to regulate her behaviour, but they gradually become internalized. What was spoken aloud at 4 and 5 becomes an internal dialogue by 6 or 7. Inner speech is the ultimate binding of language and thought. It is involved in the development of planning and self-regulation, and facilitates learning.

© Oshchepkov Dmitry/Shutterstock

© Gelpi/Shutterstock

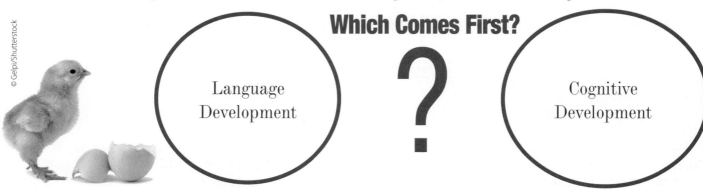

Which Comes First?

Language Development

?

Cognitive Development

Most parents

want preschoolers to develop a sense of responsibility and develop into well-adjusted individuals.

8

Early Childhood: Social and Emotional Development

Learning Outcomes

LO1 Describe the dimensions of child rearing and styles of parenting

LO2 Explain how siblings, birth order, peers, and other factors affect social development during early childhood

LO3 Discuss personality and emotional development during early childhood, focusing on the self, Erikson's views, and fears

LO4 Discuss the development of gender roles and sex differences

DID YOU KNOW?

D1 Firstborn children are more highly motivated to achieve than later-born children.

D2 Children who are physically punished are more likely to be aggressive than children who are not physically punished.

D3 Children who watch 2 to 4 hours of TV a day will see 8,000 murders and another 100,000 acts of violence by the time they have finished elementary school.

D4 Children mechanically imitate the aggressive behaviour they view in the media.

D5 Fears may change from infancy to middle childhood, but they remain a significant hurdle for children.

Preschoolers usually spend most of their time with the family. Most parents want preschoolers to develop a sense of responsibility and develop into well-adjusted individuals. They want them to acquire social skills. How do parents try to achieve these goals? What role do siblings play? How do children's peers influence social and emotional development?

LO1 Dimensions of Child Rearing

Parents have different approaches to rearing their children. Investigators of parental patterns of child rearing have found it useful to classify them according to two broad dimensions: warmth–coldness and restrictiveness–permissiveness (Baumrind, 1989, 2005).

Warm parents are affectionate toward their children. They tend to hug and kiss them and smile at them frequently. Warm parents are caring and supportive. They communicate their enjoyment in being with their children. Warm parents are less likely than cold parents to use physical discipline (Bender et al., 2007).

Cold parents may not enjoy their children and may have few feelings of affection for them. They are likely to complain about their children's behaviour, saying they are naughty or have "minds of their own."

It requires no stretch of the imagination to conclude that it is better to be warm than cold toward children. The children of parents who are warm and accepting are more likely to develop internal standards of conduct, a moral sense or conscience (Bender et al., 2007; Lau et al., 2006). Parental warmth also is related to the child's social and emotional well-being (Lau et al., 2006; Leung et al., 2004).

Where does parental warmth come from? Some of it reflects parental beliefs about how to best rear children, and some reflects parents' tendencies to imitate the behaviour of their own parents. But research by Hetherington and her colleagues (Feinberg et al., 2001) suggests that genetic factors may also be involved.

Parents decide how restrictive they will be. How will they respond when children make excessive noise, play with dangerous objects, damage property, mess up their rooms, hurt others, or masturbate? Parents who are restrictive tend to impose rules and to watch their children closely.

It is not true that parents who are strict and demand mature behaviour wind up with rebellious children. Consistent control and firm enforcement of rules can have positive consequences for the child, particularly when combined with strong support and affection (Grusec, 2006). This parenting style is termed the *authoritative style*. On the other hand, if "restrictiveness" means physical punishment, interference, or intrusiveness, it can give rise to disobedience, rebelliousness, and lower levels of cognitive development (Paulussen-Hoogeboom et al., 2007; Rudy & Grusec, 2006).

Permissive parents supervise their children less closely than restrictive parents do. Permissive parents allow their children to do what is "natural," such as make noise, treat toys carelessly, and experiment with their bodies. They may also allow their children to show some aggression, intervening only when another child is in danger.

HOW PARENTS ENFORCE RESTRICTIONS

Regardless of their general approaches to child rearing, most parents are restrictive now and then, even if only when they are teaching their

> Consistent control and firm enforcement of rules can have positive consequences for the child, particularly when combined with strong support and affection.

children not to run into the street or to touch a hot stove. Parents tend to use the methods of induction, power assertion, and withdrawal of love.

Inductive methods aim to teach knowledge that will enable children to generate desirable behaviour on their own. The main inductive technique is "reasoning," or explaining why one kind of behaviour is good and another is not. Reasoning with a 1- or 2-year-old can be basic. "Don't do that—it hurts!" qualifies as reasoning with toddlers. "It hurts!" is an explanation, though brief. The inductive approach helps the child understand moral behaviour and fosters prosocial behaviour such as helping and sharing (Paulussen-Hoogeboom et al., 2007).

Power-assertive methods include physical punishment and denial of privileges. Parents often justify physical punishment with sayings such as "Spare the rod, spoil the child." Parents may insist that power assertion is necessary because their children are noncompliant. However, use of power-assertion is related to parental authoritarianism as well as children's behaviour (Roopnarine et al., 2006; Rudy & Grusec, 2006). Parental power assertion is associated with lower acceptance by peers, poorer grades, and more antisocial behaviour in children. The more parents use power-assertive techniques, the less children appear to develop internal standards of conduct. Parental punishment and rejection are often linked with aggression and delinquency.

Some parents control children by threatening withdrawal of love. They isolate or ignore misbehaving children. Because most children need parental approval and contact, loss of love can be more threatening than physical punishment. Withdrawal of love may foster compliance but also instill guilt and anxiety (Grusec, 2002).

© Vadim Ponomarenko/Shutterstock

Preschoolers more readily comply when asked to do something than when asked to *stop* doing something (Kochanska et al., 2001). One way to manage children who are doing something wrong or bad is to involve them in something else.

HELLO
my name is

Because I say so!

authoritative a child-rearing style in which parents are restrictive and demanding yet communicative and warm.

authoritarian demanding submission and obedience.

permissive–indulgent a child-rearing style in which parents are warm and not restrictive.

rejecting–neglecting a child-rearing style in which parents are neither restrictive and controlling nor supportive and responsive.

PARENTING STYLES: HOW PARENTS TRANSMIT VALUES AND STANDARDS

Diana Baumrind (1989, 1991b) focused on the relationship between parenting styles and the development of competent behaviour in young children. She used the dimensions of warmth–coldness and restrictiveness–permissiveness to develop a grid of four parenting styles based on whether parents are high or low in each dimension (see Table 8.1).

The parents of the most capable children are rated high in both dimensions (see Table 8.1). They are highly restrictive and make strong demands for maturity. However, they also reason with their children and show strong support and feelings of love. Baumrind applies the label **authoritative** to these parents; they know what they want their children to do but also respect their children and are warm toward them.

Compared with other children, the children of authoritative parents tend to show self-reliance and independence, high self-esteem, high levels of activity and exploratory behaviour, and social competence. They are highly motivated to achieve and do well in school (Baumrind, 1989, 1991b; Grusec, 2006).

"Because I say so" could be the motto of parents that Baumrind labels **authoritarian**. Authoritarians value obedience for its own sake. They have strict guidelines for right and wrong and demand that their children accept them without question. Like authoritative parents, they are controlling. But unlike authoritative parents, their enforcement methods rely on force. Moreover, authoritarian parents do not communicate well with their children or respect their children's viewpoints. Most researchers find them to be generally cold and rejecting (Grusec, 2002).

Baumrind found the sons of authoritarian parents to be relatively hostile and defiant and the daughters to be low in independence and dominance (Baumrind, 1989). Other researchers have found that the children of authoritarian parents are less competent socially and academically than those of authoritative parents. They are anxious, irritable, and restrained in their social interactions (Grusec, 2002). As adolescents, they may be conforming and obedient but have low self-reliance and self-esteem.

Baumrind found two types of parents who are permissive as opposed to restrictive. One is permissive–indulgent and the other rejecting–neglecting. **Permissive–indulgent** parents are low in their attempts to control their children and in their demands for mature behaviour. They are easygoing and unconventional. Their brand of permissiveness is accompanied by high nurturance (warmth and support).

Rejecting–neglecting parents are also low in their demands for mature behaviour and attempts to control their children. Unlike indulgent parents, they are low in support and responsiveness. The children of neglectful parents are the least competent, responsible, and mature. The children of permissive–indulgent parents, like those of neglectful parents, are less competent in

TABLE 8.1
Baumrind's Patterns of Parenting

PARENTAL STYLE	PARENTAL BEHAVIOUR PATTERNS	
	RESTRICTIVENESS AND CONTROL	WARMTH AND RESPONSIVENESS
Authoritative	↑	↑
Authoritarian	↑	↓
Permissive–Indulgent	↓	↑
Rejecting–Neglecting	↓	↓

school and show more misconduct and substance abuse than children of more restrictive, controlling parents. But children from permissive–indulgent homes, unlike those from neglectful homes, are fairly high in social competence and self-confidence (Baumrind, 1991a).

EFFECTS OF THE SITUATION AND THE CHILD ON PARENTING STYLES

Parenting styles are not merely a one-way street, from parent to child. Parenting styles also depend partly on the situation and partly on the characteristics of the child (Grusec, 2006). For example, parents are most likely to use power-assertive techniques when dealing with aggressive behaviour (Casas et al., 2006; Lipman et al., 2006). Parents prefer power assertion to induction when they believe that children understand the rules they have violated and are capable of acting appropriately. Stress also contributes to use of power.

Baumrind's research suggests that we can make an effort to avoid some of the pitfalls of being authoritarian or overly permissive. Some recommended techniques that parents can use to help control and guide their children's behaviour are listed in Table 8.2.

LO2 Social Behaviours

during early childhood, children make tremendous advances in social skills and behaviour. Their play increasingly involves other children. They learn how to share, cooperate, and comfort others. But young children, like adults, can be aggressive as well as loving and helpful.

INFLUENCE OF SIBLINGS

Siblings serve many functions, including giving physical care, providing emotional support and nurturance, offering advice, serving as role models, providing social interaction that helps develop social skills, making demands, and imposing restrictions (McHale et al., 2006; Parke & Buriel, 2006).

TABLE 8.2
Advice for Parents in Guiding Young Children's Behaviour

DO …

- Reward good behaviour with praises, smiles, and hugs.
- Give clear, simple, realistic rules appropriate to the child's age.
- Enforce rules with reasonable consequences.
- Ignore annoying behaviour such as whining and tantrums.
- Childproof the house, putting dangerous and breakable items out of reach. Then establish limits.
- Be consistent.

DON'T …

- Pay attention only to a child's misbehaviour.
- Issue too many rules or enforce them haphazardly.
- Try to control behaviour solely in the child's domain, such as thumb sucking, which can lead to frustrating power struggles.
- Nag, lecture, shame, or induce guilt.
- Yell or spank.
- Be overly permissive.

© Ryan McVay/Photodisc/Getty Images

In early childhood, siblings' interactions have positive aspects (cooperation, teaching, nurturance) and negative aspects (conflict, control, competition) (Parke & Buriel, 2006). Older siblings tend to be more caring but also more dominating than younger siblings. Younger siblings are more likely to imitate older siblings and accept their direction.

In many cultures, older girls care for younger siblings (Clark, 2005). Parents often urge their children to stop fighting among themselves, and at times, these conflicts look deadly (and occasionally they are). But garden-variety sibling conflict can enhance their social competence, their development of self-identity (who they are and what they stand for), and their ability to rear their own children (Ross et al., 2006).

There is more conflict between siblings when the parents play favourites (Scharf et al., 2005). Conflict between siblings is also greater when the relationships between the parents or between the parents and children are troubled (Kim et al., 2006).

Adjusting to the Birth of a Sibling

The birth of a sister or brother is often a source of stress for preschoolers because of changes in family relationships (Volling, 2003). When a new baby comes into the home, the mother pays relatively more attention to that child and spends less time with the older child. As a result, the older child may feel displaced and resentful.

Children show a mixture of negative and positive reactions to the birth of a sibling. They include **regression** to baby-like behaviours, such as increased clinging, crying, and toilet accidents. Anger and naughtiness may increase. But the same children may also show increased independence and maturity, insisting on feeding or dressing themselves and helping to care for the baby (Volling, 2003). Parents can help a young child cope with the arrival of a baby by explaining in advance what is to come (Kavcic & Zupancic, 2005).

BIRTH ORDER

Differences in personality and achievement have been linked to birth order. Firstborn children, as a group,
are more highly motivated to achieve than later-born children (Latham & Budworth, 2007). Firstborn and only children perform better academically and are more cooperative (Healy & Ellis, 2007). They are more adult-oriented and less aggressive than later-born children (Beck et al., 2006; Zajonc, 2001). They obtain higher standardized test scores, including IQ and SAT scores (Kristensen & Bjerkedal, 2007; Sulloway, 2007). On the negative side, firstborn and only children show greater anxiety and are less self-reliant than later-born children.

regression a return to behaviour characteristic of earlier stages of development.

D1 Firstborn children are more highly motivated to achieve than later-born children.
As a group, this is true, but individual variances always occur.

Later-born children may learn to act aggressively to compete for the attention of their parents and older siblings (Carey, 2007b). Their self-concepts tend to be lower than those of firstborn or only children, but the social skills later-born children acquire from dealing with their family position seem to translate into greater popularity with peers (Carey, 2007b). They also tend to be more rebellious and liberal than firstborn children (Beck et al., 2006; Zweigenhaft & Von Ammon, 2000).

By and large, parents are more relaxed and flexible with later-born children. Many parents see that the firstborn child is turning out well and perhaps they assume that later-born children will also turn out well.

PEER RELATIONSHIPS

Peer interactions foster social skills—sharing, helping, taking turns, and dealing with conflict. Groups teach children how to lead and how to follow. Physical and cognitive skills develop through peer interactions. Peers also provide emotional support (Dishion & Stormshak, 2007b; Grusec, 2006).

© Shauna Longmuir

dramatic play play in which children enact social roles.

nonsocial play solitary forms of play.

social play play in which children interact with and are influenced by others.

By about 2 years of age, children imitate one another's play and engage in social games such as follow the leader (Fontaine, 2005; Kavanaugh, 2006). By the age of 2, children show preferences for particular playmates— an early sign of friendship (Sherwin-White, 2006). Friendship is characterized by shared positive experiences and feelings of attachment (Grusec, 2002). Even early friendships can be fairly stable (Rubin et al., 2006).

When preschoolers are asked what they like about their friends, they typically mention the toys and activities they share (Gleason & Hohmann, 2006). Primary-school children usually report that their friends are the children with whom they do things and have fun (Gleason & Hohmann, 2006). Not until late childhood and adolescence do friends' traits and notions of trust, communication, and intimacy become important.

PLAY—CHILD'S PLAY, THAT IS

Play is more than fun; it is also meaningful, voluntary, and internally motivated (Elkind, 2007). Play helps children develop motor skills and coordination. It contributes to social development, because children learn to share play materials, take turns, and, through **dramatic play**, try on new roles (Elkind, 2007). It supports the development of such cognitive qualities as curiosity, exploration, symbolic thinking, and problem solving. Play may even help children learn to control impulses (Elkind, 2007).

Play and Cognitive Development

Play contributes to and expresses milestones in cognitive development. Jean Piaget (1962 [1946]) identified kinds of play, each characterized by increasing cognitive complexity:

- *Functional play.* Beginning in the sensorimotor stage, the first kind of play involves repetitive motor activity, such as rolling a ball or running and laughing.
- *Symbolic play.* Also called pretend play, imaginative play, or dramatic play, symbolic play emerges toward the end of the sensorimotor stage and increases during early childhood. In symbolic play, children create settings, characters, and scripts (Kavanaugh, 2006).

- *Constructive play.* Children use objects or materials to draw something or make something, such as a tower of blocks.
- *Formal games.* Games with rules include board games, which are sometimes enhanced or invented by children, and games involving motor skills, such as marbles and hopscotch, ball games involving sides or teams, and video games. Such games may involve social interaction as well as physical activity and rules. People play such games for a lifetime.

Mildred Parten focused on the social dimensions of play.

Parten's Types of Play

In classic research on children's play, Mildred Parten (1932) observed the development of six types of play among 2- to 5-year-old nursery-school children: unoccupied play, solitary play, onlooker play, parallel play, associative play, and cooperative play (see Table 8.3). Solitary play and onlooker play are considered **nonsocial play**, that is, play in which children do not interact socially. Nonsocial play occurs more often in 2- and 3-year-olds than in older preschoolers. Parallel play, associative play, and cooperative play are considered **social play**. In each case, children are influenced by other children as they play. Parten found that associative play and cooperative play become common by age 5. They are more likely to be found among older and more experienced preschoolers (Dyer & Moneta, 2006). Girls are slightly more likely than boys to engage in social play (Zheng & Colombo, 1989).

But there are exceptions. Nonsocial play can involve educational activities that foster cognitive development. In fact, many 4- and 5- year-olds spend a good deal of time in parallel constructive play. For instance, they may work on puzzles or build with blocks near other children. Parallel constructive players are frequently perceived by teachers to be socially skillful and are popular with their peers (Coplan et al., 1994). Two-year-olds who have older siblings or who have group experience may engage in advanced social play.

Lisa Serbin and her colleagues (2001) explored infants' visual preferences for gender-stereotyped toys using the assumption that infants spend more time looking at objects that are of greater interest. They found that both girls and boys showed significant preferences for gender-stereotyped toys by 18 months of age. Although preferences for gender-typed toys are well developed by the ages of 15 to 36 months, girls

TABLE 8.3
Parten's Categories of Play

CATEGORY	NONSOCIAL OR SOCIAL?	DESCRIPTION
Unoccupied play	Nonsocial	Children do not appear to be playing. They may engage in random movements that seem to be without a goal. Unoccupied play appears to be the least frequent kind of play in nursery schools.
Solitary play	Nonsocial	Children play with toys by themselves, independently of the children around them. Solitary players do not appear to be influenced by children around them. They make no effort to approach them.
Onlooker play	Nonsocial	Children observe other children who are at play. Onlookers frequently talk to the children they are observing and may make suggestions, but they do not overtly join in.
Parallel play	Social	Children play with toys similar to those of surrounding children. However, they treat the toys as they choose and do not directly interact with other children.
Associative play	Social	Children interact and share toys. However, they do not seem to share group goals. Although they interact, individuals still treat toys as they choose. The association with the other children appears to be more important than the nature of the activity. They seem to enjoy each other's company.
Cooperative play	Social	Children interact to achieve common, group goals. The play of each child is subordinated to the purposes of the group. One or two group members direct the activities of others. There is also a division of labour, with different children taking different roles. Children may pretend to be members of a family, animals, space monsters, and all sorts of creatures.

are more likely to stray from the stereotypes (Bussey & Bandura, 1999). Girls ask for and play with "boys' toys" such as cars and trucks more often than boys choose dolls and other "girls' toys."

Sex Differences in Play

Girls and boys differ not only in toy preferences but also in their choice of play environments and activities. During the preschool and early elementary school years, boys prefer vigorous physical outdoor activities such as climbing, playing with large vehicles, and rough-and-tumble play (Else-Quest et al., 2006). In middle childhood, boys spend more time than girls in play groups of five or more children and in competitive play (Crombie & Desjardins, 1993; Else-Quest et al., 2006). Girls are more likely than boys to engage in arts and crafts and domestic play. Girls' activities are more closely directed and structured by adults (A. Campbell et al., 2002). Girls spend more time than boys playing with one other child or a small group (Crombie & Desjardins, 1993).

Why do children show these early preferences for gender-stereotyped toys and activities? Biological

factors may play a role, for example, boys' slightly greater strength and activity levels and girls' slightly greater physical maturity and coordination. But adults treat girls and boys differently. They provide gender-stereotyped toys and room furnishings and encourage gender typing in play and household chores (Leaper, 2002). Children, moreover, tend to seek out information on which kinds of toys and play are "masculine" or "feminine" and then to conform to the label (Martin & Ruble, 2004).

Some studies find that children who "cross the line" by showing interest in toys or activities considered appropriate for the other sex are often teased, ridiculed, rejected, or ignored by their parents, teachers, other adults, and peers. Boys are more likely than girls to be criticized (Fagot & Hagan, 1991; Garvey, 1990).

Another well-documented finding is that many children begin to prefer playmates of the same sex by the age of 2. Girls tend to develop this preference earlier than boys (Fagot, 1990; Hay et al., 2004). This tendency strengthens during middle childhood.

Eleanor Maccoby (1990b) believes that two factors are involved in the choice of the sex of playmates in early childhood. One is that boys' play is more oriented toward dominance, aggression, and rough play. The second is that boys are not very responsive to girls' polite suggestions. Boys may avoid girls because they see them as inferior (Caplan & Larkin, 1991).

PROSOCIAL BEHAVIOUR

Prosocial behaviour, also known as *altruism,* is intended to benefit another without expectation of reward. Prosocial behaviour includes sharing, cooperating, and helping and comforting others in distress (Strayer & Roberts, 2004). It is shown by the preschool and early school years (Knafo & Plomin, 2006a, 2006b) and is linked to the development of empathy and perspective taking.

Empathy

Empathy is sensitivity to the feelings of others and is connected with sharing and cooperation. Infants frequently begin to cry when they hear other children crying, although this early agitated response may be largely reflexive (Strayer & Roberts, 2004). Empathy promotes prosocial behaviour and decreases aggressive behaviour, and these links are evident by the second year (Hastings et al., 2000). During the second year, many children approach other children and adults who are in distress and try to help them. They may hug a crying child or tell the child not to cry. Toddlers who are rated as emotionally unresponsive to the feelings of others are more likely to behave aggressively throughout their school years (Olson et al., 2000).

Girls show more empathy than boys (Strayer & Roberts, 2004). It is unclear whether this sex difference reflects genetic factors or the socialization of girls to be attuned to the emotions of others.

Perspective Taking

According to Piaget, preoperational children tend to be egocentric. They tend not to be able to see things from the vantage points of others. Various cognitive abilities, such as being able to take another person's perspective, are related to knowing when someone is in need or distress. Perspective-taking skills improve with age, and so do prosocial skills. Among children of the same age, those with better developed perspective-taking ability also show more prosocial behaviour and less aggressive behaviour (Hastings et al., 2000).

© Pixland/Jupiterimages

© Brand X Pictures/Jupiterimages

Influences on Prosocial Behaviour

Although altruistic behaviour is defined as prosocial behaviour that occurs in the absence of rewards or the expectations of rewards, it is influenced by rewards and punishments. The peers of nursery-school children who are cooperative, friendly, and generous respond more positively to them than they do to children whose behaviour is self-centred (Hartup, 1983). Children who are rewarded for acting prosocially are likely to continue these behaviours (Knafo & Plomin, 2006a, 2006b).

Parents foster prosocial behaviour when they use inductive techniques such as explaining how behaviour affects others ("You made Josh cry. It's not nice to hit."). Parents of prosocial children are more likely to expect mature behaviour from their children. They are less likely to use power-assertive techniques of discipline (Strayer & Roberts, 2004).

DEVELOPMENT OF AGGRESSION

Children, like adults, can not only be loving and altruistic but can also be aggressive. Some children, of course, are more aggressive than others. Aggression refers to behaviour intended to hurt or injure another person.

Aggressive behaviour, similar to other social behaviour, seems to follow developmental patterns. The aggression of preschoolers is frequently instrumental or possession oriented (Persson, 2005). Younger preschoolers tend to use aggression to obtain the toys and situations they want, such as a favoured seat at the table or in the car. Older preschoolers are more likely to resolve conflicts over toys by sharing rather than fighting (Caplan et al., 1991). Anger and aggression in preschoolers usually cause other preschoolers to reject them (Henry et al., 2000; Walter & LaFreniere, 2000).

By age 6 or 7, aggression becomes hostile and person oriented. Children taunt and criticize one another and call one another names; they also attack one another physically.

Aggressive behaviour appears to be generally stable and predictive of social and emotional problems later on, especially among boys (Nagin & Tremblay, 2001; Tapper & Boulton, 2004). Toddlers who are perceived as difficult and defiant are more likely to behave aggressively throughout their school years (Olson et al., 2000). A longitudinal study of more than 600 children found that aggressive 8-year-olds tended to remain more aggressive than their peers 22 years later, at age 30 (Eron et al., 1991). Aggressive children of both sexes are more likely to have criminal convictions as adults, to abuse their spouses, and to drive while drunk.

THEORIES OF AGGRESSION

What causes some children to be more aggressive than others? Aggression in childhood appears to result from a complex interplay of biological factors and environmental factors such as reinforcement and modelling.

Evidence suggests that genetic factors may be involved in aggressive behaviour, including criminal and antisocial behaviour (Hicks et al., 2007; Lykken, 2006a; E. O. Wilson, 2004). There is a greater concordance (agreement) rate for criminal behaviour between monozygotic (MZ) twins, who fully share their genetic code, than dizygotic (DZ) twins, who, like other brothers and sisters, share only half of their genetic code (Tehrani & Mednick, 2000). If genetics is involved in aggression, genes may do their work at least in part through the male sex hormone testosterone. Testosterone is apparently connected with feelings of self-confidence, high activity levels, and—the negative side—aggressiveness (Archer, 2006; Cunningham & McGinnis, 2007; Popma et al., 2007).

Cognitive research with primary-school children finds that children who believe in the legitimacy of aggression are more likely to behave aggressively when they are presented with social provocations (Tapper & Boulton, 2004). Aggressive children are also often found to be lacking in empathy and the ability to see things from the perspective of other people (Hastings et al., 2000). They fail to conceptualize the experiences of their victims and are thus less likely to inhibit aggressive impulses.

Social cognitive explanations of aggression focus on environmental factors such as reinforcement and observational learning. When children repeatedly push, shove, and hit to grab toys or break into line, other children usually let them have their way (Kempes et al., 2005). Children who are thus rewarded for acting aggressively are likely to continue to use aggressive means, especially if they do not have alternative means to achieve their ends. Aggressive children may also associate with peers who value and encourage aggression (Stauffacher & DeHart; 2006).

Children who are physically punished are more likely to be aggressive themselves than children who are not physically punished (Patterson, 2005). Physically aggressive parents serve as models for aggression and also stoke their children's anger.

> **D2** Children who are physically punished are more likely to be aggressive than children who are not physically punished. This is true, which raises important discipline issues.

Media Influences

Real people are not the only models of aggressive behaviour in children's lives. A classic study by Albert Bandura and his colleagues (1963) suggested that televised models had a powerful influence on children's aggressive behaviour. One group of preschoolers observed a film of an adult model hitting and kicking an inflated Bobo doll, whereas a control group saw an aggression-free film. The experimental and control children were then left alone in a room with the same doll as hidden observers recorded their behaviour. The children who had observed the aggressive model showed significantly more aggressive behaviour toward the doll themselves (see Figure 8.1). Many children imitated bizarre attack behaviours devised for the model in this experiment, behaviours they would not have thought up themselves.

Television is a fertile source of aggressive models (Villani, 2001). Children are routinely exposed to TV scenes

greenland/Shutterstock

FIGURE 8.1
Photos from Albert Bandura's Classic Experiment in the Imitation of Aggressive Models

In the top row, an adult model strikes a clown doll. The second and third rows show a boy and a girl imitating the aggressive behaviour.

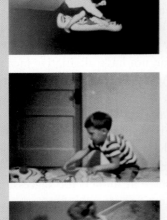

© Albert Bandura/Dept. of Psychology, Stanford University

of murder, beating, and sexual assault. Children who watch 2 to 4 hours of TV a day will see 8,000 murders and another 100,000 acts of violence by the time they have finished elementary school (Eron, 1993).

> **D3** Children who watch 2 to 4 hours of TV a day will see 8,000 murders and another 100,000 acts of violence by the time they have finished elementary school.
> What are our children watching?

Consider a number of ways in which depictions of violence contribute to violence:

- *Observational learning.* Children learn from observation (Holland, 2000). TV violence supplies models of aggressive "skills," which children may acquire.

- *Disinhibition.* Punishment inhibits behaviour. Conversely, media violence may **disinhibit** aggressive behaviour, especially when characters "get away" with it.

- *Increased arousal.* Media violence and aggressive video games increase viewers' level of arousal. We are more likely to be aggressive under high levels of arousal.

- *Priming of aggressive thoughts and memories.* Media violence "primes" or arouses aggressive ideas and memories (Bushman, 1998; Meier et al., 2006).

- *Habituation.* We become used to repeated stimuli. Children exposed to violence are more likely to assume that violence is acceptable or normal and become desensitized to it (Holland, 2000).

Though exposure to violence in the media increases the probability of violence by viewers, there is no simple one-to-one connection between media violence and violence in real life. According to social cognitive theory, we also choose whether to imitate the behaviour we observe.

> **D4** Children mechanically imitate the aggressive behaviour they view in the media.
> According to social cognitive theory, a direct connection cannot be drawn between exposure to media violence and violence in real life. But what are the indirect effects?

LO3 Personality and Emotional Development

in early childhood, children's sense of self—who they are and how they feel about themselves—develops and grows more complex. They begin to acquire a sense of their own abilities and their increasing mastery of the environment. As they move out into the world, they also face new experiences that may cause them to feel fearful and anxious.

disinhibit to stimulate a response that has been suppressed by showing a model engaging in that response.

categorical self definitions of the self that refer to external traits.

THE SELF

The sense of self, or the self-concept, emerges gradually during infancy. Infants and toddlers visually begin to recognize themselves and differentiate from other individuals such as their parents (remember the red dot study on page 120).

In the preschool years, children continue to develop their sense of self. Almost as soon as they begin to speak, they describe themselves in terms of certain categories, such as age groupings (baby, child, adult) and sex (girl, boy). Self-definitions that refer to concrete external traits have been called the **categorical self**.

Children as young as 3 years are able to describe themselves in terms of behaviours and internal states that occur often and are fairly stable over time (Eder,

© Mitch Diamond/Photolibrary

NEL

CHAPTER 8: EARLY CHILDHOOD: SOCIAL AND EMOTIONAL DEVELOPMENT   157

1989, 1990). For example, in response to the question "How do you feel when you're scared?" young children frequently respond, "Usually like running away" (Eder, 1989). In answer to the question "How do you usually act around grown-ups?" a typical response might be, "I mostly been good with grown-ups."

One aspect of the self-concept is self-esteem. Children with high self-esteem are more likely to be securely attached and have parents who are attentive to their needs (Booth-LaForce et al., 2006; Patterson & Bigler, 2006). They also are more likely to show prosocial behaviour (Salmivalli et al., 2005).

By the age of 4, preschool children begin to make evaluative judgments about two different aspects of themselves (Harter & Pike, 1984). One is their cognitive and physical competence (e.g., being good at puzzles, counting, swinging, tying shoes), and the second is their social acceptance by peers and parents (e.g., having lots of friends, being read to by Mom). But preschoolers do not yet clearly distinguish between different areas of competence. A preschooler is not likely to report being good in school but poor in physical skills. One is either "good at doing things" or not (Clark & Symons, 2000; Piek et al., 2006).

INITIATIVE VERSUS GUILT

As preschoolers continue to develop a separate sense of themselves, they increasingly move out into the world and take the initiative in learning new skills. Erik Erikson (1963) refers to these early childhood years as the stage of initiative versus guilt.

Children in this stage strive to achieve independence from their parents and master adult behaviours. They are curious, try new things, and test themselves. Children learn that not all their plans, dreams, and fantasies can be realized. Adults prohibit children from doing certain things, and children begin to internalize adult rules. Fear of violating the rules may cause the child to feel guilty and may curtail efforts to master new skills. Parents can help children develop and maintain a healthy sense of initiative by encouraging their attempts to learn and explore and by not being unduly critical and punitive.

FEARS: THE HORRORS OF EARLY CHILDHOOD

In Erikson's view, fear of violating parental prohibitions can be a powerful force in the life of a young child. Children's fears change as they move from infancy

© AFP/Getty Images

into the preschool years. The number of fears seems to peak between 2½ and 4 years and then taper off (Miller et al., 1990b). The preschool period is marked by a decline in fears of loud noises, falling, sudden movement, and strangers. Fear of social disapproval is not the most common fear among preschoolers. Preschoolers are most likely to fear animals, imaginary creatures, the dark, and personal danger (Field, 2006; Muris et al., 2003). The fantasies of young children frequently involve stories they are told and media imagery. Frightening images of imaginary creatures can persist. Many preschoolers are reluctant to have the lights turned off at night for fear that such creatures may assault them, or simply appear. Real objects and situations also cause many preschoolers to fear for their personal safety—lightning, thunder and other loud noises, high places, sharp objects and being cut, blood, unfamiliar people, strange people, and stinging and crawling insects.

During middle childhood, children become less fearful of imaginary creatures, but fears of bodily harm and injury remain common. Children grow more fearful of failure and criticism in school and in social relationships (Ollendick & King, 1991). Girls report more fears and higher levels of anxiety than boys (Weems et al., 1999).

> **stereotype** a fixed, conventional idea about a group.
>
> **gender role** a cluster of traits and behaviours that are considered stereotypical of females and males.

LO4 Development of Gender Roles and Sex Differences

I am woman, hear me roar ... I am strong
I am invincible
I am woman

these lyrics are from the song "I Am Woman" by Helen Reddy and Ray Burton. They caught attention because they counter the **stereotype** of the vulnerable woman who needs the protection of a man. The stereotype of the vulnerable woman is a fixed, oversimplified, and conventional idea. So is the stereotype of the chivalrous, protective man. Unfortunately, these stereotypes create demands and limit opportunities for both sexes.

Cultural stereotypes of males and females are broad expectations of behaviour that we call **gender roles**. In our culture, the feminine gender-role stereotype includes such traits as dependence, gentleness, helpfulness, warmth, emotionality, submissiveness, and a home orientation. The masculine gender-role stereotype includes aggressiveness, self-confidence, independence, competitiveness, and competence in business, math, and science (Miller et al., 2006).

Gender-role stereotypes develop in stages. First, children learn to label the sexes. At about 2 to 2½ years of age, they can identify pictures of girls and boys (Fagot & Leinbach, 1993). By age 3, they display knowledge of gender stereotypes for toys, clothing, work,

and activities (Campbell et al., 2004). Children of this age generally agree that boys play with cars and trucks, help their fathers, and tend to hit others. They agree that girls play with dolls, help their mothers, and do not hit others (Cherney et al., 2006). One study found that preschool boys but not girls were rejected by their peers when they showed distress (Walter & LaFreniere, 2000).

Children become increasingly traditional in their stereotyping of activities, jobs, and personality traits between the ages of 3 and 9 or 10 (Miller et al., 2006). For example, traits such as "cruel" and "repairs broken things" are viewed as masculine, and traits such as "often is afraid" and "cooks and bakes" are seen as feminine.

Children and adolescents perceive their own sex in a slightly better light. For example, girls perceive other girls as nicer, more hardworking, and less selfish than boys. Boys, on the other hand, think that they are nicer, more hardworking, and less selfish than girls (Matlin, 2008; Miller et al., 2006).

SEX DIFFERENCES

Clearly, females and males are anatomically different. And according to gender-role stereotypes, people believe that females and males also differ in their behaviours, personality characteristics, and abilities. Sex differences in infancy are small and rather inconsistent. Preschoolers display some differences in their choices of toys and play activities. Boys engage in more rough-and-tumble play and are more aggressive. Girls tend to show more empathy and to report more fears. Girls show slightly greater verbal ability than boys, whereas boys show slightly greater visual–spatial ability than girls.

Genes bestow traits that help individual organisms survive and reproduce.

© Eliza Snow/iStockphoto.com

THEORIES OF THE DEVELOPMENT OF SEX DIFFERENCES

Why is it that little girls (often) grow up to behave according to the cultural stereotypes of what it means to be female? Why is it that little boys (often) grow up to behave like male stereotypes?

The Roles of Evolution and Heredity

According to evolutionary psychologists, sex differences were fashioned by natural selection in response to problems in adaptation that were repeatedly encountered by humans over thousands of generations (Buss & Duntley, 2006; Geary, 2006). The story of the survival of our ancient ancestors is etched in our genes. Genes that bestow attributes that increase an organism's chances of surviving to produce viable offspring are most likely to be transmitted to future generations. We thus possess the genetic codes for traits that helped our ancestors survive and reproduce. These traits include structural sex differences, such as those found in the brain, and differences in body chemistry, such as hormones.

The question is whether evolution has also etched social and psychological sex differences into our genes. Consider a sex difference. Males tend to place relatively more emphasis on physical appearance in mate selection than females do, whereas females tend to place relatively more emphasis on personal factors such as financial status and reliability (Brase, 2006). We pursue this question in Chapter 14.

Organization of the Brain

The organization of the brain is largely genetically determined (Collins et al., 2000; Maccoby, 2000). The hemispheres of the brain are specialized to perform certain functions, as noted in Chapter 7. Both males and females have a left hemisphere and a right hemisphere, but the question is whether they use them in quite the same way. Consider the **hippocampus**, a brain structure that is involved in the formation of memories and the relay of incoming sensory information to other parts of the brain (Ohnishi et al., 2006). Matthias Riepe and his colleagues (Grön et al., 2000) have studied the ways in which humans and rats use the hippocampus when they are navigating mazes. Males use the hippocampus in both hemispheres when they

hippocampus a brain structure that is involved in the formation of memories and the relay of incoming sensory information to other parts of the brain.

are navigating (Grön et al., 2000). Women, however, rely on the hippocampus in the right hemisphere along with the right prefrontal cortex, an area of the brain that evaluates information and makes plans. Riepe and his colleagues wonder whether different patterns of brain activities might contribute to preference for using landmarks or maps.

Sex Hormones

Sex hormones and other chemical substances stoke the prenatal differentiation of sex organs. Toward the end of the embryonic stage, androgens—male sex hormones—sculpt the male genital organs. These chemicals may also "masculinize" or "feminize" the brain; that is, give rise to behavioural tendencies that are in some ways consistent with gender-role stereotypes (Cohen-Bendahan et al., 2004; Pei et al., 2006).

Social Cognitive Theory

Social cognitive theorists consider both the roles of rewards and punishments (reinforcement) in gender typing and the ways in which children learn from observing others and decide which behaviours are appropriate for them. Children learn much about what society considers "masculine" or "feminine" by observing and imitating models of the same sex. These models may be their parents, other adults, other children, even characters in electronic media such as TV and video games.

Socialization also plays a role. Parents, teachers, other adults—even other children—provide children with information about the gender-typed behaviours expected of them (Sabattini & Leaper, 2004). Children are rewarded with smiles and respect and companionship when they display "gender-appropriate" behaviour. Children are punished with frowns and loss of friends when they display "inappropriate" behaviour.

Boys are encouraged to be independent, whereas girls are more likely to be restricted. Boys are allowed to roam farther from home at an earlier age and are more likely to be left unsupervised after school (Miller et al., 2006).

Primary-school children show less stereotyping if their mothers frequently engage in traditionally "masculine" tasks such as washing the car, taking children to ball games, or assembling toys (Powlishta, 2004). Maternal employment is associated with less polarized gender-role concepts for girls and boys (Sabattini & Leaper, 2004; Powlishta, 2004).

Cognitive-Developmental Theory

Lawrence Kohlberg (1966) proposed a cognitive-developmental view of gender typing. According to this perspective, children form concepts about gender and then fit their behaviour to the concepts (Martin & Ruble, 2004). These developments occur in stages and are entwined with general cognitive development.

According to Kohlberg, gender typing involves the emergence of three concepts: gender identity, gender stability, and gender constancy. The first step in gender typing is attaining **gender identity**. Gender identity is the knowledge that one is male or female. At 2 years, most children can say whether they are boys or girls. By the age of 3, many children can discriminate anatomic sex differences (Campbell et al., 2004; Ruble et al., 2006).

At around age 4 or 5, most children develop the concept of **gender stability**, according to Kohlberg. They recognize that people retain their sexes for a lifetime. Girls no longer believe that they can grow up to be daddies, and boys no longer think that they can become mommies.

By the age of 5 to 7 years, Kohlberg believes that most children develop the more sophisticated concept of **gender constancy** and recognize that people's sex does not change, even if they change their dress or behaviour. A woman who cuts her hair short remains a woman. A man who dons an apron and cooks remains a man. Once children have

established concepts of gender stability and constancy, they seek to behave in ways that are consistent with their sex (Martin & Ruble, 2004).

Cross-cultural studies in the United States, Samoa, Nepal, Belize, and Kenya have found that the concepts of gender identity, gender stability, and gender constancy emerge in the order predicted by Kohlberg (Leonard & Archer, 1989; Munroe et al., 1984). However, gender constancy and gender-typed play emerge earlier than predicted by Kohlberg. Girls show preferences for dolls and soft toys and boys for hard transportation toys by the age of 1½ to 3 (Alexander, 2003; Campbell et al., 2004; Powlishta, 2004). At this age, children may have a sense of gender identity, but gender stability and gender constancy remain a year or two away.

Gender-Schema Theory

Gender-schema theory proposes that children use sex as one way of organizing their perceptions of the world (Campbell et al., 2004; Martin & Ruble, 2004). A gender schema is a cluster of concepts about male and female physical traits, behaviours, and personality traits. For example, consider the dimension of strength–weakness. Children learn that strength is linked to the male gender-role stereotype and weakness to the female stereotype. They also learn that some dimensions, such

gender identity knowledge that one is female or male.

gender stability the concept that one's sex is unchanging.

gender constancy the concept that one's sex remains the same despite changes in appearance or behaviour.

gender-schema theory the view that one's knowledge of the gender schema in one's society guides one's assumption of gender-typed preferences and behaviour patterns. Psychologically androgynous children and adolescents have better social relations, superior adjustment, and greater creativity.

as strength–weakness, are more relevant to one gender than the other—in this case, to males.

From the viewpoint of gender-schema theory, gender identity alone can inspire "gender-appropriate" behaviour (Ruble et al., 2006). As soon as children understand the labels "girl" and "boy," they seek information concerning gender-typed traits and try to live up to them. A boy may fight back when provoked because boys are expected to do so. A girl may be gentle and kind because that is expected of girls. Both boys' and girls' self-esteem will depend on how they measure up to the gender schema.

Studies indicate that children organize information according to a gender schema. For example, boys show better memory for "masculine" toys, activities, and occupations, whereas girls show better memory for "feminine" toys, activities, and occupations (Martin & Ruble, 2004). However, gender-schema theory does not address the issue of whether biological forces also play a role in gender typing.

PSYCHOLOGICAL ANDROGYNY

Cultural stereotypes tend to polarize females and males. They tend to push females and males to the imagined far ends of a continuum of gender-role traits (Rathus et al., 2008). It is common to label people as masculine or feminine. It

is also common to assume that the more feminine people are, the less masculine they are, and vice versa. That is, the female Canadian Forces helicopter pilot usually is not conceptualized as wearing lipstick or baking. The tough male business executive is not usually conceptualized as changing diapers and playing peek-a-boo. An "emotional" boy who also shows the "feminine" traits of nurturance and tenderness is probably thought of as less masculine than other boys. Outspoken, competitive girls are likely to be seen as not only masculine but also as unfeminine.

However, the traits that supposedly characterize masculinity and femininity can be found within the same individual. That is, people (male or female) who obtain high scores on measures of masculine traits on personality tests can also score high on feminine traits. People with both stereotypical feminine and masculine traits are termed **psychologically androgynous**. People who are high in only stereotypical masculine traits are typed as masculine. People who are high in only stereotypical feminine traits are typed as feminine (Bem, 1993).

Some psychologists suggest that promoting psychological androgyny in children is worthwhile because they will be able to summon up a wider range of traits to meet the challenges in their lives (Lefkowitz & Zeldow, 2006). For example, compared with their masculine or feminine peers, androgynous children and adolescents have better social relations, superior adjustment, greater creativity (Norlander et al., 2000), and more willingness to pursue occupations stereotyped as "belonging" to the other sex (Hebert, 2000).

> As soon as children understand the labels "girl" and "boy," they seek information concerning gender-typed traits and try to live up to them.

Monkey Business Images/Shutterstock

Boys are slightly heavier

and taller than girls through the age of 9 or 10. Girls then begin their adolescent growth spurt.

9

Middle Childhood: Physical and Cognitive Development

Learning Outcomes

LO1 Describe trends in physical development in middle childhood

LO2 Describe changes in motor development in middle childhood

LO3 Discuss ADHD and learning disabilities

LO4 Describe Piaget's concrete-operational stage

LO5 Discuss Piaget's and Kohlberg's theories of moral development

LO6 Describe developments in information processing in middle childhood

LO7 Describe intellectual development in middle childhood, focusing on theories of intelligence

LO8 Describe language development in middle childhood, including reading and bilingualism

LO1 Growth Patterns

following the growth trends of early childhood, boys and girls continue to gain a little over 5 cm (2 in.) in height per year until the adolescent **growth spurt** (see Figure 9.1). The average gain in weight between the ages of 6 and 12 is 2.25 to 3 kg (5 to 7 lb.) a year, but children grow less stocky and more slender (Kuczmarski et al., 2000).

NUTRITION AND GROWTH

In middle childhood, the average child's body weight doubles. Children also spend a good deal of energy in physical activity and play. To fuel this growth and activity, schoolchildren eat more than preschoolers. The average 4- to 6-year-old needs 1,400 calories per day, but the average 7- to 10-year-old requires 2,000 calories, though healthy choices from the Canada Food Guide should be the highest priority when considering nutritional needs in middle childhood.

Nutrition involves more than calories. Good nutrition includes making healthful choices from the Canada Food Guide, including fruits and vegetables, fish, poultry (without skin), and whole grains. Limit the intake of fats, sugar, and starches. However, most foods in school cafeterias and elsewhere are heavy in sugar, animal fats, and salt (Bauer et al., 2004). Portions have also grown over the decades, especially at fast-food restaurants (Nielsen & Popkin, 2003).

> **growth spurt** a period during which growth advances at a dramatically rapid rate compared with other periods.

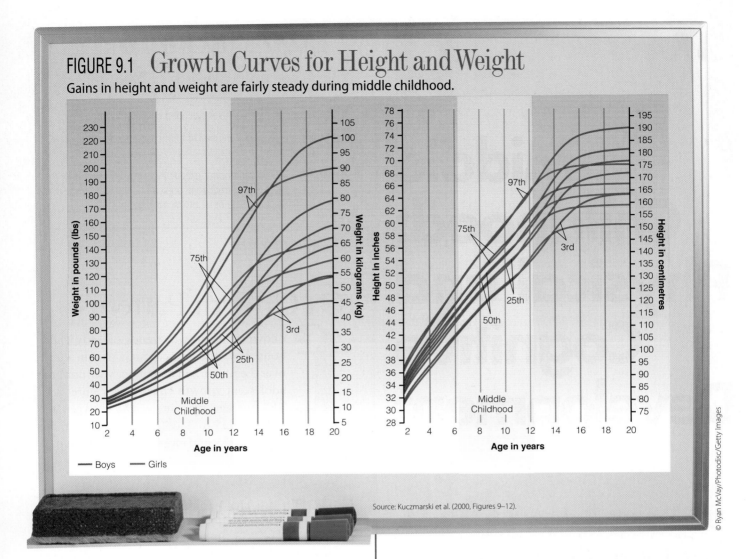

FIGURE 9.1 Growth Curves for Height and Weight

Gains in height and weight are fairly steady during middle childhood.

Boys —— Girls ——

Source: Kuczmarski et al. (2000, Figures 9–12).

© Ryan McVay/Photodisc/Getty Images

Sex Similarities and Differences in Physical Growth

Boys are slightly heavier and taller than girls through the age of 9 or 10 (see Figure 9.1). Girls then begin their adolescent growth spurt and surpass boys in height and weight until about age 13 or 14, when boys spurt and grow taller and heavier than girls. The steady gains in height and weight in middle childhood are paralleled by increased muscle strength in both sexes. Beginning at about age 11, boys develop relatively more muscle, and girls develop relatively more fat.

OVERWEIGHT IN CHILDREN

The Canadian Heart and Stroke Foundation (2008) reports that, in 2004, 8 percent of Canadian children and youth (ages 6 to 11) were obese, and 18 percent were overweight, representing 1 child in 4, or 26 percent (see Figure 9.2). Although parents often assume

D1 "Baby fat" in early childhood can remain a lifelong struggle.
Statistically, most overweight children become overweight adults.

that heavy children will "outgrow" their "baby fat," most overweight children become overweight adults (Daniels, 2006).

Overweight children are often rejected by peers or become a focus of ridicule (Storch et al., 2007). They are usually poor at sports and less likely to be considered attractive in adolescence (Storch et al., 2007). Overweight children are at greater risk of health problems throughout life (American Heart Association, 2007).

© Mike Kemp/Rubberball/Getty Images

Causes of Overweight

Heredity plays a role in being overweight. Some people inherit a tendency to burn up extra calories, whereas others inherit a tendency to turn extra calories into fat (Kolata, 2007).

Family, peers, and environmental factors play roles in children's eating habits (Moens et al., 2007). Overweight parents may serve as examples of poor exercise habits, encourage overeating, and keep unhealthful foods in the home. Dining out frequently can become an unhealthy family habit. Children who watch TV extensively burn fewer calories and are more likely to become overweight adolescents than children who exercise frequently (Schumacher & Queen, 2007).

LO2 Motor Development

the school years are marked by increases in the child's speed, strength, agility, and balance. These developments lead to more skillful motor activities.

GROSS MOTOR SKILLS

Throughout middle childhood, children show steady improvement in their ability to perform gross motor skills. Children are hopping, jumping, and climbing by age 6 or so; by age 6 or 7, they are usually capable of pedalling and balancing on a bicycle. By the ages of 8 to 10, children are showing the balance, coordination, and strength that allow them to engage in gymnastics and team sports. During these years, muscles grow stronger, and neural pathways that connect the cerebellum to the cortex become more myelinated. Experience refines sensorimotor abilities, but some differences are inborn. For example, some people are born with better visual acuity, depth perception, or coordination than others.

Reaction time is basic to the child's timing a swing of the bat or hitting a tennis ball. It gradually improves (decreases) from early childhood to about age 18, but individual differences are common (Karatekin et al., 2007). Reaction time increases again in adulthood.

> **reaction time** the amount of time required to respond to a stimulus.

FINE MOTOR SKILLS

By the age of 6 to 7, children can usually tie their shoelaces, in spite of Velcro, and hold pencils as adults do. Their abilities to fasten buttons, zip zippers, brush teeth, wash themselves, coordinate a knife and fork, and use chopsticks all develop during the early school years and improve during childhood (Beilei et al., 2002).

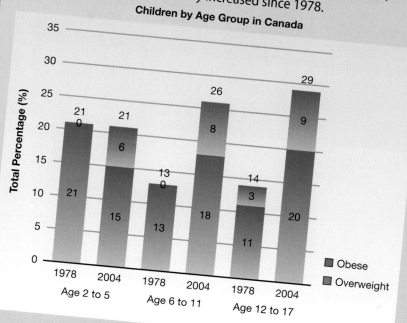

FIGURE 9.2

Overweight Children in Canada

The percentage of overweight and obese children in the age groups of 6–11 and 12–17 has dramatically increased since 1978.

Children by Age Group in Canada

Source: Fig 9.2 Statistics Canada. Overweight and obesity rates, by age group, household population aged 2 to 17, Canada excluding territories, 1978/79 and 2004. 2004 Canadian Community Health Survey: Nutrition; Canada Health Survey 1978/79. http://www.statcan.gc.ca/pub/82-620-m/2005001/c-g/child-enfant/4053584-eng.htm .

SEX DIFFERENCES

Throughout middle childhood, boys and girls perform similarly in most motor activities. Boys show slightly greater strength, especially in their forearms, which aids them in swinging a bat or throwing a ball (Butterfield & Loovis, 1993). Girls show slightly greater limb coordination and overall flexibility, which are valuable in dancing, balancing, and gymnastics (Abdelaziz et al., 2001; Cumming et al., 2005).

At puberty, sex differences favouring boys increase (Smoll & Schultz, 1990). But prior to puberty, boys are more likely than girls to receive social encouragement and opportunities in sports (A. M. Thompson et al., 2003). Between middle childhood and adolescence, children increasingly stereotype physical activities as being masculine (e.g., football) or feminine (e.g., dance) (Meaney et al., 2002).

EXERCISE AND FITNESS

Exercise reduces the risk of heart disease, stroke, diabetes, and certain forms of cancer (Atkinson & Davenne, 2007). Physically active adolescents also have a better self-image and coping skills than those who are inactive (Kirkcaldy et al., 2002). Over half of Canadians aged 5 to 17 are not active enough for optimal growth and development (Heart and Stroke Foundation of Canada, 1993).

Cardiac and muscular fitness are developed by participation in aerobic exercises, such as running, walking quickly, swimming laps, bicycling, or jumping rope for several minutes at a time. However, Canadian schools have seen physical education programming declining over several decades (Physical and Health Education Canada, 2009).

LO3 Children with Disabilities

Certain disabilities of childhood are most apt to be noticed in the middle childhood years, when the child enters school. The school setting requires that a child sit still, pay attention, and master certain academic skills. But some children have difficulty with these demands.

ATTENTION-DEFICIT/HYPERACTIVITY DISORDER (ADHD)

Nine-year-old Eddie is a problem in class. His teacher complains that he is so restless and fidgety that the rest of the class cannot concentrate on their work. He . . . is in constant motion, roaming the classroom, talking to other children while they are working. He has been suspended repeatedly for outrageous behaviour, most recently swinging from a fluorescent light fixture. . . . He has never needed much sleep and always awakened before anyone else in the family, . . . wrecking things in the living room and kitchen. Once, at the age of 4, he unlocked the front door and wandered into traffic, but was rescued by a passerby.

Psychological testing shows Eddie to be average in academic ability but to have a "virtually nonexistent" attention span. He shows no interest in television or in games or toys that require some concentration.

—Adapted from Spitzer et al., 2002

A child who has **attention-deficit/hyperactivity disorder (ADHD)** shows excessive inattention, impulsivity, and **hyperactivity**. The degree of hyperactive behaviour is crucial because many normal children are overactive and fidgety from time to time.

ADHD typically occurs by age 7. The hyperactivity and restlessness impair children's ability to function in school. They cannot sit still and have difficulty getting along with others. ADHD is diagnosed in about 1–5 percent of school-age children and is many times more common in boys than girls.

ADHD is sometimes "overdiagnosed" (Weisler & Sussman, 2007). Some children who misbehave in school are diagnosed with ADHD and medicated to encourage more acceptable behaviour (Reddy & De Thomas, 2007).

Causes of ADHD

ADHD may have a genetic component, involving the brain chemical dopamine (Thapar et al., 2007; Walitza et al., 2006). Studies in brain imaging have found differences in the brain chemistry of children with ADHD.

Though in the 1970s a widely held view was that ADHD was related to food additives, researchers now generally agree that food colouring and preservatives do not cause ADHD (Cruz & Bahna, 2006). Joel Nigg and his colleagues (2006) note that ADHD is due to a lack of executive control of the brain over motor and more primitive functions.

> **D2** Chemical food additives are not a cause of hyperactivity.
> Though in the 1970s a widely held view was that ADHD was related to food additives, researchers now generally agree that food colouring and preservatives do not cause ADHD.

Treatment and Outcome

Stimulants such as Ritalin are the most widespread treatment for ADHD. These stimulants promote the activity of the brain chemicals dopamine and noradrenaline, which stimulate the "executive centre" of the brain to control more primitive areas of the brain. Stimulants increase children's attention span and improve their academic performance (Posey et al., 2007). Most children with ADHD continue to have problems in attention, conduct, or learning in adolescence and adulthood (Nigg et al., 2004).

> **D3** Stimulants are often used to treat children who are already hyperactive.
> Stimulants such as Ritalin are the most widespread treatment for ADHD.

LEARNING DISABILITIES

Some children who are intelligent and provided with enriched home environments encounter difficulties learning how to read (**dyslexia**) or when attempting to solve simple math problems. Many such children have **learning disabilities**. Learning-disabled children may show problems in math, writing, or reading, in spite of scoring in the average range for intelligence on IQ tests. Some have difficulties in articulating the sounds of speech or in understanding spoken language. Others have problems in motor coordination. Children are usually diagnosed with a learning disability when they are performing below the level expected for their age and intelligence, and when the child shows no evidence of other handicaps such as vision or hearing problems, retardation, or socioeconomic disadvantage (Joshi, 2003; Lyon et al., 2003). Learning disabilities may persist through life, but early recognition and remediation can help many

children to learn how to compensate for their disability (Vellutino et al., 2004).

According to the Canadian Dyslexia Centre (CDC) (n.d.), an estimated 1 in 6 Canadians has dyslexia. Many more, however, may have undiagnosed dyslexia, which is a major cause of illiteracy. Figure 9.3 shows a writing sample from a dyslexic child.

stimulants drugs that increase the activity of the nervous system.

dyslexia a reading disorder characterized by letter reversals, mirror reading, slow reading, and reduced comprehension.

learning disabilities disorders characterized by inadequate development of specific academic, language, and speech skills.

Origins of Dyslexia

Theories of dyslexia focus on the ways in which sensory and neurological problems may contribute to the reading problems we find in dyslexic individuals. Genetic factors appear to be involved; 25–65 percent of children who have one dyslexic parent are dyslexic themselves (Plomin & Walker, 2003). About 40 percent of the siblings of children with dyslexia are dyslexic.

Genetic factors may give rise to neurological problems or circulation problems in the left hemisphere of the brain (Grigorenko, 2007). The circulation problems would result in oxygen deficiency. The part of the brain

FIGURE 9.3
Writing Sample of a Dyslexic Child
Dyslexic children may perceive letters as upside down (confusing *w* with *m*) or reversed (confusing *b* with *d*), leading to rotations or reversals in writing, as shown here.

called the angular gyrus "translates" visual information, such as written words, into auditory information (sounds). Problems in the angular gyrus may give rise to reading problems by making it difficult for the reader to associate letters with sounds (Grigorenko, 2007; Shaywitz et al., 2006b).

Most researchers also focus on *phonological processing*. That is, dyslexic children may not discriminate sounds as accurately as other children do (Halliday & Bishop, 2006). As a result, *b*'s and *d*'s and *p*'s may be hard to tell apart, creating confusion that impairs reading ability (Shaywitz et al., 2006a).

EDUCATING CHILDREN WHO HAVE DISABILITIES

In childhood, treatment of dyslexia focuses on remediation (Bakker, 2006). Children are given highly structured exercises to help them become aware of how to blend sounds to form words, such as by identifying word pairs that rhyme and do not rhyme. Later in life, the focus tends to be on accommodation rather than on remediation. For example, postsecondary students who have dyslexia may be allowed extra time to do the reading involved in taking tests.

Evidence is mixed on whether placing children with disabilities in separate classes can also stigmatize them and segregate them from other children. In **mainstreaming**, children with disabilities are placed in regular classrooms that have been adapted to their needs. Most students who have mild learning disabilities spend most of their school day in regular classrooms (Fergusson, 2007).

LO4 Cognitive Development

did you hear the one about the judge who pounded her gavel and yelled, "Order! Order in the court!"? "A hamburger and French fries, Your Honour," responded the defendant. Such children's jokes are based on ambiguities in the meanings of words and phrases. Most 7-year-olds will find the joke about order in the court funny because

they recognize that the word *order* has more than one meaning. At about the age of 11, children can understand ambiguities in grammatical structure. Children make enormous strides in their cognitive development during middle childhood as their thought processes and language become more logical and complex.

© Florin C/Shutterstock

PIAGET: THE CONCRETE-OPERATIONAL STAGE

According to Jean Piaget, the typical child is entering the stage of **concrete operations** by the age of 7. In this stage, which lasts until about 12, children show the beginnings of adult logic but generally focus on tangible objects rather than abstract ideas, which is why they are known as "concrete" operations.

Concrete-operational thought is reversible and flexible. Adding the numbers 2 and 3 to get 5 is an operation. Subtracting 2 from 5 to get 3 reverses the operation. Subtracting 3 from 5 to get 2 demonstrates flexibility.

Concrete-operational children are less egocentric than preoperational children. They recognize that people see things in different ways because of different situations and values. Concrete-operational children also engage in **decentration**. They can focus on multiple parts of a problem at once.

Conservation

Concrete-operational children show understanding of the laws of conservation. A 7-year-old child would say that the flattened ball of clay from the example in

Chapter 7 still has the same amount of clay as the round one "because you can roll it up again." The concrete-operational child knows that objects can have several properties or dimensions. By attending to both the height and the width of the clay, the child recognizes that the loss in height compensates for the gain in width.

Transitivity

If your parents are older than you are, and you are older than your children, are your parents older than your children? The answer, of course, is yes. But how did you arrive at this answer? If you said yes simply on the basis of knowing that your parents are older than your children (e.g., 58 and 56 compared with 5 and 3), your answer did not require concrete-operational thought. One aspect of concrete-operational is the principle of **transitivity**: If A exceeds B in some property (say, age or height) and if B exceeds C, then A must also exceed C.

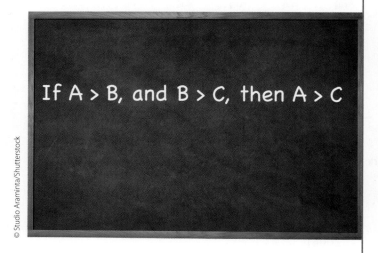

If A > B, and B > C, then A > C

© Studio Araminta/Shutterstock

Researchers can assess whether children understand the principle of transitivity by asking them to place objects in a series, or order, according to some property, such as lining up one's family members according to age, height, or weight. Placing objects in a series is termed **seriation**. Consider some examples with pre-operational and concrete-operational children.

Piaget assessed children's abilities at seriation by asking them to place 10 sticks in order of size. Children who are aged 4 to 5 usually place the sticks in a random sequence, or in small groups, as in small, medium, or large. But consider the approach of 7- and 8-year-olds who are capable of concrete operations. They look over the array, then select either the longest or shortest and place it at the point from which they will begin. Then they select the next longest (or shortest) and continue until the task is complete.

Concrete-operational children also have the decentration capacity to allow them to seriate in two dimensions at once, unlike pre-operational children. Consider a seriation task used by Piaget and Inhelder. In this test, children are given 49 leaves and asked to classify them according to size and brightness (from small to large and from dark to light) (see Figure 9.4 on page 172). As the grid is completed from left to right, the leaves become lighter. As the grid is filled in from top to bottom, the leaves become larger.

transitivity the principle that if A > B and B > C, then A > C.

seriation placing objects in an order or series according to a property or trait.

Class Inclusion

In Chapter 7, a 4-year-old was shown pictures of four cats and six dogs. When asked whether there were more dogs or more animals, she said more dogs. This pre-operational child apparently could not focus on the two subclasses (dogs and cats) and the larger subclass (animals) at the same time. But concrete-operational children can do so. Therefore, they are more likely to correctly answer the question about the dogs and the animals (Chapman & McBride, 1992).

Applications of Piaget's Theory to Education

Piaget believed that learning involves active discovery. Also, instruction should be geared to the child's level of development. When teaching a concrete-operational child about fractions, for example, the teacher should not only lecture but should also allow the child to divide concrete objects into parts. Third, Piaget believed that learning to take into account the perspectives of others is a key ingredient in the development of both cognition and morality.

LO5 Moral Development: The Child as Judge

On a cognitive level, moral development concerns the basis on which children judge that an act is right or wrong. Jean Piaget and Lawrence Kohlberg believed that moral reasoning undergoes the same cognitive-developmental pattern around the world. The moral considerations that children weigh at a given age may be influenced by the values of the cultural settings in which they are reared, but also reflect the orderly unfolding of cognitive processes (Lapsley, 2006). Moral reasoning is related to the child's overall cognitive development.

PIAGET'S THEORY OF MORAL DEVELOPMENT

Piaget observed children playing games such as marbles and making judgments on the seriousness of the wrongdoing of characters in stories. On the basis of these observations, he concluded that children's moral judgments develop in two overlapping stages: moral realism and autonomous morality (Piaget, 1932).

The first stage is usually referred to as the stage of **moral realism**, or **objective morality**. During this stage, which emerges at about the age of 5, children consider behaviour correct when it conforms either to authority or to the rules of the game. When asked why something should be done in a certain way, the 5-year-old may answer "Because that's the way to do it" or "Because my Mommy says so." Five-year-olds perceive rules as embedded in the structure of things. Rules, to them, reflect ultimate reality, hence the term *moral realism*. Rules and the notions of right and wrong are seen as absolute, not as deriving from people to meet social needs.

Another consequence of viewing rules as embedded in the fabric of the world is **immanent justice**, or automatic retribution. This view involves thinking that negative experiences are punishment for prior misdeeds,

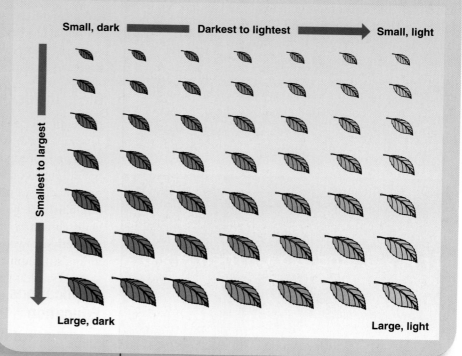

FIGURE 9.4
A Grid for Demonstrating the Development of Seriation

To classify these leaves, children must focus on two dimensions at once: size and lightness. They must also understand the principle of *transitivity*—that if A > B and B > C, then A > C.

Small, dark — Darkest to lightest → Small, light

Smallest to largest

Large, dark   Large, light

even when realistic causal links are absent (Callan et al., 2006).

Preoperational children tend to focus on only one dimension at a time. Therefore, they judge the wrongness

For a 5-year-old, rules reflect ultimate reality.

© Alan Crosthwaite/World of Stock

of an act only in terms of the amount of damage done, not in terms of the intentions of the wrongdoer. Consider children's response to Piaget's story about the broken cups. Piaget told children a story in which one child breaks 15 cups accidentally and another child breaks one cup deliberately. Children in the stage of moral realism typically say that the child who did the most damage is the naughtiest and should be punished most (Piaget, 1932).

Piaget found that when children reach the ages of 9 to 11, they begin to show **autonomous morality**. Their moral judgments tend to become more self-governed, as children come to view social rules as social agreements that can be changed, or even negotiated. Children realize that circumstances can warrant breaking rules. Children who show autonomous morality can focus simultaneously on multiple dimensions, so they consider social rules and the motives of the wrongdoer.

Children in this stage also show a greater capacity to take the point of view of others, to empathize with them. Decentration and increased empathy prompt children to weigh the intentions of the wrongdoer more heavily than the amount of damage done. The child who broke one cup deliberately may be seen as deserving of more punishment than the child who broke 15 cups accidentally. Accidents are less likely to be considered crimes.

KOHLBERG'S THEORY OF MORAL DEVELOPMENT

Kohlberg (1981, 1985) advanced the cognitive-developmental theory of moral development by elaborating on the kinds of information children use and on the complexities of moral reasoning. Before we discuss Kohlberg's views, read the tale that Kohlberg used in his research and answer the questions that follow.

In Europe, a woman was near death from a special kind of cancer. There was one drug that the doctors thought might save her. It was a form of radium that a druggist in the same town had recently discovered. The drug was expensive to make, but the druggist was charging 10 times what the drug cost him to make. He paid $200 for the radium and charged $2,000 for a small dose of the drug. The sick woman's husband, Heinz, went to everyone he knew to borrow the money, but he could only get together about $1,000 which was half of what it cost. He told the druggist that his wife was dying and asked him to sell it cheaper or let him pay later. But the druggist said: "No, I discovered the drug and I'm going to make money from it." So

Heinz got desperate and broke into the man's store to steal the drug for his wife.
—*Kohlberg (1969)*

autonomous morality
the second stage in Piaget's cognitive-developmental theory of moral development, in which children base moral judgments on the intentions of the wrongdoer and on the amount of damage done.

Kohlberg emphasized the importance of being able to view the moral world from the perspective of another person (Krebs & Denton, 2005). Look at this situation from Heinz's perspective. What do you think? Should Heinz have tried to steal the drug? Was he right or wrong? As you can see from Table 9.1, the issue is more complicated than a simple yes or no. Heinz is caught in a moral dilemma in which legal or social rules (in this case, laws against stealing) are pitted against a strong human need (Heinz's desire to save his wife). According to Kohlberg's theory, children and adults arrive at yes or no answers for different reasons. These reasons can be classified according to the level of moral development they reflect.

Children (and adults) are faced with many moral dilemmas. Consider cheating in school. When children fear failing a test, they may be tempted to cheat. Different children may decide not to cheat for different reasons. One child may fear getting caught. Another may decide that it is more important to live up to her moral principles than to get the highest possible grade. In each case, the child's decision is not to cheat. However, the decisions reflect different levels of reasoning.

TABLE 9.1
Kohlberg's Levels and Stages of Moral Development

STAGE OF DEVELOPMENT	EXAMPLES OF MORAL REASONING THAT SUPPORT HEINZ'S STEALING THE DRUG	EXAMPLES OF MORAL REASONING THAT OPPOSE HEINZ'S STEALING THE DRUG
LEVEL I: PRECONVENTIONAL—TYPICALLY BEGINS IN EARLY CHILDHOOD[a]		
Stage 1: Judgments guided by obedience and the prospect of punishment (the consequences of the behaviour)	It is not wrong to take the drug. Heinz did try to pay the druggist for it, and it is only worth $200, not $2,000.	Taking things without paying is wrong because it is against the law. Heinz will get caught and go to jail.
Stage 2: Naively egoistic, instrumental orientation (things are right when they satisfy people's needs)	Heinz ought to take the drug because his wife really needs it. He can always pay the druggist back.	Heinz should not take the drug. If he gets caught and winds up in jail, it won't do his wife any good.
LEVEL II: CONVENTIONAL—TYPICALLY BEGINS IN MIDDLE CHILDHOOD		
Stage 3: Good-boy/good-girl orientation (moral behaviour helps others and is socially approved)	Stealing is a crime, so it is bad, but Heinz should take the drug to save his wife or else people would blame him for letting her die.	Stealing is a crime. Heinz should not just take the drug because his family will be dishonoured and they will blame him.
Stage 4: Law-and-order orientation (moral behaviour is doing one's duty and showing respect for authority)	Heinz must take the drug to do his duty to save his wife. Eventually, he has to pay the druggist for it, however.	If we all took the law into our own hands, civilization would fall apart, so Heinz should not steal the drug.
LEVEL III: POSTCONVENTIONAL—TYPICALLY BEGINS IN ADOLESCENCE[b]		
Stage 5: Contractual, legalistic orientation (one must weigh pressing human needs against society's need to maintain social order)	This situation is complicated because society has a right to maintain law and order, but Heinz has to take the drug to save his wife.	I can see why Heinz feels he has to take the drug, but laws exist for the benefit of society as a whole and cannot simply be cast aside.
Stage 6: Universal ethical principles orientation (people must follow universal ethical principles and their own conscience, even if it means breaking the law)	In this case, the law comes into conflict with the principle of the sanctity of human life. Heinz must take the drug because his wife's life is more important than the law.	If Heinz truly believes that stealing the drug is worse than letting his wife die, he should not take it. People have to make sacrifices to do what they think is right.

[a]Tends to be used less often in middle childhood.
[b]May not develop at all.

Kohlberg argued that the developmental stages of moral reasoning follow the same sequence in all children. Children progress at different rates, and not everyone reaches the highest stage. But children must experience Stage 1 before Stage 2, and so on. Kohlberg theorizes three levels of moral development and two stages within each level.

The Preconventional Level

At the **preconventional level**, children base their moral judgments on the consequences of their behaviour. Stage 1 is oriented toward obedience and punishment. Good behaviour means being obedient so one can avoid punishment. In Stage 2, good behaviour allows people to satisfy their own needs and, perhaps, the needs of others. In a study of children age 7 through 16, Kohlberg (1963) found that Stage 1 and 2 types of moral judgments were offered most frequently by 7- and 10-year-olds. Stage 1 and 2 judgments fell off steeply after age 10.

The Conventional Level

At the **conventional level** of moral reasoning, right and wrong are judged by conformity to conventional (family, religious, societal) standards of right and wrong. According to the Stage 3 "good-boy/good-girl orientation," it is good to meet the needs and expectations of others. Moral behaviour is what is "normal," what the majority does. In Stage 4, moral judgments are based on rules that maintain the social order. Showing respect for authority and duty is valued highly. Many people do not develop beyond the conventional level. Kohlberg (1963) found that Stage 3 and 4 types of judgments emerge during middle childhood. They are all but absent among 7-year-olds. However, they are reported by about 20 percent of 10-year-olds and by a higher percentages of adolescents.

The Postconventional Level

At the **postconventional level**, moral reasoning is based on the person's own moral standards. If this level of reasoning develops at all, it is found among adolescents and adults (see Table 9.1).

LO6 Information Processing: Learning, Remembering, Problem Solving

Key elements in children's information processing include the following (Pressley & Hilden, 2006):

- Development of selective attention
- Development of the capacity of memory and of children's understanding of the processes of memory
- Development of the ability to solve problems, such as by finding the correct formula and applying it

DEVELOPMENT OF SELECTIVE ATTENTION

Children's ability to focus their attention and screen out distractions advances steadily through middle childhood (Rubia et al., 2006). Preoperational children engaged in problem solving tend to focus (or centre) their attention on one element of the problem at a time, which is a major reason they lack conservation. Concrete-operational children can attend to multiple aspects of the problem at once, permitting them to conserve number and volume.

An experiment illustrates how selective attention and the ability to ignore distraction develop during middle childhood. The researchers (Strutt et al., 1975) asked children between 6 and 12 years of age to sort a deck of cards as quickly as possible on the basis of the figures depicted on each card (e.g., circle versus square). In one condition, only the relevant dimension (i.e., form) was shown on each card. In another condition, a dimension not relevant to the sorting also was present (e.g., a horizontal or vertical line in the figure). In a third condition,

preconventional level according to Kohlberg, a period during which moral judgments are based largely on expectations of rewards or punishments.

conventional level according to Kohlberg, a period during which moral judgments largely reflect social rules and conventions.

postconventional level according to Kohlberg, a period during which moral judgments are derived from moral principles and people look to themselves to set moral standards.

sensory memory the structure of memory first encountered by sensory input. Information is maintained in sensory memory for only a fraction of a second.

sensory register another term for sensory memory.

working memory the structure of memory that can hold a sensory stimulus for up to 30 seconds after the trace decays.

encode to transform sensory input into a form that is more readily processed.

rehearse repeat.

long-term memory the memory structure capable of relatively permanent storage of information.

two irrelevant dimensions were present (e.g., a star above or below the figure, in addition to a horizontal or vertical line in the figure). As seen in Figure 9.5, the irrelevant information interfered with sorting ability for all age groups, but older children were much less affected than younger children.

DEVELOPMENTS IN THE STORAGE AND RETRIEVAL OF INFORMATION

Psychologists use the term *memory* to refer to the processes of storing and retrieving information. Many psychologists divide memory functioning into three major processes or structures: sensory memory, working memory, and long-term memory (see Figure 9.6).

Sensory Memory

When we look at an object and then blink our eyes, the visual impression of the object lasts for a fraction of a second in what is called **sensory memory**, or the **sensory register**. Then the "trace" of the stimulus decays. The concept of sensory memory applies to all the senses. For example, when we are introduced to somebody, the trace of the sound of the name also decays, but we can remember the name by focusing on it.

Working Memory (Short-Term Memory)

When children focus on a stimulus in the sensory register, it tends to be retained in **working memory** (also called *short-term memory*) for up to 30 seconds after the trace of the stimulus decays. Ability to maintain information in short-term memory depends on cognitive strategies and on capacity to continue to perceive a vanished stimulus. Memory function in middle childhood seems largely adult-like in organization and strategies and shows only quantitative improvement through early adolescence (Alloway et al., 2004; Archibald & Gathercole, 2006).

Auditory stimuli can be maintained longer in short-term memory than visual stimuli. For this reason, one strategy for promoting memory is to **encode** visual stimuli as sounds. Then the sounds can be repeated out loud or mentally. In Figure 9.6, mentally repeating or **rehearsing** the sound of Linda's name helps the other girl remember it.

Long-Term Memory

Think of **long-term memory** as a vast storehouse of information containing names, dates, places, what Johnny did to you in Grade 2, what Alyssa said about you when you were 12. Long-term memories may last days, years, or, for practical purposes, a lifetime.

There is no known limit to the amount of information that can be stored in long-term memory. From time to time, we

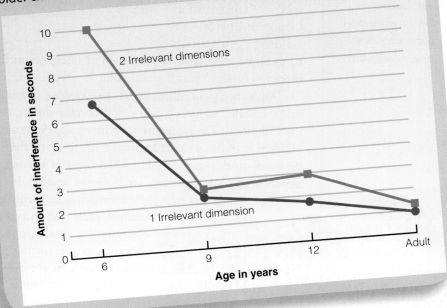

FIGURE 9.5
Development of the Ability to Ignore Distractions

Irrelevant information interfered with sorting ability for all age groups, but older children are less affected than younger ones.

Source: Strutt et al. (1975).

FIGURE 9.6
The Structure of Memory

Many psychologists divide memory into three processes or "structures." Sensory information enters sensory memory, where memory traces are held briefly before decaying. If we attend to the information, much of it is transferred to working memory (also called short-term memory), where it may decay or be displaced if it is not transferred to long-term memory. We may use rehearsal (repetition) or elaborative strategies to transfer memories to long-term memory, from which memories can be retrieved with the proper cues.

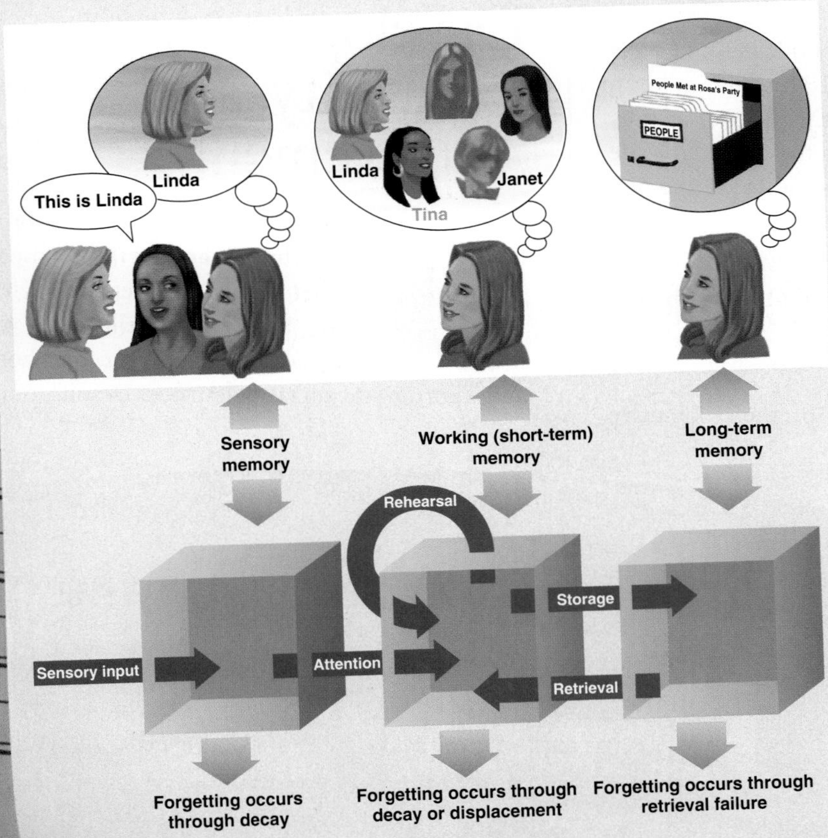
This is Linda
Linda
Linda
Janet
Tina
People Met at Rosa's Party
PEOPLE
Sensory memory
Working (short-term) memory
Long-term memory
Rehearsal
Storage
Sensory input
Attention
Retrieval
Forgetting occurs through decay
Forgetting occurs through decay or displacement
Forgetting occurs through retrieval failure

HDEV *Go to www.icanhdev.com to access an interactive version of this figure.*

may seem to have forgotten, or lost, a long-term memory, such as the names of elementary or high school classmates. But it is more likely that we cannot find the right cues to retrieve it. It is "lost" in the same way we misplace an object but know it is still in the house.

Older children are more likely than younger children to use rote rehearsal, or repetition, to try to remember information (Saito & Miyake, 2004; Towse & Cowan, 2005). A more effective method than rote rehearsal is to purposefully relate new material to well-known information, making it meaningful. Relating new material to known material is called an **elaborative strategy**. English teachers use an elaborative strategy when they have children use new words in sentences to help remember them.

elaborative strategy a method for increasing retention of new information by relating it to well-known information.

Organization in Long-Term Memory

As children's knowledge of concepts advances, the storehouse of their long-term memory becomes organized according to categories. Preschoolers tend to organize their memories by grouping objects that share the same function (Lucariello et al., 2004; Towse, 2003). "Toast" may be grouped with "peanut butter sandwich" because both are edible. In middle childhood toast and peanut butter are likely to be joined as foods.

When items are correctly categorized in long-term memory, children are more likely to recall accurate information about them. For instance, do you remember whether whales breathe underwater? If you did not know that whales are mammals or if you knew nothing about mammals, a correct answer might depend on an instance of rote learning. If children have incorrectly classified whales as fish, they might search their memories and construct the wrong answer.

Knowledge in a particular area increases the capacity to store and retrieve related information. Chess experts are superior to amateurs at remembering where chess pieces have been placed on the board (Gobet & Simon, 2000). In these studies, the experts were 8- to 12-year-old children and the amateurs were adults!

metacognition awareness of and control of one's cognitive abilities.

metamemory knowledge of the functions and processes involved in one's storage and retrieval of information.

intelligence defined by Wechsler as the "capacity … to understand the world [and the] resourcefulness to cope with its challenges."

DEVELOPMENT OF RECALL MEMORY

Children's memory is a good overall indicator of their cognitive ability (Gathercole et al., 2004a, 2004b; Towse & Cowan, 2005). In an experiment on categorization and memory, researchers placed objects that fell into four categories (furniture, clothing, tools, fruit) on a table before Grade twos and Grade fours (Hasselhorn, 1992). The children were allowed 3 minutes to arrange the pictures as they wished and to remember as many as they could. Grade fours were more likely to categorize and recall the pictures than Grade twos.

DEVELOPMENT OF METACOGNITION AND METAMEMORY

Children's knowledge and control of their cognitive abilities is termed **metacognition**. The development of metacognition is shown by the ability to formulate problems, awareness of the processes required to solve a problem, activation of cognitive strategies, maintaining focus on the problem, and checking answers.

When a sixth-grader decides which homework assignments to do first, memorizes the provincial and territorial capitals for tomorrow's test, and then tests herself to see which ones she needs to study more, she is displaying metacognition (Flavell et al., 2002; Stright et al., 2001). **Metamemory** is an aspect of metacognition that refers to children's awareness of the functioning of their memory. Older students are more likely to accurately assess their knowledge. As a result, older

children store and retrieve information more effectively (Towse & Cowan, 2005).

Older children also show more knowledge of strategies that can be used to facilitate memory. Preschoolers will usually use rehearsal if someone suggests they use it, but not until about the age of 6 or 7 do children use it on their own (Flavell et al., 2002). As children develop, they are more likely to use selective rehearsal to remember important information.

LO7 Intellectual Development, Creativity, and Achievement

a t an early age, we gain impressions of how **intelligent** we are compared with other family members and schoolmates. We associate intelligence with academic success, advancement on the job, and appropriate social behaviour. Despite our sense of

Children's Eyewitness Testimony

J ean Piaget distinctly "remembered" an attempt to kidnap him from his baby carriage as he was being wheeled along the Champs Élysées. He recalled the excited throng, the abrasions on the face of the nurse who rescued him, the police officer's white baton, and the flight of the assailant. Although Piaget's memories were graphic, they were false. Years later, the nurse admitted that she had made up the tale.

The child witness is typically asked questions to prompt information. But such questions may be "leading"; that is, they may suggest an answer. For example, "What happened at school?" is not a leading question, but "Did your teacher touch you?" is. Can children's testimony be distorted by leading questions? It appears that by the age of 10 or 11, children are no more suggestible than adults, but younger children are more likely to be misled (Bruck et al., 2006; Krackow & Lynn, 2003). Research also indicates that repeated questioning may lead children to make up events that never happened to them (Roebers & Schneider, 2002).

What, then, are investigators to do when the only witnesses to criminal events are children? Maggie Bruck and her colleagues (2006) recommend that interviewers avoid leading or suggestive questions to minimize influencing the child's response.

Newfoundland and Labrador - St. John's

Nova Scotia - Halifax

Prince Edward Island - Charlottetown

New Brunswick - Fredericton

Quebec - Quebec City

Ontario - Toronto

Manitoba - Winnipeg

Saskatchewan - Regina

Alberta - Edmonton

British Columbia - Victoria

Yukon Territories - Whitehorse

Northwest Territories - Yellowknife

Nunavut - Iqaluit

© Nicole Hill/Rubberball/Jupiterimages

familiarity with the concept of intelligence, intelligence cannot be seen, touched, or measured physically. For this reason, intelligence is subject to various interpretations.

Intelligence is usually perceived as a child's underlying competence or *learning ability*, whereas **achievement** involves a child's acquired competencies or *performance*. Most psychologists also would agree that many of the competencies underlying intelligence are seen during middle childhood, when most children are first exposed to formal schooling.

THEORIES OF INTELLIGENCE

Let's consider some theoretical approaches to intelligence. Then we will see how researchers and practitioners assess intellectual functioning.

Factor Theories

Many investigators view intelligence as consisting of one or more major mental abilities, or factors. In 1904, Charles Spearman suggested that the behaviours we consider intelligent have a common underlying factor g—"general intelligence," which represents broad reasoning and problem-solving abilities, and that specific capacities, or s factors, account for certain individual abilities, like music or poetry (Lubinski, 2004).

Psychologist Louis Thurstone (1938) believed that intelligence consists of several specific factors, or *primary mental abilities*, such as the ability to learn the meaning of words and visual–spatial abilities.

Thurstone's research suggested that these factors tended to be independent.

Sternberg's Theory of Intelligence

Psychologist Robert Sternberg (Sternberg, 2000) constructed a three-part, or "triarchic," theory of intelligence. The parts are *analytical intelligence*, *creative intelligence*, and *practical intelligence* (see Figure 9.7). Analytical intelligence is academic ability. Creative intelligence is defined by the abilities to cope with novel situations and to profit from experience. Practical intelligence, or "street smarts," enables people to adapt to the demands of their environment, including the social environment.

Gardner's Theory of Multiple Intelligences

Psychologist Howard Gardner (1983, 2006), like Sternberg, believes that intelligence—or intelligences—reflect more than academic ability. Gardner refers to each kind of intelligence in his theory as "an intelligence" because each differs in quality (see Figure 9.8 on page 181).

Three of Gardner's intelligences are verbal ability, logical–mathematical reasoning, and spatial intelligence (visual–spatial skills). Others include bodily–kinesthetic intelligence (as shown by dancers and gymnasts), musical intelligence, interpersonal intelligence (as shown by empathy and ability to relate to others), and personal knowledge (self-insight). Individuals may show great "intelligence" in one area without notable abilities in others. Critics agree that many people have special talents, as in music, but they question whether such talents are "intelligences" (Neisser et al., 1996).

MEASUREMENT OF INTELLECTUAL DEVELOPMENT

Although people may disagree about the nature of intelligence, thousands of intelligence tests are administered by psychologists and educators every day.

The Stanford–Binet Intelligence Scale (SBIS) and the Wechsler scales for children and adults are the most widely used and well-respected intelligence tests. The SBIS and Wechsler scales yield scores called **intelligence quotients (IQs)**. The concept of intelligence per se is more difficult to define. The SBIS and Wechsler scales

> **achievement** that which is attained by one's efforts and presumed to be made possible by one's abilities.
>
> **intelligence quotient (IQ)** (1) a ratio obtained by dividing a child's mental age on an intelligence test by his or her chronological age; (2) a score on an intelligence test.

FIGURE 9.7
Sternberg's Triarchic Theory of Intelligence

Robert Sternberg views intelligence as three-pronged: as having analytical, creative, and practical aspects.

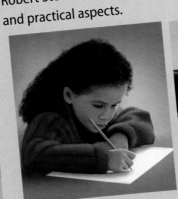

Analytical intelligence
(academic ability)
Abilities to solve problems, compare and contrast, judge, evaluate, and criticize

Creative intelligence
(creativity and insight)
Abilities to invent, discover, suppose, and theorize

Practical intelligence
("street smarts")
Abilities to adapt to the demands of one's environment and apply knowledge in practical situations

have been carefully developed and revised over the years. Each of them has been used to make vital decisions about children's education. In many cases, children whose test scores fall below or above certain scores are placed in special classes for cognitively challenged or gifted children, respectively.

The Stanford–Binet Intelligence Scale

The SBIS originated about a century ago, when Frenchmen Alfred Binet and Theodore Simon worked for the French public school system. Binet assumed that intelligence increased with age. Therefore, older children should answer more items correctly. Thus, Binet arranged a series of questions in order of difficulty, from easier to harder. These questions have since undergone revision and refinement.

The Binet–Simon scale yielded a score called a **mental age (MA)**. The MA shows the intellectual level at which a child is functioning. A child with an MA of 6 is functioning, intellectually, like the average 6-year-old child.

Louis Terman adapted the Binet–Simon scale for use with American children in 1916. Because Terman carried out his work at Stanford University, it is now named the Stanford–Binet Intelligence Scale. The SBIS yielded an intelligence quotient, or IQ, rather than an MA. The SBIS today can be used with children from the age of 2 up to adults. Table 9.2 on page 182 shows the kinds of items associated with various ages.

The IQ states the relationship between a child's mental age and his or her actual or **chronological age (CA)**. An MA of 8 is an above-average score for a 6-year-old but a below-average score for a 10-year-old.

The IQ is computed by the formula

$$IQ = \frac{\text{Mental Age (MA)}}{\text{Chronological Age (CA)}} \times 100$$

According to this formula, a child with an MA of 6 and a CA of 6 would have an IQ of 100. Furthermore, because of the factor of chronological age in the formula, children of different ages might answer the same items on a test in the same way but end up receiving different IQ scores.

Today, IQ scores on the SBIS are derived by comparing children's and adults' performances with those of other people of the same age. People who answer more items correctly than the average for their age group attain IQ scores above 100, and people who answer fewer items correctly attain scores below 100.

In 1905, in France, Alfred Binet and Theodore Simon introduced the idea of measuring intelligence. This version of the test was produced in 1937 by Lewis Terman and Maude Merrill in the United States and was specifically designed for younger children.

© SSPL/The Image Works

FIGURE 9.8

Gardner's Theory of Multiple Intelligences

Gardner argues that there are many intelligences, and that each has its neurological bases in its own parts of the brain.

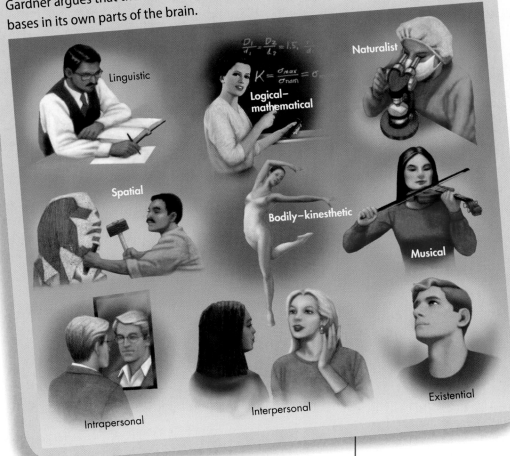

Linguistic

Logical–mathematical

Naturalist

Spatial

Bodily–kinesthetic

Musical

Intrapersonal

Interpersonal

Existential

cultural bias a factor hypothesized to be present in intelligence tests that provides an advantage for test takers from certain cultural backgrounds.

culture-free descriptive of a test in which cultural biases have been removed.

type of task (such as defining words) with another (such as using blocks to construct geometric designs). The Wechsler scales thus suggest children's strengths and weaknesses and provide overall measures of intellectual functioning.

Wechsler described some subtests as measuring verbal tasks and others as assessing performance tasks. In general, verbal subtests require knowledge of verbal concepts, whereas performance subtests (see Figure 9.9 on page 184) require familiarity with spatial-relations concepts. Wechsler's scales permit the computation of verbal and performance IQs.

Figure 9.10 on page 185 indicates the labels that Wechsler assigned to various IQ scores and the approximate percentages of the population who attain IQ scores at those levels. Most children's IQ scores cluster around the average. Only about 5 percent of the population have IQ scores above 130 or below 70.

D4 Two children can answer exactly the same items on an intelligence test correctly, yet one can be above average in intelligence and the other below average.
This is true, because IQ tests include both mental age and chronological age as factors when calculating IQ.

The Wechsler Scales

David Wechsler (1975) developed a series of scales for use with school-age children (Wechsler Intelligence Scale for Children; WISC), younger children (Wechsler Preschool and Primary Scale of Intelligence; WPPSI), and adults (Wechsler Adult Intelligence Scale; WAIS).

The Wechsler scales group test questions into subtests (such as those shown in Table 9.3 on page 183) which measure different intellectual tasks. For this reason, subtests compare a person's performance on one

The Testing Controversy

Most psychologists and educational specialists consider intelligence tests to be at least to some degree biased against minority groups and members of lower social classes (Snyderman & Rothman, 1990). If scoring well on intelligence tests requires a certain type of cultural experience, the tests are said to have a **cultural bias**. For this reason, psychologists have tried to construct **culture-free** or culture-fair intelligence tests.

Some tests do not rely on expressive language at all. For example, Raymond Cattell's (1949) Culture-Fair Intelligence Test evaluates reasoning ability through the child's

TABLE 9.2
Items Similar to Those on the Stanford–Binet Intelligence Scale

AGE	ITEM
2 years	1. Children show knowledge of basic vocabulary words by identifying parts of a doll, such as the mouth, ears, and hair.
	2. Children show counting and spatial skills and visual–motor coordination by building a tower of four blocks to match a model.
4 years	1. Children show word fluency and categorical thinking by filling in the missing words when they are asked questions such as "Father is a man; mother is a _____?" and "Hamburgers are hot; ice cream is _____?"
	2. Children show comprehension by answering correctly when they are asked questions such as "Why do people have automobiles?" and "Why do people have medicine?"
9 years	1. Children can point out verbal absurdities, as in this question: "In an old cemetery, scientists unearthed a skull, which they believed was the skull of George Washington when he was only 5 years of age. What is silly about that?"
	2. Children display fluency with words, as shown by answering questions such as "Can you tell me a number that rhymes with snore?" and "Can you tell me a colour that rhymes with glue?"
Adult	1. Adults show knowledge of the meanings of words and conceptual thinking by correctly explaining the differences between word pairs such as "sickness and misery," "house and home," and "integrity and prestige."
	2. Adults show spatial skills by correctly answering questions such as "If a car turned to the right to head north, in what direction was it heading before it turned?"

comprehension of the rules that govern a progression of geometric designs, as shown in Figure 9.11 on page 185.

But culture-free tests have not lived up to their promise. First, middle-class children still outperform lower-class children on these tests (Rushton et al., 2003). Middle-class children, for example, are more likely to have basic familiarity with materials such as blocks and pencils and paper. They are also more likely to have played with blocks (a practice relevant to the Cattell test). Second, culture-free tests do not predict academic success as well as other intelligence tests do, and scholastic aptitude remains the central concern of educators (Keogh & Whyte, 2006).

PATTERNS OF INTELLECTUAL DEVELOPMENT

Intellectual growth seems to occur in at least two major spurts. The first occurs at about the age of 6. It coincides with entry into school and also with the shift from preoperational to concrete-operational thought. School may help crystallize intellectual functioning at this time. The second spurt occurs at about age 10 or 11.

Once children reach middle childhood, they appear to undergo relatively more stable patterns of

TABLE 9.3
Kinds of Items Found on Wechsler's Intelligence Scales

VERBAL ITEMS	NONVERBAL–PERFORMANCE ITEMS
Information: "What is the capital of Canada?" "Who was Shakespeare?"	**Picture completion:** Pointing to the missing part of a picture.
Comprehension: "How is a pen similar to a pencil?" "What does 'A stitch in time saves 9' mean?"	**Picture arrangement:** Arranging cartoon pictures in sequence so that they tell a meaningful story.
Arithmetic: "If 3 chocolate bars cost 25 cents, how much will 18 chocolate bars cost?"	**Block design:** Copying pictures of geometric designs using multicoloured blocks.
Similarities: "How are good and bad alike?" "How are peanut butter and jelly alike?"	**Object assembly:** Putting pieces of a puzzle together so that they form a meaningful object.
Vocabulary: "What does canal mean?"	**Coding:** Rapid scanning and drawing of symbols that are associated with numbers.
Digit span: Repeating a series of numbers, presented by the examiner, forward and backward.	**Mazes:** Using a pencil to trace the correct route from a starting point to home.

Katrina Brown/Shutterstock

Ruslan Ivantsova/Shutterstock

Note: Items for verbal subtests are similar but not identical to actual test items on the Wechsler intelligence scales.

gains in intellectual functioning, although some spurts still occur (Deary et al., 2004). As a result, intelligence tests gain greater predictive power. In a classic study by Marjorie Honzik and her colleagues (1948), intelligence test scores taken at the age of 9 correlated strongly (+0.90) with scores at the age of 10 and more moderately (+0.76) with scores at the age of 18. Testing at age 11 even shows a moderate to high relationship with scores at the age of 77 (Deary et al., 2004).

Despite the increased predictive power of intelligence tests during middle childhood, individual differences exist. In the classic Fels Longitudinal Study (see Figure 9.12 on page 186), two groups of children (Groups 1 and 3) made reasonably consistent gains in intelligence test scores between the ages of 10 and 17, whereas three groups declined. Group 4, children who had shown the most intellectual promise at age 10, went on to show the most precipitous decline, although they still wound up in the highest 2–3 percent of the population (McCall et al., 1973). Many factors influence changes in IQ scores, including changes in the home, socioeconomic circumstances, and education (Deary et al., 2004).

> A limitation can be referred to as retardation but a person should never be called a "retard."

DIFFERENCES IN INTELLECTUAL DEVELOPMENT

The average IQ score for Canadian children is 103.34 (101.4 verbal and 104.96 performance). About half the children in Canada attain IQ scores in the broad average range from 90 to 110. Nearly 95 percent attain scores between 70 and 130. Children who attain IQ scores below 70 are generally labelled "intellectually deficient" or "mentally retarded." Children who attain scores of 130 or above are usually labelled "gifted."

Mental Retardation

Mental retardation refers to limited functioning in intellectual performance and adaptive skills. This term has been quite controversial in Canada and is used in limited circumstances. Terminology has evolved from *mental retardation* to *developmental challenge*, to *intellectual delay* to the more currently used term, *global disability*. Describing the limitation as retardation is appropriate, but an individual should never be referred to as "retarded" or a "retard." This is an insensitive term with degrading social implications.

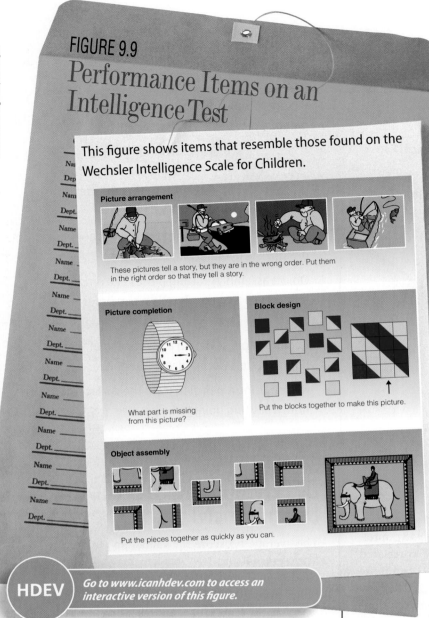

FIGURE 9.9
Performance Items on an Intelligence Test

This figure shows items that resemble those found on the Wechsler Intelligence Scale for Children.

Picture arrangement

These pictures tell a story, but they are in the wrong order. Put them in the right order so that they tell a story.

Picture completion

What part is missing from this picture?

Block design

Put the blocks together to make this picture.

Object assembly

Put the pieces together as quickly as you can.

HDEV Go to www.icanhdev.com to access an interactive version of this figure.

cultural–familial retardation substandard intellectual performance stemming from lack of opportunity to acquire knowledge and skills.

cultural–familial retardation, children are biologically normal but do not develop age-appropriate behaviour at the normal pace because of an impoverished home environment. These children may have little opportunity to interact with adults or play with stimulating toys.

Giftedness

Giftedness involves more than achieving excellence on the tasks provided by standard intelligence tests. In determining who is gifted, most educators include children who have outstanding abilities; those who are capable of high performance in a specific academic area, such as language or mathematics; and those who show creativity, leadership, and distinction in the visual or performing arts, or bodily talents, as in gymnastics and dancing.

Socioeconomic and Ethnic Differences in IQ

Research has found differences in IQ scores between socioeconomic and ethnic groups. Lower-class children obtain IQ scores some 10 to 15 points lower than those obtained by middle- and upper-class children. African North American, Latino and Latina North American, and Native North American children all tend to score below the norms for European North Americans (Neisser et al., 1996). Youth of Asian descent frequently outscore youth of European backgrounds on achievement tests in math and science, including the math portion of the SAT (Dandy & Nettelbeck, 2002; Stevenson et al., 1993).

Asian students and their mothers tend to attribute academic success to hard work (Randel et al., 2000), whereas North American mothers are more likely to attribute academic success to natural ability (Basic Behavioural Science Task Force, 1996). Thus Asian students may work harder. Controversial Canadian research conducted by J. Philippe Rushton and Arthur R. Jensen (2005) argues that denying cognitive differences between different races is not only poor science, it is injurious to unique individuals. Others fear that such research will support systemic discrimination.

Most of the children (more than 80 percent) who are retarded are mildly retarded. Mildly retarded children are the most capable of adjusting to the demands of educational institutions and to society at large. Many mildly retarded children are mainstreamed in regular classrooms rather than placed in special-needs classes.

Some causes of retardation are biological, stemming from chromosomal abnormalities, such as Down's syndrome; genetic disorders such as phenylketonuria (PKU); and brain damage (AAIDD, 2007). Brain damage can have many origins, including childhood accidents and problems during pregnancy such as maternal alcohol abuse, malnutrition, or diseases. In

FIGURE 9.10

Variations in IQ Scores

IQ scores generally vary according to a bell-shaped, or "normal," curve.

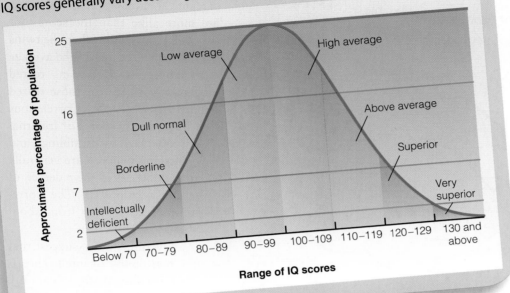

creativity a trait characterized by flexibility, ingenuity,
and originality.

convergent thinking a
thought process that attempts
to focus on the single best
solution to a problem.

divergent thinking free
and fluent association to the
elements of a problem.

Children mainly use convergent thinking to arrive at the correct answers on intelligence tests. In **convergent thinking**, thought is limited to present facts; the problem solver narrows his or her thinking to find the best solution. A child uses convergent thinking to arrive at the right answer to a multiple-choice question or to a question on an intelligence test.

Creative thinking tends to be divergent rather than convergent (Vartanian et al., 2003). In **divergent thinking**, the child associates freely to the elements of the problem. (We use divergent thinking when we are trying to generate ideas to answer an essay question or to find keywords to search on the Internet.) Tests of creativity determine the flexibility, fluency, and originality

CREATIVITY AND INTELLECTUAL DEVELOPMENT

Creativity is the ability to do things that are novel and useful (Sternberg, 2007). Creative children and adults can solve problems that have no preexisting solutions and no tried and tested formulas (Simonton, 2006). Creative children take chances (Milgram & Livne, 2006; Sternberg, 2006): They refuse to accept limitations. They appreciate art and music. They challenge social norms. They examine ideas that other people accept at face value.

Some scientists argue that creativity and innovation require high levels of general intelligence (Heilman et al., 2003), but the tests we use to measure intelligence and creativity tend to show only a moderate relationship between IQ scores and measures of creativity (Sternberg & Williams, 1997). Some children who obtain average IQ scores excel in creative areas such as music or art.

FIGURE 9.11

Sample Items from Cattell's Culture-Fair Intelligence Test

Culture-fair tests attempt to exclude items that discriminate on the basis of cultural background rather than intelligence.

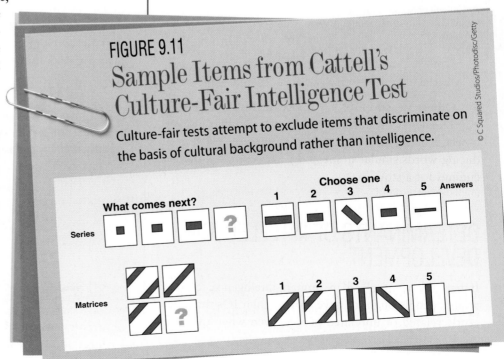

FIGURE 9.12

Five Patterns of Change in IQ Scores for Children in the Fels Longitudinal Study

In the Fels Longitudinal Study, IQ scores remained stable between the ages of 2½ and 17 for only one of five groups, Group 1.

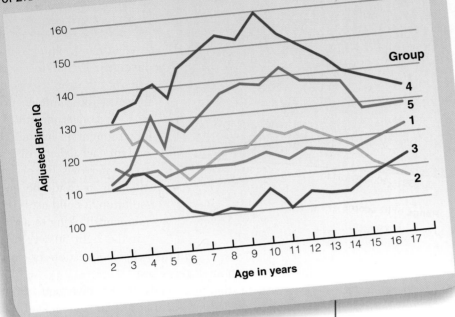

Source: McCall et al. (1973).

heritability the degree to which the variations in a trait from one person to another can be attributed to genetic factors.

reared separately. Figure 9.13 shows the averaged results of more than 100 studies of IQ and heredity (T. J. Bouchard et al., 1990). The IQ scores of identical (monozygotic; MZ) twins are more alike than the scores for any other pairs, even when the twins have been reared apart. The average correlation for MZ twins reared together is +0.85; for those reared apart, it is +0.67. Correlations between the IQ scores of fraternal (dizygotic; DZ) twins, siblings, and parents and children are generally comparable, as is their degree of genetic relationship. The correlations tend to vary from about +0.40 to +0.59.

Overall, studies suggest that the **heritability** of intelligence is between 40 and 60 percent (T. J. Bouchard et al., 1990; Neisser et al., 1996). About half of the difference between your IQ score and those of others can be explained in terms of genetic factors.

Let's return to Figure 9.13. Note that genetic pairs (such as MZ twins) reared together show higher correlations between IQ scores than similar genetic pairs (such as other MZ twins) who were reared apart. This finding holds for MZ twins, siblings, parents, children, and unrelated people. For this reason, the same group of studies that suggests that heredity plays a role in determining IQ scores also suggests that the environment plays a role.

of a person's thinking. A measure of creativity might ask how many ways you can classify the following group of names:

Martha   Paul   Jeffry   Sally   Pablo   Joan

Other measures of creativity include suggesting improvements or unusual uses for a familiar toy or object, naming items that belong in the same class, producing words similar in meaning, and writing different endings for a story.

DETERMINANTS OF INTELLECTUAL DEVELOPMENT

If heredity is involved in human intelligence, closely related people ought to have more similar IQs than distantly related or unrelated people, even when they are

Leonardo da Vinci's sketches for the wings of a glider appear to be based on his studies of bat wings. What aspects of creative thinking can you see in da Vinci's designs?

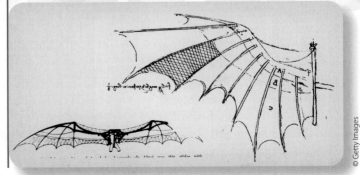

© Getty Images

Classic projects involving adopted children in Colorado, Texas, and Minnesota (Coon et al., 1990; Scarr, 1993; Turkheimer, 1991) have found a stronger relationship between the IQ scores of adopted children and their biological parents than between the IQ scores of adopted children and their adoptive parents.

Studies of environmental influences on IQ use several research strategies, including discovering situational factors that affect IQ scores, exploring children's abilities to rebound from early deprivation, and exploring the effects of positive early environments. Children whose parents are responsive and provide appropriate play materials and varied experiences during the early years attain higher IQ and achievement test scores (Bradley, 2006). Graduates of Head Start and other preschool programs also show significant gains in IQ and other test scores (Phillips & Styfco, 2007).

Many psychologists believe that heredity and environment interact to influence intelligence (Lubinski & Benbow, 2000; Winner, 2000). An impoverished environment may prevent some children from living up to their potential. An enriched environment may encourage others to realize their potential.

LO8 Language Development and Literacy

Children's language ability grows more sophisticated in middle childhood. During this stage, children begin learning to read. Many children are exposed to a variety of linguistic experiences, and these experiences affect cognitive development.

VOCABULARY AND GRAMMAR

By the age of 6, the child's vocabulary has expanded to nearly 10,000 words. By 7 to 9 years of age, most children realize that words can have different meanings, and they become entertained by riddles and jokes that require semantic sophistication. (Remember the joke at the beginning of the section on cognitive development.) By the age of 8 or 9, children are able to form "tag questions," in which the question is tagged on to the end of a declarative sentence, such "You want more ice cream, don't you?" and "You're sick, aren't you?" (Weckerly et al., 2004).

Children make subtle advances in articulation and in the capacity to use complex grammar. Preschoolers have difficulty understanding passive sentences such as "The truck was hit by the car," but children in the middle years have less difficulty interpreting them (Aschermann et al., 2004).

During these years, children develop the ability to use connectives, as illustrated by the sentence "I'll eat my spinach, but I don't want to." They also learn to form indirect object–direct object constructions (e.g., "She showed her sister the toy.").

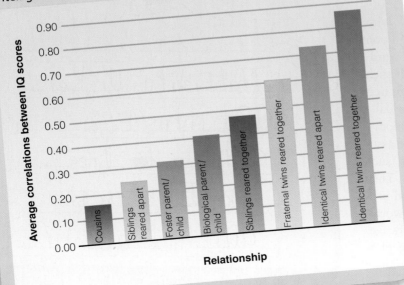

FIGURE 9.13
Findings of Studies of the Relationship Between IQ Scores and Heredity

Correlations are stronger for persons who are more closely related and for persons who are reared together or living together, thus supporting both genetic and environmental hypotheses of the origins of intelligence.

Relationship (x-axis): Cousins, Siblings reared apart, Foster parent/child, Biological parent/child, Siblings reared together, Fraternal twins reared together, Identical twins reared apart, Identical twins reared together

Average correlations between IQ scores (y-axis): 0.00 to 0.90

Source: T. J. Bouchard, et al. (1990).

READING SKILLS AND LITERACY

Reading involves perceptual, cognitive, and linguistic processes (Smolka & Eviatar, 2006). It relies on the integration of visual and auditory information. Children must accurately perceive the sounds in their language and make basic visual discriminations (Levinthal & Lleras, 2007). Children must perceive the visual differences between letters such as *b* and *d* and *p* and *q*.

How do children become familiar with their own written languages? More and more today, Canadian children are being exposed to TV programs such as *Sesame Street*. Children are exposed to books, street signs, names of stores and restaurants, and the writing on packages. Children from homes where books and other sources of stimulation are plentiful learn to read more readily. Reading storybooks with parents in the preschool years helps prepare a child for reading (Raikes et al., 2006).

METHODS OF TEACHING READING

Children read by integrating visual and auditory information (they associate what they see with sounds), whether they use the word-recognition method or the phonetic method. The **word-recognition method** associates visual stimuli such as *cat* and *Robert* with the sound combinations that produce the spoken words. This capacity is usually acquired by rote learning, or extensive repetition.

In the **phonetic method**, children learn to associate written letters and letter combinations (such as *ph* or *sh*) with the sounds they indicate. Then they sound out words. The phonetic method provides skills children can use to decode new words, but some children learn more rapidly at early ages through the word-recognition method. The phonetic method can slow them down with familiar words. Most children and adults read familiar words by word recognition and make some effort to sound out new words.

Some English words can be read only by recognition, as with *one* and *two*. This method is useful when it comes to words such as *danger, stop, poison,* and a child's name, because it provides children with a basic **sight vocabulary**. But decoding skills help children read new words on their own.

BILINGUALISM: LINGUISTIC PERSPECTIVES ON THE WORLD

According to the 2001 Census of Canada, more than 100 mother tongues are spoken in Canada in addition to our indigenous languages and our official languages of English and French. Sixty-one percent of immigrants who arrived in the 1990s use a nonofficial language as the first language spoken at home (Office of the Commissioner of Official Languages, 2005) (see Table 9.4).

Used with permission of the New England Aquarium / © Image Source

TABLE 9.4
Top Ten Languages Spoken at Home in Canada

1. English
2. French
3. Chinese
4. Italian
5. German
6. Punjabi
7. Spanish
8. Portuguese
9. Polish
10. Arabic

Fancy/Jupiter Images

One in five Canadians (and more than two in five Torontonians) is an allophone whose mother tongue is neither English nor French. Allophones comprise 20.1 percent of the population; anglophones, 57.8 percent, and francophones, 22.1 percent.

Sources: *Canadian Geographic.* (2010). Who we are: Canada by demographics—Top 10 languages. *The Canadian Atlas Online.* Retrieved from http://magazine.canadiangeographic.ca/Atlas/themes. aspx?id=whoweare&sub=whoweare_demographics_work&lang=En; Statistics Canada. (2009c). *2006 Census: The evolving linguistic portrait, 2006 Census: Sharp increase in population with a mother tongue other than English or French.* Retrieved from http://www12.statcan.ca/census-recensement/2006/as-sa/97-555/p2-eng.cfm

Bilingual children do not encounter more academic problems than children who speak only one language. Nevertheless, a century ago, many believed that children reared in bilingual homes were disadvantaged in their cognitive development. The theory was that mental capacity is limited, so people who store two linguistic systems are crowding their mental abilities. Bilingual children experience some "mixing" of languages (Gonzalez, 2006), but they can generally separate the two languages at an early age.

Today, most linguists consider it advantageous for children to be bilingual because knowledge of more than one language contributes to the complexity of the child's cognitive processes (Bialystok & Craik, 2007). For example, bilingual children are more likely to understand that the symbols used in language are arbitrary. Monolingual children are more likely to think erroneously that the word *dog* is somehow intertwined with the nature of the beast. Bilingual children therefore tend to have more cognitive flexibility.

> **bilingual** using or capable of using two languages with nearly equal or equal facility.

MANDY GODBEHEAR/Shutterstock

In the years

between 6 and 12, peers take on greater importance and friendships deepen.

10

Middle Childhood: Social and Emotional Development

In the years between 6 and 12, the child's social world expands. Peers take on greater importance and friendships deepen. Entry into school exposes the child to the influence of teachers. Relationships with parents change as children develop greater independence.

latency stage in psychoanalytic theory, the fourth stage of psychosexual development, characterized by repression of sexual impulses and development of skills.

Learning Outcomes

LO1 Explain theories of social and emotional development in middle childhood

LO2 Discuss the influences of the family on social development in middle childhood

LO3 Discuss the influences of peers on social development in middle childhood

LO4 Discuss the influence of the school on development in middle childhood

LO5 Discuss social and emotional problems that tend to develop in middle childhood

LO1 Theories of Social and Emotional Development in Middle Childhood

the major theories of personality have had less to say about this age group than about the other periods of childhood and adolescence. Nevertheless, common threads emerge.

PSYCHOANALYTIC THEORY

According to Freud, children in the middle years are in the **latency stage**. Freud believed that sexual feelings remain repressed (unconscious) during this period. Children use this period to focus on developing intellectual, social, and other culturally valued skills.

Erik Erikson, like Freud, saw the major developmental task of middle childhood as the acquisition of cognitive and social skills. Erikson labelled this stage **industry versus inferiority**. Children who are able to master the challenges of the middle years develop a sense of industry or competence. Children who have difficulties in school or with peer relationships may develop a sense of inferiority.

SOCIAL COGNITIVE THEORY

Social cognitive theory focuses on the importance of rewards and modelling in middle childhood. During these years, children depend less on external rewards and punishments and increasingly regulate their own behaviour. Children are exposed to an increasing variety of models. Not only parents but also teachers, other adults, peers, and symbolic models (such as TV characters or the heroine in a story) serve as influential models (Anderson et al., 2007; Oates & Messer, 2007).

COGNITIVE-DEVELOPMENTAL THEORY AND SOCIAL COGNITION

According to Piaget, middle childhood coincides with the stage of concrete operations and is partly characterized by a decline in egocentrism and an expansion of the capacity to view the world and oneself from the perspective of others. This cognitive advance affects the child's social relationships (Mischo, 2004; Zan & Hildebrandt, 2003).

Social cognition refers to perception of the social world, and our concern is the development of children's perspective-taking skills. Robert Selman and his colleagues (Selman, 1980; Selman & Dray, 2006) studied the development of these skills by presenting children with a social dilemma such as the following:

Holly is an 8-year-old girl who likes to climb trees. She is the best tree climber in the neighbourhood. One day while climbing down from a tall tree, she falls off the bottom branch but does not hurt herself. Her father sees her fall. He is upset and asks her to promise not to climb trees any more. Holly promises. Later that day, Holly and her friends meet Sean. Sean's kitten is caught up in a tree and can't get down. Something has to be done right away, or the kitten may fall. Holly is the only one who climbs trees well enough to reach the kitten and get it down, but she remembers her promise to her father (Selman, 1980, p. 36).

The children then were asked questions such as "How will Holly's father feel if he finds out she climbed the tree?" Using the children's responses, Selman (1976) described five levels of perspective-taking skills in childhood (see Table 10.1). Children with better perspective-taking skills tend to have better peer relationships (Selman & Dray, 2006).

DEVELOPMENT OF THE SELF-CONCEPT IN MIDDLE CHILDHOOD

In early childhood, children's self-concepts focus on concrete external traits, such as appearance, activities, and living situations. But as children undergo the cognitive developments of middle childhood, more abstract internal traits, or personality traits, begin to play a role. Social relationships and group memberships take on significance (Harter, 2006; Thompson, 2006).

An investigative method called the **Twenty Statements Test** bears out this progression. Children are given a sheet of paper with the question "Who am I?" and 20 spaces in which to write answers. Consider the answers of a 9-year-old boy and an 11-year-old girl:

The nine-year-old boy: My name is Bruce C. I have brown eyes. I have brown hair. I have brown eyebrows. I'm 9 years old. I LOVE? sports. I have 7 people in my family. I have great? eye site. I have lots! of friends. I live on 1923 Pinecrest Drive. I'm going on 10 in September. I'm a boy. I have a uncle that is almost 7 feet tall. My school is Pinecrest. My teacher

© Efremova Irina/Shutterstock

TABLE 10.1
Levels of Perspective Taking

LEVEL	APPROXIMATE AGE (YEARS)	WHAT HAPPENS
0	3–6	**Children are egocentric** and do not realize that other people have perspectives different from their own. A child of this age will typically say that Holly will save the kitten because she likes kittens and that her father will be happy because he likes kittens too. The child assumes that everyone feels as she does.
1	5–9[a]	Children understand that people in **different situations may have different perspectives**. The child still assumes that only one perspective is "right." A child might say that Holly's father would be angry if he did not know why she climbed the tree. But if she told him why, he would understand. The child recognizes that the father's perspective may differ from Holly's because of lack of information. But once he has the information, he will assume the "right" perspective (i.e., Holly's).
2	7–12[a]	The child understands that people may think or feel differently because they have **different values or ideas**. The child also recognizes that others are capable of understanding the child's own perspective. Therefore, the child is better able to anticipate reactions of others. The typical child of this age might say that Holly knows that her father will understand why she climbed the tree and that he therefore will not punish her.
3	10–15[a]	The child finally realizes that both she and another person can **consider each other's point of view at the same time**. The child may say something similar to this reasoning: Holly's father will think that Holly shouldn't have climbed the tree. But now that he has heard her side of the story, he would feel that she was doing what she thought was right. Holly realizes that her father will consider how she felt.
4	12 and above[a]	The child realizes that **mutual perspective taking does not always lead to agreement**. The perspectives of the larger social group also must be considered. A child of this age might say that society expects children to obey their parents and therefore that Holly should realize why her father might punish her.

Source: Selman (1976).
[a]Ages may overlap.

is Mrs. V. I play hockey! I'm also the smartest boy in the class. I LOVE! food. I love fresh air. I LOVE school.

The eleven-year-old girl: My name is A. I'm a human being. I'm a girl. I'm a truthful person. I'm not pretty. I do so-so in my studies. I'm a very good cellist. I'm a very good pianist. I'm a little bit tall for my age. I like several boys. I like several girls. I'm old fashioned. I play tennis. I am a very good musician. I try to be helpful. I'm always ready to be friends with anybody.

Mostly I'm good, but I lose my temper. I'm not well liked by some girls and boys. I don't know if boys like me or not.

—Montemayor & Eisen (1977, pp. 317–318)

Only the 9-year-old lists his age and address, discusses his family, and focuses on physical traits, such as eye colour, in his self-definition. The 9-year-old mentions his likes, which can be considered rudimentary psychological traits, but they are tied to the concrete, as would be expected of a concrete-operational child. The 9- and 11-year-olds list their competencies. The 11-year-old's struggle to bolster her self-esteem—her insistence on her musical abilities despite her qualms about her attractiveness—shows a greater concern with psychological traits and social relationships.

Self-Esteem

As children enter middle childhood, they evaluate their self-worth in many different areas (Tassi et al., 2001). Preschoolers tend to see themselves as either generally "good at doing things" or not. But by 5 to 7 years of age, children are able to judge their performance in seven different areas: physical ability, physical appearance, peer relationships, parent relationships, reading, math, and general school performance. They also report a general self-concept (Harter, 2006).

Children's self-esteem declines throughout middle childhood, reaching a low ebb at 12 or 13. Self-esteem then increases during adolescence (Harter, 2006). What accounts for the decline? Because preschoolers are egocentric, their self-concepts may be unrealistic. By middle childhood, children can compare themselves with other children and arrive at a more honest and critical self-appraisal. Whereas girls tend to have more positive self-concepts regarding reading, general academics, and helping others, boys tend to have more positive self-concepts in math, physical ability, and physical appearance (Jacobs et al., 2005; Wang, 2005).

Authoritative parenting apparently contributes to children's self-esteem (Baumrind, 1991a, 1991b; Supple & Small, 2006). Children with a favourable self-image tend to have parents who are restrictive, involved, and loving. Children with low self-esteem are more likely to have authoritarian or rejecting–neglecting parents.

Social acceptance by peers is related to self-perceived competence in academic, social, and athletic domains (Nesdale & Lambert, 2007). Parents and classmates have an equally strong effect on children's self-esteem in middle childhood. Friends and teachers have relatively less influence but also matter (Harter, 2006).

 D1 Children's self-esteem tends to decline in middle childhood.

Children's self-esteem declines throughout middle childhood, reaching a low ebb at age 12 or 13 and rising again in adolescence.

Learned Helplessness

One outcome of low self-esteem in academics is known as **learned helplessness**. Learned helplessness is the acquired belief that one is unable to obtain the rewards that one seeks. "Helpless" children tend to quit following failure, whereas children who believe in their own ability tend to persist or change their strategies (Zimmerman, 2000). One reason for this difference is that "helpless" children believe that success is due more to ability than effort and that they have little ability in a particular area. Consequently, persistence seems futile (Bandura et al., 2001). Helpless children typically obtain lower grades and lower scores on IQ and achievement tests (Goldstein & Brooks, 2005).

A sex difference emerges in mathematics (Simpkins et al., 2006). Researchers have found that even when girls are performing as well as boys in math and science, they have less confidence in their ability (Anderman et al., 2001). Why? Many parents hold the stereotype that girls have less math ability than boys despite their daughters' abilities, and children tend to reflect this perception.

LO2 The Family

n middle childhood, the family continues to play a key role in socializing the child, although peers, teachers, and other outsiders begin to play a greater role (Harter, 2006).

PARENT–CHILD RELATIONSHIPS

Parent–child interactions focus on some new concerns during middle childhood. They include school-related matters, assignment of chores, and peer activities (Collins et al., 2003). Parents do less monitoring of children's activities and provide less direct feedback than they did in the preschool years. Control is gradually transferred from parent to child in a process known as **co-regulation** (Maccoby, 2002; Wahler et al., 2001). Children begin to internalize the standards of their parents.

Children and parents spend less time together in middle childhood than they did in the preschool years. Children typically spend more time with their mother than with their father. Mothers' interactions with school-age children continue to revolve around caregiving; fathers are relatively more involved in recreational activities (Wolfenden & Holt, 2005).

Because of their developing cognitive ability, 10- to 12-year-olds evaluate their parents more harshly than

© GeoM/Shutterstock

adjustment of children of lesbian and gay parents is comparable to that of children of heterosexual parents. Despite the stigma attached to homosexuality, lesbians and gay men often sustain positive family relationships (Wainright et al., 2004).

What of the sexual orientation of the children of lesbian and gay parents? Green (1978) observed 37 children and young adults, age 3 to 20, who were being reared—or had been reared—by lesbians or **transsexuals**. All but one of the children reported or recalled preferences for toys, clothing, and friends (male or female) that were typical for their sex and age. All the 13 older children who reported sexual fantasies or sexual behaviour were heterosexually oriented. Gay and lesbian families are becoming much more mainstream in Canadian society, enabling better access for conducting current research.

they did in early childhood (Selman & Dray, 2006). But throughout middle childhood, children rate their parents as their best source of emotional support (Cowan & Cowan, 2005; Katz et al., 2005).

LESBIAN AND GAY PARENTS

"Where did you get that beautiful necklace?" I asked the little girl in the pediatrician's office. "From my Moms," she answered. It turned out that her parents were two women, each of whom had a biological child, one girl and one boy.

Research on lesbian and gay parenting has fallen into two general categories: the general adjustment of children and whether the children of lesbian and gay parents are more likely than other children to be lesbian or gay themselves. Research by Charlotte Patterson (2006) has generally found that the psychological

GENERATION X OR GENERATION EX? WHAT HAPPENS TO CHILDREN WHOSE PARENTS GET DIVORCED?

Is this the time of "Generation Ex"—a generation characterized by ex-wives and ex-husbands? Much of our popular culture information about divorce comes from the United States but Canadians do not divorce at the same rates as our neighbours. The Canadian divorce rate has remained fairly stable, at 37.6 divorces per 100 marriages by the 30th wedding anniversary in 2002 and 38.3 in 2003. Divorce rates for remarried individuals are higher (Statistics Canada, 2005).

Divorce may be tough on parents; it can be even tougher on children (Amato, 2006). No longer do children participate in daily activities, such as eating, with both parents. No longer do children go to ball games, movies, or Disneyland with both parents. The parents are now often supporting two households, resulting in fewer resources for the children (Tashiro et al., 2006). Many children who live with their mothers scrape by—or fail to scrape by—in poverty. The mother who was once available may become an occasional visitor, spending more time at work and placing the kids in day care for extended periods.

Most children live with their mothers after a divorce (Amato, 2006). Some fathers remain devoted to their children despite the split, but others tend to spend less time with their children as time goes on. Not only does the drop-off in paternal attention deprive children of activities and social interactions but it also saps their self-esteem: "Why doesn't Daddy love me anymore? What's wrong with me?"

The children of divorce are more likely to have conduct disorders, drug abuse, and poor grades in school (Amato, 2006). Their physical health may decline (Troxel & Matthews, 2004). By and large, the fallout for children is worst during the first year after the breakup. Children tend to rebound after a couple of years or so (Malone et al., 2004). Focused parenting is key to successfully making this significant social adjustment.

Life in Stepfamilies: His, Hers, Theirs, and …

The rule of thumb about the effects of living in stepfamilies is there is no rule of thumb (Coleman et al., 2000). Many stepparents have loving and rewarding relationships with their stepchildren (Marsiglio, 2004). Living in stepfamilies also has some risks, such as the greater risk of being physically abused by stepparents than by biological parents (Adler-Baeder, 2006). Stepchildren are also at a significantly higher risk—by a factor of eight—of being sexually abused by their stepparents than by their natural parents.

Why do we find these risks in stepfamilies? According to evolutionary psychologists, people often behave as though they want their genes to flourish in the next generation. Thus, stepparents could be less devoted to rearing other people's children.

Should We Remain Married "for the Sake of the Children"?

Many readers believe—for moral reasons—that marriage and family life must be permanent, no matter what. Readers will have to consider the moral aspects of divorce in the light of their own value systems. But—from a purely psychological perspective—what should bickering parents do? The answer seems to depend largely on how they behave in front of the children. Research shows that severe parental bickering is linked to the same kinds of problems that children experience when their parents get separated or divorced (Troxel & Matthews, 2004). When children are exposed to adult or marital conflict, they display a biological "alarm reaction": their heart rate, blood pressure, and sweating rise sharply (El-Sheikh, 2007). Therefore, Hetherington and her colleagues suggest that divorce can be a positive alternative to family conflict (Hetherington, 1989; Wallerstein et al., 2005).

THE EFFECTS OF MATERNAL EMPLOYMENT

Canadian women have traditionally been assigned the role of homemaker, but this stereotype is changing. In 2006, 73 percent of all women with children younger than age 16 living at home were part of the employed workforce. This number is up from 39 percent in 1976 (Almey, 2007).

Many commentators have voiced concerns about the effects of maternal employment on children. In part, their concerns are typically based on more traditional values that argue that the mother ought to remain in

© Photos.com

© ClassicStock/Alamy

NEL

the home. But concern has also been based on research findings that suggest maternal employment (and non-maternal care) have some negative effects on children (Belsky, 2006b).

One common belief is that mothers being in the workforce rather than in the home leads to delinquency. Researchers using data on 707 adolescents, age 12 to 14, from the National Longitudinal Survey of Youth examined whether the occupational status of a mother was connected with delinquent behaviour (Vander Ven & Cullen, 2004). They found that maternal employment made little difference, but delinquency was connected with lack of supervision.

Maternal employment has benefits. Daughters of employed women are more achievement oriented and set higher career goals for themselves than daughters of nonworking women (Hangal & Aminabhavi, 2007). Children of working mothers also tend to be more prosocial, less anxious, and more flexible in their gender role stereotypes (Nomaguchi, 2006; Wright & Young, 1998).

> **D2** The daughters of employed women are more achievement oriented and set higher career goals for themselves than the daughters of unemployed women.
> This is likely due to the role modelling that takes place between mother and daughter.

L○3 Peer Relationships

amilies exert the most powerful influences on a child during his or her first few years. But as children move into middle childhood, peers take on more importance.

PEERS AS SOCIALIZATION INFLUENCES

Parents can only provide children with experience relating to adults. Children profit from experience with peers because peers have interests and skills that reflect the child's generation (Molinari & Corsaro, 2000).

Peers provide practice in cooperating, relating to leaders, and coping with aggressive impulses, including their own. Peers can be important confidants (Dunn et al., 2001; Hanlon et al., 2004). Peers, like parents, help children learn what types of impulses—affectionate, aggressive, and so on—they can safely express. Children

who are at odds with their parents can turn to peers as sounding boards, for comparing their feelings and experiences. When children share troubling ideas and experiences with peers, they realize they are normal and not alone (Barry & Wentzel, 2006).

PEER ACCEPTANCE AND REJECTION

Acceptance or rejection by peers is important in childhood because problems with peers affect adjustment later on (Wentzel et al., 2004). Popular children tend to be attractive, mature for their age, and successful in sports or academics, although attractiveness seems to be more important for girls than boys (Langlois et al., 2000). Socially speaking, popular children are friendly, nurturant, cooperative, helpful, and socially skillful (Xie et al., 2006). They also have high self-esteem.

Children who are aggressive and disrupt group activities are more likely to be rejected by peers (Boivin et al., 2005). Most rejected children do not learn to conform. Instead, they remain on the fringes of the group and may find aggressive friends (A. J. Rose et al., 2004).

> **D3** In middle childhood, popular children tend to be attractive and relatively mature for their age.
> This is true, though more so for girls in the case of attractiveness.

DEVELOPMENT OF FRIENDSHIPS

In the preschool years and early years of middle childhood, friendships are based on geographic closeness or proximity. Friendships are superficial; quickly formed, easily broken. What matters are shared activities and who has the swing set or sandbox (Berndt, 2004; Gleason et al., 2005).

Between the ages of 8 and 11, children recognize the importance of friends meeting each other's needs and possessing desirable traits (Zarbatany et al., 2004). They are more likely to say that friends are nice and share their interests. They increasingly pick friends who are similar in behaviour and personality. Trustworthiness, mutual understanding, and a willingness to disclose personal information characterize friendships in middle childhood and beyond (Hamm, 2000; Rotenberg et al., 2004). Girls tend to develop closer friendships than boys, to seek confidants (Zarbatany et al., 2000).

TABLE 10.2
Stages in Children's Concepts of Friendship

STAGE	NAME	APPROXIMATE AGE (YEARS)	WHAT HAPPENS
0	Momentary physical interaction	3–6	Children remain egocentric. Their concept of a friend is someone who likes to play with the same things and lives nearby.
1	One-way assistance	5–9[a]	Children are less egocentric but view a friend as someone who does what they want.
2	Fair-weather cooperation	7–12[a]	Friends are viewed as doing things for one another, but the focus remains on self-interest.
3	Intimate and mutual sharing	10–15[a]	The focus is on the relationship rather than on the individuals separately. Friendship is viewed as providing mutual support over a long period of time.
4	Autonomous interdependence	12 and above[a]	Children (adolescents, and adults) understand that friendships grow and change as people change and that they may need different friends to satisfy different needs.

Source: Selman (1980).
[a] Ages may overlap

Robert Selman (1980) described five stages in children's changing concepts of friendship (see Table 10.2). The stages correspond to the levels of perspective-taking skills discussed earlier.

School-age friends are more verbal, attentive, relaxed, and responsive to each other during play than are mere acquaintances (Cleary et al., 2002). Conflicts can occur among friends, but when they do, they tend to be minor disagreements and are typically resolved in positive ways (Wojslawowicz Bowker et al., 2006).

Children in middle childhood will typically say they have more than one "best" friend (Berndt et al., 1989). Nine-year-olds report an average of four best friends (Lewis & Feiring, 1989). Best friends tend to be more alike than other friends.

In middle childhood, boys tend to play in larger groups than girls. Children's friendships are almost exclusively with others of the same sex, continuing the trend of sex segregation (Hartup, 1983).

miskolin/Shutterstock

LO4 The School

the school exerts a powerful influence on many aspects of the child's development. Schools, like parents, set limits on behaviour, make demands for mature behaviour, attempt to communicate, and are oriented toward nurturing positive physical, social, and cognitive development. Schools influence children's IQ scores, achievement motivation, and career aspirations (Aber et al., 2007; Woolfolk, 2008). Schools also influence social and moral development (Killen & Smetana, 2006).

Schools are also competitive environments, and children who do too well—and students who do not do well enough—may incur the resentment or ridicule of others.

ENTRY INTO SCHOOL

Children must master many new tasks when they start school—new academic challenges, new school and teacher expectations, fitting into a new peer group, coping with extended separation from parents, and developing increased self-control and self-help skills.

Some children enter school less well prepared than others. Kindergarten teachers report that many students begin school unprepared to learn (Slavin, 2006; Woolfolk, 2008). Most teachers say that children often lack the language skills needed to succeed. Poor health care and nutrition, and lack of adequate parental stimulation and support place many children at risk for academic failure before they enter school.

THE SCHOOL ENVIRONMENT: SETTING THE STAGE FOR SUCCESS, OR . . .

Research summaries (Slavin, 2006; Woolfolk, 2008) indicate that an effective school has the following characteristics:

- An active, energetic principal
- Empowerment of teachers through community decision making

Bullying and Pink Shirt Day

Ten-year-old Stephanie did not want to go to school. As with many other children who refuse school, she showed anxiety at the thought of leaving home. But Stephanie was not experiencing separation anxiety from her family. She, and her classmate Susan, had disagreed about something, and Susan had told her she was going to make sure that everyone hated Stephanie, leaving her with no one to hang out with. To highlight her warning, Susan had shoved Stephanie across the hall.

Bullying transforms the perception of school from a safe place into a violent place (Batsche & Porter, 2006). It is estimated that 70–75 percent of students have been bullied (LI, 2007).

Public Safety Canada (2010) defines bullying as acts of intentional harm, repeated over time, in a relationship characterized by an imbalance of power. Bullying includes physical actions (i.e. punching, kicking), verbal actions (i.e. threats and insults) and social exclusion (i.e. spreading rumours and excluding).

Bullying is not an act of anger but an act of contempt for the target. The bully views the victim as worthless and undeserving of respect. The complex circle of bullying consists of the bully, the followers, the supporters, disengaged onlookers, possible and actual defenders and the target (Olweus Bullying Prevention Program, 2010).

One day a student in Nova Scotia was bullied for wearing a pink shirt to school. To protest the bullying, two students purchased 50 pink T-shirts and handed them out in school the next day. They wanted to support the target and diffuse the power of the bullies. It was the first Pink Shirt Day.

On April 14th each year, many students and schools across Canada participate in the growing social trend known as Pink Shirt Day. The pink shirts are worn to symbolize intolerance toward bullying. Pink Shirt Day promotes awareness, understanding, and openness about the problem of bullying in a shared commitment to a community solution. Visit www.pinkshirtday.ca for more information or to organize Pink Shirt Day in your school.

• Teachers that provide a structured learning environment with high expectations that children will learn

• Empowerment of students that participate in setting goals and establishing learning activities

One key school environment factor is class size. Smaller classes permit students to receive more individual attention and are particularly useful in teaching the "basics"—reading, writing, and arithmetic—to students at risk for academic failure (Slavin, 2006; Woolfolk, 2008).

TEACHERS

Teachers, like parents, set limits, make demands, communicate values, and foster development. They are powerful role models and dispensers of reinforcement. After all, children spend several hours each weekday with teachers.

Teacher Influences on Student Performance

Achievement is enhanced when teachers expect students to master the curriculum, allocate most of the available time to academic activities, and manage the classroom effectively. Students learn more in classes when they are actively instructed or supervised by teachers than when they are working on their own. The most effective teachers ask questions, give personalized feedback, and provide opportunities for drill and practice (Slavin, 2006).

Student achievement also is linked to the emotional climate of the classroom (Slavin, 2006; Woolfolk,

> In education, teachers often find what they are looking for.

2008). Students do not do as well when teachers rely heavily on criticism, ridicule, threats, or punishment. Achievement is high in classrooms with a pleasant, friendly—but not overly warm—atmosphere.

Teacher Expectations

There is a saying that "you find what you're looking for." Consider the so-called **Pygmalion effect** in education. In Greek mythology, the sculptor Pygmalion breathed life into a beautiful statue he had carved. Teachers also try to bring out positive traits they believe dwell within their students. A classic experiment by Robert Rosenthal and Lenore Jacobson (1968) suggested that teacher expectations can become **self-fulfilling prophecies**. Rosenthal and Jacobson (1968) first gave students a battery of psychological tests. Then they informed teachers that a handful of the students, although average in performance to date, were about to blossom forth intellectually in the current school year.

In fact, the tests indicated nothing about the "chosen" children. These children had been selected at random. The purpose of the experiment was to determine

© Cheryl Casey/Shutterstock

What are some of the ways that teachers can help motivate all students to do their best? Anita Woolfolk (2008) suggests the following:

- Make the classroom safe and pleasant, and the lessons interesting and inviting.

- Recognize that students' backgrounds can give rise to diverse patterns of needs.

- Help students take appropriate responsibility for their successes and failures.

- Encourage students to perceive the links between their own efforts and their achievements.

- Help students set attainable short-term goals.

whether enhancing teacher expectations could affect student performance. It did; the identified children made significant gains in IQ scores.

In subsequent research, however, results have been mixed. Some studies have found support for the Pygmalion effect (Madon et al., 2001; Sarrazin et al., 2005a, 2005b). Others have not. But these findings have serious implications for children from ethnic minority and low-income families because there is some indication that teachers expect less from children in these groups (Slavin, 2006; Woolfolk, 2008). Teachers who expect less may "find what they are looking for," spending less time encouraging and working with children.

Sexism in the Classroom

Although girls were systematically excluded from formal education for centuries, today we do not expect to encounter **sexism** among teachers. Teachers, after all, are generally well educated. They are also trained to be fair minded and sensitive to the needs of their young charges in today's changing society.

However, according to a classic review of more than 1,000 research publications about girls and education, girls are treated unequally by their teachers, their male peers, and the school curriculum (American Association of University Women, 1992). The reviewers concluded the following:

- Many teachers pay less attention to girls than boys, especially in math, science, and technology classes.

- Many girls are subjected to **sexual harassment**—unwelcome verbal or physical conduct of a sexual nature—from male classmates, and many teachers ignore it.

- Some textbooks still stereotype or ignore women, portraying males as the shakers and movers in the world.

In a widely cited study, Myra Sadker and David Sadker (Sadker & Silber, 2007) observed students in fourth-, sixth-, and eighth-grade classes, from a variety

> **sexism** discrimination or bias against people based on their sex.
>
> **sexual harassment** unwelcome verbal or physical conduct of a sexual nature.

of cultural, urban, suburban, and rural backgrounds. In almost all cases, the findings were depressingly similar. Boys generally dominated classroom communication, whether the subject was math (a traditionally "masculine" area) or language arts (a traditionally "feminine" area). Despite the stereotype that girls are more likely to talk or even chatter, boys were eight times more likely than girls to call out answers without raising their hands. So far, it could be said, we have evidence of a sex difference, but not of sexism. However, teachers were less than impartial in responding to boys and girls when they called out. Teachers, male and female, were more likely to accept calling out from boys. Girls were more likely to be reminded that they should raise their hands and wait to be called on. Boys, it appears, are expected to be impetuous, but girls are reprimanded for "unladylike behaviour." Until they saw videotapes of themselves, the teachers were largely unaware they were treating girls and boys differently.

LO5 Social and Emotional Problems

many Canadian students suffer from emotional or behavioural problems that could benefit from professional treatment. This requires a focus on conduct disorders, depression, and anxiety.

CONDUCT DISORDERS

David is a 16-year-old high school dropout. He has just been arrested for the third time in 2 years for stealing video equipment and computers from people's homes. Acting alone, David was caught in each case when he tried to sell the stolen items. In describing his actions in each crime, David expressed defiance and showed a lack of remorse. In fact, he bragged about how often he had gotten away with similar crimes.

—Adapted from Halgin & Whitbourne (1993, p. 335)

conduct disorders disorders marked by persistent breaking of the rules and violations of the rights of others.

David has a **conduct disorder**. Children with conduct disorders persistently break rules or violate the rights of others. They exhibit behaviours such as lying, stealing, fire setting, truancy, cruelty to animals, and fighting (American Psychiatric Association, 2000). Conduct disorders typically emerge by 8 years of age and are much more common in boys than girls (Nock et al., 2006).

Children with conduct disorders are often involved in sexual activity before puberty and smoke, drink, and abuse other substances. They have a low tolerance for frustration and may have temper flare-ups. They tend to blame other people for their issues. Academic achievement is usually below grade level, but intelligence is usually at least average. Many children with conduct disorders also are diagnosed with ADHD (Chronis et al., 2007).

Origins of Conduct Disorders

Conduct disorders may have a genetic component (Scourfield et al., 2004). Other contributors include antisocial family members, deviant peers, inconsistent discipline, parental insensitivity to the child's behaviour, physical punishment, and family stress (Black, 2007).

Treatment of Conduct Disorders

The treatment of conduct disorders is challenging, but cognitive-behavioural techniques involving parent training seem to hold promise (Kazdin, 2000; Sukhodolsky et al., 2005). Children profit from interventions in which their behaviour is monitored closely, they face consequences (such as time-outs) for unacceptable behaviour, physical punishment is avoided, and positive social behaviour is rewarded (Cavell, 2001).

CHILDHOOD DEPRESSION

Kristin, age 11, feels "nothing is working out for me." For the past year, she has been failing in school, although she previously had been a B student. She has trouble sleeping, feels tired all the time, and has started refusing to go to school. She cries easily and thinks her peers are making fun of her because she is "ugly and stupid." Her mother recently found a note written by Kristin that said she wanted to jump in front of a car "to end my misery."

—Adapted from Weller & Weller (1991, p. 655)

Many children, like Kristin, are depressed. Depressed children may feel sad, blue, and down in the dumps. They may show poor appetite, insomnia, lack of energy and inactivity, loss of self-esteem, difficulty concentrating, loss of interest in people and activities they usually enjoy, crying, feelings of hopelessness and helplessness, and thoughts of suicide (American Psychiatric Association, 2000).

But many children do not recognize depression in themselves until the age of 7 or so. When children cannot report their feelings, depression is inferred from behaviour, such as withdrawal from social activity. In some cases, childhood depression is masked by conduct disorders, physical complaints, academic problems, and anxiety.

It has been estimated that between 5 and 9 percent of children are seriously depressed in any given year. Depression occurs equally often in girls and boys.

Origins of Depression

The origins of depression are complex and varied. Psychological and biological explanations have been proposed.

Some social cognitive theorists explain depression in terms of relationships between competencies (knowledge and skills) and feelings of self-esteem. Children who gain academic, social, and other competencies usually have high self-esteem. Perceived low levels of competence are linked to helplessness, low self-esteem, and depression. Longitudinal studies have found that problems in academics, socializing, physical appearance, and sports can predict feelings of depression (Kistner, 2006). Some competent children might not credit themselves because of excessive parental expectations. Or children may be perfectionistic themselves. Perfectionistic children may be depressed because they cannot meet their own standards.

© Sam Cornwell/Shutterstock

A tendency to blame oneself (an internal attribution) or others (an external attribution) is called a child's **attributional style**. Certain attributional styles can contribute to helplessness and hopelessness and hence to depression (Kagan et al., 2004; Runyon & Kenny, 2002).

It is true that some children blame themselves for all the problems in their lives, whether they deserve the blame or not. Research shows that children who are depressed are more likely to attribute the causes of their failures to internal, stable, and global factors, which they are relatively helpless to change (Lewinsohn et al., 2000b). Helplessness triggers depression. Consider the case of two children who do poorly on a math test. John thinks, "I'm a loser! I'm just no good in math! I'll never learn." Jim thinks, "That test was tougher than I thought it would be. I'll have to work harder next time." John is perceiving the problem as global (he's "a loser") and stable (he'll "never learn"). Jim perceives the problem as specific rather than global (related to the type of math test the teacher makes up) and as unstable rather than stable (he can change the results by working harder). In effect, John thinks "It's me" (an internal attribution). By contrast, Jim thinks "It's the test" (an external attribution).

> **D4** Some children blame themselves for all the problems in their lives, whether they deserve the blame or not.
> Children who are depressed are more likely to attribute the causes of their failures to internal, stable, and global factors that they are relatively helpless to change.

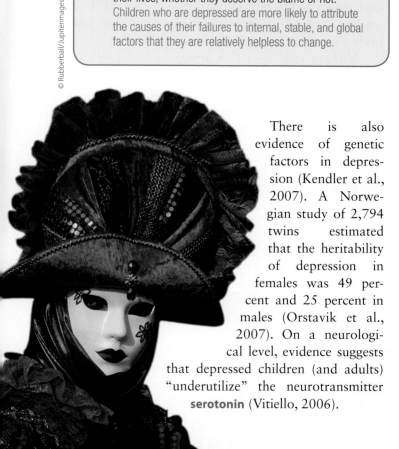

© Rubberball/Jupiterimages

There is also evidence of genetic factors in depression (Kendler et al., 2007). A Norwegian study of 2,794 twins estimated that the heritability of depression in females was 49 percent and 25 percent in males (Orstavik et al., 2007). On a neurological level, evidence suggests that depressed children (and adults) "underutilize" the neurotransmitter **serotonin** (Vitiello, 2006).

Treatment of Depression

Parents and teachers can help to alleviate relatively mild feelings of depression among children—involve them in enjoyable activities, encourage them to develop skills, praise them when appropriate, and point out when they are being too hard on themselves. But if feelings of depression persist, treatment is called for.

Psychotherapy for depression tends to be cognitive-behavioural today. Children (and adolescents) are encouraged to do enjoyable things and build social skills. They are made aware of their tendencies to minimize their accomplishments, exaggerate their problems, and overly blame themselves for shortcomings (e.g., Ellis & Dryden, 1996).

Because depressed children may underutilize serotonin, drugs that increase the action of serotonin in the brain (selective serotonin reuptake inhibitors, or SSRIs, such as Luvox, Prozac, and Zoloft) are sometimes used to treat childhood depression. Although SSRIs are often effective, a link may exist between their use and suicidal thinking in children (Harris, 2004).

CHILDHOOD ANXIETY

Children may show many kinds of anxiety disorders, which are accompanied by depression in 50–60 percent of children (Kendler et al., 2007). Yet many children show anxiety disorders, such as **generalized anxiety disorder (GAD)**, in the absence of depression (Kearney & Bensaheb, 2007). Other anxiety disorders shown by children include **phobias**, such as **separation anxiety disorder (SAD)**, and stage fright. (Beidel & Turner, 2007).

Separation Anxiety Disorder

Children sometimes show anxiety when they are separated from their caregivers. Separation anxiety is

attributional style the way in which one is disposed toward interpreting outcomes (successes or failures), as in tending to place blame or responsibility on oneself or on external factors.

serotonin a neurotransmitter that is involved in mood disorders such as depression.

generalized anxiety disorder (GAD) an anxiety disorder in which anxiety appears to be present continuously and is unrelated to the situation.

phobia an irrational, excessive fear that interferes with one's functioning.

separation anxiety disorder (SAD) an extreme form of otherwise normal separation anxiety characterized by anxiety about separating from parents; SAD often takes the form of refusal to go to school.

normal and begins during the first year. But the sense of security that is usually provided by bonds of attachment encourages children to explore their environment and become progressively independent.

It is normal for children to sometimes feel anxious when separated from loved ones or when entering an unfamiliar situation. When this interferes with normal life, there could be a more serious issue. Approximately 12 percent of children will suffer from some form of **separation anxiety disorder** (SAD) before they reach age 18. Separation Anxiety Disorder has three peaks: between ages 5 and 6, 7 and 9, and 12 and 14 (Anxiety B.C., 2010).

SAD is diagnosed when separation anxiety is persistent and excessive, when it is inappropriate for the child's developmental level, and when it interferes with activities or development tasks, such as attending school. Children with SAD tend to cling to their parents and follow them around the house. They may voice concerns about death and dying and insist that someone stay with them at bedtime. They may complain of nightmares and have "stomachaches" on school days. They may throw tantrums or plead with their parents not to leave the house.

SAD may occur before middle childhood, preventing adjustment to day care or nursery school. SAD usually becomes a significant problem in middle childhood, when children are expected to adjust to school.

Separation Anxiety Disorder, School Phobia, and School Refusal

SAD is an extreme form of separation anxiety. It is characterized by anxiety about separating from parents and may be expressed as **school phobia**—fear of school—or refusal to go to school (which can stem from fear or other factors). Separation anxiety is not behind all instances of school refusal. Some children refuse school because they perceive it as unpleasant, unsatisfying, or hostile, which it may be. Some children are concerned about doing poorly in school or being asked questions in class (in which case, they may have stage fright). High parental expectations may heighten children's anxieties, as may problems with classmates.

Treatment of School Phobia or School Refusal

It is usually not better for children with school phobia to remain at home until the origins of the problem are uncovered and resolved. Most professionals agree that the first rule in the treatment of school phobia is: Get the child back into school. The second rule is: Get the child back into school. And the third rule…you get the idea. The disorder often disappears once the child is back in school on a regular basis.

There is nothing wrong with trying to understand why a child refuses to attend school. Knowledge of the reasons for refusal can help parents and educators devise strategies for assisting the child. But perhaps such understanding need not precede insistence that the child return to school. In Figure 10.1, you can find a list of things that parents can do to get a child back into school.

Antidepressant medication has been used—often in conjunction with cognitive-behavioural methods—with much success (Pine et al., 2001; Walkup et al., 2001). However, drugs do not teach children how to cope. Many health professionals suggest that the drugs are best used only when psychological treatments have proven to be ineffective (Masi et al., 2001).

It seems unfortunate to depart middle childhood following a discussion of social and emotional problems. Most Canadian children come through middle childhood quite well, in good shape for the challenges and dramas of adolescence.

> **D5** Children with school phobia should return to school as soon as possible.
> Though understanding the problem can be helpful, getting the child back in school is the most important first step.

FIGURE 10.1
How Parents Can Help a Child Return to School

- Have the child return to school as quickly as possible.
- Secure the cooperation of the child's teacher, principal, or a Board of Education social worker.
- If the child has a specific school-related problem, such as an overly strict teacher, help the child—and teacher—find ways to handle the situation.
- Reward the child for attending school.

Adolescents

may be old enough to reproduce and may be as large as their parents, yet they may not be allowed to get a driver's licence until they turn 16 or 17. They cannot attend some movies until they turn 18.

11

Adolescence: Physical and Cognitive Development

Learning Outcomes

LO1 Describe the key events of puberty and their relationship to social development

LO2 Discuss health in adolescence, focusing on causes of death and eating disorders

LO3 Discuss adolescent cognitive development and the key events of Piaget's stage of formal operations

LO4 Discuss sex differences in cognitive abilities

LO5 Discuss Kohlberg's theory of moral development in adolescence

LO6 Discuss the roles of the school in adolescence, focusing on dropping out

LO7 Discuss career development and work experience during adolescence

Perhaps no other period of life is as exciting—and bewildering—as adolescence. Except for infancy, more changes occur during adolescence than any other time of life. Adolescence is a time of being in between. Adolescents may be old enough to reproduce and may be as large as their parents, yet they may not be allowed to get a driver's licence until they turn 16 or 17, and they cannot attend R-rated films. Given the restrictions placed on adolescents, their growing yearning for independence, and a sex drive heightened by high levels of sex hormones, it is not surprising that adolescents are occasionally in conflict with their parents.

puberty the biological stage of development characterized by changes that lead to reproductive capacity.

The idea that adolescence is an important and separate developmental stage was proposed by G. Stanley Hall (1904). Hall believed that adolescence is marked by turmoil and used the German term *Sturm und Drang* ("storm and stress") to refer to the conflicts of adolescence. Contemporary theorists no longer see adolescent storm and stress as inevitable (Smetana, 2005). Instead, they see adolescence as a period when biological, cognitive, social, and emotional functioning are reorganized. Nevertheless, adolescents need to adapt to numerous changes.

LO1 Puberty: The Biological Eruption

Puberty is a stage of development characterized by reaching sexual maturity and the ability to reproduce. The onset of adolescence coincides with the advent of puberty. Puberty is controlled

Sturm und Drang

Wolfe Larry/Shutterstock

feedback loop a system in which glands regulate each other's functioning through a series of hormonal messages.

primary sex characteristics the structures that make reproduction possible.

secondary sex characteristics physical indicators of sexual maturation—such as changes to the voice and growth of bodily hair—that do not directly involve reproductive structures.

by a **feedback loop** involving the hypothalamus, pituitary gland, the gonads—the ovaries in females and the testes in males—and hormones. The hypothalamus signals the pituitary gland, which, in turn, releases hormones that control physical growth and the gonads. The gonads respond to pituitary hormones by increasing their production of sex hormones (androgens and estrogens). The sex hormones further stimulate the hypothalamus, perpetuating the feedback loop.

The sex hormones also trigger the development of primary and secondary sex characteristics. The **primary sex characteristics** are the structures that make reproduction possible. In girls, these are the ovaries, vagina, uterus, and fallopian tubes. In boys, they are the penis, testes, prostate gland, and seminal vesicles. The **secondary sex characteristics** are physical indicators of sexual maturation that are not directly involved in reproduction. They include breast development, deepening of the voice, and the appearance of facial, pubic, and underarm hair.

THE ADOLESCENT GROWTH SPURT

The stable growth patterns in height and weight that characterize early and middle childhood end abruptly with the adolescent growth spurt. Girls start to spurt

FIGURE 11.1
Spurts in Growth

The adolescent growth spurt begins at about 10½ for girls and 13 for boys.

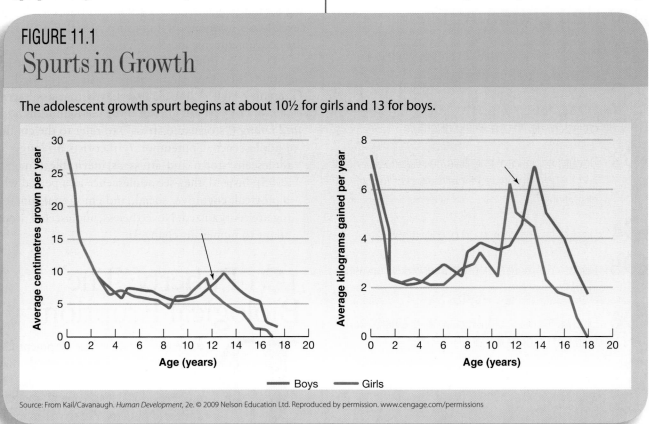

Boys —— Girls ——

Source: From Kail/Cavanaugh. *Human Development*, 2e. © 2009 Nelson Education Ltd. Reproduced by permission. www.cengage.com/permissions

in height sooner than boys, at an average age of a little older than 10. Boys start to spurt about 2 years later. Girls and boys reach their peak growth in height about 2 years after the growth spurt begins (see Figure 11.1). The spurt in height for both girls and boys continues for about another 2 years at a gradually declining pace. Boys add nearly 10 cm (4 in.) per year during the fastest year of the spurt compared with slightly more than 7.5 cm (3 in.) per year for girls. Overall, boys add an average of 37 cm (14½ in.) during the spurt and girls add a little more than 33 cm (13 in.) (Tanner, 1991a).

Adolescents begin to spurt in weight about half a year after they begin to spurt in height. The period of peak growth in weight occurs about a year and a half after the onset of the spurt. As with height, the growth spurt in weight then continues for a little more than 2 years. Because the spurt in weight lags the spurt in height, many adolescents are relatively slender compared with their preadolescent stature. However, adolescents tend to eat enormous quantities of food to fuel their growth spurts. Active 14- and 15-year-old boys may consume 3,000 to 4,000 calories a day without becoming obese.

Girls' and boys' body shapes begin to differ during adolescence. Girls develop relatively broader hips compared with their shoulders, whereas the opposite is true for boys. A girl's body shape is more rounded than a boy's because girls gain almost twice as much fatty tissue as boys. Boys gain twice as much muscle tissue as girls.

Asynchronous Growth

Adolescents may be awkward and gawky due to **asynchronous growth**; different parts of the body grow at different rates. The hands and feet mature before the arms and legs do. As a consequence, adolescent girls and boys may complain of big hands or feet. Legs reach their peak growth before the shoulders and chest. Boys stop growing out of their pants about a year before they stop growing out of their jackets (Tanner, 1989).

The Secular Trend

During the 20th century, children in the Western world grew dramatically more rapidly and ended up taller than children from earlier times (Sun et al., 2005). This historical trend toward increasing adult height was also accompanied by an earlier onset of puberty, and is known as the **secular trend**. Figure 11.2 on page 210 shows that Swedish boys and girls grew more rapidly in 1938 and 1968 than they did in 1883 and ended up several centimetres taller. At the age of 15, boys were more than 15 cm (6 in.) taller and girls were more than 7.5 cm (3 in.) taller, on average, than their counterparts from the previous century (Tanner, 1989). The occurrence of a secular trend in height and weight has been documented in nearly all European countries and in the United States and Canada.

However, children from middle- and upper-class families in developed nations, including Canada, no longer grow taller, whereas their poorer counterparts continue to gain in height from generation to generation (Tanner, 1989). Improved nutrition likely plays a key role. Healthy teenagers in more affluent countries seem to have reached their growth threshold.

© James Worrell/Getty Images

asynchronous growth imbalanced growth, such as the growth that occurs during the early part of adolescence and causes many adolescents to appear gawky.

secular trend a historical trend toward increasing adult height and earlier puberty.

CHANGES IN BOYS

At puberty, the pituitary gland stimulates the testes to increase their output of testosterone, leading to further development of the male genitals. The first visible sign of puberty is accelerated growth of the testes, which begins at an average age of about 11½, plus or minus 2 years. Testicular growth further accelerates testosterone production and other pubertal changes. The penis spurts about a year later, and still later, pubic hair begins to spurt.

Underarm and facial hair appears at about age 15. Only half of Canadian boys shave (of necessity) by age 17. At age 14 or 15, the voice deepens because of growth of the "voice box," or larynx, and the lengthening of the vocal cords. The process is gradual, and adolescent boys sometimes encounter an embarrassing cracking of the voice (see Figure 11.3 on page 211).

Testosterone also triggers the development of acne, which afflicts 75–90 percent of adolescents (Goldstein, 2004). Severe acne is manifested by

semen the fluid that contains sperm and substances that nourish and help transport sperm.

nocturnal emission emission of seminal fluid while asleep.

gynecomastia enlargement of breast tissue in males.

epiphyseal closure the process by which the cartilage that separates the long end of a bone from the main part of the bone turns to bone.

pimples and blackheads on the face, chest, and back. Although boys are more prone to acne, we cannot say that girls suffer less from it. A smooth complexion has a higher value for girls.

Males can have erections in early infancy, but erections are infrequent until age 13 or 14. Adolescent males may experience unwanted erections. The organs that produce **semen** grow rapidly, and boys typically ejaculate seminal fluid by age 13 or 14. About a year later, they begin to have **nocturnal emissions**, also called wet dreams because of the myth that emissions necessarily accompany erotic dreams. Mature sperm are found in ejaculatory emissions by about the age of 15.

Nearly half of all boys experience enlargement of the breasts, or **gynecomastia**, which usually declines in a year or two. Gynecomastia stems from the small amount of female sex hormones (estrogen) secreted by the testes.

At age 20 or 21, men stop growing taller because testosterone causes **epiphyseal closure**, which prevents the long bones from making further gains in length. Puberty for males draws to a close.

CHANGES IN GIRLS

In girls, the pituitary gland signals the ovaries to boost estrogen production at puberty. Estrogen may

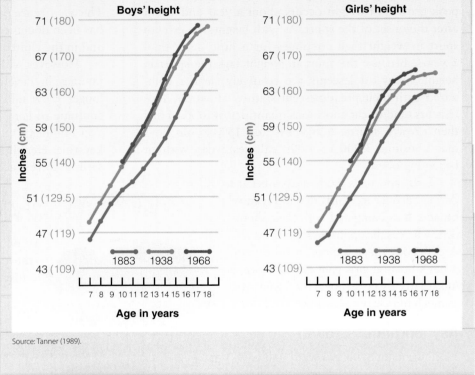

FIGURE 11.2
Are We Still Growing Taller than Our Parents?

Twentieth-century children grew taller than children in preceding centuries. Children from affluent families are no longer growing taller than their parents, but children from the lower part of the socioeconomic spectrum still do so.

Source: Tanner (1989).

FIGURE 11.3

Average Timing of Pubertal Changes in North American Youth

Girls are taller and heavier than boys from about age 9 or 10 until about age 13 because their growth spurt occurs earlier. Once boys begin their spurt, they catch up with girls and eventually become taller and heavier.

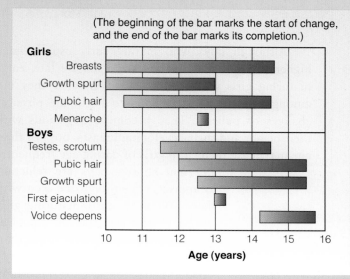

(The beginning of the bar marks the start of change, and the end of the bar marks its completion.)

Age (years)

Source: From Kail/Cavanaugh. *Human Development*, 2e. © 2009 Nelson Education Ltd. Reproduced by permission. www.cengage.com/permissions

stimulate the growth of breast tissue ("breast buds") as early as the ages of 8 or 9, but the breasts usually begin to enlarge during the 10th year. The development of fatty tissue and ducts elevates the areas of the breasts surrounding the nipples and causes the nipples to protrude. The breasts typically reach full size in about 4 years, but the *mammary glands* do not mature fully until a woman has a baby. Estrogen also promotes the growth of the fatty and supporting tissue in the hips and buttocks, which, along with the widening of the pelvis, causes the hips to round. Beginning at about the age of 10½ or 11, girls develop pubic and underarm hair (see Figure 11.3 on this page).

Estrogen causes the labia, vagina, and uterus to develop during puberty, and androgens cause the clitoris to develop. The vaginal lining varies in thickness according to the amount of estrogen in the bloodstream. Estrogen typically brakes the female growth spurt some years before testosterone brakes the growth spurt of males.

Menarche

Menarche (first menstruation) commonly occurs between the ages of 11 and 14, plus or minus 2 years (Capron et al., 2007; Mendle et al., 2006). The average age of menarche for a Canadian girl is 12½. During the past 150 years, menarche has occurred at progressively earlier ages in Western nations, another example of the secular trend (see Figure 11.4 on page 212; Tanner, 1991b).

menarche the onset of menstruation.

What accounts for the earlier age of puberty? One hypothesis is that girls must reach a certain body weight to trigger pubertal changes such as menarche. Body fat could trigger the changes because fat cells secrete a protein that signals the brain to secrete hormones that raise estrogen levels. Menarche comes later to girls who have a lower percentage of body fat, such as athletes and girls with eating disorders (Bosi & de Oliveira, 2006; Frisch, 1997). The average body weight for triggering menarche depends on the girl's height (Frisch, 1994). Today's girls are larger than those of the early 20th century because of improved nutrition and health care. As a result, menarche now occurs earlier than it did for previous generations.

Regulation of the Menstrual Cycle

Testosterone levels remain fairly stable in boys, but estrogen and progesterone levels in girls vary markedly and regulate the menstrual cycle.

Following menstruation—the sloughing off of the endometrium—estrogen levels increase, leading once more to the growth of endometrial tissue. Girls usually begin to ovulate only 12 to 18 months after menarche. After an ovum is released, if it is not fertilized, estrogen and progesterone levels drop suddenly, triggering menstruation once again.

The average menstrual cycle is 28 days, but variations are common. Girls' cycles are often irregular for a few years after menarche but later become more regular. Most cycles during the first 2 years or so after menarche occur without ovulation.

> **D1** Girls are not usually fertile immediately after their first menstrual period.
>
> Girls should not assume they cannot become pregnant at this time because variations in the timing of ovulation are common.

EARLY VERSUS LATE MATURERS

Early maturing boys tend to be more popular than their late-maturing peers and more likely to be leaders in school (Graber et al., 2004). They are more poised, more relaxed, and good-natured. Their edge in sports and the admiration of their peers heighten their sense of worth. On the negative side, early maturation is associated with greater risks of aggression and delinquency (Lynne et al., 2007) and abuse of alcohol and other drugs (Costello et al., 2007). Coaches may expect too much of early maturing boys in sports, and peers may want them to fight their battles. Sexual opportunities may create demands before they know how to respond (Lam et al., 2002).

Late maturers have the "advantage" of not being rushed into maturity. On the other hand, late-maturing boys often feel dominated by early-maturing boys. They have been found to be more dependent and more insecure and may be more easily influenced by peer pressure (Ge et al., 2003).

© BlueMoon Stock/Alamy

Although boys who mature early usually have higher self-esteem than those who mature late, early maturing girls may feel awkward, because they are among the first of their peers to begin the physical changes of puberty. They become conspicuous with their height and their developing breasts. Boys of their age may tease them. Tall girls of dating age frequently find that shorter boys are reluctant to approach them or to be seen with them. All in all, early maturing girls are at greater risk for psychological problems and substance abuse than girls who mature later on (Ge et al., 2003; Lynne et al., 2007). Many girls who mature early obtain lower grades in school and are involved in sexual activity earlier (Lam et al., 2002). For reasons such as these, the parents of early maturing girls may increase their vigilance and restrictiveness, leading to new child–parent conflicts.

Body Image

Adolescents tend to be concerned about their physical appearance, particularly in early adolescence during the rapid physical changes of puberty (Jones & Crawford, 2006). By the age of 18, girls and boys are more satisfied with their bodies (Eisenberg et al., 2006). Adolescent females in our society tend to be more preoccupied with body weight and slimness than adolescent males (Paxton

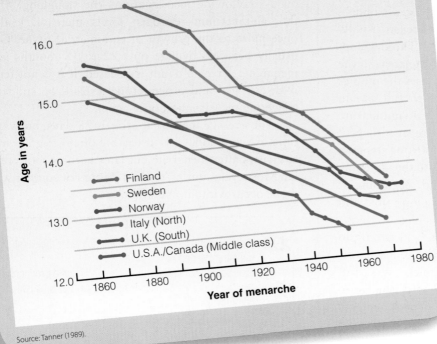

FIGURE 11.4
The Decline in Age at Menarche

The age at menarche has been declining since the mid-1800s among girls in Western nations, apparently because of improved nutrition and health care.

Age in years

- Finland
- Sweden
- Norway
- Italy (North)
- U.K. (South)
- U.S.A./Canada (Middle class)

Year of menarche

Source: Tanner (1989).

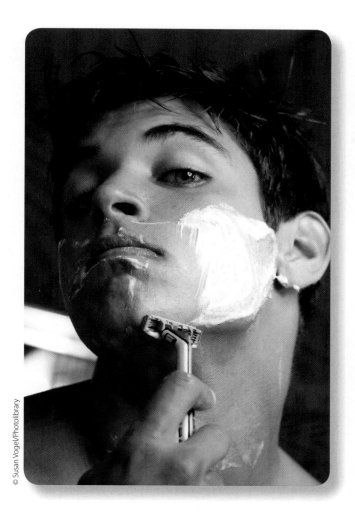

Yet about 18 percent of the nation's adolescents have at least one serious health problem (Bloom et al., 2006).

DEATH AND INJURIES

Death rates are low in adolescence, but they are nearly twice as great for male adolescents as female adolescents. Unintentional injury is the number one cause of death (73 percent) with 1 youth dying every 5 hours in Canada. Motor vehicle accidents cause 60 percent of these deaths. According to MacDonald, Yanchar, and Hebert (2007), this overwhelming rate of teen deaths can be traced to teenagers' increased likelihood of taking chances, their tendency to act impulsively, their overestimation of their skills, and their feeling of invincibility.

> **D3** Accidents are the number one cause of death for Canadian adolescents.
> Each week, 32 Canadian youths die in motor vehicle accidents (MacDonald et al., 2007).

NUTRITION

Physical growth occurs more rapidly in the adolescent years than at any other time after birth, with the exception of the first year of infancy. To fuel the adolescent growth spurt, the average girl needs 1,800 to 2,400 calories per day, and the average boy needs 2,200 to 3,200 calories (USDA, 2005). The nutritional

> **D2** Physical maturity influences boys' and girls' self esteem differently.
> Though boys who mature early often have higher self-esteem, early maturing girls can encounter negative social experiences.

et al., 2006). Many adolescent males want to gain weight to build their muscle mass (Stanford & McCabe, 2005).

LO2 Health in Adolescence

most Canadian adolescents are healthy. Few are chronically ill or miss school. Injuries tend to heal quickly.

needs of adolescents vary according to their activity level and stage of pubertal development. At the peak of the growth spurt, adolescents use twice as much calcium, iron, zinc, magnesium, and nitrogen as during other years of adolescence (USDA, 2005). Calcium intake is particularly important for females to build bone density and help prevent **osteoporosis** later in life, but most teenagers do not consume enough calcium. Adolescents are also likely to obtain less vitamin A, thiamine, and iron but more fat, sugar, and sodium than recommended (USDA, 2005).

One reason for adolescents' nutritional deficits is irregular eating patterns. Breakfast is often skipped, especially by dieters (Niemeier et al., 2006). Teenagers may rely on fast food and junk food, which are convenient but also high in fat and calories. A diet heavy in junk food can lead to being overweight, and being overweight in adolescence can lead to chronic illness and premature death in adulthood (Niemeier et al., 2006).

EATING DISORDERS

The Canadian ideal has slimmed down to where most Canadian females of normal weight are dissatisfied with the size and shape of their bodies (Paxton et al., 2005). In the section on cognitive development, we will see that adolescents also tend to think that others are paying a great deal of attention to their appearance. Because of cultural emphasis on slimness and the psychology of the adolescent, they are highly vulnerable to eating disorders, which are characterized by gross disturbances in patterns of eating.

Anorexia Nervosa

Anorexia nervosa is a life-threatening eating disorder characterized by extreme fear of being heavy, dramatic weight loss, a distorted body image, and resistance to eating enough to maintain a healthful weight. Anorexia nervosa afflicts males as well as females, but most studies put the female-to-male ratio at 10 to 1 or greater (Kjelsås et al., 2004). By and large, anorexia nervosa afflicts women during adolescence and young adulthood (Polivy et al., 2005). The typical person with anorexia is a young European Canadian female of higher socioeconomic status (Striegel-Moore et al, 2003). Affluent females are more likely to read the magazines that idealize slender bodies and shop in the stores that cater to females with slim figures (Forbush et al., 2007).

Females with anorexia nervosa can drop 25 percent or more of their weight within a year. Severe weight loss triggers abnormalities in the endocrine system (i.e., with hormones) that prevent ovulation (Nielsen & Palmer, 2003). General health declines. Problems arise in the respiratory system (Forman-Hoffman et al., 2006) and the cardiovascular system (Katzman, 2005). Females with anorexia are at risk for premature development of osteoporosis (Katzman, 2005). The mortality rate for anorexic females is about 4–5 percent.

Girls often develop anorexia nervosa to lose weight after fat gains from menarche (Shroff et al., 2006). Dieting and exercise continue well after the weight has been lost, and even after others say things are going too far. Denial is a major factor of anorexia nervosa. Distortion of the body image is also a major feature of the disorder.

© Kristian Dowling/Getty Images

Bulimia Nervosa

Bulimia nervosa is characterized by recurrent cycles of binge eating and purging. Binge eating often follows on the heels of dieting (Williams, 2004). There are various methods of purging. Vomiting is common. Other avenues include strict dieting or fasting, the overuse of laxatives, and engaging in demanding exercise regimes. Individuals with eating disorders will not settle for less than their idealized body shape and weight (Kaye et al., 2004). Bulimia, like anorexia, can lead to irregular menstrual cycles (Edler et al., 2007) and tends to afflict women during adolescence and young adulthood (Nolen-Hoeksema et al., 2007). Eating disorders are upsetting and dangerous in themselves, but are also related to depression (Nolen-Hoeksema et al., 2007).

Perspectives on Eating Disorders

The Canadian adolescent lives in a society of quick fixes and immediate feedback. Adolescents may turn to eating disorders as an immediate way to obtain their ideal body image. Unhealthy eating habits and excessive exercise patterns quickly take hold, placing the adolescent's health in danger.

A particularly disturbing risk factor for eating disorders in adolescent females is a history of child abuse, particularly sexual abuse (Corstorphine et al., 2007). One study found a history of childhood sexual abuse in about half of women with bulimia nervosa, as opposed to a rate of about 7 percent among women without the disorder (Deep et al., 1999).

Certainly young women have a very slender social ideal set before them in women such as Megan Fox. As the cultural ideal slenderizes, women who, according to the health charts, have a normal body weight, feel fat, and heavy women feel huge (Winzelberg et al., 2000).

Eating disorders tend to run in families, which raises the possibility of genetic involvement. Genetic factors will not directly cause eating disorders, but might lead to obsessionistic and perfectionistic personality traits (Wade et al., 2000).

Treatment

Eating disorders can lead to serious health problems, and the low weight of individuals with anorexia can be life-threatening. Some adolescent girls are admitted to the hospital for treatment against their will (Brunner et al., 2005). When the individual with anorexia does not—or cannot—eat adequately through the mouth, measures such as tube feeding may be used. Antidepressants (selective serotonin reuptake inhibitors) are often used to treat eating disorders because they stir the appetite of anorexic individuals and decrease binge eating in bulimic individuals (Grilo et al., 2005; Walsh et al., 2006). Cognitive-behavioural therapy has been used to help anorexic and bulimic individuals challenge their perfectionism and distorted body images.

bulimia nervosa an eating disorder characterized by cycles of binge eating and vomiting as a means of controlling weight gain.

formal operations the fourth stage in Piaget's cognitive-developmental theory, characterized by the capacity for flexible, reversible operations concerning abstract ideas and concepts, such as symbols, statements, and theories.

LO3 Cognitive Development: Piaget's Stage of Formal Operations

Concrete-operational children are bound by the facts as they are, but the adolescent and the adult can ponder abstract ideas and see the world as it could be. As many parents are aware, adolescents develop the skill of finding arguments for things they believe in, and things that they do not believe in.

The stage of **formal operations** is the top level in Jean Piaget's theory. Adolescents in this stage have reached cognitive maturity, even if rough edges remain. Yet for many children in developed nations, the stage of formal operations can begin at about the time of puberty, 11 or 12 years

© Images.com/Corbis

old. But some reach this stage a little later, and some not at all. Piaget describes the accomplishments of the stage of formal operations in terms of the individual's increased ability to classify objects and ideas, engage in logical thought, and hypothesize, just as researchers make hypotheses in their investigations. The adolescent can group and classify symbols, statements, and even theories. Adolescents can follow and formulate arguments from their premises to their conclusions and back once more, even if they do not believe in them. Hypothetical thinking, the use of symbols to represent other symbols, and deductive reasoning allow the adolescent to more fully comprehend the real world and to play with the world that dwells within the mind alone.

HYPOTHETICAL THINKING

In formal-operational thought, adolescents discover the concept of "what might be." Adolescents can project themselves into situations that transcend their immediate experience and become wrapped up in fantasies. Adolescents can think ahead, systematically trying out various possibilities in their minds. They "conduct research" to see whether their hypotheses about themselves and their friends and teachers are correct, for example, "trying on" different clothes and attitudes to see which work best for them.

In terms of career decisions, the wealth of possible directions leads some adolescents to experience both anxiety about whether they will pick the career that is the best fit and a sense of loss because they may be able to choose only one.

SOPHISTICATED USE OF SYMBOLS

Children in elementary school can understand what is meant by abstract symbols such as 1 and 2. They can also perform operations in which numbers are added, subtracted, and so on. But consider x, the primary algebraic symbol for variables. Children up to the age of 11 or 12 or so usually cannot fully understand the symbolic meaning of this concept, even if they can be taught the mechanics of solving for x in simple equations. But formal-operational children can grasp intuitively what is meant by x. Formal-operational children, or adolescents, can perform mental operations with symbols that stand for nothing in their own experience.

These symbols include those used in geometry. Adolescents work with points that have no dimensions, lines that have no width and are infinite in length, and circles that are perfectly round, even though such things are not found in nature. The ability to manipulate these symbols will permit them to work in theoretical physics or math or to obtain jobs in engineering or architecture.

Formal-operational individuals can understand, appreciate, and sometimes produce metaphors—figures of speech in which words or phrases that ordinarily signify one thing are applied to another. We find metaphors in literature, but consider how everyday figures of speech enhance our experience: *squeezing* out a living, *basking in the sunshine* of fame or glory, *hanging by a thread*, or *jumping* to conclusions.

Enhanced cognitive abilities can backfire when adolescents adamantly advance their religious, political, and social ideas without recognition of the subtleties and practical issues that might give pause to adults. For example, let's begin with the premise, "Industries should not be allowed to pollute the environment." If Industry A pollutes the environment, an adolescent may argue to shut down Industry A, at least until it stops polluting. The logic is reasonable and the goal is noble, but Industry A may be indispensable to the nation, or many thousands of people may be put out of work if it is shut down. More experienced people might prefer to seek a compromise.

ADOLESCENT EGOCENTRISM

Adolescents show a new egocentrism in which they comprehend the ideas of other people, but have difficulty sorting out those things that concern other people from the things that concern themselves.

The Imaginary Audience

Many adolescents fantasize about becoming rock stars or movie stars who are adored by millions. The concept of the **imaginary audience** achieves part of that fantasy, sort of. It places the adolescent on stage, but surrounded by critics more than by admirers. Adolescents assume that other people are concerned with their appearance and behaviour, more so than they really are (Elkind, 1967, 1985). The self-perception of adolescents as being on stage may account for their intense desire for privacy and their preoccupation with their appearance.

The Personal Fable

Spider-Man and the Fantastic Four: Stand aside! Because of the **personal fable**, many adolescents become action heroes, at least in their own minds. In the personal fable, one believes that one's thoughts and emotions are special and unique (Aalsma et al., 2006). It also refers to the common adolescent belief that one is invulnerable.

The personal fable is connected with such behaviours as showing off and risk taking (Omori & Ingersoll, 2005). Many adolescents assume that they can smoke with impunity. Cancer? "It can't happen to me." They drive recklessly. They engage in spontaneous unprotected sexual activity, assuming that sexually transmitted infections (STIs) and unwanted pregnancies happen to other people, not to them.

Many adolescents believe that their parents and other adults—even their peers—could never feel what they are feeling or know the depth of their passions. "You just don't understand me!" claims the adolescent. But, at least often enough, we do.

> **D4** It is normal for adolescents to think of themselves as action heroes and to act as though they are made of steel. High-risk behaviours seem to disregard the need to keep one's self safe. Bad things won't happen to me!

© Emanuele Taroni/Getty Images

LO4 Sex Differences in Cognitive Abilities

> **personal fable** the belief that our feelings and ideas are special and unique and that we are invulnerable; one aspect of adolescent egocentrism.

although females and males do not differ noticeably in overall intelligence, beginning in childhood, sex differences appear in certain cognitive abilities (Johnson & Bouchard, 2007). Females tend to be superior to males in verbal ability. Males tend to be superior in visual–spatial skills. The picture for mathematics is more complex, with females excelling in some areas and males in others.

VERBAL ABILITY

Verbal abilities include reading, spelling, grammar, oral comprehension, and word fluency. As a group, females surpass males in verbal ability (Halpern, 2003, 2004). These differences show up early. Girls seem to acquire language faster than boys. They make more prelinguistic vocalizations, utter their first word sooner, and develop larger vocabularies. Boys in Canada are more likely than girls to be dyslexic and to read below grade level (Halpern, 2003, 2004).

Why do females excel in verbal abilities? Biological factors such as the organization of the brain may play a role, but do not discount cultural factors—whether a culture stamps a skill as gender-neutral, masculine, or feminine (Goldstein, 2005). In Nigeria and England, reading is looked on as a masculine activity, and boys traditionally surpass girls in reading ability. But in the United States and Canada, reading tends to be stereotyped as feminine, and girls tend to excel.

VISUAL–SPATIAL ABILITY

Visual–spatial ability refers to the ability to visualize objects or shapes and to mentally manipulate and rotate them. This ability is important in such fields as art, architecture, and engineering. Boys begin to outperform girls on many types of visual–spatial tasks starting at age 8 or 9, and the difference persists into adulthood (Johnson & Bouchard, 2007). The sex difference is particularly notable on tasks that require imagining how objects will look if they are rotated in space (see Figure 11.5 on page 218; Delgado & Prieto, 2004).

Some researchers link visual–spatial performance to evolutionary theory and sex hormones. Visual–spatial ability may be related to a genetic tendency to create and defend a territory (Ecuyer-Dab & Robert, 2004). High levels of prenatal androgens have also been linked to better performance on visual–spatial and arithmetic tasks among 4- and 6-year-old girls (Finegan et al., 1992; Jacklin et al., 1988).

One environmental theory is that gender stereotypes influence the spatial experiences of children. Gender-stereotyped "boys' toys," such as blocks, Legos, and Erector sets, provide more practice with spatial skills than gender-stereotyped "girls' toys." Boys are also more likely to engage in sports, which involve moving balls and other objects through space (Halpern, 2004).

MATHEMATICAL ABILITY

For half a century or more, we have believed that male adolescents generally outperform females in mathematics, and research has tended to support that belief (Collaer & Hill, 2006; Halpern, 2004). For example, in a review of 100 studies involving more than 3 million individuals, Janet Hyde and her colleagues (1990) found a slight superiority for girls in computational skills in the elementary and middle-school years, but boys began to perform better in word problems in high school and college. There were no sex differences in understanding math concepts at any age. However, a more recent study by Hyde and her colleagues (2008) of some

FIGURE 11.5
Examples of Tests Used to Measure Visual–Spatial Ability

No sex differences are found on the spatial visualization tasks in part (a). Boys tend to perform better than girls on the tasks measuring spatial perception in part (b). The sex difference is greatest on the mental rotation tasks in part (c). What are some possible reasons for these differences?

a. Spatial visualization
Embedded-figure test. Study the figure on the left. Then cover it up and try to find where it is hidden in the figure on the right. The left-hand figure may need to be shifted in order to locate it in the right-hand figure.

b. Spatial perception
Water-level test. Examine the glass of water on the left. Now imagine that it is slightly tilted, as on the right. Draw in a line to indicate the location of the water level.

c. Mental rotation
Mental-rotation test. If you mentally rotate the figure on the left, which of the five figures on the right would you obtain?

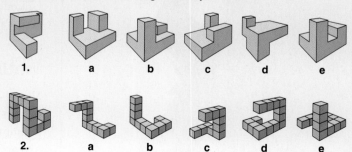

Answers: a. 1: Orient the pattern as if it were a tilted capital M, with the left portion along the top of the white triangle. 2: This pattern fits along the right sides of the two black triangles on the left. 3: Rotate this figure about 100° to the right, so that it forms a Z, with the top line coinciding with the top line of the top white triangle. **b.** The line should be horizontal, not tilted. **c.** 1: c; 2: d.

Go to www.icanhdev.com to access an interactive version of this figure.

TABLE 11.1
Kohlberg's Postconventional Level of Moral Development

STAGE	EXAMPLES OF MORAL REASONING THAT SUPPORT HEINZ'S STEALING THE DRUG	EXAMPLES OF MORAL REASONING THAT OPPOSE HEINZ'S STEALING THE DRUG
Stage 5: *Contractual, legalistic orientation:* One must weigh pressing human needs against society's need to maintain social order.	This issue is complicated because society has a right to maintain law and order, but Heinz has to take the drug to save his wife.	I can see why Heinz feels he has to take the drug, but laws exist for the benefit of society as a whole and cannot simply be cast aside.
Stage 6: *Universal ethical principles orientation:* People must follow universal ethical principles and their own conscience, even if it means breaking the law.	In this case, the law comes into conflict with the principle of the sanctity of human life. Heinz must take the drug because his wife's life is more important than the law.	If Heinz truly believes that stealing the drug is worse than letting his wife die, he should not take it. People have to make sacrifices to do what they think is right.

7 million Grade twos through Grade elevens found no sex differences for performance in mathematics on standardized tests. The complexity of the test items apparently made no difference. Nevertheless, most North Americans have different expectations for boys and girls, and these expectations may still dissuade girls from entering fields in science and math (Hyde et al., 2008).

LO5 Moral Development

Children in early childhood tend to view right and wrong in terms of rewards and punishments. Lawrence Kohlberg referred to such judgments as *preconventional*. In middle childhood, *conventional* thought tends to emerge, and children usually begin to judge right and wrong in terms of social conventions, rules, and laws (see Table 9.1 on page 174). In adolescence, many—not all—individuals become capable of formal-operational thinking, which allows them to derive conclusions about what they should do in various situations by reasoning from ethical principles. And many of these individuals engage in *postconventional* moral reasoning. They *deduce* proper behaviour.

THE POSTCONVENTIONAL LEVEL

In the **postconventional level**, moral reasoning is based on the person's own moral standards. Consider once more the case of Heinz that was introduced in Chapter 9 (see page 173). Moral judgments are derived from personal values, not from conventional standards or authority figures. In the contractual, legalistic orientation of Stage 5, it is recognized that laws stem from agreed-on procedures and that many rights have great value and should not be violated (see Table 11.1). But under exceptional circumstances, such as in the case of Heinz, laws cannot bind the individual. A Stage 5 reason for stealing the drug might be that it is the right thing to do, even though it is illegal. Conversely, it could be argued that if everyone in need broke the law, the legal system and the social contract would be destroyed.

Stage 6 thinking relies on supposed universal ethical principles, such as those of human life, individual dignity, justice, and reciprocity. Behaviour that is consistent with these principles is considered right. If a law is seen as unjust or contradicts the right of the individual, it is wrong to obey it.

In the case of Heinz, it could be argued from the perspective of Stage 6 that the principle of preserving life takes precedence over laws prohibiting stealing. Therefore, it is morally necessary for Heinz to steal the drug, even if he must go to jail. It could also be asserted, from the principled orientation, that if Heinz finds the social contract or the law to be the highest

postconventional level according to Kohlberg, a period during which moral judgments are derived from moral principles and people look to themselves to set moral standards.

FIGURE 11.6

Age and Type of Moral Judgment

The incidence of preconventional reasoning declines from more than 90 percent of moral statements at age 7 to less than 20 percent of statements at age 16. Conventional moral statements increase with age between the ages of 7 and 13 but then level off to account for 50–60 percent of statements at ages 13 and 16. Postconventional moral statements are all but absent at ages 7 and 10 but account for about 20–25 percent of statements at ages 13 and 16.

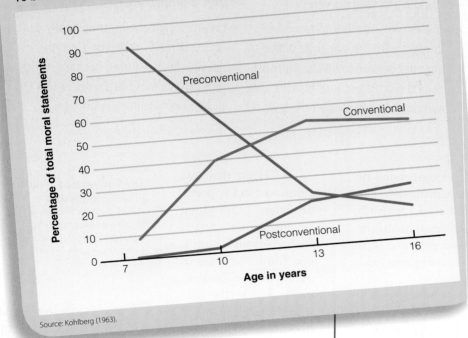

Source: Kohlberg (1963).

principle, he must remain within the law, despite the consequences.

Stage 5 and 6 moral judgments were virtually absent among the 7- and 10-year-olds in Kohlberg's (1963) sample of American children. They increased in frequency during the early and middle teens. By age 16, Stage 5 reasoning was shown by about 20 percent of adolescents and Stage 6 reasoning was demonstrated by about 5 percent of adolescents. However, Stage 3 and 4 judgments were made more frequently at all ages—7 through 16—studied by Kohlberg and other investigators (Commons et al., 2006; Rest, 1983) (see Figure 11.6).

MORAL BEHAVIOUR AND MORAL REASONING

Are individuals whose moral judgments are more mature more likely to engage in moral behaviour? The answer seems to be yes (Emler et al., 2007). Adolescents with higher levels of moral reasoning are more likely to exhibit moral behaviour (Maclean et al., 2004). Studies have also found that group discussion of moral dilemmas elevates delinquents' level of moral reasoning (Smetana, 1990).

EVALUATION OF KOHLBERG'S THEORY

Evidence supports Kohlberg's view that the moral judgments of children develop in an upward sequence (Boom et al., 2007), even though most children do not reach postconventional thought. Postconventional thought, when found, first occurs during adolescence, apparently because formal-operational thinking is a prerequisite for it (Patenaude et al., 2003).

Kohlberg believed that the stages of moral development follow the unfolding of innate sequences and are therefore universal. But he may have underestimated the influence of social, cultural, and educational institutions (Dawson, 2002).

Postconventional thinking is all but absent in developing societies (Snarey, 1994). Perhaps postconventional reasoning reflects Kohlberg's personal ideals and not a natural, universal stage of development (Helwig, 2006). In his later years, Kohlberg (1985) dropped Stage 6 reasoning from his theory in recognition of this possibility.

LO6 The Adolescent in School

how can we emphasize the importance of the school to the development of the adolescent? Adolescents are highly influenced by the opinions of their peers and their teachers. Their self-esteem rises or falls with the pillars of their skills.

The transition to junior high or high school generally involves a shift from a smaller neighbourhood elementary

Sex Differences in Moral Development

Do males reason at higher levels of moral development than females? Kohlberg and Kramer (1969) reported that the average stage of moral development for men was Stage 4, which emphasizes justice, law, and order. The average stage for women was reported to be Stage 3, which emphasizes caring and concern for others.

Carol Gilligan (Gilligan, 1982) argues that this sex difference reflects patterns of socialization: 11-year-old Jake views Heinz's dilemma as a math problem. He sets up an equation showing that life has greater value than property. Heinz should thus steal the drug. But 11-year-old Amy notes that stealing the drug and letting Heinz's wife die are both wrong. She searches for alternatives, such as getting a loan, saying that it wouldn't be wise for Heinz to go to jail and no longer be around to help his wife.

Although Gilligan sees Amy's reasoning as being as sophisticated as Jake's, it shows a lower level of moral development according to Kohlberg's system. Gilligan and other researchers (Jorgensen, 2006) agree that Amy, like other girls, has been socialized into caring about the needs of others and foregoing simplistic judgments of right and wrong. But to Jake, clear-cut conclusions are to be derived from a set of premises.

But does this difference mean that girls reason at a lower level than boys do?

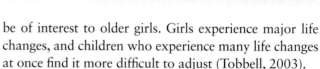

school to a larger, more impersonal setting with more students and different teachers for different classes. These changes may not fit the developmental needs of early adolescents. For example, adolescents express a desire for increased autonomy, yet teachers in junior high and high school typically allow less student input and exert more control than teachers in elementary school (Tobbell, 2003).

The transition to the new school setting is often accompanied by a decline in grades and less participation in school activities. Students may also experience a drop in self-esteem and an increase in stress (Rudolph & Flynn, 2007).

The transition from elementary school appears to be more difficult for girls than boys. Girls are more likely to be undergoing puberty and to earn the attention of boys in higher grades, whereas younger boys are not likely to be of interest to older girls. Girls experience major life changes, and children who experience many life changes at once find it more difficult to adjust (Tobbell, 2003).

But transition need not be that stressful (Rudolph et al., 2001). Elementary and middle schools can help ease the transition. Some middle schools create a more intimate, caring atmosphere by establishing smaller schools within the school building. Others have "bridge programs" during the summer that introduce students to the new school culture and strengthen their academic skills.

DROPPING OUT

Completing high school is a critical developmental task. The consequences of dropping out can be grim. Dropouts are more likely to be unemployed or have low incomes (Wald & Losen, 2007). Dropouts are more likely to develop delinquency, criminal behaviour, and substance abuse (Donovan & Wells, 2007).

Excessive school absence and reading below grade level are two predictors of school dropout (Lever et al., 2004). Other risk factors include low grades, low self-esteem, problems with teachers, substance abuse, being old for one's grade level, and being male (South et al., 2007). Adolescents who adopt adult roles early, especially marrying at a young age or becoming a parent, are also more likely to drop out (Bohon et al., 2007). Students from low-income households or large urban areas are at greater risk (National Center for Education Statistics, 2007).

Preventing Dropping Out

Many programs have been developed to prevent school dropout. Successful programs have some common characteristics (Bost & Riccomini, 2006; Reschly & Christenson, 2006): early preschool interventions (such as Head Start); identification and monitoring of high-risk students; small class size, individualized instruction, and counselling; vocational components that link learning and community work experiences; involvement of families or community organizations; and clear and reasonable educational goals.

Unfortunately, most intervention efforts are usually not introduced until students are on the verge of dropping out—when it is usually too late.

LO7 Career Development and Work Experience

deciding what job or career we will pursue after completion of school is one of the most important choices we make.

CAREER DEVELOPMENT

Children's first career aspirations may not be practical; however, they become increasingly realistic as children mature and gain experience. In adolescence, ideas about the kind of work one wants to do tend to become more firmly established, but a particular occupation may not be chosen until the postsecondary years or later (Rottinghaus et al., 2003).

© Design Pics/Kristy-Anne Glubish

Holland's Career Typology

John Holland's (1997) RIASEC method of predicting adjustment in a career matches six personality types to various kinds of careers: realistic, investigative, artistic, social, enterprising, and conventional. Within each "type" of career, some are more sophisticated than others and require more education and training.

- Realistic people are concrete in their thinking and are mechanically oriented. They tend to be best adjusted in occupations that involve motor activity, such as attending gas stations, farming, auto repairs, or construction work.

- Investigative people are abstract in their thinking, creative, and open to experience. They tend to do well in higher-level education and in research.

- Artistic people also tend to be creative and open to experience. They are emotional and intuitive. They tend to be content in the visual and performing arts.

- Socially oriented people tend to be outgoing (extraverted) and concerned for social welfare. They gravitate toward occupations in teaching (kindergarten through high school), counselling, and social work.

- Enterprising people tend to be adventurous, outgoing, and dominant. They gravitate toward leadership roles in industry and organizations.

- Conventional people thrive on routine and have needs for order, self-control, and social approval. They gravitate toward occupations in banking, accounting, clerical work, and the military.

Many people combine several vocational types (Nauta, 2007). For example, a copywriter in an advertising agency might be both artistic and enterprising.

Realistic

© Morgan Lane Photography/Shutterstock

Holland's Vocational Preference Inventory assesses these personality types, as do various vocational tests used in high schools, colleges, and universities.

All in all, thousands of occupations are available, but most young people choose from a relatively small range of traditional occupations on the basis of their personalities, experiences, and opportunities (Nauta, 2007).

ADOLESCENTS IN THE WORKFORCE

Life experiences help shape vocational development One life experience common among most North American teenagers is holding a job.

Prevalence of Adolescent Employment

According to Statistics Canada (2008a), in 2004–05, 46 percent of high-school students between the ages of 15 and 17 held a job. Those not working reported preferring to focus on schoolwork or other activities.

Artistic

Pros and Cons of Adolescent Employment

The potential benefits of adolescent employment include developing a sense of responsibility, self-reliance, and discipline; learning to appreciate the value of money and education; acquiring positive work habits and values; and enhancing occupational aspirations (Porfeli,

2007). Working a reasonable amount of time per week (less than 10 hours) prompts students to schedule their study time appropriately and lends structure to the week. On the other hand, most working adolescents are in jobs with low pay, high turnover, little authority, and little chance for advancement (Staff et al., 2004). Some question the benefits of such jobs. Students who work lengthy hours—more than 11 to 13 hours per week—report lower grades, higher rates of drug and alcohol use, more delinquent behaviour, lower self-esteem, and higher levels of psychological problems than students who do not work or who work only a few hours (Brandstätter & Farthofer, 2003). Students working 30 hours or more per week were the most likely to drop out of high school (Statistics Canada, 2008a). Perhaps the most prudent course is for parents and educators to limit the number of hours adolescents work, particularly during the school year.

> **D5** The number of hours worked after school can affect school performance.
> This is true. Working 30 hours per week or more places students at a high risk to drop out of school. Working less than 10 hours can prompt students to manage their time productively.

© R. Gino Santa Maria/Shutterstock

Adolescents are

preoccupied not only with their present selves but also with what they
want to become.

12

Adolescence: Social and Emotional Development

DID YOU KNOW?

D1 ▸ Canadian adolescent males are as concerned about occupational choices as Canadian adolescent females are.

D2 ▸ The idea of adolescents being in a constant state of rebellion against their parents is a stereotype that is no longer true.

D3 ▸ Parents should not necessarily fear peer pressure.

D4 ▸ Teen sexual activity has been declining in Canada since the early 1990s.

D5 ▸ Suicide is the second leading cause of death among Canadian adolescents.

What am I like as a person? Complicated! I'm sensitive, friendly and outgoing, though I can also be shy, self-conscious, and even obnoxious. . . . I'm responsible, even studious every now and then, but on the other hand I'm a goof-off too, because if you're too studious, you won't be popular. . . . Sometimes I feel phony, especially around boys. . . . I'll be flirtatious and fun-loving. And then everybody else is looking at me . . . Then I get self-conscious and embarrassed and become radically introverted, and I don't know who I really am! I can be my true self with my close friends. I can't be my real self with my parents. They don't understand me. They treat me like I'm still a kid. That gets confusing, though. I mean, which am I, a kid or an adult?

—Adapted from Harter (1990, pp. 352–353)

These thoughts of a 15-year-old girl illustrate a key aspect of adolescence: the search for an answer to the question "Who am I?" She is struggling to reconcile contradictory traits and behaviours to determine the "real me." Adolescents are preoccupied not only with their present selves but also with what they want to become.

Learning Outcomes

LO1 Discuss the formation of identity in adolescence

LO2 Discuss relationships with parents and peers during adolescence

LO3 Discuss sexuality during adolescence, focusing on sexual identity and teenage pregnancy

LO4 Discuss the statistics specific to youth in conflict with the law and measures that can reduce youth crime in Canada

LO5 Discuss risk factors in adolescent suicide

LO1 Development of Identity: "Who Am I?"

in this chapter, we explore social and emotional development in adolescence. We begin with the formation of identity.

ERIKSON AND IDENTITY DEVELOPMENT

Erik Erikson's fifth stage of psychosocial development is called identity versus identity diffusion. The primary task is for adolescents to develop **ego identity**: a sense of who they are and what they stand for. They are faced with choices about their future occupation, political and religious beliefs, and gender roles. Because of formal-operational thinking, adolescents can weigh options they have not directly experienced (Roeser et al., 2006).

One aspect of identity development is a **psychological moratorium** during which adolescents experiment with different roles, values, beliefs, and relationships (Erikson, 1968). During this time, adolescents undergo an **identity crisis** in which they examine their values and make decisions about their life roles. Should they attend college or university? What career should they pursue? Should they become sexually active? With whom? Adolescents in developed nations may feel overwhelmed by their options.

In their search for identity, many—not all—adolescents join "in" groups, slavishly imitating their peers' clothing, speech, hairstyles, and ideals (Erikson, 1963). Those who successfully resolve their identity crisis develop a strong sense of who they are and what they stand for. Those who do not may be intolerant of people who are different and blindly follow people who adhere to convention.

IDENTITY STATUSES

Building on Erikson's approach, James Marcia (1991) theorized four identity statuses that represent the four possible combinations of the dimensions of exploration and commitment that Erikson believed were critical to the development of identity (Schwartz, 2001) (see Table 12.1). *Exploration*

Who do I want to become?

© Image Source/Jupiterimages

involves active questioning and searching among alternatives to establish goals, values, and beliefs. *Commitment* is a stable investment in one's goals, values, and beliefs.

Identity diffusion is the least advanced status and includes adolescents who neither have commitments nor are trying to form them (Berzonsky, 2005). This stage is characteristic of younger adolescents and of older adolescents who drift through life or become alienated and rebellious (Snarey & Bell, 2003).

In the **foreclosure** status, individuals make commitments without considering alternatives. These commitments are usually established early in life and are often based on identification with parents, teachers, or religious leaders who have made a strong impression (Saroglou & Galand, 2004).

The **moratorium** status refers to a person who is actively exploring alternatives in an attempt to make choices (Akman, 2007). Such individuals are often anxious and intense.

Identity achievement refers to those who have explored alternatives and developed relatively firm commitments. They generally have high self-esteem and self-acceptance (Adams et al., 2006).

Development of Identity Statuses

Before high school, children show little interest in questions of identity. Most are either in identity diffusion or foreclosure statuses. During the high school and post-secondary years, adolescents increasingly move from the

TABLE 12.1
The Four Identity Statuses of James Marcia

COMMITMENT		EXPLORATION	
		Yes	**No**
Yes		**Identity Achievement** • Most developed in terms of identity • Has experienced a period of exploration • Has developed commitments • Has a sense of personal well-being, high self-esteem, and self-acceptance • Cognitively flexible • Sets goals and works toward achieving them	**Foreclosure** • Has commitments without considering alternatives • Commitments based on identification with parents, teachers, or other authority figures • Often authoritarian and inflexible
No		**Moratorium** • Actively exploring alternatives • Attempting to make choices with regard to occupation, ideological beliefs, and so on • Often anxious and intense • Ambivalent feelings toward parents and authority figures	**Identity Diffusion** • Least developed in terms of identity • Lacks commitments • Not trying to form commitments • May be carefree and uninvolved or unhappy and lonely • May be angry, alienated, rebellious

diffusion and foreclosure statuses to the moratorium and achievement statuses (Snarey & Bell, 2003). The greatest gains in identity formation occur in college and university (Berzonsky & Kuk, 2005). College and university students are exposed to a variety of lifestyles, beliefs, and career choices, which spur consideration of identity issues. Are you a student who has changed majors once or twice (or more)? If so, you have most likely experienced the moratorium identity status, which is common among postsecondary students. College and university seniors have a stronger sense of identity than first-year students as a result of resolving identity crises (Lewis, 2003).

ETHNICITY AND DEVELOPMENT OF IDENTITY

The development of self-identity is a key task for all adolescents. The task is more complex for adolescents who are members of ethnic minority groups (Phinney

& Ong, 2007). Adolescents who belong to the dominant culture—in this country, European Canadians of Christian heritage—are usually faced with assimilating one set of cultural values into their identities. However, adolescents who belong to ethnic minority groups, such as Black Canadians and Islamic Canadians, confront two sets of cultural values: the values of the dominant culture and those of their particular ethnic group (Phinney & Alipuria, 2006). If the cultural values conflict, the adolescent needs to sort out which values are most meaningful and incorporate them into his or her identity. Some adolescents do it cafeteria style; they take a little bit of this and a little bit of that. For example, a young Catholic woman may

© FoodPix/JupiterImages/Getty Images

ethnic identity a sense of belonging to an ethnic group.

unexamined ethnic identity the first stage of ethnic identity development; similar to the diffusion or foreclosure identity statuses.

ethnic identity search the second stage of ethnic identity development; similar to the moratorium identity status.

achieved ethnic identity the final stage of ethnic identity development; similar to the identity achievement status.

decide to use artificial means of birth control even though doing so conflicts with her religion's teachings.

Adolescents from ethnic minority groups also often experience prejudice and discrimination. Their cultural heroes may be ignored. A relative scarcity of successful role models can be a problem, particularly for youth who live in poverty. Identifying too strongly with the dominant culture may also lead to rejection by the minority culture. On the other hand, rejecting the dominant culture's values for those of the minority group may limit opportunities for advancement in the larger society.

Some researchers hypothesize three stages in the development of **ethnic identity** (Phinney, 2006). The first is **unexamined ethnic identity**, which is similar to Marcia's ego identity statuses of diffusion or foreclosure. In the second stage, the adolescent embarks on an **ethnic identity search**. This second stage, similar to Marcia's moratorium, may be based on some incident that makes the adolescent aware of her ethnicity. During this stage, the adolescent may explore her ethnic culture, participating in cultural events, reading, and discussion. In the third stage, individuals have an **achieved ethnic identity** that involves self-acceptance as a member of one's ethnic group.

SEX AND DEVELOPMENT OF IDENTITY

Erikson believed that sex differences affected the development of identity, and his views reflected the times in which he wrote. Identity development relates both to relationships and occupational choice, among other matters. Erikson (1968, 1975) assumed that relationships were more important to women's development of identity, whereas occupational and ideological matters were relatively more important to men's identity development. He believed that a young woman's identity was intimately bound up with her roles as wife and mother. Studies today show that both adolescent females and males are concerned about occupational choices, even though females remain more likely to integrate their occupational and family plans (Berzonsky, 2004). This sex difference

may persist because females continue to assume primary responsibility for child rearing, even though most women are employed outside the home (Anthis et al., 2004).

D1 Canadian adolescent males are as concerned about occupational choices as Canadian adolescent females are. Though females remain more likely to integrate their occupational and family plans, studies show an equal concern for occupational choices.

DEVELOPMENT OF THE SELF-CONCEPT

Before adolescence, children describe themselves primarily in terms of their physical characteristics and their actions. As they approach adolescence, children begin to incorporate psychological characteristics and social relationships into their self-descriptions (Damon, 1991).

The self-concept becomes more differentiated; adolescents add more categories to their self-description. Also, social roles begin to enter self-descriptions. Adolescents may describe themselves as anxious or sarcastic with parents but talkative and cheerful with friends. Such contradictions and conflicts in self-description reach their peak at about age 14 and then decline (Harter & Monsour, 1992). The advanced formal-operational skills of the older adolescent allow her to integrate contradictory aspects of the self. The older adolescent might say: "I'm very adaptable.

How would you describe yourself?

√ anxious
√ sarcastic
√ caring
√ talkative
√ cheerful
√ adaptable
√ quiet

© Radius Images/Jupiterimages

NEL

When I'm around my friends, who think that what I say is important, I'm very talkative; but around my family, I'm quiet because they're not interested enough to really listen to me" (Damon, 1991, p. 988).

SELF-ESTEEM

Self-esteem tends to decline as the child progresses from middle childhood to about the age of 12 or 13 (Harter & Whitesell, 2003). The growing cognitive maturity of young adolescents makes them increasingly aware of the disparity between their ideal self and their real self, especially in terms of physical appearance (Durkin et al., 2007; Seidah & Bouffard, 2007). Boys might fantasize having the physiques of the warriors they see in video games or in the media (Konijn et al., 2007). Most girls want to be thin, thin, thin (O'Dea, 2006).

After hitting a low point at about age 12 or 13, self-esteem gradually improves (Harter & Whitesell, 2003). Perhaps adolescents adjust their ideal selves to better reflect reality. Also, as adolescents develop academic, physical, and social skills, they may grow less self-critical (Shirk et al., 2003).

For most adolescents, low self-esteem produces temporary discomfort (Harter & Whitesell, 2003). For others, low self-esteem has serious consequences. For example, low self-esteem is often found in teenagers who are depressed or suicidal (Shirk et al., 2003).

Emotional support from parents and peers is important in maintaining self-esteem. Adolescents who feel highly regarded by family and friends are more likely to feel positive about themselves (Costigan et al., 2007). In early adolescence, support from parents is as important as peer support. By late adolescence, peer support carries more weight.

LO2 Relationships with Parents and Peers

adolescents coping with the task of establishing a sense of identity and direction in their lives are heavily influenced both by parents and peers.

RELATIONSHIPS WITH PARENTS

During adolescence, children spend much less time with their parents than they did in childhood (Larson & Richards, 1991). Adolescents continue to interact more

with their mothers than their fathers. Teenagers have more conflicts with their mothers than their fathers, but they also view their mothers as being more supportive and knowing them better (Costigan et al., 2007). Adverse relationships with fathers are often associated with depression in adolescents (Sheeber et al., 2007), but good relations with fathers contribute to psychological well-being (Flouri & Buchanan, 2003).

The decrease in time spent with family may reflect the adolescents' striving for independence. A certain degree of distancing from parents may be adaptive, as adolescents form relationships outside the family. However, adolescents continue to maintain love, loyalty, and respect for their parents (Collins & Laursen, 2006). And adolescents who feel close to their parents have more self-reliance and self-esteem, better school performance, and fewer adjustment problems (Costigan et al., 2007).

The relationship between parents and teens is not always rosy, of course. Early adolescence, in particular, is characterized by increased bickering and a decrease in both shared activities and expressions of affection (Smetana et al., 2006). Conflicts typically centre on the everyday details of family life, such as chores, homework, curfews, personal appearance, finances, and dating—often because adolescents believe they should manage matters that were previously controlled by parents (Costigan et al., 2007). But parents, especially mothers, continue to believe they should retain control in most areas, such as encouraging adolescents to do their homework and clean their rooms. As adolescents get older, they and their parents are more likely to compromise (Smetana et al., 2006). On the other hand, parents and adolescents are usually quite similar in their values and beliefs regarding social, political, religious,

and economic issues (Collins & Laursen, 2006). Even though the notion of a generation gap between adolescents and their parents may persist as a stereotype, there is little evidence of such a gap.

As adolescents grow older, parents are more likely to relax controls and less likely to use punishment (Smetana et al., 2006). Although parent–child relationships change, most adolescents feel that they are close to and get along with their parents, even though they may develop a less idealized view of them (Collins & Laursen, 2006).

> **D2** The idea of adolescents being in a constant state of rebellion against their parents is a stereotype that is no longer true.
> Parents and adolescents are usually quite similar in their values and beliefs regarding social, political, religious, and economic issues (Collins & Laursen, 2006).

Parenting Styles

Differences in parenting styles continue to influence the development of adolescents (Costigan et al., 2007). Adolescents from authoritative homes—whose parents are willing to exert control and explain the reasons for doing so—show the most competent behaviour. They are more self-reliant, do better in school, have better mental health, and show the lowest incidence of psychological problems and misconduct, including drug use.

RELATIONSHIPS WITH PEERS

The transition from childhood to adolescence is accompanied by a shift in the relative importance of parents and peers. Although relationships with parents generally remain positive, the role of peers increases as a source of activities, influence, and support. Parents are perceived as the most frequent providers of social and emotional support by Grade fours, but by Grade 7, friends of the same sex are seen to be as supportive as parents. By Grade 10, same-sex friends are viewed as providing more support than parents (Furman & Buhrmester, 1992).

Friendships in Adolescence

Adolescents have more friends than younger children do (Feiring & Lewis, 1991). Most adolescents have one or two "best friends" and several good friends. Teenagers see their friends frequently, usually several hours a day (Hartup, 1983). And when teenagers are not with their friends, you can often find them talking on the phone, texting, or "Facebooking" one another.

Friendships in adolescence differ from the friendships of childhood. Adolescents are more likely to stress acceptance, intimate self-disclosure, and mutual understanding (González et al., 2004). One Grade 8 girl described her best friend this way: "I can tell her things and she helps me talk. And she doesn't laugh at me if I do something weird—she accepts me for who I am" (Berndt & Perry, 1990, p. 269). Second, adolescents stress loyalty and trustworthiness (Rotenberg et al., 2004). They may consider a friend as someone who will "stick up for you in a fight" and will "not talk about you behind your back." Finally, adolescents are more likely than younger children to share with friends and less likely to compete with them.

Adolescents and their friends are similar in many respects. They typically are the same age and the same race. They almost always are the same sex. Even though romantic attachments increase during the teen years, most adolescents still choose members of their own sex as best friends (Hartup, 1993). Friends are often alike in school attitudes, educational aspirations, and grades. Friends also tend to have similar attitudes about drinking, drug use, and sexual activity (Youniss & Haynie, 1992).

Friendship contributes to a positive self-concept and psychological adjustment. Adolescents who have a close friend have higher self-esteem than adolescents who do not (Berndt, 1992).

Intimacy and closeness appear to be more central to the friendships of girls than of boys (Schraf & Hertz-Lazarowitz, 2003). Adolescent and adult females also are generally more likely than males to disclose secrets, personal problems, thoughts, and feelings to their friends (Dindia & Allen, 1992).

Friendship networks among girls are smaller and more exclusive than networks among boys (Schraf & Hertz-Lazarowitz, 2003). Girls tend to have one or two close friends, whereas boys tend to congregate in larger, less intimate groups. The activities of girls' and boys' friendship networks also differ. Girls are more likely to engage in unstructured activities, such as talking and listening to music. Boys are more likely to engage in organized group activities, games, and sports.

© David J. Green - technology / Alamy

Peer Groups

Most adolescents belong to one or more peer groups: *cliques* and

Adolescent peer groups function with less adult guidance or control than childhood peer groups.

© Purestock/Jupiterimages

clique a group of five to ten individuals who hang around together and who share activities and confidences.

crowd a large, loosely organized group of people who may or may not spend much time together and who are identified by the activities of the group.

crowds (Henzi et al., 2007). **Cliques** consist of five to ten individuals who hang around together and share activities and confidences. **Crowds** are larger groups that may or may not spend much time together and are identified by their activities or attitudes. Crowds are usually given labels by other adolescents such as "jocks," "brains," "druggies," or "nerds." The most negatively labelled groups ("druggies" and "rejects") show higher levels of alcohol and drug abuse, delinquency, and depression.

Adolescent peer groups function with less adult guidance or control than childhood peer groups (Staff et al., 2004). Adolescent peer groups may include members of the other sex, which sharply contrasts with the sex segregation of childhood peer groups. Such associations may lead to dating and romantic relationships.

Dating and Romantic Relationships

Romantic relationships usually begin during early and middle adolescence, and most adolescents start dating or going out by the time they graduate from high school (Florsheim, 2003). For heterosexuals, the development of dating typically takes the following sequence: putting oneself in situations where peers of the other sex probably will be present (e.g., hanging out at the mall), group activities including peers of the other sex (e.g., school dances or parties), group dating (e.g., joining a mixed-sex group at the movies), and then traditional two-person dating (Connolly et al., 2004).

Dating serves a number of functions. First and foremost, people date to have fun. Dating, especially in early adolescence, also serves to enhance prestige with peers. Dating gives adolescents additional experiences in learning to relate to people. Finally, dating prepares adolescents for adult courtship (Florsheim, 2003).

Dating relationships tend to be casual and short-lived in early adolescence. In late adolescence, relationships tend to become more stable and committed (Connolly et al., 2000). Eighteen-year-olds are more likely than 15-year-olds to mention love, trust, and commitment when describing romantic relationships (Feiring, 1993).

Peer Influence

Peer pressure is fairly weak in early adolescence. It peaks during midadolescence and declines after about age 17 (Reis & Youniss, 2004). Peer influence may increase during adolescence because peers provide a standard by which adolescents measure their own behaviour as they develop independence from the family (Foster-Clark & Blyth, 1991). Peers also provide support in times of trouble (Kirchler et al., 1991).

Parents often worry that their teenage children will fall in with the wrong crowd and be persuaded by peers to engage in self-destructive or immoral behaviour. Despite the widespread assumption that peer influences and parental influences will be in conflict, with peers exerting pressure on adolescents to engage in negative behaviours such as alcohol and drug abuse, research paints a more complex picture. Parents and peers are usually complementary rather than competing influences (Reis & Youniss, 2004).

Parents and peers also seem to exert influence in different domains. Adolescents are more likely to conform to peer standards in matters pertaining to style and taste, such as clothing, hairstyles, speech patterns, and music (Camarena, 1991). They are more likely to agree with their parents on moral principles and future educational and career goals (Savin-Williams & Berndt, 1990).

Adolescents influence each other positively and negatively. In many cases, peer pressure to finish high school and achieve academically can be stronger than pressures to engage in misconduct (Brown et al., 1993; Steinberg,

homosexual an erotic orientation toward members of one's own sex.

1996). Yet many times adolescents discourage one another from doing well or from doing too well in school. Adolescents who smoke, drink, use drugs, and engage in sexual activity also often have friends who engage in these behaviours, but

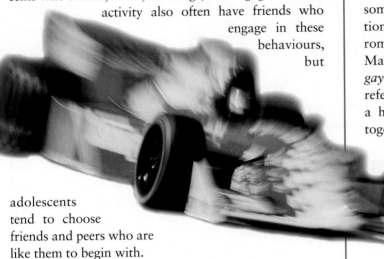

adolescents tend to choose friends and peers who are like them to begin with.

> **D3** Parents should not necessarily fear peer pressure. Parents and peers are usually complementary rather than competing influences (Reis & Youniss, 2004).

LO3 Sexuality

My first sexual experience occurred in a car after the Grade 10 Christmas dance. We were both virgins, very uncertain but very much in love. We had been going together since Grade 8. The experience was somewhat embarrassing. I remember wondering if I would look different to my mother the next day. I guess I didn't because nothing was said.

because of the flood of sex hormones, adolescents tend to experience a powerful sex drive. In addition, they are bombarded with sexual messages in the media, including scantily clad hip-grinding, crotch-grabbing pop stars; print ads for barely there underwear; and countless articles on "How to tell if your boyfriend has been (insert teen drama here . . .)" and "The 10 things that will drive your girlfriend wild." Teenagers are strongly motivated to follow the crowd, yet they are also influenced by the views of their parents and teachers. So what is a teen to do?

Sexual activity in adolescence can take many forms. In this section, we consider sexual identity, sexual behaviour, and teenage pregnancy.

SEXUAL IDENTITY

Most people, including the great majority of adolescents, have a heterosexual sexual identity. They are sexually attracted to and interested in forming romantic relationships with people of the other sex. However, some people have a **homosexual** identity or orientation. They are attracted to and interested in forming romantic relationships with people of their own sex. Males with a homosexual orientation are referred to as *gay males*. Females with a homosexual orientation are referred to as *lesbians*. However, males and females with a homosexual orientation are sometimes categorized together as "gay people," or "gays." *Bisexual* people are attracted to both females and males.

According to Ritch Savin-Williams and Lisa Diamond (2004; Savin-Williams, 2007), the development of sexual identity in gay males and lesbians involves several steps: attraction to members of the same sex, self-labelling as gay or lesbian, sexual contact with members of the same sex, and eventual disclosure of one's sexual orientation to other people. Generally, about a 10-year gap occurs between initial attraction to members of the same sex, which tends to occur at about the age of 8 or 9, and disclosure of one's orientation to other people, which usually occurs at about age 18. But some gay males and lesbians never disclose their sexual orientations to anyone or to certain people, such as their parents.

The process of "coming out"—that is, accepting one's homosexual orientation and declaring it to others—may be a long and painful struggle (Bagley & D'Augelli, 2000). Gay adolescents may be ostracized and rejected by family and friends. Depression and suicide rates are higher among gay youth than among heterosexual adolescents. As many as one in three gay, lesbian, or bisexual adolescents has attempted suicide (Hershberger & D'Augelli, 2000). Homosexual adolescents often engage in substance abuse, run away from home, and do poorly in school (Russell, 2006). As Canadian society becomes more inclusive and open to sexual diversity, social pressures lessen, potentially reducing many of these negative outcomes.

"Coming out to others" sometimes means an open declaration to the world. More often, an adolescent feels more comfortable telling a couple of close friends. Before they inform family members, gay adolescents often fear their family's negative reactions, including denial, anger, and rejection (Bagley & D'Augelli, 2000). Yet many families are more accepting.

MASTURBATION

Masturbation, or sexual self-stimulation, is the most common sexual outlet in adolescence. Surveys indicate that most adolescents masturbate at some time. The Kinsey studies, published in the mid-20th century (Kinsey et al., 1948, 1953), suggested that masturbation was nearly universal among male adolescents but less common among adolescent females. Boys who masturbate do so more frequently than girls who masturbate. Beliefs that masturbation is harmful and guilt about masturbation lessen the incidence of masturbation (Ortega et al., 2005), although masturbation has not been shown to be physically harmful.

MALE–FEMALE SEXUAL BEHAVIOUR

Adolescents today start dating and going out earlier than in past generations. Teens who date earlier are more likely to engage in sexual activity during high school (Guttmacher, 2007). Teens who initiate sexual activity earlier are also less likely to use contraception and more likely to become pregnant. But early dating does not always lead to early sex, and early sex does not always lead to unwanted pregnancies.

Sexual touching is practically universal among Canadian adolescents and has been for many generations. Adolescents use touching to express affection, satisfy their curiosities, heighten their sexual arousal, and reach orgasm while avoiding pregnancy and maintaining virginity. Many adolescents do not see themselves as having sex if they stop short of vaginal intercourse (Guttmacher, 2007). Girls are more likely than boys to be coerced into touching and to feel guilty about it (Larsson & Svedin, 2002).

Surveys show that since the early 1990s, the percentage of high school students who have engaged in sexual intercourse has been gradually declining in spite of social misperceptions (see Table 12.2, on p. 234). The incidences of kissing, touching, oral sex, and sexual intercourse all increase with age. For example, according to a survey by the Centers for Disease Control and Prevention, 42 percent of girls of ages 15 to 17 reported engaging in oral sex compared with 72 percent of girls aged 18 to 19 (Mosher et al., 2005).

Effects of Puberty

The hormonal changes of puberty are probably partly responsible for the onset of sexual activity. In boys, levels of testosterone are associated with sexual behaviour. In girls, however, testosterone levels are linked to sexual interests but not to sexual behaviour. Social factors may therefore play a greater role in regulating girls' sexual behaviour than that of boys (Browning et al., 2000; O'Donnell et al., 2003).

masturbation sexual self-stimulation.

The physical changes associated with puberty also may trigger the onset of sexual activity. For example, the development of secondary sex characteristics, such as breasts in girls and muscles and deep voices in boys, may make them more sexually attractive. Early maturing girls are more likely to have older friends, who may draw them into sexual relationships.

Parental Influences

Teenagers who have close relationships with their parents are less likely to initiate sexual activity at an early age (Bynum, 2007). Adolescents who communicate well with their parents also delay the onset of sexual activity (Aspy et al., 2007). If these youngsters do have sexual intercourse, they are more likely to use birth control and have fewer partners.

Peer Influences

A good predictor of sexual activity for adolescents is the sexual activity of their best friends (Dishion & Stormshak, 2007). When teenagers are asked why they do not wait to have sex until they are older, the main reason reported is usually peer association (O'Donnell et al., 2003). Peers, especially those of the same sex, also serve as a key source of sex education for adolescents. Adolescents report that they are more likely to receive information about sex from friends and media sources—TV shows, films, magazines, and the Internet—than from sex education classes or their parents (Kaiser Family Foundation et al., 2003).

TEENAGE PREGNANCY

In Canada, a persistent and steady decline in teen pregnancy rates for both younger (aged 15–17) and older (aged 18–19) teens is evident (Society of Obstetricians and Gynaecologists of Canada, 2009a). Most young women in developed nations defer pregnancy until after they have completed some or all of their education. Many wait until they are well into their careers and in their late 20s, their 30s, even their 40s. Why do adolescents get pregnant? For one thing, adolescent

TABLE 12.2

Number of 15- to 19-Year-Olds Who Have Had Sexual Intercourse at Least Once (1996/97, 2003, and 2005)

	1996/97		2003		2005	
	'000	%	'000	%	'000	%
TOTAL	920	47*	862	45	868	43
Gender						
Males	434	43	437	46	432	43
Females	486	51‡*	425	45	435	43
Age Group						
15 to 17†	380	32	348	30	362	29
18 to 19	540	70‡	514	68‡	506	65‡
Province						
Newfoundland and Labrador	23	46	19	54‡	17	49
Prince Edward Island	4ᴱ	37ᴱ	5	52*	3	35
Nova Scotia	16ᴱ	31‡*ᴱ	29	49	29	49
New Brunswick	28ᴱ	43ᴱ	24	52*‡	19	43
Quebec	297	59‡	252	62‡	263	58‡
Ontario	269	41*‡	302	40‡	302	37‡
Manitoba	30	39‡	31	43	27	39
Saskatchewan	38ᴱ	54	27	39‡	28	43
Alberta	82	44	80	39‡	77	39
British Columbia	133	47	93	37‡	103	40‡

† reference category
* significantly different from corresponding estimate for 2005 (p < 0.05)
‡ significantly different from estimate for reference category or within year rest of Canada (p < 0.05)
ᴱ use with caution (coefficient of variation 16.6 to 33.3%)
Note: Because of rounding, counts may not add to total.
Sources: Rotermann, M. (2008). Trends in teen sexual behaviour and condom use. Health Reports, September 2008. (Statistics Canada, Catalogue no. 82-003-XPE.) Retrieved from http://www.statcan.gc.ca/pub/82-003-x/2008003/article/10664-eng.pdf

girls, especially younger adolescents, do not have access to contraceptive devices. Among those who do, fewer than half use them reliably (Buston et al., 2007).

Some teenage girls purposefully get pregnant to try to force their partners to make a commitment to them. Some are rebelling against their parents or the moral standards of their communities. Others simply want to love and be loved. But most girls are impregnated because they and their partners miscalculate the odds of getting pregnant (Buston et al., 2007).

The teenage abortion rate has been steadily decreasing, from 21.5 per 1,000 teenage females in 1995 to 15.3 in 2005 (the latest year on record) (Sex Information and Education Council of Canada, 2010).

Consequences of Teenage Pregnancy

Actually, the outcome of teenage pregnancies is generally good for young women who want their babies and have the resources to nurture them (Rathus et al., 2008). Females tend to be healthy in late adolescence. However, the medical, social, and economic costs of *unplanned* or *unwanted* pregnancies among adolescents are enormous, both to the mothers and to the children. Adolescent mothers are more likely to experience medical complications during the months of pregnancy and their labour is likely to be prolonged. The babies are at greater risk of being premature and of low birth weight (Mathews & MacDorman, 2007). These medical problems are not necessarily because of the age of the mother, but rather because teenage mothers—especially poor teenage mothers—are less likely to access prenatal care or to obtain adequate nutrition. Despite universal health

girls typically get little advice in school or at home about how to deal with boys' sexual advances. Another reason is failure to use contraception. Some initiate sex at very early ages, when they are least likely to use contraception (Buston et al., 2007). Many adolescent

> **D4** Teen sexual activity has been declining in Canada since the early 1990s.
> Despite social misperceptions, the self-reported incidence of teen sexual activity is gradually declining.

Sexuality & U

The Society of Obstetricians and Gynaecologists of Canada (SOGC)

www.sexualityandu.ca  **S**exuality and **U**.ca

This website on contraception, sexually transmitted infections, and healthy sexuality is evidence-based, with the content developed and approved by distinguished health care professionals from the Society of Obstetricians and Gynaecologists of Canada. The site is designed to support teens, adults, parents, teachers, and health professionals.

Legal Age of Sexual Consent in Canada

➢ Age of consent in Canada recently changed from 14 to 16 (with some exceptions).

➢ Twelve- and 13-year-olds can consent to sexual activity with peers who are less than two years older than they are.

➢ Fourteen- and 15-year-olds can consent to sexual activity with persons who are within 5 years of their age.

➢ The age of consent is 18 years if the sexual activity "exploits the young person" (e.g., prostitution, pornography, or a relationship of trust or authority, such as with a teacher or coach).

➢ Many fear that raising the age of consent will harm young people by driving their sexual activity underground and, as a result, restricting their access to medical help and information on sexuality.

Source: Department of Justice Canada. (2010). Age of consent to sexual activity. Retrieved from http://www.justice.gc.ca/eng/dept-min/clp/faq.html

onime/Shutterstock

Sexual Experience

➢ The average age at which both male and female Canadians have their first sexual experience is 16.5 (sexualityandu, 2006).

➢ Teenage pregnancy rates have been declining but close to 40,000 teens become pregnant each year. Most of these pregnancies are unintended (SIECCAN, 2004).

➢ Oral contraceptives (i.e., the pill) are the most common method of contraception used by sexually active Canadian women (32 percent), followed by condom use (21 percent).

➢ Of young people who reported in 2003 that they had engaged in sexual activity with multiple partners within the past year, approximately 3 in 10 did not use a condom the last time they had sexual intercourse.

© cisale/iStockphoto

Sources: sexualityandu website; Sexual Information and Education Council of Canada (SIECCAN). (2004). Sexual health education in the schools: Questions and answers. *Canadian Journal of Human Sexuality*, 13(3–4): 129–144. Retrieved from http://www.sieccan.org/pdf/sexual_health_qs.pdf

Sexually Transmitted Infections (STIs)

➢ There are more than 25 classifications of STIs (sexualityandu, 2006).

➢ STI rates among Canadian teens are unacceptably high and have been increasing in recent years (SIECCAN, 2004).

(continued)

(continued)

➤ An estimated 75 percent of Canadians will have at least one human papillomavirus (HPV) in their lifetime.

➤ Chlamydia is the most commonly reported sexually transmitted infection (STI) in Canada with most people reporting no symptoms (sexualityandu, 2006).

➤ Two-thirds of all reported cases of chlamydia occur in the 15–24 age group.

➤ Gonorrhea is the second most reported STI in Canada, and most people report no symptoms.

➤ Women account for 57 percent of all chlamydia cases, and men account for 60 percent of all gonorrhea cases.

Sources: sexualityandu website; Sexual Information and Education Council of Canada (SIECCAN). (2004). Sexual health education in the schools: Questions and answers. *Canadian Journal of Human Sexuality,* 13(3–4): 129–144. Retrieved from http://www.sieccan.org/pdf/sexual_health_qs.pdf

youth in conflict with the law a child or adolescent whose behaviour is characterized by illegal activities.

care in Canada, teenagers need to travel to access health services, and they must be willing to attend their appointments.

The teenage mother is less likely than her peers to graduate from high school or move on to postsecondary education. Therefore, she will likely earn less and be in greater need of public assistance. Few teenage mothers obtain assistance from the babies' fathers. The fathers typically cannot support themselves, much less a family.

Preventing Teenage Pregnancy

The past several decades have seen a dramatic increase in programs to help prevent teenage pregnancies. Prevention efforts include educating teenagers about sexuality and contraception and providing family planning services (Santelli et al., 2003). An overwhelming majority of Canadian parents want their children to have sex education in the schools.

How successful are sex education programs? The better programs increase students' knowledge about sexuality. Despite fears that sex education will increase sexual activity in teenagers, some

programs seem to delay the onset of sexual activity (Bennett & Assefi, 2005; Santelli et al., 2003). Among teenagers who already are sexually active, sex education is associated with the increased use of effective contraception.

LO4 Youth in Conflict with the Law

t he term **youth in conflict with the law** refers to children or adolescents who engage in illegal activities and come into contact with the criminal justice system. At the most extreme end, youth in conflict with the law display behaviours that lead to assault (sexual and physical), robbery, or the selling of drugs. Less serious offences, such as truancy, underage drinking, running away from home, and sexual promiscuity, are considered illegal only when performed by minors. Hence, these activities are termed *status offences*.

Antisocial and criminal behaviours show a dramatic increase in many societies during adolescence and then taper off during adulthood. Whenever possible, the

Canadian legal system encourages alternative means to custody punishment, called *extrajudicial measures*, which reduce the long-term effects of being in conflict with the law. Extrajudicial measures can include a police warning, a formal caution, or a referral to an agency that can help the young person to make better decisions in the future (Department of Justice Canada, 2009).

Many criminal acts do not result in arrest or conviction. And when adolescents are arrested, their cases may be disposed of informally, as by referral to a mental health agency (Snyder & Sickmund, 2006).

YOUTH CRIME IN CANADA

Few social issues receive as much attention in Canada as youth crime. The following newspaper headline from a Toronto newspaper likely sounds familiar: "Another outbreak of street gang fighting has reawakened citizens to the extent of the problems that these young people present." Do you remember this story? Probably not—the shooting incident and the newspaper account occurred in 1949. The youths' behaviour was attributed to broken homes and declining moral standards. Sound familiar? Violent TV shows and heavy metal had not yet become fallback scapegoats (Olivo et al., 2007).

Youth crime remains a front-line social issue. In 2006, Canada's national crime rate decreased 3 percent over the previous year; however, the youth crime rate was up 3 percent from the previous year. Media sources often neglect to report that the youth crime rate in 2005

was substantially lower than in the early 1990s. But the crime statistics still remain a concern.

Property crime is down but still accounts for 4 in 10 youth crimes. The youth violent crime rate has increased 12 percent in the years between 1997 and 2006, with assault representing nearly 80 percent of those charged under this category. Drug charges have nearly doubled since 1997, and 84 percent of the charges involve cannabis. Youth crimes at school have also risen, though some would argue that the increase in charges is due to enhanced supervision and a heightened interest in the safety of school environments (Olivo et al., 2007).

FACTORS ASSOCIATED WITH YOUTH CRIME IN CANADA

Relatively few studies have explored the link between ethnicity and youth crime in Canada but the studies that have been completed indicate that the important link to youth crime is not race or ethnicity but socioeconomic deprivation, particularly a lack of either employment or education. Having criminals for parents also increases the likelihood that children will commit offences, and criminal activity as a youth can lead to adult crime (Olivo et al., 2007).

REDUCING YOUTH CRIME

Contrary to popular Canadian thought, little research evidence supports the use of punitive sanctions, such as incarceration, as effective in reducing youth crime. Although some offenders need to be incarcerated, many criminologist experts argue that more offenders need to be engaged in community programs that build character, increase self-esteem, and develop life skills. Several studies have demonstrated that youth sport can reduce youth crime. The organized sport programs that are successful at reducing youth crime appear to develop feelings of competence, connectedness, and empowerment (Carmichael, 2008). Developing these feelings is one of the primary philosophies of the Youth Criminal Justice Act, which came into force in 2003.

ABORIGINAL CULTURE AND COMMUNITY JUSTICE

Borrowing from Canadian Aboriginal culture, the Youth Criminal Justice Act relies heavily on the

The important link to youth crime is not race or ethnicity but socioeconomic deprivation.

D5 Suicide is the second leading cause of death among Canadian adolescents.
Motor vehicle accidents are the number one cause of death among Canadian adolescents.

effectiveness of restorative justice. Restorative justice is a philosophy that holds community healing as its cornerstone. It acknowledges and repairs harm that victims experience while also holding young people accountable for their actions in meaningful ways (Centre for Research on Youth at Risk, n.d.). Restorative justice views crime as a violation of one person by another, not simply as a breaking of the law. Community ownership and involvement gives people a voice to address the harm crime brings to victims, offenders, the families and friends of both, and society.

LO5 Suicide: When the Adolescent Has Nothing—Except Everything—to Lose

adolescence is such an exciting time of life. For many, the future is filled with promise and dreams of what lies ahead. One of the tragedies of teenage suicide is the loss of potential years of life. Canadian suicide rates are at the highest levels in Canadian history, and the actual number of suicides in Canada is likely underreported as a death is only certified as suicide by authorities when the victim's intent is clearly proven (Shaver, 1990).

Photos.com

RISK FACTORS IN SUICIDE

Most suicides among adolescents and adults are linked to feelings of depression and hopelessness (Cheng & Chan, 2007). Jill Rathus and her colleagues (Rathus & Miller, 2002) have found that suicidal adolescents experience four areas of psychological problems: (1) confusion about the self, (2) impulsiveness, (3) emotional instability, and (4) interpersonal problems. Some suicidal teenagers are highly achieving, rigid perfectionists who have set impossibly high expectations for themselves (Miller et al., 2000). Many teenagers throw themselves into feelings of depression and hopelessness by comparing themselves negatively with others, even when the comparisons are inappropriate. Esteem should be rooted in being good at an interest rather than putting yourself down because you aren't the best.

Adolescent suicide attempts are more common after stressful life events, especially events that entail loss of social support, such as the death of a parent or friend, breaking up with a boyfriend or girlfriend, or a family member's leaving home (Cooper et al., 2002). Other contributors to suicidal behaviour include concerns over sexuality, school grades, problems at home, and substance abuse (Conner & Goldston, 2007; Cuellar & Curry, 2007). Suicide is not always precipitated by a stressful event itself, but, instead, is often triggered by the adolescent's anxiety or fear of being "found out" for something, such as failing a course or getting arrested.

Suicide tends to run in families (National Center for Injury Prevention and Control, 2007). Do genetic factors play a role, possibly leading to psychological disorders, such as depression, that are related to suicide? Could it be that socially challenging family environments infuse several family members with conditions that create a sense of hopelessness? Or does the suicide of one family member simply give others the idea that suicide is an acceptable way to manage problems?

Researchers have found the following warning signs of suicide among adolescents:

- Belief that it is acceptable to kill oneself (Joe et al., 2007)
- Drug abuse and other kinds of conflict with the law (Cuellar & Curry, 2007; Thompson et al., 2007)
- Victimization by bullying (Klomek et al., 2007)
- Stress (Cheng & Chan, 2007)
- Hostility (Dervic et al., 2007)
- Depression and other psychological disorders (Smarty & Findling, 2007)
- Low self-esteem (Wong et al., 2007)
- Increasing age from 11 to 21 (Conner & Goldston, 2007)

Females are 3 times more likely to attempt suicide and males are 6 times more likely to complete suicide.

CULTURE, SEX, AND SUICIDE

In Canada, Aboriginal teenagers are 10 times more likely to commit suicide than their peers. Culturally specific prevention methods have shown significant success in reducing this trend. Teen suicide rates among Canadian males are 57 percent higher than in the United States. Antoon Leenaars, of the Canadian Association for Suicide Prevention, attributes this higher rate to cultural theory, claiming that Canadians are more likely to kill themselves and Americans are more likely to kill each other. Within Canada, Quebec has the highest rate of teen suicide among all of the provinces. The director of the Montreal General Hospital's Adolescent Crisis Intervention Team suggests that Quebec is a society that values the quality of life rather than its quantity. No matter what the teen group, being male raises the odds of suicide in Canada. Attempted suicide is three times more common among females but males are six times more likely to die. The higher male mortality rate is likely due to the more lethal and immediate methods of suicide chosen by males (i.e., hanging versus overdose) (Shaver, 1990).

Visit **icanhdev.com** to find the resources you need today!

Located at the back of the textbook are rip-out Chapter Review cards. Make sure you also go online to check out other tools that HDEV offers to help you successfully pass your course.

- Flashcards
- Glossary
- Interactive Practice

- Build a Summary
- Games
- Interactive Quizzing

Adulthood

is usually defined in terms of what people do rather than how old they are.

13

Early Adulthood: Physical and Cognitive Development

Learning Outcomes

LO1 Discuss the (theoretical) stage of emerging adulthood

LO2 Describe trends in physical development in early adulthood

LO3 Discuss health in early adulthood, focusing on causes of death, diet, exercise, and substance abuse

LO4 Discuss sexuality in early adulthood, focusing on homosexuality, STIs, menstrual problems, and sexual coercion

LO5 Discuss cognitive development in early adulthood, focusing on "postformal" developments and effects of college life

LO6 Describe career choice and development during early adulthood

DID YOU KNOW?

D1 Leading causes of death vary among Canadian men and women.

D2 Young people are the fastest growing group to be infected with HIV.

D3 Menstrual discomfort is normal.

D4 The majority of sexual assaults are committed by someone the victim knows.

D5 Million-dollar lottery winners often feel aimless and dissatisfied if they quit their jobs after striking it rich.

When our mothers were our age, they were engaged. They at least had some idea what they were going to do with their lives. I, on the other hand, will have a dual degree in majors that are ambiguous at best and impractical at worst (English and political science), no ring on my finger and no idea who I am, much less what I want to do. Under duress, I will admit that this is a pretty exciting time. Sometimes, when I look out across the wide expanse that is my future, I can see beyond the void. I realize that having nothing ahead to count on means I now have to count on myself; that having no direction means forging one of my own.

—*Kristen, age 22 (Page 1999, pp. 18, 20)*

Well, Kristen has some work to do: She needs to forge her own direction. Kristen is accumulating information about herself and the world outside. In earlier days, adolescents made a transition directly into adulthood. Now many young people in affluent nations have abundant opportunities to spend time in what some theorists consider a new period of development roughly spanning the ages of 18 to 25: *emerging adulthood* (Arnett, 2007).

Adulthood is usually defined in terms of what people do rather than how old they are. Over the years, developmentalists have considered marriage to be a key standard for adulthood (Carroll et al., 2007). Other criteria include holding a full-time job and living independently. Today, the transition to adulthood is mainly marked by adjustment issues, such as settling on one's values and beliefs, accepting self-responsibility, becoming financially independent, and establishing an equal relationship with one's parents (Gottlieb et al., 2007).

Adulthood itself has been divided into stages, and the first of these, early adulthood, has been largely seen as the period of life when people focus on establishing careers

emerging adulthood a theoretical period of development, spanning the ages of 18 to 25, in which young people in developed nations engage in extended role exploration.

or pathways in life. The transition to adulthood can be rapid or piecemeal. Many individuals in their late teens and early 20s remain dependent on parents and are reluctant or unable to make enduring commitments in terms of identity formation or intimate relationships. The question is whether there is another stage of development that bridges adolescence and early adulthood. Many developmental theorists believe we can, including Jeffrey Arnett (2007), who terms this stage emerging adulthood.

LO1 Emerging Adulthood

emerging adulthood is theorized to be a distinct period of development found in societies that allow young people an extended opportunity to explore their roles in life. Some parents are affluent enough to continue to support their children through their postsecondary education. Some students will receive assistance from the government by qualifying for student loans. These supports allow young people the luxury of sorting out identity issues and creating meaningful life plans. But even in Canada, of course, many people cannot afford the luxury of exploring educational opportunities in emerging adulthood.

Young Canadians seem to be generally aware of the issues involved in defining the transition from adolescence to adulthood. When individuals in their late teens and early 20s are asked whether they think they have become adults, about three in five say something like, "In some respects yes and in other respects no" (Arnett, 2000). Many think they have developed beyond the conflicts and exploratory voyages of adolescence, but they have not yet assumed the responsibilities they associate with adulthood.

LO2 Physical Development

physical development peaks in early adulthood, when most are at their height of sensory sharpness, strength, reaction time, and cardiovascular fitness. Young adults are at their tallest,

and their height remains stable through middle adulthood, declining slightly in late adulthood. A higher percentage of men's body mass is made of muscle, and men are typically stronger than women. Physical strength in both men and women peaks in their 20s and early 30s, then slowly declines (Markham, 2006).

Sensory sharpness also peaks in the early 20s (Fozard & Gordon-Salant, 2001). Visual acuity remains good until middle adulthood, when a gradual decline leads to farsightedness and, in many people, a need for reading glasses. Hearing tends to decline once people reach their late 20s and early 30s, particularly for tones that are high in pitch.

The changes of aging in the cardiovascular, respiratory, and immune systems begin in early adulthood, but they are gradual. The heart muscle becomes more rigid, decreasing the maximum heart rate and reducing the ability of the heart to pump enough blood to provide oxygen for stressful exercise. But regular exercise increases cardiovascular and respiratory capacity from what they would otherwise be at any age. As people age, the immune system produces fewer white blood cells, and the disease-fighting ability of those that remain declines.

Fertility in both sexes declines as early adulthood progresses. After age 35, women are usually advised to have their fetuses checked for Down's syndrome and other chromosomal abnormalities. Older men may also contribute to chromosomal abnormalities. A major problem in women is a reduced number of ova (egg cells) and a decline in their quality. But because of advances in reproductive technology, many women today give birth to healthy children, including their first children, in their 30s and 40s.

Both sexes may find their hair thinning and greying by the end of early adulthood. Toward the end of early adulthood, and almost certainly in middle adulthood, the skin begins to loosen, grow less elastic, and wrinkle, more so in women than in men.

© Pixland/Jupiterimages

LO3 Health and Fitness

s a group, young adults tend to be healthy. Their immune systems are generally functioning well. As Table 13.1 shows, the leading cause of death for young adults in Canada in 2004 was accidents. The percentage of deaths due to accidents declines from the younger to the relatively older age group and differs between men and women.

Suicide rates are also quite high and, as pointed out earlier, suicide rates may be underreported. Heart disease and cancer, the major killers in late adulthood, become significant sources of health concern. Interestingly, cancer rates are significantly higher for women than for men. HIV and AIDS have not made the list, possibly because these conditions take many years to overwhelm the body's immune system.

Given that so many young adults are in excellent or good health, it is ironic that many are careless about their health or put it on the "back burner." Many are concerned about their careers, their education, or their social lives and think of health issues—diet, smoking, sedentary living, excessive drinking—as something they can get to later on.

Consider the results of a poll by the Centers for Disease Control and Prevention (CDC) that reported

TABLE 13.1
Five Leading Causes of Death in Canada for Young Adults by Age Group

YOUNG MEN		YOUNG WOMEN	
(ages 15–24)	(ages 25–34)	(ages 15–24)	(ages 25–34)
Accidents 43.7 %	Accidents 31.2 %	Accidents 39.4 %	Cancer 22.0 %
Suicide 23.6 %	Suicide 25.3 %	Suicide 16.4 %	Accidents 21.4 %
Cancer 6 %	Cancer 9.2 %	Cancer 10.2 %	Suicide 13.6 %
Assault 5.8 %	Heart Disease 5.6 %	Heart Disease 4.1 %	Heart Disease 5.6 %
Heart Disease 2.1 %	Assault 4.6 %	Assault 2.9 %	Assault 3.8 %

Source: Statistics Canada. (2008a). *Leading causes of death in Canada*. (Statistics Canada, Catalogue no. 84-215-X). Table 1-3 and Table 1-4. Retrieved from www.statcan.gc.ca/pub/84-215-x/2008000/hl-fs-eng.htm#3

D1 Leading causes of death vary between Canadian men and women.
Accidents are the leading cause of death, followed by suicide and then cancer.

© Dawn Liljenquist/iStockphoto

on the health-related behaviour patterns of more than 18,000 young adults aged 18–24 (McCracken et al., 2007). More than three respondents in four (78 percent) ate fewer than the recommended five fruits and vegetables each day. Forty-three percent reported either no or insufficient physical activity. More than one in four (29 percent) were smokers, and 30 percent reported binge drinking—having five drinks in a row on single occasions. About one respondent in four (26 percent) was *overweight* (having a body-mass index [BMI] of 25.0–29.9; see Figure 13.1, on page 244), and another 14 percent were *obese* (having a BMI of 30.0 or above).

DIET AND WEIGHT

The percentage of Canadians who are overweight or obese has risen dramatically in recent years, mirroring a worldwide phenomenon. According to the Canadian Community Health Survey, 23.1 percent of Canadians aged 18 or older had a BMI of 30 or more, indicating that they were obese. Another 36.1 percent were overweight (Tjepkema, 2005).

Why are so many young adults overweight and obese? Many biological and psychological factors are involved. Being overweight tends to run in families. Studies of monkeys (Kavanagh et al., 2007) and of human twins

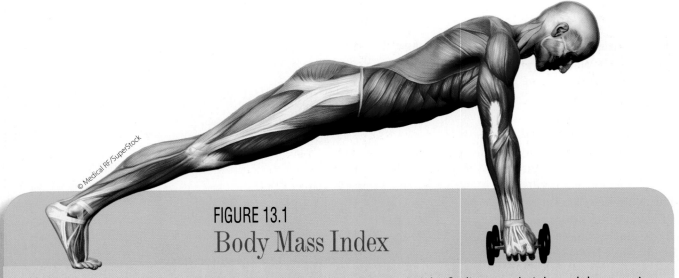

FIGURE 13.1
Body Mass Index

Your BMI is based on your height and weight. You can locate your own BMI by finding your height and then running your finger until you find your weight. Health professionals consider a BMI of 25 to 29 to be overweight, and 30 or above to be obese.

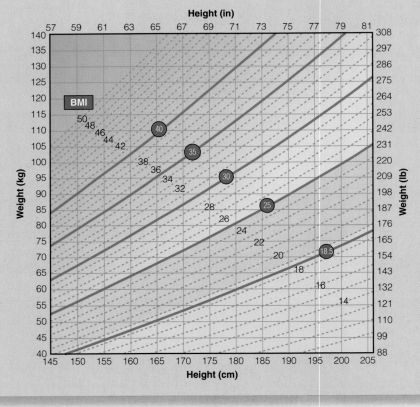

Source: Body Mass Index (BMI) Nomogram 2003. Health Canada. Reproduced with the permission of the Minister of Public Works and Government Services Canada 2010

adaptive thermogenesis the process by which the body converts food energy (calories) to heat at a lower rate when a person eats less, because of, for example, famine or dieting.

(Silventoinen et al., 2007) suggest that heredity plays a strong role in being overweight. Efforts by overweight and obese people to maintain a slender profile may be sabotaged by a mechanism that helps to preserve life in times of famine—**adaptive thermogenesis**. This mechanism causes the body to produce less energy (burn fewer calories) when less food is consumed (Major et al., 2007). This does not mean that overweight people will not lose weight by dieting; it means that weight loss will likely take longer than expected.

Fatty tissue in the body also metabolizes (burns) food more slowly than muscle. For this reason, a person with a high fat-to-muscle ratio metabolizes food more

The Skinny on Weight Control

The most effective and healthful weight-control programs involve improving nutritional knowledge, decreasing calorie intake, exercising, and changing eating habits by reducing portion sizes and eating less saturated fat and cholesterol. Most health professionals believe that Canadians eat too much animal fat and not enough fruits and vegetables. Dieting plus exercise is more effective for controlling weight than dieting alone. Exercise burns calories and builds muscle tissue, which metabolizes more calories than fatty tissue does.

Cognitive-behavioural methods such as the following also help:

- Establish calorie-intake goals and keep track of whether you are meeting them.
- Eat preplanned low-calorie snacks.
- Take a five-minute break between helpings. Ask yourself, "Am I still hungry?" If not, stop eating.
- Avoid temptations. Plan your meal before entering a restaurant. Shop from a list.
- When you meet your calorie goals, reward yourself (not with food).
- Mentally rehearse solutions to problems. Plan what you will do when cake is handed out at the office party or when you visit relatives who try to stuff you with food.
- If you binge, don't give up. Resume dieting the next day.

slowly than a person of the same weight with more muscle. Psychological factors, such as observational learning, stress, and emotional states also contribute to obesity.

EXERCISE

Adults 18 and older need 30 minutes of physical activity five or more days a week to be healthy (*Physical Activity Fact Sheet*, 2005). Significant benefits can be reaped from a moderate amount of activity, such as 30 minutes of brisk walking or raking leaves, 15 minutes of

In general, mankind, since the improvement of cookery, eats twice as much as nature requires.

HELLO
my name is
Benjamin
Franklin

running, or 45 minutes of volleyball. You can break 30 to 60 minutes of physical activity into smaller segments of 10 or 15 minutes through the day.

This amount of activity can substantially reduce the risk of developing or dying from cardiovascular disease, type 2 diabetes, and certain cancers, such as colon cancer. Exercise also benefits the brain and cognitive performance (Stein et al., 2007). Exercise may even help with psychological disorders such as anxiety and depression (Stein et al., 2007). The "trick" for most young adults is to integrate exercise into their daily routine, perhaps by means of moderately vigorous activities for 15 minutes two times a day or for 10 minutes three times a day.

SUBSTANCE ABUSE AND DEPENDENCE

People use drugs not only to cope with medical problems but also to deal with daily tensions, social anxiety, run-of-the-mill depression, even boredom. Where does the use of a drug or substance end and substance abuse begin? According to the American Psychiatric Association (2000), **substance abuse** is the ongoing use of a substance despite the social, occupational, psychological,

> **substance abuse** a persistent pattern of use of a substance characterized by frequent intoxication and impairment of physical, social, or emotional well-being.

substance dependence a persistent pattern of use of a substance that is accompanied by physiological addiction.

tolerance habituation to a drug such that increasingly higher doses are needed to achieve similar effects.

abstinence syndrome a characteristic cluster of symptoms that results from a sudden decrease in the level of usage of a substance.

or physical problems it causes. When young adults miss school or work because they are intoxicated or "sleeping it off," they are abusing alcohol.

A person who is dependent on a substance loses control over using it. **Substance dependence** means that having it in the body becomes the norm.

Tolerance develops as the body becomes habituated to the substance; as a result, more of it may be needed to achieve the same effects. A number of substances are physically addictive, so when the dosage is lowered, withdrawal symptoms, also known as **abstinence syndrome**, occur. When addicted individuals lower their intake of alcohol, they may experience symptoms such as tremors (shakes), high blood pressure, rapid heart and pulse rate, anxiety, restlessness, and weakness. Three of the most common types of abused substances are depressants, stimulants, and hallucinogens.

Effects of Depressants

Depressants slow the activity of the nervous system. Depressants include alcohol, narcotics derived from the opium poppy (such as heroin, morphine, and codeine), and sedatives (such as barbiturates and methaqualone).

Alcohol lessens inhibitions so that drinkers may do things when drinking that they might otherwise resist (Donohue et al., 2007). Alcohol is also an intoxicant: It distorts perceptions, impairs concentration, hinders coordination, and slurs the speech. Alcohol use is most prevalent among 21- to 34-year-olds. More than one million students between the ages of 18 and 24 are accidentally injured each year while under the influence, assaulted by other students who have been drinking, or sexually assaulted by men who have been drinking.

The major medical use of heroin, morphine, and other opioids is relief from pain. But it also can provide a euphoric "rush." Heroin is addictive, and regular users develop tolerance. *Barbiturates* are depressants with various legitimate medical uses, such as relief from pain, anxiety, and tension, but people can become rapidly dependent on them.

Effects of Stimulants

Stimulants speed up the heartbeat and other bodily functions. Nicotine, cocaine, and amphetamines are

Do You Have a Problem with Alcohol?

How can *you* tell whether you may have a drinking problem? Answering the following four questions can help you find out (NIAAA, 2005):

Yes No   Have you ever felt you should cut down on your drinking?

Yes No   Have people annoyed you by criticizing your drinking?

Yes No   Have you ever felt bad or guilty about your drinking?

Yes No   Have you ever had a drink first thing in the morning (as an "eye opener") to steady your nerves or get rid of a hangover?

Just one "yes" answer suggests a possible alcohol problem. Two or more "yeses" make it highly likely that a problem exists. In either case, it is advisable to discuss your answers with your doctor or another health care provider.

the most common stimulants. Nicotine is the addictive chemical in tobacco (Nonnemaker & Homsi, 2007). According to Lung Cancer Canada (2008), 45,000 Canadians die from smoking-related deaths each year, which is the same as 1 in 5 deaths. For long-time smokers, the chance of dying from a smoking-related cause is, on average, 1 in 2.

Cocaine accelerates the heart rate, spikes the blood pressure, constricts the arteries of the heart, and thickens the blood, a combination that can cause cardiovascular and respiratory collapse (Mitchell, 2006). Overdoses can cause restlessness, insomnia, tremors, and even death. Amphetamines can keep users awake for long periods and reduce their appetites. Tolerance for amphetamines develops rapidly. The powerful amphetamine called methamphetamine may be physically addictive (Jonkman, 2006). Methamphetamine abuse can cause brain damage, leading to problems in learning and memory.

Effects of Hallucinogenics

Hallucinogenics give rise to perceptual distortions called hallucinations, which sometimes can be so strong that they are confused with reality. Marijuana, ecstasy, LSD, and PCP are hallucinogenic drugs. Marijuana, which is typically smoked, helps users relax, elevates their mood, increases sensory awareness, and can induce visual hallucinations, for example, time seeming to slow down. Marijuana carries health risks such as impairing perceptual–motor coordination and short-term memory (Egerton et al., 2006; Lamers et al., 2006). Research suggests that regular users may experience withdrawal, which is a sign of addiction (Budney et al., 2007).

Ecstasy, a popular "party" drug, provides the boost of a stimulant and mild hallucinogenic effects. The combination appears to free users from inhibitions and awareness of the consequences of risky behaviour, such as unprotected sex. Ecstasy can also impair working memory, increase anxiety, and lead to depression (Lamers et al., 2006). LSD is the acronym for lysergic acid diethylamide, another hallucinogenic drug. High doses of hallucinogenics can impair coordination and judgment (driving while using hallucinogenic drugs poses grave risks), change the mood, and cause paranoid delusions.

STRESS AND HEALTH

According to a national poll taken by Ipsos Reid (2006), nearly half (45 percent) of Canadians feel that they do

Many Canadians report that stress negatively affects their lives (BC Partners for Mental Health and Addictions Information, 2004). In a survey, Canadians reported the areas of their lives that were negatively affected by stress:

48 % reported sleep quality

41 % reported personal health

33 % reported home or family lives

23 % reported quality of sex life

23 % reported quality of work

not have the control over their stress levels that they would like. Stress has a negative impact on people's psychological and physical health, and on their social, academic, and vocational lives (see Figure 13.2 on page 248).

> **hallucinogenics** drugs that give rise to hallucinations.

LO4 Sexuality

Sexual activity with a partner usually peaks in one's 20s. Why does this age group have sex most frequently? The answer is a combination of youth and opportunity. Men and women in this age group are still experiencing the flood of sex hormones that affected them as adolescents. Now, however, they are of an age at which they are likely to be in sexual relationships.

Table 13.2, on page 249, explores a global study that examined the number of reported sex partners in a lifetime. Clearly, Canadians, as a social group, are comfortable with their sexuality when compared with populations from other countries. Canadians are known for their toques, maple syrup, and hockey, and for being polite and cautious. Apparently, we have been overlooked globally when it comes to our sexuality. Canadians have more sex partners in a lifetime than people in most other countries, and we are also more sexually adventurous, spending more time on foreplay and intercourse, according to a 2007–08 "Durex Sexual Wellbeing Global Survey" (Lunau, 2009).

THE ORIGINS OF SEXUAL ORIENTATION

According to Statistics Canada (2009a), 1 percent of Canadians aged 18 to 59 reported they consider themselves to be homosexual (gay or lesbian), and 0.7 percent reported they consider themselves bisexual. But these numbers depend on the willingness of respondents to identify themselves as belonging to a sexual category. Only 94 percent of respondents identified themselves as heterosexual. Surveys find that about 3 percent of males and 2 percent of females in the United States identify themselves as homosexual (Laumann et al., 1994). Psychology seeks to examine the possible origins of sexual orientation. Nature and nurture explore the

FIGURE 13.2
Evaluation of Amount of Stress Experienced

Reported sources of stress:

finances 44 %

work 37 %

unchecked emails and phone messages 17 %

Many Canadians reported positive influences of stress:

46 % reported exercising in response to stress

48 % reported that stress is proof they they have important responsibilities

31 % reported that stress improves the quality of their work

BC Partners for Mental Health and Addictions Information. (2004). *Wellness module 2: Stress and well-being.* Retrieved from http://www.heretohelp.bc.ca/skills/module2

[All Respondents (n=1848)]

■ HIGH STRESS   ■ MODERATE STRESS   ☐ LOW STRESS

Age group	HIGH STRESS	MODERATE STRESS	LOW STRESS
18.34 (N=439)	29%	57%	14%
35.54 (N=786)	39%	50%	11%
55+ (N=623)	25%	54%	21%

Source: American Psychological Association. (2007a). Stress in America: Mind/body health: For a healthy mind and body, talk to a psychologist. Washington, DC: American Psychological Association.

nito/Shutterstock

Red = Life
Orange = Healing
Yellow = Sun
Green = Nature
Royal Blue = Harmony
Violet = Spirit

biological makeup of the individual and environmental influences.

Learning theorists study the roles of factors such as reinforcement, which might come in the form of sexual behaviour with members of one's own sex or childhood sexual abuse by someone of the same sex. But critics point out that most individuals become aware of their sexual orientation before they have sexual contacts with people of either sex (Laumann et al., 1994).

Some evidence suggests genetic factors play a role in sexual orientation (Kohl, 2007; Sefcek et al., 2007). Twin studies have indicated that about 52 percent of identical (monozygotic) twin pairs are "concordant" (in agreement) for a gay male sexual orientation, compared with 22 percent for fraternal (dizygotic) twins (Bailey & Pillard, 1991). Monozygotic twins fully share their genetic heritage, whereas dizygotic twins, like other pairs of siblings, have a 50 percent overlap.

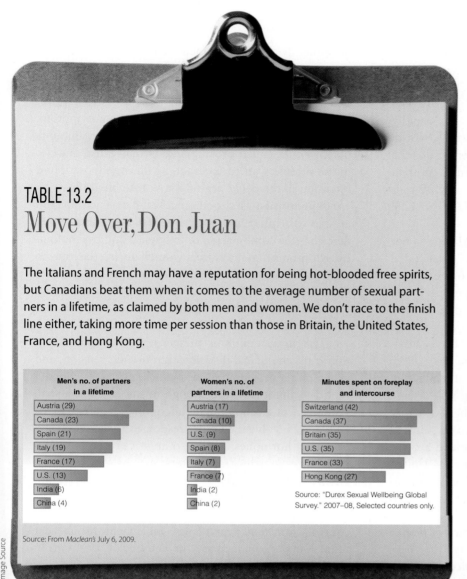

TABLE 13.2
Move Over, Don Juan

The Italians and French may have a reputation for being hot-blooded free spirits, but Canadians beat them when it comes to the average number of sexual partners in a lifetime, as claimed by both men and women. We don't race to the finish line either, taking more time per session than those in Britain, the United States, France, and Hong Kong.

Men's no. of partners in a lifetime	Women's no. of partners in a lifetime	Minutes spent on foreplay and intercourse
Austria (29)	Austria (17)	Switzerland (42)
Canada (23)	Canada (10)	Canada (37)
Spain (21)	U.S. (9)	Britain (35)
Italy (19)	Spain (8)	U.S. (35)
France (17)	Italy (7)	France (33)
U.S. (13)	France (7)	Hong Kong (27)
India (6)	India (2)	
China (4)	China (2)	

Source: "Durex Sexual Wellbeing Global Survey." 2007–08, Selected countries only.

Source: From *Maclean's* July 6, 2009.

© Image Source

Sex hormones promote the development of male and female sex organs and regulate the menstrual cycle. They also fuel the sex drive and may influence *whom* one will find to be sexually attractive (Huang, 2007). One thing is for certain, pride festivities are celebrated and supported in increasing numbers throughout Canadian towns and cities. The rainbow flag, which symbolizes the inclusion of all, is as colourful as the individuals who populate this community. Canadians have experienced a significant paradigm shift in promoting the diversity of sexuality among our citizens. Our legislation on marriage and adoption reflects social acceptance and inclusion of the Canadian LGBTQ (lesbian, gay, bisexual, trans [gendered, sexual, twin-spirited], and questioning) community, but we still have significant social barriers to overcome. According to a Statistics Canada (2009a) survey, the number of gays, lesbians, and bisexuals who reported having experienced

discrimination was 3 times higher than that of heterosexuals. We must continue to work together to build a community that all Canadians can be proud of.

SEXUALLY TRANSMITTED INFECTIONS (STIs)

The Canadian Federation for Sexual Health (2007) reports that between 1997 and 2004, reported rates of sexually transmitted infections (STIs) in Canada increased dramatically. Rates of STIs among young people (aged 15–24) showed the most dramatic rise (in both the homosexual and heterosexual communities). The number of nationally reported cases likely represents only a fraction of the actual number of cases because many of the infections are asymptomatic (Signal Hill, 2009). Chlamydia, a bacterial infection of the vagina or urinary tract that can result in sterility, is the most commonly occurring STI in young Canadians, followed by gonorrhea, genital warts, genital herpes, syphilis, and HIV/AIDS (Society of Obstetricians and Gynaecologists of Canada, 2009b). Because of its lethality, HIV/AIDS tends to capture most of the headlines. However, other STIs are more widespread and can also be deadly.

More than two-thirds of chlamydia cases occur among youth, although they represent only 14 percent of the population (Signal Hill, 2009). Chlamydia is a major cause of pelvic inflammatory disease (PID), which often leads to infertility.

Human papillomavirus (HPV) is transmitted through vaginal, oral, or anal sex, or by skin-to-skin contact. HPV can cause skin warts, genital warts, and pre-cancerous lesions, which can lead to certain types of cancers. An estimated 75 percent of Canadians will have at least one HPV infection in their lifetime (Society of Obstetricians and Gynaecologists of Canada, 2009b). A controversial vaccine is available that prevents most young women from being infected with HPV and is best administered before they become sexually active (Pichichero, 2006).

HIV/AIDS

HIV/AIDS is the most devastating STI. If left untreated, it is lethal, and the long-term prospects of those who

dysmenorrhea painful menstruation.

prostaglandins hormones that cause muscles in the uterine wall to contract, as during labour.

amenorrhea the absence of menstruation.

premenstrual syndrome (PMS) the discomforting symptoms that affect many women during the 4–6 day interval preceding their periods.

premenstrual dysphoric disorder (PMDD) a condition similar to but more severe than PMS.

do receive treatment remain unknown. HIV—the virus that causes AIDS—is spreading rapidly around the world. By the end of the 20th century, it had infected nearly 39 million people (UNAIDS, 2006).

HIV/AIDS is not a disease associated with race or gender or sexual orientation. It is a human disease that can affect any person who has been sexually active. Young Canadians between the ages of 19 and 30, especially college and university students, are at a particularly high risk for contracting this disease because they tend to be at the height of their sexuality and have opportunities to have several partners during a short period of time. In fact, young people are the fastest growing group to be infected with HIV. United Nations AIDS estimates that half of all infections to date have been in the 15- to 24-year-old age group (Burmaster, 1996).

Health Canada estimates that 27 percent of people living with HIV do not know that they have the virus. Awareness is the key to making the choices that will protect you and keep you healthy (HIV Edmonton, 2010). Although knowledge about HIV/AIDS is widespread among youth, only about half modify their sexual practices as a result of it (Santelli et al., 2000). Major risk factors include sex with multiple partners, failure to use condoms, and drug and alcohol abuse (UNAIDS, 2006). The causes, methods of transmission, symptoms, and treatment—where it exists—of STIs are described in Table 13.3.

 D2 Young people are the fastest growing group to be infected with HIV.
Only about half of adolescents with knowledge of how HIV is transmitted actually change their sexual practices.

MENSTRUAL PROBLEMS

Fifty percent to 75 percent of women experience at least some discomfort prior to or during menstruation, including dysmenorrhea, menstrual migraines, amenorrhea, premenstrual syndrome (PMS), and premenstrual dysphoric disorder (PMDD) (Sommerfeld, 2000). **Dysmenorrhea** is the most common menstrual problem, and pelvic cramps are the most common symptom. Cramps are most often brought about by high amounts of hormones called **prostaglandins** that cause muscles in the uterine wall to contract, as during labour. Fluid retention in the pelvic region may cause bloating.

Amenorrhea is the absence of menstruation and a sign of infertility. **Premenstrual syndrome (PMS)** describes the combination of biological and psychological symptoms that may affect women during the four- to six-day interval that precedes their menses each month. **Premenstrual dysphoric disorder (PMDD)** is more severe than PMS and a technical term used as a diagnostic category by the American Psychiatric Association (2000).

The most common premenstrual symptoms are minor psychological discomfort, muscular tension, and aches or pains, but only a small minority of women report symptoms severe enough to impair their social, academic, or occupational functioning. The causes of PMS may involve the body's responses to changing levels of sex hormones. PMS also appears to be linked to imbalances in neurotransmitters, such as serotonin and GABA, which are related to the appetite, anxiety, and mood changes (Bäckström et al., 2003). Many treatment options are available for PMS: exercise, dietary control, hormone treatments, and medications that reduce anxiety or increase the activity of serotonin in the nervous system. Check with your gynecologist.

 D3 Menstrual discomfort is normal.
Statistically speaking, some form of menstrual discomfort is a normal monthly experience.

SEXUAL ASSAULT: THE MOST INTIMATE CRIME OF VIOLENCE

It is difficult to accurately report statistics on sexual assaults that occur in Canada. According to the Canadian Centre for Justice Statistics, victimization data suggests that fewer than 1 in 10 incidents of sexual assault are reported to police. Further, 94 percent of incidents of sexual touching go unreported, compared with 78 percent of sexual attacks. Although victims may not report these crimes to the police, many do seek support from informal sources, such as friends (72 percent),

TABLE 13.3
Overview of Sexually Transmitted Infections (STIs)

STI AND CAUSE	TRANSMISSION	SYMPTOMS	DIAGNOSIS	TREATMENT
Gonorrhea ("clap," "drip"): Gonococcus bacterium (*Neisseria gonorrhoeae*)	Vaginal, oral, or anal sex . To newborns passing through the birth canal of an infected mother.	In men, yellowish, thick discharge, burning urination. Women may be symptom-free or have vaginal discharge, burning urination, or irregular menstruation.	Clinical inspection. Culture of discharge.	Antibiotics.
Syphilis: *Treponema pallidum*	Vaginal, oral, or anal sex. Touching an infectious chancre. Congenital.	Hard, painless chancre appears at site of infection within 2–4 weeks. May progress through additional stages if untreated.	Clinical inspection or examination of fluid from a chancre. Blood test.	Antibiotics.
Chlamydia and non-gonococcal urethritis: caused by *Chlamydia trachomatous* bacterium in women	Vaginal, oral, or anal sex. To newborns passing through birth canal of infected mother.	Women and men may be symptom-free or frequent and painful urination and a discharge.	Analysis of cervical smear in women. Analysis of penile fluid in men.	Antibiotics.
Genital herpes: caused by Herpes simplex virus-type 2 (HSV-2)	Vaginal, oral, or anal sex.	Painful, reddish bumps around the genitals, thigh, or buttocks. Bumps become blisters that fill with pus and break, shedding viral particles. Fever, aches, and pains possible.	Clinical inspection of sores. Culture and examination of fluid drawn from sore.	Antiviral drugs may provide relief and help with healing but are not cures.
HIV/AIDS: Acronym for human immuno-deficiency virus, the cause of acquired immunodeficiency syndrome	Vaginal or anal sex. Infusion of contaminated blood by needle sharing or from mother to baby during childbirth. Breast feeding.	Usually symptom-free for many years. Swollen lymph nodes, fever, weight loss, fatigue, diarrhea. Deadly "opportunistic infections."	Blood, saliva, or urine tests detect HIV antibodies. Other tests confirm the presence of HIV itself.	There is no cure for HIV/AIDS. A "cocktail" of highly active antiviral therapy (HAART) prolongs life in many people living with HIV/AIDS.
HPV/Genital warts: caused by human papilloma virus (HPV)	Sexual contact. Contact with infected towels or clothing.	Painless warts resembling cauliflowers on the genitals or anus or in the rectum. Associated with cervical cancer.	Clinical inspection.	A vaccine can prevent infection in most young women. Warts removed by freezing, topical drugs, burning, and surgery.
Pubic lice ("crabs"): *Pthirus pubis* (an insect, not a crab)	Sexual contact. Contact with an infested towel, sheet, or toilet seat.	Intense itching in pubic area and other hairy regions to which lice can attach.	Clinical inspection.	Topical drugs containing pyrethrins or piperonal butoxide.

Walk a Mile in Her Shoes is an international event in which men, figuratively and literally, walk a mile in women's shoes to raise money and awareness to stop violence against women.

Social Attitudes, Myths, and Cultural Factors That Encourage Sexual Assaults

Many people believe a number of myths about sexual assault, such as "Women say no when they mean yes" and "The way women dress, they are just asking to have sex" (Maxwell et al., 2003). Yet another myth is that deep down inside, women want to be overpowered and forced into sex by men. These myths have the effect of justifying sexual assault in assailants' and the public's minds.

Males are also often reinforced from childhood for aggressive and competitive behaviour, as in sports. Gender typing may lead men to reject "feminine" traits such as tenderness and empathy that might restrain aggression (Yost & Zurbriggen, 2006).

SEXUAL HARASSMENT

Sexual harassment occurs everywhere: in schools, in the workplace, in the military, and online. It victimizes 40–60 percent of working women and similar percentages of female students in colleges and universities (American Psychological Association, 1998).

For legal purposes, sexual harassment in the workplace is usually defined as deliberate or repeated unwanted comments, gestures, or physical contact. Sexual harassment makes the workplace or other setting a hostile place. Examples range from unwelcome sexual jokes, suggestive comments, verbal abuse, leering at or ogling a person's body, unwelcome physical contact, outright sexual assault, or demands for sex accompanied by threats concerning one's job or student status.

Charges of sexual harassment are often ignored or trivialized by co-workers and employers. The victim may hear, "Why make a big deal out of it? It's not like you were attacked in the street." Yet evidence shows that people who are sexually harassed suffer from it. Some become physically ill (Rospenda et al., 2005). Some find harassment on the job so unbearable that they resign (Sims et al., 2005). College women have dropped courses, switched majors, and have even quit medical residency programs to avoid it (Stratton et al., 2005).

One reason that sexual harassment is so stressful is that blame tends to fall on the victim. Some harassers

---

sexual harassment deliberate or repeated unwanted comments, gestures, or physical contact.

family (41 percent), co-workers (33 percent), and doctors and nurses (13 percent). According to the general survey, most (93 percent) sexual assaults did not result in a physical injury to the victim. The Alberta Association of Sexual Assault Centres reports that 39 percent of Canadian women have experienced at least one incident of sexual assault since the age of 16 (Brennan & Taylor-Butts, 2008).

Types of Sexual Assault

Sexual assault includes any form of sexual activity without a person's consent, including kissing, touching, and intercourse. Stalking refers to being followed, receiving threatening or unwanted communications, and being spied on. Stalking acts often occur repeatedly and cause the persons being stalked to fear for their own safety.

> **D4** The majority of sexual assaults are committed by someone the victim knows.
> According to the Ontario Women's Directorate, 69 percent of women who are sexually assaulted know the person who assaults them. Only 1 percent of these women will report the assault to the police.

> Sexual harassment involves deliberate or repeated unwanted comments, gestures, or physical contact.

argue that charges of harassment were exaggerated. In our society, women are often demonized if they assert themselves, but they remain victimized if they don't (Witkowska & Gådin, 2005).

Sexual harassment sometimes has more to do with the abuse of power than sexual desire (Finkelman, 2005). This is especially so in work settings that are traditional male preserves, such as the firehouse, the construction site, or the military academy (Stratton et al., 2005). The Canadian justice system recognizes sexual harassment as a form of sex discrimination and holds that employers are accountable if harassment creates a hostile or abusive work environment.

LO5 Cognitive Development

as with physical development, people are at the height of their cognitive powers during early adulthood. Some aspects of cognitive development, such as memory, show a general decline as people age, yet people typically retain their verbal skills and may even show improvement in vocabulary and general knowledge (Fair, 2007). Performance on tasks that require reasoning or problem-solving speed and visual–spatial skills, such as piecing puzzles together, tends to decline.

Consider the difference between **crystallized intelligence** and **fluid intelligence**. Crystallized intelligence represents one's lifetime of intellectual attainments and generally increases with age. Fluid intelligence, defined by mental flexibility—the ability to process information rapidly—is more susceptible to the effects of aging (Lachman, 2004).

How then should we think of cognitive development in relation to early adulthood? Piaget did not propose a fifth stage of cognitive development, beyond formal-operational thought, and post-conventional thought, the final stage in Kohlberg's theory of moral development, often develops in adolescence.

In terms of brain development, most verbal and quantitative capacities may have developed by late adolescence and early adulthood. However, adolescence carries with

Aristotle

it a certain egocentrism that can impair judgment, problem solving, and other areas of cognition. Certain experiences of early adulthood can lead to further cognitive developments, but these experiences are not universal, and many people become set in their cognitive ways long before the arrival of early adulthood.

COGNITION AND SOCIETAL DEVELOPMENTS

K. Walter Schaie sought to separate the effects of age-related changes within the individual from cohort effects. To do so, he introduced a developmental model that elevated the study of age-related changes above simple longitudinal and cross-sectional studies (Bergeman & Boker, 2006). He used successive repeated and independent sampling of age cohorts across the decades of a longitudinal study. The resulting data permitted many comparisons within and across age groups and birth cohorts.

Using his method, Schaie (2002; Schaie & Zanjani, 2006) found that the cognitive development of the individual is strongly tied in to the societal developments of the day. While late adolescents are likely to have the broadest general knowledge of the sciences, young adults are more focused in their *use* of scientific expertise than adolescents are. Many adolescents acquire general scientific knowledge in biology, chemistry, and physics during high school. And now, more than ever, girls keep pace with boys in these classes. The same is generally true in algebra, geometry, and, for the few, precalculus and calculus.

PERRY'S THEORY OF EPISTEMIC COGNITION

William Perry's (1981, 1970/1998) theory of **epistemic cognition** concerns our ideas about how we arrive at our beliefs,

crystallized intelligence one's intellectual attainments, as shown, for example, by vocabulary and accumulated knowledge.

fluid intelligence mental flexibility; the ability to process information rapidly.

epistemic cognition thought processes directed at considering how we arrive at our beliefs, facts, and ideas.

© The London Art Archive/Alamy

© Rubberball/Jupiterimages

dualistic thinking dividing the cognitive world into opposites, such as good and bad, or us versus them.

relativistic thinking recognition that judgments are often not absolute but made from a certain belief system or cultural background.

pragmatic thought decision making characterized by willingness to accept reality and compromise.

cognitive–affective complexity a mature form of thinking that permits people to harbour positive and negative feelings about their career choices and other matters.

facts, and ideas. Young adults may wonder why their beliefs differ from others' and may seek to justify or revise their thinking and their conclusions. College students' views on what they know and how they get to know what they know become more complex as they are exposed to the complexities of postsecondary thinking (King & Kitchener, 2004; Magolda, 2004). Cognitive development in postsecondary schooling rests not only on exposure to "great books"; it is also fostered by being challenged by students from different backgrounds and by instructors who have views that differ from those of students (Moshman, 2005).

Students often enter their postsecondary years assuming there are right and wrong answers and that the world can be divided easily into black versus white, good versus bad, and us versus them. This type of thinking is termed **dualistic thinking**. After a while, in a multicultural society or on a school campus, students may realize that judgments of good or bad are often rooted in a certain belief system, such as a religion or a cultural background, so that such judgments actually represent **relativistic thinking** rather than absolute judgments (Vukman, 2005). For example, some world cultures may believe they put women "on pedestals" by restricting their activities outside the home. The newly "relativistic" college student may be hard-pressed to take issue with this argument, but as thought deepens, adults may become capable of *commitment within relativistic thinking*. That is, the more cognitively mature person can say, "Yes, I understand where you're coming from when you say you're putting women on pedestals by preventing them from going outdoors unless they are chaperoned, but my bottom line is that you're treating them like second-class citizens and would never allow them to do the same to you."

Numerous studies show that college and university life encourage cognitive development through broadened experiences.

LABOUVIE-VIEF'S THEORY OF PRAGMATIC THOUGHT

Gisella Labouvie-Vief's (2006) theory of **pragmatic thought** notes that adults must typically narrow possibilities into choices, whether these are choices about careers, school, or life partners. The "cognitively healthy" adult is more willing than the egocentric adolescent to compromise and cope within the world as it is, not the world as she or he would like it to be. To deal with the real world, adults need to be able to accept living with mixed feelings about their goals. As people mature, Labouvie-Vief found that they tend to develop a **cognitive–affective complexity** that enables them to harbour both positive and negative feelings about their career choices ("I may never get rich, but when I wake up in the morning, I'll look forward to what I'm doing that day") and their partners ("Okay, he may not be a hunk, but he's stable and he won't abuse me"). Adults function best when they accept reality but choose goals that allow them to experience positive feelings (Labouvie-Vief & González, 2004).

POSTFORMAL THINKING

Most developmentalists agree that the cognitive processes of young adults are in many ways more advanced than the cognitive processes of adolescents—at least in our cultural setting (Commons, 2004; Gurba, 2005). Young adults maintain most of the benefits of their general secondary educations, and some may have gathered specialized knowledge and skills through opportunities in higher education. Many have gained knowledge and expertise in the career world as well.

The thinking of young adults tends to be *less* egocentric than that of adolescents. Young adults are less likely to see the world in black and white. They are more relativistic, but ideally capable of making commitments in their relativistic worlds. A 24-year-old television production coordinator committed herself to an editor who was nice-looking and loyal but somewhat "quiet" after years of dating handsome but more emotional and less predictable men.

What developmentalists do not agree on is whether they should consider the cognitive abilities of young adults to be a fifth stage of cognitive development, perhaps a *postformal* stage that would extend beyond Piaget's stage of formal operations.

EDUCATION AND COGNITIVE DEVELOPMENT

Emily, 22, in her second year of college, was describing her placement abroad in South Africa. Her face lit up as she painted a picture—not at all rosy—of her experiences working in HIV/AIDS education programs. She discussed the conditions of South African poor and the "insanely deplorable" treatment of workers in the diamond mine. Emily's experiences cannot be evaluated by a grade, but the experience clearly had a major impact on her cognitive development.

Numerous studies show that college and university life encourages cognitive development through broadened experience (Pascarella et al., 2003). Halawah (2006), conducting his research in the United Arab Emirates, found that informal student–faculty relationships were as important, and perhaps more important, than coursework in promoting higher levels of reflective reasoning.

The Diverse Culture of Postsecondary Education

Emily's semester abroad took full advantage of the diversity students can experience in postsecondary education. Some students attend schools that are close to home, culturally if not necessarily geographically. Others attend schools that are more diverse. Diversity speaks to the differences we find between groups of people: ethnic and cultural diversity (race, religion, country of origin, language), socioeconomic level, gender, age, and sexual orientation. Many students find more kinds of people on campus than they "dreamt of" before they began college or university. They meet people from other backgrounds, places, and walks of life—among them, their instructors.

The following ideas adapted from the Association of American Colleges & Universities (2007) suggest how students can benefit from diversity on their campus to achieve cognitive growth:

- Recognize that your way of looking at the world is not universal
- Embrace opportunities for encountering people who are different

- Recognize that your initial reaction to cultural difference may be defensive
- Understand what makes other people's cultural views and traits valuable to them
- Listen carefully to others' descriptions of cultural differences and concerns
- Immerse yourself in a different culture (as Emily did) for an extended period of time
- Commit yourself to understanding a given situation from another point of view

LO6 Career Development

Work is a major part of life, and early adulthood is the time when most of us become established in our careers. We will consider how this happens, but, "What motivates people to work in the first place?"

The first reason people work is obvious: earning a living, fringe benefits, and ensuring future security all inspire people to pursue careers and employment. These external benefits of working are called *extrinsic motives*; however, extrinsic motives alone do not explain why people work. Work can also satisfy many internal or *intrinsic motives*, including the opportunities to engage in stimulating and satisfying

"Work is the refuge of people who have nothing better to do."
—*Oscar Wilde*

© Image Source Pink/Jupiterimages

CHOOSING A CAREER AND STAGES OF CAREER DEVELOPMENT

For most of us, career development has a number of stages. Our discussion is informed by psychologist Donald Super's theory of career development, but we have made some changes to reflect contemporary realities.

The first or *fantasy stage* involves the child's unrealistic conception of self-potential and of the world of work, which dominates from early childhood until about age 11. Young children focus on glamour professions, such as acting, medicine, sports, and law enforcement (Auger et al., 2005). They show little regard for the fit between these occupations and their abilities. During the second or *tentative choice stage*, from about age 11 through high school, children base their choices on their interests, abilities, and limitations, as well as glamour.

Beyond age 17 or so, in the *realistic choice stage*, choices become narrowed as students weigh job requirements and rewards against their interests, abilities, and values (Nauta, 2007). They may direct their educational plans to ensure they obtain the knowledge and skills they need to enter their intended occupation. Some follow the paths of role models such as parents or respected members of the community (Auger et al., 2005). Many "fall into" careers not because of particular skills and interests, but because of what is available at the time, family pressures, or the lure of high income or a certain lifestyle. Others may "job hop" through several different career paths before finally finding one that fits well.

During the *maintenance stage*, we begin "settling" into our career role, which often happens in the second half of our 30s. Although we may change positions within a company or within a career, as in moving from marketing to management, we often have a sense of our careers continuing to develop, a feeling of forward motion. Of course, people can also get "trapped" into dead-end jobs during this stage (Savickas, 2002).

Here is where we diverge from the traditional view of career development. Because of corporate downsizing, mergers and acquisitions, many employees no longer feel the loyalty to their employers that workers once did. Thus they are more likely to "job hop" when the opportunity arises. People are also living longer, healthier lives in rapidly changing times. They are staying in school longer and returning to school for education,

activities and to develop one's talents (Ryan & Deci, 2000). Many million-dollar lottery winners who quit their jobs encounter feelings of aimlessness and dissatisfaction afterward (Corliss, 2003). Moreover, within a year of cashing their cheques, lottery winners generally report happiness (or unhappiness) levels corresponding to their pre-winning levels (Corliss, 2003). Despite folk wisdom, money does not always buy happiness; many people seek more in life than extrinsic rewards such as a paycheque and financial security. They also want intrinsic rewards, such as engaging in challenging activities, broadening their social contacts, and filling their days with meaningful activity.

 D5 Million-dollar lottery winners often feel aimless and dissatisfied if they quit their jobs after striking it rich.
This is true—wouldn't it be nice to be in a position to conduct this research firsthand!

Intrinsic reasons for working include (Duffy & Sedlacek, 2007):

- *The work ethic.* The view that we are morally obligated to avoid idleness.
- *Self-identity.* Our occupational identity can become intertwined with our self-identity.
- *Self-fulfillment.* We often express our personal needs and interests through our work.
- *Self-worth.* Recognition and respect for a job well done contribute to self-esteem.
- *Socialization.* The workplace extends our social contacts.
- *Public roles.* Work roles help define our functions in the community.

training, and retraining. Today it is the norm, rather than the exception, for people to switch jobs more than once. That said, vocational interests tend to be stable over the life course (Rottinghaus et al., 2007). Though people may switch jobs, they generally seek jobs that reflect stable interests.

The final stage in Super's scheme is the *retirement stage*, during which the individual severs bonds with the workplace. In the chapters on late adulthood, we will see that retirement today is far from final. Retirees often become restless and undertake second or third careers.

DEVELOPMENTAL TASKS IN BEGINNING A CAREER

One of the challenges of early adulthood is becoming established in the career world. Different careers hold different challenges, but many challenges are common, such as the following (Bozionelos & Wang, 2006; Quigley & Tymon, 2006):

- Learning to carry out the job tasks.
- Accepting your subordinate status within the organization or profession.
- Learning to get along with your co-workers and supervisor.
- Showing that you can maintain the job, make improvements, and show progress.
- Finding a sponsor or mentor to "show you the ropes."
- Defining the boundaries between the job and other areas of life. Not taking home your troubles on the job.
- Evaluating your occupational choice in the light of measurable outcomes of your work.
- Learning to cope with daily hassles on the job, frustrations, and successes and failures.

Visit **icanhdev.com** to find the resources you need today!

Located at the back of the textbook are rip-out Chapter Review cards. Make sure you also go online to check out other tools that HDEV offers to help you successfully pass your course.

- Flashcards
- Glossary
- Interactive Practice

- Build a Summary
- Games
- Interactive Quizzing

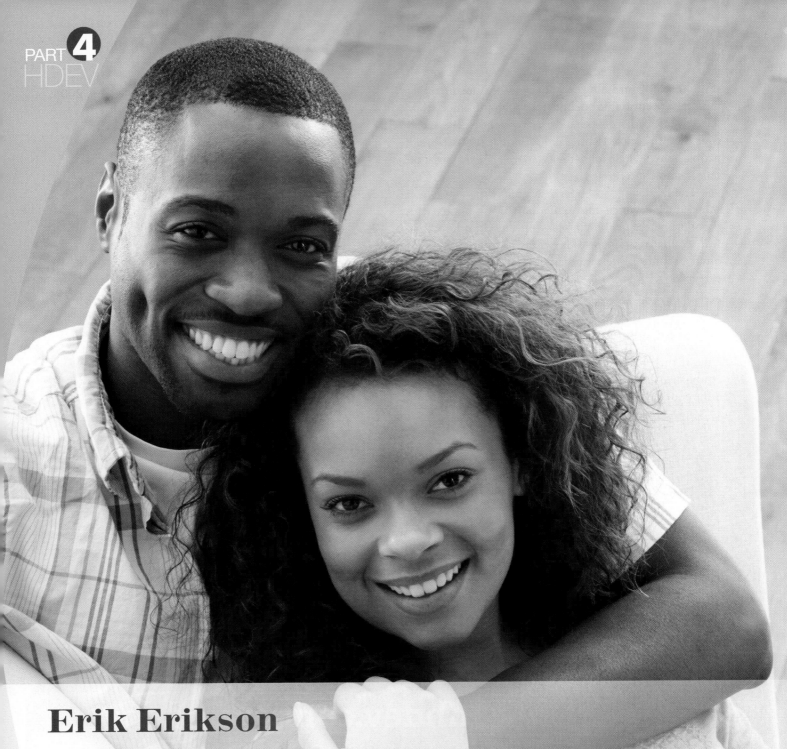

Erik Erikson

saw the establishment of intimate relationships as the key "crisis," or challenge, of early adulthood.

14

Early Adulthood: Social and Emotional Development

Learning Outcomes

LO1 Examine the issues involved in early adulthood separation

LO2 Describe the conflict between intimacy and isolation

LO3 Discuss the stage of life for entry into adulthood

LO4 Examine the emotional forces of attraction and love

LO5 Explain why people get lonely and what they do in response

LO6 Discuss the lifestyle of being single

LO7 Describe the practice of cohabitation

LO8 Describe the practice of marriage

LO9 Discuss the state of parenthood

LO10 Discuss divorce and its repercussions

Early adulthood generally covers the two decades from ages 20 to 40, although some theorists begin at 17 or 18, and others extend the period to age 44 or 45. The traditional view of development in early adulthood was laid down by developmental psychologist Robert Havighurst (1972) nearly 40 years ago. He believed that each stage of development involved accomplishing certain "tasks," and the tasks he describes for early adulthood include the following:

☑ 1. Getting started in an occupation

☑ 2. Selecting and courting a mate

☑ 3. Learning to live contentedly with one's partner

☑ 4. Starting a family and becoming a parent

☑ 5. Assuming the responsibilities of managing a home

☑ 6. Assuming civic responsibilities

☑ 7. Finding a congenial social group

Many "sophisticated" young adults will laugh at this list of tasks. Others will think that it doesn't sound too bad at all. It is brought to your attention simply as a traditional view of an ideal world of past generations that ignores some realities of human diversity and contemporary life. For example, many young adults (and older adults) remain single. Some may choose stable and long-term relationships but not the traditional label of marriage to legitimize these relationships. Some couples choose not to have children, and others may discover they are infertile. For some, civic responsibilities are not a priority. Havighurst did not list *separation* from one's family of origin, which we consider next.

LO1 Separation

Young adults leave home at different ages and for different reasons, and some never had a traditional home life to begin with. The typical developmental milestones seem distant to young adults who have spent years in orphanages, bounced about from one foster home to another, or have spent time in detention or in the homes of grandparents or other relatives because their parents could not provide a home (Minkler & Fuller-Thomson, 2005).

individuation the young adult's process of becoming an individual by means of integrating his or her own values and beliefs with those of his or her parents and society at large.

Young adults who enter the job market out of high school, or without completing high school, may live at home for a while to save up some money before venturing out on their own. When they do, they may move in with roommates or to a poorer neighbourhood than their parents' so that they can afford independent living. Even so, parents may contribute cash.

Other young adults may leave home to go to college or university, or enlist in the military. If the college and university students are attending a local school, they may stay at home or move in with roommates so they can afford it. When young adults attend school away from home, a room is often kept for them at home and is relatively untouched. Psychologically, the "nest" remains if and when they need it. Highly traditional or insecure parents may find a son's or daughter's leaving to attend school elsewhere to be so stressful that departure damages the parent–child relationship (Steele, 2005). The departure tends to be relatively more stressful when a daughter leaves.

Those who enlist in the military have their housing needs taken care of. Their rupture from home and neighbourhood is sudden and complete, although they can return when they are on leave or their service is finished.

If young adults are working within commuting distance of their homes of origin, even after graduating, they may return home to live for financial reasons. Entry-level jobs often do not pay well, or the young adult may want to try to save enough for a down payment on an apartment or a house. Some young adults get married and then move in with a set of parents. And sometimes a couple who are living together without being married move in with a set of tolerant parents.

SEPARATION–INDIVIDUATION

Whether or not young adults leave the nest, they need to separate from their parents psychologically. Psychologists and educators refer to the relevant processes as *separation* and **individuation**—that is, becoming an individual by means of integrating one's own values and beliefs with those of one's parents and one's society.

Most men in our society consider separation and individuation to be key goals of personality development in early adulthood (Blazina et al., 2007). But many psychologists argue that the priorities are different for women—that for women, the establishment and maintenance of social relationships are also of primary importance (Gilligan et al., 1990; Jordan et al., 1991). Nevertheless, women need to become their own persons in the sense of separating from their mothers (Brockman, 2003). Males are more likely to show a struggle or a fight for independence (Levpušcek, 2006).

© Radius Images/Jupiterimages

The transition to college, university, or to the workplace can play roles in separation and individuation. Employment and financial independence can lessen feelings of connectedness with parents, whereas college or university can maintain these feelings (Buhl et al., 2003). Feelings of connectedness are related to the amount of financial and emotional support students receive from parents (Tanner, 2006).

LO2 Intimacy versus Isolation

erik Erikson was aware that young adults have issues separating from parents. He was a psychoanalyst, and many of the young women who opened their hearts to him complained of difficulties in disappointing their mothers whose values were different and usually more traditional than their own. However, Erikson focused on one central conflict for each stage of life, and the core conflict he chose for early adulthood was **intimacy versus isolation.**

Erikson (1963) saw the establishment of intimate relationships as the key "crisis" of early adulthood. Young adults who have evolved a firm sense of identity during adolescence are now ready to "fuse" their identities with those of other people through marriage and abiding friendships. Erikson warned that we might not be able to commit ourselves to others until we have achieved ego identity, or established stable life roles. Lack of identity is related to the high divorce rate in young marriages. Erikson argued that young adults who do not reach out to develop intimate relationships risk retreating into isolation and loneliness.

Erikson, like Havighurst, has been criticized for suggesting that young adults who choose to remain celibate or single are not developing normally (Hayslip et al., 2006). Similarly, Erikson appeared to make similar traditional demands of people in middle and late adulthood.

intimacy versus isolation according to Erik Erikson, the central conflict or life crisis of early adulthood, in which a person develops an intimate relationship with a significant other or risks heading down a path toward social isolation.

LO3 Seasons of Life

n the basis of their in-depth interviews of adult men and women, Yale psychologist Daniel Levinson and his colleagues (Levinson, 1996; Levinson et al., 1978), formulated a theory of adult development in which people shape their lives according to the goals they consider to be most important. Levinson considers the ages of 17 to 33 to be the entry phase of adulthood for young men—when they leave their parents' home, enter the military, college or university, or the job market, and become emotionally and financially independent. Many young adults also adopt what Levinson

© Stuart Miles/Shutterstock

calls "**the dream**"— the drive to become someone, to leave their mark on history— which serves as a tentative blueprint for life. Levinson (1996) found that women undergo similar developments, but experience more social constraints, both from their families of origin and society in general. Thus women may take longer to leave home, and may feel more pressure to go from one home (their parents') to another (their husband's).

Levinson labelled the ages of 28 to 33 the *age-30 transition*. For men and women, he found that the late twenties and early thirties are commonly characterized by reassessment: "Where is my life going?" "Why am I doing this?"

Levinson and his colleagues also found that the later thirties were often characterized by settling down or planting roots. At this time, many people felt a need to make a financial and emotional investment in their home. Their concerns became focused on promotion or tenure, career advancement, mortgages, and, in many or most cases, raising their own families.

Today, Levinson's views seem rather archaic, at least when they are applied to young women (Hayslip et al., 2006). It is now acceptable and widespread for women to lead independent, single lives, for as long as they wish. And, truth be told, the great majority of career women in sizeable Canadian cities simply would not care what anyone thinks about their marital status or living arrangements. And given the mobility young adults have in Canada today, many will not live in places where people frown upon their styles of life.

LO4 Attraction and Love: Forces That Bind?

Young adults separate from their families of origin and (often, not always) join with others. In developed nations, they are free to choose the people with whom they will associate and develop friendships and romantic relationships. The emotional forces that fuel these associations are *attraction* and *love*.

ATTRACTION

Investigators define feelings of attraction as psychological forces that draw people together. Some researchers find that physical appearance is the key factor in consideration of partners for dates, sex, and long-term relationships (Wilson et al., 2005). We might like to claim that sensitivity, warmth, and intelligence are more important to us, but we may never learn about other people's personalities if they do not meet minimal standards for attractiveness (Langlois et al., 2000; Strassberg & Holty, 2003).

Is Beauty in the Eye of the Beholder?

Are our standards of beauty subjective, or do we have broad agreement on what is attractive? In certain African tribes, long necks and round, disk-like lips are signs of feminine beauty. Women thus stretch their necks and lips to make themselves more appealing (Ford & Beach, 1951).

In our culture, taller men are considered to be more attractive by women (Kurzban & Weeden, 2005;

PAUL NEVIN/Ticket/Photolibrary

Pawlowski & Koziel, 2002). Young women prefer their dates to be about 15 cm (6 in.) taller than they are. Young men, on the average, prefer women who are about 11.5 cm (4½ in.) shorter (Gillis & Avis, 1980). Tall women are not viewed so positively.

In our culture, "thin is in," especially for females (Furnham et al., 2005; Wilson et al., 2005).

Most men in our society are attracted to women with ample bustlines (Hill et al., 2005). In one study, men rated a continuum of female figures that differed only in the size of their bust (Thompson & Tantleff, 1992). Men preferred women with larger but not "huge" busts.

An experiment manipulated men's voices and asked women to rate them for attractiveness. Women at the fertile phase of the menstrual cycle found men with more "masculine"—deeper—voices to be more attractive (Jones et al., 2008).

Nonphysical Traits Affect Perceptions of Physical Beauty

Although our culture has physical standards for beauty, nonphysical traits also affect our perceptions. For example, the attractiveness of a partner is likely to be enhanced by traits such as familiarity, liking, respect, and sharing of values and goals (Kniffin & Wilson, 2004). People also rate the attractiveness of faces higher when they are smiling than when they are not smiling (O'Doherty et al., 2003).

> **D1** People are considered to be more attractive when they are smiling. Studies seem to indicate that this is true.

Sex Differences in Perceptions of Attractiveness

Gender-role expectations may affect perceptions of attractiveness. For example, women are more likely to be attracted to socially dominant men than men are to be attracted to socially dominant women (Buunk et al., 2002). Women who viewed videos of prospective dates found men who acted outgoing and self-expressive more appealing than men who were

passive (Riggio & Woll, 1984). Yet men who viewed videos in the Riggio and Woll (1984) study were put off by outgoing, self-expressive behaviour in women.

Susan Sprecher and her colleagues (1994) surveyed a representative sample of more than 13,000 adults. In one section of their questionnaire, they asked respondents how willing they would be to marry someone who was older, younger, of a different religion, not likely to hold a steady job, not good-looking, and so forth. Each item was followed by a 7-point scale in which 1 meant "not at all" and 7 meant "very willing." As shown in Table 14.1, women were more willing than men to marry someone who was not good looking. On the other hand, women were less willing to marry someone not likely to hold a steady job.

Are Preferences Concerning Attractiveness Inborn?

Evolutionary psychologists believe that evolutionary forces favour the continuation of sex differences in preferences for mates because certain preferred traits provide reproductive advantages (Buss, 2005). Some physical features are universally appealing to both females and males, such

TABLE 14.1
Sex Differences in Preferences for Mates

HOW WILLING WOULD YOU BE TO MARRY SOMEONE WHO—	MEN	WOMEN
Was not "good looking"?	3.41	4.42**
Was older than you by 6 or more years?	4.15	5.29**
Was younger than you by 6 or more years?	4.54	2.80**
Was not likely to hold a steady job?	2.73	1.62**
Would earn much less than you?	4.60	3.76**
Would earn much more than you?	5.19	5.93**
Had more education than you?	5.22	5.82**
Had less education than you?	4.67	4.08**
Had been married before?	3.35	3.44
Already had children?	2.84	3.11*
Was of a different religion?	4.24	4.31
Was of a different race?	3.08	2.84*

Source: Based on information in Susan Sprecher, Quintin Sullivan, & Elaine Hatfield (1994). Mate Selection Preferences: Gender Differences Examined in a National Sample. *Journal of Personality and Social Psychology*, 66(6), 1074–1080.
*Difference statistically significant at the .01 level of confidence.
**Difference statistically significant at the .001 level of confidence.

attraction–similarity hypothesis the view that people tend to develop romantic relationships with people who are similar to themselves in physical attractiveness and other traits.

reciprocity the tendency to respond in kind when we feel admired and complimented.

romantic love a form of love fuelled by passion and feelings of intimacy.

> **D2** "Opposites attract" has been proven to be a false notion.
> People who are similar are usually more likely to be attracted to one another.

as cleanliness, good complexion, clear eyes, good teeth, good hair, firm muscle tone, and a steady gait. Perhaps these features are markers of reproductive potential (Buss, 2005). Age and health may be relatively more important to a woman's appeal because these characteristics tend to be associated with her reproductive capacity: the "biological clock" limits her reproductive potential. Physical characteristics associated with a woman's youthfulness, such as smooth skin, firm muscle tone, and lustrous hair, may thus have become more closely linked to a woman's appeal (Buss, 2005). A man's reproductive value, however, may depend more on how well he can provide for his family than on his age or physical appeal. The value of men as reproducers, therefore, is more intertwined with factors that contribute to a stable environment for child rearing—such as economic status and reliability. Evolutionary psychologists argue that these sex differences in mate preferences may have been passed down through the generations as part of our genetic heritage (Buss, 2005).

The Attraction–Similarity Hypothesis: Do "Opposites Attract" or "Do Birds of a Feather Flock Together"?

Do not despair if you are less than magnificent in appearance, along with most of us mere mortals. You may be saved from permanently blending in with the wallpaper by the effects of the **attraction–similarity hypothesis**. This hypothesis holds that people tend to develop romantic relationships with people who are similar to themselves in attractiveness

and other traits (Klohnen & Luo, 2003; Morry & Gaines, 2005). Look around and do some informal research of your own. What do you see?

Researchers have found that people who are involved in committed relationships are more likely to be similar to their partners in their attitudes and cultural attributes (Amodio & Showers, 2005). Our partners tend to be like us in race and ethnicity, age, level of education, and religion.

Reciprocity: If You Like Me, You Must Have Excellent Judgment

Has anyone told you that you are good-looking, brilliant, and emotionally mature to boot? That your taste is excellent? Ah, what amazing judgment! When we feel admired and complimented, we tend to return these feelings and behaviours. This tendency is called **reciprocity**. Reciprocity is a potent determinant of attraction (Levine, 2000; Sprecher, 1998). Perhaps the power of reciprocity has enabled many couples to become happy with one another and reasonably well adjusted.

Attraction can lead to feelings of love. Let us now turn to that most fascinating topic.

LOVE

The experience of **romantic love** as opposed to attachment or sexual arousal occurs within a cultural context in which the concept is idealized (Berscheid, 2003, 2006). Western culture has a long tradition of idealizing the

---

An American survey (Michael et al., 1994) found that:

- The sex partners of nearly 94 percent of single European American men are European American women.
- About 2 percent of single European American men are partnered with Latina American women, 2 percent with Asian American women, and less than 1 percent with African American women.
- The sex partners of nearly 82 percent of African American men are African American women.
- Nearly 8 percent of African American men are partnered with European American women. Less than 5 percent are partnered with Latina American women.
- About 83 percent of the women and men in the study chose partners within 5 years of their own age and of the same or a similar religion.
- Of all the women in the study, not one with a graduate college degree had a partner who had not finished high school.
- Men with a college degree almost never had sexual relationships with women with much more or much less education than they had.

Do you believe the results would be different if the survey was conducted here in multicultural Canada?

© Ryan McVay/Photodisc/Getty Images

Prince Charming or just another toad?

concept of romantic love, as represented, for instance, by romantic fairy tales that have been passed down through the generations. In fact, our exposure to the concept of romantic love may begin with hearing those fairy tales, and later perhaps, continue to blossom through exposure to romantic novels, television and film scripts, and the heady tales of friends and relatives.

Researchers have found that love is a complex concept, involving many areas of experience (Berscheid, 2003, 2006). Let us consider two psychological perspectives on love, both of which involve emotional arousal.

Love as Appraisal of Arousal

Social psychologists Ellen Berscheid and Elaine Hatfield (Berscheid, 2003, 2006; Hatfield & Rapson, 2002) define romantic love in terms of a state of intense physiological arousal and the cognitive appraisal of that arousal as love. The arousal may be experienced as a pounding heart, sweaty palms, and butterflies in the stomach when one is in the presence of, or thinking about, one's love interest. Cognitive appraisal of the arousal means attributing it to some cause, such as fear or love. The perception that one has fallen in love is thus derived from: (1) a state of intense arousal in relation to an appropriate love object (that is, a person, not an event like a rock concert), (2) a cultural setting that idealizes romantic love, and (3) the attribution of the arousal to feelings of love to the person.

Sternberg's Triangular Theory of Love

Robert Sternberg's (2006) "triangular theory" of love includes three building blocks, or components, of loving experiences:

1. **Intimacy:** The experience of warmth toward another person that arises from feelings of closeness and connectedness, and the desire to share one's inmost thoughts.
2. **Passion:** Intense romantic or sexual desire, accompanied by physiological arousal.
3. **Commitment:** Commitment to maintain the relationship through good times and bad.

> **intimacy** the experience of warmth toward another person that arises from feelings of closeness and connectedness.
>
> **passion** intense sexual desire for another person.
>
> **commitment** the decision to devote oneself to a cause or another person.

Sternberg's model is triangular in that various kinds of love can be conceptualized in terms of a triangle in which each vertex represents one of the building blocks (Figure 14.1, on page 266). In Sternberg's model, couples are well matched if they possess corresponding levels of passion, intimacy, and commitment (Drigotas et al., 1999; Sternberg, 2006). According to the model, various combinations of the building blocks of love characterize different types of love relationships (see Table 14.2 on page 267). For example, infatuation (passionate love) is typified by sexual desire but not by intimacy and commitment.

"Being in love" can refer to states of passion or infatuation, whereas friendship is usually based on shared interests, liking, and respect. Friendship and passionate love do not necessarily overlap. Nothing prevents people in love from becoming good friends, however—perhaps even the best of friends. Sternberg's model recognizes that the intimacy we find in true friendships and the passion we find in love are blended in two forms of love—romantic love and consummate love. These love types differ along the dimension of commitment, however.

Romantic love has both passion and intimacy but lacks commitment. Romantic love may burn brightly and then flicker out. Or it may develop into a more complete love, called consummate love, in which all three components flower. Consummate love is an ideal toward which many Westerners strive. Sometimes a love relationship has both passion and commitment but lacks intimacy. Sternberg calls this *fatuous* (foolish) *love*. Fatuous love is associated with whirlwind courtships that burn brightly but briefly as the partners realize they are not well matched. In companionate love, intimacy and commitment are strong, but passion is lacking. Companionate love typifies long-term relationships and marriages in which passion has ebbed but a deep and abiding friendship remains (Hatfield & Rapson, 2002).

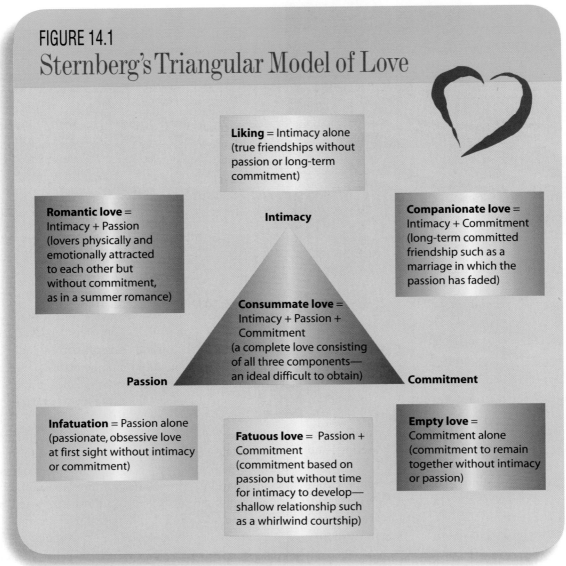

FIGURE 14.1
Sternberg's Triangular Model of Love

Liking = Intimacy alone (true friendships without passion or long-term commitment)

Romantic love = Intimacy + Passion (lovers physically and emotionally attracted to each other but without commitment, as in a summer romance)

Companionate love = Intimacy + Commitment (long-term committed friendship such as a marriage in which the passion has faded)

Intimacy

Consummate love = Intimacy + Passion + Commitment (a complete love consisting of all three components— an ideal difficult to obtain)

Passion

Commitment

Infatuation = Passion alone (passionate, obsessive love at first sight without intimacy or commitment)

Fatuous love = Passion + Commitment (commitment based on passion but without time for intimacy to develop— shallow relationship such as a whirlwind courtship)

Empty love = Commitment alone (commitment to remain together without intimacy or passion)

Sternberg, Robert J. (1986, April) A triangular theory of love. *Psychological Review, 93*(2), 119–135.

D3 Couples can remain in love after passion fades.
With companionate love, couples can remain "in love" after passion fades.

Jealousy

O! beware, my lord, of jealousy;
It is the green-ey'd monster . . .

William Shakespeare, *Othello*

Thus was Othello, the Moor of Venice, warned of jealousy in the Shakespearean play that bears his name. Yet Othello could not control his feelings and wound up killing his beloved (and innocent) wife, Desdemona. Partners can become jealous when others show sexual interest in their partners or when their partners show interest in another.

Jealousy can lead to loss of feelings of affection, feelings of insecurity and rejection, anxiety and loss of self-esteem, and feelings of mistrust. Jealousy, therefore, can be one reason that relationships fail. In extreme cases jealousy can cause depression or give rise to spouse abuse, suicide, or, as with Othello, murder (Puente & Cohen, 2003; Vandello & Cohen, 2003).

Many young adults—including many college students—play jealousy games. They let their partners know that they are attracted to other people. They flirt openly or manufacture tales to make their partners pay more attention to them, to test the relationship, to inflict pain, or to take revenge for a partner's disloyalty.

D4 Jealousy can be destructive to a relationship.
Some milder forms of jealousy may have the positive effect of revealing how much one cares for one's partner. User beware!

TABLE 14.2
Sternberg's Typology of Love

1. Nonlove	A relationship in which all three components of love are absent. Characterizes casual interactions or acquaintances.
2. Liking	Intimacy without passion and commitment, as found in friendship.
3. Infatuation	"Love at first sight" in which one experiences passionate desire for another person in the absence of intimacy and commitment.
4. Empty love	Characterized by commitment to maintain the relationship in the absence of passion and intimacy. Describes stagnant relationships that no longer involve emotional intimacy or physical attraction.
5. Romantic love	Characterized by the combination of passion and intimacy but without commitment.
6. Companionate love	Characterized by intimacy and commitment. It often occurs in long-term relationships in which passion has waned and been replaced by committed friendship.
7. Fatuous love	Associated with whirlwind romances and "quickie marriages." Passion and commitment are present, but intimacy is not.
8. Consummate love	Combination of passion, intimacy, and commitment. The ideal form of love in our society.

Sternberg, Robert J. (1986, April) A triangular theory of love. *Psychological Review, 93*(2), 119–135.

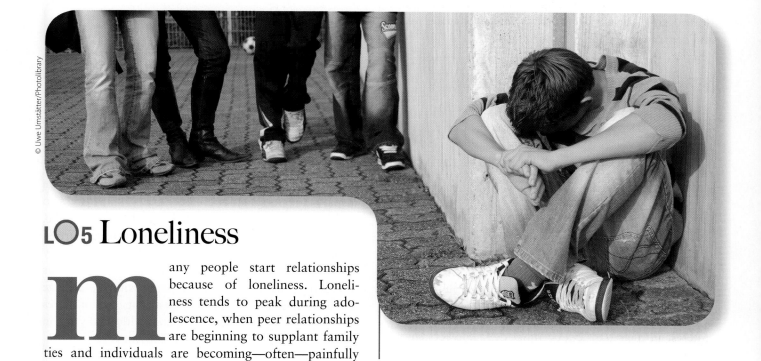

LO5 Loneliness

many people start relationships because of loneliness. Loneliness tends to peak during adolescence, when peer relationships are beginning to supplant family ties and individuals are becoming—often—painfully aware of how other adolescents may be more successful at making friends and earning the admiration of others. A study of 90 adolescents aged 16 to 18 found that feelings of loneliness were related to low self-confidence, introversion, unhappiness, and emotional instability (Cheng & Furnham, 2002). Loneliness is also often related to feelings of depression. A study of 101 dating couples with a mean age of 21 found that poor relationships contributed to feelings of loneliness and to depression—even though the individuals had partners (Segrin et al., 2003).

Research shows consistently that social support helps people cope with stress, and that stress can lead to a host of health problems (Pressman et al., 2005). Therefore, it is not surprising that loneliness is associated with physical health problems and depression. One study, for example, found that lonely people had higher blood pressure than people who were not lonely (Hawkley et al., 2003). Social isolation has also been shown to predict cancer, cardiovascular disease, and a higher mortality rate (Tomoka et al., 2006).

The causes of loneliness are many and complex. Lonely people tend to have several of the following characteristics: lack of social skills, lack of interest in other people, and lack of empathy (Cramer, 2003). The fear of rejection is often connected with self-criticism of social skills and expectations of failure in relating to others (Vorauer et al., 2003). Lonely people also fail to disclose personal information to potential friends (Solano et al., 1982), are cynical about human nature (for example, seeing people as only out for themselves), and demand too much too soon.

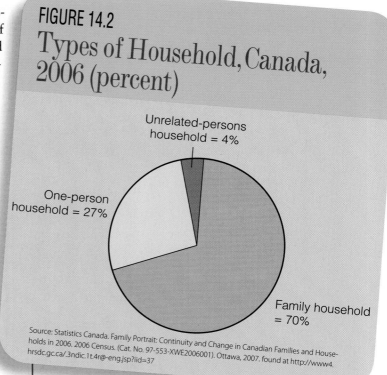

FIGURE 14.2

Types of Household, Canada, 2006 (percent)

Unrelated-persons household = 4%

One-person household = 27%

Family household = 70%

Source: Statistics Canada. Family Portrait: Continuity and Change in Canadian Families and Households in 2006. 2006 Census. (Cat. No. 97-553-XWE2006001). Ottawa, 2007. found at http://www4.hrsdc.gc.ca/.3ndic.1t.4r@-eng.jsp?iid=37

D5 Many people remain lonely because they fear being rejected by others.
Being alone is very different from being lonely. Studies show that being lonely is a significant and complex issue for young adults.

LO6 The Single Life

married people became the minority in Canada for the first time, according to the census information released by Statistics Canada in its "family portrait" from data collected in 2006. Unmarried persons are defined as those who are divorced, separated, widowed, or have never married. In 2006, 51.5 percent of the population age 16 or older were unmarried, compared with 38.6 percent just 20 years earlier (CBC News, 2007a).

D6 Being single has become a more common Canadian lifestyle over the past few decades.
The evolution of relationships has seen acceptance of a variety of different lifestyle choices.

In 2006, single persons represented 27 percent (more than 1 in 4) of all Canadian households (see Figure 14.2). Several factors contribute to the increased proportion of singles. More young adults are postponing marriage to pursue educational and career goals. Many are also deciding to "live together" (cohabit), at least for a while, rather than get married. Also people are getting married later, with average ages of first marriages varying widely across the provinces. In 2003, the average age of grooms in Quebec was 31.9 years, compared with the average age of 29.3 in Saskatchewan. The average age of brides in Quebec was 30.4 years, compared with 27.0 years in Saskatchewan (Statistics Canada, 2007a).

> There is nothing I would not do
> If you would be my POSSLQ
>
> —Charles Osgood

Andresr/Shutterstock

According to the "family portrait" compiled by Statistics Canada, in 2006, 26 percent of families with children were headed by a lone parent. Of those families, about 20 percent were headed by men, representing a large gender disparity. The number of lone-parent families headed by men is growing more than twice as fast as those headed by women (Statistics Canada, 2007b).

Single people encounter less social stigma today. They are less likely today to be perceived as socially inadequate or as failures. On the other hand, many young adults do not choose to be single. Some have not yet found Mr. or Ms. Right. But many young adults see being single as an alternative, open-ended way of life—not a temporary stage that precedes marriage. As career options for women have expanded, they are not as financially dependent on men as their mothers and grandmothers were.

Being single is not without its problems. Many single people are lonely. Some singles would like to have a steady, meaningful relationship. Others, usually women, worry about their physical safety. Some young adults who are living alone find it difficult to satisfy their needs for intimacy, companionship, and sex. Despite these concerns, most singles are well adjusted.

There is no distinct "singles scene." Single people differ in their sexual interests and lifestyles. Many achieve emotional and psychological security through a network of intimate relationships with friends. Many are sexually active and practice **serial monogamy** (Kulick, 2006). Others have both a primary sexual relationship with one steady partner and occasional flings. A few pursue casual sexual encounters. By contrast, some singles remain celibate, either by choice or lack of opportunity. Some choose **celibacy** for religious reasons, to focus on work or another cause, because they find sex unalluring, or because they fear STIs.

> **serial monogamy** a series of exclusive sexual relationships.
>
> **celibacy** abstention from sexual activity, whether from choice or lack of opportunity.
>
> **cohabitation** living together with a romantic partner without being married.

LO7 Cohabitation: Darling, Would You Be My POSSLQ?

POSSLQ? POSSLQ is the unromantic abbreviation used by statisticians to refer to **cohabitation**. It stands for People of Opposite Sex Sharing Living Quarters and applies to unmarried couples who live together.

Some social scientists believe that cohabitation has become accepted within the social mainstream. Whether or not this is so, society in general has become more tolerant (Laumann et al., 2007). We seldom hear cohabitation referred to as "living in sin" or "shacking up" as we once did. People today are more likely to refer to cohabitation with value-free expressions such as "living together."

According to the 2006 census, the number of common-law couples surged 18.9 percent since 2001. Same-sex married couples were also counted for the first time in this census, reflecting the legalization of same-sex marriage across Canada. The census enumerated 45,345 same-sex couples, of which 16.5 percent were married couples (Statistics Canada, 2007b).

Frazer Harrison/Getty Images

TABLE 14.3

Proportion of Cohabiting Couples

COUNTRY	YEAR	AS % OF ALL COUPLES
Sweden	2000	30.0
Norway	2000	24.5
Finland	2000	18.5
Mexico	2000	18.7
New Zealand	2001	18.3
France	1999	17.5
Canada	**2001**	**16.0**
Quebec	**2001**	**29.8**
Other Provinces	**2001**	**11.7**
United States	2000	8.2

Source: Nunavut Bureau of Statistics at http://www.eia.gov.nu.ca/stats/Publications/Cenpub/StatsUpdate,%20Families,%20Marital%20Status,%20Households%20and%20Dwellings,%202006%20Census.pdf page 2. Adapted from Statistics Canada, Profile of Marital Status, Common-law Status, Families, Dwellings and Households, 2006 Census, 94-576-XCB2006001, Census year 2006 Released September 12, 2007; and Statistics Canada, Profile of Marital Status, Common-law Status, Families, Dwellings and Households, 2001 Census, 95F0487XCB2001001, Census year 2001 Released October 22, 2002

Interestingly, cohabitation rates vary internationally (see Table 14.3). Quebec seems to keep pace with non-traditional European countries, whereas the rest of Canada aligns more closely with the statistics from the United States.

So, when couples cohabit before marriage, are they less likely to divorce? The answer is no. In fact, on average, such couples are more likely to divorce, not only in Canada but also in the United States and Great Britain. Women between the ages of 20 to 30 were 63 percent more likely to separate if they had cohabited first, compared with 33 percent of women who hadn't cohabited first (Ambert, 2005).

Young adults cohabit for many reasons. Cohabitation, like marriage, is an alternative to living alone. Romantic partners may have deep feelings for each other but not be ready to get married. Some couples prefer cohabitation because it provides an abiding relationship without the legal entanglements of marriage (Hussain, 2002; Marquis, 2003).

Willingness to cohabit is related to less traditional views of marriage and gender roles (Hussain, 2002; Marquis, 2003). For example, divorced people are more likely than people who have never been married to cohabit. Perhaps the experience of divorce leaves some people more willing to share their lives than

their bank accounts. Cohabitants are less likely than noncohabitants to say that religion is very important to them (Bramlett & Mosher, 2002). Tradition aside, many cohabitants are simply less committed to their relationships than married people are (Hussain, 2002; Marquis, 2003). Moreover, men are more often the one unwilling to make a commitment (Peplau, 2003).

Economic factors also come into play. Young adults may decide to cohabit because of the economic advantages of sharing household expenses. Cohabiting individuals who receive public assistance risk losing support if they get married (Hussain, 2002; Marquis, 2003). College and university students may cohabit secretly to maintain the parental support they might lose if they were to reveal their living arrangements.

Cohabiting couples may believe that cohabitation will strengthen eventual marriage by helping them iron out the kinks in their relationship. Yet some studies suggest that the likelihood of divorce within 10 years of marriage is nearly twice as great among married couples who cohabited before marriage (Smock, 2000). Why?

We cannot conclude that cohabitation necessarily causes divorce. We must be cautious about drawing causal conclusions from correlational data. Selection factors—the factors that led some couples to cohabit and others not to cohabit—may explain the results. For example, cohabitors tend to be less traditional and less religious than noncohabitors (Hussain, 2002; Marquis, 2003), and thus tend to be less committed to the values and interests traditionally associated with the institution of marriage. Therefore, the attitudes of cohabitors and not necessarily cohabitation itself are likely to be responsible for their higher rates of divorce.

LO8 Marriage: Tying the Knot

families, for all of their different descriptions and labels, remain our most common form of Canadian lifestyle. Young adults are quite likely to get married in a traditional sense of the word. They are mature enough to have completed graduate school or to have established careers. They are also young enough not to have generally suffered being widowed.

WHY DO PEOPLE GET MARRIED?

Even in this era of serial monogamy and cohabitation, people get married. Marriage meets many personal and cultural needs. For traditionalists, marriage legitimizes sexual relations. Marriage provides an institution in which children can be supported and socialized. Marriage (theoretically) restricts sexual relations so that a man can be assured—or assume—that his wife's children are his. Unless one has signed

TABLE 14.4
Happy Marriages

Percentage of Married Persons Age 18 and Older Who Said Their Marriages Were "Very Happy," by Period

PERIOD	MEN	WOMEN
1973–1976	69.6	68.6
1977–1981	68.3	64.2
1982–1986	62.9	61.7
1987–1991	66.4	59.6
1993–1996	63.2	59.7
1998–2004	64.4	60.4

Source: The General Social Survey, conducted by the National Opinion Research Center of the University of Chicago. Reprinted from Whitehead & Popenoe, 2006, Figure 4.

a prenuptial agreement to the contrary, marriage permits the orderly transmission of wealth from one family to another and one generation to another.

Today, because more people believe that premarital sex is acceptable between two people who feel affectionate toward each other, the desire for sex is less likely to motivate marriage. But marriage provides a sense of security and opportunities to share feelings, experiences, and ideas with someone with whom one forms a special attachment. Most young adults agree that marriage is important

monogamy marriage between one man and one woman.

polygyny marriage between one man and more than one woman. (A form of *polygamy*, in which one partner has more than one partner of the other sex.)

polyandry marriage between one woman and more than one man. (A form of *polygamy*.)

gay marriage marriage between two gay males or between two lesbians.

homogamy the practice of people getting married to people who are similar to them.

for people who plan to spend the rest of their lives together (Jayson, 2008).

The Future Families Project (Bibby, 2004) was a survey of Canadian values conducted by Reginald Bibby of the University of Lethbridge. Many people want to get married because they believe they will be happier. According to Table 14.4, most married men and women are happier, though their numbers have decreased since the 1970s.

TYPES OF MARRIAGE

Among couples, two types of marriage are possible: monogamy and polygamy. In **monogamy**, a husband and wife are wed only to each other. In polygamy, a person has more than one spouse (of the other sex) and is permitted sexual access to each of them.

Polygyny has been the most prevalent form of polygamy among the world's preliterate societies (Ford & Beach, 1951; Frayser, 1985). **Polyandry** is relatively rare. In polygynous societies, such as Bounty, British Columbia, men are married to multiple wives, but their unions have not been deemed legal in Canadian society.

Arranged Marriage

In the Broadway musical *Fiddler on the Roof*, Tevye, the Jewish father of three girls of marriageable age in 19th-century Russia, demands that his daughters marry Jewish men to perpetuate their families' religious and cultural traditions. Traditional societies such as those of modern-day India (Myers et al., 2005) and Pakistan (Zaidi & Shuraydi, 2002) and olden Europe (Seward, 2005) frequently use/used arranged marriages, in which the families of the bride and groom more or less arrange for the union.

As in *Fiddler*, one of the purposes of arranged marriage is to ensure the bride and groom share similar backgrounds so they will carry on their traditions. Supporters of arranged marriage also argue that it is wiser to follow family wisdom than one's own heart, especially since the attraction couples feel is often infatuation and not a deep, abiding love. Proponents also claim a lower divorce rate for arranged marriages than for "self-

arranged marriages," but couples who enter arranged marriages are generally more traditional to begin with.

Gay Marriage

In churches and in politics, the debate about homosexuality has focused recently on **gay marriage**—that is, whether gay males and lesbians should be allowed to marry. Although Canada recognizes the equality rights of gay and lesbian citizens, such is not the case in many areas of the United States and throughout the world.

Only a small number of countries permit same-sex marriage, including the Netherlands, Sweden, Portugal, Canada, and Argentina. Committed gay and lesbian couples who cannot legally marry may enter into civil unions, domestic partnerships, or registered partnerships in various places. These options offer varying degrees of the benefits of marriage and are available in countries such as Brazil, France, Germany, the United Kingdom, Australia, and in several states in the United States. Canada is very much a front runner in the domain of gay rights but we need to remember that legal equality must also be supported by social equality.

WHOM DO WE MARRY: ARE MARRIAGES MADE IN HEAVEN OR IN THE NEIGHBOURHOOD?

Although the selection of a mate is (officially) free in our society, factors such as race, social class, and religion often determine the categories of people within which we seek mates (Laumann et al., 2007). Young adults tend to marry others from the same area and social class. Parental approval may not be formally required but is often viewed as desirable. Since neighbourhoods often comprise people from a similar social class, storybook marriages like Cinderella's are the exception to the rule.

Young adults tend to marry people who are similar in physical attractiveness, attitudes, background, and interests (Blackwell & Lichter, 2004). Young adults are more often than not similar to their mates in height, weight, personality traits, intelligence, educational level, religion, even in use of alcohol and tobacco (Myers, 2006; Reynolds et al., 2006). As Canada continues to diversify and embrace a philosophy of multiculturalism, mixed marriages and mixed common-law relationships are becoming an increasing trend, having risen nearly 30 percent between 2001 and 2006, according to Statistics Canada (Weeks, 2009). Mixed unions comprise only about 4 percent of all relationships but they reflect our multicultural mosaic. The concept of "like marrying like" is termed **homogamy**.

Research shows that marriages between people from similar backgrounds tend to be more stable (Myers, 2006), perhaps because partners are more likely to share values and attitudes (Willetts, 2006).

Most people also tend to follow *age homogamy*—to select a partner who falls in their own age range, with bridegrooms two to five years older than their wives (Buss, 1994; Michael et al., 1994). But age homogamy reflects the tendency to marry in early adulthood. Persons who marry late or who remarry tend not to select partners so close in age.

MARITAL SATISFACTION

The nature of romantic relationships and the satisfaction of the partners strongly affect the well-being of each member of the couple at various stages throughout adulthood (Bertoni et al., 2007). An Italian study of married couples found that the partners' confidence in their ability to influence their relationship for the better contributed to the quality of the marriage (Bertoni et al., 2007). In turn, the quality of the marital relationship appeared to positively affect individuals' physical and psychological health. Another study found that intimacy, which is fuelled by trust, honesty, and the sharing of innermost feelings, is strongly related to marital satisfaction (Patrick et al., 2007). So is the psychological support of one's spouse.

Satisfaction with one's career is positively correlated with marital satisfaction, and both are related to general life satisfaction (Perrone et al., 2007). Perhaps general tendencies toward happiness (or depression) manifest themselves in various walks of life, including one's vocational life and romantic relationships. Or perhaps doing very well in one arena can cast a positive glow on other parts of life.

© Walt Disney/Courtesy: Everett Collection

Cinderella and Prince Charming: According to homogamy theory their marriage might have had a very tough time surviving in the real world.

When one marital partner is a heavy drinker and the other is not, marital satisfaction declines over time (Homish & Leonard, 2007). It doesn't matter who is the heavy drinker, the man or the woman; in either case, satisfaction declines. Another study followed 172 newly wed couples over four years and found that physical aggression preceded sharp declines in marital satisfaction (Lawrence & Bradbury, 2007). Interestingly, the union was more likely to be dissolved when the woman was the aggressor.

Researchers in one study investigated the effects of infants' sleep patterns and crying on marital satisfaction in 107 first-time parent couples during the first year following birth. In general, marital satisfaction decreased as the year wore on, and the baby's crying was apparently the main source of the problem (Meijer & van den Wittenboer, 2007). Parental loss of sleep compounded the difficulties.

Satisfaction in the Relationships of Heterosexual, Gay Male, and Lesbian Couples

Numerous researchers have studied the factors that predict satisfaction in a relationship or the deterioration and ending of a relationship. Much of this research has sought to determine whether there are differences in the factors that satisfy heterosexual and homosexual couples. The interesting finding is that we are hard pressed to find differences. One difference that stands out favours the gay and lesbian couples: they tend to distribute household chores evenly and not in terms of gender role stereotypes (Kurdek, 2005, 2006). Now for the similarities: gay, lesbian, and male–female couples are all more satisfied when they receive social support from their partners, they share power in the relationship, they fight fair, and they perceive their partners to be committed to the relationship (Mathews et al., 2006; Twist, 2005). But a couple of differences favour stability in the relationships of the male–female couples: they are more likely to have the support of their families and less likely to be stigmatized by society at large. As the attitudes of Canadian society become more inclusive, these disparities are likely to disappear.

LO9 Parenthood

Becoming a parent is a major life event that requires changes in nearly every sphere of life: personal, social, financial, and academic (Redshaw & van den Akker, 2007). In fact, many individuals and couples in contemporary developed nations no longer think of parenthood as a necessary part of marriage or a relationship (Doherty et al., 2007).

Just as people are getting married in their later 20s today, they are also delaying parenthood into their later 20s (Arnett, 2007; Popenoe & Whitehead, 2006). And many women do not bear children until they are in their 30s or their 40s. But bearing children in developed nations is generally seen as ideally occurring in early adulthood, although teenage pregnancy remains a Canadian reality.

> **D7** Research indicates that having a child will not necessarily save a troubled marriage.
> In fact, a newborn can often add stress to a couple's relationship.

Why do people have children? Reliable birth control methods have separated sex acts from reproduction. Except for women living under the most "traditional" circumstances or for couples who make a "mistake," becoming pregnant is a choice. In developed nations, most couples report that they choose to have children for personal happiness or well-being (Dyer, 2007). In more traditional societies, people report having children to strengthen marital bonds, provide social security, assist with labour (as in having more farm hands), provide social status, maintain the family name and lineage, secure property rights and inheritance, and in some places, improve the odds of—yes—reincarnation (Dyer, 2007). Of these reasons, having children to care for one in one's old age ("social security") looms large. In Canada, the Canadian Pension Plan helps support older people, but how many middle-aged people (typically daughters) are running in one direction to rear their children and in another direction to provide emotional and other supports for elderly parents and other relatives?

Having a child is unlikely to save a marriage. Numerous studies show that with the added stress of caring for a new baby, the quality of a couple's adjustment often declines significantly throughout the year following delivery (e.g., Lawrence et al., 2007; Simonelli et al., 2007).

PARENTHOOD AND ROLE OVERLOAD

Some research has focused on the effects of newborns entering the lives of working-class families, especially when the mother must return to work shortly after the birth (e.g., Perry-Jenkins et al., 2007). In such cases, the parents are frequently

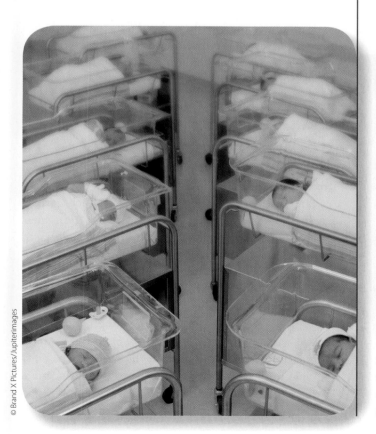

© Brand X Pictures/Jupiterimages

depressed, and conflict often emerges. Although fathers in such cases may give lip service to helping with the baby and do a few things to help out here and there, the mother is almost always the primary caregiver (Wall & Arnold, 2007) and thus encounters role overload. That is, the mother suffers from playing roles as both primary caregiver and, in our demanding economy, one of two primary breadwinners. Role overload is one of the primary reasons that Canada has instituted supportive maternity and paternity leave programs.

Yet a longitudinal study of 45 couples expecting their first child showed that family life does not have to be this stressful (McHale & Rotman, 2007). The couples were assessed during pregnancy and from their child's infancy through toddlerhood—at 3, 12, and 30 months after birth. Parents who generally agreed on their beliefs about parenting, and on which parent should do what, experienced a postnatal adjustment that was largely solid and remained stable. In other words, when both members of the couple believed they should share caregiving equally and they lived up to it, their adjustment was good. If they believed that one parent should be primarily responsible for caregiving and abided by that scenario, adjustment was also good. Consistency between their expressed beliefs and their behaviour predicted adjustment.

PARENTHOOD IN DUAL-EARNER FAMILIES

The financial realities of contemporary life, and the women's movement, have made the move of women into the workplace the norm in Canadian society. Thus young adults with children, who are married or cohabiting, more often than not make up dual-earner families.

Studies find that the mothers in dual-earner families encounter more stress than the fathers do (Schneewind & Kupsch, 2007; Wall, 2007). Evidence of a powerful sex difference in dual-earner families is also found in analysis of longitudinal survey data on 884 dual-earner couples (Chesley & Moen, 2006). Caring for children was related to declines in well-being for dual-earner women, but, ironically, with increases in well-being for dual-earner men. Perhaps the men were relieved of much stress by the second income. Dual-earner women with flexible work schedules encountered less stress than women with fixed schedules, apparently because they were more capable of managing their role overload.

What happens in the workplace doesn't necessarily stay in the workplace. A study of 113 dual-earner couples found that problems in the workplace contributed to tension in the couples, health problems, and dissatisfaction with the relationship (Matthews et al., 2006).

Because of problems balancing work and family life, usually the mother and not the father cuts back on work or drops out of the workforce altogether when dual-earner families can no longer afford to have a parent out of the home (Wall, 2007). Because of experience with dual-earner families around them, a sample of 194 adolescents from dual-earner families generally expected that they (if they were female) or their partners (if they were male) would be the ones to cut back or quit work in the future, at least temporarily, if the couple had a child (Weinshenker, 2006). The responses showed little insight into the problems raised by interrupting careers. On the other hand, having a working mother encouraged the adolescents—female and male—to say they believed in gender egalitarianism.

> *Whenever I date a guy, I think, is this the man I want my children to spend their weekends with?*
>
> —Rita Rudner

Studies find that the mothers in dual-earner families encounter more stress than the fathers do.

© Jamie Grill/Corbis

LO 10 Divorce: Breaking Bonds

When Reginald Bibby (2004) surveyed Canadian teenagers, 90 percent said they expected to marry and stay with the same partner for life. Yet we know that 38 percent of married Canadians will be divorced by their 30th wedding anniversary. This number increases to 48.4 percent in Quebec and decreases to 21.6 percent in Newfoundland and Labrador (Ambert, 2009). Divorce rates sharply increased in 1968 when a new Divorce Act was passed, broadening the grounds for divorce. The increased economic independence of women has also contributed to the divorce rate. More women today have the economic means to leave a troubled marriage. Today, more people consider marriage an alterable condition than in prior generations.

Canadians today also want more from marriage than did their grandparents and are not as willing to accept less. They expect marriage to be both personally fulfilling and a foundation for family life and rearing children. The most common reasons given for a divorce today are problems in communication and a lack of understanding. Key complaints today include a husband's criticism, defensiveness, contempt, and stonewalling—not lack of financial support (Carrère et al., 2000; Gottman et al., 1998).

THE COST OF DIVORCE

Divorce is usually related to financial and emotional problems. When a household splits, the resources often cannot maintain the earlier standard of living for each partner. Divorce hits women in the wallet harder than men. Ambert (2009) warns that divorce brings an increased risk of poverty for mothers and children, whereas 29 percent of men's incomes increase because they are less likely to receive custody of their children and thus avoid many child-related expenses. Women who have not pursued a career may struggle to compete with younger, more experienced workers when seeking work. Divorced mothers often face the combined stress of the sole responsibility for child rearing and the need to increase their incomes. Divorced fathers may find it difficult to pay alimony and child support while establishing a new lifestyle.

My wife and I were considering a divorce, but after pricing lawyers we decided to buy a new car instead.

—Henny Youngman

Divorce can also prompt feelings of failure as a spouse and parent, loneliness and uncertainty about the future, and depression. Married people appear to be better able to cope with the stresses and strains of life, perhaps because they can lend each other emotional support. Divorced and separated people have the highest rates of physical and mental illness (Carrère et al., 2000; Lorenz et al., 2006). They also have high rates of suicide (Donald et al., 2006; Lorant et al., 2005). These variables can also be the result of pre-existing conditions and may have contributed to the marital breakdown. On the other hand, divorce may permit personal growth and renewal and the opportunity to take stock of oneself and establish a new, more rewarding life. But as noted in Chapter 10, children tend to be the biggest losers when parents divorce.

Some theorists

view middle age as a time of peak performance, whereas others portray it as a time of crisis or decline.

NEL

15

Middle Adulthood: Physical and Cognitive Development

Learning Outcomes

LO1 Describe trends in physical development in middle adulthood

LO2 Discuss the major health concerns of middle adulthood, including cancer and heart disease

LO3 Discuss the functioning of the immune system

LO4 Discuss sexuality in middle adulthood, focusing on menopause and sexual dysfunctions

LO5 Describe cognitive development in middle adulthood, distinguishing between crystallized and fluid intelligence

LO6 Discuss opportunities for exercising creativity and continuing education in middle adulthood

DID YOU KNOW?

D1 Canadians are proud of their health care system.

D2 Sexuality continues to be an important part of a middle-aged woman's life.

D3 Sexual dysfunctions are not rare.

D4 The average IQ score of a nation may increase as a reflection of social changes.

D5 Scores on the verbal subtests of standardized intelligence tests can increase for a lifetime.

D6 Not all types of memory functioning decline in middle adulthood.

D7 Creativity continues well into middle adulthood.

In 1992, 1,200 people were asked when middle age begins. Forty-six percent said it occurred when you realize you don't know who the new music groups are (Beck, 1992). If they had been polled today, perhaps they would have said that middle age begins when you don't know who won American Idol or who received the rose in this season's *The Bachelor*. In chronological terms, developmentalists consider middle adulthood to span the years from 40 to 65, with 60 to 65 as a transition period to late adulthood. But some developmentalists assert that we are truly becoming only as old as we feel, that 65 is the new 55, and so on.

Some theorists view middle age as a time of peak performance, and others have portrayed it as a time of crisis or decline (Lachman, 2004). Physically speaking,

George Pimentel/WireImage/Getty Images

we are at our peak in early adulthood, but in general, those who eat right and exercise will in many ways undergo only a gradual and relatively minor physical decline in middle adulthood. As we age, we become more vulnerable to a variety of illnesses, but we also become less prone to irresponsible behaviour that may result in injury or death. On the other hand, some sensory and sexual changes might well become major issues. Cognitively speaking, we are at our peak in many intellectual functions in middle adulthood, but may experience some loss of processing speed and some lapses in memory. Even so, these declines are often made up for in expertise.

LO1 Physical Development

no two people age in the same way or at the same rate. This phenomenon is called **interindividual variability**. But whatever individual differences may exist, physiological aging is defined by changes in the body's integumentary system (the body's system of skin, hair, and nails), senses, reaction time, and lung capacity. These changes may well be unavoidable. Changes in metabolism, muscle mass, strength, bone density, aerobic capacity, blood-sugar tolerance, and ability to regulate body temperature may be moderated and sometimes reversed through exercise and diet.

Skin and Hair

Hair usually begins to grey in middle adulthood as the production of *melanin*, the pigment responsible for hair colour, decreases. Hair loss also accelerates with aging, especially in men. Much wrinkling associated with aging is caused by exposure to ultraviolet (UV) rays.

Beginning gradually in early adulthood, the body produces fewer proteins that give the skin its elasticity. The body also produces fewer *keratinocytes*—the cells in the outer layer of the skin that are regularly shed and renewed, leaving the skin dryer and more brittle.

Sensory Functioning

Normal age-related changes in vision begin to appear by the mid-30s and assert themselves as significant problems in middle adulthood. **Presbyopia** (Latin for "old vision") refers to loss of elasticity in the lens that makes it harder to focus on, or accommodate to, nearby objects or fine print. Cataract, glaucoma, and hearing loss are usually problems of late adulthood.

Reaction Time

Reaction time—the amount of time it takes to respond to a stimulus—increases with age, mainly because of changes in the nervous system. At age 25 or so, we begin to lose neurons, which are responsible for sensing signals such as sights and sounds and for coordinating our muscular responses.

Lung Capacity

Lung tissue stiffens with age, diminishing the lungs' capacity to expand, such that breathing capacity may decline by half between early and late adulthood. Regular exercise can offset much of this loss, and beginning

© Polka Dot Images/Jupiterimages

to exercise regularly in middle adulthood can expand breathing capacity beyond what it was earlier in life.

Lean-Body Mass and Body Fat

Beginning at age 20, we lose nearly 3.2 kg (7 lb.) of lean-body mass with each decade. The rate of loss accelerates after age 45. Fat replaces lean-body mass, which includes muscle. Consequently, the average person's body mass index (BMI) rises.

Muscle Strength

Loss of muscle reduces strength. However, the change is gradual, and in middle adulthood, exercise can readily compensate, by increasing the size of remaining muscle cells. Exercise will not re-achieve the prowess of the athlete in early adulthood, but will contribute to vigour, health, and a desirable body shape.

Metabolism

Metabolism is the rate at which the body processes or "burns" food to produce energy. The resting metabolic rate—also called the *basal metabolic rate (BMR)*—declines as we age. Fatty tissue burns fewer calories than muscle, and the decline in BMR is largely attributable to the loss of muscle tissue and the corresponding increase in fatty tissue. Since we require fewer calories to maintain our weight as we age, middle-aged people (and older adults) are likely to gain weight if they eat as much as they did as young adults.

Bone Density

Bone, which consists largely of calcium, begins to lose density and strength at around the age of 40. As bones lose density, they become more brittle and prone to fracture. Bones in the spine, hip, thigh (femur), and forearm lose the most density as we age. We discuss osteoporosis in Chapter 17.

Aerobic Capacity

As we age, the cardiovascular system becomes less efficient. Heart and lung muscles shrink. Aerobic capacity declines as less oxygen is taken into the lungs and the heart pumps less blood. The maximum heart rate declines, but exercise expands aerobic capacity at *any* age.

Blood-Sugar Tolerance

Blood sugar, or glucose, is the basic fuel and energy source for cells. The energy from glucose supports

cell activities and maintains body temperature. Glucose circulates in the bloodstream and enters cells with the help of insulin, a hormone secreted by the pancreas.

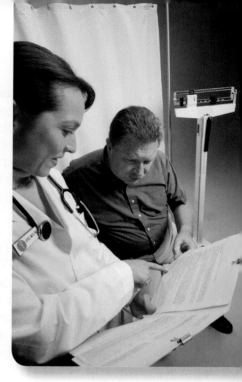
© Creatas Images/Jupiterimages

As we age, the tissues in our body become less capable of taking up glucose from the bloodstream. Body tissues lose their sensitivity to insulin; the pancreas must thus produce more insulin to achieve the same effect. Therefore, blood-sugar levels rise, increasing the risk of adult-onset diabetes.

LO2 Health

the health of people aged 40–65 in developed nations such as Canada is better than ever. Nearly everyone has been vaccinated for preventable diseases. Many, perhaps the majority, practice preventive health care. Once people reach 40, they are advised to have annual physical checkups. More is known today about curing or treating illnesses than we have ever known.

Racial, ethnic, and sex differences affect the incidence and treatment of various diseases. People from certain groups appear to be more likely to develop certain chronic conditions, such as hypertension and specific types of cancer. Canadians are very proud of their health care system but reduced access and lengthy wait times make it apparent that much work is needed to restore health care to the level of our pride.

As we consider the health of people in middle adulthood, we focus on many things that can go wrong. For

> **D1** Canadians are proud of their health care system.
> Reduced access and lengthy wait times make it clear that we need to focus on our health care system if we wish to protect it.

metastasis the transference of malignant or cancerous cells to other parts of the body.

most of us, things go quite well if we get regular medical checkups, pay attention to our diets, exercise, avoid smoking, drink in moderation if at all, regulate stress, and—ideally—enjoy supportive relationships.

LEADING CAUSES OF DEATH

In early adulthood the leading causes of death, accidents and suicide, screamed out their preventability. In middle adulthood, diseases come to the fore (see Table 15.1). Cancer and heart disease are numbers one and two, and accidents are now in third place. Cancer and heart disease are also preventable to some degree, of course. According to the American Cancer Society (2007), people should start being screened for prostate cancer (men around age 50), breast cancer (women around age 40), and cancer of the colon and rectum (men and women around age 50). Most men should have digital rectal exams (in which the doctor uses a gloved finger to feel the prostate gland) and blood tests for prostate-specific antigen (PSA) at age 50. However, African Canadian men are at greater risk of developing prostate cancer and are advised to start screening at age 45. The American Cancer Society recommends women begin having mammograms to screen for breast cancer at age 40. A baseline electrocardiogram (abbreviated EKG or ECG), which is one measure of the health of the heart, is usually done around the age of 50 and repeated every two to three years.

CANCER

Although heart disease is the nation's number one cause of death, cancer is the overall leading cause of death in middle adulthood (see Table 15.2). (Not indicated in Table 15.2 is women's sharply increased incidence of death due to heart disease after menopause.) In many cases, cancer can be controlled or cured, especially when detected early.

Cancer is a chronic, noncommunicable disease characterized by uncontrolled growth of cells, which form masses of excess tissue called tumours. Tumours can be *benign* (noncancerous) or *malignant* (cancerous). Benign tumours do not spread and rarely pose a threat to life. Malignant

TABLE 15.1
Leading Causes of Death in Middle Adulthood*

AGE GROUP	45–54	55–64
Cancer	119.0	333.4
Heart diseases	90.2	218.8
Accidents	40.7	33.2
Chronic liver diseases	18.0	22.6
Suicide	16.6	13.8
Strokes & other cerebrovascular diseases	14.9	34.3
Diabetes	13.4	37.1
Chronic respiratory diseases	8.4	40.4
Blood poisoning	5.4	12.9
Kidney diseases	5.0	13.6
Homicide	4.8	3.0
Influenza & pneumonia	4.6	10.8

*Annual deaths per 100,000 people.
Source: Arialdi M. Minino, Melanie P. Heron, Sherry L. Murphy, & Kenneth D. Kochanek. (2007, October 10). Deaths: Final data for 2004. *National vital statistics reports*, 55(19). Adapted from Table 9, pp. 27–29. http://www.cdc.gov/nchs/data/nvsr/nvsr55/nvsr55_19.pdf.

tumours invade and destroy surrounding tissue. Cancerous cells in malignant tumours may also break away from the primary tumour and travel through the bloodstream or lymphatic system to form new tumours, called **metastases**, elsewhere in the body. Metastases damage vital body organs and systems and in many cases lead to death. The

TABLE 15.2
Deaths Due to Cancer and Heart Disease in Middle Adulthood and Late Adulthood*

AGE GROUP	45–54	55–64	65–74	75–84	85 AND OVER
Cancer	119.0	333.4	755.1	1,280.4	1,653.3
Heart diseases	90.2	218.8	541.6	1,506.3	4,895.9

*Annual deaths per 100,000 people.
Source: Arialdi M. Minino, Melanie P. Heron, Sherry L. Murphy, & Kenneth D. Kochanek. (2007, October 10). Deaths: Final data for 2004. *National vital statistics reports*, 55(19). Adapted from Table 9, pp. 27–29. http://www.cdc.gov/nchs/data/nvsr/nvsr55/nvsr55_19.pdf.

TABLE 15.3
Lifetime Risk of Being Diagnosed with Cancer

SITE	MEN	WOMEN
All kinds	1 in 2	1 in 3
Prostate	1 in 6	—
Breast	1 in 909	1 in 7
Lung and bronchus	1 in 13	1 in 18
Colon/rectum	1 in 17	1 in 18
Melanoma	1 in 53	1 in 78
Urinary bladder	1 in 28	1 in 88
Non-Hodgkin's lymphomas	1 in 46	1 in 56
Leukemia	1 in 68	1 in 96
Kidney and renal pelvis	1 in 68	1 in 114
Cervix	—	1 in 125
Ovary	—	1 in 58
Pancreas	1 in 80	1 in 80
Oral cavity and pharynx	1 in 71	1 in 147

Source: Adapted from Fay, M. P. (2004). *Estimating Age-Conditional Probability of Developing Cancer Using a Piecewise Mid-Age Joinpoint Model to the Rates.* Statistical Research and Applications Branch, NCI, Technical Report # 2003-03, 2004.

arteriosclerosis hardening of the arteries.

colorectal cancer incidence and death rates (Health Disparities, 2004). African Canadians have twice the average death rate from prostate cancer. The incidence of cervical cancer in Latina Canadian women is higher than that of other demographic groups. Only 52 percent of indigenous women age 40 years and over have had a recent mammogram. Indigenous populations have the poorest survival rate from cancer.

Much of the difference in mortality rates can be attributed to lack of early detection and treatment (Health Disparities, 2004). Many members of minority groups avoid screening by the health care system, which they see as impersonal, insensitive, and racist.

Despite the many causes of cancer (see Table 15.4, on p. 284) and risk factors that vary among population groups, two out of three cancer deaths are the result of two controllable factors: smoking and diet (Willett, 2005). According to the Canadian Cancer Society, cigarette smoking causes 84 percent of lung cancer deaths in Canada. On average, 300 Canadians die each week from lung cancer caused by smoking (Canadian Cancer Society, 2007). Diet may account for about 30 percent of all cancers in Western cultures. However, many cases of cancer also involve family history, or heredity (Kauff & Offit, 2007).

Traditional methods for treating cancer are surgery (surgical removal of cancerous tissue), radiation (high-dose X-rays or other sources of high-energy radiation to kill cancerous cells and shrink tumours), chemotherapy (drugs that kill cancer cells or shrink tumours), and hormonal therapy (hormones that stop tumour growth). These methods have their limitations. Anticancer drugs and radiation kill both healthy tissue and malignant tissue. They also have side effects, such as nausea, vomiting, loss of appetite, loss of hair, and weakening of the immune system.

HEART DISEASE

Every 7 minutes, a Canadian dies of heart disease or stroke (Heart and Stroke Foundation, 2010). In heart disease, the flow of blood to the heart is insufficient to supply the heart with the oxygen it needs. Heart disease most commonly results from **arteriosclerosis** or *hardening of the arteries*, which impairs circulation and increases the risk of a blood clot (thrombus). The most common

incidence of cancer increases dramatically with age (see Table 15.2). Table 15.3 shows the lifetime risk of being diagnosed with various kinds of cancer.

Cancer begins when a cell's DNA, its genetic material, changes such that the cell divides indefinitely. The change is triggered by mutations in the DNA, which can be caused by internal or external factors. Internal factors include heredity, problems in the immune system, and hormonal factors. External agents, called carcinogens, include some viruses, chemical compounds in tobacco and elsewhere, and ultraviolet (UV) solar radiation.

About one man in two and one woman in three will eventually develop cancer if they live long enough (Fay, 2004). The incidence of death from cancer almost triples in the decade of 55–64 as compared with the decade of 45–54 (see Table 15.2).

Although cancer cuts across all racial and ethnic groups, African Canadian have higher than average

TABLE 15.4
Factors in Heart Disease and Cancer

© GoodShoot/Jupiterimages

HEART DISEASE

Biological:
Family history
Physiological conditions:
- Obesity
- High serum cholesterol
- Hypertension

Psychological (personality and behaviour):
Type A behaviour
Hostility and holding in feelings of anger
Job strain
Chronic fatigue, stress, anxiety, depression, and emotional strain
Patterns of consumption:
- Heavy drinking (but a drink a day may be helpful with heart disease)
- Smoking
- Overeating
Sudden stressors
Physical inactivity

Sociocultural:
African Canadians are more prone to hypertension and heart disease than European Canadians
Access to health care
Timing of diagnosis and treatment

CANCER

Biological:
Family history
Physiological conditions:
- Obesity

Psychological (personality and behaviour):
Patterns of consumption:
- Smoking
- Drinking alcohol (especially in women)
- Eating animal fats
Unprotected sun exposure (risk of skin cancer)
Prolonged depression
Prolonged stress

Sociocultural:
Socioeconomic status
Access to health care
Timing of diagnosis and treatment
Higher death rates are found in nations with higher rates of fat intake

---

atherosclerosis the buildup of fatty deposits (*plaque*) on the lining of arteries.

leukocyte white blood cell.

form of arteriosclerosis is **atherosclerosis**—the buildup of fatty deposits called *plaque* in the lining of arteries (see Figure 15.1). Plaque results in the heart receiving insufficient blood and can cause a heart attack.

The risk factors for heart disease are shown in Table 15.4. Several of these risk factors are beyond the control of the individual (age, race/ethnicity, and sex), but people can have some control over others (smoking, exercise, diet, and regular medical checkups).

LO3 The Immune System

he immune system is the body's defence against infections and other sources of disease. The immune system combats disease in several ways, one of which is the production of white blood cells, which engulf and kill worn-out and cancerous body cells and pathogens such as bacteria, fungi, and viruses. The technical term for white blood cells is **leukocytes**.

Leukocytes recognize foreign substances by their shapes. The foreign substances are termed *antigens* because the body reacts to them by generating specialized proteins, or *antibodies*. Antibodies attach themselves to the foreign substances, deactivating them and marking them for destruction. The immune system "remembers" how to battle antigens by maintaining their antibodies in the bloodstream, often for years.

Inflammation is another function of the immune system. When injury occurs, blood vessels in the area first contract (to stem bleeding) and then dilate. Dilation increases the flow of blood, cells, and natural chemicals to the damaged area, causing redness, swelling, and warmth. The increased blood supply floods the region with white blood cells to combat invading microscopic life forms such as bacteria, which otherwise might use the local damage as a port of entry into the body.

FIGURE 15.1
Atherosclerosis

In atherosclerosis, fatty deposits called *plaque* build up along artery walls. As arteries narrow, blood flow becomes constricted, setting the stage for heart attacks or strokes. In this figure, (a) shows a fully open artery, (b) shows moderate build-up of plaque, and (c) shows dangerous build-up of plaque.

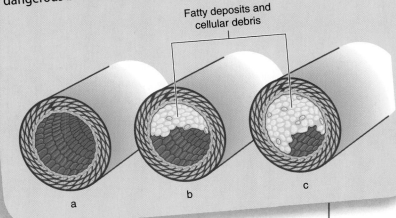

Fatty deposits and cellular debris

a   b   c

STRESS AND THE IMMUNE SYSTEM

Stress suppresses the immune system, as measured by the presence of substances in the blood that make up the immune system (Arranz et al., 2007; Thornton et al., 2007), leaving us more vulnerable to infections such as the common cold (Barnard et al., 2005; Cohen, 2003).

The stress hormones connected with anger—steroids, epinephrine, and norepinephrine—can constrict the blood vessels to the heart, leading to a heart attack in people who are vulnerable (Monat et al., 2007). The stress

of chronic hostility and anger is related to higher cholesterol levels and a greater risk of heart disease (Richards et al., 2000).

LO4 Sexuality

most people in middle adulthood lead rich sex lives (Duplassie & Daniluk, 2007; Vares et al., 2007). Table 15.5, on page 286, compares the frequency of sex in early adulthood with that in middle adulthood. Generally, the frequency of sexual activity tends to decline in middle adulthood (Michael et al., 1994), but the decline is gradual. Note that a significant percentage of 50- to 59-year-old women become sexually inactive. This drop-off may reflect lack of opportunity. Women in this age group are increasingly likely to be widowed. Also, as divorced women grow older, they are less likely to remarry.

In the latter part of middle adulthood, the years of 57 to 64, nearly three-quarters of adults remain sexually active (Lindau et al., 2007), but sexual problems often work their way into relationships. The most common problems among women are lack of sexual desire and difficulty becoming sexually aroused (Goldstein et al., 2006; Lindau et al., 2007). The most common problem among men is erectile dysfunction (Johannes et al., 2000).

But it is misleading to focus on the negative. Even women in middle adulthood whose partners use Viagra to obtain erections generally report heightened sexual satisfaction as a result and often have an increase in sexual desire (Vares et al., 2007). Many middle-aged women who have chosen to remain single also report satisfying sex lives (Bridges, 2007).

MENOPAUSE, PERIMENOPAUSE, AND THE CLIMACTERIC

Menopause, or the "change of life," is the cessation of menstruation. Menopause is a normal process that most commonly occurs between the ages of 46 and 50

© Blend Images/Jupiterimages

TABLE 15.5
Frequency of Sex in the Past 12 Months According to Age (by Percentage)

AGE	NOT AT ALL	A FEW TIMES PER YEAR	A FEW TIMES PER MONTH	2 OR 3 TIMES A WEEK	4 OR MORE TIMES A WEEK
MEN					
25–29	7	15	31	36	11
30–39	8	15	37	33	6
40–49	9	18	40	27	6
50–59	11	22	43	20	3
WOMEN					
25–29	5	10	38	37	10
30–39	9	16	36	33	6
40–49	15	16	44	20	5
50–59	30	22	35	12	2

Note: Percentages for 18- to 24-year-olds are excluded because they are likely to reflect sexual opportunity as well as sexual interest and biological factors.

Source: Robert T. Michael, John H. Gagnon, Edward O. Laumann, & Gina Kolata. (1994). *Sex in America: A definitive survey.* New York: Warner Books, Table 8, p. 117.

perimenopause the beginning of menopause, usually characterized by 3 to 11 months of amenorrhea or irregular periods.

climacteric the gradual decline in reproductive capacity of the ovaries, generally lasting about 15 years.

and lasts for about two years. **Perimenopause** refers to the beginning of menopause and is usually characterized by 3 to 11 months of amenorrhea (lack of menstruation) or irregular periods.

Menopause is a specific event in a longer term process known as the **climacteric** ("critical period"), the gradual decline in the reproductive capacity of the ovaries due to a decline in production of estrogen. The climacteric generally lasts about 15 years, from about age 45 to 60. After age 35 or so, the menstrual cycles of many women shorten, from an average of 28 days to 25 days at age 40 and to 23 days by the mid-40s. By the end of her 40s, a woman's cycles may become erratic, with some periods shortened and others missed.

The estrogen deficit may lead to unpleasant perimenopausal sensations, such as night sweats, hot flashes (suddenly feeling hot), and hot flushes (suddenly looking reddened). Hot flashes and flushes may alternate

with cold sweats, feeling suddenly cold and clammy. All of these sensations reflect *vasomotor instability*, disruptions in the body mechanisms that dilate or constrict the blood vessels to maintain an even body temperature. Additional signs of estrogen deficiency include dizziness, headaches, joint pain, tingling in the hands or feet, burning or itchy skin, and heart palpitations. The skin usually becomes drier. There is some loss of breast tissue and decreased vaginal lubrication during sexual arousal. However, menopause does not signal an end to women's sexual appetite.

Long-term estrogen deficiency has been linked to brittleness and porosity of the bones—osteoporosis. Osteoporosis can be handicapping, even life threatening. The brittleness of the bones increases the risk of serious fractures, especially of the hip, and many older women never recover from such injuries (Marwick, 2000). Estrogen deficiency also can impair cognitive functioning and feelings of psychological well-being (Ross et al., 2000; Yaffe et al., 2000).

 D2 Sexuality continues to be an important part of a middle-aged woman's life.
Some women feel liberated because of the separation of sex from reproduction.

Hormone Replacement Therapy

Some women with severe physical symptoms have been helped by hormone replacement therapy (HRT), which typically consists of synthetic estrogen and progesterone. HRT may reduce the hot flushes and other symptoms brought about by hormonal deficiencies (den Tonkelaar & Oddens, 2000). Estrogen replacement also lowers the risks of osteoporosis (Grady, 2003a, 2003b) and colon cancer (Solomon & Dluhy, 2003).

HRT is controversial. The Women's Health Initiative study of some 16,600 postmenopausal women aged 50 to 79 found that exposure to a combination of estrogen and progestin appears to significantly increase the risk of breast cancer and of blood clots, which can lead to strokes (Chlebowski et al., 2003).

Because of the Chlebowski study and studies with similar findings, the number of women using HRT has dropped significantly over the past few years (Rabin, 2007), and many women are considering alternatives. Breast cancer specialist Larry Norton (cited in Duenwald, 2002) notes that progestin alone prevents or lessens hot flashes in about 70 percent of women. Selective serotonin reuptake inhibitors (SSRIs) are also of help (Stearns et al., 2003).

DO MEN UNDERGO AN "ANDROPAUSE"?

For women, menopause is a time of relatively distinct age-related declines in sex hormones and fertility. In men, the decline in the production of male sex hormones and fertility is more gradual (Tan & Culberson, 2003). Thus, a man in his 70s or older can father a child. However, many men in their 50s experience problems in achieving and maintaining erections (Conrad, 2007), which may reflect circulatory problems, hormone deficiencies, or other factors (Charlton, 2004).

To help with these symptoms, physicians write many prescriptions for testosterone and related drugs each year, but the benefits are not fully proven, and the risks, including heightened risks of prostate cancer and heart disease, should inspire caution (Tan, 2002; Vastag, 2003).

SEXUAL DYSFUNCTIONS

Sexual dysfunctions are persistent or recurrent problems in becoming sexually aroused or reaching orgasm. Many of us have sexual problems on occasion, but sexual dysfunctions are chronic and cause significant distress.

We do not have precise figures on the occurrence of sexual dysfunctions. The most accurate information may be based on the National Health and Social Life Survey (Laumann et al., 1994) (see Table 15.6), in which the researchers found that sexual dysfunctions are quite common. Women more often reported painful sex, lack of pleasure, inability to reach orgasm, and lack of desire. Men were more likely to report reaching orgasm too soon ("premature ejaculation") and performance anxiety.

sexual dysfunction
a persistent or recurrent problem in becoming sexually aroused or reaching orgasm.

> **D3** Sexual dysfunctions are not rare.
> According to some studies, sexual dysfunctions are actually common.

Premature ejaculation is most likely to affect men in early adulthood. Dysfunctions that tend to begin or be prominent in men's middle adulthood include lack of interest in sex and erectile dysfunction.

Lack of desire is more common among women than men (Goldstein et al., 2006). Nevertheless, the belief that men are always eager for sex is only a myth. The lack of desire is often limited to one partner. When one member of a couple is more interested in sex than the other, sex therapists often recommend that couples try to compromise and try to resolve problems in the relationship that may dampen sexual ardour (Moore &

TABLE 15.6

Sexual Dysfunctions Reported within the Past Year, According to the National Health and Social Life Survey

	MEN (%)	WOMEN (%)
Pain during sex	3.0	14.4
Sex not pleasurable	8.1	21.2
Unable to reach orgasm	8.3	24.1
Lack of interest in sex	15.8	33.4
Anxiety about performance*	17.0	11.5
Reaching climax too early	28.5	10.3
Unable to keep an erection**	10.4	—
Having trouble lubricating	—	18.8

Source: Adapted from Tables 10.8A and 10.8B, pages 370 and 371, in Laumann, E. O., Gagnon, J. H., Michael, R. T., & Michaels, S. (1994). *The social organization of sexuality: Sexual practices in the United States*. Chicago: University of Chicago Press.
*Anxiety about performance is not itself a sexual dysfunction. However, it figures prominently in sexual dysfunctions.
**Incidence increases with age, and the NHSLS figures may be an underestimate.

Heiman, 2006). Couples usually find that sex is no better than other facets of their relationship (Matthews et al., 2006).

Repeated erectile problems, characterized by persistent difficulty in achieving or maintaining an erection during sexual activity, may make men anxious: when sexual opportunities arise, they expect failure rather than pleasure. As a result, they may avoid sex (Bancroft et al., 2005a, 2005b). Their partners may also avoid sexual contact because of their own frustration. The incidence of erectile disorder increases with age. A study of men aged 40–69 in Massachusetts found that nearly half reported problems in obtaining and maintaining erections. Men in the 50- to 59-year-old age group reported erectile problems two-thirds as frequently as men in the 60- to 69-year-old age group (Johannes et al., 2000).

The reduction in testosterone levels that occurs in middle and later adulthood may in part explain men's gradual loss of sexual desire—along with some loss of muscle mass and strength (Janssen, 2006). But women's sexual desire may also decline with age because of physical and psychological changes (Goldstein et al., 2006; Hayes & Dennerstein, 2005). Some medications, especially those used to control anxiety, depression, or hypertension, may also reduce desire. Viagra has helped a number of women whose sexual response has been hindered by antidepressants (Nurnberg et al., 2008).

Fatigue may lead to erectile disorder in men, and to inadequate lubrication in women, which can lead to her experiencing painful sex. But these will be isolated incidents unless the couple attaches too much meaning to them and becomes concerned about future performances. Painful sex, however, can also reflect underlying infections or medical conditions.

Biological causes of erectile disorder affect the flow of blood to and through the penis, a problem that becomes more common as men age or experience damage to nerves involved in erection (Goldstein, 1998, 2000). Erectile problems can arise when clogged or narrow arteries leading to the penis deprive the penis of oxygen (Thompson et al., 2005).

Similarly, aging can affect the sexual response of women. Perimenopausal and postmenopausal women usually produce less vaginal lubrication than younger women, and the vaginal walls thin, which can render sex painful (Dennerstein & Goldstein, 2005) and possibly create performance anxiety (McCabe, 2005; Schultz et al., 2005). In such cases, artificial lubrication can help supplement the woman's own production, and estrogen replacement may halt or reverse some of the sexual changes of aging (Goldstein & Alexander, 2005). But partners also need to have realistic expectations and consider enjoyable sexual activities they can engage in without discomfort or high demands (McCarthy & Fucito, 2005).

Middle-aged and older men might try weight control and regular exercise, which may ward off erectile dysfunction (Derby, 2000). Exercise seems to lessen clogging of arteries, keeping them clear for the flow of blood into the penis. Oral medications—Viagra, Levitra, and Cialis—are commonly used to treat erectile disorder.

LO5 Cognitive Development

Middle-aged adults continue to develop cognitively in various ways (Schaie, 2005; Willis & Schaie, 2006). For example, the overall Wechsler Adult Intelligence Scale score of a 53-year-old farmer in Saskatchewan decreases from the age of 27. His "verbal intelligence," as measured mainly by his knowledge of the meaning of words, remains pretty much the same, but his "performance subtest" scores, or his ability to perform on timed spatially related subtests, declines. A woman in her mid-40s, who had been "all-business" through her mid-20s in college, moved to Montreal at age 29 and is now extremely knowledgeable in art history and opera. She knew absolutely nothing about these areas as an undergraduate, when her math ability was at its height. A 55-year-old practical nurse is "lost" when he tries to understand the science behind a new medical test presented at a professional meeting in Vancouver; nevertheless, he learns how to interpret a report based on results from the test and discovers, to his relief, that most of his peers are in the same boat. A 47-year-old woman returns to college to complete her social work diploma. At first she is fearful of competing with the "kids," but she finds out quickly enough that her sense of purpose more than compensates for what she thinks of as any "loss in brainpower."

CHANGES IN INTELLECTUAL ABILITIES

Intellectual development in adulthood shows multidirectionality, interindividual variability, and plasticity. The concept of **multidirectionality** underscores the finding that some aspects of intellectual functioning may improve while others remain stable or decline. Rather than being measured strictly by academic degrees, intellectual functioning reflects the interaction of heredity and environmental factors—and, as discussed, personal choice to engage in further study to increase one's facility in certain intellectual areas.

We discussed *interindividual variability* in terms of physical development, and we find it in cognitive development as well. People mature in different cultural settings. Some still frown on education for women. Some areas have better schools than others. Some youth find themselves in subcultures in which their peers disapprove if they earn high grades or seek approval from teachers. We also find interindividual variability in middle adulthood. Some people find themselves or allow themselves to be in "ruts" in which they gain little if any new knowledge. Others are hungry for the new and so read, travel, and visit museums in any spare moment they can find.

Plasticity refers to people's intellectual abilities not being absolutely fixed but being able to be modified under certain conditions at almost any time in life. The ideal period for language learning may be childhood, but you can pick up a new language in your 40s, 50s, or even later. You learn the meanings of new words for a lifetime (unless you lock yourself in a closet).

Consider the so-called "Flynn Effect." Philosopher and researcher John Flynn (2003) found that IQ scores increased some 18 points in the United States between the years 1947 and 2002. Psychologist Richard Nisbett (2007) argues that our genetic codes could not possibly have changed enough in half a century to account for this enormous difference and concludes that the reasons for the change must be social and cultural factors such as the penetration of better educational systems and mass media.

> **multidirectionality** in the context of cognitive development, the notion that some aspects of intellectual functioning may improve while others remain stable or decline.
>
> **plasticity** the capability of intellectual abilities to be modified, as opposed to being absolutely fixed.

> **D4** The average IQ score of a nation may increase as a reflection of social changes.
> I.Q. scores in Canada have actually risen over the past couple of generations.

© Brand X Images/Jupiterimages

Cohort Effects

The people who were middle-aged in 1947 and those who were middle-aged in 2002 belong to different cohorts. Figure 15.2 shows some cohort effects from the Seattle Longitudinal Study, begun in 1956 by K. Warner Schaie. Participants were tested every seven years, and Schaie and his colleagues were able to assess both cohort effects and longitudinal effects on intellectual functioning. The figure shows that groups of adults born more recently were superior to those born at earlier times in four of five mental abilities assessing inductive reasoning, verbal meaning, spatial orientation, and word fluency (Schaie, 1994). The cohorts born earlier performed better in numeric ability. Schaie notes that the intellectual functioning of the members of a society reflects that society's technology and social functioning (Charness & Schaie, 2003). This study also indicates that the younger cohorts were actually exposed to a better educational system—one that encouraged them to think abstractly (*inductive reasoning*), learn the meaning of words (*verbal meaning, word fluency*), and interact with geometric figures (*spatial orientation*).

Crystallized Intelligence versus Fluid Intelligence

Some might ask whether math ability and vocabulary size are accurate measures of "intelligence," when they are merely the types of items we find on intelligence tests, and a person's scores on intelligence tests can change as a result of experience. But John Horn came up with a distinction that may be of some use. He spoke about the difference between crystallized and fluid intelligence.

Crystallized intelligence is defined as the knowledge and skills that depend on accumulated information and experience, awareness of social conventions, and the capacity to make good decisions and judgments. Crystallized intelligence includes knowledge of a field's specialized vocabulary; an English major, for example, might know the meaning of the terms *iambic pentameter, rhetoric,* and *onomatopoeia.* We know it is socially desirable to look a business associate in the eye in a Canadian board room, but did you know that this behaviour is considered hostile in Japan? Choosing to eat healthful foods could also be considered a sign of crystallized intelligence.

Fluid intelligence involves a person's skills at processing information. Let's do a quick comparison to a computer. Your crystallized intelligence is like the amount of information you have in storage. Your fluid intelligence is like the sizes of your processor and your memory (meaning *working memory*—how much you can keep in mind at once), which work together to access and manipulate information and arrive at answers quickly and accurately. Whereas researchers suggest a powerful role for environmental factors in the genesis of crystallized intelligence, they theorize a relatively stronger role for neurological factors in fluid intelligence (Horn & Noll, 1997; Salthouse & Davis, 2006).

Studies show that crystallized intelligence tends to increase with age through middle adulthood. In the absence of senile dementias, crystallized intelligence commonly increases throughout the lifespan, along with the verbal subtests of standardized intelligence tests. The same studies that indicate crystallized intelligence tends to increase throughout adulthood also tend to show

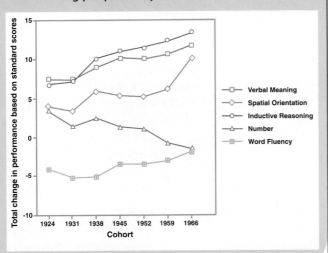

FIGURE 15.2
Differences in Intellectual Abilities across Cohorts

More recently born cohorts in the Seattle Longitudinal Study show greater intellectual abilities in all areas except for numeric abilities. What technological factors might contribute to a decrease in numerical skills among people today?

Source: K. Warner Schaie. (1994). The course of adult intellectual development. *American Psychologist, 49,* 304–313. Copyright © American Psychological Association. Reprinted by permission.

a decline for fluid intelligence (Escorial et al., 2003; Salthouse, 2001). K. Warner Schaie's (1994) longitudinal data (see Figure 15.3) shows that the intellectual factor of perceptual speed, which is most strongly related to fluid intelligence, is also the factor that drops off most dramatically from early adulthood to late adulthood. Spatial orientation and numeric ability, both related to fluid intelligence, also decline dramatically in late adulthood. Verbal ability and inductive reasoning, which are more related to crystallized intelligence, show gains through middle adulthood and hold up in late adulthood.

> **D5** Scores on the verbal subtests of standardized intelligence tests can increase for a lifetime.
> This is true and is evidence that an old dog can learn new tricks.

Figure 15.3 reveals group trends, despite interindividual variations. Schaie and his colleagues (2004) found that circumstances such as the following tend to stem cognitive decline in advanced late adulthood:

- Good physical health
- Favourable environmental conditions, such as decent housing
- Remaining intellectually active through reading and keeping up with current events
- Being open to new ideas and new styles of life

© Ray Massey/Getty Images

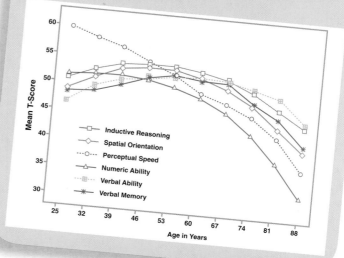

Source: K. Warner Schaie. (1994). The course of adult intellectual development. *American Psychologist, 49*, 304–313. Copyright © American Psychological Association. Reprinted by permission.

FIGURE 15.3
Longitudinal Changes in Six Intellectual Abilities, Ages 25–88

Most intellectual abilities show gains or remain largely stable from early adulthood through middle adulthood. Numeric ability shows a modest decline throughout middle adulthood, and perceptual speed shows a more dramatic drop-off.

- Living with a partner who is intellectually active
- Being satisfied with one's achievements

When these factors are present, they can help individuals maximize their potential at any age.

INFORMATION PROCESSING

One of the interesting things about aging is that it can become more difficult to keep new information in working memory even when long-term memory remains relatively intact. Many older adults know too well the meaning of "in one ear and out the other."

Speed of Information Processing

The speed of information processing can be measured in several ways. One is simply physical: *reaction time*, which is the time it takes to respond to a stimulus. If you touch a hot stove, how long does it take to pull your hand away? In one assessment of reaction time, people push a button when a light is flashed. Compared with

fluid intelligence

crystallized intelligence

CHAPTER 15: MIDDLE ADULTHOOD: PHYSICAL AND COGNITIVE DEVELOPMENT young adults, those in middle adulthood respond to the light more slowly—their reaction time is greater (Hartley, 2006). The difference in reaction time is only a fraction of a second, but it is enough to keep the typical middle-aged adult out of the firing line in the military and on the sidelines of professional sports (Salthouse & Berish, 2005). It can also make a difference when trying to avoid an accident on the highway.

Reaction time is only one aspect of processing speed. The broad cognitive aspect of perceptual speed is also intertwined with fluid intelligence. As with reaction time, the changes in middle adulthood are not that dramatic, but are measurable. Because of continuous experience with reading and writing, an educated person in middle adulthood may be better than ever at doing crossword puzzles (largely dependent on crystallized intelligence), but she might find it more difficult to navigate new cities than when she was younger (largely dependent on fluid intelligence) (Salthouse & Siedlecki, 2007).

Most researchers believe that the decline in processing speed reflects changes in the integrity of the nervous system. Having said that, hypotheses run rampant, from the death of neurons in the brain to changes in specific parts of the brain and changes in the secretion of neurotransmitters (Hartley, 2006).

Memory

K. Warner Schaie's (1994) longitudinal research found that memory is one intel-

lectual factor that showed improvement through most of the years of middle adulthood and stability from age 53 to 60. Not all researchers agree. Researchers use several kinds of memory

tasks, which do not necessarily lead to the same results (Salthouse et al., 2006). Despite Schaie's results, most researchers conclude that people in middle adulthood and late adulthood perform less well than young adults at memorizing lists of words, numbers, and passages of prose (Salthouse & Davis, 2006).

The main strategies for memorization are *rote rehearsal* and *elaborative rehearsal*. Once we are in the latter part of middle adulthood, we are less likely than when we were younger to be able to learn new information by rote repetition (Salthouse & Babcock, 1991). We are also less capable of screening out distractions (Radvansky et al., 2005). Elaborative rehearsal may also suffer because we are also apparently less capable of rapid classification or categorization (Hultsch et al., 1998).

We have been speaking of working or short-term memory. Let's look at storage or long-term memory. Not all types of memory functions decline in middle adulthood. We are typically more likely to retain or expand our general knowledge in middle adulthood (Prull et al., 2000; Zacks et al., 2000), such as by learning more about an area in which we have little knowledge or experience.

Procedural memory is a kind of motor memory of how to do things—how to ride a bicycle, how to use a keyboard, how to write with a pen, how to drive a car. One of my favourite photos is of the older Jean Piaget riding a bicycle. The student of children looks childlike, but the message for the student of psychology or education is that we can maintain procedural memories for a lifetime.

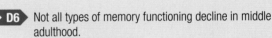

D6 Not all types of memory functioning decline in middle adulthood.
Long-term memory and general knowledge often improve with age.

Expertise and Practical Problem Solving

Any employer with some knowledge of human development would want to hire someone in middle adulthood. Middle-aged people have verbal abilities that match or exceed those of younger people, have lost very little in the way of fluid intelligence, and have a greater store of expertise and practical problem-solving skills (Leclerc & Hess, 2007). Despite interindividual variations, as a group, middle-aged adults show their skills every day in every way.

Over the years they have acquired social skills that enable them to deal better with subordinates and with supervisors. They have a better feeling for other people's limitations and potentials, and they have a better understanding of how to motivate them. They may also have experience that will help them to remain calm in stressful situations.

The parent who was so distraught when the first child cried may now be relaxed when the grandchildren cry. Part of the difference may be the "distance"—the generation of removal. But it is also the result of learning that the children will survive and develop into normal human beings (whatever that means) whether or not they cry as children.

In terms of vocations, the initial training or education of middle-aged people has now had the benefits of years of experience. People in middle adulthood have learned what works and what does not work for them. In the cases of the professions, for instance, "book learning" and perhaps internships have been supplemented by years of experience in the real world. Pianist Arthur Rubenstein became so accomplished as the years wore on that he often practised "mentally"—he needed the physical keyboard only intermittently. Although he lost some speed when playing rapid passages, he compensated by slowing before beginning those passages, and he created drama when he escalated his pacing.

LO6 Creativity and Learning

middle adulthood offers numerous opportunities for exercising creativity, expanding knowledge, and intellectual experience.

CREATIVITY

People in middle adulthood can be creative, and many middle-aged adults are at the height of their creativity. At age 56, Pablo Picasso painted *Guernica*, which protested the Spanish civil war and is one of the best known images in art. Author Toni Morrison wrote the Pulitzer Prize–winning novel

Beloved at age 57. Inventor Thomas Edison built the kinetoscope, an early peephole method for watching films, at age 44. Yet researchers have found some differences in creativity among young adults and middle-aged people. Aspects of creativity that are relatively more likely to be found among young adults include creativity in music, mathematics, and physics (Norton et al., 2005; Simonton, 2006). Wolfgang Amadeus Mozart, considered by many critics to be the greatest composer in history, died at the age of 35. Albert Einstein published his general theory of relativity at the age of 36.

Writers and visual artists often continue to improve into middle adulthood, although their most emotional and fervent works may be produced at younger ages. The most emotionally charged works of poets tend to be penned in early adulthood (Simonton, 2007).

> **D7** Creativity continues well into middle adulthood.
> Pablo Picasso, Toni Morrison, and Thomas Edison all had great creative achievements during middle age.

MATURE LEARNERS

For most adults, learning is a perpetual process. We learn when a new store opens in the neighbourhood or when we watch or listen to the media. We learn when we hear what is happening with a family member or observe a pet. But when psychologists and educators use the term "adult learning," they are usually speaking of learning as it occurs within some formal educational setting.

Even when we limit our discussion to educational settings, we find vast diversity and interindividual variation. But research on mature learners suggests that they are likely to have some things in common: They are apt to be highly motivated, and they are more likely than

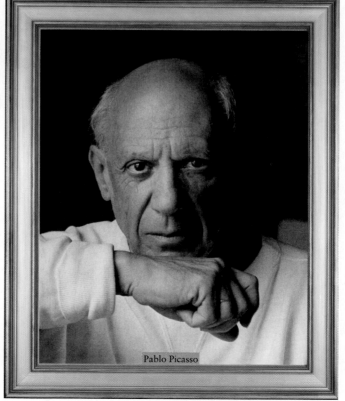

Pablo Picasso

> Research on mature learners suggests that they are apt to be highly motivated, and they are more likely than younger learners to find the subject matter interesting *for its own sake.*

younger learners to find the subject matter interesting for its own sake (Bye et al., 2007).

In 2007, a higher percentage of women (69 percent) than men (62 percent) aged 25–44 had completed a college or university program. Canada has the highest rate of postsecondary attainment in the world (Lambert et al., 2004). You might assume that women who have families and returned to school would be the women with the least exacting combinations of family and work demands. Actually, it's the other way around (Hostetler et al., 2007). Women with the greatest demands on them from family and work are those most likely to return to school. But once they're back, their major source of stress is time constraints; those who receive the emotional support of their families and employers experience the least stress and do best (Kirby et al., 2004).

Government assistance programs, such as Ontario's Second Careers, report an increasing number of laid-off adult workers are enrolling in postsecondary schools. Others in middle adulthood may choose to pursue educational goals that were not realized in their youth. When returning students come to campus, they often feel a bit on the periphery of things because rules, regulations, and activities are generally designed for younger students (Brady, 2007). The returning students are often unsure whether to share their thoughts or perspectives with the class; perhaps, they may think, their ideas are out of date. Then again, some returning students have achieved commanding positions at work or in social roles and may find it difficult to accept their subordinate status in the teacher–student relationship (Marron & Rayman, 2002). However, all in all, research suggests that both younger and returning students, and instructors, benefit from the mix of views that includes returning students (Brady, 2007).

Learning . . . The Perpetual Process

© Shauna Longmuir

Many of us

"launch" our children into the outside world during middle adulthood and help them establish themselves.

16

Middle Adulthood: Social and Emotional Development

Learning Outcomes

LO1 Discuss theories of development in middle adulthood

LO2 Discuss stability and change in social and emotional development in middle adulthood

LO3 Discuss career developments typical of middle adulthood

LO4 Discuss trends in relationships in middle adulthood, focusing on grandparenting and being in the "sandwich generation"

In the 1950s, a TV sitcom called *Father Knows Best* (don't laugh) featured upright Jim Anderson as the title character. He was an insurance agent who was apparently born in a suit and wore it 24 hours a day. His wife was apparently born in an apron and wore it proudly all day long. The series caught them in middle age, with three children, presumably because they could not have the average 2.4 children. The older two, teenagers, were called Bud and Princess. They lived in a spacious, clean suburban house and had a spacious, clean suburban car. Such a "fine," "typical" American family may have been what Robert Havighurst had in mind when he proposed his "developmental tasks" of middle adulthood in the 1970s.

Havighurst's vision of normalcy has no room for gay men and lesbians, for people who cannot or choose not to have children, for people who choose the single life, and for people who do not undertake "meaningful" social and civic responsibilities. Having said that, we must admit that Havighurst did arrive at a list of issues that affect many of us at midlife, many of which we will discuss in this chapter.

Many of us do "launch" our children into the outside world during our middle adulthood, and we do help them establish themselves—sometimes for much longer than we might have anticipated. We may find that our preferences in leisure activities have changed over the years, or we may continue activities we have long enjoyed—athletic, cultural, and social pursuits.

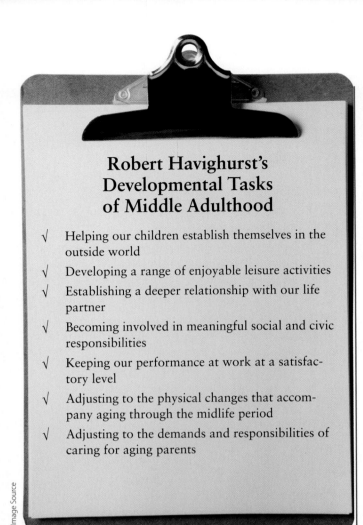

Robert Havighurst's Developmental Tasks of Middle Adulthood

√ Helping our children establish themselves in the outside world

√ Developing a range of enjoyable leisure activities

√ Establishing a deeper relationship with our life partner

√ Becoming involved in meaningful social and civic responsibilities

√ Keeping our performance at work at a satisfactory level

√ Adjusting to the physical changes that accompany aging through the midlife period

√ Adjusting to the demands and responsibilities of caring for aging parents

© Image Source

Some of us are establishing deeper relationships with life partners, but some are living alone, having never partnered or perhaps having divorced, and some are living with stepfamilies and possibly struggling along. Some of us are involved in meaningful social or civic activities, but some of us are loners, and, as we will see, going it alone can have negative consequences for our mental and physical well-being.

Havighurst sounds pessimistic about work—keeping our performance at a satisfactory level. Many of us reach our peak performance or first come into our own in middle adulthood. We have gained expertise, as noted in Chapter 15, and our abilities remain generally intact.

Yes, we may have issues in adjusting to physical aging. Our bodies will be changing. We may encounter illnesses we really weren't thinking all that much about during young adulthood. We may indeed have to come to the aid of aging parents. On the other hand, we may also find new rewards in our relationships with our aging parents once we are both quite "grown up."

LO1 Theories of Development in Middle Adulthood

theories of development in middle adulthood largely deal with the issue of whether we can consider middle adulthood to be a distinct stage or phase of life. According to Erikson's theory of psychosocial development, middle adulthood is characterized by a particular life crisis. We shall describe that crisis and consider the evidence, pro and con. Daniel Levinson spoke of a specific midlife transition and a midlife crisis (not to be confused with Erikson's *life crises*). Again we shall consider the evidence. Then we will take a broader look at the ways in which personality appears to change—or not change—during middle adulthood.

ERIK ERIKSON'S THEORY OF PSYCHOSOCIAL DEVELOPMENT

Erikson believed that the major psychological challenge of the middle years is *generativity versus*

© Digital Vision/Getty Images

stagnation. **Generativity** is the ability to generate or produce. Erikson (1980) saw psychosocial generativity as being based in an instinctual drive toward procreativity—that is, being bearing and rearing children. To him, the negative counterpart of generativity meant rejection or suppression of this natural drive and would lead to **stagnation**. He did recognize that some people could not have children of their own and that social or interpersonal conditions made it difficult for some people to bear children. Under such circumstances, substitutes were possible that might not be as naturally or as fully satisfying but that could work for the individual. For example, a person or couple without children (or even with children) might contribute to the teaching or welfare of other people's children, or might make things of lasting value such as objects of art, or might contribute to charity or to civic works. Erikson and others (e.g., Thiele & Whelan, 2006) also note that grandparenthood provides additional opportunities for satisfying generativity in middle adulthood. Today, of course, some writers note that environmentalists are acting in a generative manner when they take steps to care for future generations (de St. Aubin et al., 2004). Generativity not only contributes to future generations; it also enhances one's self-esteem and sense of meaning in life (Marushima, 2000).

Erikson argued that people who do not engage in generative behaviour risk stagnating and falling into routines that can strip their lives of meaning and purpose. This particular point remains murky. For example, Van Hiel and colleagues (2006) administered a battery of psychological tests to nearly 200 middle-aged adults, many of whom were identified as high in generativity and many of whom were identified as high in stagnation. The more generative group scored significantly higher in the personality variable of conscientiousness, and the more stagnating group scored significantly higher on the personality variable of neuroticism. Neuroticism was measured in the study by the NEO Personality Inventory and is defined as emotional instability—an enduring tendency to experience negative feelings such as anxiety, anger, guilt, and depression. So the first question we might ask is whether some people stagnate "because of" less generative behaviour or whether their lower generativity is related to personality traits such as

neuroticism. The Van Hiel group also found, with a group of 457 middle-aged adults, that generativity and stagnation are independent dimensions rather than opposites. In other words, middle-aged people can be low in both generativity and stagnation. Other researchers will doubtlessly replicate or challenge this research.

DANIEL LEVINSON'S SEASONS

According to Daniel Levinson and his colleagues, the years from 40 to 45 comprise a **midlife transition**—a psychological shift into middle adulthood that is often accompanied by a crisis during which people fear they have more to look back upon than forward to. This crisis is termed a **midlife crisis** and is defined as a time of dramatic self-doubt and anxiety during which people sense the passing of their youth and become preoccupied with concern about the imminence of their own mortality. Levinson believed that marker events such as menopause, the death of a parent or a friend, or a child's leaving "the nest" could trigger the crisis.

Once beset by the crisis, some people attempt to deny the realities of aging, such as by having an extramarital affair to prove to themselves they are still sexually attractive, buying a sports car (red, of course), or suddenly shifting careers. Many people, however, view the years from age 45 onward as a type of second adulthood, filled with opportunities for new direction and fulfillment.

generativity ability to generate or produce, as in bearing children or contributing to society.

stagnation the state of no longer developing, growing, or advancing.

midlife transition a psychological shift into middle adulthood that is theorized to occur between the ages of 40 and 45 as people begin to believe they have more to look back upon than forward to.

midlife crisis a time of dramatic self-doubt and anxiety during which people sense the passing of their youth and become concerned with their own aging and mortality.

Generativity

Stagnation

> **D1** The midlife crisis is the creation of Hollywood more than of real life.
>
> A midlife crisis may be more the exception than the rule.

© Jeffrey Coolidge/Getty Images

For many people today, the so-called midlife crisis is imposed from the outside in the form of a career crash resulting from corporate *downsizing*—the thinning of the ranks of middle managers. But people who are flexible enough to make the transition to other careers can find increased satisfaction.

The 50s are often more relaxed and productive than the 40s. Yet many people in their 50s need to adjust to the children leaving home (the "empty nest"), the effects of aging, and competition from younger workers. But we will also see that the last child's leaving home can more often than not be a positive event.

ENTERING MIDLIFE: CRISIS, TURNING POINT, OR PRIME OF LIFE?

Theorists have made much of turning 35 or 40, or of entering midlife. We mention the age of 35 because it was crucial to journalist Gail Sheehy in her popular book *Passages*, published in the 1970s. She interviewed numerous adult women and men and reported that the women seemed to enter middle age about five years earlier than the men, at about the age of 35. Why 35? In the 1970s, 35 was the age that women were usually advised to stop using the birth-control pill and to start using amniocentesis to check for chromosomal abnormalities in the fetus if they were pregnant. At this age, their "biological clocks" were also running out. Today we could say that 40 or so is the new 30 or 35 and that most women at 35 can still safely use "the pill." Many women, in fact, do become pregnant in their late 30s and early 40s. However, amniocentesis is still usually recommended for women who become pregnant at age 35 or older.

With people nowadays more likely to live into their late 70s or their 80s, 40 has become a much more realistic halfway point than that of the traditional 70 year human lifespan—or, as some might label it, a turning point (Wetherington et al., 2004). When people turn 40, they often realize they have as much to look back upon as they have to look forward to.

Daniel Levinson and his colleagues (1978) considered the transition to midlife at about the age of 40 a crisis, a midlife crisis, characterized by taking stock and often recognizing that one has fallen short of one's Dream or dreams. The promising ballerina in her 20s never danced *The Nutcracker* with the Royal Winnipeg Ballet. The Queen's University business major never sat at the Fortune 500 merger that brought in $25 million. The police college graduate at the top of her class never made RCMP commissioner. Thus, argues Becker

(2006), the value of psychotherapy at this time of life should not be minimized.

These portraits are negative, to say the least. Other observers of adult development note that while some theorists present portraits of middle-aged people suddenly focusing on tragedy, loss, or doom, others find people to be in or entering the "prime of life" (Almeida & Horn, 2004; Lachman, 2004). People can develop certain illnesses at almost any time of life, but as described in Chapter 15, most people in middle adulthood encounter little decline in physical prowess. Only professionals who rely on peak performance, such as athletes and dancers, will find the loss compelling enough to shuttle them into new life directions. Intellectually, moreover, little fluid intelligence, if any, is lost, and crystallized intelligence is growing—especially among professionals who continue to develop skills in their chosen fields.

Middle-aged adults, especially professionals, are also often earning more money than young adults. They are more likely to be settled geographically and vocationally, although they may experience midlife career changes and movement from one organization or business to another. By now, many have built systems of social support and may be involved in enduring romantic and social relationships and have children. The flip side, as we will see, may be overwhelming responsibility, such as caring for adolescent children, a spouse, aging parents, and remaining in the workplace all at once— quite a juggling act! But many in middle adulthood are at the height of their productivity and resilience, despite these challenges.

THE LIFE-EVENTS APPROACH

The life-events approach to middle age focuses on the particular challenges and changes that people are likely to face at this time of life rather than

Who's Having a Crisis?

According to psychiatrist Richard A. Friedman (2008), one excuse for human messing up is "my dog ate my homework." Another is "I'm going through a midlife crisis." As mortality begins to loom on the horizon, some people experience the impulse to do things in denial of their age, such as buy a new, fast, expensive car; suddenly quit a job; or leave a loyal spouse for a younger version.

Friedman reports on the experiences of middle-aged men who cheated on their wives, claiming to have midlife crises. They may say that they love their wives and don't know what got into them, but they're usually seeking novelty and risking too much for a few moments of fun. Being bored with routine is not what is meant by the term midlife crisis.

phases or stages of life. Numerous researchers have found that the most stressful life events of middle adulthood tend to include the death of a spouse or a child; the death of a parent or a sibling; marital divorce or separation, or separation from a cohabitant; hospitalization or change in the health status of oneself, one's child, one's parent, or one's sibling; the need to care for one's parents; a change in the relationship with one's children; financial difficulties; concern about one's appearance, weight, or aging; moving; change or loss of employment; a change in a relationship with an important friend; or a change in responsibilities at work (Etaugh & Bridges, 2006; Lorenz et al., 2006).

One common change in middle adulthood occurs when the last child leaves the home. Though we once assumed that women without children in the home would experience a painful "**empty nest syndrome**," this time can just as often be a positive stage (Etaugh & Bridges, 2006). Today, many middle-aged women in developed nations find they are "as young as they feel." Most are in the workforce and find life satisfaction in activities other than childrearing and homemaking.

> **D2** Modern mothers no longer experience an "empty-nest syndrome" when the last child leaves home.
> Having the last child leave home is often a positive event for middle-aged women.

As sources of stress, negative life events, including physical illness and depression, have been shown to be harmful to people's health in middle adulthood (Lorenz et al., 2006; Ryff et al., 2002). Some stressed people resort to a host of medicines, both prescribed and over-the-counter (Outram et al., 2006). An accumulation of stressful life events even seems capable of accelerating age-related declines in memory functioning (VonDras et al., 2005).

Nevertheless, middle-aged people's situations—such as having understanding and helpful family members or friends—and attitudes can have moderating effects on stressors (Etaugh & Bridges, 2006). A sense of control has been shown to override the effects of stress and foster feelings of well-being among midlife adults (Windsor et al., 2008). Middle-aged adults who perceive negative life events as specific rather than global problems and as capable of being changed are less likely to be depressed by them (Adler et al., 2006).

> **empty nest syndrome**
> a feeling of loneliness or loss of purpose that parents, and especially the mother, are theorized to experience when the youngest child leaves home.

Life Events

√ Death of a spouse

√ Marriage

√ Illness

√ Financial problems

√ Marital separation or divorce

√ Change in appearance

√ Loss of a job

© Image Source

LO2
Stability and Change in Middle Adulthood

What will their personalities be like in 20 years?

STABILITY   CHANGE

© Stuart McClymont/Getty Images

a number of researchers have been using five basic factors of personality isolated by Robert McCrae and Paul Costa and their colleagues to study stability and change in the personality development of adults over several decades (McCrae & Costa, 2006; Terracciano et al., 2006). These factors include extraversion, agreeableness, conscientiousness, neuroticism (emotional instability), and openness to experience (see Table 16.1). Cross-cultural research has found that these five factors appear to define the personality structure of North American, German, Portuguese, Hebrew, Chinese, Korean, and Japanese people (McCrae & Costa, 1997). A study of more than 5,000 German, British, Spanish, Czech, and Turkish people suggests that the factors are related to people's basic temperaments, which are considered to be largely inborn (McCrae et al., 2000). The researchers interpret the results to suggest that our personalities tend to mature rather than be shaped by environmental conditions, although the expression of personality traits is certainly affected by culture. (A person who is "basically" open to new experience is likely to behave less openly in a traditional, fundamentalist society than in an open society.)

ARE THERE SUDDEN SHIFTS IN PERSONALITY?

The notions of crises or turning points in emotional development also suggest that people undergo rather sudden changes or shifts in personality. As pointed out by Robert McCrae and Paul Costa, Jr. (2006), we have widely assumed that our personalities are deeply affected by adult life events such as getting married, working our way up in a vocation, and having and rearing children. However, according to two decades of longitudinal research, the

TABLE 16.1
The "Big Five": The Five-Factor Model of Personality

FACTOR	NAME	TRAITS
I	Extraversion	Contrasts talkativeness, assertiveness, and activity with silence, passivity, and reserve
II	Agreeableness	Contrasts kindness, trust, and warmth with hostility, selfishness, and distrust
III	Conscientiousness	Contrasts organization, thoroughness, and reliability with carelessness, negligence, and unreliability
IV	Neuroticism	Contrasts nervousness, moodiness, and sensitivity to negative stimuli with coping ability
V	Openness to experience	Contrasts imagination, curiosity, and creativity with shallowness and lack of perceptiveness

HDEV *Go to www.icanhdev.com to access an interactive version of this figure.*

"big five" personality traits tend to show a good deal of stability over time, at least after age 30 (Roberts & DelVecchio, 2000). McCrae and Costa suggest that this stability brings into question whether it makes sense for developmentalists, such as the Levinson group (1978), to suggest that phases or stages of adult development are predictable.

> **D3** The events of middle adulthood do not tend to cause major shifts in personality.
> According to two decades of longitudinal research, the "big five" personality traits tend to show a good deal of stability over time (Roberts & DelVecchio, 2000).

Longitudinal and cross-sectional research has shown some consistent trends of group personality change over the years, but by and large, those who are, say, most extraverted in young adulthood will remain most extraverted in middle adulthood (Roberts & DelVecchio, 2000; Roberts et al., 2006). However, for adults as a group, male and female, the traits of agreeableness and conscientiousness tend to increase from young adulthood to middle adulthood. Neuroticism declines throughout the same period, meaning that people become more emotionally stable. Extraversion and openness to new experience either remain the same or decline slightly in middle adulthood, suggesting again greater stability in personality, or "maturity." The trait of being open to new experience decreases once more in late adulthood.

PERSONALITY THEMES AMONG COLLEGE-EDUCATED WOMEN

Abigail Stewart, Joan Ostrove, and Ravenna Helson (2001) developed scales to assess a number of personality themes among women, as shown in Table 16.2. Alyssa Zucker and her colleagues (2002) administered these scales to three cohorts of college-educated women: women in their 20s, 40s, and 60s. As shown in Figure 16.1, scores on three of the scales were higher for women in their 40s than women in their 20s, and then higher again for women in their 60s: identity certainty, confident power, and concern about aging. Generativity was higher in the 40s than in the 20s, but the generativity of the cohort in their 60s was much the same. Despite increasing concern with aging, personal distress was lower among older women, suggesting, perhaps, that older women are more settled. Remember, however, that these samples are of college-educated women, who are less likely than the general population to incur certain financial and health problems in late adulthood that may be more common among people on the lower rung of the socioeconomic ladder.

> **"big five" personality traits** basic personality traits derived from contemporary statistical methods: extraversion, agreeableness, conscientiousness, neuroticism (emotional instability), and openness to experience.

TABLE 16.2

Themes Used on Scales to Assess Development of Personality in Women from Young Adulthood through Late Adulthood

THEME	ITEMS ASSESS FEELINGS SUCH AS THE FOLLOWING:
Identity certainty	Feeling that I am my own person; believing that I will seize my opportunities; being of a clear mind about what I can accomplish
Confident power	Having self-confidence; having a sense of authority and power; believing that others respect me
Concern with aging	Looking old; thinking about death a great deal; feeling less attractive than I used to look; feeling that men are no longer interested in me
Generativity	Having a sense of being needed; helping younger people learn and develop; trying to make positive changes in society; having interests beyond my immediate family
Personal distress	Feeling depressed or disillusioned; feeling angry at men or women; having feelings of incompetence; feeling alone; feeling exploited

Source: Stewart, A. J., Ostrove, J. M., & Helson, R. (2001). Middle aging in women: Patterns of personality change from the 30s to the 50s. Journal of Adult Development, 8, 23–37.

I've "learned the ropes" now.

© Comstock Images/Jupiterimages

adulthood (Hochwarter et al., 2001). The gains were greatest for men, and especially for men who were white-collar workers, for example, professors. Some workers—particularly blue-collar workers—reported feelings of alienation and dissatisfaction. Some complain that supervisors treated them with disrespect and failed to ask them how to improve working conditions and productivity (Judge & Klinger, 2008). These feelings are particularly painful for middle-aged workers when the supervisors are young adults. Women are often balancing the demands of the workplace and a family, and they may still experience a "glass ceiling" on the job (Casini & Sanchez-Mazas, 2005). Although women may be sought out in the hiring process, they will not necessarily have an easy time advancing. Still, most women and blue-collar workers reported more satisfaction on the job throughout middle age—just not as much as white-collar men.

D4 Women who have a college or university education do not typically experience increased personal distress as they advance from middle adulthood to late adulthood. Aside from increased concern with aging, this is generally true.

D5 Job satisfaction increases throughout middle adulthood. A study of more than 2,000 university employees found that job satisfaction increased steadily throughout middle adulthood (Hochwarter et al., 2001).

LO3 Work in Middle Adulthood

as suggested by Erikson and Levinson, many workers are at their peak in middle adulthood. They have had years to "learn the ropes," and many have advanced into the highest ranks of their trades or professions. One's work can continue to provide social benefits, a sense of identity, and self-esteem.

JOB SATISFACTION

Canadians are among the most satisfied workers in the world. In a global study of 23 countries, only workers in Denmark and Norway had a higher satisfaction level with their current employer (Fortier, 2010).

A study of more than 2,000 university employees found that job satisfaction increased steadily throughout middle

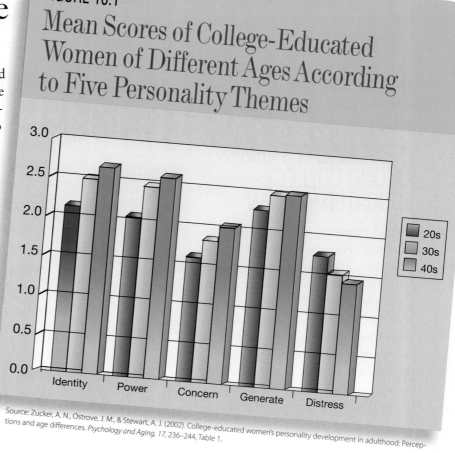

FIGURE 16.1
Mean Scores of College-Educated Women of Different Ages According to Five Personality Themes

Source: Zucker, A. N., Ostrove, J. M., & Stewart, A. J. (2002). College-educated women's personality development in adulthood: Perceptions and age differences. *Psychology and Aging, 17*, 236–244, Table 1.

The growing job satisfaction throughout middle age can be linked to factors such as increased expertise and income. Workers in middle adulthood may also have more realistic perceptions of their career goals. They may have come to terms with recognition that (most of them) will never be the CEO of Apple, Inc., the lead singer in a famous rock band, or the first person to set foot on Mars.

CAREER CHANGE IN MIDDLE ADULTHOOD

People change careers for many reasons, such as more money, more job security, greater prestige, and more stimulation (Jepsen & Choudhuri, 2001; Sullivan et al., 2003). Most people who change their careers do so in young adulthood. By middle adulthood, people tend to have greater responsibilities and to have become more "entrenched" in their pursuits. They may also wonder whether they have the time and the ability to start over.

For reasons such as these, most career changes in midlife involve shifts into related fields (Shultz & Adams, 2007). In the entertainment world, an actor might become a director or a producer. In the field of education, a teacher might move into educational administration. More radical shifts can occur, and they can also be successful (Hall, 2004). A laboratory chemist who has spent 20 years working for a pharmaceuticals company might decide she wants to work with people and to have more time for herself, so she might move into teaching high-school chemistry and travelling during the summers. We know of a social worker who decided to become a rabbi at the age of 43 and undertook several years of study. She said that she didn't feel she was really changing much at all, just getting better at Hebrew.

These are all "voluntary," planned changes. Some middle-aged people change careers following a personal crisis such as a divorce, conflict with co-workers, or being fired. In such cases middle-aged people

sometimes pick up whatever work they can to sustain themselves (Shultz & Adams, 2007).

UNEMPLOYMENT

Our friend lost her executive position in her late 40s, when her company was bought out and a new management team came in. She knew she was in a vulnerable position because the company taking over usually "chops off the head" of the acquired company; still, she thought she might be low enough on the totem pole to escape notice. Not so. New management cut in half the number of professionals at her level. At first she focused on the fact that her severance package was good. She thought she would take a month off to relax and then use the head-hunting firm hired by the company to relocate. However, she soon found that hers was a relatively small industry, and very few openings approximated her level. Former work friends clustered around her at first, but began to drift away. After four months, she had sunk into a deep clinical depression.

One group of researchers (McKee-Ryan et al., 2005) used meta-analysis to average out the finding of 104 studies of the effects of unemployment on the health of young and middle-aged adults. Unemployed subjects had lower physical and psychological well-being than employed subjects, and unemployed middle-aged subjects had lower well-being than unemployed young adults. Within the samples of unemployed middle-aged adults, those who fared worst were those for whom work was more important, who had lesser financial resources and social support, and who tended to blame themselves for losing their jobs. Those who fared best were those who had emotional and financial resources and social support, who could structure their time, and who had realistic strategies for job hunting or finding substitutes for jobs.

A study of small samples of unemployed men, 22 men aged 15–30 and 11 men aged 40–60, parallels the findings of the McKee-Ryan group (Broomhall & Winefield, 1990). The groups had been out of work for an average of 18 to 20 months. Men in the middle-aged group were significantly less satisfied with their lives and in poorer psychological health than the younger men.

When we consider women who are unemployed, we find age differences in the intensity

© AFP/Getty Images

*After working for more than 15 years as a television and film actor, Clint Eastwood made his directorial debut with **The Beguiled** in 1971.*

of their search for employment and their willingness to accept certain kinds of jobs. In a study of married women in four age groups, post-adolescents (up to age 21) spent more time trying to find employment than did women aged 22–35, 36–49, or 50–62 (Kulik, 2000). (As in the Broomhall & Winefield study, the groupings do not perfectly fit the definitions of young adulthood and middle adulthood.) The women aged 50–62 were most likely to accept jobs low in pay, as long as they liked the work, and those aged 22–49 were most likely to reject jobs because they conflicted with family life or because of work conditions. As in the study by McKee-Ryan and her colleagues (2005), the older women in the study were more likely to experience declines in their well-being following the loss of employment. On the other hand, the older women were least likely to suffer financial strain. We certainly cannot generalize this finding to single women who, as a group, would presumably have fewer financial resources.

LO4 Relationships in Middle Adulthood

t he term *middle adulthood* is a convenient term for describing people whose ages lie between young adulthood and late adulthood. In terms of their family relationships, their generation is in the middle in another way—often "sandwiched" in, as we will see, between their own children (and grandchildren) and their parents.

EVOLVING PARENT–CHILD RELATIONSHIPS

Infants are completely dependent on their parents. Children are also dependent. Adolescents strive for independence, and, as they mature and gain experience, parents generally begin to share control with them. As a matter of fact, it is stressful for parents when adolescents do not exert self-control, and parents must direct them in many areas of life—getting them up in time for school, urging them to maintain their personal hygiene, fighting

with them over their choice of clothing, and coaxing them to complete their homework.

Once their children become emerging adults or young adults, most parents in Canada are content to "launch" their children to live on their own or with roommates. In many cases, the children remain at least partly financially dependent, sometimes for several years (Aquilino, 2005). Children who have been close to their parents may also remain in some ways emotionally dependent once they are out on their own—or at the very least, they may be hurt when their parents disapprove of their personal choices.

Parents are usually satisfied with their children living apart from them, providing they call or e-mail regularly and drop by (or allow the parents to drop by) with some sort of reasonable frequency. Parents often try to find a balance between staying in touch and "interfering," especially once their children have partners or children of their own.

In some traditional societies, young adults do not usually leave the home of origin until they are married or some other key event takes place. When Alessandra Rusconi (2004) compared the common practice in Germany and Italy, he found that Germans normally left home to set up independent homes prior to marriage. In Italy, however, the picture was mixed. In large industrial cities, young adults tended to follow the German model, whereas more rural and Southern Italians tended to remain in the home until they got married. Similarly, parents in some traditional societies assume that their adult children will live nearby; moving to another part of the country is not only painful for parents but also can create an embarrassment for them among their extended family and community.

When children take partners or get married, new challenges can emerge for their parents. First of all, parents may feel that nobody can be "good enough" for their child, but, sometimes, their child does apparently make a poor choice—or at least a poor match. The parents must then deal with the issues as to whether, and how, they express their feelings about it. Regardless of the partner or spouse chosen by their child, parents must deal with in-laws and the extended family of the in-laws. Sometimes the families of both partners have a good match, but more often the families would not

© maxstockphoto/Shutterstock

© Peter Menzel/Hungry Planet: What the World Eats

have chosen each other as friends. Still, for the sake of the child, the parents usually try to act friendly on the occasions when the families are together. But it can be another source of stress.

And then the children may have children.

GRANDPARENTING

Let's begin this section by selecting one of the following two statements. Which statement will you live by (or forever destroy your relationship with your child by)?:

- As a grandparent, you have the right to tell your son or daughter how to raise your grandchild.

- As a grandparent, you have to keep your mouth tightly shut when you see your son-in-law or daughter-in-law doing the wrong thing with your grandchild.

One of the most challenging jobs of the newly minted grandparent is to navigate carefully between the treacherous rocks of reckless interference and painful neglect.

Young adulthood is the time of life when most of those who will bear children do so, and middle adulthood is the time of life when most of us who will become grandparents begin that role. Having and relating to grandchildren, like having and relating to one's children, has its pluses and its minuses. But research generally finds that the balance is more positive in the case of having grandchildren. For example, a study of grandparenting conducted in China, Greece, and Poland found that having grandchildren was viewed as an overwhelmingly positive event in each culture and was beneficial to grandparents, both socially and psychologically (Filus, 2006). The study also found that grandparents, like parents, participated in the care of grandchildren and in their recreational

and educational activities. But the balance differed, as it does in Canada. Parents spend a higher proportion of their time with their children in child care, whereas grandparents spend relatively more time in recreational and educational activities. We are speaking, of course, of situations in which the grandparents do not live in the same household with the grandchildren.

Cross-cultural studies also find gender differences in grandchildren's relationships with their grandparents that tend to parallel their relationships with their parents. Studies in the United States, Poland, Greece, Germany, and China all find that grandchildren through adolescence spend more time involved in activities with their grandmothers than with their grandfathers (Filus, 2006; Höpflinger & Hummel, 2006). Grandchildren are also relatively more involved with their mother's parents than their father's parents. It may come as a surprise, but the sex of the grandchild has little effect on these overall findings. Even male grandchildren, who would toss the football back and forth with the grandfather and not the grandmother, tend to generally gravitate more toward contacts with grandmothers than with grandfathers. Despite the greater involvement with

Lesbians and Bisexual Women as Grandparents

One study that relied on extensive interviews of lesbian and bisexual grandmothers found that the experiences of these women were in some ways similar to those of heterosexual people, and in other ways quite different (Orel, 2006). Like most heterosexual grandparents, the lesbian and bisexual grandmothers believed that they were important sources of emotional support for their grandchildren. They also reported that their children either helped (facilitated) or hindered (discouraged) their relationships with their grandchildren, and that the pattern might shift from time to time. On the other hand, all of the grandmothers in the study were concerned about whether or not they should disclose their sexual orientations to their grandchildren and exactly how they should go about it.

grandmothers, grandchildren say they value their grandfathers just as highly—but researchers are not about to devise an experiment that would put children's lip service to the test!

One of the "hyped" advantages of being a grandparent is being able to play with one's grandchildren but then go home, leaving the "work" to the children's parents. In many cases, however, this mindset assumes plentiful sources of money and leisure time. It hardly addresses all the complications of family separations or divorce, or loss of identity as a family unit, which is so common today (Bridges et al., 2007; Soliz, 2007). It also doesn't address the fact that some grandparents hardly—or never—see their grandchildren because of geographical separation or harsh feelings following family conflict.

The notion of grandparents enjoying the best of the grandchild while escaping responsibility also ignores the thousands of grandparents who bear the primary responsibility for rearing grandchildren (Goodman, 2007a; Hayslip & Kaminski, 2006).

Grandparents in Charge

In most cases, one or two biological parents determine the course of child-rearing of grandchildren. But sometimes grandparents play a major role—or *the* major role (Goodman, 2007a). For example, an Israeli study of immigrants from Ethiopia and Eastern European countries found that grandparents who lived with single parents and their grandchildren had a strong influence on their grandchildren and contributed to the overall adjustment of the family (Doron & Markovitzky, 2007).

Many studies (e.g., Doron & Markovitzky, 2007; Goodman, 2007b) show that grandparents have less influence when they live with couples and their grandchildren; under these circumstances, they are less likely to contribute to the adjustment of the family. Rather than "filling a hole," they frequently become a source of discord between their son or daughter and their son- or daughter-in-law.

In some cases grandparents are the sole caregivers of their grandchildren. These arrangements typically begin

Most grandparents do enjoy their roles in their grandchildren's lives. Their grandchildren value them deeply, even when they do not see them as often as they might wish.

when the grandchild has a single parent (Hayslip & Kaminski, 2006; Park & Greenberg, 2007). Now and then, that single parent dies. The single parent may be in the military and be sent on a tour of duty. The parent may place the child with grandparents while she or he "tries" living in another location, with or without a new job, and the time extends. The parent may run off, perhaps mired in personal troubles or involved in criminal activity.

Regardless of the reasons that grandparents—usually grandmothers—assume the responsibility for parenting grandchildren, becoming a parent, again, in middle adulthood, can be particularly stressful (Gerard et al., 2006; Leder et al., 2007). Do they attend school meetings with young parents and continually make explanations? If they are at the height of their careers, where do they find the time for all the chores (Ludwig et al., 2007)? Do they have to become current with the new crop of children's TV programs? It's a far cry from playing with the grandchildren, or taking them to a museum, and then going home—leaving the "work" to the parents!

But let us not forget that most grandparents do enjoy their roles in their grandchildren's lives. Their grandchildren value them deeply, even when they do not see them as often as they might wish (Bridges et al., 2007). Grandparents' greater fund of child-rearing experience often allows them to relate to their grandchildren in a more relaxed way than parents can.

© Pat Canova/Photolibrary

MIDDLE-AGED CHILDREN AND AGING PARENTS

Because of increasing life expectancy, more than half of the middle-aged people in developed nations have at least one living parent, and they frequently go on to experience late adulthood together (Callahan, 2007; U.S. Bureau of the Census, 2008). In Far Eastern nations such as China, Japan, and Korea, older parents tend to live with their children and their grandchildren, but not so in Canada and the United States (Kwok, 2006).

The relationships between middle-aged and older parents can grow quite close, especially as tensions and expectations from earlier years tend to slip into history. If an older mother had been disappointed in her now middle-aged daughter's choice of a husband, the marriage may have since ended or worked itself out, or there might be grandchildren to focus on. The passing years and other events place relationships in perspective.

If the aging parents require assistance, in the United States and Canada the task usually falls to a middle-aged daughter, who then becomes what has been dubbed part of the **sandwich generation**. She is "sandwiched" between several generations, caring for or contributing to the support of her own children at the same time she is caring for one or two parents (Grundy & Henretta, 2006). She may also be helping out with grandchildren. If she is fortunate, a sibling living in the vicinity can share the task. Given that she is also likely to be in the workforce, her role overload is multiplied (Gans & Silverstein, 2006).

In other societies, such as that of Hong Kong, where aging parents usually live with a son's family, it is more often than not the son who assumes the major responsibility for caring for his parents, emotionally and financially (Kwok, 2007). In this patriarchal society, the son's priorities often run like this: first, his own children; second, his parents; third, his wife.

SIBLINGS

Sibling relationships continue into late adulthood for most North Americans. The majority of people in middle adulthood have at least one living brother or sister. Most adult sibling relationships are close, but they tend to reflect the nature of sibling relationships in childhood. Then, too, sisters tend to have more intimate relationships than brothers (Bedford & Avioli, 2006). Yet now and then, sibling relationships that were antagonistic or competitive in childhood or adolescence grow closer in middle adulthood if the siblings cooperate in caring for a disabled parent (Leone, 2000). Conversely, a sibling relationship that had been close can grow distant if one sibling allows another to do all the work in caring for a parent.

sandwich generation the term given middle-aged people who need to meet the demands of their own children and of aging parents.

FRIENDS

Adolescents often belong to cliques and crowds, and young adults often have large numbers of friends. In middle adulthood, the number of friends tends to dwindle, and couples and individuals tend to place more value on the friends they keep (Adams & Ueno, 2006). In midlife, people become less willing to spend their time with "just anybody"; therefore, their remaining friends are still more likely to be "close matches" in terms of interests, activities, and, often, years of mutual experience. For this reason, the loss of a friend is felt more deeply. But as in earlier years, friendships have sex differences. Male friends are more likely to be competitive and less likely to be intimate than female friends (Adams & Ueno, 2006; Muhlbauer & Chrisler, 2007).

Toni Antonucci and Kira Burditt (2004) report that men are more likely than women not to have friends or other close social relationships, and that social isolation is related to poorer physical and psychological health and with mortality. In a survey of 1,421 men ranging in age from 20 to 93, men without close social ties were found to be significantly more depressed than men with relationships.

© Blend Images/Jupiterimages

D6 Middle-aged people tend to have fewer friends than young adults do.
Middle-aged people tend to have fewer friends than young adults, but they have more in common with the friends who remain.

People age 65

and older are the most rapidly growing segment of the Canadian population.

17

Late Adulthood: Physical and Cognitive Development

An Agequake Is Coming. People age 65 and older are the most rapidly growing segment of the Canadian population. So many people are living longer that we are in the midst of a "greying of Canada," an aging of the population that is having significant effects on many aspects of society.

> **life span (longevity)** the maximum amount of time a person can live under optimal conditions.

LO1 Physical Development

in 1900, only 1 person in 25 was over the age of 65. Today, that figure has more than tripled, to 1 in 8 of us. By mid-century, more than 1 in 5 North Americans will be 65 years of age or older. By the year 2050, we expect the percentage of North Americans over the age of 75 will have doubled (Kawas & Brookmeyer, 2001). To put these numbers in historical context, consider that through virtually all of human history, until the beginning of the 19th century, only a small fraction of humans lived to the age of 50.

LONGEVITY AND LIFE EXPECTANCY

One's **life span**, or **longevity**, is the length of time one can live under the best of circumstances. The life span of a species, including humans, depends on its genetic programming. With the right genes and environment,

Learning Outcomes

LO1 Discuss physical development in late adulthood

LO2 Compare programmed and cellular damage theories of aging

LO3 Identify common health concerns associated with late adulthood

LO4 Discuss cognitive development in late adulthood

life expectancy the amount of time a person can actually be expected to live in a given setting.

and with the good fortune to avoid serious accidents or illnesses, people have a life span of about 115 years.

One's **life expectancy** refers to the number of years a person in a given population group can actually expect to live. The average European American child born 100 years ago in the United States could expect to live 47 years. The average African American could expect a shorter life of 35.5 years (Andersen & Taylor, 2009). Great strides have been made in increasing life expectancy. A century ago, lower life expectancy rates were, in part, the result of high infant mortality rates due to diseases such as German measles, smallpox, polio, and diphtheria. These diseases have since been brought under control or eradicated. Other major killers, including bacterial infections such as tuberculosis, are now largely controlled by antibiotics. Factors that contribute to longevity include public health measures such as safer water supplies, improved dietary habits, and more accessible health care. Table 17.1 shows the life expectancy of males and females born in 2002 in various regions and countries of the world.

Distant Cousins?

It is interesting to note the considerable differences in life expectancy among the different countries of the world, as indicated in Table 17.1. Perhaps most surprising is the difference between Canada and the United States. Our lifelong experiences are very similar, yet our life expectancy is relatively higher. Life expectancy of Canadians (see Table 17.1) continues to rise, according to numbers released by Statistics Canada. Though the study did not examine why people are living longer, such factors as access to health care, advances in medicine, better diets, and access to clean water all play a role (CBC News, 2008).

> **D1** Canadians have a higher life expectancy than our neighbours in the United States.
> This difference is likely due largely to the differences in our health care systems.

It is also interesting to note the variations in life expectancy across Canada. British Columbia residents are expected to live to 81.2, whereas people in Canada's

TABLE 17.1
Life Expectancy at Birth, by Sex, by Province

	MALES	FEMALES
	(in years)	
Canada		
1920 to 1922	59	61
1930 to 1932	60	62
1940 to 1942	63	66
1950 to 1952	66	71
1960 to 1962	68	74
1970 to 1972	69	76
1980 to 1982	72	79
1990 to 1992	75	81
2000 to 2002	**77**	**82**
2005 to 2007		
Canada	78	83
Newfoundland and Labrador	76	81
Prince Edward Island	78	83
Nova Scotia	77	82
New Brunswick	77	83
Quebec	78	83
Ontario	79	83
Manitoba	77	82
Saskatchewan	77	82
Alberta	78	83
British Columbia	79	84

Source: Statistics Canada. (2010b). Life expectancy, at birth and at age 65, by sex, Canada, provinces and territories, annual (years). (CANSIM, table 102-0512.) Retrieved from http://cansim2.statcan.gc.ca/cgi-win/cnsmcgi.exe?Lang=E&RootDir=CII/&Detail=1&ResultTemplate=CII/CII___&TblDetail=1&C2SUB=HEALTH&Array_Pick=1&ArrayId=102-0512; Statistics Canada. (2006). Life tables, Canada, provinces and territories. (Statistics Canada Catalogue no. 84-537-XIE.) Retrieved from http://www.heartandstroke.com/site/c.iklQLcMWJtE/b.3483991/k.34A8/Statistics.htm

three northern territories, with a predominantly indigenous ethnicity, have a life expectancy of only 76.3. Within regions of our own country, we have disparities in health care and living conditions.

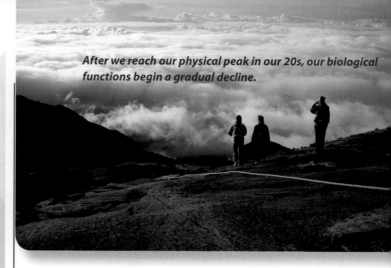

After we reach our physical peak in our 20s, our biological functions begin a gradual decline.

Life expectancy varies from province to province and between the provinces and the territories.

© Emma Wood/Alamy

Sex Differences in Life Expectancy

Although the longevity gap between men and women is narrowing, life expectancy among men trails that among women by about 4.7 years (78 years for men versus 82.7 years for women) (CBC News, 2008).

Why the gap? For one thing, heart disease typically develops later in life in women than in men because estrogen provides women some protection against heart disease. Also, men are more likely to die from accidents, cirrhosis of the liver, strokes, suicide, homicide, HIV/AIDS, and some forms of cancer. Many of these causes of death reflect unhealthful habits that are more typical of men, such as drinking, reckless behaviour, and smoking.

Many men are also reluctant to have regular physical examinations or to talk about health concerns with their doctors. Many men avoid medical attention until problems that could have been easily prevented or treated become serious or life-threatening. For example, women are more likely to examine themselves for signs of breast cancer than men are to examine their testicles for unusual lumps.

PHYSICAL AND SOCIAL CHANGES

After we reach our physical peak in our 20s, our biological functions begin a gradual decline. Aging also involves adapting to changing physical and social realities. "Newbies" in the workplace become the "old guard." One-time newlyweds come to celebrate their silver and golden anniversaries. Yet aging can involve more than adjustment; it can also bring about personal growth and exciting changes in direction. Even advanced age can bring greater harmony and integration to our personalities. However, we must learn to adapt to changes in our mental skills and abilities. Though older people's memories and fluid intelligence may not be as keen as they once were, maturity and experience frequently make them sources of wisdom.

Aging also has social aspects. Our self-concepts and behaviour as "young," "middle-aged," or "old" stem in large measure from cultural beliefs. In historical times, "mature" people had great prestige, leading men to routinely claim to be older than they were. Women, whose reproductive capacity was valued, did not want to be viewed as being older than they were. By contrast, the modern era has been marked by **ageism**—prejudice against people because of their age. Stereotypes that paint older people as crotchety, sluggish, forgetful, and fixed in their ways shape the way people respond to older people and actually impair their performance (Horton, 2008).

ageism prejudice against people because of their age.

D2 In historical times, aging was viewed so positively that men often claimed to be older than they actually were.
Maturity was considered a mark of prestige but asking job applicants their age is illegal in Canada.

In Chapter 15, we reviewed several physical changes that occur as people advance from early adulthood to middle adulthood and, in a number of cases, to late adulthood (changes in the skin, hair, and nails; senses; reaction time; lung capacity; metabolism; muscle strength; bone density; aerobic capacity; blood-sugar tolerance; and ability to regulate body temperature). Here we revisit and highlight changes in sensory functioning and bone density as they apply to late adulthood.

Changes in Sensory Functioning

Beginning in middle age, the lenses of the eyes become brittle, leading to presbyopia, as discussed in Chapter 15. Chemical changes of aging can lead to vision disorders

Ten Ways to Recognize Hearing Loss

The following questions from the NIDCD* will help you determine whether you need to have your hearing evaluated by a medical professional:

1. Do you have a problem hearing over the telephone?
2. Do you have trouble following the conversation when two or more people are talking at the same time?
3. Do people complain that you turn the TV volume up too high?
4. Do you strain to understand conversation?
5. Do you have trouble hearing in a noisy background?
6. Do you find yourself asking people to repeat themselves?
7. Do many people you talk to seem to mumble (or not speak clearly)?
8. Do you misunderstand what others are saying and respond inappropriately?
9. Do you have trouble understanding the speech of women and children?
10. Do people get annoyed because you misunderstand what they say?

If you answered "yes" to three or more of these questions, you may want to schedule a hearing evaluation with an ear, nose, and throat specialist or an audiologist.

*NIDCD (National Institute on Deafness and Other Communication Disorders). (2008, April 16). Ten Ways to Recognize Hearing Loss. http://www.nidcd.nih.gov/health/hearing/10ways.asp

such as **cataracts** and **glaucoma**. Cataracts cloud the lenses of the eyes, reducing vision. Today, outpatient surgery for correcting cataracts is routine. If performed before the condition progresses too far, the outcome for regained sight is excellent. Glaucoma is a buildup of fluid pressure inside the eyeball. Glaucoma can lead to tunnel vision (lack of peripheral vision) or blindness. Glaucoma rarely occurs before age 40, but affects about 1 in 250 people over the age of 40, and 1 in 25 people over 80. Rates are higher among diabetics than nondiabetics. Glaucoma is treated with medication or surgery.

The sense of hearing, especially the ability to hear higher frequencies, also declines with age. **Presbycusis** is age-related hearing loss that affects about 1 person in 3 over the age of 65 (Sommers, 2008). Hearing ability tends to decline more quickly in men than in women. Hearing aids magnify sound and can compensate for hearing loss. The Ten Ways to Recognize Hearing Loss questionnaire from the NIDCD shows how to recognize hearing loss.

Taste and smell become less acute as we age. Our sense of smell decreases almost ninefold from youth to advanced late adulthood. We also lose taste buds in the tongue with aging. As a result, foods must be more strongly spiced to yield the same flavour.

Bone Density

Bones begin to lose density in middle adulthood, becoming more brittle and vulnerable to fracture. Bones in the spine, hip, thigh, and forearm lose the most density as we age. **Osteoporosis** is a disorder in which bones lose so much calcium that they become dangerously prone to breakage. Osteoporosis can lead to bone fractures, the most serious of which are hip fractures, that is, breaks in the thigh bone, just below the hip joint. Hip fractures often result in hospitalization, loss of mobility, and, as is often the case in people in advanced late adulthood, death from complications. Fifteen to 20 percent of the people who sustain a hip fracture die within a year (Brunner et al., 2003).

Osteoporosis can shorten one's stature by centimetres and deform one's posture, causing the curvature in the spine known as "dowager's hump." Both men and women are at risk of osteoporosis, but women are at greater risk. Men typically have a larger bone mass, which provides greater protection against the disorder. Following the decline in bone density that women experience after menopause, women stand about twice the risk of hip fractures and about eight times the risk of spine fractures that men do. But older women who engage in walking as a form of regular exercise are less likely than their sedentary counterparts to suffer hip fractures (USDHHS, 2005).

Facts and Stats from Osteoporosis Canada:

- In adults over age 50, 1 in 4 women and at least 1 in 8 men have osteoporosis (the gender difference is due to drops in estrogen).
- Osteoporotic hip fractures consume more hospital bed days than strokes or heart attacks.
- Adults aged 19–50 need 1000 mg of calcium a day. Adults older than age 50 need 1200 mg of calcium a day (see the calculator on the Osteoperosis Canada website).
- Routine Vitamin D supplementation is recommended for all Canadian adults.
- Regular physical activity, in particular weight-bearing activities, can help build and maintain bone mass throughout life.
- Smoking and excess alcohol consumption contribute to bone loss.
- It is never too late to take steps to reduce further bone loss.

Source: Osteoporosis Canada web site www.osteoporosis.ca; Osteoporosis Canada. (2010). Facts and statistics: About osteoporosis. Retrieved from http://www.osteoporosis.ca/index.php/ci_id/8867/la_id/1.htm. Used with permission.

Evgeny Tomeev/Shutterstock

Canoneer/Shutterstock

SLEEP

Older people need about 7 hours of sleep per night, yet sleep disorders such as insomnia and **sleep apnea** become more common in later adulthood (Wickwire et al., 2008). Sleep apnea sufferers stop breathing repeatedly during the night, causing awakenings. Apnea may be more than a sleep problem. For reasons not entirely clear, apnea is linked to increased risk of heart attacks and strokes.

Sleep problems in late adulthood may involve physical changes that bring discomfort. Sometimes they symptomize psychological disorders such as depression, anxiety, or dementia. Men with enlarged prostate glands commonly need to urinate during the night, causing awakening. Other contributing factors include loneliness,

especially after the death of a close friend, spouse, or life partner.

sleep apnea temporary suspension of breathing while asleep.

Sleep medications are the most common treatment for insomnia (Wickwire et al., 2008). Alternatives may include keeping a regular sleep schedule, calming exaggerated worries about the consequences of remaining awake, using relaxation techniques, and exercise. Sleep apnea may be treated with surgery to widen the upper airways that block breathing or by the use of devices such as a nose mask that maintains pressure to keep airway passages open while sleeping (Wickwire et al., 2008).

SEXUALITY

People do not lose their sexuality as they age.

Even in the aftermath of the sexual revolution of the 1960s, many people still tie sex to reproduction. Therefore, they assume that sex is an activity only for the young. According to unfounded cultural myths, older people are sexless and older men with sexual interests are "dirty old men."

If older people believe these myths, they may renounce sex or feel guilty if they remain sexually active. Older women are handicapped by a double standard of greater tolerance of continued sexuality among men.

However, people do not lose their sexuality as they age (Laumann et al., 2006). Sexual daydreaming, sex drive, and sexual activity all tend to decline with age, but sexual satisfaction may remain high (Barnett & Dunning, 2003). Older people with partners usually remain sexually active (Laumann et al., 2006). Most older people report that they like sex. Sexual activity among older people, as among other groups, is influenced not only by physical structures and changes but also by psychological well-being, feelings of intimacy, and cultural expectations (Laumann et al., 2006).

Although many older people retain the capacity to respond sexually, physical changes do occur. But if older people fine-tune their expectations, they may find themselves leading some of their most sexually fulfilling years (Trudel et al., 2007).

Changes in Women

Many of the physical changes in older women stem from a decline in estrogen production. The vaginal walls lose much of their elasticity and grow paler and thinner. Thus, sexual activity may become irritating. The thinning of the walls may also place greater pressure against the bladder and urethra during sex, sometimes leading to urinary urgency and a burning sensation during urination.

The vagina also shrinks. The labia majora lose much of their fatty deposits and become thinner. The vaginal opening constricts, and penile entry may become difficult. Following menopause, women also produce less vaginal lubrication, and lubrication may take minutes, not seconds, to appear. Lack of adequate lubrication is a key reason for painful sex. Women's nipples still become erect as they are sexually aroused, but the spasms of orgasm become less powerful and fewer in number. Thus, orgasms may feel less intense, even though the experience of orgasm may remain just as satisfying. Despite these changes, women can retain their ability to reach orgasm well into their advanced years. Nevertheless, the uterine contractions that occur during orgasm may become discouragingly painful for some older women.

Changes in Men

Age-related changes tend to occur more gradually in men than in women and are not clearly related to any one biological event (Barnett & Dunning, 2003). Male adolescents may achieve erection in seconds.

After about age 50, men take progressively longer to achieve erection. Erections become less firm, perhaps because of lowered testosterone levels (Laumann et al., 2006).

Testosterone production usually declines gradually from about age 40 to age 60, and then begins to level off. However, the decline is not inevitable and may be related to a man's general health. Sperm production tends to decline, but viable sperm may be produced by men in their 70s, 80s, and 90s.

Nocturnal erections diminish in intensity, duration, and frequency as men age, but they do not normally disappear altogether (Perry et al., 2001). An adolescent may require but a few minutes to regain erection and ejaculate again after a first orgasm, whereas a man in his 30s may require half an hour. Past age 50, regaining erection may require several hours.

Older men produce less ejaculate, and the contractions of orgasm become weaker and fewer. Still, an older male may enjoy orgasm as thoroughly as he did at a younger age. Following orgasm, erection subsides more rapidly than in a younger man.

> **D3** Age-related sexual changes occur more gradually for men. Unlike many women's changes, which are related to menopause, men's changes are not clearly related to one biological event.

Patterns of Sexual Activity

Despite decline in physical functions, older people can lead fulfilling sex lives. Years of sexual experience may more than compensate for any lessening of physical response (Laumann et al., 2006). Frequency of sexual activity tends to decline with age because of hormonal changes, physical problems, boredom, and cultural attitudes. Yet sexuality among older people is variable (Laumann et al., 2006). Many older people engage in sexual activity as often as or more often than when younger; some develop an aversion to sex; others lose interest.

Couples may adapt to the physical changes of aging by broadening their sexual repertoire to include more diverse forms of stimulation. The availability of a sexually interested and supportive partner may be the most important determinant of continued sexual activity (Laumann et al., 2006). The Internet has opened new doors of access and creativity for the older generation, just as it has for today's younger generations.

LO2 Theories of Aging

So far, everyone who has lived has aged—which may not be a bad fate, considering the alternative. Although we can list all the things that happen as we age, we don't know exactly why they happen. Theories of aging fall into two broad categories:

- *Programmed theories* see aging as the result of genetic instructions.
- *Cellular damage theories* propose that aging results from damage to cells.

PROGRAMMED THEORIES OF AGING

Programmed theories propose that aging and longevity are determined by a biological clock that ticks at a rate governed by genes. That is, the seeds of our own demise are carried in our genes. Evidence supporting a genetic link to aging comes in part from studies showing that longevity tends to run in families (Perls, 2005). For example, the siblings of centenarians are more likely than members of the general population to live to be 100 themselves (Perls et al., 2002).

But why should organisms carry "suicidal" genes? Programmed aging theorists believe that it would be adaptive for species to survive long enough to reproduce and transmit their genes to future generations. From the evolutionary perspective, a species has no advantage (and probably a disadvantage given limited food supplies) by being able to repair cell machinery and body tissues to maintain life indefinitely.

Cellular clock theory focuses on the built-in limits of cell division. After dividing about 50 times, human cells cease dividing and eventually die (Hayflick, 1996). Researchers find clues to the limits of cell division in **telomeres**, the protective segments of DNA at the tips of chromosomes. Telomeres shrink each time cells divide. When the loss of telomeres reaches a critical point after a number of cell divisions, the cell may no longer be able to function (Epel et al., 2006). The length of the telomeres for a species may determine the number of times a cell can divide and survive.

Hormonal stress theory focuses on the endocrine system, which releases hormones into the bloodstream. Hormonal changes foster age-related changes such as puberty and menopause. As we age, stress hormones, including corticosteroids and adrenaline, are left at elevated levels following illnesses, making the body more vulnerable to chronic conditions such as diabetes, osteoporosis, and heart disease. The changes in production of stress hormones over time may be preprogrammed by genes.

Immunological theory holds that the immune system is preset to decline by an internal biological clock. For example, the production of antibodies declines with age, rendering the body less able to fight off infections. Age-related changes in the immune system also increase the risk of cancer and may contribute to general deterioration.

CELLULAR DAMAGE THEORIES OF AGING

Programmed theories assume that internal bodily processes are preset to age by genes. Cellular damage theories propose that internal bodily changes and external environmental assaults (such as carcinogens

cellular clock theory a theory of aging focusing on the limits of cell division.

telomeres protective segments of DNA located at the tips of chromosomes.

hormonal stress theory a theory of aging that hypothesizes that stress hormones, left at elevated levels, make the body more vulnerable to chronic conditions.

immunological theory a theory of aging that holds that the immune system is preset to decline by an internal biological clock.

Twins Gin Kanie (left) and Kin Narita lived to the ages of 108 and 107.

© Yoshida-Fujifotos/The Image Works

and toxins) cause cells and organ systems to malfunction, leading to death. For example, the **wear-and-tear theory** suggests that over the years, our bodies—as machines that wear out through use—become less capable of repairing themselves.

The **free-radical theory** attributes aging to damage caused by the accumulation of unstable molecules called *free radicals.* Free radicals are produced during metabolism by oxidation, possibly damaging cell proteins, membranes, and DNA (Sierra, 2006). Most free radicals are naturally disarmed by nutrients and enzymes called *antioxidants.* Most antioxidants are either made by the body or found in food. As we age, our bodies produce fewer antioxidants (Rattan et al., 2006). People whose diets are rich in antioxidants are less likely to develop heart disease and some cancers.

As we age, cell proteins bind to one another in a process called *cross-linking,* thereby toughening tissues. Cross-linking stiffens collagen—the connective tissue supporting tendons, ligaments, cartilage, and bone. One result is coarse, dry skin. (Flavoured animal collagen is called gelatin, better known by the brand name *Jell-O.*) **Cross-linking theory** holds that the stiffening of body proteins accelerates and eventually breaks down bodily processes, leading to some of the effects of aging (Rattan et al., 2006). The immune system combats cross-linking, but becomes less able to do so as we age.

When considering the many theories of aging, remember that aging is an extremely complex biological process that may not be explained by any single theory or cause. Aging likely involves a combination of these and other factors.

LO3 Health Concerns and Aging

though aging takes a toll on our bodies, many gerontologists believe that disease is not inevitable. They distinguish between *normal aging* and *pathological aging.* In normal aging, physiological processes decline slowly

Free radicals may also be produced by exposure to environmental agents such as ultraviolet light, extreme heat, pesticides, and air pollution.

with age and the person is able to enjoy many years of health and vitality into late adulthood. In pathological aging, chronic diseases or degenerative processes, such as heart disease, diabetes, and cancer, lead to disability or premature death. Older persons typically need more health care than younger persons. Though people over the age of 65 make up about 12 percent of the population, they occupy 25 percent of the hospital beds. As the numbers of older people increase in the 21st century, so will the cost of health care. Maintaining a strong and cost-efficient health care system remains a key political priority for most Canadians.

It is not true that most older adults require institutional care, such as nursing homes or residential care facilities. More than two of three adults age 65 and older live in their own homes. Less than 10 percent of older adults live in nursing homes or other long-term care facilities. The population of nursing homes is made up largely of people age 80 and older. Yet if older adults live long enough, nearly half will eventually require some form of nursing or home health care.

> **D4** Most older adults remain living independently.
> More than 2/3 of adults over the age of 65 live in their own homes.

It is also untrue that most older Canadians spend their later years in a retirement community. The majority of older adults remain in their own communities after retirement. Moreover, despite beliefs that most older people are impoverished, Canadians aged 65 and older are actually less likely than the general population to live under the poverty level.

In 1900, older people were more likely to die from infectious diseases such as influenza and pneumonia than they are today. Today, older people are at greater risk of dying from chronic diseases such as heart disease and

Is Calorie Restriction the Fountain of Youth?

Restricting calories by approximately 30 percent may trigger anti-aging responses that evolved to increase the chances of survival when food is scarce. For example, calorie restriction in humans, non-human primates, and other mammals lowers blood pressure, cholesterol, and blood-sugar and insulin levels. It strengthens the immune system and lowers the fat mass (Roth et al., 2004). Calorie restriction also fends off Alzheimer-like symptoms in rhesus monkeys.

In laboratory experiments, mice were fed a diet that was 30–40 percent lower in calories than normal but contained all necessary nutrients. The development of chronic diseases and cancers was retarded, and the mice lived 50 percent beyond their normal life spans (Hursting et al., 2003).

Raising levels of the hormone DHEAS (dehydroepiandrosterone sulfate) may be one way that calorie restriction reduces the risk of cancer and improves immune system functioning. DHEAS production usually begins to decline after approximately age 30, dipping to as low as 5–15 percent of peak levels by age 60. DHEAS levels are higher than normal in long-lived men and in rhesus monkeys with calorie-restricted diets (Chong et al., 2004).

It remains to be seen whether, and to what degree, calorie restriction extends the life span of people who have access to modern health care. Moreover, many people have difficulty keeping their weight within normal limits. How willing would we be to lower our calorie intake further? Researchers are therefore also seeking alternative ways of triggering the anti-aging responses caused by calorie restriction.

---

cancer. More than four out of five people over the age of 65 have at least one chronic health problem (Heron, 2007). Some health issues, such as varicose veins, are minor. Others, such as heart disease, pose serious health risks. Figure 17.1, on page 320, shows the percentages of people age 65 and older who are affected by common chronic health conditions. While longevity is increasing, so too are the number of years older persons are living with one or more chronic health problems.

HEART DISEASE, CANCER, AND RESPIRATORY DISEASE

The three major causes of death of Canadians age 65 and older are heart disease, cancer, and respiratory disease (see Table 17.2, on page 320). Cancer is the leading cause of death in men and women over the age of 65, followed by heart disease and respiratory disease.

As we age, the risk of most cancers rises because the immune system becomes less able to rid the body of precancerous and cancerous cells. Many older people are not adequately screened or treated for cancer or

heart disease. One reason for the gap in diagnosis and treatment is *elder bias* (Ludwick & Silva, 2003), or discrimination against the elderly on the part of some health professionals.

arthritis inflammation of the joints.

Among the top chronic conditions listed in Figure 17.1, several are also leading causes of death or pose significant risk factors for mortality. Hypertension, which affects about 50 percent of Canadians over the age of 65, is a major risk factor for heart attacks and strokes. Diabetes, the fifth most common chronic illness, is the fifth leading cause of death. Other chronic conditions, such as cataracts, chronic sinusitis, visual impairment, and varicose veins, are rarely fatal but can lead to disability and reduced quality of life.

ARTHRITIS

Arthritis is joint inflammation that results from conditions affecting the structures inside and surrounding the joints. Symptoms progress from redness to heat, swelling,

FIGURE 17.1

Chronic Health Conditions among People Age 65 and Over

The leading chronic health conditions affecting people in late adulthood are hypertension, heart disease, and arthritis.

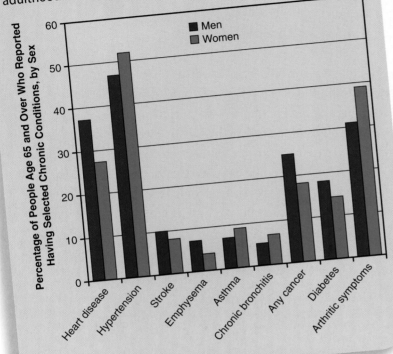

Source: Melanie P. Heron. (2007). *National Vital Statistics Reports, 50*(5) Centers for Disease Control and Prevention. www.cdc.gov/nchs/data/nvsr/nvsr56/nvsr56_05

three have the disease. The joints most commonly affected are in the knees, hips, fingers, neck, and lower back. Osteoarthritis is caused by erosion of cartilage, the pads of fibrous tissue that cushion the ends of bones. As cartilage wears down, bones grind together, causing pain (Axford et al., 2008). Osteoarthritis is more common among obese people because excess weight adds to the load on the hip and knee joints. Health professionals suggest using over-the-counter anti-inflammatory drugs (aspirin, acetaminophen, ibuprofen, naproxen) and prescription anti-inflammatory drugs to help relieve pain and discomfort (Axford et al., 2008). In severe cases, joint replacement surgery may be needed. Specific exercises are also sometimes prescribed.

Rheumatoid arthritis is characterized by chronic inflammation of the membranes that line the joints as a result of the body's immune system attacking its own tissues. The condition affects the entire body. It can produce unrelenting pain and eventually lead to severe disability. Bones and cartilage may also be affected. Onset of the disease usually occurs between the ages of 40 and 60. Anti-inflammatory drugs are used to treat it.

osteoarthritis a painful, degenerative disease characterized by wear and tear on joints.

rheumatoid arthritis a painful, degenerative disease characterized by chronic inflammation of the membranes that line the joints.

pain, and loss of function. Children can also be affected by arthritis, but it is more common with advancing age. Arthritis is more common in women than men. Osteoarthritis and rheumatoid arthritis are the two most common forms of arthritis.

Osteoarthritis is a painful, degenerative disease characterized by wear and tear on joints. By the age of 60, more than half of Canadians show some signs of the disease. Among people over the age of 65, two of

TABLE 17.2

Ten Leading Causes of Death in Canada by Gender, 65 Years and Over

MEN	WOMEN
1. Cancer	1. Cancer
2. Heart disease	2. Heart disease
3. Respiratory disease	3. Respiratory disease
4. Brain disease	4. Brain disease
5. Diabetes	5. Diabetes
6. Accidents	6. Accidents
7. Liver Disease	7. Pneumonia
8. Aneurysm	8. Alzheimer's disease
9. Pneumonia	9. Liver disease
10. Nephritis	10. Nephritis

Source: Statistics Canada. (2009b). Ten leading causes of death by selected age groups, by sex, Canada — 65 to 74 years. Retrieved from http://www.statcan.gc.ca/pub/84-215-x/2008000/tbl/t008-eng.htm

SUBSTANCE ABUSE

Abuse of medication (prescription and over-the-counter drugs), much of which is unintentional, poses a serious health threat to older Canadians. In 2005, pharmacists dispensed an average of 35 prescriptions per person aged 60 to 79, and 74 prescriptions per person aged 80 or older (Ramage-Morin, 2009). Among the most commonly used drugs are blood pressure medication, tranquilizers, sleeping pills, and antidepressants. Taken correctly, prescription drugs can be of help. If used incorrectly, they can be harmful.

It is not true that substance abuse is rare in late adulthood. Millions of older adults are addicted to, or risk becoming addicted to, prescription drugs, especially tranquilizers.

According to the Centre for Addiction and Mental Health, medication issues in older adults are a significant problem. An estimated 50 percent of prescriptions are not taken properly. In addition, up to 20 percent of Canadian hospitalizations are the result of problems with medication. Further, the following signs of medication issues are sometimes mistaken for signs of aging: slurred speech, increased confusion, lethargy or sleepiness, and stumbling and falls (Centre for Addiction and Mental Health, 2009).

> **D5** Medication issues are common in older adults.
> Medication issues can be confused for signs of aging.

Although alcohol consumption is lower overall among older people, compared with among younger adults, many older adults suffer from long-term alcoholism. However, the health risks of alcohol abuse increase with age. The slowdown in the metabolic rate reduces the body's ability to metabolize alcohol, increasing the likelihood of intoxication. The combination of alcohol and other drugs, including prescription drugs, can be dangerous or even lethal. Alcohol can also either diminish or intensify the effects of prescription drugs.

ACCIDENTS

Though accidents can occur at any age, older people face greater risks of unintentional injuries from falls, motor vehicle accidents, residential fires, and nonfatal poisoning. Accidents are the sixth leading cause of death among older Canadians. Falls are especially dangerous for older adults who have osteoporosis because of their increased risks of fractures (Facts about Falling, 2008).

© Sean Murphy/Getty Images

Many accidents involving older adults can be prevented by equipping the home with safety features, such as railings and nonskid floors. Wearing proper glasses and using hearing aids can reduce the risk of accidents resulting from vision or hearing problems, including many motor vehicle accidents. Adherence to safe driving speeds is especially important among older drivers because they have slower reaction times than younger drivers.

dementia a condition characterized by deterioration of cognitive functioning.

Alzheimer's disease (AD) a severe form of dementia characterized by memory lapses, confusion, emotional instability, and progressive loss of cognitive functioning.

DEMENTIA AND ALZHEIMER'S DISEASE

Dementia is a condition characterized by dramatic deterioration of mental abilities involving thinking, memory, judgment, and reasoning. Dementia is not a consequence of normal aging (see Figure 17.3 on page 322), but of disease processes that damage brain tissue. Some causes of dementia include brain infections such as meningitis, HIV infection, and encephalitis; and chronic alcoholism, infections, strokes, and tumors (Lippa, 2008; see Figure 17.2, on page 322). The most common cause of dementia (about 63 percent) is **Alzheimer's disease (AD)** (Alzheimer

FIGURE 17.2
Causes of Dementia
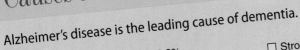

Alzheimer's disease is the leading cause of dementia.

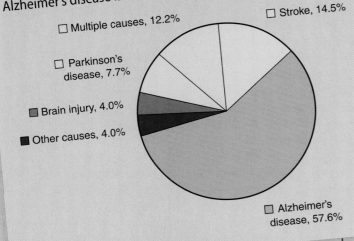

☐ Multiple causes, 12.2%

☐ Parkinson's disease, 7.7%

■ Brain injury, 4.0%

■ Other causes, 4.0%

☐ Stroke, 14.5%

☐ Alzheimer's disease, 57.6%

Source: Melanie P. Heron. (2007). *National Vital Statistics Reports, 56*(5). Centers for Disease Control and Prevention. www.cdc.gov/nchs/data/nvsr/nvsr56/nvsr56_05

They may experience hallucinations or paranoid delusions, believing that others are attempting to harm them. People with AD may eventually become unable to walk or communicate, rendering them completely dependent on others.

Although the cause or causes of AD remain a mystery, scientists believe that both environmental and genetic factors are involved (Goldman et al., 2008; Tomiyama et al., 2008). The accumulation of plaque may cause the memory loss and other symptoms of AD; however, experiments with non-humans suggest that memory deficits may precede the formation of significant deposits of plaque (Jacobsen et al., 2006).

Medicines can help improve memory functions in people with AD, but their effects are modest. Researchers are investigating whether regular use of anti-inflammatory drugs and antioxidants may lower the risk of developing AD by preventing the brain inflammation

Society, 2009). Approximately 500,000 Canadians have dementia. The authors of *Rising Tide: The Impact of Dementia on Canadian Society* forecast that, within a generation, dementia will affect 1.1 million Canadians who will require 756 million hours of care, at an estimated cost of $153 billion (Alzheimer Society, 2010).

Although some dementias may be reversible, especially those caused by tumours and treatable infections and those resulting from depression or substance abuse, the dementia resulting from AD is progressive and irreversible (Lippa, 2008).

AD progresses in several stages. At first subtle cognitive and personality changes occur, in which people with AD have trouble managing finances and recalling recent events. As AD progresses, people with AD find it harder to manage daily tasks, select clothes, recall names and addresses, and drive. Later, they have trouble using the bathroom and maintaining hygiene. They no longer recognize family and friends or speak in full sentences. They may become restless, agitated, confused, and aggressive. They may get lost in stores, parking lots, even their own homes.

FIGURE 17.3
Rates of Alzheimer's Disease among Older Adults

Though Alzheimer's disease is not a consequence of normal aging, the risk of Alzheimer's disease is greatest among people in the 75- to 84-year age range.

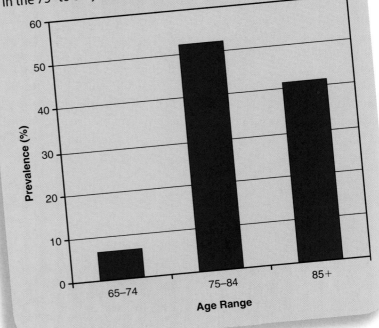

Source: Herbert, L. E., et al. (2003). Alzheimer's Disease in the U.S. Population: Prevalence Estimates Using the 2000 Census. *Archives of Neurology, 60*, 1119–1122.

associated with AD (Gray et al., 2008; Meinert & Breitner, 2008). Calorie restriction may prevent the accumulation of plaque (Qin et al., 2006). Researchers are also investigating whether cognitive training that focuses on the enhancement of memory and processing speed can delay or prevent the development of AD (Acevedo & Loewenstein, 2007; Vellas et al., 2008).

LO4 Cognitive Development

When artist Jack Tworkov was in his 30s, his paintings were realistic. In his 50s, his works were abstract expressionistic, like those of Jackson Pollock. In his 60s, his painting remained abstract and became hard-edged with geometric precision. At the age of 79, a year before his death, he was experimenting with a loosely flowing calligraphic style that he never showed to the public. It was in the early stages of development.

Although Tworkov's body was in decline, he once commented, "Every morning I go to the easel in a fever." He wore a T-shirt and blue jeans, the clothing typical of a teenager. But Tworkov seemed more at ease in his attire at 79 than many are at 16.

Tworkov was fortunate in that his cognitive processes were clear. Given the scores of new works in his later years, his processing speed had remained good—or at least good enough. His visual and motor memory and his capacity to rivet his attention to a task all remained superb. All these skills are part of what we labelled *fluid intelligence* in Chapter 15, and they are most vulnerable to decline in late adulthood (Saggino et al., 2006). We have no personal way of comparing his skills in late adulthood with what they were 20 or 40 years earlier, but based simply on what can be observed, his abilities were stunning.

Crystallized intelligence can continue to improve throughout much of late adulthood (Mangina & Sokolov, 2006). However, if you have another look at Figure 15.3 on page 291, you will see that all cognitive skills, on average, tend to decline in advanced age.

MEMORY: REMEMBRANCE OF THINGS PAST—AND FUTURE

In a classic study of memory, Harry Bahrick and his colleagues (1975) sought to learn how well

"Who is the author of the play Hamlet? That is the question."

high-school graduates would recognize photographs of their classmates. Some of their subjects had graduated 15 years earlier, and others had been out of school for some 50 years. The experimenters interspersed photos of actual classmates with four times as many photos of strangers. People who had graduated 15 years earlier correctly recognized persons who were former schoolmates 90 percent of the time. But those who had graduated about 50 years earlier still recognized former classmates 75 percent of the time. A chance level of recognition would have been only 20 percent (one photo in five was of an actual classmate). Thus, the visual recognition memories had lasted half a century in people who were now in late adulthood.

Developmentalists speak of various kinds of memories. First we can distinguish between retrospective and prospective memories—memories of the past ("retro") and memories of the things we plan to do in the future. We can then divide retrospective memories into explicit and implicit memories. Explicit memories are of specific information, such as things we did or things that happened to us (called episodic or autobiographical memories) and general knowledge, such as the author of *Hamlet* (semantic memory). Implicit memories are more automatic and recall the performance of tasks such as reciting the alphabet or multiplication tables, riding a bicycle, or using a doorknob.

Explicit versus Implicit Memories

Older adults often complain that they struggle to remember the names of people they know, even people they know very well. They are frustrated by the awareness that they knew the name yesterday, perhaps even a half hour ago, but "now" it is gone. When they do recall it, or another person reminds them of the name, they think, "Of course!" and perhaps belittle themselves for forgetting. An experiment with young adults and adults in their 70s found that the older adults did

implicit memory automatic memories based on repetition and apparently not requiring any conscious effort to retrieve.

have a disproportionate difficulty identifying public figures from photographs, but little difficulty when asked to identify uncommon objects (Rendell et al., 2005). The working memories of older adults seem to hold less information simultaneously than the working memories of young adults. Perhaps, then, when older adults picture the person whose name they forget, or think about that person engaged in some activity, the picture or activity momentarily displaces the name (Braver & West, 2008).

The temporal memory of older adults—that is, their recall of the order in which events have occurred—may become confused (Dumas & Hartman, 2003; Hartman & Warren, 2005). Older adults may have difficulty discriminating actual events from illusory events (Rybash & Hrubi-Bopp, 2000).

Older adults usually do not fare as well as younger adults in tasks that measure explicit memory, but they tend to do as well, or nearly as well, in tasks that assess **implicit memory** (Mitchell & Bruss, 2003). Implicit memory tasks tend to be automatic and do not require any conscious effort. They may reflect years of learning and repetition. Implicit memory includes remembering multiplication tables or the alphabet. We could ask you which letter comes after *p* or to recite the alphabet. The second task would be easier because that is the way you learned, and overlearned, the 26 letters of the alphabet. It is said that you never forget how to ride a bicycle or use a keyboard; these are also implicit memories—in these cases, sensorimotor habits.

Daniel Schacter (1992) illustrates implicit memory with the story of a woman with amnesia who was found wandering the streets. The police picked her up and found that she could not remember who she was or anything else about her life, and she had no identification. After extensive fruitless questioning, the police hit on the idea of asking her to dial phone numbers—any number at all. Although the woman did not "know" what she was doing, she dialled her mother's number. She could not make her mother's number explicit, but dialling it was a habit, and she remembered it *implicitly*.

Associative Memory

We use associative learning, and associative memory, to remember that the written letter *A* has the sound of an "A." We also use associative memory to develop a sight

> It is said that you never forget how to ride a bicycle or use a keyboard: these are also implicit memories—in these cases, sensorimotor habits.

vocabulary; that is, we associate the written *the* with the sound of the word; we do not decode it as we read. In these cases we usually learn by rote rehearsal, or repletion. But we also often use elaborative rehearsal, which is a more complex strategy that makes learning meaningful, to retrieve the associated spellings for spoken words. For example, we may remember to recall the rule "*i* before *e* except after *c*" to retrieve the correct spelling of *retrieve*.

It turns out that aging has more of a detrimental effect on associative memory than on memory for single items (Naveh-Benjamin et al., 2007). For example, older adults have greater difficulty discriminating between new and already experienced combinations of items on an associative recognition task—that is, recognizing pairs of words that have been presented before—than between new and already experienced single items on an item recognition task (Light et al., 2004). Various possibilities have been hypothesized to explain the age-related deficit in associative memory. One is an impairment in the initial binding or learning phase of individual pieces of information when the individual is attempting to encode them (Naveh-Benjamin et al., 2003). According to the binding hypothesis, older adults are impaired primarily in associating items with one another, but not in remembering individual items (Cohn et al., 2008). A second hypothesis states that the specific impairment is in recollection when the individual attempts to retrieve the information (Yonelinas, 2002), which may reflect poor binding during encoding, poor use of strategic processes during retrieval, or both.

Research by Melanie Cohn and her colleagues (2008) suggests that impairments in associative memory among older adults represent problems in binding information, recollection, and use of effective strategies for retrieval (such as creating sentences that use both members of a pair of words as they are presented). For example, if one member of a pair is "man" and another is "cigarette," an elaborative strategy for

FIGURE 17.4
The Aging Brain

In the aging brain, atrophy in the frontal lobe and in the middle (medial) part of the temporal lobe may account for deficits in associative memory.

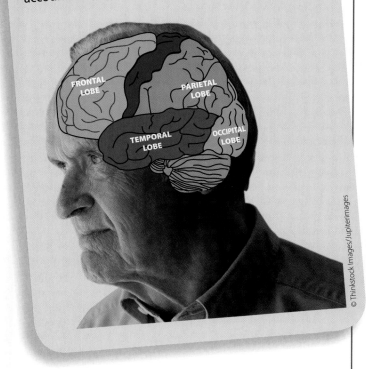

FRONTAL LOBE

PARIETAL LOBE

TEMPORAL LOBE

OCCIPITAL LOBE

© Thinkstock Images/Jupiterimages

recollecting the pair could be to rapidly construct the sentence, "The man refuses to smoke a cigarette." Cohn and her colleagues believe that these cognitive developments "are consistent with neurobiological models" of memory that focus on the frontal and medial temporal lobes of the brain (see Figure 17.4). The frontal regions—the executive centre of the brain—are involved in directing one's attention and organizing information and strategic processes. The medial temporal lobe binds elements to form memory traces, recovers information in response to use of proper memory cues, and is therefore a key to recollection. Neurological research shows that deterioration is evident in aging in the frontal lobes and to a lesser degree in the medial temporal lobe, thus logically impairing binding, recollection, and the use of effective strategies for the retrieval of information.

Long-Term Memory

Long-term memory has no known inherent limits, as noted in Chapter 9. Memories may reside there for a lifetime, to be recalled with the proper cues. But long-term memories are also subject to distortion, bias, and even decay.

Harry Bahrick and his colleagues (2008) administered questionnaires to 267 alumni of Ohio Wesleyan University, who had graduated anywhere from 1 to 50 years earlier. Subjects thus ranged in age from early adulthood to late adulthood. They were asked to recall their college grades, and their recollections were checked against their actual grades. Of 3,967 grades, 3,025 were recalled correctly. Figure 17.5, on page 326, relates the correct responses to the age of the respondent. The number of correct recollections fell off with the age of the respondent, due, generally, to errors of omission—that is, leaving items blank rather than entering the wrong grade. As a matter of fact, graduates who were out of school more than 40 years entered no more wrong grades, on average, than those who were out of school 8 years or so. The researchers found a grade-inflation bias: 81 percent of commission errors inflated the true grade.

In typical studies of long-term memory, researchers present older adults with timelines that list ages from early childhood to the present day and ask them to fill in key events and to indicate how old they were at the time. Using this technique, people seem to recall events from the second and third decades of life in greatest detail and with the most emotional intensity (Glück & Bluck, 2007). These include early romances (or their absence), high-school days, music groups and public figures, sports heroes, "life dreams," and early disappointments. Many psychologists look to psychological explanations for these findings, and, considering "coming of age" and the development of "identity" are common characteristics of the second and third decades of life, they may be correct in their pursuit. But note that sex hormones also have their strongest effects in adolescence and early adulthood and that the secretion of these hormones is related to the release of neurotransmitters involved in memory formation (Lupien et al., 2007).

Prospective Memory

Why do we need electronic organizers, desk calendars, and shopping lists? To help us remember the things we have planned to do. Retrospective memory helps us retrieve information from the past. **Prospective memory** aids us in remembering things we have planned to do in the future, despite the passage of time and despite the occurrence of interfering events.

prospective memory memory of things one has planned for the future.

FIGURE 17.5
Memory for College Grades, One to Fifty-Four Years Later

Mean number of correctly recalled grades, omission errors, and commission errors as a function of retention interval.

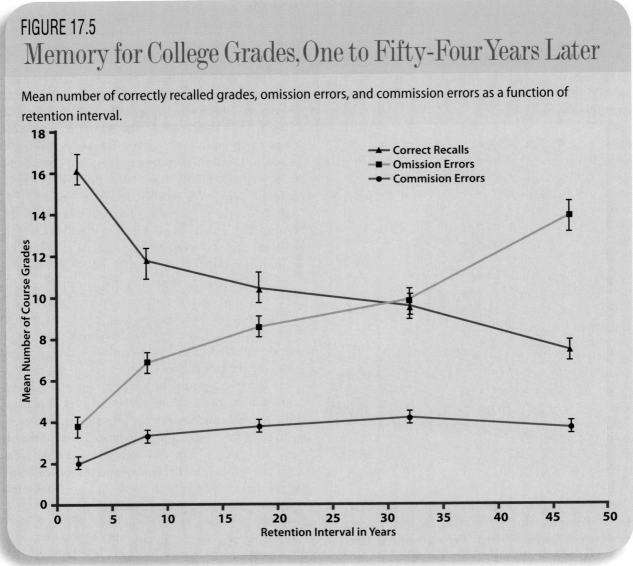

Source: Harry P. Bahrick, Lynda K. Hall, & Laura A. Da Costa. (2008). Fifty years of memory of college grades: Accuracy and distortions. *Emotion, 8*(1), 13–22.

In order for prospective memory to succeed, we need to have foolproof strategies, such as alarm reminders on our cell phones, or we need to focus our attention and keep it focused. Distractibility will prevent us from reaching the goal.

A Swiss study examined the relationships between processing speed, working memory (the amount of information a person can keep in mind at once), prospective memory, and retrospective memory among 361 people between the ages of 65 and 80 (Zeintl et al., 2007). It was found that age-related declines in processing speed and working memory—aspects of fluid intelligence—had important effects on retrospective memory. However, some age-related declines in prospective memory appeared to be independent of processing speed and working memory. In other words, even if fluid intelligence remained intact, prospective memory might decline, suggestive of powerful roles for attention and distractibility.

Another study found that the age-related decline in prospective memory is greatest when the task to be completed is not crucial and the cues used to jog the memory are not very prominent (Kliegel et al., 2008). When the task is important and older adults use conspicuous cues to remind them, age-related declines in prospective memory tend to disappear. However, the adults need to be sufficiently cognitively aware to plan the strategy.

LANGUAGE DEVELOPMENT

People aged 75 and older tend to show a decline in reading comprehension that is related to a decrease in the scope of working memory (De Beni et al., 2007). Because of the decline in working memory and because of impairments in hearing, many older adults find it more difficult to understand the spoken language (Burke & Shafto, 2008). However, when the speaker slows down and articulates more clearly, comprehension increases (Gordon-Salant et al., 2007).

Older adults may also show deficiencies in language production. Although they may retain their receptive vocabularies, they often show a gradual decline in their expressive vocabularies—that is, the number of words they produce (Hough, 2007). Declines in associative memory and working memory appear to decrease the likelihood that words will "be there" when older people try to express ideas (Burke & Shafto, 2008). Similarly, older people are more likely to experience the frustrating "tip-of-the-tongue" phenomenon, in which they know a word but temporarily cannot produce it (Shafto et al., 2007).

PROBLEM SOLVING

Figure 17.6 shows the so-called Duncker Candle Problem, which is sometimes used to challenge problem-solving skills. The goal is to attach the candle to the wall, using only the objects shown, so that it will burn properly. Rather than be concerned about whether or not you can solve the problem, notice the types of thoughts you have already had as you have surveyed the objects in the figure. Even if you haven't arrived at a solution yet, you have probably used mental trial and error to visualize what might work. (You will find the answer to the Duncker Candle Problem in Figure 17.7, on page 328.)

These standard problem-solving methods require executive functioning to select strategies, working memory to hold the elements of the problem in mind, and processing speed to accomplish the task while the elements remain in mind, all of which have fluid components that tend to decline with age (Hassing & Johanssom, 2005). Experiments with young and older adults consistently show that the older adults use fewer strategies and display slower processing speed in solving

FIGURE 17.6
The Duncker Candle Problem

Can you use the objects shown on the table to attach the candle to the wall of the room so that it will burn properly? You can find the answer on page 328.

> Because of the decline in working memory and because of impairments in hearing, many older adults find it more difficult to understand the spoken language.

complex math problems (Allain et al., 2007; Lemaire & Arnaud, 2008).

How important, you might wonder, is it for older people to solve complex math problems or "teasers" like the Duncker Candle Problem? The answer depends on what people are attempting to accomplish in life. However, research suggests that for the vast majority of older adults, abstract problem-solving ability, as in complex math problems, is not related to their quality of life. "Real-world" or everyday problem-solving skills are usually of greater concern (Gilhooly et al., 2007).

Moreover, when older adults encounter interpersonal conflicts, they tend to regulate their emotional responses differently from young and middle-aged adults. Whereas younger groups are relatively more likely to express feelings of anger or frustration, to seek support from other people, or to solve interpersonal problems, older adults are more likely to focus on remaining calm and unperturbed (Coats & Blanchard-Fields, 2008). The difference appears to be partially due to older adults' decreased tendency to express anger and increased priority on regulating emotion. Perhaps the older adults do not wish to be "jarred," but it also sounds a bit like wisdom.

WISDOM

We may seek athletes who are in their 20s, but we prefer coaches who are decades older. It may be desirable to hire high-school teachers and college and university professors who have recently graduated, but we usually seek high-school principals and department chairpersons who are older. It is helpful to have 18-year-olds who are bursting with energy knocking on doors to get out the vote, but we want our presidential candidates to be older. Why? Because we associate age with *wisdom*.

Among the numerous cognitive hazards of aging, older people tend to be more distractible than young adults. Developmental psychologist Lynn Hasher (2008) suggests that distractibility can enable older adults to take a broader view of various situations: "A broad attention span may enable older adults to ultimately know more about a situation and . . . what's going on than their younger peers. . . . [This] characteristic may play a significant role in why we think of older people as wiser."

Kunzmann and Baltes (2005) note that wise people approach life's problems in a way that addresses the meaning of life. They consider not only the present, but also the past and the future, as well as the contexts in which the problems arise. They tend to be tolerant of other people's value systems and to acknowledge that life holds uncertainties and that one can only attempt to find workable solutions in an imperfect world. Ardelt

Great love and great achievements involve great risk. Dalai Lama

(2008a, 2008b) adds emotional and philosophical dimensions to the definition of wisdom. She suggests that wise people tend to possess an unselfish love for others and tend to be less afraid of death.

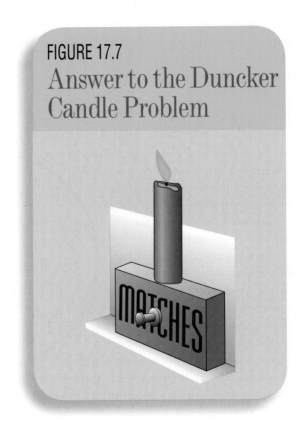

FIGURE 17.7
Answer to the Duncker Candle Problem

For many people,

the later years are the best years—especially when they are filled with

meaningful activity.

18

Late Adulthood: Social and Emotional Development

Learning Outcomes

LO1 Evaluate various theories of social and emotional development in late adulthood

LO2 Discuss psychological development in late adulthood, focusing on self-esteem and maintaining independence

LO3 Discuss the social contexts in which people age, focusing on housing, religion, and family

LO4 Discuss factors that contribute to adjustment to retirement

LO5 Discuss factors in "successful aging"

For many people, the later years are the best years—especially when they are filled with meaningful activity. The stresses involved in building and maintaining a career, selecting a mate, and rearing children may have receded. Questions of identity may have become settled.

Troubling emotions such as depression and anxiety tend to decline as we age, whereas positive emotions remain fairly steady (Charles et al., 2001). On the whole, older Canadians are at least as happy as younger people. According to the National Health Interview Survey, the majority of people 65 and older consider themselves to be in "excellent," "very good," or "good" overall health when compared with other people of their age (Kart & Kinney, 2001).

Yet, as we will see, aging has its challenges. Older people are more likely to be bereaved by the loss of spouses and close friends. Older people may need to cope with declining health, retirement, and relocation.

LO1 Theories of Social and Emotional Development in Late Adulthood

Late adulthood differs from the phases of life that come before it. Previous phases or stages focus on growth and gains, or at least on stability, in most areas. In late adulthood, we must also cope with decline and death. Theories of development in late adulthood deal with the ways in which we can approach our relationships with our changing bodies, our mental capacities, transitions in intimate relationships, our families, society at large, and voluntary and involuntary relocations.

ERIK ERIKSON'S PSYCHOSOCIAL THEORY AND OFFSHOOTS

Erikson labelled his eighth or final stage of life the stage of **ego integrity or despair.** Erikson believed that people who achieved positive outcomes to earlier life crises would be more likely to obtain ego integrity than despair in late adulthood. Each earlier stage unfolds into the next for the final stage in life's developmental journey.

Ego Integrity versus Despair

The basic challenge in the crisis of ego integrity versus despair is to maintain the belief that life is meaningful and worthwhile despite physical

ego integrity or despair
Erikson's eighth life crisis, defined by maintenance of the belief that life is meaningful and worthwhile despite physical decline and the inevitability of death versus depression and hopelessness.

decline and the inevitability of death. Ego integrity derives from wisdom, as well as from the acceptance of one's lifespan being limited and occurring at a certain point in the sweep of history. We spend most of our lives accumulating things and relationships. Erikson argued that adjustment in the later years requires the wisdom to let go.

Robert Peck's Developmental Tasks

Robert Peck (1968) amplified Erikson's stage of ego integrity versus despair by outlining three developmental tasks that people face in late adulthood:

- *Ego differentiation versus work-role preoccupation.* After retirement, people need to find new ways of defining their self-worth outside of their achievements in the workplace, perhaps in terms of roles in the community, activities with friends and family, or in spiritual undertakings.

- *Body transcendence versus body preoccupation.* At some point in late adulthood, people face inevitable physical decline, and it is in their best interests to come to terms with it by placing more value on cognitive activities and social relationships. Some people, of course, run into chronic illnesses or disabilities years earlier and must face the need to transcend body preoccupation prior to late adulthood.

- *Ego transcendence versus ego preoccupation.* Ego transcendence means preparing in some way to go beyond the physical limitations of one's own lifespan. As death comes nearer, some prepare to transcend death by helping secure the futures of their children or grandchildren. Others work more broadly to benefit their church, synagogue, or mosque, or to leave planet Earth in "better shape" than they found it.

Based on extensive interviews with small samples, Monika Ardelt (2008b) writes that ego transcendence grows out of self-reflection and willingness to learn from experience. She believes ego transcendence—which she also calls *the quieting of the ego*—is characterized by a concern for the well-being of humankind in general, not only for the self and close loved ones.

The Life Review

Daniel Levinson theorized that one aspect of the "midlife crisis" was that people realized they had more to look back on than forward to. In Chapter 16, we saw that that the existence of the midlife crisis is in dispute;

© SuperStock/Getty Images

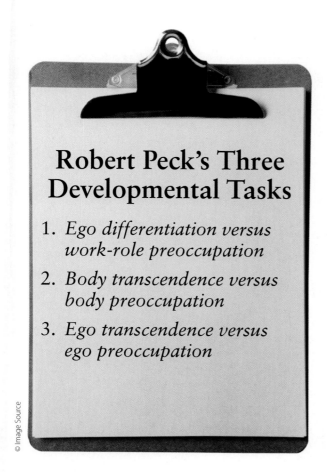

Robert Peck's Three Developmental Tasks

1. *Ego differentiation versus work-role preoccupation*

2. *Body transcendence versus body preoccupation*

3. *Ego transcendence versus ego preoccupation*

© Image Source

however, no one can argue that people in late adulthood have more to look back on than forward to. In fact, one of the complaints younger people sometimes level at older relatives is that they too often engage in reminiscence—that is, relating stories from the distant past. At times, some older people may seem to live in the past, possibly in denial of current decline and the approach of death.

Reminiscence was once considered a symptom of dementia, but contemporary researchers consider it to be a normal aspect of aging (Kunz, 2007). In working with healthy older volunteers as individuals and in groups, Robert Butler (2002) found that life reviews can be complex and nuanced, incoherent and self-contradictory, or even replete with irony, tragedy, and comedy. Butler believes that older people engage in life reviews to attempt to make life meaningful, to move on with new relationships as contemporaries pass on, and to help them find ego integrity and accept the end of life.

Butler (2002) also argues that health care professionals rely far too much on drugs to ease the discomforts of older adults. Pilot programs suggest that therapists may be able to relieve depression and other psychological problems in older adults by helping them reminisce about their lives (Bohlmeijer et al., 2005).

© Andrea Pistolesi/Getty Images

DISENGAGEMENT THEORY

According to **disengagement theory**, older people and society mutually withdraw from one another as older people approach death (Cumming & Henry, 1961). People in late adulthood focus more on their inner lives, preparing for the inevitable. Because of retirement, government or industry now supports them through pensions or charity rather than vice versa. Family members expect less from them.

How accurate is this theory? Probably not very. It seems that well-being among older adults is generally predicted by pursuing goals, rather than withdrawal (Frazier et al., 2007). Goals might need to be adjusted to be consistent with one's physical and cognitive abilities, but disengagement does not appear to be the path to adjustment. Moreover, relationships between children and parents change as the parents travel the years of late adulthood, but children—who are now middle-aged—often maintain close, supportive ties with aging parents, and despite some diminished capacities, the aging parents may become sources of wisdom.

ACTIVITY THEORY

Activity theory states, in contrast to disengagement theory, that older adults are better adjusted when they are more active and involved in physical and social activities. Activity theory places many of the barriers to such activity in social attitudes such as beliefs that older people should "take it easy," and in structural matters such

socioemotional selectivity theory the view that we place increasing emphasis on emotional experience as we age but limit our social contacts to regulate our emotions.

as forced retirement, rather than the desires of the individual.

Research shows that physical activity is associated with a lower mortality rate in late adulthood (Talbot et al., 2007). Leisure and informal social activities contribute to life satisfaction among retired people (Joung & Miller, 2007). An Israeli study found particular benefits for life satisfaction in activities involving the next generation, the visual and performing arts, and spiritual and religious matters (Nimrod, 2007). However, value was also found in independent activities in the home.

SOCIOEMOTIONAL SELECTIVITY THEORY

Socioemotional selectivity theory addresses the development of older adults' social networks. Laura Carstensen (Charles & Carstensen, 2007) hypothesizes that increasing emphasis is placed on emotional experience as we age. As we age, we are more focused on emotionally fulfilling experiences. Figure 18.1 shows the results of an experiment by Carstensen and her colleagues (1999), in which research participants aged 20 to 83 read two pages from a popular novel. The subjects then spent an hour on meaningless activities before being asked to recall everything they could about the pages they had read. Their recollections were classified as emotional or nonemotional. The proportion of emotional material recalled increased with the age group, showing a greater emotional response of the older subjects.

In order to regulate their emotional lives as they grow older, people limit their social contacts to a few individuals who are of major importance. By the time older adults reach their 80s, they are likely to have whittled their social networks down to a few family members and friends. This does not mean that older adults are antisocial. It means, rather, that they see themselves as having less time to waste and that they are more risk-averse; that is, they do not want to involve themselves in painful social interactions.

Carstensen and her colleagues (Ersner-Hershfield et al., 2008) also note that older people's perceived limitation on future time increases their appreciation for life, which brings about positive emotions. On the other hand, the same constraints on future time heighten awareness that such positive experiences will

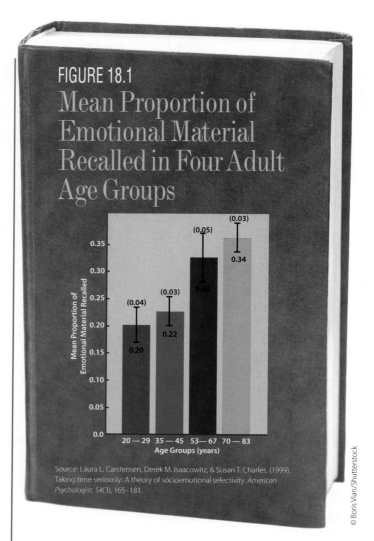

FIGURE 18.1

Mean Proportion of Emotional Material Recalled in Four Adult Age Groups

Source: Laura L. Carstensen, Derek M. Isaacowitz, & Susan T. Charles. (1999). Taking time seriously: A theory of socioemotional selectivity. *American Psychologist, 54*(3), 165–181.

© Boris Vian/Shutterstock

be drawing to a close, thus giving rise to mixed emotional states that have a poignant quality.

LO2 Psychological Development

Various psychological issues affect older adults, including self-esteem and the factors that contribute to self-esteem in late adulthood. Self-esteem, as we will see, is tied to both independence and dependence. Also, the psychological problems of depression and anxiety can affect us at any age, but they warrant special focus in late adulthood.

SELF-ESTEEM

To study the lifespan development of self-esteem, Richard Robins and his colleagues (2002) recruited more than 300,000 individuals to complete an extensive on-line questionnaire that provided demographic information (age, sex, ethnic background, and so forth) and measures of self-esteem. Two-thirds of the respondents were from the United States, and 57 percent were female. Results are shown in Figure 18.2. Generally, the self-esteem of males was higher than that of females. Self-esteem was highest in childhood (likely an inflated estimate) and dipped precipitously with entry into adolescence, a finding consistent with studies reported in Chapter 12. Self-esteem then rose gradually throughout middle adulthood and declined in late adulthood, with most of the decline occurring between the ages of 70 and 85. However, this is all relative. Even for people in their 80s, self-esteem levels were above the mid-point of the questionnaire.

Robins and Trzesniewski (2005) suggest a couple of possible reasons for the drop in self-esteem they found among people in their 80s. The first is that life changes such as retirement, loss of a spouse or partner, reduced social support, declining health, and downward movement in socioeconomic status account for the drop in self-esteem. The other hypothesis is more optimistic, namely that older people are wiser and more content.

FIGURE 18.2
Mean Level of Self-Esteem as a Function of Age, for Total Sample, Males, and Females

Self-esteem is highest in childhood, dips in adolescence, rises gradually throughout middle adulthood, and declines in late adulthood (Robins & Trzesniewski, 2005).

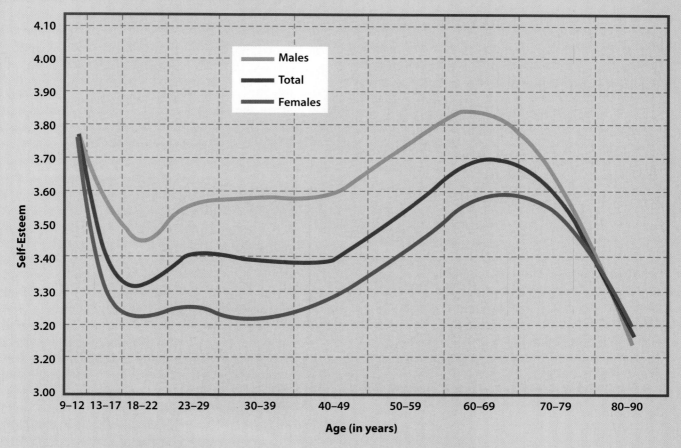

Source: Richard W. Robins, Kali H. Trzesniewski, Jessica L. Tracy, Samuel D. Gosling, & Jeff Potter. (2002). Global self-esteem across the lifespan. *Psychology and Aging, 17*(3), 423–434.

Erikson (1968) and other theorists suggest the possibility that ego transcendence occurs in this stage of life, such that people come to accept themselves as they are, "warts and all," and no longer need to inflate their self-esteem.

As the years wear on in late adulthood, people express progressively less "body esteem"—that is, less pride in the appearance and functioning of their bodies. There is also a gender difference, with older men expressing less body esteem than older women do (Kaminski & Hayslip, 2006). Men are more likely to accumulate fat around the middle, whereas women accumulate fat in the hips. Sexual arousal problems are usually more distressing for men. Older adults with poor body esteem tend to withdraw from sexual activity, which often frustrates their partners (Mohan & Bhugra, 2005).

INDEPENDENCE VERSUS DEPENDENCE

Being able to care for oneself appears to be a core condition of successful aging. Older people who are independent tend to think of themselves as leading a "normal life," whereas those who are dependent on others, even if they are only slightly dependent, tend to worry more about aging and encountering physical disabilities and stress (Sousa & Figueiredo, 2002). A study of 441 healthy people aged 65 to 95 found that dependence on others to carry out the activities of daily living increased with age (Perrig-Chiello et al., 2006). A particularly

sensitive independence issue is toileting, as found in a study of stroke victims (Clark & Rugg, 2005). Interviews found that independence in toileting is especially important in enabling older people to avoid a loss in their self-esteem.

PSYCHOLOGICAL PROBLEMS

Problems in coping with aging are associated with psychological problems, including depression and anxiety.

Volunteering and the Older Adult in Canada

B eing able to care for oneself is important but apparently caring for others is also a key factor in personal well-being. Volunteering helps charitable and nonprofit organizations deliver needed programs and services and also provides a social outlet and structure that allow older generations to feel valuable and involved in the community where they live.

In 2004, Canadians volunteered about 2 billion hours. Although both men and women volunteer a similar amount of time, according to Human Resources and Skills Development Canada (2010b), the average number of hours volunteered increases with age. Those in the youngest age group (aged 15–24) volunteered, on average, 63 hours per year, whereas those 65 years and older volunteered an average of 111 hours.

People in later life contribute significantly to the communities in which they live.

Depression

Depression affects some 10 percent of people aged 65 and older (Kvaal et al., 2008). Depression in older people can be either a continuation of depression from earlier periods of life, or a new development (Fiske, 2006). Depression can be related to the personality factor of neuroticism (Duberstein et al., 2008), possible structural changes in the brain (Ballmaier et al., 2008), and a possible genetic predisposition to imbalances of the neurotransmitter norepinephrine (Togsverd et al., 2008). Researchers are also investigating links between depression and physical illnesses such as Alzheimer's disease, heart disease, stroke, Parkinson's disease, and cancer. Depression is also associated with the loss of friends and loved ones, but depression is a mental disorder that goes beyond sadness or bereavement. The loss of companions and friends will cause profound sadness, but mentally healthy people bounce back within approximately a year and find new sources of pleasure and support. Inability to bounce back is a symptom of depression.

> **D2** When friends and loved ones die, sadness is a normal reaction; depression is not.
> It is normal to be sad when we suffer loss. Depression is a mental disorder.

Depression often goes undetected and untreated in older people (Cochran, 2005). Depression may be overlooked because its symptoms are masked by physical complaints such as low energy, loss of appetite, and insomnia. Health care providers also tend to focus more on older people's physical health than their mental health. Many older people are reluctant to admit to depression because when they were young, psychological problems carried a stigma. Depression is also associated with memory lapses and other cognitive impairment, such as difficulty concentrating (Ballmaier et al., 2008). Some cases of depression are wrongly attributed to the effects of aging or are misdiagnosed as dementia or Alzheimer's disease. Depression in older people can usually be treated successfully, using the same means that work in younger people, such as antidepressant drugs and cognitive-behavioural psychotherapy (Schuurmans et al., 2006).

Untreated depression can lead to suicide, which is not uncommon among older people. The highest rates of suicide are found among older men who have lost their wives or partners, lost their social networks, or who fear the consequences of physical illnesses and loss

of freedom (Johnson et al., 2008; Schmidtke et al., 2008). Though fewer older adults suffer from depression than younger adults, suicide is more frequent among older adults, especially Caucasian males (Eddleston et al., 2006).

Anxiety Disorders

generalized anxiety disorder general feelings of dread and foreboding.

phobic disorder irrational, exaggerated fear of an object or situation.

panic disorder recurrent experiencing of attacks of extreme anxiety in the absence of external stimuli that usually evoke anxiety.

agoraphobia fear of open, crowded places.

Anxiety disorders affect at least 3 percent of people aged 65 and older, but co-exist with depression in about 8–9 percent of older adults (Kvaal et al., 2008). Older women are approximately twice as likely to be affected than older men (Stanley & Beck, 2000). The most common anxiety disorders among older adults are **generalized anxiety disorder** and **phobic disorders**. **Panic disorder** is rare. Most cases of **agoraphobia** affecting older adults tend to be of recent origin and may involve the loss of social support systems due to the death of a spouse or close friends. Then again, some older individuals who are frail may have realistic fears of falling on the street and may be misdiagnosed as agoraphobic if they refuse to leave the house alone. Generalized

© The Copyright Group/SuperStock

anxiety disorder may arise from the perception that one lacks control over one's life.

Anxiety disorders can be harmful to older people's physical health. When older adults with anxiety disorders are subjected to stress, their levels of cortisol (a stress hormone) rise, and they take some time to subside (Chaudieu et al., 2008). Cortisol suppresses the functioning of the immune system, making people more vulnerable to illness.

Mild tranquilizers (such as Valium) are commonly used to quell anxiety in older adults. Psychological interventions, such as cognitive-behaviour therapy, have proven beneficial and do not carry the risk of side effects or potential dependence (Caudle et al., 2007).

LO3 Social Contexts of Aging

People do not age within a vacuum, but within social and communal contexts, including their living arrangements, facilities and services within their communities, religious affiliations, and family and social relationships.

COMMUNITIES AND HOUSING FOR OLDER PEOPLE

There's no place like home. According to surveys, older people consistently report that they prefer to remain in their homes as long as their physical and mental conditions allow them to do so (Sabia, 2008). Most likely to remain in their homes are older people who have plentiful financial resources, large amounts of equity in their homes, and strong ties to their communities. Conversely, most likely to need to consider residing elsewhere are older people with declining health conditions, changes in their family composition, and significant increases in property taxes and costs of utilities (Sabia, 2008). In many suburban communities, for example, property taxes have been skyrocketing to keep pace with the costs of public education. Older people no longer have children in the schools nor—more crucially—sufficient income to pay the increased taxes, and so they sell their homes.

Older people who live in urban areas are highly concerned about exposure to crime, particularly crimes of violence. Ironically, people aged 80 and older are significantly less likely to be victimized than people

Older adults may be reluctant to relocate to nursing homes because nursing homes signify the loss of independence.

in other age groups (Beaulieu et al., 2008). Social support helps older people cope with their concerns about victimization (Beaulieu et al., 2008). If they are victimized, social support helps them avoid some of the problems that characterize post-traumatic stress disorder, such as intrusive thoughts and nightmares (Sexton, 2008).

> **D3** Despite experiencing heightened anxiety about being exposed to crime, older people are less likely than younger peoplel to be victims of crime.
> It is still important to take steps so that older people feel safe in their homes.

When older people can no longer manage living on their own, they may consider utilizing the services of home care aides and visiting nurses to help them remain in the home. Others may move in with adult children. Still others may move into assisted living residences, in which they have their own apartments, community dining rooms, 24-hour nursing aid, and on-call physician care.

When older adults relocate to residences for the elderly, whether or not they have facilities for assisted living, existing social networks tend to be disrupted, and they are challenged to find new friends and create new networks (Dupuis-Blanchard, 2008). Such residences often have communal dining facilities and organized activities, including transportation to nearby shopping and entertainment. Residents typically take time in engaging with other people socially and are selective in forming new relationships (Dupuis-Blanchard, 2008).

Older adults may be reluctant to relocate to nursing homes because nursing homes signify the loss of independence. Surveys indicate that older adults are relatively more willing to enter nursing homes when they perceive themselves to be in poor health and when one or more close family members live near the nursing home (Jang et al., 2008).

There are frightening stories of what happens in nursing homes, and there are heartening stories. Occasionally, cases of elder abuse occur, in which staff act harshly toward residents, sometimes in response to cognitively impaired residents acting aggressively toward the staff (Rosen et al., 2008). However, a well-selected and well-trained staff can deal well with impaired residents, many of whom are disoriented and frightened (Kazui et al., 2008).

RELIGION

Religion involves beliefs and practices centred on claims about the nature of reality and moral behaviour, usually codified as rituals, religious laws, and prayers. Religions also usually encompass cultural traditions and myths, faith, spiritual experience, and communal as well as private worship. Nearly half the people in the world identify with one of the "Abrahamic" religions: Judaism, Christianity, or Islam. These religions, and many others, teach that there is a life after death, and that moral living will enable one to experience the benefits of the afterlife.

We discuss religion as part of the social context in which older adults (and others) dwell because religion often involves, in addition to worshiping, participating in the social, educational, and charitable activities of a congregation. Therefore, religion and religious activities provide older adults with a vast arena for social networking.

Religion also has a special allure as people approach the end of life. As people undergo physical decline, religion asks them to focus, instead, on moral conduct and spiritual "substance" such as the soul. People who experience physical suffering in this world are advised to look forward to relief in the next.

Therefore, it is not surprising that studies find that religious involvement in late adulthood is usually associated with less depression (Braam et al., 2008) and more life satisfaction (Korff, 2006). Frequent churchgoing has also been shown to be associated with fewer problems in the activities of daily living among older people (Park et al., 2008). Here, of course, we can assume that older people reap benefits from social networking as well as from church attendance per se.

Consider some of the benefits of frequent churchgoing found in studies of older African Americans. Older African Americans who attend services more than once a week live 13.7 years longer, on average, than their counterparts who *never* attend church (Marks et al., 2005). In-depth interviews with the churchgoers found several reasons for their relative longevity, including avoidance of negative coping methods such as aggressive behaviour and drinking alcohol, evading being victimized by violence, a sense of hopefulness, and social support.

> **D4** African Americans who attend church more than once a week live more than 13 years longer than African Americans who never attend.
> This is true on average.

FAMILY AND SOCIAL RELATIONSHIPS

Family and social relationships provide some of the most obvious—and most important—elements in the social lives of older adults.

Marriage

Approximately 38 percent of Canadian marriages end in divorce, but for many people, marriage lasts, like the traditional words, "until death do us part." Married people face very different life tasks as young adults, middle-aged adults, and older adults (Baltes, 1997), and the qualities in relationships that help them fulfill these tasks may also vary from stage to stage. Core issues in early adulthood are the selection of a partner, the development of a shared life, and emotional intimacy. Given these needs, similarity in personality may foster feelings of attachment and intimacy and provide a sense of equity in contributing to the relationship (Shiota & Levenson, 2007).

By middle adulthood, the partners' concerns appear to shift toward meeting shared and individual responsibilities (Moen et al., 2001). The partnership needs to handle tasks such as finances, household chores, and

© Shauna Longmuir

parenting. Conflicts may easily arise over a division of labour unless the couple can divide the tasks readily (Hatch & Bulcroft, 2004; Shiota & Levenson, 2007). At this stage, similarity in personality may work against the couple, with each partner competing to handle or avoid the same task. For example, as found by Shiota and Levenson (2007) in a study of the Big Five personality factors in middle-aged and older adults and marital satisfaction, *difference rather than similarity* in conscientiousness and extraversion predicts marital satisfaction in the decade of the 40s, whereas similarity does just as well in the decade of the 60s.

Shiota and Levenson (2007) suggest that conscientious people want to get things done, but by middle adulthood they have their own way of doing things. When two people in close quarters each want a task completed in their own way, conflicts are likely. The relationship is likely smoother if one partner is detail-oriented while the other is more easygoing. It is also useful if one partner is the workaholic and the other is the "people person" or social butterfly. They each then have their domains of expertise and are less likely to clash.

Are you a social butterfly? What's your area of expertise?

When couples reach their 60s, many midlife responsibilities such as childrearing and work have declined, allowing the partners to spend more time together. As a result, intimacy becomes a central issue once more. In this stage, couples report less disagreement over finances, household chores, and parenting (or grandparenting), but may have concerns about emotional expression and companionship (Hatch & Bulcroft, 2004). As compared with couples in midlife, older couples show more affectionate behaviour when they discuss conflicts, and, in general, they disagree with one another less (Carstensen et al., 1995). Similarity in personality is less of a contributor to conflict than it is in midlife, consistent with the finding that similarity in conscientiousness and extraversion is no longer strongly associated with marital dissatisfaction.

On the other hand, older couples may complain they spend too much time together, especially women whose husbands have just retired (Shiota & Levenson, 2007). If similarity in personality is a problem in this stage of life, perhaps it is because highly similar spouses become bored with one another (Amato & Previti, 2003).

In a study of 120 older Israeli couples, Kulik (2004) found that sharing power in the relationship and dividing household tasks contributed to satisfaction in the relationships. Past assistance from one's spouse in a time of need also affected the quality of the marriage and life satisfaction for both partners in the relationship.

Divorce, Cohabitation, and Remarriage

Having worked out most of the problems in their relationships and having learned to live with those that remain, older adults are less likely than younger adults to seek divorce. The ideal of lifelong marriage retains its strength (Amato et al., 2007). Because of fear of loss of assets, family disruption, and relocation, older adults do not undertake divorce lightly. When they do, it is often because they belong to an aberrant marriage, which is particularly puni-

© Dole/Shutterstock

© Michael Krasowitz/Getty Images

> **D5** Older married couples are focused on each other, and intimacy becomes a primary focus of their relationship. Because work and child rearing are removed from the relationship, many couples can now focus primarily on each other and intimacy.

tive or because one of the partners has taken up a relationship with an outsider (Bengtson et al., 2005).

Older people are increasingly likely to cohabit today, making up about 4 percent of the unmarried population (Brown et al., 2006). Nearly 90 percent of them had been married, and they are less likely than younger people to wish to remarry (Mahay & Lewin, 2007). Although they are less likely than younger cohabiters to marry their partners, older cohabiters report being in more intimate, stable relationships (King & Scott, 2005). Whereas younger cohabiters often see their lifestyle as a prelude to marriage, older cohabiters are more likely to see their relationship as an alternative lifestyle. They cite reasons for avoiding remarriage, such as concern about ramifications for pensions and disapproval by adult children, who may be concerned about their inheritance (King & Scott, 2005). Yet when older partners do remarry, as when they decide to cohabit, they usually make a strong commitment to one another and form a stable relationship (Kemp & Kemp, 2002).

Gay and Lesbian Relationships

Most of the research on gay men and lesbians has focused on adolescents and young adults (Grossman et al., 2003). However, a growing body of information about older gay males and lesbians has shown that, as with heterosexuals, gay men and lesbians in long-term partnerships tend to enjoy higher self-esteem, less depression, fewer suicidal urges, and less alcohol and drug abuse (D'Augelli et al., 2001). Gay men in long-term partnerships are also less likely to incur sexually transmitted infections (Wierzalis et al., 2006).

An interesting pattern has emerged, in which gay men or lesbians sometimes form long-term intimate relationships with straight people of the other sex (Muraco, 2006). These relationships do not involve sexual activity, but the couples consider themselves to be "family" and are confidants.

Widowhood

Losing one's spouse in late adulthood is certainly one of the most traumatic—if not the most traumatic—experiences of one's life. The couple may have been together for half a century or more, and most of the rough edges of the relationship will likely have been smoothed. Men in their 70s seem to have the most difficulty coping, especially when they have retired and had been expecting to spend more time with their wives

during the coming years (Lund & Caserta, 2001). In contrast, middle-aged male widowers are relatively more capable of dealing with their loss (Lund & Caserta, 2001).

Once widowed, men and women both need to engage in the activities of daily living by taking care of their personal hygiene, assuming the responsibilities that had been handled by their spouse, and remaining connected to the larger social community, whether that community mostly involves kin, friends, or people at their place of worship (Caserta & Lund, 2007). Yet the involuntary nature of being widowed is much more likely to lead to social isolation than marital separation (Glaser et al., 2006). The reasons for isolation are physical, cognitive, and emotional. Widowhood leads to a decline in physical and mental health, including increased mortality and deterioration in memory functioning (Aartsen et al., 2005). Loss of a spouse also heightens the risks of depression and suicide among older adults, and more so among men than women (Ajdacic-Gross et al., 2008).

Men who are widowed are more likely than women to remarry, or at least to form new relationships with the opposite sex. One reason is simply that women tend to outlive men, so more older women are available. Also, women, more so than men, make use of the web of kinship relations and close friendships available to them. Men may also be less adept than women at various aspects of self and household care, and therefore seek that help from a new partner.

Singles and Older People without Children

Single, never-married, and non-cohabiting adults without children make up a small minority of the adult Canadian population. According to data from the United States, Japan, Europe, Australia, and Israel, single older adults without children are just as likely as people who have had children—married or not—to be socially active and involved in volunteer work (Wenger et al., 2007). They also tend to maintain close relationships with siblings and long-time friends. Very old (mean age = 93) mothers and women who have not had children report equally positive levels of well-being (Hoppmann & Smith, 2007).

On the other hand, married older men without children appear to be especially dependent on their spouses (Wenger et al., 2007). Parents also seem to be more likely than people without children to

> The involuntary nature of being widowed is much more likely than marital separation to lead to social isolation.

have a social network that permits them to avoid nursing homes or other residential care when their physical health declines (Wenger et al., 2007).

Siblings

By and large, older sibling pairs tend to shore each other up with emotional support (Taylor et al., 2008). This is especially true among sisters (as women are more likely than men to talk about feelings) who are close in age and geographically near one another. After a spouse dies, the widowed person's siblings (and children) tend to ramp up their social contacts and emotional support (Guiaux et al., 2007). The widowed person's sibling, especially a sister, often takes the place of a spouse as a confidant (Wenger & Jerrome, 1999).

A lifespan developmental study of twin relationships found that, compared with other sibling relationships, twin relationships were more intense in terms of frequency of contacts, intimacy, conflict, and emotional support (Neyer, 2002). Frequency of contact and emotional closeness declined from early to middle adulthood, but increased again in late adulthood (mean age at time of study = 71.5 years).

Friendships

You can't pick your relatives—at least not your blood relatives—but you can choose your friends. Older people have often narrowed their friendships to friends who are most like them and enjoy the same kinds of activities. As a way of regulating their emotions, they tend to avoid people with whom they have had conflict over the years. Friends serve many functions in the lives of older adults, including providing social networks, acting as confidants, and offering emotional closeness and support, especially when a family member or another friend dies.

Adult Children and Grandchildren

In late adulthood, one's grandchildren typically reach adulthood. The generation of removal that grandparents had from their grandchildren in middle adulthood continues to provide a perspective on the behaviour and achievements of their grandchildren that they might not have had with their own children. Although grandparent–adult grandchild relationships have great variation, research suggests that both cohorts view each other in a positive light and see their ties as deep and meaningful (Kemp, 2005). They conceptualize their relationships as distinct family connections that involve unconditional love, emotional support, obligation, and respect. Grandparents and adult grandchildren often act as friends and confidants. As they experience life events together, their relationships can seem precious and capable of being cut short at any time.

LO4 Retirement

Once upon a time, when it was assumed that work was, by definition, mind-numbing, it was also assumed that people retired as soon as they could afford to do so, usually at age 65. According to the Statistics Canada data surveyed earlier in this text, at age 65, the average person has two decades of life to look forward to. That number has been increasing and is likely to continue to increase. Moreover, because of medical advances, 65-year-olds are more and more likely to be robust. Therefore, many people, especially professionals, are working beyond the age of 65.

RETIREMENT PLANNING

One of the keys of a successful retirement is retirement planning (Reitzes & Mutran, 2004). Retirement planning may include regularly putting money aside in plans such as RRSPs and various pension plans in the workplace; investing in stocks, bonds, or a second home; and, perhaps, investigating the kinds of recreational activities available in other geographic areas of interest. People who are thinking about moving or extended travelling will also be interested in learning about the weather (including effects on allergies) and crime statistics.

People who live alone may do their retirement planning as individuals. However, couples in relationships—

including married heterosexuals, cohabiting heterosexuals, and gay and lesbian couples—usually make their retirement plans collaboratively (Mock et al., 2006; Moen et al., 2006). By and large, the greater the satisfaction in the relationship, the more likely the partners are to make their retirement plans together (Mock & Cornelius, 2007). Phyllis Moen and her colleagues (2006) found that in married couples, husbands more often than wives tended to be in control of the plans, although control was also related to the partner's workload and income level. Men in same-sex couples are more likely than women in same-sex couples to do retirement planning, but women who do such planning are more likely to do it collaboratively.

ADJUSTMENT TO RETIREMENT

Let's begin this section with two questions: Is the key to retirement doing as little as possible? Does adjustment to retirement begin with retirement? The answer to both questions is no.

Research has consistently shown that older adults who are best adjusted to retirement are highly involved in a variety of activities, such as community activities and organizations (Kloep & Hendry, 2007). In the case of community activities, the experience and devotion of retirees renders their participation an important asset for the community, and the activities promote the adjustment of older adults into retirement.

> **D6** The key to successful retirement is knowing how to relax.
> This is true. However, "relaxing" does not necessarily mean doing as little as possible.

Pinquart and Schindler (2007) found in a retirement study that retirees could be divided into three groups, according to their satisfaction with retirement and various other factors. The group that was most satisfied with retirement maintained leisure and other non-work-related activities as sources of life satisfaction, or replaced work with more satisfying activities. They retired at a typical retirement age and had a wealth of resources to compensate for the loss of work: they were married, in good health, and of high socioeconomic status. The majority of a second group retired at a later age and tended to be female; the majority of the third group retired at

a younger age and tended to be male. The second and third groups were not as satisfied with retirement. They were in poorer health, less likely to be married, and lower in socioeconomic status than the first group. The third group had a spotty employment record. Another way to look at this data is to suggest that retirement per se didn't change these people's lives in major ways.

A 2-year longitudinal study found that the adjustment of older retirees was affected by their pre-retirement work identities (Reitzes & Mutran, 2006). For example, upscale professional workers continued to be well-adjusted and had high self-esteem. They weren't simply "retirees"; they were retired professors or retired doctors or retired lawyers and the like. On the other hand, hourly wage earners and other blue collar workers tended to have lower self-esteem and were more likely to think of themselves as simply "retirees."

Data from Dutch and American retirees found that the following factors impeded adjustment to retirement: a lengthy attachment to work, lack of control over the transition to retirement (e.g., forced retirement at age 65), worrying prior to retirement about what retirement would bring, and lack of self-confidence (Reitzes & Mutran, 2004; van Solinge & Henkens, 2005). Nevertheless, a wide range of feelings about giving up work surface just before retirement. Some people are relieved; others are worried—about finances, about surrendering their work roles, or both. Even so, most retirees report that their well-being has increased a year after they have retired, and that much of the stress they felt before retiring has diminished (Nuttman-Shwartz, 2007).

LEISURE ACTIVITIES AND RETIREMENT

Once people retire, they have the opportunity to fill most of their days with recreational and leisure activities. Research has shown that engaging in recreational and leisure activities is essential for retirees' physical and psychological health (Hansen et al., 2008). A recent Japanese study found that older men's failure to engage in leisure activities with neighbours, social organizations, and friends was strongly associated with feelings of depression (Arai et al., 2007). Similarly, older women appeared to need to engage in leisure activities with social groups, children, and grandchildren in order to avoid depression.

Joint leisure activities also contribute to the satisfaction of marital and other intimate partners and to family well-being (Ton & Hansen, 2001). They reduce stress (Melamed et al., 1995) and help retirees avert boredom (Sonnentag, 2003). Contributing to civic activities or volunteering at hospitals and the like also enhances retirees' self-esteem and fosters feelings of self-efficacy (Siegrist et al., 2004).

Kleiber and Kelly (1980) proposed a model of leisure development in which the final period includes retirement and aging. Leisure takes on special importance after retirement and may become central to the retiree's identity and self-acceptance. If the retiree's health remains robust, leisure activities tend to carry over from working days and may ease the transition to retirement. On the other hand, the physical aspects of aging and the death of companions can force changes in the choice of activities and diminish the level of satisfaction gotten from them.

A British study of adults with an average age of 72 reported that nearly three in four (73 percent) engaged in leisure activities (Ball et al., 2007); 23 percent engaged in "active leisure" (sailing, walking); 18 percent "passive leisure" (listening to music, watching television); 24 percent, social activities; 20 percent, hobbies; and 15 percent, other activities. The key motives for leisure activity were pleasure and relaxation.

Jo-Ida Hansen and her colleagues (Hansen et al., 2008) administered a questionnaire about leisure activities to 194 retirees, also with an average age of 72. They mathematically correlated the respondents' self-reported leisure activities and found that they fell into three clusters or factors, as shown in Table 18.1. Factor I included athletic, competitive, and outdoor activities. Factor II involved artistic, cultural, and self-expressive activities. Partying was the sole activity that defined Factor III. Partying isn't just for youngsters.

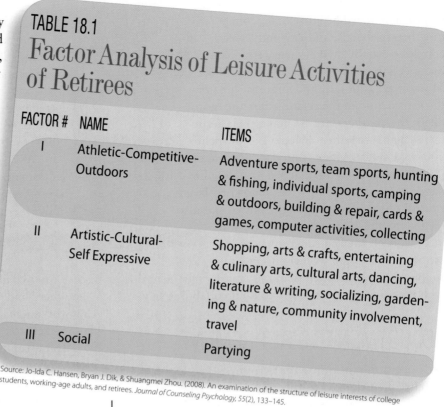

TABLE 18.1

Factor Analysis of Leisure Activities of Retirees

FACTOR #	NAME	ITEMS
I	Athletic-Competitive-Outdoors	Adventure sports, team sports, hunting & fishing, individual sports, camping & outdoors, building & repair, cards & games, computer activities, collecting
II	Artistic-Cultural-Self Expressive	Shopping, arts & crafts, entertaining & culinary arts, cultural arts, dancing, literature & writing, socializing, gardening & nature, community involvement, travel
III	Social	Partying

Source: Jo-Ida C. Hansen, Bryan J. Dik, & Shuangmei Zhou. (2008). An examination of the structure of leisure interests of college students, working-age adults, and retirees. *Journal of Counseling Psychology, 55*(2), 133–145.

(Volz, 2000). According to a poll of some 1,600 adults, 75 percent of older people say they feel younger than their years (Stewart & Armet, 2000).

There have been many definitions of successful aging. One journal article identified 28 studies with 29 definitions of the concept (Depp & Jeste, 2006). By and large, the definitions included physical activity, social contacts, self-rated good health, the absence of cognitive impairment and depression, nonsmoking, and the absence of disabilities and chronic diseases such

LO5 Successful Aging

despite the stereotype of "grumpy old men and women," a recent study found that most people in their 70s report being generally satisfied with their lives according to a recent study.

© Brand X Pictures/Jupiterimages

as arthritis and diabetes. According to these common criteria, 35 percent of the older people sampled in these studies could be said to be aging successfully. Other researchers define successful aging as good physical health, cognitive functioning, and social networking (Andrews et al., 2002).

SELECTIVE OPTIMIZATION WITH COMPENSATION

A different view of successful aging is being advanced by researchers who focus on the processes by which individuals attempt to provide better person–environment fits to the changing physical, cognitive, and social circumstances of late adulthood (e.g., Baltes & Baltes, 1990). From this point of view, often referred to as **selective optimization with compensation**, older people manage to maximize their gains while minimizing their losses.

Margaret Baltes and Laura Carstensen (2003) note that a good deal of the research carried on by developmentalists focuses on decline and loss as major themes associated with late adulthood, and therefore tends to direct attention away from the fact that many older people experience late adulthood as a satisfying and productive stage of life. The concept of selective optimization with compensation is related to socioemotional selectivity theory and is a key theme in adaptive aging (now also known as successful aging). In keeping with socioemotional selectivity theory, successful agers tend to seek emotional fulfillment by reshaping their lives to concentrate on what they find to be important and meaningful. Baltes and Carstensen (2003) define the process of selection as a narrowing of the array of goals and arenas to which older people direct their resources. In fact, Baltes and Carstensen go so far as to consider selective optimization with compensation to be the "cardinal principle of lifespan development" (2003).

Research about people aged 70 and older reveals that successful agers form emotional goals that bring them satisfaction (Löckenhoff & Carstensen, 2004). In applying the principle of selective optimization with compensation, successful agers may no longer compete in certain athletic or business activities (Bajor & Baltes, 2003; Freund & Baltes, 2002). Instead, they focus on matters that allow them to maintain a sense of control over their own lives.

Successful agers also tend to be optimistic. Such an outlook may be derived from transcendence of the ego, from spirituality, or sometimes from one's genetic heritage. (Yes, there is a genetic component to happiness [Lykken & Csikszentmihalyi, 2001].) However, retaining social contacts and building new ones also contributes to a positive outlook, as does continuing with one's athletic activities, where possible, and one's artistic and cultural activities.

The stereotype is that retirees look forward to late adulthood as a time when they can rest from life's challenges. But sitting back and allowing the world to pass by is a prescription for depression, not for living life to its fullest. In one experiment, Sandman and Crinella (1995) randomly assigned people (average age = 72) either to a foster grandparent program with neurologically impaired children or to a control group. They followed both groups for 10 years. The foster grandparents carried out physical challenges, such as walking a few miles each day, and also engaged in new kinds of social interactions. Those in the control group did not engage in these activities. After 10 years, the foster grandparents showed superior overall cognitive functioning, including memory functioning, and better sleep patterns, compared with those in the control group.

In the more normal course of events, many successful agers challenge themselves by taking up new pursuits such as painting, photography, or writing. Some travel to new destinations. Others return to school, taking special courses for older students, sitting in on regular college or university classes, or participating in seminars on special topics of interest. What will your retirement years look like?

selective optimization with compensation reshaping of one's life to concentrate on what one finds to be important and meaningful in the face of physical decline and possible cognitive impairment.

Though late adulthood is often viewed as a time to sit back and rest, it is an excellent opportunity to engage in new challenges and activities, such as going back to school.

© Journal-Courier/Clayton Stalter/The Image Works

Today, only a small minority

of Canadians—typically those who are in advanced old age or who are gravely or terminally ill—die in their own homes.

19

Life's Final Chapter

DID YOU KNOW?

D1 A person may stop breathing and have no heartbeat but still be alive.

D2 The five stages of dying provide insight into the dying process but they should not be used as a template.

D3 Even the medical community is divided on the hot-button issue of physician-assisted suicide.

D4 People with living wills can hope their wishes will be carried out if they become unable to speak for themselves.

D5 When helping someone cope with a death, don't expect to have all of the answers.

When we are young and our bodies are supple and strong, it may seem that we will live forever. All we have to do is eat right, exercise, and avoid smoking and driving recklessly. We may have but a dim awareness of our own mortality. We parcel thoughts about death and dying into a mental file cabinet to be opened later in life, along with items like retirement, Old Age Security, and varicose veins. But death can occur at any age—by accident, violence, or illness. We can also be affected deeply at any stage of life through the deaths of others.

The denial of death is deeply embedded in our culture. Many people prefer not to think about death or plan ahead for their eventual demise, as though thinking about it or planning for it might bring it about sooner. Elisabeth Kübler-Ross (1969) wrote that "We use euphemisms, we make the dead look as if they were asleep, we ship the children off to protect them from the anxiety and turmoil around the house if the [person] is fortunate enough to die at home, [and] we don't allow children to visit their dying parents in the hospitals." When we consider death and dying, a number of questions arise:

- How do we know when a person has died?
- Are there stages of dying?
- What is meant by the "right to die"? Do people have a right to die?
- What is a living will?
- Is there a proper way to mourn? Are there stages of grieving?

This chapter addresses these questions and many more.

Learning Outcomes

LO1 Define death and dying, and evaluate views on stages of dying

LO2 Identify settings in which people die, distinguishing between hospitals and hospices

LO3 Discuss various kinds of euthanasia and controversies about them

LO4 Discuss people's perspectives on death at various stages of development

LO5 Discuss coping with death, focusing on the funeral and possible stages of grieving

LO1 Understanding Death and Dying

death is commonly defined as the cessation of life. Many people think of death as a part of life, but death is the termination of life and not a part of life. **Dying**, though, is a part of life. It is the universal end-stage of life in which bodily processes decline, leading to death. Yet life holds significance and meaning even in the face of impending death.

CHARTING THE BOUNDARIES BETWEEN LIFE AND DEATH

How do we know when a person has died? Is it the stoppage of their hearts? Of their breathing? Of their brain activity?

Medical authorities generally use **brain death** as the basis for determining that a person has died (Appel, 2005). The most widely used criterion for establishing brain death is the absence of activity of the cerebral cortex, as shown by a flat EEG recording. When there is no activity in the cortex, consciousness—the sense of self and all psychological functioning—has ceased. The broader concept of **whole brain death** includes death of the brain stem, which is responsible for certain automatic functions, such as the reflex of breathing. Thus a person who is "brain dead" can continue to breathe. On the other hand, in some cases people have been kept "alive," even though they were whole-brain-dead, by life-support equipment that took over their breathing and circulation.

Death is also a legal matter. In Canada, a person is considered legally dead when there is an irreversible cessation of breathing and circulation or when an irreversible cessation of brain activity occurs, including activity in the brain stem, which controls breathing (Appel, 2005).

> **death** the irreversible cessation of vital life functions.
>
> **dying** the end-stage of life in which bodily processes decline, leading to death.
>
> **brain death** cessation of activity of the cerebral cortex.
>
> **whole brain death** cessation of activity of the cerebral cortex and brain stem.

ARE THERE STAGES OF DYING?

Our overview of the process of dying has been influenced by the work of Elisabeth Kübler-Ross (1969).

> **D1** A person may stop breathing and have no heartbeat but still be alive.
> People whose hearts and lungs have ceased functioning can often be revived using cardiopulmonary resuscitation (CPR).

From her observations of terminally ill patients, Kübler-Ross found some common responses to news of impending death. She hypothesized that dying patients pass through five stages of dying. She suggested that older people who suspect that death is near may undergo similar responses:

1. *Denial.* In this stage, people think, "It can't be me. The diagnosis must be wrong." Denial can be flat and absolute, or it can fluctuate so that one minute the patient accepts the medical verdict, and the next, the patient chats animatedly about future plans.

2. *Anger.* Denial usually gives way to anger and resentment toward the young and healthy, and, sometimes, toward the medical establishment: "It's unfair. Why me?" or "They didn't catch it in time."

3. *Bargaining.* People may bargain with God to postpone death, promising, for example, to do good deeds if they are given another six months, or another year.

4. *Depression.* With depression come feelings of grief, loss, and hopelessness—at the prospect of leaving loved ones and life itself.

5. *Final acceptance.* Ultimately, inner peace may come as a quiet acceptance of the inevitable. This "peace" is not contentment; it is nearly devoid of feeling. The patient may still fear death, but comes to accept it with a sense of peace and dignity.

Much current "death education" suggests that hospital staff and family members can help support dying people by understanding the stages they are going through, by not imposing their own expectations, and by helping patients to achieve final acceptance when they are ready to do so. But critics note that staff may be imposing Kübler-Ross's expectations.

Another critic, Joan Retsinas (1988), notes that Kübler-Ross's stages are limited to cases in which people receive a diagnosis of a terminal illness. As Retsinas points out, most people die because of their advanced years, not because of a specific terminal diagnosis. Thus, Kübler-Ross's approach may not be much use in helping us understand reactions under circumstances other than terminal illness.

Life and Death Issues: A Blurring Line

Because of medical advances, people are now able to live longer and delay death. But the ability to live longer does not necessarily walk hand in hand with quality of life. Such is the case for those suffering degenerative or incurable diseases.

In 1992, Sue Rodriquez, suffering from amyotrophic lateral sclerosis (ALS, or Lou Gehrig's disease), sought the right to secure physician-assisted suicide in Canada. She argued that her right to "life, liberty, and security of the person" included individual control over the circumstances and the timing of her inevitable death. The Supreme Court denied her argument, stating that to allow this act would erode the belief of the Canadian people in the sanctity of life. The state would not condone suicide and would protect the rights of the vulnerable.

Nancy B. was a young woman suffering from an incurable disease (Guillaine-Barré syndrome) and bedridden for life. She requested that doctors disconnect the respirator keeping her alive, arguing that no one can be made to undergo treatment without consent. The courts allowed this request in 1992, stating that the doctors would not be aiding the patient to commit suicide because Nancy B.'s death would result from the underlying disease.

The line becomes even blurrier when we consider legal advanced directives known as "living wills."

An *instruction directive* sets out what types of treatment a person does not want in the event that these decisions cannot be voiced at the appropriate time. A *proxy directive* allows an individual to select, in advance, someone who can make health care decisions on his or her behalf.

So the lines blur, and questions surround the laws of Canada. The lines are drawn between active and passive assistance and the timing of clearly thought-out decisions that are documented in advance of a medical crisis.

These issues are not new philosophical discussions and are likely to continue to be challenged in Canadian public and legal arenas (Tidermann & Valiquet, 2008).

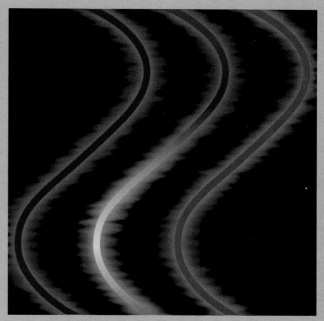

Edwin Shneidman (1977) acknowledges that dying people may have feelings such as those described by Kübler-Ross, but his research shows that individuals behave in dying more or less as they behaved during earlier periods when they experienced stress, failure, and threat. A gamut of emotional responses and psychological defences emerge, especially denial, and can be observed in every death. However, the process of dying does not necessarily follow any progression of stages, as suggested by Kübler-Ross. The key factors that appear to affect the adjustment of the dying individual include the type and extent of organic cerebral impairment, pain and weakness, the time or phase of the person's life, the person's philosophy of life (and death), and prior experiences with crises.

LO2 Where People Die

a hundred years ago, most people died in their homes, surrounded by family members. Today, only a small minority of Canadians—typically those who are in advanced old age or who are gravely or terminally ill—die in their own homes. When asked, most people respond that they would prefer to die at home with loved ones, yet 70 percent of Canadians die in a hospital (Canadian Hospice Palliative Care Association, 2010). Many people, of course, die suddenly wherever they happen to be at the time, either because of accidents, heart attacks, or other unanticipated events.

IN THE HOSPITAL

Hospitals are impersonal places to die. Hospitals function to treat diseases, not to help prepare patients and their families for death. Instead of dying in familiar surroundings, comforted by family and friends, patients in hospitals often face death alone, cut off from their usual supports. On the other hand, patients and their families may assume that going to the hospital gives them the best chance of averting death.

HOSPICE CARE

Depending on where they live in Canada, only 16–30 percent of Canadians who die will have access to or receive hospice services (Canadian Hospice Palliative Care Association, 2010). Because of our rapidly aging population, demand for these services will continue to rise. Increasing numbers of dying people and their families are turning to **hospices** to help make their final days as meaningful and

hospice an organization that treats dying patients by focusing on palliative care rather than curative treatment.

pain-free as possible. The word *hospice* derives from the Latin *hospitium*, meaning "hospitality," the same root of the words *hospital* and *hospitable*. The derivation is fitting, as hospices provide a homelike atmosphere to help terminally ill patients approach death with a maximum of dignity and a minimum of pain and discomfort. When necessary, hospices can provide care in inpatient settings, such as a hospitals, nursing facilities, or hospice centres, but most hospice care is provided in the patient's home.

Hospice workers typically work in teams that include physicians, nurses, social workers, mental health or pastoral counsellors, and home care aides who provide physical, medical, spiritual, and emotional support to the entire family, not just the patient. Bereavement specialists assist the family to prepare for the loss and help them through grieving after the death. In contrast to hospitals, hospices provide the patient and family with as much control over decision making as possible. The patient's wishes not to be resuscitated or not to be kept alive on life-support equipment are honoured. Patients are given ample amounts of pain-killing narcotics to alleviate suffering.

Hospices not only provide a more supportive environment for the patient and family, they are also less

The hospice considers the unit of care to be the entire family, not just the patient.

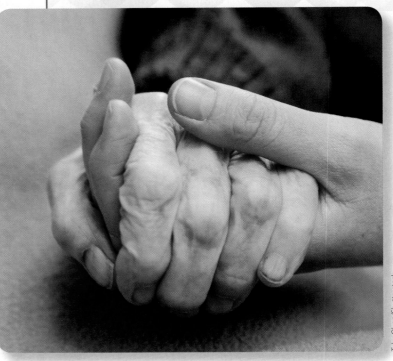

Tyler Olson/Shutterstock

Characteristics of Hospice Care

✓ offers palliative and not curative care

✓ treats the person, not the disease

✓ emphasizes quality, rather than length of life

✓ considers the entire family, not just the patient

✓ help and support is available around the clock

costly than hospital treatment, especially home-based care.

Hospice care has the following characteristics:

- Hospices offer **palliative care**, rather than curative treatment. They control pain and symptoms to enable the patient to live as fully and comfortably as possible.

- Hospices treat the person, not the disease. The hospice team addresses the medical, emotional, psychological, and spiritual needs of patients, family, and friends.

- Hospices emphasize quality, rather than length of life, neither hastening nor postponing death.

- The hospice considers the unit of care to be the entire family, not just the patient. Bereavement counselling is provided after the death.

- Help and support is available to the patient and family around the clock.

SUPPORTING A DYING PERSON

First of all, you must be there for the person who is dying. Put yourself at the same eye level and don't withhold touching. Be available to listen, to talk, and to share experiences. Give the person the opportunity to talk about death and to grieve, but don't be afraid to also talk about the ongoing lives of mutual acquaintances. People who are dying often need to focus on topics other than impending death, and some enjoy humorous stories. They may be comforted to hear about your life experiences—your concerns and worries as well as your joys, hopes, and dreams. But be aware of the person's emotional state on any given day. Some days

are better than others. Don't attempt to minimize the person's emotional pain or need to grieve by refusing to acknowledge it or changing the subject. Be sensitive to the person's feelings, and offer consolation and support. People with cognitive impairment may repeat certain thoughts many times; you can go with it or gently guide the conversation in another direction now and then. He or she may repeatedly ask whether certain tasks have been taken care of, and a simple yes may do each time.

palliative care treatment focused on the relief of pain and suffering rather than cure.

euthanasia the purposeful taking of life to relieve suffering.

active euthanasia the administration of a lethal treatment (usually a drug) to cause a quick and painless death.

voluntary active euthanasia the intentional administration of lethal drugs or other means of producing a painless death with the person's informed consent.

LO3 Euthanasia: Is There a Right to Die?

the word **euthanasia**, literally meaning "good death," is derived the Greek roots *eu* ("good") and *thanatos* ("death"). Also called "mercy killing," it refers to the purposeful taking of a person's life through gentle or painless means to relieve pain or suffering. There are several types of euthanasia.

ACTIVE EUTHANASIA: MERCY KILLING OR MURDER?

In **active euthanasia**, a lethal treatment (usually a drug) is administered to cause a quick and painless death. Usually a spouse or family member administers it.

Voluntary Active Euthanasia

When euthanasia is carried out with the patient's consent, it is called **voluntary active euthanasia** or assisted suicide. Voluntary active euthanasia remains illegal in Canada, although legal challenges to Canadian laws are working their way through the courts. It is not illegal in some other countries, such as The Netherlands, though protocols must be followed.

Dubbed "Dr. Death," Dr. Jack Kevorkian assisted in more than 100 suicides in the United States.

Physician-Assisted Suicide

involuntary active euthanasia the intentional administration of lethal drugs or other means of producing a painless death without the person's informed consent.

In some cases of active voluntary euthanasia, physicians in the United States have legally assisted patients who had terminal or incapacitating illnesses and wished to die. These physicians provided lethal doses of drugs and sometimes administered the drugs when the patients were too ill to administer the drugs themselves. The best-known cases of physician-assisted suicides involved Dr. Jack Kevorkian, a retired pathologist dubbed "Dr. Death," who claimed to have assisted in more than 100 patient suicides. Following an assisted suicide that was aired on *60 Minutes*, Kevorkian was convicted of second-degree homicide in Michigan and served 8 years of a 10- to 25-year prison sentence. Unlike Kevorkian, most physicians who assist in patient suicides do so without publicity because they fear legal prosecution and sanctions by medical societies, which remain ethically opposed to the practice.

Involuntary Active Euthanasia

Involuntary active euthanasia stands on shakier moral, ethical, and legal ground than voluntary euthanasia. In involuntary active euthanasia, one person causes the death of another person without that person's informed consent. Cases of involuntary euthanasia usually involve patients who are comatose or otherwise incapacitated, and whose guardians believe the patient would have wanted to die if he or she had retained the capacity to make the decision. Still, in the eyes of the law, it is considered homicide.

Terminal Sedation

Terminal sedation is an alternative to euthanasia. It is the practice of relieving distress in a terminally ill patient in the last hours or days of his or her life, usually by means of a continuous intravenous infusion of a sedative drug, such as a tranquilizer. Terminal sedation is not intended to hasten death, although whether it has that effect is often debated (Cellarius, 2008).

Attitudes Toward Physician-Assisted Suicide in the United States

In the United States, issue of physician-assisted suicide continues to be debated among physicians and in the lay community, even though the American Medical Association stands strongly against it. Physicians themselves are split on the question of whether this form of active euthanasia is ever justified. Physicians opposing assisted suicides often cite the belief that such actions go against thousands of years of the medical tradition of treating patients.

Euthanasia is legal in The Netherlands, but is not undertaken lightly. For example, when a patient or a patient's family requests euthanasia to relieve a terminally ill patient's suffering, about half of the physicians try to avoid the issue because their values oppose it or they find it emotionally burdensome (Georges et al., 2008). Many of these physicians suggest that patients' suffering can be alleviated without hastening their death (Rietjens et al., 2008). Physicians who are open to euthanasia explain that patients' suffering sometimes cannot be alleviated by using medicine.

Euthanasia, defined as performance of the death-inducing act by another person (such as a physician), is illegal everywhere in the United States. However, in 1997, Oregon enacted a Death with Dignity Act, which enables terminally ill patients to ask physicians to prescribe lethal doses of medication. The medication is then administered by patients themselves (Facts about the Death with Dignity Act, 2007). Euthanasia and physician-assisted suicide are illegal throughout Canada and are subject to legal prosecution.

A nationally representative survey of American physicians found that 69 percent object to physician-assisted suicide, 18 percent object to terminal sedation, but only 5 percent object to withdrawal of artificial life support (Curlin et al., 2008). Religion played a role in physicians' attitudes, as is illustrated in Figure 19.1: 84 percent of highly religious physicians objected to physician-assisted suicide, as compared with 55 percent of physicians who were not particularly religious; 25 percent of highly religious physicians objected to terminal sedation, as compared with 12 percent of less religious physicians. Even

FIGURE 19.1

Percent of Physicians Who Object to Physician-Assisted Suicide or Terminal Sedation, According to Religiosity

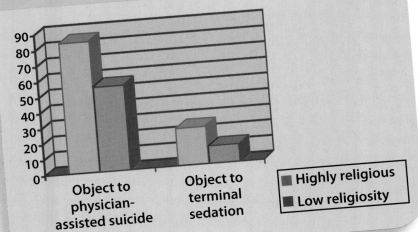

Object to physician-assisted suicide	Object to terminal sedation
■ Highly religious
■ Low religiosity

the medical community remains divided on this philosophical life and death issue.

A survey of 988 terminally ill patients found that 60.2 percent said they supported euthanasia or physician-assisted suicide in general, but only 10.6 percent reported seriously considering it for themselves (Emanuel et al., 2000). Patients who were aged 65 and older and who felt more appreciated by others were less likely to consider euthanasia and suicide. Not surprisingly, depression, pain, and substantial caregiving needs all contributed to consideration of suicide.

> **D3** Even the medical community is divided on the hot-button issue of physician-assisted suicide.
> Eighty-four percent of highly religious physicians object to physician-assisted suicide.

PASSIVE EUTHANASIA

Passive euthanasia involves actions that hasten death by means of withholding potentially life-saving treatments, such as failing to resuscitate a terminally ill patient who stops breathing, or withdrawing medicine, food, or life-support equipment (such as respirators) from a comatose patient. The legal status of passive euthanasia varies with the circumstances. One form of passive euthanasia that is legal throughout the United States and Canada

is the withholding or withdrawing of life-sustaining equipment or techniques in terminally ill people who have clearly specified their wish not to be kept alive by aggressive or heroic treatment. The declaration of these wishes may be in the form of a living will, which specifies the conditions under which the person desires to have life-sustaining treatment withdrawn or withheld.

> **passive euthanasia** the withholding or withdrawal of life-sustaining treatment to hasten death.

THE LIVING WILL

Pierre suffers a tragic accident that leaves him in an irreversible coma and dependent on artificial life support—a respirator to maintain his breathing and feeding tubes to supply his body with nutrients. Would Pierre want his life to be maintained by whatever means were at the disposal of modern medicine, or would he prefer doctors to withdraw life support, allowing him to die naturally?

Keisha has been in pain day after day. She suffers from a terminal disease and her heart suddenly stops due to cardiac arrest. Would she want the doctors to resuscitate her by whatever means were necessary in order to prolong her life for another few days or weeks? Who is to decide when it is time for her to die—Keisha or the doctors managing her care?

DO NOT RESUSCITATE

© Creatas Images/Jupiterimages

living will a document prepared when a person is well, directing medical care providers to terminate life-sustaining treatment in the event of incapacitation or inability to speak.

A **living will** often contains a health care directive, which is a legal document that people draft when they are well that directs health care workers not to use aggressive medical procedures or life-support equipment to prolong vegetative functioning in the event they became permanently incapacitated and unable to communicate their wishes. Terminally ill patients can insist, for example, that "Do Not Resuscitate" orders be included in their charts, directing doctors not to use CPR in the event they suffer cardiac arrest.

The withdrawal of life-sustaining treatment is a form of passive euthanasia. Unlike active euthanasia, death is not induced by administering a drug or assisting in the patient's suicide.

Living wills must be drafted in accordance with provincial or territorial laws (see Figure 19.2). The living will takes effect only when people are unable to speak for themselves. For this reason, living wills usually identify a proxy, such as the next of kin, who can make decisions in the event that the signer cannot communicate.

Still, many living wills are ignored. Some are disregarded by proxies, often because the proxies don't judge the patient's wishes accurately or because they can't bear the emotional burden of "pulling the plug." Physicians, too, may not comply with advance directives, perhaps because the directives weren't available when needed or weren't clear. Physicians are more likely to follow specific advance directives (e.g., "Do not resuscitate") than general guidelines.

> **D4** People with living wills can hope their wishes will be carried out if they become unable to speak for themselves.
> A living will may not be carried out for many reasons. Specific advance directives have a better chance of being carried out than general guidelines.

LO4 Lifespan Perspectives on Death

Psychologists have found interesting developments in people's understanding of and reactions to death. Children, for example, seem to follow something of a Piagetan route in their cognitive

Organ Donation: The Gift of Life

One winter day, I lost a dear student and friend to a sudden brain aneurism. Greg died as he had lived, with dignity and with charity. Upon his death, seven people received a gift of life because Greg had previously arranged to donate his strong and healthy organs. One donor can save up to eight lives.

Donating your organs for transplant surgery after your death keeps a part of you alive while helping someone else in need. Living donors—usually family members—can be used for some transplants. For most procedures, such as those involving liver, heart, lung, and corneal transplants, organs must be taken from donors shortly after death. Only organs that were healthy at the time of death and remain intact after death are suitable for transplantation. The donor must also be free of infectious diseases.

In Canada in 2008:

4,330 people were on the waiting list for an organ transplant

215 people died while waiting for an organ transplant

2,083 transplants took place

1,541 of those transplants were made possible because of deceased donors (Organ Donation and Transplant Association of Canada, 2009).

Organ donations save lives but regardless of your decision, make your wishes known to your family to relieve them of the burden of this decision in the time of their grief.

Organ donation. The gift of life.

© Peter Scholey/Alamy

development although reversibility is reversed—in other words, they begin by thinking of death as reversible and by about the time they enter school, they see it as irreversible (Poltorak & Glazer, 2006). People who truly understand what death is appear to take some reasonable steps to avert it, even "risk-taking" adolescents (Mills et al., 2008).

FIGURE 19.2
Health Care Directive

Health Care Directive

Please type or print legibly

Manitoba 🐃

This is the Health Care Directive of:

Name_____

Address_____ City_____

Province_____ Postal Code_____ Telephone ( )_____

Part 1 - Designation of Health Care Proxy

You may name one or more persons who will have the power to make decisions about your medical treatment when you lack the ability to make those decisions yourself. If you do not wish to name a proxy, you may skip this part.

I hereby designate the following persons(s) as my Health, Care Proxy:

Proxy 1

Name_____

Address_____

_____

City_____

Province_____ Postal Code _____

Telephone ( )_____

Proxy 2

Name_____

Address_____

_____

City_____

Province_____ Postal Code _____

Telephone ( )_____

(*Check ✓ one choice **only**.*) *For an explanation of "consecutively" and "jointly" please see the reverse side of this form.*

**If I have named more than one proxy,
I wish them to act:**
❏ **consecutively**   OR   ❏ **jointly**

My Health Care Proxy may make medical decisions on my behalf when I lack the capacity to do so for myself
(*check ✓ on choice **only***):

❏ With **no restrictions**

❏ With **restrictions as follows:**

_____

_____

_____

_____

_____

Part 2 - Treatment Instructions

In this part, you may set out your instructions concerning medical treatment that you do or do not wish to receive and the circumstances in which you do or do not wish to receive that treatment. REMEMBER—your instructions can only be carried out if they are set out clearly and precisely. If you do not wish to provide any treatment instructions, you may skip this part.

_____

_____

_____

_____

_____

Part 3 - Signature and Date

You must sign and date this Health Care Directive, No witness is required.

Signature_____

Date_____

If you are unable to sign yourself, a substitute may sign on your behalf. The substitute must sign in your presence and in the presence of a witness. The proxy or the proxy's spouse cannot be the substitute or witness.

Name of substitute:_____

Address_____

_____

Signature_____

Date_____

Name of witness:_____

Address_____

_____

Signature_____

Date_____

Permission to reprint this document is provided by the Queen's Printer for Manitoba.

MG-3598 (Rev. 05/04)

Source: Province of Manitoba.

Without taking sides in what we might think of as a religious debate, we can note that many people at most ages assume, or are encouraged to assume, a form of spiritual reversibility in their thinking about death (Balk et al., 2007; Lattanzi-Licht, 2007). Religious traditions inform them that the soul of the person who has passed on will dwell in heaven or in Paradise forever, or that it will be reincarnated on Earth.

CHILDREN

Younger children lack the cognitive ability to understand the permanent nature of death (Slaughter & Griffiths, 2007). Preschoolers may think that death is reversible or temporary, a belief reinforced by cartoon characters that die and come back to life (Poltorak & Glazer, 2006). Nevertheless, their thinking becomes increasingly realistic as they progress through the ages of 4, 5, and 6 (Li-qi & Fu-xi, 2006). Children's understanding of death appears to increase as they learn about the biology of the human body and how various organs contribute to the processes of life (Slaughter & Griffiths, 2007).

Loss is difficult to bear for children, especially when a parent dies (Greidanus, 2007). Death of a loved one strikes at the core of a child's sense of security and well-being. Older children may feel guilty because of the mistaken belief that they brought about the death by once wishing for the person to die. The loss of security may lead to anger, which may be directed toward surviving family or expressed in aggressive play. They may show regressive or infantile behaviours, such as talking "baby talk" or becoming more demanding of food or attention. Some children may persist for several weeks in maintaining the belief that the deceased person is still alive. Though child psychiatrists believe this response is normal, prolonged denial can be a harbinger of more severe problems (Crenshaw, 2007).

When children learn about death, it is normal for them to fear it. But children in various cultures are also taught that it is possible to survive death, either through reincarnation, as in some Eastern religions, or as in the transcendence of the soul, as in Christianity. Children in North America are sometimes told "Your father is now in heaven and you will see him there again. Meanwhile, he is watching over you." The concept of surviving death renders death less permanent and less frightening to many children—and adults (Lattanzi-Licht, 2007).

Encourage children to express all of their emotions honestly and openly. Watch for danger signs including:

✓ loss of sleep or appetite
✓ depressed mood for several weeks
✓ the development of excessive fears (e.g, the fear of being alone)
✓ refusal to go to school
✓ withdrawal from friends

How can you help a child cope with grief? First, don't force a frightened child to attend a funeral. Another kind of service or observance may be more appropriate, such as lighting a candle, saying a prayer, or visiting a gravesite at another time. Many helping professionals suggest avoiding the use of euphemisms, such as "Aunt Jane is sleeping comfortably now," which deny the reality that children face. They also suggest responding to children's questions and worries as honestly and openly as possible, but in a way that reassures them that you are available to help them cope with their loss. But here of course, we again run into the issue of what the reality of death is; the person who believes in an afterlife, the agnostic, and the atheist all have different versions.

Professionals generally advise letting children know they can express their feelings openly and freely without fear of criticism. Spend time with them, providing emotional support and reassurance. Also, be aware of danger signals—such as loss of sleep or appetite, depressed mood for several weeks, excessive fears (such as fear of being alone), withdrawal from friends, a sharp decline in school performance or refusal to attend school—that indicate the child may need professional help.

Many have debated whether the best approach is to encourage children to let go of their ties to the person who has died, reach some sort of "closure," and "move on" with their own lives (Greidanus, 2007). Research suggests that children can maintain their bond with the deceased person even while they continue to grieve, invest in other relationships and new activities, and learn to live under the changed circumstances (Sasaki, 2007).

ADOLESCENTS

Adolescents are "in between" in many ways. They know full well that when life functions come to an end, they cannot be restored, yet they are not beyond constructing magical, spiritual, or pseudoscientific theories as to how some form of life or thought might survive (Balk et al., 2007). Adolescents also speak of death in terms of concepts such as light, darkness, transition, and nothingness (Oltjenbruns & Balk, 2007).

As compared with young children, adolescents also become increasingly exposed to death among older family members such as grandparents, and even among fellow adolescents, some of whom have died of illness or from accidents, suicide, or foul play. Adolescents are more likely than young children to attend funerals, including funerals with open caskets. These experiences challenge the adolescent sense of immortality that is associated with the personal fable (see Chapter 11; Noppe & Noppe, 2004). Even though adolescents come to recognize that the concept of death applies to them, they continue to engage in riskier behaviour than adults do. On the other hand, those adolescents who perceive certain behaviours to be highly risky are less likely to engage in them (Mills et al., 2008).

> Even though adolescents come to recognize that the concept of death applies to them, they continue to engage in riskier behaviour than adults do.

ADULTS

Most young adults in developed nations need not spend much time thinking about the possibility of their death. The leading causes of death in early adulthood are accidents and suicide. In middle adulthood, heart disease and cancer have become the leading causes of death. People are advised to become proactive in their screenings for cardiovascular problems and for several kinds of cancer. Some cancers have sex differences, but educated women and men are aware that age is a risk factor in both heart disease and cancer, and they are likely aware of middle-aged people who died "untimely" deaths from one or the other.

Heart disease and cancer remain the leading causes of death in late adulthood. As people move into advanced old age, many should no longer be driving due to loss of sensory acuity and slowed reaction time. Older adults are also more prone to falls, Alzheimer's disease, and other dementias. Some older people come to fear disability and discomfort nearly as much as death.

Theorists of social and emotional development in late adulthood suggest that ego transcendence, or concern for the well-being of humankind in general, enables some people to begin to face death with an inner calm (see Chapter 18; Ardelt, 2008b). On the other hand, continuing with physical, leisure, and informal social activities are all associated with greater life satisfaction among older, retired people (Joung & Miller, 2007; Talbot et al., 2007). There is no single formula for coping with physical decline and the approach of death.

LO5 Coping with Death

for most of us, coping with death is at best complicated, and at worst painful and disorienting. Losing a loved one is generally considered to be the most stressful life change we can endure.

WHAT TO DO WHEN SOMEONE DIES

If you are present at someone's death, call the family doctor, the police, or 911. A doctor is needed to complete the death certificate and to indicate the cause of death. If the cause of death cannot be readily determined, a coroner or medical examiner may become involved to determine the cause of death. Once the body has been examined by the doctor and the death certificate has been completed, a funeral director may be contacted to remove the body from the home or the hospital and

to make arrangements for burial, cremation, or placement in a mausoleum. If death occurs unexpectedly or foul play is involved or suspected, an autopsy may be performed to determine the cause and circumstances of death. Sometimes an autopsy is performed, with the family's consent, if the knowledge gained from the procedure could benefit medical science.

Funeral Arrangements

Funerals respond to death in an organized way that is tied to religious custom and cultural tradition. Funerals offer family and community a ritual for grieving publicly and saying farewell to the person who died. Funerals grant a closure that can help observers begin to move on with their lives.

Family members of the deceased decide how simple or elaborate they prefer the funeral to be, whether they want embalming, and whether the deceased's body should be buried or cremated. Sometimes these matters are spelled out by religious or family custom. Sometimes family members fight over them.

After their homes, automobiles, and children's educations, funerals may be a Canadian family's next largest expense. Consider these guidelines to arrange a funeral that meets your needs and remains in your budget. Have a good friend, who will be able to make decisions, go with you to arrange the funeral. Funerals can be expensive. Make decisions based on reason and good sense, not on emotions or guilt. If a funeral home has not yet been selected, shop around; you can and should ask about services and costs. Be aware that

Funerals can be expensive. Make decisions based on reason and good sense, not on emotions or guilt.

some cemeteries offer the plot for free but then make their profit from charging exorbitant maintenance fees, opening and closing fees, costs for monuments, and other fees. Caskets are often the major burial expense and can range from $500 to $50,000 or more! Recognize that the type of casket you choose makes no difference to the deceased person, and tell the funeral director to show you models that fall within the price range that you are comfortable paying.

Legal and Financial Matters

Many legal and financial matters require attention following a death. Family members will need to deal with issues concerning estates, inheritance, outstanding debts, insurance, and amounts owed for funeral expenses. Focusing on these matters can be difficult during a time of grief. Family members should seek legal counsel to protect their own financial interests and for guidance on handling the deceased person's affairs. An attorney is

Different cultures often have very different approaches to funerary traditions. Compare these musicians, for example, who are part of a cremation ceremony in Bali, Indonesia, to the mourners in black on page 359.

© Sylvain Grandadam/Getty Images

© Mark Weiss/Getty Images

usually needed to settle the estate, especially if it is size-able or if complex matters arise in sorting through the deceased person's affairs.

GRIEF AND BEREAVEMENT

The death of a close friend or family member can be a traumatic experience. It typically leads to a state of **bereavement**, an emotional state of longing and depriva-tion characterized by feelings of **grief** and a deep sense of loss. **Mourning** is synonymous with grief over the death of a person, but also describes culturally prescribed ways of displaying grief. Different cultures prescribe different periods of mourning and different rituals for expressing grief. The tradition of wearing unadorned black clothing for mourning dates at least to the Roman Empire. In rural parts of Mexico, Italy, and Greece, widows are often still expected to wear black for the remainder of their lives. In England and the United States, the wearing of black is on the decline, replaced by wearing joyous colours as the life of the deceased person is celebrated.

Coping with loss requires time and the ability to come to terms with the loss and move ahead with one's life. Having a supportive social network is important in navigating this major transition.

Grieving

There is no one right way to grieve, nor a fixed period of time for which grief should last. In some cases, especially for parents who have lost a child, grief never ends, though people do learn over time to live with the loss. People grieve in different ways. Some grieve more pub-licly, while others reveal their feelings only in private. You may not always know when someone is grieving.

The Widow Who Wasn't a Bride

What do you call a widow who isn't a widow? Part of the problem, according to Shatz (2006), is that we have no word for a woman who has cohabited with a man who has died, even if she has been with him for decades. In her doc-toral dissertation, Shatz describes the experiences of nine women who experienced "disenfranchised grief" following the loss of their partners. The bereaved women felt marginalized by society and cut off from their partners' biological children. Not only had these men taken care of their children in their wills, to the exclusion of their cohabitants, but they had arranged to be buried next to their late spouses at some time in the past but had never changed that arrangement. Apparently these men did not want to be thought of badly by their biological children.

Grief usually involves a combination of emotions, especially depression, loneliness, feelings of emptiness, disbelief and numbness, apprehension about the future ("What will I do now?"), guilt ("I could have done something."), even anger ("They could have handled this better."). Grief may also be punctuated by relief that the deceased person is no longer suffering intense pain and by a heightened awareness of one's own mortality. Grief may also compromise the immune system, leaving the person more vulnerable to disease. Researchers also find that the death of a loved puts one at greater risk of committing suicide, especially during the first weeks following the loss (Ajdacic-Gross et al., 2008).

ARE THERE STAGES OF GRIEVING?

John Bowlby (1961), the attachment theorist, was the first to propose

bereavement the state of deprivation brought about by the death of a family member or close friend.

grief emotional suffering resulting from a death.

mourning customary methods of expressing grief.

a stage theory of grief for coping with bereavement. It included four stages: shock-numbness, yearning-searching, disorganization-despair, and reorganization. Elisabeth Kübler-Ross (1969) adapted Bowlby's stage theory to describe her five-stage reaction of terminally ill patients to knowledge of their own impending death: denial-isolation, anger, bargaining, depression, and acceptance. The stage theory of grief has become generally accepted when applied to various kinds of losses, including children's responses to parental separation, adults' responses to marital separation (Gray et al., 1991), and hospital staffs' responses to the death of an inpatient. Medical education currently relies heavily on the Kübler-Ross (Kübler-Ross & Kessler, 2005) model of grief (Maciejewski et al., 2007).

Jacobs (1993) modified the stage theory of grief to include the following stages: numbness-disbelief, separation distress (yearning-anger-anxiety), depression-mourning, and recovery. Jacobs' stage theory, like the theories that preceded it, is largely based on anecdotes and case studies.

To test Jacobs' theory, Paul Maciejewski and his colleagues (2007) administered five items measuring disbelief, yearning, anger, depression, and acceptance of death to 233 bereaved individuals from 1 to 24 months following their losses. The results are shown visually in Figure 19.3. Several findings are clear. Disbelief was highest just after the loss and gradually waned over the course of two years. Acceptance of the loss shows the opposite course, being nonexistent at the outset, growing gradually, and peaking two years later. Yearning, anger, and depression rise suddenly in the predicted order and then each wanes gradually.

Maciejewski and his colleagues (2007) believe they found support for the theory, and to some degree they did. The predicted feelings were present and arose in the predicted order. However, others reviewing the same data noted that the investigators tested for only these five emotions; the emotions they neglected could have been more powerful (Bonanno & Boerner, 2007; Silver & Wortman, 2007). Also, given their overlap, one wonders just how stage-like these emotions are. But no

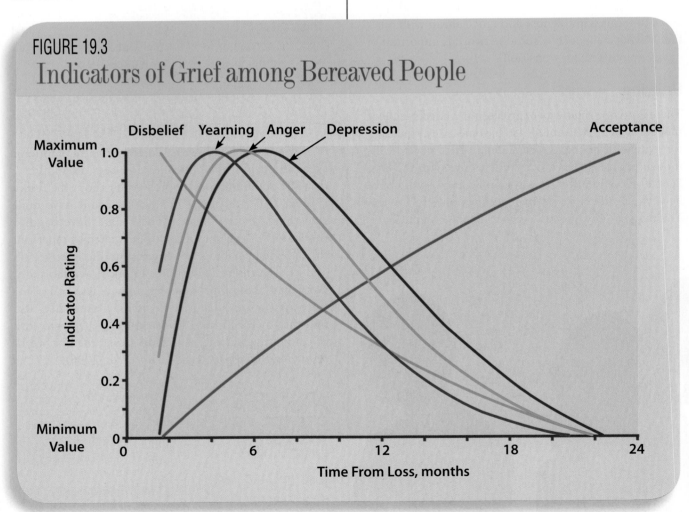

FIGURE 19.3
Indicators of Grief among Bereaved People

Source: Maciejewski, P. K., Zhang, B., Block, S. D., & Prigerson, H. G. (2007). An empirical examination of the stage theory of grief. *Journal of the American Medical Association, 297*, 716–723.

observer can deny that, in this sample, all five emotions are present and occur in a predictable order.

ADVICE FOR COPING

What can you do if you are faced with the death of someone who is close to you? Consider some combination of the following: First, take care of yourself. When you are grieving, you can become so absorbed with your loss that you fail to attend to your own personal needs. Some people do not eat or bathe. They may feel guilty doing things for themselves and avoid any pleasurable experiences. Remember, you can grieve without withdrawing from life.

Allow yourself to feel your loss. Some people prefer to bottle up their feelings, but covering up feelings or trying to erase them with tranquilizers may prolong grieving. When you feel the time is right, turning to a trusted friend or a counsellor may help you to get in touch with your feelings.

Don't reject offers of help from friends and family. If they don't know how they can help, tell them what you need.

Don't command yourself to get over it. Give yourself time. There is no fixed timetable for grief to run its course. Don't let other people push you into moving on "to the next stage" unless you are prepared to do so.

Join a bereavement support group. You will find that you are not alone in your suffering. Sharing experiences can help you to cope better and to work through your grief in a supportive environment.

Advice for Helping a Bereaved Friend or Relative Cope

When someone you know has lost a loved one, you will naturally want to reach out to them. Yet you may not know how to help, or you may fear that you'll say the wrong thing. *Don't worry about what to say.* Just spending time with the bereaved person can help. Nor should you expect to have all the answers; sometimes there are no answers. Sometimes what matters is simply being a good listener. Don't be afraid to talk about the deceased person. Take your cue from the bereaved person. Not talking about the departed person brings down a curtain of silence that can make it more difficult for the bereaved person to work through feelings of grief. By the same token, don't force the bereaved to talk about their feelings. Keep in touch regularly, but don't assume that because you don't get a call, the person doesn't want to talk. The bereaved person may be too depressed or lack the energy to reach out. Offer to help with chores such as shopping, running errands, and babysitting.

Don't minimize the loss, and avoid clichés like, "You're young, you can have more children," or "It was for the best."

D5 When helping someone cope with a death, don't expect to have all of the answers.
Sometimes there are no right answers. Simply listening and being supportive is a wise course of action.

Bereaved persons can find comfort knowing that they are not alone in their suffering; sharing experiences can help bereaved persons to cope and process what they are feeling.

LOOK TO FIND THE LESSON

Death is a universal developmental event that we all encounter. Some of us fear the shadow that it casts, while others embrace the lessons that come from the loss of our loved ones. Fittingly, those that have taken us by the hand in life—in death—often serve as our most insightful teachers.

Randy Pausch is an excellent example of this. A famous lecture series asks the question, "if you knew you were going to die, and you had one last lecture, what would you say to your students?" Randy brought an interesting perspective to this question as he was dying of pancreatic cancer when he delivered his famous last lecture at Carnegie Mellon University on September 18, 2007. He chose not to speak about death, but about the lessons to be learned in life.

Randy spoke about moments that change our lives forever. He explored the notion that lessons are learned through disappointment, and that we need to realize that brick walls aren't designed to keep us out but to show us how badly we want to achieve something. Experience is what we get when we don't get what we want. Randy talked about embracing the negative feedback that you receive in life because when people stop saying anything to you anymore, they have given up on you. Finally, Randy challenged us to determine if we are "Tiggers" or "Eeyores". Do we search for the fun in every situation, or do we choose to wallow in self misery (The Last Lecture, 2008)?

> Death holds the gift of wisdom.

As our loved ones pass—and as we ultimately take our final journey into death—we must look to find the lesson. Death holds the gift of wisdom. Death teaches us that, through memories, loved ones live on forever.

Visit **icanhdev.com** to find the resources you need today!

Located at the back of the textbook are rip-out Chapter Review cards. Make sure you also go online to check out other tools that HDEV offers to help you successfully pass your course.

- Flashcards
- Glossary
- Interactive Practice

- Build a Summary
- Games
- Interactive Quizzing

AAIDD. (2007). American Association on Intellectual and Developmental Disabilities. Available at www.aamr.org. Accessed May 24, 2007.

Aalsma, M. C., Lapsley, D. K., & Flannery, D. J. (2006). Personal fables, narcissism, and adolescent adjustment. *Psychology in the Schools, 43*(4), 481–491.

Aartsen, M. J., et al. (2005). Does widowhood affect memory performance of older persons? *Psychological Medicine, 35*(2), 217–226.

Abdelaziz, Y. E., Harb, A. H., & Hisham, N. (2001). *Textbook of Clinical Pediatrics.* Philadelphia: Lippincott Williams & Wilkins.

Aber, J. L., Bishop-Josef, S. J., Jones, S. M., McLearn, K. T., & Phillips, D. A. (Eds.). (2007). *Child development and social policy: Knowledge for action. APA Decade of Behavior volumes.* Washington, DC: American Psychological Association.

Abravanel, E., & DeYong, N. G. (1991). Does object modeling elicit imitative-like gestures from young infants? *Journal of Experimental Child Psychology, 52,* 22–40.

Acevedo, A., & Loewenstein, D. A. (2007). Nonpharmacological cognitive interventions in aging and dementia. *Journal of Geriatric Psychiatry and Neurology, 20*(4), 239–249.

Active Healthy Kids Canada. (2010). *Healthy habits start earlier than you think: The Active Healthy Kids Canada report card on physical activity for children and youth.* Toronto: Author. Retrieved from http://www.activehealthykids.ca/ecms.ashx/2010 ActiveHealthyKidsCanadaReportCardlongform.pdf

Adams, G. R., Berzonsky, M. D., & Keating, L. (2006). Psychosocial resources in first-year university students: The role of identity processes and social relationships. *Journal of Youth and Adolescence, 35*(1), 81–91.

Adams, R. G., & Ueno, K. (2006). Middle-aged and older adult men's friendships. In V. H. Bedford & B. Formaniak Turner (Eds.), *Men in relationships: A new look from a life course perspective* (pp. 103–124). New York: Springer Publishing Co.

Adler, J. M., Kissel, E. C., & McAdams, D. P. (2006). Emerging from the CAVE: Attributional style and the narrative study of identity in midlife adults. *Cognitive Therapy and Research, 30*(1), 39–51.

Adler-Baeder, F. (2006). What do we know about the physical abuse of stepchildren? A review of the literature. *Journal of Divorce & Remarriage, 44*(3–4), 67–81.

Adolph, K. E., & Berger, S. E. (2005). Physical and motor development. In M. H. Bornstein & M. E. Lamb (Eds.), *Developmental science: An advanced textbook* (5th ed.) (pp. 223–281). Hillsdale, NJ: Erlbaum.

Aguiar, A., & Baillargeon, R. (2002). Developments in young infants' reasoning about occluded objects. *Cognitive Psychology, 45*(2), 267–336.

Ainsworth, M. D. S. (1989). Attachments beyond infancy. *American Psychologist, 44,* 709–716.

Ainsworth, M. D. S., Blehar, M. C., Waters, E., & Wall, S. (1978). *Patterns of attachment: A psychological study of the Strange Situation.* Hillsdale, NJ: Erlbaum.

Ainsworth, M. D. S., & Bowlby, J. (1991). An ethological approach to personality development. *American Psychologist, 46*(4), 333–341.

Ajdacic-Gross, V., et al. (2008). Suicide after bereavement. *Psychological Medicine, 38*(5), 673–676.

Akman, Y. (2007). Identity status of Turkish university students in relation to their evaluation of family problems. *Social Behavior and Personality, 35*(1), 79–88.

Alberta SBS Prevention Campaign. (2010). Parents and caregivers of young children. Retrieved from http://www.shakenbaby.ca

Alexander, G. M. (2003). An evolutionary perspective of sex-typed toy preferences: Pink, blue, and the brain. *Archives of Sexual Behavior, 32*(1), 7–14.

Alfirevic, Z., Sundberg, K., & Brigham, S. (2003). Amniocentesis and chorionic villus sampling for prenatal diagnosis. *Cochrane Database of Systematic Reviews,* DOI: 10.1002/14651858.CD003252.

Allain, P., Kauffmann, M., Dubas, F., Berrut, G., & Le Gall, D. (2007). Executive functioning and normal aging: A study of arithmetic word-problem-solving. *Psychologie & NeuroPsychiatrie Du Vieillissement, 5*(4), 315–325.

Alloway, T. P., Gathercole, S. E., Willis, C., & Adams, A. (2004). A structural analysis of working memory and related cognitive skills in young children. *Journal of Experimental Child Psychology, 87*(2), 85–106.

Almeida, D. M., & Horn, M. C. (2004). Is daily life more stressful during middle adulthood? In O. G. Brim, C. D. Ryff, & R. C. Kessler (Eds.), *How healthy are we?: A national study of well-being at midlife* (pp. 425–451). *The John D. and Catherine T. MacArthur foundation series on mental health and development. Studies on successful midlife development.* Chicago: University of Chicago Press.

Almey, M. (2007). Women in Canada:Work chapter updates, 2006. (Statistics Canada, Catalogue no. 89F0133XIE). Retrieved from http://www.statcan.gc.ca/pub/89f0133x/89f0133x2006000-eng.htm

Alzheimer Society. (2010). *Rising tide: The impact of dementia on Canadian society.* Retrieved from http://www.alzheimer.ca/english/rising_tide/rising_tide_summary.htm

Amato, P. R. (2006). Marital discord, divorce, and children's well-being: Results from a 20-year longitudinal study of two generations. In A. Clarke-Stewart & J. Dunn (Eds.), *Families count: Effects on child and adolescent development. The Jacobs Foundation series on adolescence* (pp. 179–202). New York: Cambridge University Press.

Amato, P. R., Booth, A., Johnson, D. R., & Rogers, S. J. (2007). *Alone together: How marriage in America is changing.* Cambridge, MA: Harvard University Press.

Amato, P. R., & Previti, D. (2003). People's reasons for divorcing. *Journal of Family Issues, 24,* 602–626.

Ambert, A.-M. (2005). *Cohabitation and marriage: How are they related.* Contemporary Family Trends series. Ottawa: The Vanier Institute of the Family. Retrieved from http://www.vifamily.ca/sites/default/files/cohabitation_and_marriage.pdf

Ambert, A.-M. (2009). *Divorce: Facts, causes & consequences* (3rd. ed.). Ottawa: Vanier Institute of the Family. Retrieved from http://www.vifamily.ca/node/80

American Academy of Pediatrics. (2007, February 7). *A woman's guide to breastfeeding.* Available at http://www.aap.org/family/brstguid.htm.

American Association of University Women. (1992). *How schools shortchange women: The AAUW report.* Washington, DC: AAUW Educational Foundation.

American Cancer Society. (2007). www.cancer.org.

American Fertility Association. (2007). Available at http://www.theafa.org/fertility/malefactor/index.html. Accessed February 6, 2007.

American Heart Association. (2007). Overweight in children. Available at http://www.americanheart.org/presenter.jhtml?identifier=4670. Accessed May 18, 2007.

American Psychological Association (1998, March 16). Sexual harassment: Myths and realities. APA Public Information Home Page; www.apa.org.

American Psychological Association. (2007a). Stress in America: *Mind/body health: For a healthy mind and body, talk to a psychologist.* Washington, DC: American Psychological Association.

American Psychological Association. (2007b). Stress tip sheet. American Psychological Association Help Center Media Room, Page A, Item 42.

Ammaniti, M., Speranza, A. M., & Fedele, S. (2005). Attachment in infancy and in early and late childhood: A longitudinal study. In K. A Kerns & R. A. Richardson (Eds.), *Attachment in middle childhood* (pp. 115–136). New York: Guilford.

Amodio, D. M., & Showers, C. J. (2005). "Similarity breeds liking" revisited: The moderating role of commitment. *Journal of Social and Personal Relationships, 22*(6), 817–836.

Anderman, E. M., et al. (2001). Learning to value mathematics and reading: Relations to mastery and performance-oriented instructional practices. *Contemporary Educational Psychology, 26*(1), 76–95.

Andersen, M. L., & Taylor, H. H. (2009). *Sociology: The essentials* (5th ed.). Belmont, CA: Wadsworth.

Anderson, C. A., Gentile, D. A., & Buckley, K. E. (2007). *Violent video game effects on children and adolescents: Theory, research, and public policy.* New York: Oxford University Press.

Andreou, G., Krommydas, G., Gourgoulianis, K. I., Karapetsas, A., & Molyvdas, P. A. (2002). Handedness, asthma, and allergic disorders: Is there an association? *Psychology, Health, and Medicine, 7*(1), 53–60.

Andrews, G., Clark, M., & Luszcz, M. (2002). Successful aging in the Australian longitudinal study of aging: Applying the MacArthur

Model cross-nationally. *Journal of Social Issues, 58,* 749–765.

Angier, N. (2007, June 12). Sleek, fast, and focused: The cells that make dad dad. *New York Times,* pp. F1, F6.

Annett, M. (1999). Left-handedness as a function of sex, maternal versus paternal inheritance, and report bias. *Behavior Genetics, 29*(2), 103–114.

Annett, M., & Moran, P. (2006). Schizotypy is increased in mixed-handers, especially right-handed writers who use the left hand for primary actions. *Schizophrenia Research, 81*(2–3), 239–246.

Anthis, K. S., Dunkel, C. S., & Anderson, B. (2004). Gender and identity status differences in late adolescents' possible selves. *Journal of Adolescence, 27*(2), 147–152.

Antonucci, T. C., & Birditt, K. S. (2004). Lack of close relationships and well-being across the life span. Paper presented to the American Psychological Association.

Anxiety BC. (2010). Separation anxiety. Retrieved from http://www.anxietybc.com/parent/separation.php

Appel, J. M. (2005). Defining death. *Journal of Medical Ethics, 31*(11), 641–642.

Aquilino, W. S. (2005). Impact of family structure on parental attitudes toward the economic support of adult children over the transition to adulthood. *Journal of Family Issues, 26*(2), 143–167.

Arai, A., et al. (2007). Association between lifestyle activity and depressed mood among home-dwelling older people. *Aging & Mental Health, 11*(5), 547–555.

Archer, J. (2006). Testosterone and human aggression: An evaluation of the challenge hypothesis. *Neuroscience & Biobehavioral Reviews, 30*(3), 319–345.

Archibald, L. M. D., & Gathercole, S. E. (2006). Short-term memory and working memory in specific language impairment. In T. P. Alloway & S. E. Gathercole (Eds.), *Working memory and neurodevelopmental disorders* (pp. 139–160). New York: Psychology Press.

Ardelt, M. (2008a). Wisdom, religiosity, purpose in life, and death attitudes of aging adults. In A. Tomer, G. T. Eliason, T. Grafton, & P. T. P. Wong (Eds.), *Existential and spiritual issues in death attitudes* (pp. 139–158). Mahwah, NJ: Erlbaum.

Ardelt, M. (2008b). Self-development through selflessness: The paradoxical process of growing wiser. In H. A. Wayment, & J. J. Bauer (Eds.), *Transcending self-interest: Psychological explorations of the quiet ego. Decade of behavior* (pp. 221–233). Washington, DC: American Psychological Association.

Arija, V., et al. (2006). Nutritional status and performance in test of verbal and non-verbal intelligence in 6-year-old children. *Intelligence, 34*(2), 141–149.

Arnett, J. J. (2000). Emerging adulthood. *American Psychologist, 55*(5), 469–480.

Arnett, J. J. (2007). Socialization in emerging adulthood: From the family to the wider world, from socialization to self-socialization. In J. E. Grusec & P. D. Hastings (Eds.), *Handbook of socialization: Theory and research* (pp. 208–231). New York: Guilford.

Arnon, S., et al. (2006). Live music is beneficial to preterm infants in the neonatal intensive care unit environment. *Birth: Issues in Perinatal Care, 33*(2), 131–136.

Arranz, L., Guayerbas, N., & De la Fuente, M. (2007). Impairment of several immune functions in anxious women. *Journal of Psychosomatic Research, 62*(1), 1–8.

Aschermann, E., Gülzow, I., & Wendt, D. (2004). Differences in the comprehension of passive voice in German- and English-speaking children. *Swiss Journal of Psychology, 63*(4), 235–245.

Ash, D. (2004). Reflective scientific sense-making dialogue in two languages: The science in the dialogue and the dialogue in the science. *Science Education, 88*(6), 855–884.

Aslin, R. N., & Schlaggar, B. L. (2006). Is myelination the precipitating neural event for language development in infants and toddlers? *Neurology, 66*(3), 304–305.

Aspy, C. B., et al. (2007). Parental communication and youth sexual behaviour. *Journal of Adolescence, 30*(3), 449–466.

Association of American Colleges & Universities. (2007). Case Study Facilitation Guidelines: February Fifth Forum: Cultivating Community. Available at http://www.diversityweb.org/diversity_innovations/institutional_leadership/institutional_statements_plans/knox.cfm. Accessed November 1, 2007.

Atkinson, G., & Davenne, D. (2007). Relationships between sleep, physical activity and human health. *Physiology & Behavior, 90*(2–3), 229–235.

Auger, R. W., Blackhurst, A. E., & Wahl, K. H. (2005). The development of elementary-aged children's career aspirations and expectations. *Professional School Counseling, 8*(4), 322–329.

August, D., Carlo, M., Dressler, C., & Snow, C. (2005). The critical role of vocabulary development for English language learners. *Learning Disabilities Research & Practice, 20*(1), 50–57.

Autism Society of Canada. (2009). What are autism spectrum disorders? Retrieved from http://www.autismsocietycanada.ca/understanding_autism/what_are_asds/index_e.htm

Axford, J., Heron, C., Ross, F., & Victor, C. R. (2008). Management of knee osteoarthritis in primary care: Pain and depression are the major obstacles. *Journal of Psychosomatic Research, 64*(5), 461–467.

Bäckström T., et al. (2003). The role of hormones and hormonal treatments in premenstrual syndrome. *CNS Drugs, 17*(5), 325–342.

Bagley, C., & D'Augelli, A. R. (2000). Suicidal behaviour in gay, lesbian, and bisexual youth. *British Medical Journal, 320,* 1617–1618.

Bahrick, H. P., Bahrick, P. O., & Wittlinger, R. P. (1975). Fifty years of memory for names and faces: A cross-sectional approach. *Journal of Experimental Psychology: General, 104*(1), 54–75.

Bahrick, H. P., Hall, L. K., & Da Costa, L.A. (2008). Fifty years of memory of college grades: Accuracy and distortions. *Emotion, 8*(1), 13–22.

Bailey, J. M., & Pillard, R. C. (1991). A genetic study of male sexual orientation. *Archives of General Psychiatry, 48,* 1089–1096.

Bajor, J. K., & Baltes, P. B. (2003). The relationship between selection optimization with compensation, conscientiousness, motivation, and performance. *Journal of Vocational Behavior, 63*(3), 347–367.

Bakalar, N. (2005, November 22). Premature births increase along with C–sections. *New York Times,* p. F8.

Bakker, D. J. (2006). Treatment of developmental dyslexia: A review. *Pediatric Rehabilitation, 9*(1), 3–13.

Balk, D., Wogrin, C., Thornton, G., & Meagher, D. (2007). *Handbook of thanatology.* New York: Routledge/Taylor & Francis Group.

Ball, V., Corr, S., Knight, J., & Lowis, M. J. (2007). An investigation into the leisure occupations of older adults. *British Journal of Occupational Therapy, 70*(9), 393–400.

Ballmaier, M., et al. (2008). Hippocampal morphology and distinguishing late-onset from early-onset elderly depression. *American Journal of Psychiatry, 165*(2), 229–237.

Baltes, P. B. (1997). On the incomplete architecture of human ontogeny: Selection, optimization, and compensation as foundation of developmental theory. *American Psychologist, 52,* 366–380.

Baltes, P. B., & Baltes, M. M. (1990). Psychological perspectives on successful aging: The model of selective optimization with compensation. In P. B. Baltes & M. M. Baltes (Eds.), *Successful aging: Perspectives from the behavioral sciences* (pp. 1–34). New York: Cambridge University Press.

Baltes, M., & Carstensen, L. L. (2003). The process of successful aging: Selection, optimization and compensation. In U. M. Staudinger, & U. Lindenberger (Eds.), *Understanding human development: Dialogues with lifespan psychology* (pp. 81–104). Dordrecht, Netherlands: Kluwer Academic Publishers.

Bancroft, J., Carnes, L., & Janssen, E. (2005a). Unprotected anal intercourse in HIV-positive and HIV-negative gay men: The relevance of sexual arousability, mood, sensation seeking, and erectile problems. *Archives of Sexual Behavior, 34,* 299–305.

Bancroft, J, Carnes, L. & Janssen, E., Goodrich, D., & Long, J. S. (2005b). Erectile and ejaculatory problems in gay and heterosexual men. *Archives of Sexual Behavior, 34,* 285–297.

Bandura, A. (1986). *Social foundations of thought and action: A social-cognitive theory.* Englewood Cliffs, NJ: Prentice Hall.

Bandura, A. (2006a). Going global with social cognitive theory: From prospect to paydirt. In S. I. Donaldson, D. E. Berger, & K. Pezdek (Eds.), *Applied psychology: New frontiers and rewarding careers* (pp. 53–79). Hillsdale, NJ: Lawrence Erlbaum Associates Publishers.

Bandura, A. (2006b). Toward a psychology of human agency. *Perspectives on Psychological Science, 1*(2), 164–180.

Bandura, A., Barbaranelli, C., Vittorio Caprara, G., & Pastorelli, C. (2001). Self-efficacy beliefs as shapers of children's aspirations and career trajectories. *Child Development, 72*(1), 187–206.

Bandura, A., Ross, S. A., & Ross, D. (1963). Imitation of film-mediated aggressive models. *Journal of Abnormal and Social Psychology, 66,* 3–11.

Barnard, C. J., Collins, S. A., Daisley, J. N., & Behnke, J. M. (2005). Maze performance and immunity costs in mice. *Behaviour, 142*(2), 241–263.

Barnett, J. E., & Dunning, C. (2003). Clinical perspectives on elderly sexuality. *Archives of Sexual Behavior, 32*(3), 295–296.

Barr, R. G., Paterson, J. A., MacMartin, L. M., Lehtonen, L., & Young, S. N. (2005). Prolonged and unsoothable crying bouts in infants with and without colic. *Journal of Developmental & Behavioral Pediatrics, 26*(1), 14–23.

Barr, R., Rovee-Collier, C., & Campanella, J. (2005). Retrieval protracts deferred imitation by 6-month-olds. *Infancy, 7*(3), 263–283.

Barry, C. M., & Wentzel, K. R. (2006). Friend influence on prosocial behavior: The role of motivational factors and friendship characteristics. *Developmental Psychology, 42*(1), 153–163.

Basic Behavioral Science Task Force of the National Advisory Mental Health Council. (1996). Basic behavioral science research for mental health: Sociocultural and environmental practices. *American Psychologist, 51,* 722–731.

Batsche, G. M., & Porter, L. J. (2006). Bullying. In G. G. Bear & K. M. Minke (Eds.), *Children's needs III: Development, prevention, and intervention* (pp. 135–148). Washington, DC: National Association of School Psychologists.

Bauer, K. W., Yang, Y. W., & Austin, S. B. (2004). "How can we stay healthy when you're throwing all of this in front of us?" Findings from focus groups and interviews in middle schools on environmental influences on nutrition and physical activity. *Health Education and Behavior, 31*(1), 33–46.

Bauman, M. L., Anderson, G., Perry, E., & Ray, M. (2006). Neuroanatomical and neurochemical studies of the autistic brain: Current thought and future directions. In S. O. Moldin & J. L. R. Rubenstein (Eds.), *Understanding autism: From basic neuroscience to treatment* (pp. 303–322). Boca Raton, FL: CRC Press.

Baumrind, D. (1989). Rearing competent children. In W. Damon (Ed.), *Child development today and tomorrow.* San Francisco: Jossey-Bass.

Baumrind, D. (1991a). The influence of parenting style on adolescent competence and substance use. *Journal of Early Adolescence, 11,* 56–95.

Baumrind, D. (1991b). Parenting styles and adolescent development. In J. Brooks-Gunn, R. Lerner, & A. C. Petersen (Eds.), *Encyclopedia of adolescence.* New York: Garland.

Baumrind, D. (2005). Taking a stand in a morally pluralistic society: Constructive obedience and responsible dissent in moral/character education. In L. Nucci (Ed.), *Conflict, contradiction, and contrarian elements in moral development and education* (pp. 21–50). Mahwah, NJ: Erlbaum.

BC Partners for Mental Health and Addictions Information. (2004). *Wellness module 2: Stress and well-being.* Retrieved from http://www.heretohelp.bc.ca/skills/module2

Bearce, K. H., & Rovee-Collier, C. (2006). Repeated priming increases memory accessibility in infants. *Journal of Experimental Child Psychology, 93*(4), 357–376.

Beaulieu, M-D., et al. (2008). When is knowledge ripe for primary care? *Evaluation & the Health Professions, 31*(1), 22–42.

Beck, E., Burnet, K. L., & Vosper, J. (2006). Birth-order effects on facets of extraversion. *Personality and Individual Differences, 40*(5), 953–959.

Beck, M. (1992, December 7). The new middle age. *Newsweek.* 50–56.

Becker, D. (2006). Therapy for the middle-aged: The relevance of existential issues. *American Journal of Psychotherapy, 60*(1), 87–99.

Bedford, V. H., & Avioli, P. S. (2006). "Shooting the bull": Cohort comparisons of fraternal intimacy in midlife and old age. In V. H. Bedford & B. Formaniak Turner (Eds.),

Men in relationships: A new look from a life course perspective (pp. 81–101). New York: Springer Publishing Co.

Beidel, D. C., & Turner, S. M. (2007). Clinical presentation of social anxiety disorder in children and adolescents. In D. C. Beidel & S. M. Turner (Eds.), *Shy children, phobic adults: Nature and treatment of social anxiety disorders* (2nd ed.) (pp. 47–80). Washington, DC: American Psychological Association.

Beilei, L., Lei, L., Qi, D., & von Hofsten, C. (2002). The development of fine motor skills and their relations to children's academic achievement. *Acta Psychologica Sinica, 34*(5), 494–499.

Belmonte, M. K., & Carper, R. A. (2006). Monozygotic twins with Asperger syndrome: Differences in behaviour reflect variations in brain structure and function. *Brain and Cognition, 61*(1), 110–121.

Belsky, J. (2006a). Determinants and consequences of infant–parent attachment. In L. Balter & C. S. Tamis-LeMonda (Eds.), *Child psychology: A handbook of contemporary issues* (2nd ed.) (pp. 53–77). New York: Psychology Press.

Belsky, J. (2006b). Early child care and early child development: Major findings of the NICHD Study of Early Child Care. *European Journal of Developmental Psychology, 3*(1), 95–110.

Belsky, J., et al. (2007). Are there long-term effects of early child care? *Child Development, 78*(2), 681–701.

Bem, S. L. (1993). *The lenses of gender.* New Haven, CT: Yale University Press.

Bender, H. L., et al. (2007). Use of harsh physical discipline and developmental outcomes in adolescence. *Development and Psychopathology, 19*(1) 227–242.

Bengtson, V. L., et al. (Eds.). (2005). *Sourcebook of family theory and research.* Thousand Oaks, CA: Sage Publications, Inc.

Bennett, S. E., & Assefi, N. P. (2005). School-based teenage pregnancy prevention programs: A systematic review of randomized controlled trials. *Journal of Adolescent Health, 36*(1), 72–81.

Berg, C. J., Chang, J., Callaghan, W. M., & Whitehead, S. J. (2003). Pregnancy-related mortality in the United States, 1991–1997. *Obstetrics and Gynecology, 101,* 289–296.

Bergeman, C. S., & Boker, S. M. (Eds.) (2006). *Methodological issues in aging research. Notre Dame series on quantitative methods.* Mahwah, NJ: Erlbaum.

Berndt, T. J. (1992). Friendship and friends' influence in adolescence. *Current Directions in Psychological Science, 1,* 156–159.

Berndt, T. J. (2004). Friendship and three A's (aggression, adjustment, and attachment). *Journal of Experimental Child Psychology, 88*(1), 1–4.

Berndt, T. J., Miller, K. E., & Park, K. E. (1989). Adolescents' perceptions of friends and parents' influence on aspects of their school adjustment. *Journal of Early Adolescence, 9,* 419–435.

Berndt, T. J., & Perry, T. B. (1990). Distinctive features and effects of early adolescent friendships. In R. Montemayor, G. R. Adams, & T. P. Gullotta (Eds.), *From childhood to adolescence: A transitional period?* Newbury Park, CA: Sage.

Bernstein, I. M., et al. (2005). Maternal smoking and its association with birth weight. *Obstetrics & Gynecology, 106,* 986–991.

Berscheid, E. (2003). On stepping on land mines. In Sternberg, R. J. (Ed.). Psychologists defying the crowd: Stories of those who battled the establishment and won. (pp. 33–44). Washington, DC: American Psychological Association.

Berscheid, E. (2006). Searching for the meaning of "love." In R. J. Sternberg & K. Weis (Eds.), *The new psychology of love* (pp. 171–183). New Haven, CT: Yale University Press.

Bertoni, A., et al. (2007). Stress communication, dyadic coping and couple satisfaction: A cross-sectional and cross-cultural study. *Età Evolutiva, 86,* 58–66.

Berzonsky, M. D. (2004). Identity style, parental authority, and identity commitment. *Journal of Youth and Adolescence, 33*(3), 213–220.

Berzonsky, M. D. (2005). Ego identity: A personal standpoint in a postmodern world. *Identity, 5*(2), 125–136.

Berzonsky, M. D., & Kuk, L. S. (2005). Identity style, psychosocial maturity, and academic performance. *Personality and Individual Differences, 39*(1), 235–247.

Bialystok, E., & Senman, L. (2004). Executive processes in appearance–reality tasks: The role of inhibition of attention and symbolic representation. *Child Development, 75*(2), 562–579.

Bialystok, E. K., & Craik, F. I. M. (2007). Bilingualism and naming: Implications for cognitive assessment. *Journal of the International Neuropsychological Society, 13*(2), 209–211.

Bibby, R. (2004). *The Future Families Project: A survey of Canadian hopes and dreams.* Ottawa: Vanier Institute of the Family. Retrieved from http://www.vifamily.ca/node/177

Bird, A., Reese, E., & Tripp, G. (2006). Parent–child talk about past emotional events: Associations with child temperament and goodness-of-fit. *Journal of Cognition and Development, 7*(2), 189–210.

Bissell, M., & McKay, A. (2005). Taking action on chlamydia literature review. Retrieved from http://www.toronto.ca/health/sexualhealth/checkuponchlamydia/pdf/chlamydia_research_3.pdf

Black, D. W. (2007). Antisocial personality disorder, conduct disorder, and psychopathy. In J. E. Grant, & M. N. Potenza (Eds.), *Textbook of men's mental health* (pp. 143–170). Washington, DC: American Psychiatric Publishing, Inc.

Blackwell, D. L., & Lichter, D. T. (2004). Homogamy among dating, cohabiting, and married couples. *Sociological Quarterly, 45*(4), 719–737.

Blass, E. M., & Camp, C. A. (2003). Changing determinants in 6- to 12-week-old human infants. *Developmental Psychobiology, 42*(3), 312–316.

Blazina, C., Eddins, R., Burridge, A., & Settle, A. G. (2007). The relationship between masculinity ideology, loneliness, and separation-individuation difficulties. *The Journal of Men's Studies, 15*(1), 101–109.

Bloom, B., Dey, A. N., & Freeman, G. (2006). Summary health statistics for U.S. children: National Health Interview Survey, 2005. *National Center for Health Statistics, Vital Health Stat 10*(231).

Bloom, L. (1998). Language acquisition in its developmental context. In W. Damon (Ed.), *Handbook of child psychology* (5th ed.), Vol. 2. New York: Wiley.

Bloom, M. (2006, April 19). Life expectancy gender gap narrows. *MedPage Today,* http://www.medpagetoday.com/PublicHealth-Policy/PublicHealth/tb/3121. Accessed October 5, 2008.

Bloom, P. (2002). Mind reading, communication, and the learning of names for things. *Mind and Language, 17*(1–2), 37–54.

Boccia, M., & Campos, J. J. (1989). Maternal emotional signals, social referencing, and infants' reactions to strangers. In N. Eisenberg (Ed.), *New directions for child development*, No. 44, *Empathy and related emotional responses*. San Francisco: Jossey-Bass.

Body and Health Canada. (2010). Colour blindness. Retrieved from http://bodyand-health.canada.com/condition_info_details. asp?disease_id=36

Bohlmeijer, E., Valenkamp, M., Westerhof, G., Smith, F., & Cuijpers, P. (2005). Creative reminiscence as an early intervention for depression. *Aging & Mental Health, 9*(4), 302–304.

Bohon, C., Garber, J., & Horowitz, J. L. (2007). Predicting school dropout and adolescent sexual behavior in offspring of depressed and nondepressed mothers. *Journal of the American Academy of Child & Adolescent Psychiatry, 46*(1), 15–24.

Boivin, M., Vitaro, F., & Poulin, F. (2005). Peer relationships and the development of aggressive behavior in early childhood. In R. E. Tremblay, W. W. Hartup, & J. Archer (Eds.), *Developmental origins of aggression* (pp. 376–397). New York: Guilford.

Boland, M. (2009). Exclusive breastfeeding should continue to six months. *Paediatrics & Child Health, 10*(3): 148. Retrieved from http://www.cps.ca/english/statements/n/breastfeedingmar05.htm

Bonanno, G. A., & Boerner, K. (2007). The stage theory of grief. *Journal of the American Medical Association, 297*, 2693.

Boom, J., Wouters, H., & Keller, M. (2007). A cross-cultural validation of stage development: A Rasch re-analysis of longitudinal socio-moral reasoning data. *Cognitive Development, 22*(2), 213–229.

Booth-LaForce, C., et al. (2006). Attachment, self-worth, and peer-group functioning in middle childhood. *Attachment & Human Development, 8*(4), 309–325.

Bosi, M,. L. & de Oliveira, F. P. (2006). Bulimic behavior in adolescent athletes. In P. I. Swain (Ed.), *New developments in eating disorders research* (pp. 123–133). Hauppauge, NY: Nova Science Publishers.

Bost, L. W., & Riccomini, P. J (2006). Effective instruction: An inconspicuous strategy for dropout prevention. *Remedial and Special Education, 27*(5), 301–311.

Bouchard, T. J., Jr., & Loehlin, J. C. (2001). Genes, evolution, and personality. *Behavior Genetics, 31*(3), 243–273.

Bouchard, T. J., Jr., Lykken, D. T., McGue, M., Segal, N. L., & Tellegen, A. (1990). Sources of human psychological differences: The Minnesota study of twins reared apart. *Science, 250*, 223–228.

Bower, T. G. R. (1974). *Development in infancy*. San Francisco: W. H. Freeman.

Bowlby, J. (1961). Processes of mourning. *International Journal of Psychoanalysis, 42*, 317–339.

Bowlby, J. (1988). *A secure base*. New York: Basic Books.

Bozionelos, N., & Wang, L. (2006). The relationship of mentoring and network resources with career success in the Chinese organizational environment. *International Journal of Human Resource Management, 17*(9), 1531–1546.

Braam, A. W., et al. (2008). God image and mood in old age. *Mental Health, Religion, & Culture, 11*(2), 221–237.

Bracht, M. (2007). Toilet training 101. *Parents-Canada.com*. Retrieved from http://www.parentscanada.com/developing/pre-school/articles.aspx? listingid=181

Bradley, R. H. (2006). The home environment. In N. F. Watt et al. (Eds.), *The crisis in youth mental health: Critical issues and effective programs*, Vol. 4, *Early intervention programs and policies, Child psychology and mental health* (pp. 89–120). Westport, CT: Praeger/Greenwood.

Bradley, R. H., Caldwell, B. M., & Corwyn, R. F. (2003). The child care HOME inventories: Assessing the quality of family child care homes. *Early Childhood Research Quarterly, 18*(3), 294–309.

Brady, E. M. (2007). Review of Adulthood: New Terrain. *Educational Gerontology, 33*(1), 85–86.

Bramlett, M. D., & Mosher, W. D. (2002). Cohabitation, marriage, divorce, and remarriage. National Center for Health Statistics, Vital Health Statistics, 23(22). Available at http://www.cdc.gov/nchs/data/series/sr_23/sr23_022.pdf.

Branco, J. C., & Lourenço, O. (2004). Cognitive and linguistic aspects in 5- to 6-year-olds' class-inclusion reasoning. *Psicologia Educa-ção Cultura, 8*(2), 427–445.

Brandstätter, H., & Farthofer, A. (2003). Influence of part-time work on university students' academic performance. *Zeitschrift für Arbeits- und Organisationspsychologie, 47*(3), 134–145.

Brandtjen, H., & Verny, T (2001). Short and long term effects on infants and toddlers in full time daycare centers. *Journal of Prenatal & Perinatal Psychology & Health, 15*(4), 239–286.

Brase, G. L. (2006). Cues of parental investment as a factor in attractiveness. *Evolution and Human Behavior, 27*(2), 145–157.

Braver, T. S., & West, R. (2008). Working memory, executive control, and aging. In F. I. M. Craik & T. A. Salthouse (Eds.), *The handbook of aging and cognition* (3rd ed.) (pp. 311–372). New York: Psychology Press.

Brazier, A., & Rowlands, C. (2006). PKU in the family: Working together. *Clinical Child Psychology and Psychiatry, 11*(3), 483–488.

Bremner, A., & Bryant, P. (2001). The effect of spatial cues on infants' responses in the AB task, with and without a hidden object. *Developmental Science, 4*(4), 408–415.

Brennan, S., & Taylor-Butts, A. (2008). *Sexual assault in Canada: 2004 and 2007.* (Statistics Canada Catalogue no. 85F0033M). Canadian Centre for Justice Statistics Profile Series, no. 19. Retrieved from http://www.statcan.gc.ca/pub/85f0033m/85f0033m2008019-eng.pdf

Bridges, A. J. (2007). Successful living as a (single) woman. *Psychology of Women Quarterly, 31*(3), 327–328.

Bridges, L. J., Roe, A. E. C., Dunn, J., & O'Connor, T. G. (2007). Children's perspectives on their relationships with grandparents following parental separation: A longitudinal study. *Social Development, 16*(3), 539–554.

Briones, T. L., Klintsova, A. Y., & Greenough, W. T. (2004). Stability of synaptic plasticity in the adult rat visual cortex induced by complex environment exposure. *Brain Research, 1018*(1), 130–135.

Brockman, D. D. (2003). *From late adolescence to young adulthood.* Madison, CT: International Universities Press, Inc.

Brody, L. R., Zelazo, P. R., & Chaika, H. (1984). Habituation–dishabituation to speech in the neonate. *Developmental Psychology, 20*, 114–119.

Bronfenbrenner, U., & Morris, P. A. (2006). The bioecological model of human development. In R. M. Lerner & W. Damon (Eds.), *Handbook of child psychology* (6th ed.), Vol. 1, *Theoretical models of human development* (pp. 793–828). Hoboken, NJ: Wiley.

Bronson, G. W. (1990). Changes in infants' visual scanning across the 2- to 14-week age period. *Journal of Experimental Child Psychology, 49*, 101–125.

Bronson, G. W. (1991). Infant differences in rate of visual encoding. *Child Development, 62*, 44–54.

Bronson, G. W. (1997). The growth of visual capacity: Evidence from infant scanning patterns. *Advances in Infancy Research, 11*, 109–141.

Broomhall, H. S., & Winefield, A. H. (1990). A comparison of the affective well-being of young and middle-aged unemployed men matched for length of unemployment. *British Journal of Medical Psychology, 63*(1), 43–52.

Brown, B. B., Mounts, N., Lamborn, S. D., & Steinberg, L. (1993). Parenting practices and peer group affiliation in adolescence. *Child Development, 64*, 467–482.

Brown, R. (1973). *A first language: The early stages*. Cambridge, MA: Harvard University Press.

Brown, R. (1977). Introduction. In C. A. Snow & C. Ferguson (Eds.), *Talking to children*. New York: Cambridge University Press.

Brown, S. L., Lee, G. R., & Bulanda, J. R. (2006). Cohabitation among older adults. *Journals of Gerontology: Series B: Psychological Sciences and Social Sciences, 61B*(2), S71–S79.

Brownell, C. A., & Carriger, M. S. (1990). Changes in cooperation and self-other differentiation during the second year. *Child Development, 61*, 1164–1174.

Browning, J. R., Hatfield, E., Kessler, D., & Levine, T. (2000). Sexual motives, gender, and sexual behavior. *Archives of Sexual Behavior, 29*(2), 135–153.

Bruck, M., Ceci, S. J., & Principe, G. F. (2006). The child and the law. In K. Renninger, I. E. Sigel, W. Damon, & R. M. Lerner (Eds.), *Handbook of child psychology* (6th ed.), Vol. 4, *Child psychology in practice* (pp. 776–816). Hoboken, NJ: Wiley.

Brunner, L. C., Eshilian-Oates, L., & Kuo, T. Y. (2003, February 1). Hip fractures in adults. *American Family Physician.*

Brunner, R., Parzer, P., & Resch, F. (2005). Involuntary hospitalization of patients with anorexia nervosa: Clinical issues and empirical findings. *Fortschritte der Neurologie, Psychiatrie, 73*(1), 9–15.

Bryden, P. J., Bruyn, J., & Fletcher, P. (2005). Handedness and health: An examination of the association between different handedness classifications and health disorders. *Laterality: Asymmetries of Body, Brain and Cognition, 10*(5), 429–440.

Budney, A. J., Vandrey, R. G., Hughes, J. R., Moore, B. A., & Bahrenburg, B. (2007). Oral delta-9-tetrahydrocannabinol suppresses cannabis withdrawal symptoms. *Drug and Alcohol Dependence, 86*(1), 22–29.

Bugental, D. B., & Happaney, K. (2004). Predicting infant maltreatment in low-income families: The interactive effects of maternal attributions and child status at birth. *Developmental Psychology, 40*(2), 234–243.

Buhl, H. M., Wittmann, S., & Noack, P. (2003). Child – parent relationship of university students and young employed adults. *Zeitschrift für Entwicklungspsychologie und Pädagogische Psychologie, 35*(3), 144–152.

Bunikowski, R., et al. (1998). Neurodevelopmental outcome after prenatal exposure to opiates. *European Journal of Pediatrics, 157*(9), 724–730.

Burke, D. M., & Shafto, M. A. (2008). Language and aging. In F. I. M. Craik, & T. A. Salthouse (Eds.), *The handbook of aging and cognition* (3rd ed.) (pp. 373–443). New York: Psychology Press.

Burmaster, A. (1996, July 22). HIV/AIDS: The new awareness. *The Peak*. Retrieved from http://www.peak.sfu.ca/the-peak/96-2/issue12/aidsl.html

Bushman, B. J. (1998). Priming effects of media violence on the accessibility of aggressive constructs in memory. *Personality and Social Psychology Bulletin, 24*(5), 537–545.

Bushnell, E. W. (1993, June). *A dual-processing approach to cross-modal matching: Implications for development.* Paper presented at the Society for Research in Child Development, New Orleans, LA.

Bushnell, I. W. R. (2001). Mother's face recognition in newborn infants: Learning and memory. *Infant and Child Development, 10*(1–2), 67–74.

Bushnik, T. (2006). *Child care in Canada.* (Statistics Canada, Catalogue no. 89-599-MIE — No. 003). Retrieved from http://www.statcan.gc.ca/pub/89-599-m/89-599-m2006003-eng.pdf

Buss, D. M. (1994). *The evolution of desire: Strategies of human mating.* New York: Basic Books.

Buss, D. M. (Ed.). (2005). *The handbook of evolutionary psychology.* Hoboken, NJ: John Wiley & Sons, Inc.

Buss, D. M., & Duntley, J. D. (2006). The evolution of aggression. In M. Schaller, J. A. Simpson, & D. T. Kenrick (Eds.), *Evolution and social psychology: Frontiers of social psychology* (pp. 263–285). Madison, CT: Psychosocial Press.

Bussey, K., & Bandura, A. (1999). Social cognitive theory of gender development and differentiation. *Psychological Review, 106*(4), 676–713.

Buston, K., Williamson, L., & Hart, G. (2007). Young women under 16 years with experience of sexual intercourse: Who becomes pregnant? *Journal of Epidemiology & Community Health, 61*(3) 221–225.

Butterfield, S. A., & Loovis, E. M. (1993). Influence of age, sex, balance, and sport participation on development of throwing by children in grades K–8. *Perceptual and Motor Skills, 76,* 459–464.

Butler, R. N. (2002). The life review. *Journal of Geriatric Psychology, 35*(1), 7–10.

Buunk, B. P., et al. (2002). Age and gender differences in mate selection criteria for various involvement levels. *Personal Relationships, 9*(3), 271–278.

Bye, D., Pushkar, D., & Conway, M. (2007). Motivation, interest, and positive affect in traditional and nontraditional undergraduate students. *Adult Education Quarterly, 57*(2), 141–158.

Bynum, M. S. (2007). African American mother–daughter communication about sex and daughters' sexual behavior: Does college racial composition make a difference? *Cultural Diversity & Ethnic Minority Psychology, 13*(2), 151–160.

Callahan, J. J. (2007). Sandwich anyone? *Gerontologist, 47*(4), 569–571.

Callan, M. J., Ellard, J. H., & Nicol, J. E. (2006). The belief in a just world and immanent justice reasoning in adults. *Personality and Social Psychology Bulletin, 32*(12), 1646–1658.

Calvert, S. L., & Kotler, J. A. (2003). Lessons from children's television: The impact of the Children's Television Act on children's learning. *Journal of Applied Developmental Psychology, 24*(3), 275–335.

Camarena, P. M. (1991). Conformity in adolescence. In R. M. Lerner, A. C. Petersen & J. Brooks-Gunn (Eds.), *Encyclopedia of Adolescence.* New York: Garland.

Campanella, J., & Rovee-Collier, C. (2005). Latent learning and deferred imitation at 3 months. *Infancy, 7*(3), 243–262.

Campbell, A., Shirley, L., & Caygill, L. (2002). Sex-typed preferences in three domains: Do two-year-olds need cognitive variables? *British Journal of Psychology, 93*(2), 203–217.

Campbell, A., Shirley, L., Heywood, C., & Crook, C. (2000). Infants' visual preference for sex-congruent babies, children, toys and activities: A longitudinal study. *British Journal of Developmental Psychology, 18*(4), 479–498.

Campbell, D. A., Lake, M. F. Falk, M., & Backstrand, J. R. (2006). A randomized control trial of continuous support in labor by a lay doula. *Journal of Obstetric, Gynecologic, and Neonatal Nursing, 35*(4), 456–464.

Campbell, D. W., Eaton, W. O., & McKeen, N. A. (2002). Motor activity level and behavioural control in young children. *International Journal of Behavioral Development, 26*(4), 289–296.

Campbell, S. B., et al. (2004). The course of maternal depressive symptoms and maternal sensitivity as predictors of attachment security at 36 months. *Development and Psychopathology, 16*(2), 231–252.

Campos, J. J., Hiatt, S., Ramsey, D., Henderson, C., & Svejda, M. (1978). The emergence of fear on the visual cliff. In M. Lewis & L. Rosenblum (Eds.), *The origins of affect.* New York: Plenum.

Campos, J. J., Langer, A., & Krowitz, A. (1970). Cardiac responses on the visual cliff in prelocomotor human infants. *Science, 170,* 196–197.

Camras, L. A., et al. (2007). Do infants show distinct negative facial expressions for fear and anger? Emotional expression in 11-month-old European American, Chinese, and Japanese Infants. *Infancy, 11*(2), 131–155.

Canadian Cancer Society. (2007, January 18). Smoking rates dropping, but lung cancer deaths still leading cause of cancer death. Media release. Retrieved from http://www.cancer.ca/Canada-wide/About%20us/Media%20centre/CW-Media%20releases/CW-2007/Smoking%20rates%20dropping%20%20but%20lung%20cancer%20deaths%20still%20leading%20cause%20of%20cancer%20death.aspx?sc_lang=en

Canadian Cystic Fibrosis Foundation. (2010). About cystic fibrosis. Retrieved from http://www.cysticfibrosis.ca/en/aboutCysticFibrosis/index.php

Canadian Dyslexia Centre. (n.d.). About dyslexia. Retrieved from http://www.dyslexiacentre.ca/english/about_dyslexia.htm

Canadian Federation for Sexual Health. (2007). *Sexual health in Canada: Baseline 2007.* Retrieved from http://www.cfsh.ca/files/publications/sexual_health_in_canada_baseline_2007_final.pdf

Canadian Foundation for the Study of Infant Deaths. (2010). Babies' 'flat heads' can be prevented: Health coalition—Growing public awareness of SIDS prompts concern about positional plagiocephaly. Retrieved from http://www.sidscanada.org/resource-news4html

Canadian Geographic. (2010). Who we are: Canada by demographics—Top 10 languages. *The Canadian Atlas Online.* Retrieved from http://magazine.canadiangeographic.ca/Atlas/themes.aspx?id=whoweare&sub=whoweare_demographics_work&lang=En

Canadian Hospice Palliative Care Association (2010). *Fact Sheet: Hospice palliative care in Canada.* Retrieved from http://www.chpca.net/resource_doc_library/Fact_Sheet_HPC_in_Canada.pdf

Canadian Paediatric Society. (2007). Bedwetting. Retrieved from http://www.cps.ca/caringforkids/growing&learning/bedwetting.htm

Canadian Paediatric Society. (2010, June 24). When your child is sick. Retrieved from http://www.cps.ca/caringforkids!whensick/colds.htm

Canadian PKU and Allied Disorders. (2008). About PKU. Retrieved from http://www.canpku.org/

Canadian Psychological Association. (2000). *Canadian code of ethics for psychologists* (3rd ed.). Retrieved (May 12, 2010) from http://www.cpa.ca/cpasite/userfiles/Documents/Canadian%20Code%20of%20Ethics%20for%20Psycho.pdf

Candy, T. R., Crowell, J. A., & Banks, M. S. (1998). Optical, receptoral, and retinal constraints on foveal and peripheral vision in the human neonate. *Vision Research, 38*(24), 3857–3870.

Canitano, R. (2007). Epilepsy in autism spectrum disorders. *European Child & Adolescent Psychiatry, 16*(1), 61–66.

Caplan, M., Vespo, J., Pedersen, J., & Hale, D. F. (1991). Conflict and its resolution in small groups of one and two-year-olds. *Child Development, 62,* 1513–1524.

Caplan, P. J., & Larkin, J. (1991). The anatomy of dominance and self-protection. *American Psychologist, 46,* 536.

Capron, C., Thérond, C., & Duyme, M. (2007). Brief report: Effect of menarcheal status and family structure on depressive symptoms and emotional/behavioural problems in young adolescent girls. *Journal of Adolescence, 30*(1), 175–179.

Carey, B. (2007a, March 26). Poor behavior is linked to time in day care. *New York Times online.*

Carey, B. (2007b, June 22). Research finds firstborns gain the higher I.Q. *The New York Times online.*

Carmichael, D. (2008). *Youth sport vs. youth crime.* Retrieved from http://www.isrm.co.uk/news/docs/132 Sport%20and%20Crime.pdf

Carrère, S., Buehlman, K. T., Gottman, J. M., Coan, J. A., & Ruckstuhl, L. (2000). Predicting marital stability and divorce in newlywed couples. *Journal of Family Psychology, 14*(1), 42–58.

Carroll, J. S., et al. (2007). So close, yet so far away: The impact of varying marital horizons on emerging adulthood. *Journal of Adolescent Research, 22*(3), 219–247.

Carstensen, L. L., Gottman, J. M., & Levenson, R. W. (1995). Emotional behavior in long-term marriage. *Psychology and Aging, 10,* 140–149.

Carstensen, L. L., Isaacowitz, D. M., & Charles, S. T. (1999). Taking time seriously: A theory of socioemotional selectivity. *American Psychologist, 54*(3), 165–181.

Carver, L. J., & Vaccaro, B. G. (2007). 12-month-old infants allocate increased neural resources to stimuli associated with negative adult emotion. *Developmental Psychology, 43*(1), 54–69.

Casas, J. F., et al. (2006). Early parenting and children's relational and physical aggression in the preschool and home contexts. *Journal of Applied Developmental Psychology, 27*(3), 209–227.

Caserta, M. S., & Lund, D. A. (2007). Toward the development of an Inventory of Daily Widowed Life (IDWL). *Death Studies, 31*(6), 505–534.

Casini, A., & Sanchez-Mazas, M. (2005). "This job is not for me!": The impact of the gender norm and the organizational culture on professional upward mobility. *Cahiers Internationaux de Psychologie Sociale, Sep-Dec Vol* (67–68), 101–112.

Cassia, V. M., Simion, F., & Umilta, C. (2001). Face preference at birth: The role of an orienting mechanism. *Developmental Science, 4*(1), 101–108.

Caton, D., et al. (2002). Anesthesia for childbirth: Controversy and change. *American Journal of Obstetrics & Gynecology, 186*(5), S25–S30.

Cattell, R. B. (1949). *The culture-fair intelligence test.* Champaign, IL: Institute for Personality and Ability Testing.

Caudle, D. D., et al. (2007). Cognitive errors, symptom severity, and response to cognitive behavior therapy in older adults with generalized anxiety disorder. *American Journal of Geriatric Psychiatry, 15*(8), 680–689.

Caulfield, R. (2000). Beneficial effects of tactile stimulation on early development. *Early Childhood Education Journal, 27*(4), 255–257.

Cavallini, A., et al. (2002). Visual acuity in the first two years of life in healthy term newborns: An experience with the Teller Acuity Cards. *Functional Neurology: New Trends in Adaptive and Behavioral Disorders, 17*(2), 87–92.

Cavell, T. A. (2001). Updating our approach to parent training. I. The case against targeting noncompliance. *Clinical Psychology: Science and Practice, 8*(3), 299–318.

CBC News. (2003, March 17). Father calls sickle cell anemia 'neglected' disease. Retrieved from http://www.cbc.ca/health/story/2003/03/17/sickle_cell030317.html

CBC News. (2007a, September 12). Married people outnumbered for first time: Census. Retrieved from http://www.cbc.ca/canada/story/2007/09/12/censusfamilies.html

CBC News. (2007b, April 20). *Newborn screening.* Retrieved from http://www.cbc.ca/news/background/health/newborn_screen.html

CBC News. (2008, January 14). Life expectancy hits 80.4 years: Statistics Canada. Retrieved from http://www.cbc.ca/canada/story/2008/01/14/death-stats.html

CBC News. (2009, February 5). Assisted human reproduction: Regulating and treating conception problems. Retrieved from http://www.cbc.ca/health/story/2009/02/05/f-reprotech.html

CBC News. (2010, July 13). Quebec to pay for IVF treatment. Retrieved from http://www.cbc.ca/canada/montreal/story/2010/07/13/quebec-ivf-treatment.html

Cellarius, V. (2008). Terminal sedation and the "imminence condition." *Journal of Medical Ethics, 34*(2), 69–72.

Centers for Disease Control and Prevention. (2005). National Center for Health Statistics. *America's children, 2005. America's children: Key national indicators of well-being 2005.* Childstats.gov. Available at http://www.childstats.gov/amchildren05/hea8.asp.

Centers for Disease Control and Prevention. (2006). HIV/AIDS Surveillance Report, 2005, v. 17. Atlanta: U.S. Department of Health and Human Services, Centers for Disease Control and Prevention. Available at http://www.cdc.gov/hiv/topics/surveillance/resources/reports/.

Centers for Disease Control and Prevention, the Alan Guttmacher Institute, and the Child Trends Databank, as reported in the *New York Times,* March 7, 2004. Reprinted by permission of the New York Times Co.

Central Intelligence Agency. (2004, September 17). *The World Factbook.* Available at http://www.cia.gov/cia/publications/factbook/geos/us.html#People.

Centre for Addiction and Mental Health. (2006). *Responding to older adults with substance use, mental health and gambling challenges.* Retrieved from http://www.camh.net/Publications/Resources_for_Professionals/Older_Adults/index.html

Centre for Research on Youth at Risk. (n.d.). *Restorative justice fact sheet.* Retrieved from http://www.stthomasu.ca/research/youth/restorative.htm

Cernoch, J., & Porter, R. (1985). Recognition of maternal axillary odors by infants. *Child Development, 56,* 1593–1598.

Chapman, M., & McBride, M. C. (1992). Beyond competence and performance: Children's class inclusion strategies, superordinate class cues, and verbal justifications. *Developmental Psychology, 28,* 319–327.

Charles, S. T., & Carstensen, L. L. (2007). Emotion regulation and aging. In J. J. Gross (Ed.), *Handbook of emotion regulation* (pp. 307–327). New York: Guilford Press.

Charles, S. T., Reynolds, C. A., & Gatz, M. (2001). Age-related differences and change in positive and negative affect over 23 years. *Journal of Personality and Social Psychology, 80,* 136–151.

Charlton, R. (2004). Ageing male syndrome, andropause, androgen decline or mid-life crisis? *Journal of Men's Health & Gender, 1*(1), 55–59.

Charness, N., & Schaie, K. W. (2003). *Impact of technology on successful aging.* New York: Springer.

Chaudieu, I., et al. (2008). Abnormal reactions to environmental stress in elderly persons with anxiety disorders. *Journal of Affective Disorders, 106*(3), 307–313.

Cheng, H., & Furnham, A. (2002). Personality, peer relations, and self-confidence as predictors of happiness and loneliness. *Journal of Adolescence, 25*(3), 327–339.

Cheng, S-T., & Chan, A. C. M. (2007). Multiple pathways from stress to suicidality and the protective effect of social support in Hong Kong adolescents. *Suicide and Life-Threatening Behavior, 37*(2), 187–196.

Cherney, I. D., Harper, H. J., & Winter, J. A. (2006). Nouveaux jouets: Ce que les enfants identifient comme "jouets de garçons" et "jouets de filles." *Enfance, 58*(3), 266–282.

Chesley, N., & Moen, P. (2006). When workers care: Dual-earner couples' caregiving strategies, benefit use, and psychological well-being. *American Behavioral Scientist, 49*(9), 1248–1269.

Chess, S., & Thomas, A. (1991). Temperament. In M. Lewis (Ed.), *Child and adolescent psychiatry: A comprehensive textbook.* Baltimore: Williams & Wilkins.

Chlebowski, R. T., et al. (2003). Influence of estrogen plus progestin on breast cancer and mammography in healthy postmenopausal women: The Women's Health Initiative Randomized Trial. *Journal of the American Medical Association, 289,* 3243–3253.

Chomsky, N. (1988). *Language and problems of knowledge.* Cambridge, MA: MIT Press.

Chomsky, N. (1990). On the nature, use, and acquisition of language. In W. G. Lycan (Ed.), *Mind and cognition.* Oxford: Blackwell.

Chong, L., McDonald, H., & Strauss, E. (2004). Deconstructing aging. *Science, 305*(5689), 1419.

Chou, T-L., et al. (2006). Developmental and skill effects on the neural correlates of semantic processing to visually presented words. *Human Brain Mapping, 27*(11), 915–924.

Christian, P., et al. (2003). Effects of alternative maternal micronutrient supplements on low birth weight in rural Nepal: Double blind randomised community trial. *British Medical Journal, 326,* 571.

Christophersen, E. R., & Mortweet, S. L. (2003). Establishing bedtime. In E. R. Christophersen & S. L. Mortweet (Eds.), *Parenting that works: Building skills that last a lifetime* (pp. 209–228). Washington, DC: American Psychological Association.

Chronis, A. M., et al. (2007). Maternal depression and early positive parenting predict future conduct problems in young children with attention-deficit/hyperactivity disorder. *Developmental Psychology, 43*(1), 70–82.

Cicchetti, D., Rogosch, F. A., & Toth, S. L. (2006). Fostering secure attachment in infants in maltreating families through preventive interventions. *Development and Psychopathology, 18*(3), 623–649.

Clancy, B., & Finlay, B. (2001). Neural correlates of early language learning. In M. Tomasello & E. Bates (Eds.), *Language development: The essential readings.* Malden, MA: Blackwell.

Clark, E. V. (1973). What's in a word? On the child's acquisition of semantics in his first language. In E. Moore (Ed.), *Cognitive development and the acquisition of language.* New York: Academic Press.

Clark, E. V. (1975). Knowledge, context, and strategy in the acquisition of meaning. In D. P. Date (Ed.), *Georgetown University roundtable on language and linguistics.* Washington, DC: Georgetown University Press.

Clark, J. (2005). Sibling relationships: Theory and issues for practice. *Child & Family Social Work, 10*(1), 90–91.

Clark, J., & Rugg, S. (2005). The importance of independence in toileting. *British Journal of Occupational Therapy, 68*(4), 165–171.

Clark, R. (1983). *Family life and school achievement: Why poor black children succeed or fail.* Chicago: University of Chicago Press.

Clarke-Stewart, K. A., & Beck, R. J. (1999). Maternal scaffolding and children's narrative retelling of a movie story. *Early Childhood Research Quarterly, 14*(3), 409–434.

Clayton, R., & Crosby, R. A. (2006) Measurement in health promotion. In R. A. Crosby, R. J. DiClemente, & L. F. Salazar (Eds.), *Research methods in health promotion* (pp. 229–259). San Francisco: Jossey-Bass.

Cleary, D. J., Ray, G. E., LoBello, S. G., & Zachar, P. (2002). Children's perceptions of close peer relationships: Quality, congruence and meta-perceptions. *Child Study Journal, 32*(3), 179–192.

Clode, D. (2006). Review of A left-hand turn around the world: Chasing the mystery and meaning of all things southpaw. *Laterality: Asymmetries of Body, Brain and Cognition, 11*(6) 580–581.

Cnattingius, S. (2004). The epidemiology of smoking during pregnancy: Smoking prevalence, maternal characteristics, and pregnancy outcomes. *Nicotine & Tobacco Research, 6*(Supp. l2), S125–S140.

Coats, A. H., & Blanchard-Fields, F. (2008). Emotion regulation in interpersonal problems: The role of cognitive-emotional complexity, emotion regulation goals, and expressivity. *Psychology and Aging, 23*(1), 39–51.

Cochran, S. V. (2005). Assessing and treating depression in men. In G. E. Good, & G. R. Brooks (Eds.), *The new handbook of psychotherapy and counseling with men* (pp. 121–133). San Francisco: Jossey-Bass.

Cohen, L. S., et al. (2006). Relapse of major depression during pregnancy in women who maintain or discontinue antidepressant treatment. *Journal of the American Medical Association, 295*(5), 499–507.

Cohen, S. (2003). Psychosocial models of the role of social support in the etiology of physical disease. In P. Salovey & A. J. Rothman (Eds.), *Social psychology of health* (pp. 227–244). New York: Psychology Press.

Cohen-Bendahan, C. C. C., Buitelaar, J. K., van Goozen, S. H. M., & Cohen-Kettenis, P. T. (2004). Prenatal exposure to testosterone and functional cerebral lateralization: A study in same-sex and opposite-sex twin girls. *Psychoneuroendocrinology, 29*(7), 911–916.

Cohn, M., Emrich, S. M., & Moscovitch, M. (2008). Age-related deficits in associative memory. *Psychology and Aging, 23*(1), 93–103.

Coleman, M., Ganong, L. H., & Fine, M. (2000). Reinvestigating remarriage: Another decade of progress. *Journal of Marriage & the Family, 62*(4) 1288–1307.

Coleman, P. K. (2003). Perceptions of parent–child attachment, social self-efficacy, and peer relationships in middle childhood. *Infant and Child Development, 12*(4), 351–368.

Collaer, M. L., & Hill, E. M. (2006). Large sex difference in adolescents on a timed line judgment task: Attentional contributors and task relationship to mathematics. *Perception, 35*(4), 561–572.

Collins, W. A., & Laursen, B. (2006). Parent–adolescent relationships. In P. Noller & J. A. Feeney (Eds.), *Close relationships: Functions, forms and processes* (pp. 111–125). Hove, England: Psychology Press/Taylor & Francis.

Collins, W. A., Maccoby, E. E., Steinberg, L., Hetherington, E. M., & Bornstein, M. H. (2000). Contemporary research on parenting: The case for nature and nurture. *American Psychologist, 55*(2), 218–232.

Collins, W. A., Maccoby, E. E., Steinberg, L., Hetherington, E. M., & Bornstein, M. H. (2003). Contemporary research on parenting: The case for nature and nurture. In M. E. Hertzig & E. A. Farber (Eds.), *Annual progress in child psychiatry and child development: 2000–2001* (pp. 125–153). New York: Brunner-Routledge.

Colombo, J. (1993). *Infant cognition.* Newbury Park, CA: Sage.

Commons, M. L. (2004). The state of the art on Perry and epistemological development? *Journal of Adult Development, 11*(2), 59–60.

Commons, M. L., Galaz-Fontes, J. F., & Morse, S. J. (2006). Leadership, cross-cultural contact, socio-economic status, and formal operational reasoning about moral dilemmas among Mexican non-literate adults and high school students. *Journal of Moral Education, 35*(2), 247–267

Conel, J. L. (1959). *The postnatal development of the human cerebral cortex, 5.* Cambridge, MA: Harvard University Press.

Conner, K. R., & Goldston, D. B. (2007). Rates of suicide among males increase steadily from age 11 to 21: Developmental framework and outline for prevention. *Aggression and Violent Behavior, 12*(2), 193–207.

Connolly, J., Craig, W., Goldberg, A., & Pepler, D. (2004). Mixed-gender groups, dating, and romantic relationships in early adolescence. *Journal of Research on Adolescence, 14*(2), 185–207.

Connolly, J., Furman, W., & Konarski, R. (2000). The role of peers in the emergence of heterosexual romantic relationships in adolescence. *Child Development, 71*(5), 1395–1408.

Connor, P. D., Sampson, P. D., Streissguth, A. P., Bookstein, F. L., & Barr, H. M. (2006). Effects of prenatal alcohol exposure on fine motor coordination and balance: A study of two adult samples. *Neuropsychologia, 44*(5), 744–751.

Conrad, P. (2007). *The medicalization of society: On the transformation of human conditions into treatable disorders.* Baltimore, MD: Johns Hopkins University Press.

Constantino, J. N., et al. (2006). Autistic social impairment in the siblings of children with pervasive developmental disorders. *American Journal of Psychiatry, 163*(2), 294–296.

Cooke, B. M., Breedlove, S. M., & Jordan, C. L. (2003). Both estrogen receptors and androgen receptors contribute to testosterone-induced changes in the morphology of the medial amygdala and sexual arousal in male rats. *Hormones & Behavior, 43*(2), 336–346.

Coon, H., Fulker, D. W., & DeFries, J. C. (1990). Home environment and cognitive ability of 7-year-old children in the Colorado adoption project: Genetic and environmental etiologies. *Developmental Psychology, 26*, 459–468.

Cooper, J., Appleby, L., & Amos, T. (2002). Life events preceding suicide by young people. *Social Psychiatry and Psychiatric Epidemiology, 37*(6), 271–275.

Coovadia, H. (2004). Antiretroviral agents: How best to protect infants from HIV and save their mothers from AIDS. *New England Journal of Medicine, 351*(3), 289–292.

Coplan, R. J., Rubin, K. H., Fox, N. A., Calkins, S. D., & Stewart, S. L. (1994). Being alone, playing alone, and acting alone: Distinguishing among reticence, and passive-, and active-solitude in young children. *Child Development, 65*, 129–137.

Coren, S. (1992). *The left-hander syndrome.* New York: Free Press.

Cornwell, A. A., C., & Feigenbaum, P. (2006). Sleep biological rhythms in normal infants and those at high risk for SIDS. *Chronobiology International, 23*(5), 935–961.

Corstorphine, E., Waller, G., Lawson, R., & Ganis, C. (2007). Trauma and multi-impulsivity in the eating disorders. *Eating Behaviors, 8*(1), 23–30.

Costello, E. J., Sung, M., Worthman, C., & Angold, A. (2007). Pubertal maturation and the development of alcohol use and abuse. *Drug and Alcohol Dependence, 88*, S50–S59.

Costigan, C. L., Cauce, A. M., & Etchison, K. (2007). Changes in African American mother–daughter relationships during adolescence: Conflict, autonomy, and warmth. In B. J. R. Leadbeater & N. Way (Eds.), *Urban girls revisited: Building strengths* (pp. 177–201). New York: New York University Press.

Courage, M. L., Howe, M. L., & Squires, S. E. (2004). Individual differences in 3.5-month olds' visual attention: What do they predict at 1 year? *Infant Behavior and Development, 27*(1), 19–30.

Cowan, P. A., & Cowan, C. P. (2005). Five-domain models: Putting it all together. In P. A. Cowan, C. P. Cowan, J. C. Ablow, V. K. Johnson, & J. R. Measelle (Eds.), *The family context of parenting in children's adaptation to elementary school, Monographs in parenting series* (pp. 315–333). Mahwah, NJ: Erlbaum.

Cramer, D. (2003). Facilitativeness, conflict, demand for approval, self-esteem, and satisfaction with romantic relationships. *Journal of Psychology, 137*(1), 85–98.

Crenshaw, D. A. (2007). Life span issues and assessment and intervention. In D. Balk, et al. (Eds.), *Handbook of thanatology* (pp. 227–234). New York: Routledge/Taylor & Francis Group.

Crombie, G., & Desjardins, M. J. (1993, March). *Predictors of gender: The relative importance of children's play, games, and personality characteristics.* Paper presented at the meeting of the Society for Research in Child Development, New Orleans, LA.

Crook, C. K., & Lipsitt, L. P. (1976). Neonatal nutritive sucking: Effects of taste stimulation upon sucking rhythm and heart rate. *Child Development, 47*, 518–522.

Crowther, C., et al. (2006). Neonatal respiratory distress syndrome after repeat exposure to antenatal corticosteroids: A randomised control trial. *Lancet, 367*(9526), 1913–1919.

Cruz, N. V., & Bahna, S. L. (2006). Do foods or additives cause behavior disorders? *Psychiatric Annals, 36*(10), 724–732.

Cuellar, J., & Curry, T. R. (2007). The prevalence and comorbidity between delinquency, drug abuse, suicide attempts, physical and sexual abuse, and self-mutilation among delinquent Hispanic females. *Hispanic Journal of Behavioral Sciences, 29*(1), 68–82.

Cumming, E., & Henry, W. E. (1961). *Growing old: The process of disengagement.* New York: Basic Books.

Cumming, S. P., Eisenmann, J. C., Smoll, F. L., Smith, R. E., & Malina, R. M. (2005). Body size and perceptions of coaching behaviors by adolescent female athletes. *Psychology of Sport and Exercise, 6*(6), 693–705.

Cunningham, R. L., & McGinnis, M. Y. (2007). Factors influencing aggression toward females by male rats exposed to anabolic androgenic steroids during puberty. *Hormones and Behavior, 51*(1), 135–141.

Curlin, F. A., et al. (2008). To die, to sleep: US physicians' religious and other objections to physician-assisted suicide, terminal sedation, and withdrawal of life support. *American Journal of Hospice & Palliative Medicine, 25*(2), 112–120.

D'Augelli, A. R., Grossman, A. H., Hershberger, S. L., & O' Connell, T. S. (2001). Aspects of mental health among older lesbian, gay, and bisexual adults. *Aging & Mental Health, 5*(2), 149–158.

Daman-Wasserman, M., Brennan, B., Radcliffe, F., Prigot, J., & Fagen, J. (2006). Auditory-visual context and memory retrieval in 3-month-old infants. *Infancy, 10*(3) 201–220.

Damon, W. (1991). Adolescent self-concept. In R. M. Lerner, A. C. Petersen, & J. Brooks-Gunn (Eds.), *Encyclopedia of adolescence.* New York: Garland.

Dandy, J., & Nettelbeck, T. (2002). The relationship between IQ, homework, aspirations and academic achievement for Chinese, Vietnamese and Anglo-Celtic Australian school children. *Educational Psychology, 22*(3), 267–276.

Dane, S., & Erzurumluoglu, A. (2003). Sex and handedness differences in eye–hand visual reaction times in handball players. *International Journal of Neuroscience, 113*(7), 923–929.

Dang-Vu, T. T., Desseilles, M., Peigneux, P., & Maquet, P. (2006). A role for sleep in brain plasticity. *Pediatric Rehabilitation, 19*(2) 98–118.

Daniels, S. R. (2006). The consequences of childhood overweight and obesity. *The Future of Children, 16*(1), 47–67.

Davis, L., Edwards, H., Mohay, H., & Wollin, J. (2003). The impact of very premature birth on the psychological health of mothers. *Early Human Development, 73*(1–2), 61–70.

Davis, S. R., Davison, S. L., Donath, S., & Bell, R. J. (2005). Circulating androgen levels and self-reported sexual function in women. *Journal of the American Medical Association, 294*(1), 91–96.

Dawson, T. L. (2002). New tools, new insights: Kohlberg's moral judgement stages revisited. *International Journal of Behavioral Development, 26*(2), 154–166.

De Beni, R., Borella, E., & Carretti, B. (2007). Reading comprehension in aging: The role of working memory and metacomprehension. *Aging, Neuropsychology, and Cognition, 14*(2), 189–212.

De Haan, M., & Groen, M. (2006). Neural bases of infants' processing of social information in faces. In P. J. Marshall & N. A. Fox (Eds.), *The development of social engagement: Neurobiological perspectives. Series in affective science* (pp. 46–80). New York: Oxford University Press.

de St. Aubin, E., McAdams, D. P., & Kim, T-C. (Eds.). (2004). *The generative society: Caring for future generations.* Washington, DC: American Psychological Association.

de Villiers, J. G., & de Villiers, P. A. (1999). Language development. In M. H. Bornstein & M. E. Lamb (Eds.), *Developmental psychology: An advanced textbook* (4th ed.) (pp. 313–373). Mahwah, NJ: Erlbaum.

Deary, I. J., Whiteman, M. C., Starr, J. M., Whalley, L. J., & Fox, H. C. (2004). The impact of childhood intelligence on later life: Following up the Scottish mental surveys of 1932 and 1947. *Journal of Personality and Social Psychology, 86*(1), 130–147.

DeCasper, A. J., & Fifer, W. P. (1980). Of human bonding: Newborns prefer their mothers' voices. *Science, 208,* 1174–1176.

DeCasper, A. J., & Prescott, P. A. (1984). Human newborns' perception of male voices: Preference, discrimination, and reinforcing value. *Developmental Psychobiology, 17,* 481–491.

DeCasper, A. J., & Spence, M. J. (1991). Auditorily mediated behavior during the perinatal period: A cognitive view. In M. J. Weiss & P. R. Zelazo (Eds.), *Infant attention* (pp. 142–176). Norwood, NJ: Ablex.

Deep, A. L., et al. (1999). Sexual abuse in eating disorder subtypes and control women: The role of comorbid substance dependence in bulimia nervosa. *International Journal of Eating Disorders, 25*(1), 1–10.

Dehaene-Lambertz, G., Pena, M., Christophe, A., & Landrieu, P. (2004). Phoneme perception in a neonate with a left sylvian infarct. *Brain and Language, 88*(1), 26–38.

Delgado, A. R., & Prieto, G. (2004). Cognitive mediators and sex-related differences in mathematics. *Intelligence, 32*(1), 25–32.

den Tonkelaar, I. & Oddens, B. J. (2000). Determinants of long-term hormone replacement therapy and reasons for early discontinuation. *Obstetrics & Gynecology, 95*(4), 507–512.

Dennerstein, L., & Goldstein, I. (2005). Postmenopausal female sexual dysfunction: At a crossroads. *Journal of Sexual Medicine, 2*(Suppl3), 116–117.

Dennis, W. (1960). Causes of retardation among institutional children: Iran. *Journal of Genetic Psychology, 96,* 47–59.

Dennis, W., & Dennis, M. G. (1940). The effect of cradling practices upon the onset of walking in Hopi children. *Journal of Genetic Psychology, 56,* 77–86.

Department of Justice Canada, (2009). *If your child is in trouble with the law.* Retrieved from http://www.justice.gc.ca/eng/pi/yj-jj/information/information.html

Depp, C. A., & Jeste, D. V. (2006). Definitions and predictors of successful aging: A comprehensive review of larger quantitative studies. *American Journal of Geriatric Psychiatry, 14,* 6–20.

Derby, C. A. (2000, October 2). Cited in Study finds exercise reduces the risk of impotence. *The Associated Press.*

Dervic, K., Grunebaum, M. F., Burke, A. K., Mann, J. J., & Oquendo, M. A. (2007). Cluster C personality disorders in major depressive episodes: The relationship between hostility and suicidal behavior. *Archives of Suicide Research, 11*(1), 83–90.

Dezoete, J. A., MacArthur, B. A., & Tuck, B. (2003). Prediction of Bayley and Stanford–Binet scores with a group of very low birth-weight children. *Child: Care, Health and Development, 29*(5), 367–372.

DiLalla, D. L., Gottesman, I. I., Carey, G., & Bouchard, T. J., Jr. (1999). Heritability of MMPI Harris–Lingoes and Subtle–Obvious subscales in twins reared apart. *Assessment, 6*(4), 353–366.

Dindia, K., & Allen, M. (1992). Sex differences in self-disclosure: A meta-analysis. *Psychological Bulletin, 112,* 106–124.

Dishion, T. J., & Stormshak, E. A. (2007a). Child and adolescent intervention groups. In T. J. Dishion & E. A. Stormshak (Eds.), *Intervening in children's lives: An ecological, family-centered approach to mental health care* (pp. 201–215). Washington, DC: American Psychological Association.

Dishion, T. J., & Stormshak, E. A. (2007b). Family and peer social interaction. In T. J. Dishion & E. A. Stormshak. (Eds.), *Intervening in children's lives: An ecological, family-centered approach to mental health care* (pp. 31–48). Washington, DC: American Psychological Association.

Doherty, W. J., Carroll, J. S., & Waite, L. J. (2007). In A. S. Loveless & T. B. Holman (Eds.), Supporting the institution of marriage: Ideological, research, and ecological perspectives. *The family in the new millennium: World voices supporting the "natural" clan Vol 2: Marriage and human dignity* (pp. 21–51). Praeger perspectives. Westport, CT: Praeger Publishers/Greenwood Publishing Group.

Dollfus, S., et al. (2005). Atypical hemispheric specialization for language in right-handed schizophrenia patients. *Biological Psychiatry, 57*(9), 1020–1028.

Dombrowski, M. A. S., et al. (2000). Kangaroo skin-to-skin care for premature twins and their adolescent parents. *American Journal of Maternal/Child Nursing, 25*(2), 92–94.

Donald, M. et al. (2006). Risk and protective factors for medically serious suicide attempts. *Australian and New Zealand Journal of Psychiatry, 40*(1), 87–96.

Donohue, K. F., Curtin, J. J., Patrick, C. J., & Lang, A. R. (2007). Intoxication level and emotional response. *Emotion, 7*(1), 103–112.

Donovan, D. M., & Wells, E. A. (2007). "Tweaking 12-Step": The potential role of 12-Step self-help group involvement in methamphetamine recovery. *Addiction, 102*(Suppl. 1), 121–129 .

Dorling, J., et al. (2006). Data collection from very low birthweight infants in a geographical region: Methods, costs, and trends in mortality, admission rates, and resource utilisation over a five–year period. *Early Human Development, 82*(2), 117–124.

Doron, H., & Markovitzky, G. (2007). Family structure and patterns and psychological adjustment to immigration in Israel. *Journal of Ethnic & Cultural Diversity in Social Work, 15*(1–2), 215–235.

Dragsow, E., Halle, J. W., & Phillips, B. (2001). Effects of different social partners on the discriminated requesting of a young child with autism and severe language delays. *Research in Developmental Disabilities, 22*(2), 125–139.

Drewett, R., Blair, P., Emmett, P., Emond, A., & The ALSPAC Study Team. (2004). Failure to thrive in the term and preterm infants of mothers depressed in the postnatal period: A population-based birth cohort study. *Journal of Child Psychology and Psychiatry and Allied Disciplines, 45*(2), 359–366.

Drigotas, S. M., Rusbult, C. E., & Verette, J. (1999). Level of commitment, mutuality of commitment, and couple well-being. *Personal Relationships, 6*(3) 389–409.

Duberstein, P. R., Pálsson, S. P., Waern, M., & Skoog, I. (2008). Personality and risk for depression in a birth cohort of 70-year-olds followed for 15 years. *Psychological Medicine, 38*(5), 663–671.

Duenwald, M. (2002, July 16). Hormone therapy: One size, clearly, no longer fits all. *The New York Times.*

Duffy, R. D., & Sedlacek, W. E. (2007). What is most important to students' long-term career choices. *Journal of Career Development, 34*(2), 149–163.

Duggan, A., et al. (2004). Evaluating a statewide home visiting program to prevent child abuse in at-risk families of newborns: Fathers' participation and outcomes. *Child Maltreatment: Journal of the American Professional Society on the Abuse of Children, 9*(1), 3–17.

Dumas, J. A., & Hartman, M. (2003). Adult age differences in temporal and item memory. *Psychology and Aging, 18*(3), 573–586.

Dunn, J., Davies, L. C., O'Connor, T. G., & Sturgess, W. (2001). Family lives and friendships: The perspectives of children in step-, single-parent, and nonstep families. *Journal of Family Psychology, 15*(2), 272–287.

Dunn, J., & Hughes, C. (2001). "I got some swords and you're dead!": Violent fantasy, antisocial behavior, friendship, and moral sensibility in young children. *Child Development, 72*(2), 491–505.

Duplassie, D., & Daniluk, J. C. (2007). Sexuality: Young and middle adulthood. In M S. Tepper & A. F. Owens (Eds.), *Sexual health Vol. 1: Psychological foundations* (pp. 263–289). *Praeger perspectives: Sex, love, and psychology.* Westport, CT: Praeger Publishers/Greenwood Publishing Group.

Dupuis-Blanchard, S. M. (2008). Social engagement in relocated older adults. *Dissertation Abstracts International: Section B: The Sciences and Engineering. 68*(7-B), 4387.

Durkin, S. J., Paxton, S. J., & Sorbello, M. (2007). An integrative model of the impact of exposure to idealized female images on adolescent girls' body satisfaction. *Journal of Applied Social Psychology, 37*(5), 1092–1117.

Dyer, S., & Moneta, G. B. (2006). Frequency of parallel, associative, and cooperative play in British children of different socioeconomic status. *Social Behavior and Personality, 34*(5), 587–592.

Dyer, S. J. (2007). The value of children in African countries—Insights from studies on infertility. *Journal of Psychosomatic Obstetrics & Gynecology, 28*(2), 69–77.

Dykman, R. A., Casey, P. H., Ackerman, P. T., & McPherson, W. B. (2001). Behavioral and cognitive status in school-aged children with a history of failure to thrive during early childhood. *Clinical Pediatrics, 40*(2), 63–70.

Eccles, J. S., et al. (2000). Gender-role socialization in the family: A longitudinal approach. In T. Eckes & H. M. Trautner (Eds.), *The developmental social psychology of gender* (pp. 333–360). Mahwah, NJ: Erlbaum.

Eckerman, C. O., Hsu, H.-C., Molitor, A., Leung, E. H. L., & Goldstein, R. F. (1999). Infant arousal in an en-face exchange with a new partner: Effects of prematurity and perinatal biological risk. *Developmental Psychology, 35*(1), 282–293.

Ecuyer-Dab, I., & Robert, M. (2004). Spatial ability and home-range size: Examining the relationship in Western men and women (*Homo sapiens*). *Journal of Comparative Psychology, 118*(2), 217–231.

Eddleston, M., Dissanayake, M., Sheriff, M. H. R., Warrell, D. A., & Gunnell, D. (2006). Physical vulnerability and fatal self-harm in the elderly. *British Journal of Psychiatry, 189*(3), 278–279.

Eder, R. A. (1989). The emergent personologist: The structure and content of 3½-, 5½-, and 7½-year-olds' concepts of themselves and other persons. *Child Development, 60,* 1218–1228.

Eder, R. A. (1990). Uncovering young children's psychological selves: Individual and developmental differences. *Child Development, 61,* 849–863.

Edler, C., Lipson, S. F., & Keel, P. K. (2007). Ovarian hormones and binge eating in bulimia nervosa. *Psychological Medicine, 37*(1), 131–141.

Egeland, B., & Sroufe, L. A. (1981). Attachment and early maltreatment. *Child Development, 52,* 44–52.

Egerton, A., Allison, C., Brett, R. R., & Pratt, J. A. (2006). Cannabinoids and prefrontal cortical function: Insights from preclinical studies. *Neuroscience & Biobehavioral Reviews, 30*(5), 680–695.

Eimas, P. D., Siqueland, E. R., Juscyk, P., & Vigorito, J. (1971). Speech perception in infants. *Science, 171,* 303–306.

Eisenberg, M. E., Neumark-Sztainer, D., & Paxton, S. J. (2006). Five-year change in body satisfaction among adolescents. *Journal of Psychosomatic Research, 61*(4), 521–527.

Eisner, E. W. (1990). The role of art and play in children's cognitive development. In E. Klugman & S. Smilansky (Eds.), *Children's play and learning: Perspectives and policy implications.* New York: Teachers College Press.

El-Sheikh, M. (2007). Children's skin conductance level and reactivity: Are these measures stable over time and across tasks? *Developmental Psychobiology, 49*(2), 180–186.

Elkind, D. (1967). Egocentrism in adolescence. *Child Development, 38,* 1025–1034.

Elkind, D. (1985). Egocentrism redux. *Developmental Review, 5,* 218–226.

Elkind, D. (2007). *The power of play: How spontaneous imaginative activities lead to happier, healthier children.* Cambridge, MA: Da Capo Press.

Ellis, A., & Dryden, W. (1996). *The practice of rational emotive behavior therapy.* New York: Springer.

Else-Quest, N. M., Hyde, J. S., Goldsmith, H. H., & Van Hulle, C. A. (2006). Gender differences in temperament: A meta-analysis. *Psychological Bulletin, 132*(1), 33–72.

Eltzschig, H., Lieberman, E., & Camann, W. (2003). Regional anesthesia and analgesia for labor and delivery. *New England Journal of Medicine, 348*(4), 319–332.

Emanuel, E. J., Fairclough, D. L., & Emanuel, L. L. (2000). Attitudes and desires related to euthanasia and physician-assisted-suicide among terminally ill patients and their caregivers. *JAMA: Journal of the American Medical Association, 284*(19), 2460–2468.

Emler, N., Tarry, H., & St. James, A. (2007). Postconventional moral reasoning and reputation. *Journal of Research in Personality, 41*(1), 76–89.

Epel, E. S., et al. (2006). Cell aging in relation to stress arousal and cardiovascular disease risk factors. *Psychoneuroendocrinology, 31*(3), 277–287.

Erikson, E. H. (1963). *Childhood and society.* New York: Norton.

Erikson, E. H. (1968). *Identity: Youth and crisis.* New York: Norton.

Erikson, E. H. (1975). *Life history and the historical moment.* New York: Norton.

Erikson, E. H. (1980). On the generational cycle—an address. In G. Junkers (Ed.). (2006). *Is it too late?: Key papers on psychoanalysis and ageing.* (pp. 141–159). London: Karnac Books.

Eron, L. D. (1993). Cited in T. DeAngelis (1993), It's baaack: TV violence, concern for kid viewers, *APA Monitor, 24*(8), 16.

Eron, L. D., Huesmann, L. R., & Zelli, A. (1991). The role of parental variables in the learning of aggression. In D. J. Pepler & K. H. Rubin (Eds.), *The development and treatment of childhood aggression.* Hillsdale, NJ: Erlbaum.

Ersner-Hershfield, H., Mikels, J. A., Sullivan, S. J., & Carstensen, L. L. (2008). Poignancy: Mixed emotional experience in the face of meaningful endings. *Journal of Personality and Social Psychology, 94*(1) 158–167.

Escorial, S., et al. (2003). Abilities that explain the intelligence decline: Evidence from the WAIS-III. *Psicothema, 15*(1), 19–22.

Etaugh, C. A., & Bridges, J. S. (2006). Midlife transitions. In J. Worell & C. D. Goodheart (Eds.), *Handbook of girls' and women's psychological health: Gender and well-being across the lifespan* (pp. 359–367). *Oxford series in clinical psychology.* New York: Oxford University Press.

Facts About Falling (2008, January 28). *The Washington Post.*

Facts about the Death with Dignity Act. (2007, September 22). Oregon Office of Disease Prevention and Epidemiology. Available at http://www.oregon.gov/DHS/ph/pas/faqs. shtml. Accessed October 5, 2008.

Fagot, B. I. (1990). A longitudinal study of gender segregation: Infancy to preschool. In F. F. Strayer (Ed.), *Social interaction and behavioral development during early childhood.* Montreal: La Maison D'Ethologie de Montreal.

Fagot, B. I., & Hagan, R. (1991). Observations of parent reactions to sex-stereotyped behaviors: Age and sex effects. *Child Development, 62,* 617–628.

Fagot, B. I., & Leinbach, M. D. (1993). Gender-role development in young children: From discrimination to labeling. *Developmental Review, 13,* 205–224.

Fagot, B. I., Rodgers, C. S., & Leinbach, M. D. (2000). Theories of gender socialization. In T. Eckes & H. M. Trautner (Eds.), *The developmental social psychology of gender* (pp. 65–89). Mahwah, NJ: Erlbaum.

Fair, R. C. (2007). Estimated age effects in athletic events and chess. *Experimental Aging Research, 33*(1), 37–57.

Fantz, R. L. (1961). The origin of form perception. *Scientific American, 204,* 66–72.

Fantz, R. L., Fagan, J. F., III, & Miranda, S. B. (1975). Early visual selectivity. In L. B. Cohen & P. Salapatek (Eds.), *Infant perception: From sensation to cognition,* Vol. 1. New York: Academic Press.

Farmer, A., Elkin, A., & McGuffin, P. (2007). The genetics of bipolar affective disorder. *Current Opinion in Psychiatry, 20*(1), 8–12.

Fay, M. P. (2004). *Estimating age-conditional probability of developing cancer using a piecewise mid-age joinpoint model for the rates.* Statistical Research and Applications Branch, NCI, Technical Report # 2003-03-2004.

Feijó, L., et al. (2006). Mothers' depressed mood and anxiety levels are reduced after massaging their preterm infants. *Infant Behavior & Development, 29(3),* 476–480.

Feinberg, M. E., Neiderhiser, J. M., Howe, G., & Hetherington, E. M. (2001). Adolescent, parent, and observer perceptions of parenting: Genetic and environmental influences on shared and distinct perceptions. *Child Development, 72*(4), 1266–1284.

Feiring, C. (1993, March). *Developing concepts of romance from 15 to 18 years.* Paper presented at the meeting of the Society for Research in Child Development, New Orleans, LA.

Feiring, C., & Lewis, M. (1991). The transition from middle to early adolescence: Sex differences in the social network and perceived self-competence. *Sex Roles, 24,* 489–509.

Feldman, R., & Masalha, S. (2007). The role of culture in moderating the links between early ecological risk and young children's adaptation. *Development and Psychopathology, 19*(1), 1–21.

Fergusson, A. (2007). What successful teachers do in inclusive classrooms: Research-based teaching strategies that help special learners succeed. *European Journal of Special Needs Education, 22*(1), 108–110.

Fernandez-Twinn, D. S., & Ozanne, S. E. (2006). Mechanisms by which poor early growth programs type-2 diabetes, obesity and the metabolic syndrome. *Physiology & Behavior, 88*(3), 234–243.

Féron, J., Gentaz, E., & Streri, A. (2006). Evidence of amodal representation of small numbers across visuo-tactile modalities in 5-month-old infants. *Cognitive Development, 21*(2), 81–92.

Field, A. P. (2006). The behavioral inhibition system and the verbal information pathway to children's fears. *Journal of Abnormal Psychology, 115*(4), 742–752.

Field, T. (1999). Sucking and massage therapy reduce stress during infancy. In M. Lewis & D. Ramsay (Eds.), *Soothing and stress* (pp. 157–169). Hillsdale, NJ: Erlbaum.

Field, T., Hernandez-Reif, M., Feijo, L., & Freedman, J. (2006). Prenatal, perinatal and neonatal stimulation: A survey of neonatal nurseries. *Infant Behavior & Development, 29*(1), 24–31.

Filus, A. (2006). Being a grandparent in China, Greece and Poland. *Studia Psychologiczne, 44*(1), 35–46.

Finegan, J. K., Niccols, G. A., & Sitarenios, G. (1992). Relations between prenatal testosterone levels and cognitive abilities at 4 years. *Developmental Psychology, 28,* 1075–1089.

Finkelman, J. M. (2005). Sexual harassment. In A. Barnes (Ed.). *The handbook of women, psychology, and the law.* (pp. 64–78). Hoboken, NJ: Wiley.

Fisch, S. M. (2004). *Children's learning from educational television: Sesame Street and beyond.* Mahwah, NJ: Erlbaum.

Fiske, A. (2006). The nature of depression in later life. In S. H. Qualls, & B. G. Knight (Eds.), *Psychotherapy for depression in older adults* (pp. 29–44). Hoboken, NJ: John Wiley & Sons Inc.

Fitzgerald, H. E., et al. (1991). The organization of lateralized behavior during infancy. In H. E. Fitzgerald, B. M. Lester, & M. W. Yogman (Eds.), *Theory and research in behavioral pediatrics.* New York: Plenum.

Fivush, R. (2002). Scripts, schemas, and memory of trauma. In N. L. Stein et al. (Eds.), *Representation, memory, and development: Essays in honor of Jean Mandler* (pp. 53–74). Mahwah, NJ: Erlbaum.

Fivush, R., & Hammond, N. R. (1990). Autobiographical memory across the preschool years: Toward reconceptualizing childhood amnesia. In R. Fivush & J. A. Hudson (Eds.), *Knowing and remembering in young children.* Cambridge: Cambridge University Press.

Fivush, R., Kuebli, J., & Clubb, P. A. (1992). The structure of events and event representations: A developmental analysis. *Child Development, 63,* 188–201.

Fivush, R., Sales, J, M., Goldberg, A., Bahrick, L., & Parker, J. (2004). Weathering the storm: Children's long-term recall of Hurricane Andrew. *Memory, 12*(1), 104–118.

Flavell, J. H. (1993). Young children's understanding of thinking and consciousness. *Current Directions in Psychological Science, 2,* 40–43.

Flavell, J. H., Miller, P. H., & Miller, S. A. (2002). *Cognitive development* (4th ed.). Upper Saddle River, NJ: Prentice Hall.

Florsheim, P. (Ed.). (2003). *Adolescent romantic relations and sexual behavior: Theory, research, and practical implications.* Mahwah, NJ: Erlbaum.

Flouri, E., & Buchanan, A. (2003). The role of father involvement and mother involvement in adolescents' psychological well-being. *British Journal of Social Work, 33*(3), 399–406.

Flynn, J. R. (2003). Movies about intelligence: The limitations of g. *Current Directions in Psychological Science, 12*(3), 95–99.

Foley, G. M. (2006). Self and social–emotional development in infancy: A descriptive synthesis. In G. M. Foley & J. D. Hochman (Eds.), *Mental health in early intervention: Achieving unity in principles and practice* (pp. 139–173). Baltimore: Paul H. Brookes.

Fontaine, A-M. (2005). Écologie développementale des premières interactions entre enfants: Effet des matériels de jeu. *Enfance, 57*(2), 137–154.

Food and Drug Administration. (2004, July 20). *Decreasing the chance of birth defects.* Available at http://www.fda.gov/ fdac/ features/996_bd.html.

Forbush, K., Heatherton, T. F., & Keel, P. K. (2007). Relationships between perfectionism and specific disordered eating behaviors. *International Journal of Eating Disorders, 40*(1), 37–41.

Ford, C. S., & Beach, F. A. (1951). *Patterns of sexual behavior.* New York: Harper & Row.

Forman-Hoffman, V. L., Ruffin, T., & Schultz, S. K. (2006). Basal metabolic rate in anorexia nervosa patients: Using appropriate predictive equations during the refeeding process. *Annals of Clinical Psychiatry, 18*(2), 123–127.

Fortier, J. (2010, April 10). Canada a nation of "satisfied" workers: Survey. *Financial Post.* Retrieved from http://www.working.com/ national/sectors/Canada+nation+satisfied+ workers+Survey/2901739/story.html

Foster-Clark, F. S., & Blyth, D. A. (1991). Peer relations and influences. In R. M. Lerner, A. C. Petersen, & J. Brooks-Gunn (Eds.), *Encyclopedia of adolescence.* New York: Garland.

Fouad, N. A., & Arredondo, P. (2007). Implications for Psychologists as Researchers. In N. A. Fouad & P. Arredondo (Eds.), *Becoming culturally oriented: Practical advice for psychologists and educators* (pp. 81–93). Washington, DC: American Psychological Association.

Fozard, J. L., & Gordon- Salant, S. (2001). Changes in vision and hearing with aging. In J. E. Birren, & K. W. Schaie (Eds.), *Handbook of psychology of aging* (5th ed.) (pp. 241–266). San Diego: Academic Press.

Franklin, A., Pilling, M., & Davies, I. (2005). The nature of infant color categorization: Evidence from eye movements on a target detection task. *Journal of Experimental Child Psychology, 91*(3), 227–248.

Frayser, S. (1985). *Varieties of sexual experience: An anthropological perspective on human sexuality.* New Haven, CT: Human Relations Area Files Press.

Frazier, L. D., Newman, F. L., & Jaccard, J. (2007). Psychosocial outcomes in later life. *Psychology and Aging, 22*(4), 676–689.

Freeman, M. S., Spence, M. J., and Oliphant, C. M. (1993, June). *Newborns prefer their mothers' low-pass filtered voices over other female filtered voices.* Paper presented at the meeting of the American Psychological Society, Chicago.

Frerichs, L., Andsager, J. L., Campo, S., Aquilino, M., & Dyer, C. S. (2006). Framing breastfeeding and formula-feeding messages in popular U.S. magazines. *Women & Health, 44*(1), 95–118.

Freund, A. M., & Baltes, P. B. (2002). The adaptiveness of selection, optimization, and compensation as strategies of life management. *Journals of Gerontology: Series B: Psychological Sciences & Social Sciences, 57B*(5), P426–P434.

Fried, P. A., & Smith, A. M. (2001). A literature review of the consequences of prenatal marijuana exposure: An emerging theme of a deficiency in aspects of executive function. *Neurotoxicology and Teratology, 23*(1), 1–11.

Friedman, R. A. (2008, January 15). Crisis? Maybe he's a narcissistic jerk. *The New York Times online.*

Frisch, R. (1997). Speech reported in N. Angier (1997), Chemical tied to fat control could help trigger puberty, *New York Times,* pp. C1, C3.

Frisch, R. E. (1994). The right weight: Body fat, menarche and fertility. *Proceedings of the Nutrition Society, 53,* 113–129.

Frodi, A. M. (1985). When empathy fails: Infant crying and child abuse. In B. M. Lester & C. F. Z. Boukydis (Eds.), *Infant crying.* New York: Plenum.

Fromkin, V., et al. (2004).*The development of language in Genie: A case of language acquisition beyond the "critical period."* New York: Psychology Press.

Fry, D. P. (2005). Rough-and-tumble social play in humans. In A. D. Pellegrini & P. K. Smith (Eds.), *The nature of play: Great apes and humans* (pp. 54–85). New York: Guilford Press.

Furman, W., & Buhrmester, D. (1992). Age and sex differences in perceptions of networks of personal relationships. *Child Development, 63,* 103–115.

Furman, W., Rahe, D., & Hartup, W. W. (1979). Social rehabilitation of low-interactive preschool children by peer intervention. *Child Development, 50,* 915–922.

Furnham, A., Petrides, K. V., & Constantinides, A. (2005). The effects of body mass index and waist-to-hip ratio on ratings of female attractiveness, fecundity, and health. *Personality and Individual Differences, 38*(8), 1823–1834.

Ganesh, M. P., & Magdalin, S. (2007). Perceived problems and academic stress in children of disrupted and non-disrupted families. *Journal of the Indian Academy of Applied Psychology, 33*(1), 53–59.

Gans, D., & Silverstein, M. (2006). Norms of filial responsibility for aging parents across time and generations. *Journal of Marriage and Family, 68*(4), 961–976.

Gardner, H. (1983). *Frames of mind: The theory of multiple intelligences.* New York: Basic Books.

Gardner, H. (2006). *The development and education of the mind: The selected works of Howard Gardner.* Philadelphia: Routledge/Taylor & Francis.

Garmon, L. (Writer & Director). (1997). Secret of the wild child [Television series episode]. *Nova.* Arlington, VA: PBS.

Gartstein, M. A., Slobodskaya, H. R., & Kinsht, I. A. (2003). Cross-cultural differences in temperament in the first year of life: United States of America (U.S.) and Russia. *International Journal of Behavioral Development, 27*(4), 316–328.

Garvey, C. (1990). *Developing child.* Cambridge, MA: Harvard University Press.

Gathercole, S. E., Pickering, S. J., Ambridge, B., & Wearing, H. (2004a). The structure of working memory from 4 to 15 years of age. *Developmental Psychology, 40*(2), 177–190.

Gathercole, S. E., Pickering, S. J., Knight, C., & Stegmann, Z. (2004b). Working memory skills and educational attainment: Evidence from national curriculum assessments at 7 and 14 years of age. *Applied Cognitive Psychology, 18*(1), 1–16.

Gavin, N. I., et al. (2005). Perinatal depression: A systematic review of prevalence and incidence. *Obstetrics & Gynecology, 106,* 1071–1083.

Ge, X., et al. (2003). It's about timing and change: Pubertal transition effects on symptoms of major depression among African American youths. *Developmental Psychology, 39*(3), 430–439.

Geary, D. C. (2006). Sex differences in social behavior and cognition: Utility of sexual selection for hypothesis generation. *Hormones and Behavior, 49*(3), 273–275.

Georges, J.-J., The, A. M., Onwuteaka-Philipsen, B. D., & van der Wal, G. (2008). Dealing with requests for euthanasia. *Journal of Medical Ethics, 34*(3), 150–155.

Georgiades, S., et al. (2007). Structure of the autism symptom phenotype: A proposed multidimensional model. *Journal of the American Academy of Child & Adolescent Psychiatry, 46*(2), 188–196.

Gerard, J. M., Landry-Meyer, L., & Roe, J. G. (2006). Grandparents raising grandchildren: The role of social support in coping with caregiving challenges. *International Journal of Ageing & Human Development, 62*(4), 359–383.

Geschwind, D. H. (2000). Interview cited in D. E. Rosenbaum (2000, May 16), On left-handedness, its causes and costs, *New York Times,* pp. F1, F6.

Gesell, A. (1928). *Infancy and human growth.* New York: Macmillan.

Gesell, A. (1929). Maturation and infant behavior patterns. *Psychological Review, 36,* 307–319.

Ghetti, S., & Alexander, K. W. (2004). "If it happened, I would remember it": Strategic use of event memorability in the rejection of false autobiographical events. *Child Development, 75*(2), 542–561.

Gibson, E. J. (1969). *Principles of perceptual learning and development.* New York: Appleton-Century-Crofts.

Gibson, E. J. (1991). *An odyssey in learning and perception.* Cambridge, MA: MIT Press.

Gibson, E. J., & Walk, R. D. (1960). The visual cliff. *Scientific American, 202,* 64–71.

Gilhooly, M. L., et al. (2007). Real-world problem solving and quality of life in older people. *British Journal of Health Psychology, 12*(4), 587–600.

Gilligan, C. (1982). *In a different voice.* Cambridge, MA: Harvard University Press.

Gilligan, C. (1990). Remapping the moral domain: New images of the self in relationship. In C. Zanardi (Ed.), *Essential papers on the psychology of women. Essential papers in psychoanalysis* (pp. 480–495). New York: New York University Press.

Giussani, D. A. (2006). Prenatal hypoxia: Relevance to developmental origins of health and disease. In P. Gluckman & M. Hanson (Eds.), *Developmental origins of health and disease* (pp. 178–190). New York: Cambridge University Press.

Glaser, K., Tomassini, C., Racioppi, F., & Stuchbury, R. (2006). Marital disruptions and loss of support in later life. *European Journal of Ageing, 3*(4), 207–216

Gleason, T. R. (2002). Social provisions of real and imaginary relationships in early childhood. *Developmental Psychology, 38*(6), 979–992.

Gleason, T. R. (2004). Imaginary companions and peer acceptance. *International Journal of Behavioral Development, 28*(3), 204–209.

Gleason, T. R., Gower, A. L., Hohmann, L. M., & Gleason, T. C. (2005). Temperament and friendship in preschool-aged children. *International Journal of Behavioral Development, 29*(4), 336–344.

Gleason, T. R., & Hohmann, L. M. (2006). Concepts of real and imaginary friendships in early childhood. *Social Development, 15*(1), 128–144.

Gleason, T. R., Sebanc, A. M., & Hartup, W. W. (2003). Imaginary companions of preschool children. In M. E. Hertzig & E. A. Farber (Eds.), *Annual progress in child psychiatry and child development: 2000–2001* (pp. 101–121). New York: Brunner-Routledge.

Glück, J., & Bluck, S. (2007). Looking back across the life span: A life story account of the reminiscence bump. *Memory & Cognition, 35*(8), 1928–1939.

Gobet, F., & Simon, H. A. (2000). Five seconds or sixty? Presentation time in expert memory. *Cognitive Science, 24*(4), 651–682.

Goel, P., Radotra, A., Singh, I., Aggarwal, A., & Dua, D. (2004). Effects of passive smoking on outcome in pregnancy. *Journal of Postgraduate Medicine, 50*(1), 12–16.

Golan, H., & Huleihel, M. (2006). The effect of prenatal hypoxia on brain development: Short- and long-term consequences demonstrated in rodent models. *Developmental Science, 9*(4), 338–349.

Goldberg, J, Holtz, D., Hyslop, T., & Tolosa, J. E. (2002). Has the use of routine episiotomy decreased? Examination of episiotomy rates from 1983 to 2000. *Obstetrics and Gynecology, 99*(3), 395–400.

Goldman, J. S., Adamson, J., Karydas, A., Miller, B. L., & Hutton, M. (2008). New genes, new dilemmas: FTLD genetics and its implications for families. *American Journal of Alzheimer's Disease and Other Dementias, 22*(6), 507–515.

Goldschmidt, L., Day, N. L., & Richardson, G. A. (2000). Effects of prenatal marijuana exposure on child behavior problems at age 10. *Neurotoxicology and Teratology, 22*(3), 325–336.

Goldsmith, H. H., et al. (2003). Part III: Genetics and development. In R. J. Davidson et al. (Eds.), *Handbook of affective sciences.* London: Oxford University Press.

Goldstein, E. B. (2005). *Cognitive psychology: Connecting mind, research, and everyday experience.* Belmont, CA: Wadsworth.

Goldstein, H. (2004). International comparisons of student attainment. *Assessment in Education: Principles, Policy & Practice, 11*(3), 319–330.

Goldstein, I. (1998). Cited in Kolata, G. (1998, April 4). Impotence pill: Would it also help women? *The New York Times,* pp. A1, A6.

Goldstein, I. (2000). Cited in Norton, A. (2000, September 1). Exercise helps men avoid impotence. *Reuters News Agency online.*

Goldstein, I., & Alexander, J. L. (2005). Practical aspects in the management of vaginal atrophy and sexual dysfunction in perimenopausal and postmenopausal women. *Journal of Sexual Medicine, 2*(Suppl3), 154–165.

Goldstein, I., Meston, C., Davis, S., & Traish, A. (Eds.). (2006). *Female sexual dysfunction.* New York: Parthenon.

Goldstein, S., & Brooks, R. B. (2005). *Handbook of resilience in children.* New York: Kluwer Academic/Plenum.

Gonzalez, V. (2005). Cultural, linguistic, and socioeconomic factors influencing monolingual and bilingual children's cognitive development. In V. Gonzalez & J. Tinajero (Eds.), *Review of research and practice,* Vol. 3 (pp. 67–104). Mahwah, NJ: Erlbaum.

González, Y. S., Moreno, D. S., & Schneider, B. H. (2004). Friendship expectations of early adolescents in Cuba and Canada. *Journal of Cross-Cultural Psychology, 35*(4), 436–445.

Goodman, C. G. (2007a). Intergenerational triads in skipped-generation grandfamilies. *International Journal of Ageing & Human Development, 65*(3), 231–258.

Goodman, C. G. (2007b). Family dynamics in three-generation grandfamilies. *Journal of Family Issues, 28*(3), 355–379.

Goodman, G. S., Rudy, L., Bottoms, B. L., & Aman, C. (1990). Children's concerns and memory: Issues of ecological validity in the study of children's eyewitness testimony. In R. Fivush & J. A. Hudson (Eds.), *Knowing and remembering in young children.* Cambridge: Cambridge University Press.

Gopnik, A., & Meltzoff, A. N. (1992). Categorization and naming: Basic-level sorting in eighteen-month-olds and its relation to language. *Child Development, 63,* 1091–1103.

Gopnik, A., & Slaughter, V. (1991). Young children's understanding of changes in their mental states. *Child Development, 62,* 98–110.

Gordon-Salant, S., Fitzgibbons, P. J., & Friedman, S. A. (2007). Recognition of time-compressed and natural speech with selective temporal enhancements by young and elderly listeners. *Journal of Speech, Language, and Hearing Research, 50*(5), 1181–1193.

Gormally, S., et al. (2001). Contact and nutrient caregiving effects on newborn infant pain responses. *Developmental Medicine and Child Neurology, 43*(1), 28–38.

Gottfried, G. M., Hickling, A. K., Totten, L. R., Mkroyan, A., & Reisz, A. (2003). To be or not to be a galaprock: Preschoolers' intuitions about the importance of knowledge and action for pretending. *British Journal of Developmental Psychology, 21*(3), 397–414.

Gottlieb, B. H., Still, E., & Newby-Clark, I. R. (2007). Types and precipitants of growth and decline in emerging adulthood. *Journal of Adolescent Research, 22*(2), 132–155.

Gottman, J. M., Coan, J., Carrère, S. & Swanson, C. (1998). Predicting marital happiness and stability from newlywed interactions. *Journal of Marriage and the Family, 60,* 5–22.

Graber, J. A., Seeley, J. R., Brooks-Gunn, J., & Lewinsohn, P. M. (2004). Is pubertal timing associated with psychopathology in young adulthood? *Journal of the American Academy of Child and Adolescent Psychiatry, 43*(6), 718–726.

Grady, D. (2003a). Postmenopausal hormones—Therapy for symptoms only. *New England Journal of Medicine, 348*(19), 1835–1837.

Grady, D. (2003b, June 25). Study finds new risks in hormone therapy. *The New York Times.*

Gray, C., Koopman, E., & Hunt, J. (1991). The emotional phases of marital separation: an empirical investigation. *American Journal of Orthopsychiatry, 1991*(61), 138–143.

Gray, S. L., et al. (2008). Antioxidant vitamin supplement use and risk of dementia or Alzheimer's disease in older adults. *Journal of the American Geriatrics Society, 56*(2), 291–295.

Greco, C., Rovee-Collier, C., Hayne, H., Griesler, P., & Early, L. (1986). Ontogeny of early event memory: II. Encoding and retrieval by 2- and 3-month-olds. *Infant Behavior and Development, 9,* 461–472.

Green, R. (1978). Sexual identity of 37 children raised by homosexual or transsexual parents. *American Journal of Psychiatry, 135,* 692–697.

Greene, S. M., Anderson, E. R., Doyle, E. A., Riedelbach, H., & Bear, G. G. (2006). Divorce. In K. M. Minke (Ed.), *Children's needs III: Development, prevention, and intervention* (pp. 745–757). Bethesda, MD: National Association of School Psychologists.

Greenough, W. T., Black, J. E., & Wallace, C. S. (2002). Experience and brain development. In M. H. Johnson, Y. Munakata, & R. O. Gilmore (Eds.), *Brain development and cognition: A reader* (2nd ed.) (pp. 186–216). Malden, MA: Blackwell.

Greidanus, J. A. (2007). A narrative inquiry into the experiences of bereaved children. *Dissertation Abstracts International Section A: Humanities and Social Sciences, 67*(9-A), 3447.

Grigorenko, E. L. (2007). Triangulating developmental dyslexia: Behavior, brain, and genes. In D. Coch, G. Dawson, & K. W. Fischer (Eds.). *Human behavior, learning, and the developing brain: Atypical development.* (pp. 117–144). New York: Guilford.

Grilo, C. M., Masheb, R. M., & Wilson, G. T. (2005). Efficacy of cognitive behavioral therapy and fluoxetine for the treatment of binge eating disorder: A randomized double-blind placebo-controlled comparison. *Biological Psychiatry, 57*(3), 301–309.

Grindrod, C. M., & Baum, S. R. (2005). Hemispheric contributions to lexical ambiguity resolution in a discourse context: Evidence from individuals with unilateral left and right hemisphere lesions. *Brain and Cognition, 57*(1), 70–83.

Grolnick, W. S., McMenamy, J. M., & Kurowski, C. O. (2006). Emotional self-regulation in infancy and toddlerhood. In L. Balter & C. S. Tamis-LeMonda (Eds.), *Child psychology: A handbook of contemporary issues* (2nd ed.) (pp. 3–25). New York: Psychology Press.

Grön, G., Wunderlich, A. P., Spitzer, M., Tomczak, R., & Riepe, M. W. (2000). Brain activation during human navigation: Gender-different neural networks as substrate of performance. *Nature Neuroscience, 3*(4), 404–408.

Grossmann, A. H., D'Augelli, A. R., & O'Connell, T. S. (2003). Being lesbian, gay, bisexual, and sixty or older in North America. In L. D. Garnets, & D. C. Kimmel (Eds.), *Psychological perspectives on lesbian, gay, and bisexual experiences* (2nd ed.) (pp. 629–645). New York: Columbia University Press.

Grossmann, K., et al. (2002). The uniqueness of the child–father attachment relationship: Fathers' sensitive and challenging play as a pivotal variable in a 16-year longitudinal study. *Social Development, 11*(3), 307–331.

Grundy, E., & Henretta, J. C. (2006). Between elderly parents and adult children: A new look at the intergenerational care provided by the "sandwich generation." *Ageing & Society, 26*(5), 707–722.

Grusec, J. E. (2002). Parenting socialization and children's acquisition of values. In M. H. Bornstein (Ed.), *Handbook of parenting* (2nd ed.), Vol. 5, *Practical issues in parenting* (pp. 143–167). Mahwah, NJ: Erlbaum.

Grusec, J. E. (2006). The development of moral behavior and conscience from a socialization perspective. In M. Killen & J. G. Smetana (Eds.), *Handbook of moral development* (pp. 243–265). Mahwah, NJ: Erlbaum.

Guerin, D. W., Gottfried, A. W., & Thomas, C. W. (1997). Difficult temperament and behaviour problems: A longitudinal study from 1.5 to 12 years. *International Journal of Behavioral Development, 21*(1), 71–90.

Guerrini, I., Thomson, A. D., & Gurling, H. D. (2007). The importance of alcohol misuse, malnutrition and genetic susceptibility on brain growth and plasticity. *Neuroscience & Biobehavioral Reviews, 31*(2), 212–220.

Guiaux, M., van Tilburg, T., & van Groenou, M. B. (2007). Changes in contact and support exchange in personal networks after widowhood. *Personal Relationships, 14*(3), 457–473.

Güntürkün, O. (2006). Letters on nature and nurture. In P. B. Baltes et al. (Eds.), *Lifespan development and the brain: The perspective of biocultural co-constructivism* (pp. 379–397). New York: Cambridge University Press.

Gurba, E. (2005). On the specific character of adult thought: Controversies over postformal operations. *Polish Psychological Bulletin, 36*(3), 175–185.

Gutknecht, L. (2001). Full-genome scans with autistic disorder: A review. *Behavior Genetics, 31*(1), 113–123.

Guttmacher Institute. (2007, June 8). Available at http://www.guttmacher.org/.

Guzikowski, W. (2006). Doula—a new model of delivery (continuous, nonprofessional care during the delivery). *Ceska Gynekologie, 71*(2), 103–105.

Haapasalo, J., & Moilanen, J. (2004). Official and self-reported childhood abuse and adult crime of young offenders. *Criminal Justice and Behavior, 31*(2), 127–149.

Haith, M. M. (1979). Visual cognition in early infancy. In R. B. Kearsly & I. E. Sigel (Eds.), *Infants at risk: Assessment of cognitive functioning.* Hillsdale, NJ: Erlbaum.

Haith, M. M. (1990). Progress in the understanding of sensory and perceptual processes in early infancy. *Merrill–Palmer Quarterly, 36,* 1–26.

Halawah, I. (2006). The impact of student-faculty informal interpersonal relationships on intellectual and personal development. *College Student Journal, 40*(3), 670–678.

Halgin, R. P., & Whitbourne, S. K. (1993). *Abnormal psychology.* Fort Worth, TX: Harcourt Brace Jovanovich.

Hall, D. T. (2004). The protean career: A quarter-century journey. *Journal of Vocational Behavior, 65*(1), 1–13.

Hall, G. S. (1904). *Adolescence: Its psychology and its relations to physiology, anthropology, sociology sex, crime, religion and education, Vol. II.* New York: D Appleton & Company.

Halliday, L. F., & Bishop, D. V. M. (2006). Auditory frequency discrimination in children with dyslexia. *Journal of Research in Reading, 29*(2), 213–228.

Halpern, D. F. (2003). Sex differences in cognitive abilities. *Applied Cognitive Psychology, 17*(3), 375–376.

Halpern, D. F. (2004). A cognitive-process taxonomy for sex differences in cognitive abilities. *Current Directions in Psychological Science, 13*(4), 135–139.

Hamm, J. V. (2000). Do birds of a feather flock together? The variable bases for African American, Asian American, and European American adolescents' selection of similar friends. *Developmental Psychology, 36*(2), 209–219.

Hangal, S., & Aminabhavi, V. A. (2007). Self-concept, emotional maturity, and achievement motivation of the adolescent children of employed mothers and homemakers. *Journal of the Indian Academy of Applied Psychology, 33*(1), 103–110.

Hanlon, T. E., Bateman, R. W., Simon, B. D., O'Grady, K. E., & Carswell, S. B. (2004). Antecedents and correlates of deviant activity in urban youth manifesting behavioral problems. *Journal of Primary Prevention, 24*(3), 285–309.

Hannon, P., Bowen, D. J., Moinpour, C. M., & McLerran, D. F. (2003). Correlations in perceived food use between the family food preparer and their spouses and children. *Appetite, 40*(1), 77–83.

Hansen, J. C., Dik, B. J., & Zhou, S. (2008). An examination of the structure of leisure interests of college students, working-age adults, and retirees. *Journal of Counseling Psychology, 55*(2), 133–145.

Harel, J., & Scher, A. (2003). Insufficient responsiveness in ambivalent mother–infant relationships: Contextual and affective aspects. *Infant Behavior and Development, 26*(3), 371–383.

Harlow, H. F., & Harlow, M. K. (1966). Learning to love. *American Scientist, 54,* 244–272.

Harlow, H. F., Harlow, M. K., & Suomi, S. J. (1971). From thought to therapy: Lessons from a primate laboratory. *American Scientist, 59,* 538–549.

Harris, G. (2004, September 14). *FDA links drugs to being suicidal.* Available at http://www.nytimes.com.

Harris, J. R. (2007, March 26). To the editor: Day care and a child's behavior. *New York Times online*.

Harris, S. R., Megens, A. M., Backman, C. L., & Hayes, V. E. (2005). Stability of the Bayley II Scales of Infant Development in a sample of low-risk and high-risk infants. *Developmental Medicine & Child Neurology, 47*(12), 820–823.

Hart, S. J., Davenport, M. L., Hooper, S. R., & Belger, A. (2006). Visuospatial executive function in Turner syndrome: Functional MRI and neurocognitive findings. *Brain: A Journal of Neurology, 129*(5), May, 1125–1136.

Harter, S. (1990). Self and identity development. In S. S. Feldman & G. R. Elliott (Eds.), *At the threshold: The developing adolescent*. Cambridge, MA: Harvard University Press.

Harter, S. (2006). The Self. In K. A. Renninger, I. E. Sigel, W. Damon, & R. M. Lerner (Eds.), *Handbook of child psychology* (6th ed.), Vol. 4, *Child psychology in practice* (pp. 505–570). Hoboken, NJ: Wiley.

Harter, S., & Monsour, A. (1992). Developmental analysis of conflict caused by opposing attributes in the adolescent self-portrait. *Developmental Psychology, 28*, 251–260.

Harter, S., & Pike, R. (1984). The pictorial scale of perceived competence and social acceptance for young children. *Child Development, 55*, 1969–1982.

Harter, S., & Whitesell, N. R. (2003). Beyond the debate: Why some adolescents report stable self-worth over time and situation, whereas others report changes in self-worth. *Journal of Personality, 71*(6), 1027–1058.

Hartley, A. (2006). Changing role of the speed of processing construct in the cognitive psychology of human aging. In J. E. Birren & K. W. Schaie (Eds.), *Handbook of the psychology of aging* (6th ed.) (pp. 183–207). Amsterdam, Netherlands: Elsevier.

Hartman, M., & Warren, L. H. (2005). Explaining age differences in temporal working memory. *Psychology and Aging, 20*(4), 645–656.

Hartup, W. W. (1983). The peer system. In P. H. Mussen (Ed.), *Handbook of child psychology*, Vol. 4, *Socialization, personality, and social development*. New York: Wiley.

Hasher, L. (2008, May 20). Cited in Reistad-Long, S. Older brain, wiser brain. *The New York Times online*. Accessed October 5, 2008.

Hasselhorn, M. (1992). Task dependency and the role of typicality and metamemory in the development of an organizational strategy. *Child Development, 63*, 202–214.

Hassing, L. B., & Johanssom, B. (2005). Aging and cognition. *Nordisk Psykologi, 57*(1), 4–20.

Hastings, P. D., Zahn-Waxler, C., Robinson, J., Usher, B., & Bridges, D. (2000). The development of concern for others in children with behavior problems. *Developmental Psychology, 36*(5), 531–546.

Hatch, L. R., & Bulcroft, K. (2004). Does long-term marriage bring less frequent disagreements? *Journal of Family Issues, 25*, 465–495.

Hatcher, R. A., et al. (Eds.). (2007). *Contraceptive technologies* (18th rev. ed.). New York: Ardent Media.

Hatfield, E., & Rapson, R. L. (2002). Passionate love and sexual desire: Cultural and historical perspectives. In A. L. Vangelisti, H. T. Reis, et al. (Eds.), *Stability and change in relationships. Advances in personal relationships* (pp. 306–324). New York: Cambridge University Press.

Havighurst, R. (1972). In Robert Havighurst: Developmental theorist. Available at http://faculty.mdc.edu/jmcnair/EDF3214.Topic.Outline/Robert.Havighurst.htm. Accessed October 2, 2008.

Hawkley, L. C., Burleson, M. H., Berntson, G. G., & Cacioppo, J. T. (2003). Loneliness in everyday life: Cardiovascular activity, psychosocial context, and health behaviors. *Journal of Personality & Social Psychology, 85*(1), 105–120.

Hay, D. F., Payne, A., & Chadwick, A. (2004). Peer relations in childhood. *Journal of Child Psychology and Psychiatry. 45*(1), 84–108.

Hayes, R., & Dennerstein, L. (2005). The impact of aging on sexual function and sexual dysfunction in women: A review of population-based studies. *Journal of Sexual Medicine, 2*(3), 317–330.

Hayflick, L. (1996) *How and why we age*. New York: Ballantine Books, 1994.

Hayne, H., & Fagen, J. W. (Eds.). (2003). *Progress in infancy research*, Vol. 3. Mahwah, NJ: Erlbaum.

Hayslip, B., Jr., & Kaminski, P. L. (2006). Custodial grandchildren. In G. G. Bear & K. M. Minke (Eds.), *Children's needs III: Development, prevention, and intervention* (pp. 771–782). Washington, DC: National Association of School Psychologists.

Hayslip, B., Jr., Neumann, C. S., Louden, L., & Chapman, B. (2006). Developmental stage theories. In J. C. Thomas, D. L. Segal, & M. Hersen. (Eds.), *Comprehensive handbook of personality and psychopathology, Vol. 1: Personality and everyday functioning* (pp. 115–141). Hoboken, NJ: John Wiley & Sons, Inc.

Health Canada. (2007a). Breastfeeding. Retrieved from http://www.hc-sc.gc.ca/fn-an/pubs/infant-nourrisson/nut_infant_nourrisson_term_3-eng.php

Health Canada. (2007b). *Eating well with Canada's food guide*. Retrieved from http://www.hc-sc.gc.ca/fn-an/pubs/res-educat/res-educat_3-eng.php

Health Canada. (2009). Aboriginal Head Start on Reserve. Retrieved from http://www.hc-sc.gc.ca/fniah-spnia/famil/develop/ahsor-papa_intro-eng.php

Health Disparities, Minority Cancer Awareness. (2004). Cancer Prevention and Control, National Center for Chronic Disease Prevention and Health Promotion, Centers for Disease Control.

The Health Journal. (2010). Canadian women over 30 at risk as infertility rates predicted to double. Retrieved from http://www.thehealthjournal.ca/site/content/view/136/1/

Healy, M. D., & Ellis, B. J. (2007). Birth order, conscientiousness, and openness to experience. Tests of the family-niche model of personality using a within-family methodology. *Evolution and Human Behavior, 28*(1), 55–59.

Heart and Stroke Foundation. (2008). Healthy weight in children and youth. Retrieved from http://www.heartandstroke.com/site/c.ikIQLcMWJtE/b.3484343/k.2A0B/For_Parents_Healthy_Weights_in_children.htm?gclid=CLiArI3m2aICFR5V5wod3wshyA

Heart and Stroke Foundation of Canada. (1993). *Position statement on physical activity*. Unpublished report. Ottawa: Author. Retrieved from http://www.pembinatrails.ca/program/physicaleducation/Documents/MPESA/Articles/Health%20Related/children%20stats.doc

Heart and Stroke Foundation of Canada. (2010). Statistics:Cardiovascular disease deaths. Retrieved from http://www.heartandstroke.com/site/c.ikIQLcMWJtE/b.3483991/k.34A8/Statistics.htm

Hebert, T. P. (2000). Gifted males pursuing careers in elementary education: Factors that influence a belief in self. *Journal for the Education of the Gifted, 24*(1), 7–45.

Heilman, K. M., Nadeau, S. E., & Beversdorf, D. O. (2003). Creative innovation: Possible brain mechanisms. *Neurocase, 9*(5), 369–379.

Heimann, M., et al. (2006). Exploring the relation between memory, gestural communication, and the emergence of language in infancy: A longitudinal study. *Infant and Child Development, 15*(3), 233–249.

Heindel, J. J., & Lawler, C. (2006) Role of exposure to environmental chemicals in developmental origins of health and disease. In P. Gluckman & M. Hanson (Eds.), *Developmental origins of health and disease* (pp. 82–97). New York: Cambridge University Press.

Helwig, C. C. (2006). Rights, civil liberties, and democracy across cultures. In M. Killen & J. G. Smetana (Eds.), *Handbook of moral development* (pp. 185–210). Mahwah, NJ: Erlbaum.

Henry, D., et al. (2000). Normative influences on aggression in urban elementary school classrooms. *American Journal of Community Psychology, 28*(1) 59–81.

Henzi, S. P., et al. (2007). Look who's talking: developmental trends in the size of conversational cliques. *Evolution and Human Behavior, 28*(1), 66–74.

Heron, M. P. (2007). National Vital Statistics Reports, 56(5). Centers for Disease Control and Prevention. Available at www.cdc.gov/nchs/data/nvsr/nvsr56/nvsr56_05.

Hershberger, S. L., & D'Augelli, A. R. (2000). Issues in counseling lesbian, gay, and bisexual adolescents. In R. M. Perez, K. A. De-Bord, & K. J. Bieschke (Eds.), *Handbook of counseling and psychotherapy with lesbian, gay, and bisexual clients* (pp. 225–247). Washington, DC: American Psychological Association.

Hertenstein, M. J., & Campos, J. J. (2004). The retention effects of an adult's emotional displays on infant behavior. *Child Development, 75*(2), 595–613.

Hetherington, E. M. (1989). Coping with family transition: Winners, losers, and survivors. *Child Development, 60*, 1–14.

Hetherington, E. M. (2006). The influence of conflict, marital problem solving and parenting on children's adjustment in nondivorced, divorced and remarried families. In A. Clarke-Stewart & J. Dunn (Eds.), *Families count: Effects on child and adolescent development, The Jacobs Foundation series on adolescence* (pp. 203–237). Cambridge, UK: Cambridge University Press.

Hetherington, E. M., et al. (1992). *Coping with marital transitions*. Monographs of the Society for Research in Child Development, 57(2–3, ser. 227).

Hicks, B. M., et al. (2007). Genes mediate the association between P3 amplitude and externalizing disorders. *Psychophysiology, 44*(1), 98–105.

Hill, R. A., Donovan, S., & Koyama, N. F. (2005). Female sexual advertisement reflects resource availability in twentieth-century UK society. *Human Nature, 16*(3), 266–277.

Hill, S. E., & Flom, R. (2007). 18- and 24-month-olds' discrimination of gender-consistent and inconsistent activities. *Infant Behavior & Development, 30*(1) 168–173.

Hill, S. Y., et al., (2007). Cerebellar volume in offspring from multiplex alcohol dependence families. *Biological Psychiatry, 61*(1), 41–47.

Hinojosa, T., Sheu, C., & Michel, G. F. (2003). Infant hand-use preferences for grasping objects contributes to the development of a hand-use preference for manipulating objects. *Developmental Psychobiology, 43*(4), 328–334.

HIV Edmonton. (2010.). *HIV/AIDS.* Retrieved from http://www.hivedmnton.com/hivinfo.htm

Hochwarter, W. A., Ferris, G. R., Perrewé, P. L., Witt, L. A., & Kiewitz, C. (2001). A note on the nonlinearity of the age-job-satisfaction relationship. *Journal of Applied Social Psychology, 31*(6), 1223–1237.

Hoegh, D. G., & Bourgeois, M. J. (2002). Prelude and postlude to the self: Correlates of achieved identity. *Youth and Society, 33*(4), 573–594.

Hoff, E. (2006). Language experience and language milestones during early childhood. In K. McCartney & D. Phillips (Eds.), *Blackwell handbook of early childhood development., Blackwell handbooks of developmental psychology* (pp. 233–251). Malden, MA: Blackwell.

Hoff, E. V. (2005). A friend living inside me—The forms and functions of imaginary companions. *Imagination, Cognition and Personality, 24*(2), 151–189.

Hogan, A. M., de Haan, M., Datta, A., & Kirkham, F. J. (2006). Hypoxia: An acute, intermittent and chronic challenge to cognitive development. *Developmental Science, 9*(4), 335–337.

Hogan, A. M., Kirkham, F. J., Isaacs, E. B., Wade, A. M., & Vargha-Khadem, F. (2005). Intellectual decline in children with moyamoya and sickle cell anaemia. *Developmental Medicine & Child Neurology, 47*(12), 824–829.

Holland, J. J. (2000, July 25). *Groups link media to child violence.* Available at http://www.ap.org/.

Holland, J. L. (1997). *Making vocational choices: A theory of vocational personalities and work environments* (3rd ed.). Odessa, FL: Psychological Assessment Resources.

Homer, B. D., & Nelson, K. (2005). Seeing objects as symbols and symbols as objects: Language and the development of dual representation. In B. D. Homer & C. S. Tamis- LeMonda (Eds.), *The development of social cognition and communication* (pp. 29–52). Mahwah, NJ: Erlbaum.

Homish, G. G., & Leonard, K. E. (2007). The drinking partnership and marital satisfaction: The longitudinal influence of discrepant drinking. *Journal of Consulting and Clinical Psychology, 75*(1) 43–51.

Honzik, M. P., Macfarlane, J. W., & Allen, L. (1948). The stability of mental test performance between two and eighteen years. *Journal of Experimental Education, 17*, 309–324.

Höpflinger, F., & Hummel, C. (2006). Heranwachsende Enkelkinder und ihre Großeltern: Im Geschlechtervergleich. *Zeitschrift für Gerontologie und Geriatrie, 39*(1), 33–40.

Hoppmann, C., & Smith, J. (2007). Life-history related differences in possible selves in very

old age. *International Journal of Aging & Human Development, 64*(2), 109–127.

Horn, J. L., & Noll, J. (1997). Human cognitive capabilities: Gf-Gc theory. In D. P. Flanagan, J. L. Genshaft, & P. L. Harrison (Eds.), *Contemporary intellectual assessment: Theories, tests, and issues* (pp. 53–91). New York: Guilford Press.

Horton, S. M. (2008). Aging stereotypes: Effects on the performance and health of seniors. *Dissertation Abstracts International Section A: Humanities and Social Sciences. 68*(8-A), 3540.

Hossain, M., Chetana, M., & Devi, P. U. (2005). Late effect of prenatal irradiation on the hippocampal histology and brain weight in adult mice. *International Journal of Developmental Neuroscience, 23*(4), 307–313.

Hostetler, A. J., Sweet, S., & Moen, P. (2007). Gendered career paths: A life course perspective on returning to school. *Sex Roles, 56*(1–2), 85–103.

Hough, M. S. (2007). Adult age differences in word fluency for common and goal-directed categories. *Advances in Speech Language Pathology, 9*(2), 154–161.

Howe, M. L. (2006). Developmentally invariant dissociations in children's true and false memories: Not all relatedness is created equal. *Child Development, 77*(4), 1112–1123.

Huang, J. (2007). Hormones and female sexuality. In A. F. Owens & M. S. Tepper (Eds.), *Sexual health (Vol 2): Physical foundations* (pp. 43–78). *Praeger perspectives: Sex, love, and psychology.* Westport, CT: Praeger Publishers/ Greenwood Publishing Group.

Huesmann, L. R., Dubow, E. F., Eron, L. D., & Boxer, P. (2006). Middle childhood family contextual factors as predictors of adult outcomes. In A. C. Huston & M. N. Ripke (Eds.), *Middle Childhood: Contexts of Development.* Cambridge, UK: Cambridge University Press.

Huestis, M. A., et al. (2002). Drug abuse's smallest victims: in utero drug exposure. *Forensic Science International, 128*(2), 20.

Huizink, A. C., & Mulder, E. J. H. (2006). Maternal smoking, drinking or cannabis use during pregnancy and neurobehavioral and cognitive functioning in human offspring. *Neuroscience & Biobehavioral Reviews, 30*(1), 24–41.

Hultsch, D. F., Hertzog, C., Dixon, R.A., & Small, B. J. (1998). *Memory change in the aged.* New York: Cambridge University Press.

Human Resources and Skills Development Canada. (2010a). *Family life—Age of mother at childbirth.* Retrieved from http://www4. hrsdc.gc.ca/.3ndic.1t.4r@-eng.jsp?iid=75

Human Resources and Skills Development Canada. (2010b). Indicators of Well Being in Canada: Social participation—Volunteering. Retrieved from http://www4.hrsdc. gc.ca/.3ndic.1t.4r@-eng.jsp?iid=74

Hunt, C. E., & Hauck, F. R. (2006). Sudden infant death syndrome. *Canadian Medical Association Journal, 174*(13), 1861–1869.

Huntington Society of Canada. (n.d.). What is Huntington disease? Retrieved from http:// www.huntingtonsociety.ca/english/index.asp

Hur, Y. (2005). Genetic and environmental influences on self-concept in female pre-adolescent twins: Comparison of Minnesota and Seoul data. *Twin Research and Human Genetics, 8*(4), 291–299.

Hurd, Y. L., et al. (2005). Marijuana impairs growth in mid–gestation fetuses. *Neurotoxicology and Teratology, 27*(2), 221–229.

Hursting, S. D., Lavigne, J. A., Berrigan, D., Perkins, S. N., & Barrett, J. C. (2003). Calorie restriction, aging, and cancer prevention: Mechanisms of action and applicability to humans. *Annual Review of Medicine, 54*(131–152).

Hussain, A. (2002, June 26) It's official. Men really are afraid of commitment. Reuters.

Hyde, J. S., Fennema, E., & Lamon, S. J. (1990). Gender differences in mathematics performance: A meta-analysis. *Psychological Bulletin, 107*, 139–155.

Hyde, J. S., Lindberg, S. M., Linn, M. C., Ellis, A. B., & Williams, C. C. (2008). Gender similarities characterize math performance. *Science, 321*, 494–495.

Hynes, M., Sheik, M., Wilson, H. G., & Spiegel, P. (2002). Reproductive health indicators and outcomes among refugee and internally displaced persons in postemergency phase camps. *Journal of the American Medical Association, 288*, 595–603.

Infant and Toddler Nutrition. (2007, April 10). National Institutes of Health, Department of Health and Human Services. Available at http://www.nlm.nih.gov/medlineplus/ infantandtoddlernutrition.html.

International Human Genome Sequencing Consortium (2006). A global map of p53 transcription-factor binding sites in the human genome. *Cell, 124*(1), 207–219.

Ipsos Reid. (2006). 1/2 of Canadians say they have no control over stress levels. Retrieved from http://www.marketwire.com/press-release/-of-Canadians-Say-They-Have-No-Control-Over-Stress-Levels-598798.htm

Jacklin, C. N., Wilcox, K. T., & Maccoby, E. E. (1988). Neonatal sex-steroid hormones and cognitive abilities at six years. *Developmental Psychobiology, 21*, 567–574.

Jacobs, D. M., Levy, G., & Marder, K. (2006). Dementia in Parkinson's disease, Huntington's disease, and related disorders. In M. J. Farah & T. E. Feinberg (Eds.), *Patient-based approaches to cognitive neuroscience* (2nd ed.) (pp. 381–395). Cambridge, MA: MIT Press.

Jacobs, J. E., Davis-Kean, P., Bleeker, M., Eccles, J. S., & Malanchuk, O. (2005). "I can, but I don't want to": The impact of parents, interests, and activities on gender differences in math. In A. M. Gallagher & J. C. Kaufman (Eds.), *Gender differences in mathematics: An integrative psychological approach* (pp. 246–263). New York: Cambridge University Press.

Jacobs, S. (1993). *Pathologic grief: Maladaptation to loss.* Washington, DC: American Psychiatric Press.

Jacobson, J. L., Jacobson, S. W., Padgett, R. J., Brumitt, G. A., & Billings, R. L. (1992). Effects of prenatal PCB exposure on cognitive processing efficiency and sustained attention. *Developmental Psychology, 28*, 297–306.

Jacobsen, J. S., et al. (2006). Early-onset behavioral and synaptic deficits in a mouse model of Alzheimer's disease. *Proceedings of the National Academy of Sciences, 103*, 5161–5166.

Jacobson, P. F., & Schwartz, R. G. (2005). English past tense use in bilingual children with language impairment. *American Journal of Speech-Language Pathology, 14*(4), 313–323.

James, W. 1890. *The principles of psychology.* Mineola, NY: Dover (Reprint publisher).

Jang, Y., Kim, G., Chiriboga, D. A., & Cho, S. (2008). Willingness to use a nursing home.

Journal of Applied Gerontology, 27(1), 110–117.

Janssen, E. (Ed.). (2006). *The psychophysiology of sex.* Bloomington, IN: Indiana University Press.

Jayson, S. (2008, June 8). More view cohabitation as acceptable choice. *USA Today.* Available at http://www.usatoday.com/news/nation/2008-06-08-cohabitation-study_N.htm. Accessed October 2, 2008.

Jeng, S.-F., Yau, K.-I. T., Liao, H.-F., Chen, L.-C., & Chen, P.-S. (2000). Prognostic factors for walking attainment in very low birth weight preterm infants. *Early Human Development, 59*(3), 159–173.

Jepsen, D. A., & Choudhuri, E. (2001). Stability and change in 25-year occupational career patterns. *Career Development Quarterly, 50*(1), 3–19.

Joe, S., Romer, D., & Jamieson, P. (2007). Suicide acceptability is related to suicide planning in U.S. adolescents and young adults. *Suicide and Life-Threatening Behavior, 37*(2), 165–178.

Johannes, C. B., et al. (2000). Incidence of erectile dysfunction in men 40 to 69 years old: Longitudinal results from the Massachusetts male aging study. *The Journal of Urology, 163,* 460.

Johnson, J. G., Zhang, B., & Prigerson, H. G. (2008). Investigation of a developmental model of risk for depression and suicidality following spousal bereavement. *Suicide and Life-Threatening Behavior, 38*(1), 1–12.

Johnson, W., & Bouchard, T. J., Jr., (2007). Sex differences in mental abilities: g masks the dimensions on which they lie. *Intelligence, 35*(1), 23–39.

Johnson, W., & Krueger, R. F. (2006). How money buys happiness: Genetic and environmental processes linking finances and life satisfaction. *Journal of Personality and Social Psychology, 90*(4), 680–691.

Johnson, W., McGue, M., Krueger, R. F., & Bouchard, T. J., Jr. (2004). Marriage and personality: A genetic analysis. *Journal of Personality and Social Psychology, 86*(2), 285–294.

Jones B. C., et al. (2008). Effects of menstrual cycle phase on face preferences. *Archives of Sexual Behaviour, 37*(1), 78–84.

Jones, D. C., & Crawford, J. K. (2006). The peer appearance culture during adolescence: Gender and body mass variations. *Journal of Youth and Adolescence, 35*(2), 257–269.

Jones, S. S., & Hong, H-W. (2005). How some infant smiles get made. *Infant Behavior & Development, 28*(2), 194–205.

Jonkman, S. (2006). Sensitization facilitates habit formation: Implications for addiction. *Journal of Neuroscience, 26*(28), 7319–7320.

Jordan, J. V., Kaplan, A. G., Miller, J. B., Stiver, I. P., & Surrey, J. L. (1991). *Women's growth in connection.* New York: Guilford Press.

Jorgensen, G. (2006). Kohlberg and Gilligan: Duet or duel? *Journal of Moral Education, 35*(2), 179–196.

Joshi, P. T., Salpekar, J. A., & Daniolos, P. T. (2006). Physical and sexual abuse of children. In M. K. Dulcan & J. M. Wiener (Eds.), *Essentials of child and adolescent psychiatry* (pp. 595–620). Washington, DC: American Psychiatric Publishing.

Joshi, R. M. (2003). Misconceptions about the assessment and diagnosis of reading disability. *Reading Psychology, 24*(3–4), 247–266.

Joung, H-M., & Miller, N. J. (2007). Examining the effects of fashion activities on life satisfaction of older females: Activity theory revisited. *Family & Consumer Sciences Research Journal, 35*(4), 338–356.

Judge, T. A., & Klinger, R. (2008). Job satisfaction: Subjective well-being at work. In M. Eid, & R. J. Larsen (Eds.), *The science of subjective well-being* (pp. 393–413). New York: Guilford Press.

Kagan, J., & Klein, R. E. (1973). Cross-cultural perspectives on early development. *American Psychologist, 28,* 947–961.

Kagan, L. J., MacLeod, A. K., & Pote, H. L. (2004). Accessibility of causal explanations for future positive and negative events in adolescents with anxiety and depression. *Clinical Psychology and Psychotherapy, 11*(3), 177–186.

Kaiser Family Foundation, Holt, T., Greene, L., & Davis, J. (2003). *National Survey of Adolescents and Young Adults: Sexual health knowledge, attitudes, and experiences.* Menlo Park, CA: Henry J. Kaiser Family Foundation.

Kaminski, P. L., & Hayslip, B., Jr. (2006). Gender differences in body esteem among older adults. *Journal of Women & Aging, 18*(3), 19–35.

Kaminski, R. A., & Stormshak, E. A. (2007). Project STAR: Early intervention with preschool children and families for the prevention of substance abuse. In P. Tolan, J. Szapocznik, & S. Sambrano (Eds.), *Preventing youth substance abuse: Science-based programs for children and adolescents* (pp. 89–109). Washington, DC: American Psychological Association.

Kanevsky, L., & Geake, J. (2004). Inside the zone of proximal development: Validating a multifactor model of learning potential with gifted students and their peers. *Journal for the Education of the Gifted, 28*(2), 182–217.

Karapetsas, A., & Kantas, A. (1991). Visuomotor organization in the child: A neuropsychological approach. *Perceptual and Motor Skills, 72,* 211–217.

Karatekin, C., Marcus, D. J., & White, T. (2007). Oculomotor and manual indexes of incidental and intentional spatial sequence learning during middle childhood and adolescence. *Journal of Experimental Child Psychology, 96*(2), 107–130.

Karavasilis, L., Doyle, A. B., & Markiewicz, D. (2003). Associations between parenting style and attachment to mother in middle childhood and adolescence. *International Journal of Behavioral Development, 27*(2), 153–164.

Kart, C. S., & Kinney, J. M. (2001). *The realities of aging.* Boston: Allyn & Bacon.

Katz, R., Lowenstein, A., Phillips, J., & Daatland, S. O. (2005). Theorizing inter-generational family relations: Solidarity, conflict, and ambivalence in cross-national contexts. In V. L. Bengtson et al. (Eds.), *Sourcebook of family theory & research* (pp. 393–420). Thousand Oaks, CA: Sage.

Katzman, D. K. (2005). Medical complications in adolescents with anorexia nervosa: A review of the literature. *International Journal of Eating Disorders, 37*(Suppl), S52–S59.

Kauff, N. D., & Offit, K. (2007). Modeling genetic risk of breast cancer. *Journal of the American Medical Association, 297,* 2637–2639.

Kavanagh, K., et al. (2007). Characterization and heritability of obesity and associated risk factors in vervet monkeys. *Obesity, 15*(7), 1666–1674.

Kavanaugh, R. D. (2006). Pretend play. In B. Spodek & O. N. Saracho (Eds.), *Handbook of research on the education of young children* (2nd ed.) (pp. 269–278). Mahwah, NJ: Erlbaum.

Kavcic, T., & Zupancic, M. (2005). Sibling relationship in early/middle childhood: Trait- and dyad-centered approach. *Studia Psychologica, 47*(3), 179–197.

Kawas, C. H., & Brookmeyer, R. (2001). Aging and the public health effects of dementia. *The New England Journal of Medicine, 344,* 1160–1161.

Kaye, W. H., et al. (2004). Genetic analysis of bulimia nervosa: Methods and sample description. *International Journal of Eating Disorders, 35*(4), 556–570.

Kazdin, A. E. (2000). Treatments for aggressive and antisocial children. *Child and Adolescent Psychiatric Clinics of North America, 9*(4), 841–858.

Kazui, H., et al. (2008). Association between quality of life of demented patients and professional knowledge of care workers. *Journal of Geriatric Psychiatry and Neurology, 21*(1), 72–78.

Kazui, M., Endo, T., Tanaka, A., Sakagami, H., & Suganuma, M. (2000). Intergenerational transmission of attachment: Japanese mother–child dyads. *Japanese Journal of Educational Psychology, 48*(3), 323–332.

Kearney, C. A., & Bensaheb, A. (2007). Assessing anxiety disorders in children and adolescents. In S. R. Smith & L. Handler (Eds.), *The clinical assessment of children and adolescents: A practitioner's handbook* (pp. 467–483). Mahwah, NJ: Erlbaum.

Keen, D., Rodger, S., Doussin, K., & Braithwaite, M. (2007). A pilot study of the effects of a social-pragmatic intervention on the communication and symbolic play of children with autism. *Autism, 11*(1), 63–71.

Keller, H., Kärtner, J., Borke, J., Yovsi, R., & Kleis, A. (2005). Parenting styles and the development of the categorical self: A longitudinal study on mirror self-recognition in Cameroonian Nso and German families. *International Journal of Behavioral Development, 29*(6), 496–504.

Kellman, P. J., & Arterberry, M. E. (2006). Infant visual perception. In D. Kuhn et al. (Eds.), *Handbook of child psychology: Vol. 2, Cognition, perception, and language* (6th ed.) (pp. 109–160). Hoboken, NJ: Wiley.

Kellogg, R. (1959). *What children scribble and why.* Oxford: National Press.

Kellogg, R. (1970). Understanding children's art. In P. Cramer (Ed.), *Readings in developmental psychology today.* Del Mar, CA: CRM.

Kemp, C. L. (2005). Dimensions of grandparent–adult grandchild relationships: From family ties to intergenerational friendships. *Canadian Journal on Aging, 24*(2), 161–178.

Kemp, E. A., & Kemp, J. E. (2002). *Older couples: New romances: Finding & keeping love in later life.* Berkeley, CA: Celestial Arts.

Kempes, M., Matthys, W., de Vries, H., & van Engeland, H. (2005). Reactive and proactive aggression in children: A review of theory, findings and the relevance for child and adolescent psychiatry. *European Child & Adolescent Psychiatry, 14*(1), 11–19.

Kendler, K. S., Gardner, C. O., Gatz, M., & Pedersen, N. L. (2007). The sources of comorbidity between major depression and generalized anxiety disorder in a Swedish national twin sample. *Psychological Medicine, 37*(3), 453–462.

Keogh, A. F., & Whyte, J. (2006). Exploring children's concepts of intelligence through ethnographic methods. *Irish Journal of Psychology, 27*(1–2), 69–78.

Kerns, K. A., Abraham, M. M., Schlegelmilch, A., & Morgan, T. A. (2007). Mother–child attachment in later middle childhood: Assessment approaches and associations with mood and emotion regulation. *Attachment & Human Development, 9*(1), 33–53.

Kidd, E., & Bavin, E. L. (2007). Lexical and referential influences on on-line spoken language comprehension: A comparison of adults and primary-school-age children. *First Language, 27*(1), 29–52.

Kidshealth. (2010). Infections: Toxoplasmosis. Retrieved from http://kidshealth.org/parent/infections/parasitic/toxoplasmosis.html

Killen, M., & Smetana, J. G. (Eds.). (2006). *Handbook of moral development.* Mahwah, NJ: Erlbaum.

Kim, J-Y., McHale, S. M., Osgood, D. W., & Crouter, A. C. (2006). Longitudinal course and family correlates of sibling relationships from childhood through adolescence. *Child Development, 77*(6), 1746–1761.

King, J., MacKay, M., Sirnick, A., & The Canadian Shaken Baby Group. (2003). Shaken baby syndrome in Canada: Clinical characteristics and outcomes of hospital cases. *Canadian Medical Association Journal, 168*(2), 155–159. Retrieved from http://www.cmaj.ca/cgi/content/full/168/2/155

King, P. M., & Kitchener, K. S. (2004). Reflective judgment. *Educational Psychologist, 39*(1), 5–18.

King, V., & Scott, M. E. (2005). A comparison of cohabiting relationships among older and younger adults. *Journal of Marriage and Family, 67*(2), 271–285.

Kinsbourne, M. (2003). The corpus callosum equilibrates the cerebral hemispheres. In E. Zaidel & M. Iacoboni (Eds.), *The parallel brain: The cognitive neuroscience of the corpus callosum* (pp. 271–281). Cambridge, MA: MIT Press.

Kinsey, A. C., Pomeroy, W. B., & Martin, C. E. (1948). *Sexual behavior in the human male.* Philadelphia: W. B. Saunders.

Kinsey, A. C., Pomeroy, W. B., Martin, C. E., & Gebhard, P. H. (1953). *Sexual behavior in the human female.* Philadelphia: W. B. Saunders.

Kirby, P. G., Biever, J. L., Martinez, I. G., & Gómez, J. P. (2004). Adults returning to school: The impact on family and work. *Journal of Psychology: Interdisciplinary and Applied, 138*(1), 65–76.

Kirchler, E., Pombeni, M. L., & Palmonari, A. (1991). Sweet sixteen . . . Adolescents' problems and the peer group as source of support. *European Journal of Psychology of Education, 6,* 393–410.

Kirkcaldy, B. D., Shephard, R. J., & Siefen, R. G. (2002). The relationship between physical activity and self-image and problem behaviour among adolescents. *Social Psychiatry and Psychiatric Epidemiology, 37*(11), 544–550.

Kistner, J. (2006). Children's peer acceptance, perceived acceptance, and risk for depression. In T. E. Joiner, J. S. Brown, & J. Kistner (Eds.), *The interpersonal, cognitive, and social nature of depression* (pp. 1–21). Mahwah, NJ: Erlbaum.

Kjelsås, E., Bjornstrom, C., & Götestam, K. G. (2004). Prevalence of eating disorders in female and male adolescents (14–15 years). *Eating Behaviors, 5*(1), 13–25.

Klaus, M. H., & Kennell, J. H. (1978). Parent-to-infant attachment. In J. H. Stevens Jr. & M. Mathews (Eds.), *Mother/child, father/child relationships.* Washington, DC: National Association for the Education of Young Children.

Kleiber, D. A., & Kelly, J. R. (1980). Leisure, socialization, and the life cycle. In S. E. Iso-Ahola (Ed.), *Social psychological perspectives on leisure and recreation* (pp. 91–137). Springfield, IL: Charles C. Thomas.

Kliegel, M., Jäger, T., & Phillips, L. H. (2008). Adult age differences in event-based prospective memory: A meta-analysis on the role of focal versus nonfocal cues. *Psychology and Aging, 23*(1), 203–208.

Klein, P. J., & Meltzoff, A. N. (1999). Long-term memory, forgetting and deferred imitation in 12-month-old infants. *Developmental Science, 2*(1), 102–113.

Klier, C. M. (2006). Mother–infant bonding disorders in patients with postnatal depression: The Postpartum Bonding Questionnaire in clinical practice. *Archives of Women's Mental Health, 9*(5), 289–291.

Klintsova, A. Y., & Greenough, W. T. (1999). Synaptic plasticity in cortical systems. *Current Opinion in Neurobiology, 9*(2), 203–208.

Kloep, M., & Hendry, L. B. (2007). Retirement: A new beginning? *The Psychologist, 20*(12), 742–745.

Klohnen, E. C., & Luo, S. (2003). Interpersonal attraction and personality: What is attractive–self similarity, ideal similarity, complementarity or attachment security? *Journal of Personality and Social Psychology, 85*(4), 709–722.

Klomek, A. B., et al. (2007). Bullying, depression, and suicidality in adolescents. *Journal of the American Academy of Child & Adolescent Psychiatry, 46*(1), 40–49.

Knaak, S. (2005). Breast-feeding, bottle-feeding and Dr. Spock: The shifting context of choice. *Canadian Review of Sociology and Anthropology, 42*(2), 197–216.

Knafo, A., & Plomin, R. (2006a). Parental discipline and affection and children's prosocial behavior: Genetic and environmental links. *Journal of Personality and Social Psychology, 90*(1), 147–164.

Knafo, A., & Plomin, R. (2006b). Prosocial behavior from early to middle childhood: Genetic and environmental influences on stability and change. *Developmental Psychology, 42*(5), 771–786.

Kniffin, K. M., & Wilson, D. S. (2004). The effect of nonphysical traits on the perception of physical attractiveness: Three naturalistic studies. *Evolution and Human Behavior, 25*(2), 88–101.

Kochanska, G. (2001). Emotional development in children with different attachment histories: The first three years. *Child Development, 72*(2), 474–490.

Kochanska, G., Coy, K. C., Murray, K. T. (2001). The development of self-regulation in the first four years of life. *Child Development, 72*(4), 1091–1111.

Kogan, M. D., et al. (2000). Trends in twin birth outcomes and prenatal care utilization in the United States, 1981–1997. *Journal of the American Medical Association, 284*(3), 335–341.

Kohl, C. (2004). Postpartum psychoses: Closer to schizophrenia or the affective spectrum? *Current Opinion in Psychiatry, 17*(2), 87–90.

Kohl, J. V. (2007). The mind's eyes: Human pheromones, neuroscience, and male sexual preferences. *Journal of Psychology & Human Sexuality, 18*(4), 313–369.

Kohlberg, L. (1963). Moral development and identification. In H. W. Stevenson (Ed.), *Child psychology: 62nd yearbook of the National Society for the Study of Education.* Chicago: University of Chicago Press.

Kohlberg, L. (1966). Cognitive stages and preschool education. *Human Development, 9,* 5–17.

Kohlberg, L. (1969). Stage and sequence: The cognitive-developmental approach to socialization. In D. A. Goslin (Ed.), *Handbook of socialization theory and research.* Chicago: Rand McNally.

Kohlberg, L. (1981). *The meaning and measurement of moral development.* Worcester, MA: Clark University Press.

Kohlberg, L. (1985). *The psychology of moral development.* San Francisco: Harper & Row.

Kohlberg, L., & Kramer, R. (1969). Continuities and discontinuities in childhood and adult moral development. *Human Development, 12,* 93–120.

Kohyama, J., Shiiki, T., Ohinata-Sugimoto, J., & Hasegawa, T. (2002). Potentially harmful sleep habits of 3-year-old children in Japan. *Journal of Developmental and Behavioral Pediatrics, 23*(2), 67–70.

Kolata, G. (2007, May 8). Genes take charge, and diets fall by the wayside. *New York Times online.*

Kolb, B., & Gibb, R. (2007). Brain plasticity and recovery from early cortical injury. *Developmental Psychobiology, 49*(2), 107–118.

Konijn, E. A., Bijvank, M. N., & Bushman, B. J. (2007). I wish I were a warrior: The role of wishful identification in the effects of violent video games on aggression in adolescent boys. *Developmental Psychology, 43*(4), 1038–1044.

Kopp, C. B. (1989). Regulation of distress and negative emotions: A developmental view. *Developmental Psychology, 25,* 343–354.

Korff, S. C. (2006). Religious orientation as a predictor of life satisfaction within the elderly population. *Dissertation Abstracts International: Section B: The Sciences and Engineering. 67*(1-B), 2006, 550.

Krebs, D. L., & Denton, K. (2005). Toward a more pragmatic approach to morality: A critical evaluation of Kohlberg's model. *Psychological Review, 112*(3), 629–649.

Kristensen, P., & Bjerkedal, T. (2007). Explaining the relation between birth order and intelligence. *Science, 313*(5832), 1717.

Kroeger, K. A., & Nelson, W. M., III. (2006). A language programme to increase the verbal production of a child dually diagnosed with Down syndrome and autism. *Journal of Intellectual Disability Research, 50*(2), 101–108.

Krojgaard, P. (2005). Continuity and discontinuity in developmental psychology. *Psyke & Logos, 26*(2), 377–394.

Krueger, C., Holditch-Davis, D., Quint, S., & DeCasper, A. (2004). Recurring auditory experience in the 28- to 34-week-old fetus. *Infant Behavior & Development, 27*(4), 537–543.

Kübler-Ross, E. (1969). *On death and dying.* New York: Macmillan.

Kübler-Ross, E., & Kessler, D. (2005). *On grief and grieving*. New York: Scribner.

Kuczaj, S. A., II (1982). On the nature of syntactic development. In S. A. Kuczaj II (Ed.), *Language development*, Vol. 1, *Syntax and semantics*. Hillsdale, NJ: Erlbaum.

Kuhl, P. K., et al. (1997). Cross-language analysis of phonetic units in language addressed to infants. *Science, 277*(5326), 684–686.

Kuhl, P. K., et al. (2006). Infants show a facilitation effect for native language phonetic perception between 6 and 12 months. *Developmental Science, 9*(2) F13–F21.

Kuhn, D. (2007). Editorial. *Cognitive Development, 22*(1), 1–2.

Kulick, D. (2006). Regulating sex: The politics of intimacy and identity. *Sexualities, 9*(1), 122–124.

Kulik, L. (2000). Women face unemployment: A comparative analysis of age groups. *Journal of Career Development, 27*(1), 15–33.

Kulik, L. (2004). Perceived equality in spousal relations, marital quality, and life satisfaction. *Families in Society, 85*(2), 243–250.

Kulp, J. (2007, March 27). To the editor: Day care and a child's behavior. *New York Times online*.

Kunz, J. A. (2007). The life story matrix. In J. A. Kunz, & F. G. Soltys (Eds.), *Transformational reminiscence: Life story work* (pp. 1–16). New York: Springer Publishing Co.

Kunzmann, U., & Baltes, P. B. (2005). The psychology of wisdom: Theoretical and empirical challenges. In R. J. Sternberg, & J. Jordan (Eds.), *A handbook of wisdom: Psychological perspectives* (pp. 110–135). New York: Cambridge University Press.

Kurdek, L. A. (2005). What do we know about gay and lesbian couples? *Current Directions in Psychological Science, 14*(5), 251.

Kurdek, L. A. (2006). Differences between partners from hetersosexual, gay, and lesbian cohabiting couples. *Journal of Marriage and the Family, 68*(2), 509–528.

Kurzban, R., & Weeden, J. (2005). HurryDate: Mate preferences in action. *Evolution and Human Behavior, 26*(3), 227–244.

Kvaal, K., et al. (2008). Co-occurrence of anxiety and depressive disorders in a community sample of older people. *International Journal of Geriatric Psychiatry, 23*(3) 229–237.

Kwok, H-K. (2006). A study of the sandwich generation in Hong Kong. *Current Sociology, 54*(2), 257–272.

Kwok, H. W. M. (2003). Psychopharmacology in autism spectrum disorders. *Current Opinion in Psychiatry, 16*(5), 529–534.

Labouvie-Vief, G. (2006). Emerging structures of adult thought. In J. J. Arnett & J. L. Tanner (Eds.). *Emerging adults in America.* (pp. 59–84). Washington, DC: American Psychological Association.

Labouvie-Vief, G., & González, M. M. (2004). Dynamic integration: Affect optimization and differentiation in development. In D. Y. Dai & R. J. Sternberg (Eds.), *Motivation, emotion, and cognition* (pp. 237–272). Mahwah, NJ: Erlbaum.

Labrell, F., & Ubersfeld, G. (2004). Parental verbal strategies and children's capacities at 3 and 5 years during a memory task. *European Journal of Psychology of Education, 19*(2), 189–202.

Lachman, M. E. (2004). Development in midlife. *Annual Review of Psychology, 55*, 305–331.

Laflamme, D., Pomerleau, A., & Malcuit, G. (2002). A comparison of fathers' and mothers' involvement in childcare and stimulation behaviors during free-play with their infants at 9 and 15 months. *Sex Roles, 47*(11–12), 507–518.

Lai, H-L., et al. (2006). Randomized controlled trial of music during kangaroo care on maternal state anxiety and preterm infants' responses. *International Journal of Nursing Studies, 43*(2), 139–146.

Lam, K. S. L., Aman, M. G., & Arnold, L. E. (2006). Neurochemical correlates of autistic disorder: A review of the literature. *Research in Developmental Disabilities, 27*(3), 254–289.

Lam, T. H., Shi, H. J., Ho, L. M., Stewart, S. M., & Fan, S. (2002). Timing of pubertal maturation and heterosexual behavior among Hong Kong Chinese adolescents. *Archives of Sexual Behavior, 31*(4), 359–366.

Lamb, M. E., & Ahnert, L. (2006). Nonparental child care: Context, concepts, correlates, and consequences. In K. A. Renninger, I. E. Sigel, W. Damon, & R. M. Lerner (Eds.), *Handbook of child psychology* (6th ed.), Vol. 4, *Child psychology in practice* (pp. 950–1016). Hoboken, NJ: Wiley.

Lambert, M., Zeman, K., Allen, M., & Bussière, P. (2004). *Who pursues postsecondary education, who leaves and why: Results from the youth in transition survey.* (Statistics Canada, Catalogue no. 81-595-MIE—No. 026). Culture, Tourism and the Centre for Education Statistics research paper. Ottawa: Statistics Canada. Retrieved from http://dsp-psd.pwgsc.gc.ca/Collection/Statcan/81-595-MIE/81-595-MIE2004026.pdf

Lamers, C. T. J., Bechara, A., Rizzo, M., & Ramaekers, J. G. (2006). Cognitive function and mood in MDMA/THC users, THC users and non-drug using controls. *Journal of Psychopharmacology, 20*(2), 302–311.

Lampl, M., Veldhuis, J. D., & Johnson, M. L. (1992). Saltation and stasis: A model of human growth. *Science, 258*, 801–803.

Lange, G., & Pierce, S. H. (1992). Memory-strategy learning and maintenance in preschool children. *Developmental Psychology, 28*, 453–462.

Langlois, J. H., et al. (2000). Maxims or myths of beauty? A meta-analytic and theoretical review. *Psychological Bulletin, 126*(3), 390–423.

Lansford, J. E., Malone, P. S., Castellino, D. R., Dodge, K. A., Pettit, G. S., & Bates, J. E. (2006). Trajectories of internalizing, externalizing, and grades for children who have and have not experienced their parents' divorce or separation. *Journal of Family Psychology. 20*(2), 292–301.

Lantolf, J. P., & Thorne, S. L. (2007). Sociocultural theory and second language learning. In B. VanPatten & J. Williams (Eds.), *Theories in second language acquisition: An introduction* (pp. 201–224). Mahwah, NJ: Erlbaum.

LaPointe, L. L. (Ed.). (2005). Feral children. *Journal of Medical Speech-Language Pathology, 13*(1), vii–ix.

Lapsley, D. K. (2006). Moral stage theory. In K. Killen & J. G. Smetana (Eds.), *Handbook of moral development* (pp. 37–66). Mahwah, NJ: Erlbaum.

Larroque, B., et al. (2005). Temperament at 9 months of very preterm infants born at less than 29 weeks' gestation: The Epipage study. *Journal of Developmental & Behavioral Pediatrics, 26*(1), 48–55.

Larson, R., & Richards, M. H. (1991). Daily companionship in late childhood and early adolescence: Changing developmental contexts. *Child Development, 62*, 284–300.

Larsson, I., & Svedin, C. (2002). Experiences in childhood: Young adults' recollections. *Archives of Sexual Behavior, 31*(3), 263–273.

Latham, G. P., & Budworth, M.-H. (2007). The study of work motivation in the 20th century. In L. L. Koppes, (Ed.), *Historical perspectives in industrial and organizational psychology* (pp. 353–381). Mahwah, NJ: Erlbaum.

Lattanzi-Licht, Marcia. (2007). Religion, spirituality, and dying. In D. Balk, et al. (Eds.), *Handbook of thanatology* (pp. 11–17). New York: Routledge/Taylor & Francis Group.

Lau, A. S., Litrownik, A. J., Newton, R. R., Black, M. M., & Everson, M. D. (2006). Factors affecting the link between physical discipline and child externalizing problems in Black and White families. *Journal of Community Psychology, 34*(1), 89–103.

Laumann, E. O., et al. (2006). Sexual activity, sexual disorders and associated help-seeking behavior among mature adults in five Anglophone countries from the Global Survey of Sexual Attitudes and Behaviors. *Archives of Sexual Behavior, 35*(2), 145–161.

Laumann, E. O., Gagnon, J. H., Michael, R. T., & Michaels, S. (1994). *The social organization of sexuality*. Chicago: University of Chicago Press.

Laumann, E. O., Mahay, J., & Youm, Y. (2007). Sex, intimacy, and family life in the United States. In M. Kimmel (Ed.), *The sexual self: The construction of sexual scripts* (pp. 165–190). Nashville, TN: Vanderbilt University Press.

Laurendeau, M., & Pinard, A. (1970). *The development of the concept of space in the child*. New York: International Universities Press.

Lawrence, E., Nylen, K., & Cobb, R. J. (2007). Prenatal expectations and marital satisfaction over the transition to parenthood. *Journal of Family Psychology, 21*(2), 155–164.

Lawrence, E. B., & Bradbury, T. N. (2007). Trajectories of change in physical aggression and marital satisfaction. *Journal of Family Psychology, 21*(2), 236–247.

Leaper, C. (2002). Parenting girls and boys. In M. H. Bornstein (Ed.), *Handbook of parenting* (2nd ed.), Vol. 1, *Children and parenting* (pp. 189–225). Mahwah, NJ: Erlbaum.

Lecanuet, J. P., Graniere-Deferre, C., Jacquet, A.-Y., & DeCasper, A. J. (2000). Fetal discrimination of low-pitched musical notes. *Developmental Psychobiology, 36*(1), 29–39.

Leclerc, C. M., & Hess, T. M. (2007). Age differences in the bases for social judgments: Tests of a social expertise perspective. *Experimental Aging Research, 33*(1), 95–120.

Leder, S., Grinstead, L. N., & Torres, E. (2007). Grandparents raising grandchildren: Stressors, social support, and health outcomes. *Journal of Family Nursing, 13*(3), 333–352.

Leerkes, E. M., & Crockenberg, S. C. (2006). Antecedents of mothers' emotional and cognitive responses to infant distress: The role of family, mother, and infant characteristics. *Infant Mental Health Journal, 27*(4), 405–428.

Lefkowitz, E. S., & Zeldow, P. B. (2006). Masculinity and femininity predict optimal mental health: A belated test of the androgyny hypothesis. *Journal of Personality Assessment, 87*(1), 95–101.

Legro, R. S., et al. (2007). Clomiphene, metformin, or both for infertility in the polycystic ovary syndrome. *New England Journal of Medicine, 356*(6), 551–566.

Lejeune, C., et al. (2006). Prospective multicenter observational study of 260 infants born to 259 opiate-dependent mothers on methadone or high-dose buprenophine substitution. *Drug and Alcohol Dependence, 82*(3), 250–257.

Lemaire, P., & Arnaud, L. (2008). Young and older adults' strategies in complex arithmetic. *American Journal of Psychology, 121*(1), 1–16.

Lengua, L., J., Honorado, E., & Bush, N. R. (2007). Contextual risk and parenting as predictors of effortful control and social competence in preschool children. *Journal of Applied Developmental Psychology, 28*(1), 40–55.

Lenneberg, E. H. (1967). *Biological foundations of language.* New York: Wiley.

Leonard, S. P., & Archer, J. (1989). A naturalistic investigation of gender constancy in three- to four-year-old children. *British Journal of Developmental Psychology, 7,* 341–346.

Leonardo, E. D., & Hen, R. (2006). Genetics of affective and anxiety disorders. *Annual Review of Psychology. 57,* 117–137.

Leone, J. L. (2000). Psychosocial factors leading to harmony or disharmony in sibling relationships in mid-life when faced with caregiving responsibilities for aging parents. *Dissertation Abstracts International: Section B: The Sciences and Engineering, 61*(4-B), 2245.

Letourneau, E. J., Schoenwald, S. K., & Sheidow, A. J. (2004). Children and adolescents with sexual behavior problems. *Child Maltreatment: Journal of the American Professional Society on the Abuse of Children, 9*(1), 49–61.

Leung, C., McBride-Chang, C., & Lai, B. (2004). Relations among maternal parenting style, academic competence, and life satisfaction in Chinese early adolescents. *Journal of Early Adolescence, 24*(2), 113–143.

Lever, N., et al. (2004). A drop-out prevention program for high-risk inner-city youth. *Behavior Modification, 28*(4), 513–527.

Levine, D. (2000). Virtual attraction: What rocks your boat. *CyberPsychology & Behavior, 3*(4), 565–573.

Levinson, D. J., Darrow, C. N, & Klein, E. B. (1978). *Seasons of a man's life.* New York: Knopf.

Levinson, D. J. (1996). *The seasons of a woman's life.* New York: Knopf.

Levinthal, B. R., & Lleras, A. (2007). The unique contributions of retinal size and perceived size on change detection. *Visual Cognition, 15*(1), 101–105.

Levpušcek, M. P. (2006). Adolescent individuation in relation to parents and friends: Age and gender differences. *European Journal of Developmental Psychology, 3*(3), 238–264.

Lewinsohn, P. M., Rohde, P., Seeley, J. R., Klein, D. N., & Gotlib, I. H. (2000). Natural course of adolescent major depressive disorder in a community sample: Predictors of recurrence in young adults. *American Journal of Psychiatry, 157,* 1584–1591.

Lewis, B. A., et al. (2004). Four-year language outcomes of children exposed to cocaine in utero. *Neurotoxicology and Teratology, 26*(5), 617–627.

Lewis, H. L. (2003). Differences in ego identity among college students across age, ethnicity, and gender. *Identity, 3*(2), 159–189.

Lewis, M., & Feiring, C. (1989). Early predictors of childhood friendship. In T. J. Berndt & G. W. Ladd (Eds.), *Peer relationships in child development.* New York: Wiley.

Li, Q. (2007). New bottle but old wine: A research of cyberbullying in schools. *Computers in Human Behavior, 23*(4), 1777–1791.

Lickliter, R. (2001). The dynamics of language development: From perception to comprehension. *Developmental Science, 4*(1), 21–23.

LifeCanada. Teen abortions. (n.d.), Retrieved from http://www.abortionincanada.ca/stats/teenage_abortions.html

Light, L. L., Patterson, M. M., Chung, C., & Healy, M. R. (2004). Effects of repetition and response deadline on associative recognition in young and older adults. *Memory & Cognition, 32,* 1182–1193.

Lindau, S. T., Schumm, L. P., Laumann, E. O., Levinson, W., O'Muircheartaigh, C. A., & Waite, L. J. (2007). A study of sexuality and health among older adults in the United States. *New England Journal of Medicine, 357*(8), 762–775.

Lipman, E. L. et al. (2006). Testing effectiveness of a community-based aggression management program for children 7 to 11 years old and their families. *Journal of the American Academy of Child & Adolescent Psychiatry, 45*(9), 1085–1093.

Lippa, R. L. (2008). Non-Alzheimer's dementia: Clinical features, management, and genetics. *American Journal of Alzheimer's Disease and Other Dementias, 22*(6), 454–455.

Lipsitt, L. P. (2002). Early experience and behavior in the baby of the twenty-first century. In J. Gomes-Pedro et al. (Eds.), *The infant and family in the twenty-first century* (pp. 55–78). London: Brunner-Routledge.

Lipsitt, L. P. (2003). Crib death: A biobehavioral phenomenon? *Current Directions in Psychological Science, 12*(5), 164–170.

Li-qi, Z., & Fu-xi, F. (2006). Preschool children's understanding of death. *Chinese Journal of Clinical Psychology, 14*(1), 91–93.

Löckenhoff, C. E., & Carstensen, L. L. (2004). Socioemotional selectivity theory, aging, and health: The increasingly delicate balance between regulating emotions and making tough choices. *Journal of Personality, 72*(6), 1395–1424.

Lorant, V., et al. (2005). A European comparative study of marital status and socio-economic inequalities in suicide. *Social Science & Medicine, 60*(11), 2431–2441.

Lorenz, F. O., Wickrama, K. A. S., Conger, R. D., & Elder Jr., G. H. (2006). The short-term and decade-long effects of divorce on women's midlife health. *Journal of Health and Social Behavior, 47*(2), 111–125.

Lorenz, K. (1962). *King Solomon's ring.* London: Methuen.

Lorenz, K. (1981). *The foundations of ethology.* New York: Springer-Verlag.

Lovaas, O. I. (1977). *The autistic child: Language development through behavior modification.* New York: Halstead Press.

Lovaas, O. I., Smith, T., & McEachin, J. J. (1989). Clarifying comments on the young autism study: Reply to Schapler, Short, and Mesibov. *Journal of Consulting and Clinical Psychology, 57,* 165–167.

Lubinski, D. (2004). Introduction to the Special Section on Cognitive Abilities: 100 Years After Spearman's (1904) "'General Intelligence,' Objectively Determined and Measured." *Journal of Personality and Social Psychology, 86*(1), 96–111.

Lubinski, D., & Benbow, C. P. (2000). States of excellence. *American Psychologist, 55,* 137–150.

Lucariello, J. M., Hudson, J. A., Fivush, R., & Bauer, P. J. (Eds.). (2004). *The development of the mediated mind: Sociocultural context and cognitive development.* Mahwah, NJ: Erlbaum.

Luciano, M., Kirk, K. M., Heath, A. C., & Martin, N. G. (2005). The genetics of tea and coffee drinking and preference for source of caffeine in a large community sample of Australian twins. *Addiction, 100*(10), 1510–1517.

Ludwick, R., & Silva, M. C. (2003, December 19). Ethical challenges in the care of elderly persons. *The Online Journal of Issues in Nursing.* Available at http://nursingworld.org/ojin. Accessed October 5, 2008.

Ludwig, F. M., Hattjar, B., Russell, R. L., & Winston, K. (2007). How caregiving for grandchildren affects grandmothers' meaningful occupations. *Journal of Occupational Science, 14*(1), 40–51.

Lunau, K. (2009, June 29). Are we blushing yet? *macleans.ca,* Retrieved from http://www2.macleans.ca/2009/06/29/are-we-blushing-yet/

Lund, D. A., & Caserta, M. S. (2001). When the unexpected happens: Husbands coping with the deaths of their wives. In D. A. Lund (Ed.), *Men coping with grief* (pp. 147–167). Amityville, NY: Baywood Publishing Co.

Lung Cancer Canada. (2008). Smoking. Retrieved from http://www.lungcancercanada.ca/Education/Did_you_know/Smoking.html

Lupien, S. J., Maheu, F., Tu, M., Fiocco, A., & Schramek, T. E. (2007). The effects of stress and stress hormones on human cognition: Implications for the field of brain and cognition. *Brain and Cognition, 65*(3), 209–237.

Lykken, D. T. (2006a). In C. J. Patrick (Ed.), *Psychopathic personality: The scope of the problem* (pp. 3–13). New York: Guilford.

Lykken, D. T. (2006b). The mechanism of emergenesis. *Genes, Brain & Behavior, 5*(4), 306–310.

Lykken, D. T., & Csikszentmihalyi, M. (2001). Happiness—stuck with what you've got? *Psychologist, 14*(9), 470–472.

Lynne, S. D., Graber, J. A., Nichols, T. R., Brooks-Gunn, J., & Botvin, G. J. (2007). Links between pubertal timing, peer influences, and externalizing behaviors among urban students followed through middle school. *Journal of Adolescent Health, 40*(2), 181.e7–181.e13.

Lyon, G. R., Shaywitz, S. E., & Shaywitz, B. A. (2003). A definition of dyslexia. *Annals of Dyslexia, 53,* 1–14.

Maccoby, E. E. (1990). The role of gender identity and gender constancy in sex-differentiated development. In D. Schrader (Ed.), *New directions for child development,* no. 47, *The legacy of Lawrence Kohlberg.* San Francisco: Jossey-Bass.

Maccoby, E. E. (2000). Perspectives on gender development. *International Journal of Behavioral Development, 24*(4), 398–406.

Maccoby, E. E. (2002). Parenting effects: Issues and controversies. In J. G. Borkowski et al. (Eds.), *Parenting and the child's world: Influences on academic, intellectual, and social-emotional development* (pp. 35–46). Mahwah, NJ: Erlbaum.

Maccoby, E. E., & Jacklin, C. N. (1974). *The psychology of sex differences.* Stanford, CA: Stanford University Press.

MacDonald, N., Yanchar, N., & Hebert, P. (2007). What's killing and maiming Canada's youth? *Canadian Medical Association Journal, 176*(6). Retrieved from http://www.cmaj.ca/cgi/content/full/176/6/737

Macfarlane, A. (1975). Olfaction in the development of social preferences in the human neonate. In M. A. Hofer (Ed.), *Parent–infant interaction.* Amsterdam: Elsevier.

Macfarlane, A. (1977). *The psychology of childbirth.* Cambridge, MA: Harvard University Press.

Maciejewski, P. K., Zhang, B., Block, S. D., & Prigerson, H. G. (2007). An empirical examination of the stage theory of grief. *Journal of the American Medical Association, 297,* 716–723.

Mackic-Magyar, J., & McCracken, J. (2004). Review of autism spectrum disorders: A research review for practitioners. *Journal of Child and Adolescent Psychopharmacology, 14*(1), 17–18.

Maclean, A. M., Walker, L. J., & Matsuba, M. K. (2004). Transcendence and the moral self: Identity integration, religion, and moral life. *Journal for the Scientific Study of Religion, 43*(3), 429–437.

Madon, S., et al. (2001). Am I as you see me or do you see me as I am? Self-fulfilling prophecies and self-verification. *Personality and Social Psychology Bulletin, 27*(9), 1214–1224.

Magolda, M. B. B. (2004). Evolution of a constructivist conceptualization of epistemological reflection. *Educational Psychologist, 39*(1), 31–42.

Mahay, J., & Lewin, A. C. (2007). Age and the desire to marry. *Journal of Family Issues, 28*(5), 706–723.

Mahler, M. S., Pine, F., & Bergman, A. (1975). *The psychological birth of the human infant: Symbiosis and individuation.* New York: Basic Books.

Maimburg, R. D., & Væth, M. (2006). Perinatal risk factors and infantile autism. *Acta Psychiatrica Scandinavica, 114*(4), 257–264.

Major, G. C., Doucet, E., Trayhurn, P., Astrup, A., & Tremblay, A. (2007). Clinical significance of adaptive thermogenesis. *International Journal of Obesity, 31*(2), 204–212.

Malina, R. M., & Bouchard, C. (1991). *Growth, maturity, and physical activity.* Champaign, IL: Human Kinetic Books.

Malinosky-Rummell, R., & Hansen, D. H. (1993). Long-term consequences of childhood physical abuse. *Psychological Bulletin, 114,* 68–79.

Malone, P. S., et al. (2004). Divorce and child behavior problems: Applying latent change score models to life event data. *Structural Equation Modeling, 11*(3), 401–423.

Maluccio, A. N., & Ainsworth, F. (2003). Drug use by parents: A challenge for family reunification practice. *Children and Youth Services Review, 25*(7), 511–533.

Mandler, J. M. (1990). Recall and its verbal expression. In R. Fivush & J. A. Hudson (Eds.), *Knowing and remembering in young children.* Cambridge: Cambridge University Press.

Mangina, C. A., & Sokolov, E. N. (2006). Neuronal plasticity in memory and learning abilities: Theoretical position and selective review. *International Journal of Psychophysiology, 60*(3), 203–214.

Maratsos, M. P. (2007). Commentary. *Monographs of the Society for Research in Child Development, 72*(1), 121–126.

Marcia, J. E. (1991). Identity and self-development. In R. M. Lerner, A. C. Petersen, & J. Brooks-Gunn (Eds.), *Encyclopedia of adolescence.* New York: Garland.

Marcovitch, S., & Zelazo, P. D. (2006). The influence of number of A trials on 2-year-olds' behavior in two A-not-B-type search tasks: A test of the hierarchical competing systems model. *Journal of Cognition and Development, 7*(4), 477–501.

Marean, G. C., Werner, L. A., & Kuhl, P. K. (1992). Vowel categorization by very young infants. *Developmental Psychology, 28,* 396–405.

Markham, B. (2006). Older women and security. In J. Worell & C. D. Goodheart (Eds.), *Handbook of girls' and women's psychological health: Gender and well-being across the lifespan* (pp. 388–396). *Oxford series in clinical psychology.* New York: Oxford University Press.

Marks, L., Nesteruk, O., Swanson, M., Garrison, B., & Davis, T. (2005). Religion and health among African Americans. *Research on Aging, 27*(4), 447–474.

Marquis, C. (2003, March 16). Living in sin. *The New York Times,* p. WK2.

Marron, D. J., & Rayman, J. R. (2002). Addressing the career development needs of adult students in research university settings. In S. G. Niles (Ed.), *Adult career development: Concepts, issues and practices* (3rd ed.) (pp. 321–337). Columbus, OH: National Career Development Association.

Marsiglio, W. (2004). When stepfathers claim stepchildren: A conceptual analysis. *Journal of Marriage and Family, 66*(1), 22–39.

Martin, C. L., & Ruble, D. (2004). Children's search for gender cues: Cognitive perspectives on gender development. *Current Directions in Psychological Science, 13*(2), 67–70.

Martin, C. L., Ruble, D. N., & Szkrybalo, J. (2002). Cognitive theories of early gender development. *Psychological Bulletin, 128*(6), 903–933.

Marushima, R. (2000). Relation of generativity to self-concept among middle-aged adults. *Japanese Journal of Educational Psychology, 48*(1), 52–62.

Marwick, C. (2000). Consensus panel considers osteoporosis. *Journal of the American Medical Association online, 283*(16).

Masi, G., Mucci, M., & Millepiedi, S. (2001). Separation anxiety disorder in children and adolescents: Epidemiology, diagnosis, and management. *CNS Drugs, 15*(2), 93–104.

Maternity Center Association. (2004, April). *What every pregnant woman needs to know about cesarean section.* New York: MCA.

Mathews, T.J., & MacDorman, M.F. (2007). Infant mortality statistics from the 2004 period linked birth/infant death data set. *National Vital Statistics Reports, 55* (14). Hyattsville, MD: National Center for Health Statistics.

Matlin, M. W. (2008). *The psychology of women* (8th ed.). Belmont, CA: Thomson/Wadsworth.

Matthews, A. K., Hughes, T. L., & Tartaro, J. (2006). Sexual behavior and sexual dysfunction in a community sample of lesbian and heterosexual women. In A. M. Omoto & H. S. Kurtzman (Eds.), *Sexual orientation and mental health* (pp. 185–205). Washington, DC: American Psychological Association.

Matthews, J. (1990). Drawing and individual development. In R. M. Thomas (Ed.), *The encyclopedia of human development and education: Theory, research, and studies.* Oxford: Pergamon.

Matthews, R. A., Del Priore, R. E., Acitelli, L. K., & Barnes-Farrell, J. L. (2006). Work-to-relationship conflict: Crossover effects in dual-earner couples. *Journal of Occupational Health Psychology, 11*(3), 228–240.

Maxwell, C. D., Robinson, A. L., & Post, L. A. (2003). The nature and predictors of sexual victimization and offending among adolescents. *Journal of Youth & Adolescence, 32*(6) 465–477.

McCabe, M. P. (2005). The role of performance anxiety in the development and maintenance of sexual dysfunction in men and women. *International Journal of Stress Management, 12*(4), 379–388.

McCall, R. B., Applebaum, M. I., & Hogarty, P. S. (1973). *Developmental changes in mental performance.* Monographs of the *Society for Research in Child Development, 38*(3, ser. 150).

McCarthy, B. W., & Fucito, L. M. (2005). Integrating medication, realistic expectations, and therapeutic interventions in the treatment of male sexual dysfunction. *Journal of Sex & Marital Therapy, 31*(4), 319–328.

McCartney, K., Owen, M. T., Booth, C. L., Clarke-Stewart, K. A., & Vandell, D. L. (2004). Testing a maternal attachment model of behavior problems in early childhood. *Journal of Child Psychology and Psychiatry, 45*(4), 765–778.

McClellan, J. M., & Werry, J. S. (2003). Evidence-based treatments in child and adolescent psychiatry: An inventory. *Journal of the American Academy of Child and Adolescent Psychiatry, 42*(12), 1388–1400.

McCracken, M., Jiles, R., & Blanck, H. M. (2007). Health behaviors of the young adult U.S. population: Behavioral risk factor surveillance system, 2003. *Preventing Chronic Disease, 4*(2), A25.

McCrae, R. R., & Costa, P. T., Jr. (1997). Personality trait structure as a human universal. *American Psychologist, 52,* 509–516.

McCrae, R. R., & Costa Jr., P. T. (2006). Cross-cultural perspectives on adult personality trait development. In D. K. Mroczek, & T. D. Little (Eds.), *Handbook of personality development* (pp. 129–145). Mahwah, NJ: Lawrence Erlbaum Associates Publishers.

McCrae, R. R., et al. (2000). Nature over nurture: Temperament, personality, and life span development. *Journal of Personality and Social Psychology, 78*(1), 173–186.

McDevitt, T. M., & Ormrod, J. E. (2002). *Child development and education.* Upper Saddle River, NJ: Prentice Hall.

McDonough, L. (2002). Basic-level nouns: First learned but misunderstood. *Journal of Child Language, 29*(2), 357–377.

McEwan, M. H., Dihoff, R. E., & Brosvic, G. M. (1991). Early infant crawling experience is reflected in later motor skill development. *Perceptual and Motor Skills, 72,* 75–79.

McGlaughlin, A., & Grayson, A. (2001). Crying in the first year of infancy: Patterns and prevalence. *Journal of Reproductive and Infant Psychology, 19*(1), 47–59.

McGrath, M., et al. (2005). Early precursors of low attention and hyperactivity in a preterm sample at age four. *Issues in Comprehensive Pediatric Nursing, 28*(1), 1–15.

McHale, J. P., & Rotman, T. (2007). Is seeing believing? Expectant parents' outlooks on coparenting and later coparenting solidarity. *Infant Behavior & Development, 30*(1), 63–81.

McHale, S. M., Kim, J.-Y., & Whiteman, S. D. (2006). Sibling relationships in childhood and adolescence. In P. Noller & J. A. Feeney (Eds.), *Close relationships: Functions, forms and processes* (pp. 127–149). New York: Psychology Press/Taylor & Francis.

McIlvane, W. J., & Dube, W. V. (2003). Stimulus control topography coherence theory: Foundations and extensions. *Behavior Analyst, 26*(2), 195–213.

McKee-Ryan, F., Song, Z., Wanberg, C. R., & Kinicki, A. J. (2005). Psychological and physical well-being during unemployment: A meta-analytic study. *Journal of Applied Psychology, 90*(1), 53–76.

McManus, C. (2003). Right hand, left hand: The origins of asymmetry in brains, bodies, atoms and cultures. *Cortex, 39*(2), 348–350.

McManus, I. C., et al. (1988). The development of handedness in children. *British Journal of Developmental Psychology, 6,* 257–273.

Meaney, K. S., Dornier, L. A., & Owens, M. S. (2002). Sex-role stereotyping for selected sport and physical activities across age groups. *Perceptual and Motor Skills, 94*(3), 743–749.

Meier, B. P., Robinson, M. D., & Wilkowski, B. M. (2006). Turning the other cheek: Agreeableness and the regulation of aggression-related primes. *Psychological Science, 17*(2), 136–142.

Meijer, A. M., & van den Wittenboer, G. L. H. (2007). Contribution of infants' sleep and crying to marital relationship of first-time parent couples in the first year after childbirth. *Journal of Family Psychology, 21*(1) 49–57.

Meinert, C. L., & Breitner, J. C. S. (2008). Chronic disease long-term drug prevention trials: Lessons from the Alzheimer's Disease Anti-Inflammatory Prevention Trial (ADAPT). *Alzheimer's & Dementia, 4*(1, Suppl 1), S7–S14.

Melamed, S., Meir, E. I., & Samson, A. (1995). The benefits of personality-leisure congruence. *Journal of Leisure Research, 27,* 25–40.

Meldrum, M, L. (2003). A capsule history of pain management. *Journal of the American Medical Association, 290,* 2470–2475.

Mellon, M. W. (2006). Enuresis and encopresis. In G. G.Bea, & K. M. Minke (Eds.), *Children's needs III: Development, prevention, and intervention* (pp. 1041–1053). Washington, DC: National Association of School Psychologists.

Mellon, M. W., & Houts, A. C. (2006). Nocturnal enuresis. In J. E. Fisher & W. T. O'Donohue (Eds.), *Practitioner's guide to evidence-based psychotherapy* (pp. 432–441). New York: Springer Science + Business Media.

Meltzoff, A. N. (2007). Infants' causal learning: Intervention, observation, imitation. In A. Gopnik & L. Schulz (Eds.), *Causal learning: Psychology, philosophy, and computation* (pp. 37–47). New York: Oxford University Press.

Meltzoff, A. N., & Prinz, W. (Eds.). (2002). *The imitative mind: Development, evolution, and brain bases.* New York: Cambridge University Press.

Mendle, J., et al. (2006). Family structure and age at menarche: A children-of-twins approach. *Developmental Psychology, 42*(3), 533–542.

Merrill, L. L., Crouch, J. L., Thomsen, C. J., & Guimond, J. M. (2004). Risk for intimate partner violence and child physical abuse: Psychosocial characteristics of multi-risk male and female Navy recruits. *Child Maltreatment: Journal of the American Professional Society on the Abuse of Children, 9*(1), 18–29.

Metcalfe, J. S., et al. (2005). Development of somatosensory-motor integration: An event-related analysis of infant posture in the first year of independent walking. *Developmental Psychobiology, 46*(1), 19–35.

Metzger, K. L., et al. (2007). Effects of nicotine vary across two auditory evoked potentials in the mouse. *Biological Psychiatry, 61*(1), 23–30.

Meyer, S., & Shore, C. (2001). Children's understanding of dreams as mental states. *Dreaming, 11*(4), 179–194.

Michael, R., Gagnon, J., Laumann, E., & Kolata, G. (1994). *Sex in America: A definitive survey.* Boston: Little Brown.

Milgram, R. M., & Livne, N. L. (2006). Research on creativity in Israel: A chronicle of theoretical and empirical development. In J. C. Kaufman & R. J. Sternberg (Eds.), *The international handbook of creativity* (pp. 307–336). New York: Cambridge University Press.

Millar, W. J., & Maclean, H. (2005). Breastfeeding practices. *Health Reports* (Statistics Canada, Catalogue 82-003-XIE) 16(12): 23–31. Retrieved from http://www.statcan.gc.ca/pub/82-003-x/82-003-x2004002-eng.pdf

Miller, A. L., Wyman, S. E., Huppert, J. D., Glassman, S. L., & Rathus, J. H. (2000). Analysis of behavioral skills utilized by suicidal adolescents receiving dialectical behavior therapy. *Cognitive and Behavioral Practice, 7*(2), 183–187.

Miller, C. F., Trautner, H. M., & Ruble, D. N. (2006). The role of gender stereotypes in children's preferences and behavior. In L. Balter & C. S. Tamis-LeMonda (Eds.), *Child psychology: A handbook of contemporary issues* (2nd ed.) (pp. 293–323). New York: Psychology Press.

Miller, S. M., Boyer, B. A., & Rodoletz, M. (1990). Anxiety in children: Nature and development. In M. Lewis & S. M. Miller (Eds.), *Handbook of developmental psychopathology.* New York: Plenum.

Mills, B., Reyna, V. F., & Estrada, S. (2008). Explaining contradictory relations between risk perception and risk taking. *Psychological Science, 19*(5), 429–433.

Minino, A. M., Heron, M. P., Murphy, S. L., & Kochanek, K. D. (2007, October 10). Deaths: Final data for 2004. *National vital statistics reports, 55*(19). Available at http://www.cdc.gov/nchs/data/nvsr55/nvsr55_19.pdf.

Minkler, M., & Fuller-Thomson, E. (2005). African American grandparents raising grandchildren: A national study using the Census 2000 *American Community Survey. Journals of Gerontology: Series B: Psychological Sciences and Social Sciences, 60B*(2), S82–S92.

Miscarriage. (2007, January 11). Available at http://www.nlm.nih.gov/medlineplus/ency/article/001488.htm. Accessed February 23, 2007.

Mischo, C. (2004). Fördert Gruppendiskussion die Perspektiven-Koordination? *Zeitschrift für Entwicklungspsychologie und Pädagogische Psychologie, 36*(1), 30–37.

Mitchell, A. L. (2006). Medical consequences of cocaine. *Journal of Addictions Nursing, 17*(4), 249.

Mitchell, D. D., & Bruss, P. J. (2003) Age differences in implicit memory: Conceptual, perceptual, or methodological? *Psychology and Aging, 18*(4), 807–822.

Mock, S. E., & Cornelius, S. W. (2007). Profiles of interdependence: The retirement planning of married, cohabiting, and lesbian couples. *Sex Roles, 56*(11–12), 793–800.

Mock, S. E., Taylor, C. J., & Savin-Williams, R. C. (2006). Aging together: The retirement plans of same-sex couples. In D. Kimmel, T. Rose, & S. David (Eds.), *Lesbian, gay, bisexual, and transgender aging: Research and clinical perspectives* (pp. 152–174). New York: Columbia University Press.

Moen, P., Huang, Q., Plassmann, V., & Dentinger, E. (2006). Deciding the future. *American Behavioral Scientist, 49*(10), 1422–1443.

Moen, P., Kim, J. E., & Hofmeister, H. (2001). Couples' work/retirement transitions, gender, and marital equality. *Social Psychology Quarterly, 64,* 55–71.

Moens, E., Braet, C., & Soetens, B. (2007). Observation of family functioning at mealtime: A comparison between families of children with and without overweight. *Journal of Pediatric Psychology, 32*(1), 52–63.

Mohan, R., & Bhugra, D. (2005). Literature update. *Sexual and Relationship Therapy, 20*(1), 115–122.

Molinari, L., & Corsaro, W. A. (2000). Le relazioni amicali nella scuola dell'infanzia e nella scuola elementare: Uno studio longitudinale. *Eta Evolutiva, 67,* 40–51.

Monat, A., Lazarus, R S , & Reevy, G. (Eds.). (2007). *The Praeger handbook on stress and coping* (Vol. 2). Westport, CT: Praeger Publishers/Greenwood Publishing Group.

Montemayor, R., & Eisen, M. (1977). The development of self-conceptions from childhood to adolescence. *Developmental Psychology, 13,* 314–319.

Moore, D. R. & Heiman, J. R. (2006). Women's sexuality in context: Relationship factors and female sexual functioning. In I. Goldstein, C. Meston, S. Davis, & A. Traish (Eds.), *Female sexual dysfunction.* New York: Parthenon.

Morelli, G. A., Oppenheim, D., Rogoff, B., & Goldsmith, D. (1992). Cultural variation in infants' sleeping arrangements: Questions of independence. *Developmental Psychology, 28,* 604–613.

Morrell, J., & Steele, H. (2003). The role of attachment security, temperament, maternal perception, and care-giving behavior in persistent infant sleeping problems. *Infant Mental Health Journal, 24*(5), 447–468.

Morry, M. M., & Gaines, S. O. (2005). Relationship satisfaction as a predictor of similarity ratings: A test of the attraction-similarity hypothesis. *Journal of Social and Personal Relationships, 22*(4), 561–584.

Morton, S. M. B. (2006). Maternal nutrition and fetal growth and development. In P. Gluckman & M. Hanson (Eds.), *Developmental origins of health and disease* (pp. 98–129). New York: Cambridge University Press.

Moses, L. J., & Flavell, J. H. (1990). Inferring false beliefs from actions and reactions. *Child Development, 61,* 929–945.

Mosher, W. D., Chandra, A., & Jones, J. (2005). *Sexual behavior and selected health measures: men and women 1–B 44 years of age, United States, 2002. Advance data from vital and health statistics.* Centers for Disease Control and Prevention. National Center for Health Statistics, Number 362, Figures 2 and 3.

Moshman, D. (2005). *Adolescent psychological development (2nd ed.).* Mahwah, NJ: Erlbaum.

Mueller, R., Pierce, K., Ambrose, J. B., Allen, G., & Courchesne, E. (2001). Atypical patterns of cerebral motor activation in autism: A functional magnetic resonance study. *Biological Psychiatry, 49*(8) 665–676.

Muhlbauer, V., & Chrisler, J. C. (Eds.). (2007). *Women over 50: Psychological perspectives.* New York: Springer Science + Business Media.

Munroe, R. H., Shimmin, H. S., & Munroe, R. L. (1984). Gender role understanding and sex role preference in four cultures. *Developmental Psychology, 20,* 673–682.

Muraco, A. (2006). Intentional families: Fictive kin ties between cross-gender, different sexual orientation friends. *Journal of Marriage and Family, 68*(5), 1313–1325.

Muris, P., Bodden, D., Merckelbach, H., Ollendick, T. H., & King, N. (2003). Fear of the beast: A prospective study on the effects of negative information on childhood fear. *Behaviour Research and Therapy, 41*(2), 195–208.

Myers, J. E., Madathil, J., & Tingle, L. R. (2005). Marriage satisfaction and wellness in India and the United States: A preliminary comparison of arranged marriages and marriages of choice. *Journal of Counseling & Development, 83*(2), 183–190.

Nadeau, L., et al. (2003). Extremely premature and very low birthweight infants: A double hazard population? *Social Development, 12*(2), 235–248.

Nagin, D. S., & Tremblay, R. E. (2001). Parental and early childhood predictors of persistent physical aggression in boys from kindergarten to high school. *Archives of General Psychiatry, 58*(4), 389–394.

National Center for Children in Poverty. (2004). Low-income children in the United States (2004). Available at http://cpmcnet.columbia.edu/dept/nccp/.

National Center for Education Statistics. (2007, June). Dropout rates in the United States: 2005. Available at http://nces.ed.gov/pubs2007/dropout05/. Accessed July 20, 2007.

National Center for Injury Prevention and Control, Office of Statistics and Programming, Centers for Disease Control and Prevention. (2007a, March 29). National Center for Health Statistics (NCHS), National Vital Statistics System. Accessed May 7, 2007. Available at http://webappa.cdc.gov/cgi-bin/broker.exe.

National Center for Injury Prevention and Control. (2007b, July 11). Suicide: Fact sheet. Available at http://www.cdc.gov/ncipc/factsheets/suifacts.htm.

National Guideline Clearinghouse. (2007). Use of clomiphene citrate in women. Available at http://www.guideline.gov/summary/summary.aspx?ss=15&doc_id=4843&nbr=3484. Last updated January 29, 2007. Accessed February 6, 2007.

National Institutes of Health. (2002). Available at http://cerhr.niehs.nih.gov/genpub/topics/vitamin_a-ccae.html.

National Sleep Foundation. (2007). Children's sleep habits. Available at http://www.sleepfoundation.org/site/c.huIXKjM0IxF/b.2453615/apps/nl/content3.asp?content_id={5239AA1B-DB37-42DA-B1ED-436FA086D3AC}&notoc=1.

Natsopoulos, D., Kiosseoglou, G., & Xeromeritou, A. (1992). Handedness and spatial ability in children: Further support for Geschwind's hypothesis of "pathology of superiority" and for Annett's theory of intelligence. *Genetic, Social, and General Psychology Monographs, 118*(1) 103–126.

Nauta, M. M. (2007). Career interests, self-efficacy, and personality as antecedents of career exploration. *Journal of Career Assessment, 15*(2), 162–180.

Naveh-Benjamin, M., Brav, T. K., & Levy, O. (2007). The associative memory deficit of older adults: The role of strategy utilization. *Psychology and Aging, 22,* 202–208.

Naveh-Benjamin, M., Hussain, Z., Guez, J., & Bar-On, M. (2003). Adult age differences in episodic memory: Further support for an associative-deficit hypothesis. *Journal of Experimental Psychology: Learning, Memory, and Cognition, 29,* 826–837.

Nduati, R., et al. (2000). Effect of breastfeeding and formula feeding on transmission of HIV-1. *Journal of the American Medical Association, 283,* 1167–1174.

Neisser, U., et al. (1996). Intelligence: Knowns and unknowns. *American Psychologist, 51,* 77–101.

Nelson, C. A., de Haan, M., & Thomas, K. M. (2006). Neuroscience of cognitive development: The role of experience and the developing brain. Hoboken, NJ: Wiley.

Nelson, C. A., & Luciana, M. (Eds.). (2001). *Handbook of developmental cognitive neuroscience.* Cambridge, MA: MIT Press.

Nelson, C. A., & Ludemann, P. M. (1989). Past, current, and future trends in infant face perception research. *Canadian Journal of Psychology, 43,* 183–198.

Nelson, K. (1973). *Structure and strategy in learning to talk.* Monographs for the Society for Research in Child Development, 38(1–2, ser. 149).

Nelson, K. (1981). Individual differences in language development: Implications for development of language. *Developmental Psychology, 17,* 170–187.

Nelson, K. (1990). Remembering, forgetting, and childhood amnesia. In R. Fivush & J. A. Hudson (Eds.), *Knowing and remembering in young children.* Cambridge: Cambridge University Press.

Nelson, K. (1993). Events, narratives, memory: What develops? In C. A. Nelson (Ed.), *Minnesota symposia on child psychology, Vol. 26, Memory and affect in development.* Hillsdale, NJ: Erlbaum.

Nelson, K. (2005). Cognitive functions of language in early childhood. In B. D. Homer & C. S. Tamis-LeMonda (Eds.), *The development of social cognition and communication* (pp. 7–28). Mahwah, NJ: Erlbaum.

Nelson, K. (2006). Advances in pragmatic developmental theory: The case of language acquisition. *Human Development, 49*(3), 184–188.

Nelson, K., & Fivush, R. (2004). The emergence of autobiographical memory: A social cultural developmental theory. *Psychological Review, 111*(2), 486–511.

Nesdale, D., & Lambert, A. (2007). Effects of experimentally manipulated peer rejection on children's negative affect, self-esteem, and maladaptive social behavior. *International Journal of Behavioral Development, 31*(2), 115–122.

Newburn-Cook, C. V., et al. (2002). Where and to what extent is prevention of low birth weight possible? *Western Journal of Nursing Research, 24*(8), 887–904.

Newman, R., Ratner, N. B., Jusczyk, A. M., Jusczyk, P. W., & Dow, K. A. (2006). Infants' early ability to segment the conversational speech signal predicts later language development: A retrospective analysis. *Developmental Psychology, 42*(4), 643–655.

Neyer, F. J. (2002). Twin relationships in old age. *Journal of Social and Personal Relationships, 19*(2), 155–177.

NIAAA (National Institute on Alcohol Abuse and Alcoholism). (2005). Cage questionnaire. Available at http://pubs.niaaa.nih.gov/publications/Assesing%20Alcohol/InstrumentPDFs/16_CAGE.pdf.

Nielsen, S., & Palmer, B. (2003). Diagnosing eating disorders: AN, BN, and the others. *Acta Psychiatrica Scandinavica, 108*(3), 161–162.

Nielsen, S. J., & Popkin, B. M. (2003). Patterns and trends in food portion sizes, 1977–1998. *Journal of the American Medical Association, 289*(4), 450–453.

Niemeier, H. M., Raynor, H. A., Lloyd-Richardson, E. E., Rogers, M. L., & Wing, R. R. (2006). Fast food consumption and breakfast skipping: Predictors of weight gain from adolescence to adulthood in a nationally representative sample. *Journal of Adolescent Health, 39*(6), 842–849.

Nigg, J. T., Goldsmith, H. H., & Sachek, J. (2004). Temperament and attention deficit hyperactivity disorder: The development of a multiple pathway model. *Journal of Clinical Child and Adolescent Psychology, 33*(1), 42–53.

Nigg, J. T., Hinshaw, S. P., & Huang-Pollock, C. (2006). Disorders of attention and impulse regulation. In D. Cicchetti & D. J. Cohen (Eds.), *Developmental psychopathology, Vol. 3, Risk, disorder, and adaptation* (2nd ed.) (pp. 358–403). Hoboken, NJ: Wiley.

Nimrod, G. (2007). Retirees' leisure. *Leisure Studies, 26*(1), 65–80.

Nisbett, R. E. (2007, December 9). All brains are the same color. *The New York Times online.*

Nock, M. K., Kazdin, A. E., Hiripi, E., & Kessler, R. C. (2006). Prevalence, subtypes, and correlates of DSM-IV conduct disorder in the National Comorbidity Survey Replication. *Psychological Medicine, 36,* 699–710.

Nolen-Hoeksema, S., Stice, E., Wade, E., & Bohon, C. (2007). Reciprocal relations between rumination and bulimic, substance abuse, and depressive symptoms in female adolescents. *Journal of Abnormal Psychology, 116*(1), 198–207.

Nomaguchi, K. M. (2006). Maternal employment, nonparental care, mother–child interactions, and child outcomes during preschool years. *Journal of Marriage and Family, 68*(5), 1341–1369.

Nonaka, A. M. (2004). The forgotten endangered languages: Lessons on the importance of remembering from Thailand's Ban Khor Sign Language. *Language in Society, 33*(5), 737–767.

Nonnemaker, J. M., & Homsi, G. (2007). Measurement properties of the Fagerström Test for nicotine dependence adapted for use in an adolescent sample. *Addictive Behaviors, 32*(1), 181–186.

Noppe, I. C., & Noppe, L. D. (2004). Adolescent experiences with death: Letting go of immortality. *Journal of Mental Health Counseling, 26*(2), 146–167.

Norlander, T., Erixon, A., & Archer, T. (2000). Psychological androgyny and creativity: Dynamics of gender-role and personality trait. *Social Behavior and Personality, 28*(5), 423–435.

Norton, A., et al. (2005). Are there pre-existing neural, cognitive, or motoric markers for musical ability? *Brain and Cognition, 59*(2), 124–134.

Nurnberg, H. G., et al. (2008). Sildenafil treatment of women with antidepressant-associated sexual dysfunction. *Journal of the American Medical Association, 300*(4), 395–404.

Nuttman-Shwartz, O. (2007). Is there life without work? *International Journal of Aging & Human Development, 64*(2) 129–147.

O'Boyle, M. W., & Benbow, C. P. (1990). Handedness and its relationship to ability and talent. In S. Coren (Ed.), *Left-handedness: Behavior implications and anomalies.* Amsterdam: North-Holland.

O'Dea, J. A. (2006). Self-concept, self-esteem and body weight in adolescent females: A three-year longitudinal study. *Journal of Health Psychology, 11*(4), 599–611.

O'Doherty, J., et al. (2003). Beauty in a smile: The role of medial orbitofrontal cortex in facial attractiveness. *Neuropsychologia, 41*(2), 147–155.

O'Donnell, L., et al. (2003). Long-term influence of sexual norms and attitudes on timing of sexual initiation among urban minority youth. *Journal of School Health, 23*(2), 68–75.

O'Keeffe, M. J., O'Callaghan, M., Williams, G. M., Najman, J. M., & Bor, W. (2003). Learning, cognitive, and attentional problems in adolescents born small for gestational age. *Pediatrics, 112*(2), 301–307.

O'Neill, D. K., & Chong, S. C. F. (2001). Preschool children's difficulty understanding the types of information obtained through the five senses. *Child Development, 72*(3), 803–815.

O'Neill, D. K., & Gopnik, A. (1991). Young children's ability to identify the sources of their beliefs. *Developmental Psychology, 27,* 390–397.

O'Shea, R. P., & Corballis, P. M. (2005). Binocular rivalry in the divided brain. In D. Alais & R. Blake (Eds.), *Binocular rivalry.* (pp. 301–315). Cambridge, MA: MIT Press.

Oates, J., & Messer, D. (2007). Growing up with TV. *The Psychologist, 20*(1), 30–32.

Office of National Statistics. (2006). Available at http://www.multiplebirths.org.uk/media.asp. Accessed February 6, 2007.

Office of the Commissioner of Official Languages. (2005). Bilingualism in Canada. Retrieved from http://www.ocol-clo.gc.ca/html/biling_e.php

Ogunfowora, O. B., Olanrewaju, D. M., & Akenzua, G. I. (2005). A comparative study of academic achievement of children with sickle cell anemia and their healthy siblings. *Journal of the National Medical Association, 97*(3), 405–408.

Ohnishi, T., Matsuda, H., Hirakata, M., & Ugawa, Y. (2006). Navigation ability dependent neural activation in the human brain: An fMRI study. *Neuroscience Research, 55*(4), 361–369.

Olivo, L., Cotter, R., & Bromwich, R. (2007). *Youth and the law: New approaches to criminal justice and child protection.* Toronto: Emond Montgomery Publications Ltd.

Ollendick, T. H., & King, N. J. (1991). Origins of childhood fears: An evaluation of Rachman's theory of teen-acquisition. *Behavior Research and Therapy, 29,* 117–123.

Olson, S. L., Bates, J. E., Sandy, J. M., & Lanthier, R. (2000). Early developmental precursors of externalizing behavior in middle childhood and adolescence. *Journal of Abnormal Child Psychology, 28*(2), 119–133.

Oltjenbruns, K. A., & Balk, D. E. (2007). Life span issues and loss, grief, and mourning: Part 1: The importance of a developmental context: childhood and adolescence as an example. In D. Balk, et al. (Eds.), *Handbook of thanatology* (pp. 143–163). New York: Routledge/Taylor & Francis Group.

Olweus Bullying Prevention Program. (2010). What is bullying? Retrieved from http://www.olweus.org/public/bullying.page

Omori, M., & Ingersoll, G. M. (2005). Health-endangering behaviours among Japanese college students: A test of psychosocial model of risk-taking behaviours. *Journal of Adolescence, 28*(1), 17–33.

Orel, N. (2006). Lesbian and bisexual women as grandparents: The centrality of sexual orientation in the grandparent – grandchild relationship. In D. Kimmel, T. Rose, & S. David (Eds.), *Lesbian, gay, bisexual, and transgender ageing: Research and clinical perspectives* (pp. 175–194). New York: Columbia University Press.

Organ Donation and Transplant Association of Canada. (2009). Facts. Retrieved from http://organdonations.ca/facts

Örnkloo, H., & von Hofsten, C. (2007). Fitting objects into holes: On the development of spatial cognition skills. *Developmental Psychology, 43*(2), 404–416.

Orstavik, R. E., Kendler, K. S., Czajkowski, N., Tambs, K., & Reichborn-Kjennerud, T. (2007). Genetic and environmental contributions to depressive personality disorder in a population-based sample of Norwegian twins. *Journal of Affective Disorders, 99*(1–3), 181–189.

Ortega, V., Ojeda, P., Sutil, F., & Sierra, J. C. (2005). Culpabilidad sexual en adolescentes: Estudio de algunos factores relacionados. *Anales de Psicología, 21*(2), 268–275.

Osteoporosis Canada. (2010). Facts and statistics: About osteoporosis. Retrieved from http://www.osteoporosis.ca/index.php/ci_id/8867/la_id/1.htm

Oster, H. (2005). The repertoire of infant facial expressions: an ontogenetic perspective. In J. Nadel, & D. Muir (Eds.), *Emotional development: Recent research advances* (pp. 261–292). New York: Oxford University Press.

Ouellette, G. P. (2006). What's meaning got to do with it: The role of vocabulary in word reading and reading comprehension. *Journal of Educational Psychology, 98*(3), 554–566.

Outram, S., Murphy, B., & Cockburn, J. (2006). Prevalence of and factors associated with midlife women taking medicines for psychological distress. *AeJAMH (Australian e-Journal for the Advancement of Mental Health), 5*(3), 1–13.

Oztop, E., Kawato, M., & Arbib, M. (2006) Mirror neurons and imitation: A computationally guided review. *Neural Networks, 19*(3), 254–271.

Paavola, L., Kemppinen, K., Kumpulainen, K., Moilanen, I., & Ebeling, H. (2006). Maternal sensitivity, infant co-operation and early linguistic development: Some predictive relations. *European Journal of Developmental Psychology, 3*(1), 13–30.

Page, K. (1999, May 16). The graduate. *Washington Post Magazine, 152,* 18, 20.

Pancsofar, N., & Vernon-Feagans, L. (2006). Mother and father language input to young children: Contributions to later language development. *Journal of Applied Developmental Psychology, 27*(6), 571–587.

Park, H-O. H., & Greenberg, J. S. (2007). Parenting grandchildren. In J. Blackburn, & C. N. Dulmus (Eds.), *Handbook of gerontology: Evidence-based approaches to theory, practice, and policy* (pp. 397–425). Hoboken, NJ: John Wiley & Sons, Inc.

Park, N. S., et al. (2008). Religiousness and longitudinal trajectories in elders' functional status. *Research on Aging, 30*(3), 279–298.

Parke, R. D., & Buriel, R. (2006). Socialization in the family: Ethnic and ecological perspectives. In N. Eisenberg, W. Damon, & R. M. Lerner (Eds.), *Handbook of child psychology* (6th ed.), *Vol. 3, Social, emotional, and personality development* (pp. 429–504). Hoboken, NJ: Wiley.

Parten, M. B. (1932). Social participation among preschool children. *Journal of Abnormal and Social Psychology, 27,* 243–269.

Pascarella, E. T., Wolniak, G. C., Pierson, C. T., Terenzini, P. T., & Schuh, J. H. (2003). Experiences and outcomes of first-generation students in community colleges. *Journal of College Student Development, 44*(3), 420–429.

Patenaude, J., Niyonsenga, T., & Fafard, D. (2003). Changes in students' moral development during medical school: A cohort study. *Canadian Medical Association Journal, 168*(7), 840–844.

Paterson, D. S., et al. (2006). Multiple serotonergic brainstem abnormalities in sudden infant death syndrome. *Journal of the American Medical Association, 296,* 2124–2132.

Patrick, S., Sells, J. N., Giordano, F. G., & Tollerud, T. R. (2007). Intimacy, differentiation, and personality variables as predictors of marital satisfaction. *The Family Journal, 15*(4), 359–367.

Patterson, C. J. (2006). Children of lesbian and gay parents. *Current Directions in Psychological Science, 15*(5), 241–244.

Patterson, G. R. (2005). The next generation of PMTO models. *The Behavior Therapist, 28*(2), 27–33.

Patterson, M. M., & Bigler, R. S. (2006). Preschool children's attention to environmental messages about groups: Social categorization and the origins of intergroup bias. *Child Development, 77*(4), 847–860.

Pauli-Pott, U., Mertesacker, B., & Beckmann, D. (2003). Ein Fragebogen zur Erfassung des fruhkindlichen Temperaments im Elternurteil. *Zeitschrift für Kinder- und Jugend-psychiatrie und Psychotherapie, 31*(2), 99–110.

Paulussen-Hoogeboom, M. C., Stams, G. J. J. M., Hermanns, J. M. A., & Peetsma, T. T. D. (2007). Child negative emotionality and parenting from infancy to preschool: A meta-analytic review. *Developmental Psychology, 43*(2), 438–453.

Paus, T., et al. (1999). Structural maturation of neural pathways in children and adolescents: In vivo study. *Science, 283*(5409), 1908–1911.

Pawlowski, B., & Koziel, S. (2002). The impact of traits offered in personal advertisements on response rates. *Evolution & Human Behavior, 23*(2), 139–149.

Paxton, S. J., Neumark-Sztainer, D., Hannan, P. J., & Eisenberg, M. E. (2006). Body dissatisfaction prospectively predicts depressive mood and low self-esteem in adolescent girls and boys. *Journal of Clinical Child and Adolescent Psychology, 35*(4), 539–549.

Paxton, S. J., Norris, M., Wertheim, E. H., Durkin, S. J., & Anderson, J. (2005). Body dissatisfaction, dating, and importance of thinness to attractiveness in adolescent girls. *Sex Roles, 53*(9–10), 663–675.

Peck, R. C. (1968). Psychological developments in the second half of life. In B. L. Neugarten (Ed.), *Middle age and aging* (pp. 88–92). Chicago: University of Chicago Press.

Pei, M., Matsuda, K., Sakamoto, H., & Kawata, M. (2006). Intrauterine proximity to male fetuses affects the morphology of the sexually dimorphic nucleus of the preoptic area in the adult rat brain. *European Journal of Neuroscience, 23*(5), 1234–1240.

Pelphrey, K. A., et al. (2004). Development of visuospatial short-term memory in the second half of the first year. *Developmental Psychology, 40*(5), 836–851.

Pemberton, E. F. (1990). Systematic errors in children's drawings. *Cognitive Development, 5*, 395–404.

Penn, H. E. (2006). Neurobiological correlates of autism: A review of recent research. *Child Neuropsychology, 12*(1), 57–79.

Perls, T. T. (2005). The oldest old. *Scientific American, 272*, 70–75.

Perls, T. T., et al. (2002). Life-long sustained mortality advantage of siblings of centenarians. *Proceedings of the National Academy of Sciences 99*, 8442–8447.

Perrig-Chiello, P., Perrig, W. J., Uebelbacher, A., & Stähelin, H. B. (2006). Impact of physical and psychological resources on functional autonomy in old age. *Psychology, Health & Medicine, 11*(4), 470–482.

Perrone, K. M., Webb, L. K., & Jackson, Z. V. (2007). Relationships between parental attachment, work and family roles, and life satisfaction. *The Career Development Quarterly, 55*(3), 237–248.

Perry, P. J., et al. (2001). Bioavailable testosterone as a correlate of cognition, psychological status, quality of life, and sexual function in aging males: Implications for testosterone replacement therapy. *Annals of Clinical Psychiatry, 13*(2), 75–80.

Perry, W. G. (1970/1998). *Forms of intellectual and ethical development in the college years: A scheme.* New York: Holt, Rinehart and Winston.

Perry, W. G. (1981). Cognitive and ethical growth: The making of meaning. In A. W. Chickering & Assoc. (Eds.). *The modern American college* (pp. 76–116). San Francisco: Jossey-Bass.

Perry-Jenkins, M., Goldberg, A. E., Pierce, C. P., & Sayer, A. G. (2007). Shift work, role overload, and the transition to parenthood. *Journal of Marriage and Family, 69*(1), 123–138.

Persson, G. E. B. (2005). Developmental perspectives on prosocial and aggressive motives in preschoolers' peer interactions. *International Journal of Behavioral Development, 29*(1), 80–91.

Philip, J., et al. (2004). Late first-trimester invasive prenatal diagnostic results of an international randomized trial. *Obstetrics & Gynecology, 103*(6), 1164–1173.

Phillips, D. A., & Styfco, S. J. (2007). Child development research and public policy: Triumphs and setbacks on the way to maturity. In J. L. Aber et al. (Eds.), *Child development and social policy: Knowledge for action. APA Decade of Behavior volumes* (pp. 11–27). Washington, DC: American Psychological Association.

Phinney, J. S. (2006). Ethnic identity exploration in emerging adulthood. In J. J. Arnett & J. L. Tanner (Eds.), *Emerging adults in America: Coming of age in the 21st century* (pp. 117–134). Washington, DC: American Psychological Association.

Phinney, J. S., & Alipuria, L. L. (2006). Multiple social categorization and identity among multiracial, multiethnic, and multicultural individuals: Processes and implications. In R. J. Crisp & M. Hewstone (Eds.), *Multiple social categorization: Processes, models and applications* (pp. 211–238). New York: Psychology Press.

Phinney, J. S., & Ong, A. D. (2007). Conceptualization and measurement of ethnic identity: Current status and future directions. *Journal of Counseling Psychology, 54*(3), 271–281.

Phipps, M. G., Blume, J. D., & DeMonner, S. M. (2002). Young maternal age associated with increased risk of postneonatal death. *Obstetrics and Gynecology, 100*, 481–486.

Physical Activity Fact Sheet, (2005). The President's Council on Physical Fitness and Sports, Department of Human Services.

Physical and Health Education Canada. (2009). Physical education in school. Retrieved from http://www.phecanada.ca/physical-education-school

Piaget, J. (1932). *The moral judgment of the child.* London: Kegan Paul.

Piaget, J. (1962). *Play, dreams, and imitation in childhood.* New York: Norton. (Originally published in 1946.)

Piaget, J. (1963). *The origins of intelligence in children.* New York: Norton. (Originally published in 1936.)

Piaget, J. (1976). *The grasp of consciousness: Action and concept in the young child.* Cambridge, MA: Harvard University Press.

Pichichero, M. E. (2006). Prevention of cervical cancer through vaccination of adolescents. *Clinical Pediatrics, 45*(5), 393–398.

Piek, J. P. (2006). *Infant motor development.* Champaign, IL: Human Kinetics.

Piek, J. P., Baynam, G. B., & Barrett, N. C. (2006). The relationship between fine and gross motor ability, self-perceptions and self-worth in children and adolescents. *Human Movement Science, 25*(1), 65–75.

Pierce, K. M., & Vandell, D. L. (2006). Child care. In G. G. Bear & K. M. Minke (Eds.), *Children's needs III: Development, prevention, and intervention* (pp. 721–732). Washington, DC: National Association of School Psychologists.

Pine, D. S., et al. (2001). Fluvoxamine for the treatment of anxiety disorders in children and adolescents. *New England Journal of Medicine, 344*(17), 1279–1285.

Pinker, S. (1994). *The language instinct.* New York: William Morrow.

Pinker, S., & Jackendoff, R. (2005). The faculty of language: What's special about it? *Cognition, 95*(2), 201–236.

Pinquart, M., & Schindler, I. (2007). Changes of life satisfaction in the transition to retirement. *Psychology and Aging, 22*(3), 442–455.

Pittman, G. (2010, September 1). First-time mothers drive up C-section rate: Study. *Reuters.* Retrieved from http://www.canada.com/health/First+time+mothers+drive+section+rate+Study/3470332/story.html

Plomin, R. (Ed.). (2002). *Behavioral genetics in the postgenomic era.* Washington, DC: American Psychological Association.

Plomin, R., Owen, M. J., & McGuffin, P. (1994). The genetic basis of complex human behaviors. *Science, 264,* 1733–1739.

Plomin, R., & Walker, S. O. (2003). Genetics and educational psychology. *British Journal of Educational Psychology, 73*(1), 3–14.

Polivy, J., Herman, C. P., & Boivin, M. (2005). Eating disorders. In J. E. Maddux & B. A. Winstead (Eds.), *Psychopathology: Foundations for a contemporary understanding* (pp. 229–254). Mahwah, NJ: Erlbaum.

Poltorak, D. Y., & Glazer, J. P. (2006). The development of children's understanding of death. *Child and Adolescent Psychiatric Clinics of North America, 15*(3), 567–573.

Popma, A., et al. (2007). Cortisol moderates the relationship between testosterone and aggression in delinquent male adolescents. *Biological Psychiatry, 61*(3), 405–411.

Porfeli, E. J. (2007). Work values system development during adolescence. *Journal of Vocational Behavior, 70*(1), 42–60.

Porter, R. H., Makin, J. W., Davis, L. B., & Christensen, K. M. (1992). Breast-fed infants respond to olfactory cues from their own mother and unfamiliar lactating females. *Infant Behavior and Development, 15,* 85–93.

Posey, D. J., et al. (2007). Positive effects of methylphenidate on inattention and hyperactivity in pervasive developmental disorders: An analysis of secondary measures. *Biological Psychiatry, 61*(4), 538–544.

Posner, M. I., & Rothbart, M. K. (2007). *Relating brain and mind. Educating the human brain.* Washington, DC: American Psychological Association.

Powlishta, K. K. (2004). Gender as a social category: Intergroup processes and gender-role development. In M. Bennett & F. Sani (Eds.), *The development of the social self* (pp. 103–133). New York: Psychology Press.

Powlishta, K. K., Sen, M. G., Serbin, L. A., Poulin-Dubois, D., & Eichstedt, J. A. (2001). From infancy through middle childhood: The role of cognitive and social factors in becoming gendered. In R. K. Unger (Ed.), *Handbook of the psychology of women and gender* (pp. 116–132). New York: Wiley.

Prato-Previde, E., Fallani, G., & Valsecchi, P. (2006). Gender differences in owners interacting with pet dogs: An observational study. *Ethology, 112*(1), 64–73.

Pratt, C., & Bryant, P. (1990). Young children understand that looking leads to knowing (so long as they are looking into a single barrel). *Child Development, 61,* 973–982.

Pressley, M., & Hilden, K. (2006). Cognitive strategies. In D. Kuhn, R. S. Siegler, W. Damon, & R. M. Lerner (Eds.), *Handbook of child psychology* (6th ed.), Vol. 2, *Cognition, perception, and language* (pp. 511–556). Hoboken, NJ: Wiley.

Pressman, S. D., et al. (2005). Loneliness, social network size, and immune response to influenza vaccination in college freshmen. *Health Psychology. 24*(3), 297–306.

Priner, R., Freeman, S., Perez, R., & Sohmer, H. (2003). The neonate has a temporary conductive hearing loss due to fluid in the middle ear. *Audiology & Neurotology, 8*(2), 100–110.

Province of British Columbia. (2010). *Baby's best chance: Parents' handbook of pregnancy and health care* (6th ed., 2nd rev.). Retrieved from http://www.hls.gov.bc.ca/publications/year/2010/bbc.pdf

Provence, S., & Lipton, R. C. (1962). *Infants in institutions*. New York: International Universities Press.

Prull, M. W., Gabrieli, J. D. E., & Bunge, S. A. (2000). In Craik, F. I. M., & Salthouse, T. A. (Eds.), *Age-related changes in memory: A cognitive neuroscience perspective. The handbook of aging and cognition* (2nd ed.) (pp. 91–153). Mahwah, NJ: Lawrence Erlbaum Associates Publishers.

Public Safety Canada. (2010). *Bullying prevention: Nature and extent of bullying in Canada*. Retrieved from http://www.publicsafety.gc.ca/res/cp/res/2008-bp-01-eng.aspx

Puente, S., & Cohen, D. (2003). Jealousy and the meaning (or nonmeaning) of violence. *Personality & Social Psychology Bulletin, 29*(4), 449–460.

Pugh, K. R., et al. (2000). The angular gyrus in developmental dyslexia: Task-specific differences in functional connectivity within posterior cortex. *Psychological Science, 11*(1), 51–56.

Pujol, J., et al. (2006). Myelination of language-related areas in the developing brain. *Neurology, 66*(3), 339–343.

Pulverman, R., Hirsh-Pasek, K., Golinkoff, R. M., Pruden, S., & Salkind, S. J. (2006). Conceptual foundations for verb learning: Celebrating the event. In K. Hirsh-Pasek & R. M. Golinkoff (Eds.), *Action meets word: How children learn verbs* (pp. 134–159). New York: Oxford University Press.

Qin, W., et al. (2006). Calorie restriction attenuates Alzheimer's disease type brain amyloidosis in Squirrel monkeys (Saimiri sciureus). *Journal of Alzheimer's Disease, 10*(4), 417–422.

Quigley, N. R., & Tymon, Jr., W. G. (2006). Toward an integrated model of intrinsic motivation and career self management. *Career Development International, 11*(6), 522–543.

Rabin, R. C. (2007, August 28). For a low-dose hormone, take your pick. *The New York Times online*.

Radvansky, G. A., Zacks, R. T., & Hasher, L. (2005). Age and inhibition: The retrieval of situation models. *Journals of Gerontology: Series B: Psychological Sciences and Social Sciences, 60B*(5), P276–P278.

Raikes, H., et al. (2006). Mother–child bookreading in low-income families: Correlates and outcomes during the first three years of life. *Child Development, 77*(4), 924–953.

Ramage-Morin, P. L. (2009). Medication use among senior Canadians. *Health Reports*, March 2009. (Statistics Canada, Catalogue no. 82-003-X). Retrieved from http://www.statcan.gc.ca/pub/82-003-x/2009001/article/10801/findings-resultats-eng.htm

Ramey, C. T., Campbell, F. A., & Ramey, S. L. (1999). Early intervention: Successful pathways to improving intellectual development. *Developmental Neuropsychology, 16*(3) 385–392.

Randel, B., Stevenson, H. W., & Witruk, E. (2000). Attitudes, beliefs, and mathematics achievement of German and Japanese high school students. *International Journal of Behavioral Development, 24*(2), 190–198.

Rapin, I. (1997). Autism. *New England Journal of Medicine, 337*, 97–104.

Rathus, J. H., & Miller, A. L. (2002). Dialectical Behavior Therapy adapted for suicidal adolescents. *Suicide and Life-Threatening Behavior, 32*(2), 146–157.

Rathus, S. A., Nevid, J. S., & Fichner-Rathus, L. (2008). *Human sexuality in a world of diversity* (7th ed.). Boston: Allyn & Bacon.

Rattan, S. I. S., Kristensen, P., & Clark, B. F. C. (Eds.). (2006). *Understanding and modulating aging*. Malden, MA: Blackwell Publishing.

Rebar, R. W., & DeCherney, A. H. (2004). Assisted reproductive technology in the United States. *New England Journal of Medicine, 350*(16), 1603–1604.

Reddy, L. A., & De Thomas, C. (2007). Assessment of attention-deficit/hyperactivity disorder with children. In S. R. Smith & L. Handler (Eds.), *The clinical assessment of children and adolescents: A practitioner's handbook* (pp. 365–387). Mahwah, NJ: Erlbaum.

Redshaw, M., & van den Akker, O. (2007). Editorial. *Journal of Reproductive and Infant Psychology, 25*(2), 103–105.

Reef, S., Zimmerman-Swain, L., & Coronado, V. (2004). Disease description: Rubella is a viral illness caused by a togavirus of the genus *Rubivirus*. Available at http://www.cdc.gov/nip/diseases/rubella/default.htm.

Rees, S., Harding, R., & Inder, T. (2006). The developmental environment and the origins of neurological disorders. In P. Gluckman & M. Hanson (Eds.), *Developmental origins of health and disease* (pp. 379–391). New York: Cambridge University Press.

Reijneveld, S. A., et al. (2004). Infant crying and abuse. *Lancet, 364*(9442), 1340–1342.

Reis, O., & Youniss, J. (2004). Patterns in identity change and development in relationships with mothers and friends. *Journal of Adolescent Research, 19*(1), 31–44.

Reitzes, D. C., & Mutran, E. J. (2004). The transition to retirement. *International Journal of Aging & Human Development, 59*(1), 63–84.

Reitzes, D. C., & Mutran, E. J. (2006). Lingering identities in retirement. *Sociological Quarterly, 47*(2), 333–359.

Rendell, P. G., Castel, A. D., & Craik, F. I. M. (2005). Memory for proper names in old age: A disproportionate impairment? *The Quarterly Journal of Experimental Psychology A: Human Experimental Psychology, 58A*(1), 54–71.

Representative Poetry Online. (2009). Mary Elizabeth Frye: Do not stand at my grave and weep. Retrieved from http://rpo.library.utoronto.ca/poem/2670.html

Reschly, A., & Christenson, S. L. (2006). School completion. In G. G. Bear & K. M. Minke (Eds.), *Children's needs III: Development, prevention, and intervention* (pp. 103–113). Washington, DC: National Association of School Psychologists.

Rest, J. R. (1983). Morality. In P. H. Mussen (Ed.), *Handbook of child psychology*, Vol. 3, *Cognitive development*. New York: Wiley.

Retsinas, J. (1988). A theoretical reassessment of the applicability of Kübler-Ross's stages of dying. *Death Studies, 12*(3), 207–216.

Reynolds, C. A., Barlow, T., & Pedersen, N. L. (2006). Alcohol, tobacco and caffeine use: Spouse similarity processes. *Behavior Genetics, 36*(2), 201–215.

Rice, J. (2007). Six degrees of autism. *Discover* [Discover Media LLC].

Richards, J. C., Hof, A., & Alvarenga, M. (2000). Serum lipids and their relationships with hostility and angry affect and behaviors in men. *Health Psychology, 19*(4), 393–398.

Rietjens, J., et al. (2008). Continuous deep sedation for patients nearing death in the Netherlands: Descriptive study. *British Medical Journal, 336*(7648), 810–813.

Riggio, R. E., & Woll, S. B. (1984). The role of nonverbal cues and physical attractiveness in the selection of dating partners. *Journal of Social and Personal Relationships, 1*(3), 347–357.

Rizzolatti, G., Fadiga, L., Fogassi, L., & Gallese, V. (2002). From mirror neurons to imitation: Facts and speculations. In A. N. Meltzoff & W. Prinz (Eds.), *The imitative mind: Development, evolution, and brain bases*. New York: Cambridge University Press.

Roberts, B. W., & DelVecchio, W. F. (2000). The rank-order consistency of personality traits from childhood to old age: A quantitative review of longitudinal studies. *Psychological Bulletin, 126*(1), 3–25.

Roberts, B. W., Walton, K. E., & Viechtbauer, W. (2006). Patterns of mean-level change in personality traits across the life course: A meta-analysis of longitudinal studies. *Psychological Bulletin, 132*(1). 1–25.

Robins, R. W., & Trzesniewski, K. H. (2005). Self-esteem development across the lifespan. *Current Directions in Psychological Science, 14*(3), 158–162.

Robins, R. W., Trzesniewski, K. H., Tracy, J. L., Gosling, S. D., & Potter, J. (2002). Global self-esteem across the lifespan. *Psychology and Aging, 17*(3), 423–434.

Robins Wahlin, T., Lundin, A., & Dear, K. (2007). Early cognitive deficits in Swedish gene carriers of Huntington's disease. *Neuropsychology, 21*(1), 31–44.

Roeser, R. W., Peck, S. C., & Nasir, N. S. (2006). Self and identity processes in school motivation, learning, and achievement. In P. A. Alexander & P. H. Winne (Eds.), *Handbook of educational psychology* (pp. 391–424). Mahwah, NJ: Erlbaum.

Roffwarg, H. P., Muzio, J. N., & Dement, W. C. (1966). Ontogenetic development of the human sleep–dream cycle. *Science, 152*, 604–619.

Ronald, A., et al. (2006). Genetic heterogeneity between the three components of the autism spectrum: A twin study. *Journal of the American Academy of Child & Adolescent Psychiatry, 45*(6), 691–699.

Rondal, J. A., & Ling, L. (2006). Neurobehavioral specificity in Down's Syndrome. *Revista de Logopedia, Foniatría y Audiología, 26*(1), 12–19.

Roopnarine, J. L., Krishnakumar, A., Metindogan, A., & Evans, M. (2006). Links between parenting styles, parent–child academic interaction, parent–school interaction, and early academic skills and social behaviors in young children of English-speaking Caribbean immigrants. *Early Childhood Research Quarterly, 21*(2), 238–252.

Rose, A. J., Swenson, L. P., & Carlson, W. (2004). Friendships of aggressive youth: Considering the influences of being disliked and of being perceived as popular. *Journal of Experimental Child Psychology, 88*(1), 25–45.

Rose, S. A., Feldman, J. F., & Jankowski, J. J. (2001). Visual short-term memory in the first year of life: Capacity and recency effects. *Developmental Psychology, 37*(4), 539–549.

Rose, S. A., Feldman, J. F., & Jankowski, J. J. (2004). Infant visual recognition memory. *Developmental Review, 24*(1), 74–100.

Rose, S. A., Feldman, J. F., & Jankowski, J. J. (2005). The structure of infant cognition at 1 year. *Intelligence, 33*(3), 231–250.

Rose, S. A., Feldman, J. F., & Wallace, I. F. (1992). Infant information processing in relation to six-year cognitive outcomes. *Child Development, 63*, 1126–1141.

Rosen, T., Pillemer, K., & Lachs, M. (2008). Resident-to-resident aggression in long-term care facilities. *Aggression and Violent Behavior, 13*(2), 77–87.

Rosenstein, D., & Oster, H. (1988). Differential facial responses to four basic tastes. *Child Development, 59*, 1555–1568.

Rosenthal, R., & Jacobson, L. (1968). *Pygmalion in the classroom.* New York: Holt, Rinehart & Winston.

Rospenda, K. M., et al. (2005). Is workplace harassment hazardous to your health? *Journal of Business and Psychology, 20*(1), 95–110.

Ross, H., Ross, M., Stein, N., & Trabasso, T. (2006). How siblings resolve their conflicts: The importance of first offers, planning, and limited opposition. *Child Development. 77*(6) 1730–1745.

Ross, J. L., Roeltgen, D., Feuillan, P., Kushner, H., & Cutler, W. B. (2000). Use of estrogen in young girls with Turner syndrome: Effects on memory. *Neurology, 54*(1), 164–170.

Rotenberg, K. J., et al. (2004). Cross-sectional and longitudinal relations among peer-reported trustworthiness, social relationships, and psychological adjustment in children and early adolescents from the United Kingdom and Canada. *Journal of Experimental Child Psychology, 88*(1), 46–67.

Rotermann, M. (2008). Trends in teen sexual behaviour and condom use. *Health Reports,* September 2008. (Statistics Canada, Catalogue no. 82-003-XPE). Retrieved from http://www.statcan.gc.ca/pub/82-003-x/2008003/article/10664-eng.pdf

Roth, G. S., et al. (2004). Aging in rhesus monkeys: Relevance to human health interventions. *Science, 305*(5689), 1423–1426.

Rothbart, M. K., Ellis, L. K., & Posner, M. I. (2004). Temperament and self-regulation. In R. F. Baumeister & K. D. Vohs (Eds.), *Handbook of self-regulation: Research, theory, and applications.* New York: Guilford.

Rothbart, M. K., & Sheese, B. E. (2007). Temperament and emotion regulation. In J. J. Gross (Ed.), *Handbook of emotion regulation* (pp. 331–350). New York: Guilford.

Rottinghaus, P. J., Betz, N. E., & Borgen, F. H. (2003). Validity of parallel measures of vocational interests and confidence. *Journal of Career Assessment, 11*(4), 355–378.

Rottinghaus, P. J., Coon, K. L.,Gaffey, A. R., & Zytowski, D. G. (2007). Thirty-year stability and predictive validity of vocational interests. *Journal of Career Assessment, 15*(1), 5–22.

Roulet-Perez, E., & Deonna, T. (2006). Autism, epilepsy, and EEG epileptiform activity. In R. Tuchman & I. Rapin (Eds.), *Autism: A neurological disorder of early brain development* (pp. 174–188). *International review of child neurology.* London: Mac Keith Press.

Rovee-Collier, C. (1993). The capacity for long-term memory in infancy. *Current Directions in Psychological Science, 2*, 130–135.

Rubia, K., et al. (2006). Progressive increase of frontostriatal brain activation from childhood to adulthood during event-related tasks of cognitive control. *Human Brain Mapping, 27*(12), 973–993.

Rubin, K. H., Bukowski, W. M., & Parker, J. G. (2006). Peer interactions, relationships, and groups. In N. Eisenberg, W. Damon, & R. M. Lerner (Eds.), *Handbook of child psychology* (6th ed.), Vol. 3, *Social, emotional, and personality development* (pp. 571–645). Hoboken, NJ: Wiley.

Ruble, D. N., Martin, C. L., & Berenbaum, S. A. (2006). Gender development. In N. Eisenberg, W. Damon, & R. M. Lerner (Eds.), *Handbook of child psychology* (6th ed.), Vol. 3, *Social, emotional, and personality development.* (pp. 858–932). Hoboken, NJ: Wiley.

Rudolph, K. D., & Flynn, M. (2007). Childhood adversity and youth depression: Influence of gender and pubertal status. *Development and Psychopathology, 19*(2), 497–521.

Rudolph, K. D., Lambert, S. F., Clark, A. G., & Kurlakowsky, K. D. (2001). Negotiating the transition to middle school: The role of self-regulatory processes. *Child Development, 72*(3), 929–946.

Rudy, D., & Grusec, J. E. (2006). Authoritarian parenting in individualist and collectivist groups: Associations with maternal emotion and cognition and children's self-esteem. *Journal of Family Psychology, 20*(1), 68–78.

Rumbold, A. R., et al. (2006). Vitamins C and E and the risks of preeclampsia and perinatal complications. *New England Journal of Medicine, 354*, 1796–1806.

Runyon, M. K., & Kenny, M. C. (2002). Relationship of attributional style, depression, and posttrauma distress among children who suffered physical or sexual abuse. *Child Maltreatment: Journal of the American Professional Society on the Abuse of Children, 7*(3), 254–264.

Rusconi, A. (2004). Different pathways out of the parental Home: A comparison of West Germany and Italy. *Journal of Comparative Family Studies, 35*(4), 627–649.

Rushton, J. P., & Jensen, A. R. (2005). Thirty years of research on race differences in cognitive ability. *Psychology, Public Policy and Law, 11*(2), Retrieved from http://psychology.uwo.ca/faculty/rushtonpdfs/PPPL1.pdf

Rushton, J. P., Skuy, M., & Fridjhon, P. (2003). Performance on Raven's Advanced Progressive Matrices by African, East Indian, and White engineering students in South Africa. *Intelligence, 31*(2), 123–137.

Russ, S. W. (2006). Pretend play, affect, and creativity. In P. Locher, C. Martindale, & L. Dorfman (Eds.), *New directions in aesthetics, creativity and the arts, Foundations and frontiers in aesthetics* (pp. 239–250). Amityville, NY: Baywood.

Russell, S.T. (2006). Substance use and abuse and mental health among sexual-minority youths: Evidence from add health. In A. M. Omoto & H. S. Kurtzman (Eds.), *Sexual orientation and mental health: Examining identity and development in lesbian, gay, and bisexual people* (pp. 13–35). Washington, DC: American Psychological Association.

Rutter, M. (2006). The psychological effects of early institutional rearing. In P. J. Marshall & N. A. Fox (Eds.), *The development of social engagement: Neurobiological perspectives. Series in affective science* (pp. 355–391). New York: Oxford University Press.

Ryan, R. M., & Deci, E. L. (2000). Self-determination theory and the facilitation of intrinsic motivation, social development, and well-being. *American Psychologist, 55*(1), 68–78.

Rybash, J. M., & Hrubi-Bopp, K. L. (2000). Source monitoring and false recollection: A life span developmental perspective. *Experimental Aging Research, 26*(1), 75–87.

Ryff, C. D., Singer, B. H., & Seltzer, M. M. (2002). Pathways through challenge: Implications for well-being and health. In L. Pulkkinen, & A. Caspi (Eds.), *Paths to successful development: Personality in the life course* (pp. 302–328). New York: Cambridge University Press.

Saaristo-Helin, K., Savinainen-Makkonen, T., & Kunnari, S. (2006). The phonological mean length of utterance: Methodological challenges from a crosslinguistic perspective. *Journal of Child Language, 33*(1), 179–190.

Sabattini, L., & Leaper, C. (2004). The relation between mothers' and fathers' parenting styles and their division of labor in the home: Young adults' retrospective reports. *Sex Roles, 50*(3–4), 217–225.

Sabia, J. J. (2008). There's no place like home: A hazard model analysis of aging in place among older homeowners in the PSID. *Research on Aging, 30*(1), 3–35.

Sadker, D. M., & Silber, E. S. (Eds.) (2007). *Gender in the classroom: Foundations, skills, methods, and strategies across the curriculum.* Mahwah, NJ: Erlbaum.

Sadler, T. W. (Ed.). (2005). Abstracts of papers presented at the thirty-fifth annual meeting of the Japanese Teratology Society, Tokyo, Japan. *Teratology, 52*(4), b1–b51.

Saffran, J. R., Werker, J. F., & Werner, L. A. (2006). The infant's auditory world: Hearing, speech, and the beginnings of language. In D. Kuhn, R. S. Siegler, W. Damon, & R. M. Lerner (Eds.), *Handbook of child psychology,* Vol. 2, *Cognition, perception, and language* (6th ed.) (pp. 58–108). Hoboken, NJ: Wiley.

Saggino, A., Perfetti, B., Spitoni, G., & Galati, G. (2006). Fluid intelligence and executive functions: New Perspectives. In L. V. Wesley (Ed.), *Intelligence: New research* (pp. 1–22). Hauppauge, NY: Nova Science Publishers.

Saigal, S., et al. (2006). Transition of extremely low-birth-weight infants from adolescence to young adulthood: Comparison with normal birth-weight controls. *Journal of the American Medical Association, 295*(6), 667–675.

Saiki, J., & Miyatsuji, H. (2007). Feature binding in visual working memory evaluated by type identification paradigm. *Cognition, 102*(1), 49–83.

Saito, S., & Miyake, A. (2004). On the nature of forgetting and the processing–storage relationship in reading span performance. *Journal of Memory and Language, 50*(4), 425–443.

Salapatek, P. (1975). Pattern perception in early infancy. In L. B. Cohen & P. Salapatek (Eds.), *Infant perception: From sensation to cognition.* New York: Academic Press.

Sales, J. M., Fivush, R., & Peterson, C. (2003). Parental reminiscing about positive and negative events. *Journal of Cognition and Development, 4*(2), 185–209.

Salmivalli, C., Ojanen, T., Haanpää, J., & Peets, K. (2005). "I'm OK but you're not" and other peer-relational schemas: Explaining individual differences in children's social goals. *Developmental Psychology, 41*(2), 363–375.

Salthouse, T. A. (2001). Structural models of the relations between age and measures of cognitive functioning. *Intelligence, 29*(2), 93–115.

Salthouse, T. A., & Babcock, R. L. (1991). Decomposing adult age differences in working memory. *Developmental Psychology, 27*(5), 763–776.

Salthouse, T. A., & Berish, D. E. (2005). Correlates of within-person (across-occasion) variability in reaction time. *Neuropsychology, 19*(1), 77–87.

Salthouse, T. A., & Davis, H. P. (2006). Organization of cognitive abilities and neuropsychological variables across the lifespan. *Developmental Review, 26*(1), 31–54.

Salthouse, T. A., & Siedlecki, K. L. (2007). Efficiency of route selection as a function of adult age. *Brain and Cognition, 63*(3), 279–286.

Salthouse, T. A., Siedlecki, K. L., & Krueger, L. E. (2006). An individual differences analysis of memory control. *Journal of Memory and Language, 55*(1), 102–125.

Salzarulo, P., & Ficca, G. (Eds.). (2002). *Awakening and sleep–wake cycle across development.* Amsterdam: John Benjamins.

Sandman, C., & Crinella, F. (1995). Cited in Margoshes, P. (1995). For many, old age is the prime of life. *APA Monitor, 26*(5), 36–37.

Santelli, J. S., et al. (2003). Reproductive health in school-based health centers: Findings from the 1998–99 census of school-based health centers. *Journal of Adolescent Health, 32*(6), 443–451.

Santelli, J. S., Lindberg, J. D., Abma, J., McNeely, C. S., & Resnick, M. (2000). Adolescent sexual behavior: Estimates and trends from four nationally representative surveys. *Family Planning Perspectives, 32*(4), 156–165, 194.

Santos, D. C. C., Gabbard, C., & Goncalves, V. M. G. (2000). Motor development during the first 6 months: The case of Brazilian infants. *Infant and Child Development, 9*(3), 161–166.

Saroglou, V., & Galand, P. (2004). Identities, values, and religion: A study among Muslim, other immigrant, and native Belgian young adults after the 9/11 attacks. *Identity, 4*(2), 97–132.

Sarrazin, P., Trouilloud, D., & Bois, J. (2005a). Attentes du superviseur et performance sportive du pratiquant. Amplitude et fonctionnement de l'effet Pygmalion en contexte sportif. *Bulletin de Psychologie, 58*(1), 63–68.

Sarrazin, P., Trouilloud, D., Tessier, D., Chanal, J., & Bois, J. (2005b). Attentes de motivation et comportements différenciés de l'enseignant d'éducation physique et sportive à l'égard de ses élèves: une étude en contexte naturel d'enseignement. *Revue Européenne de Psychologie Appliquée, 55*(2), 111–120.

Sasaki, C. (2007). Grounded-theory study of therapists' perceptions of grieving process in bereaved children. *Dissertation Abstracts International: Section B: The Sciences and Engineering, 68*(1-B), 635.

Saudino, K. J., & Eaton, W. O. (1993, March). *Genetic influences on activity level. II. An analysis of continuity and change from infancy to early childhood.* Paper presented at the meeting of the Society for Research in Child Development, New Orleans, LA.

Save the Children. (2004). *State of the world's mothers 2004.* Available at http://www.savethechildren.org/mothers/report_2004/index.asp. Accessed June 2004.

Savickas, M. L. (2005). The theory and practice of career construction. In S. D. Brown & R. W. Lent (Eds.). *Career development and counseling.* (pp. 42–70). Hoboken, NJ: Wiley.

Savin-Williams, R. C. (2007). Girl-on-girl sexuality. In B. J. R. Leadbeater & N. Way (Eds.), *Urban girls revisited: Building strengths* (pp. 301–318). New York: New York University Press.

Savin-Williams, R. C., & Berndt, T. (1990). Friendship and peer relations. In S. S. Feldman & G. R. Elliott (Eds.), *At the threshold: The developing adolescent.* Cambridge, MA: Harvard University Press.

Savin-Williams, R. C., & Diamond, L. M. (2004). Sex. In R. M. Lerner & L. Steinberg (Eds.), *Handbook of adolescent psychology* (2nd ed.) (pp. 189–231). Hoboken, NJ: Wiley.

Sayegh, Y., & Dennis, W. (1965). The effect of supplementary experiences upon the behavioral development of infants in institutions. *Child Development, 36*(1), 81–90.

Scarr, S. (1993, March). *IQ correlations among members of transracial adoptive families.* Paper presented at the meeting of the Society for Research in Child Development, New Orleans, LA.

Schacter, D. I. (1992). Understanding implicit memory: A cognitive neuroscience approach. *American Psychologist, 47*(4), 559–569.

Schaffer, H. R., & Emerson, P. E. (1964). *The development of social attachments in infancy.* Monographs of the Society for Research in Child Development, 29(94).

Schaie, K. W. (1994). The course of adult intellectual development. *American Psychologist, 49,* 304–313. Copyright © American Psychological Association.

Schaie, K. W. (2002). The impact of longitudinal studies on understanding development from young adulthood to old age. In. W. W. Hartup & R. K. Silbereisen (Eds.), *Growing points in developmental science* (pp. 307–328). New York: Psychology Press.

Schaie, K. W. (2005). What can we learn from longitudinal studies of adult development? *Research in Human Development, 2*(3), 133–158.

Schaie, K. W., Willis, S. L., & Caskie, G. I. L. (2004). The Seattle longitudinal study: Relationship between personality and cognition. *Aging, Neuropsychology, and Cognition, 11*(2–3), 304–324.

Schaie, K. W., & Zanjani, F. A. K. (2006). Intellectual development across adulthood. In C. Hoare (Ed.), *Handbook of adult development and learning* (pp. 99–122). New York: Oxford University Press.

Scharf, M., Shulman, S., & Avigad-Spitz, L. (2005). Sibling relationships in emerging adulthood and in adolescence. *Journal of Adolescent Research, 20*(1), 64–90.

Scheithauer, H., Hayer, T., Petermann, F., & Jugert, G. (2006). Physical, verbal, and relational forms of bullying among German students: Age trends, gender differences, and correlates. *Aggressive Behavior, 32*(3), 261–275.

Schmidtke, A., Sell, R., & Lohr, C. (2008). Epidemiology of suicide in older persons. *Zeitschrift für Gerontologie und Geriatrie, 41*(1), 3–13.

Schneewind, K. A., & Kupsch, M. (2007). Patterns of neuroticism, work-family stress, and resources as determinants of personal distress: A cluster analysis of young, dual-earner families at the individual and couple level. *Journal of Individual Differences, 28*(3), 150–160.

Schneidman, E. S. (1977). Aspects of the dying process. *Psychiatric Annals, 17*(8), 391–397.

Schonfeld, A. M., Mattson, S. N., & Riley, E. P. (2005). Moral maturity and delinquency after prenatal alcohol exposure. *Journal of Studies on Alcohol, 66*(4), 545–554.

Schoppe-Sullivan, S. J., Mangelsdorf, S. C., Brown, G. L., & Sokolowski, M. S. (2007). Goodness-of-fit in family context: Infant temperament, marital quality, and early coparenting behavior. *Infant Behavior & Development, 30*(1), 82–96.

Schraf, M., & Hertz-Lazarowitz, R. (2003). Social networks in the school context: Effects of culture and gender. *Journal of Social and Personal Relationships, 20*(6), 843–858.

Schuetze, P., Lawton, D., & Eiden, R. D. (2006). Prenatal cocaine exposure and infant sleep at 7 months of age: The influence of the caregiving environment. *Infant Mental Health Journal, 27*(4), 383–404.

Schuetze, P., Zeskind, P. S., & Eiden, R. D. (2003). The perceptions of infant distress signals varying in pitch by cocaine-using mothers. *Infancy, 4*(1), 65–83.

Schultz, D. P., & Schultz, S. E. (2008). A history of modern psychology (9th Ed.). Belmont, CA: Thomson/Wadsworth.

Schultz, W. W., et al. (2005). Women's sexual pain and its management. *Journal of Sexual Medicine, 2*(3), 301–316.

Schumacher, D., & Queen, J. A. (2007). *Overcoming obesity in childhood and adolescence: A guide for school leaders.* Thousand Oaks, CA: Corwin Press.

Schuurmans, J., et al. (2006). A randomized, controlled trial of the effectiveness of cognitive-behavioral therapy and sertraline versus a waitlist control group for anxiety disorders in older adults. *American Journal of Geriatric Psychiatry, 14*(3), 255–263.

Schwartz, S. J. (2001). The evolution of Eriksonian and neo-Eriksonian identity theory and research: A review and integration. *Identity, 1*(1), 7–58.

Scott, J. R. (2006). Preventing eclampsia. *Obstetrics & Gynecology, 108,* 824–825.

Scourfield, J., Van den Bree, M., Martin, N., & McGuffin, P. (2004). Conduct problems in children and adolescents: A twin study. *Archives of General Psychiatry, 61,* 489–496.

Secker-Walker, R. H., & Vacek, P. M. (2003). Relationships between cigarette smoking during pregnancy, gestational age, maternal weight gain, and infant birthweight. *Addictive Behaviors, 28*(1), 55–66.

Sefcek, J. A., Brumbach, B. H., Vasquez, G., & Miller, G. F. (2007). The evolutionary psychology of human mate choice: How ecology, genes, fertility, and fashion influence mating strategies. *Journal of Psychology & Human Sexuality, 18*(2–3) 125–182.

Segrin, C., Powell, H. L., Givertz, M., & Brackin, A. (2003). Symptoms of depression, relational quality, and loneliness in dating relationships. *Personal Relationships, 10*(1), 25–36.

Seidah, A., & Bouffard, T. (2007). Being proud of oneself as a person or being proud of one's physical appearance: What matters for feeling well in adolescence? *Social Behavior and Personality, 35*(2), 255–268.

Selman, R. L. (1976). Social-cognitive understanding. In T. Lickona (Ed.), *Moral development and behavior: Theory, research, and social issues.* New York: Holt, Rinehart & Winston.

Selman, R. L. (1980). *The growth of interpersonal understanding: Developmental and clinical analysis.* New York: Academic Press.

Selman, R. L., & Dray, A. J. (2006). Risk and prevention. In K. A. Renninger, I. E. Sigel, W. Damon, & R. M. Lerner (Eds.), *Handbook of child psychology* (6th ed.), Vol. 4, *Child psychology in practice* (pp. 378–419). Hoboken, NJ: Wiley.

Serbin, L. A., Poulin-Dubois, D., Colburne, K. A., Sen, M. G., & Eichstedt, J. A. (2001). Gender stereotyping in infancy: Visual preferences for and knowledge of gender-stereotyped toys in the second year. *International Journal of Behavioral Development, 25*(1), 7–15.

Seward, R. R. (2005). Family and community in Ireland. *Journal of Comparative Family Studies, 36*(2), 343–344.

Sex Information and Education Council of Canada. (2010). Have teen pregnancy rates in Canada been going up, down, or holding steady? Retrieved from http://www.sexualityandu.ca/pdfs/CTR_TeenPregnancyRates.pdf

Sexton, S. A. (2008). The influence of social support systems on the degree of PTSD symptoms in the elderly. *Dissertation Abstracts International: Section B: The Sciences and Engineering, 68*(7-B), 2008, 4846.

Shafto, M. A., Burke, D. M., Stamatakis, E. A., Tam, P. P., & Tyler, L. K. (2007). On the tip-of-the-tongue: Neural correlates of increased word-finding failures in normal aging. *Journal of Cognitive Neuroscience, 19*(12), 2060–2070.

Shatz, K. H. (2006). The widow who wasn't a bride. *Dissertation Abstracts International Section A: Humanities and Social Sciences, 67*(2-A), 739.

Shaver, A. (1990). *Teen suicide.* Government of Canada, Political and Social Affairs Division. (Background paper, issue BP-236E). Retrieved from http://dsppsd. pwgsc.gc.ca/Collection-R/LoPBdP/BP/bp236-e.htm

Shaywitz, B. A., Lyon, G. R., & Shaywitz, S. E. (2006a). The role of functional magnetic resonance imaging in understanding reading and dyslexia. *Developmental Neuropsychology, 30*(1), 613–632.

Shaywitz, S. E., Mody, M., & Shaywitz, B. A. (2006b). Neural mechanisms in dyslexia. *Current Directions in Psychological Science, 15*(6), 278–281.

Sheeber, L. B., Davis, B., Leve, C., Hops, H., & Tildesley, E. (2007). Adolescents' relationships with their mothers and fathers: Associations with depressive disorder and subdiagnostic symptomatology. *Journal of Abnormal Psychology, 116*(1), 144–154.

Sherwin-White, S. (2006). The social toddler: Promoting positive behaviour. *Infant Observation, 9*(1), 95–97.

Shiota, M. N., & Levenson, R. W. (2007). Birds of a feather don't always fly farthest. *Psychology and Aging, 22*(4), 666–675.

Shirk, S., Burwell, R., & Harter, S. (2003). Strategies to modify low self-esteem in adolescents. In M. A. Reinecke et al. (Eds.), *Cognitive therapy with children and adolescents: A casebook for clinical practice* (2nd ed.) (pp. 189–213). New York: Guilford.

Shonk, S. M., & Cicchetti, D. (2001). Maltreatment, competency deficits, and risk for academic and behavioral maladjustment. *Developmental Psychology, 37*(1), 3–17.

Shroff, H., et al. (2006) Features associated with excessive exercise in women with eating disorders. *International Journal of Eating Disorders, 39*(6), 454–461.

Shultz, K. S., & Adams, G. A. (Eds.). (2007). *Aging and work in the 21st century.* New York: Lawrence Erlbaum Associates, Inc.

SIDS Network. (2001, May 14). Available at http://www.sids-network.org.

Siegel, L. S. (1992). Infant motor, cognitive, and language behaviors as predictors of achievement at school age. In C. Rovee-Collier & L. P. Lipsitt (Eds.), *Advances in infancy research*, Vol. 7. Norwood, NJ: Ablex.

Siegler, R. S., & Alibali, M. W. (2005). *Children's thinking* (4th ed.). Upper Saddle River, NJ: Prentice Hall.

Siegrist, J., Von Dem Knesebeck, O., & Pollack, C. E. (2004). Social productivity and well-being of older people. *Social Theory & Health, 2*(1), 1–17.

Sierra, F. (2006). Is (your cellular response to) stress killing you? *Journals of Gerontology: Series A: Biological Sciences and Medical Sciences, 61A*(6), 557–561.

Signal Hill. (2009). *Healthy sexuality.* Retrieved from http://www.prolifebc.ca/hs-std.html

Signorello, L. B., & McLaughlin, J. K. (2004). Maternal caffeine consumption and spontaneous abortion: A review of the epidemiologic evidence. *Epidemiology, 15*(2), 229–239.

Silbereisen, R. K. (2006). Development and ecological context: History of the psychological science in a personal view and experience—An interview with Urie Bronfenbrenner. *Psychologie in Erziehung und Unterricht, 53*(1), 241–249.

Silventoinen, K., et al. (2007). Genetic and environmental factors in relative weight from birth to age 18: The Swedish young male twins study. *International Journal of Obesity, 31*(4), 615–621.

Silver, R. C., & Wortman, C. B. (2007). The stage theory of grief. *Journal of the American Medical Association, 297*, 2692.

Simion, F., Cassia, V. M., Turati, C., & Valenza, E. (2001). The origins of face perception: Specific versus nonspecific mechanisms. *Infant and Child Development, 10*(1–2), 59–65.

Simonelli, A., Monti, F., & Magalotti, D. (2005). The complex phenomenon of failure to thrive: Medical, psychological and relational-affective aspects. *Psicologia Clinica dello Sviluppo, 9*(2), 183–212.

Simonelli, A., Vizziello, G. F., Bighin, M., De Palo, F., & Petech, E. (2007). Transition to triadic relationships between parenthood and dyadic adjustment. *Età Evolutiva, 86*, 92–99.

Simonton, D. K. (2006a). Creative genius, knowledge, and reason: The lives and works of eminent creators. In J. C. Kaufman & J. Baer (Eds.). *Creativity and reason in cognitive development.* (pp. 43–59). New York: Cambridge University Press.

Simonton, D. K. (2006b). Creativity around the world in 80 ways ... but with one destination. In J. C. Kaufman & R. Sternberg (Eds.), *The international handbook of creativity* (pp. 490–496). New York: Cambridge University Press.

Simonton, D. K. (2007). Creative life cycles in literature: Poets versus novelists or conceptualists versus experimentalists? *Psychology of Aesthetics, Creativity, and the Arts, 1*(3), 133–139.

Simpkins, S. D., Fredricks, J. A., Davis-Kean, P. E., & Eccles, J. S. (2006). Healthy mind, healthy habits: The influence of activity involvement in middle childhood. In A. C. Huston & M. N. Ripke (Eds.), *Developmental contexts in middle childhood: Bridges to adolescence and adulthood. Cambridge studies in social and emotional development* (pp. 283–302). New York: Cambridge University Press.

Sims, C. S., Drasgow, F., & Fitzgerald, L. F. (2005). The effects of sexual harassment on turnover in the military. *Journal of Applied Psychology, 90*(6), 1141–1152.

Singer, L. T., et al. (2005). Prenatal cocaine exposure and infant cognition. *Infant Behavior & Development, 28*(4), 431–444.

Sinnema, J. (2009, March 12). Bad habits priming kids for chronic diseases: Study. *Edmonton Journal.* Retrieved from http://www.canada.com/health/healthy-living/habits+priming+kids+chronic+diseases+Study/1385622/story.html

Sirrs, S. M., et al. (2007). Normal-appearing white matter in patients with phenylketonuria: Water content, myelin water fraction, and metabolite concentrations. *Radiology, 242*, 236–243.

Skeels, H. M. (1966). *Adult status of children with contrasting early life experiences: A follow-up study.* Monographs of the Society for Research in Child Development, 31(3, ser. 105).

Skinner, B. F. (1957). *Verbal behavior.* New York: Appleton.

Skoczenski, A. M. (2002). Limitations on visual sensitivity during infancy: Contrast sensitivity, vernier acuity, and orientation processing. In J. W. Fagen & H. Hayne (Eds.), *Progress in infancy research*, Vol. 2. Mahwah, NJ: Erlbaum.

Slater, A. (2000). Visual perception in the young infant: Early organization and rapid learning. In D. Muir & A. Slater (Eds.), *Infant development: The essential readings.* Malden, MA: Blackwell.

Slater, A., Mattock, A., & Brown, E. (1990). Size constancy at birth: Newborn infants' responses to retinal and real size. *Journal of Experimental Child Psychology, 49*, 314–322.

Slaughter, V., & Griffiths, M. (2007). Death understanding and fear of death in young children. *Clinical Child Psychology and Psychiatry, 12*(4), 525–535.

Slavin, R. E. (2006). *Educational psychology: Theory and practice* (8th ed.). Boston: Allyn & Bacon.

Sloan, S., Sneddon, H., Stewart, M., & Iwaniec, D. (2006). Breast is best? Reasons why mothers decide to breastfeed or bottlefeed their babies and factors influencing the duration of breastfeeding. *Child Care in Practice, 12*(3), 283–297.

Slobin, D. I. (2001). Form/function relations: How do children find out what they are? In M. Tomasello & E. Bates (Eds.), *Language development: The essential readings.* Malden, MA: Blackwell.

Smarty, S., & Findling, R. L. (2007). Psychopharmacology of pediatric bipolar disorder: A review. *Psychopharmacology, 191*(1), 39–54.

Smetana, J. G. (1990). Morality and conduct disorders. In M. Lewis & S. M. Miller (Eds.), *Handbook of developmental psychopathology.* New York: Plenum.

Smetana, J. G. (2005). Adolescent–parent conflict: Resistance and subversion as developmental process. In L. Nucci (Ed), *Conflict, contradiction, and contrarian elements in moral development and education* (pp. 69–91). Mahwah, NJ: Erlbaum.

Smetana, J. G., Campione-Barr, N., & Metzger, A. (2006). Adolescent development in interpersonal and societal contexts. *Annual Review of Psychology, 57,* 255–284.

Smiley, P. A., & Johnson, R. S. (2006). Self-referring terms, event transitivity and development of self. *Cognitive Development, 21*(3), 266–284.

Smith, C. L., Calkins, S. D., Keane, S. P., Anastopoulos, A. D., & Shelton, T. L. (2004). Predicting stability and change in toddler behavior problems: Contributions of maternal behavior and child gender. *Developmental Psychology, 40*(1), 29–42.

Smith, P. K. (2005). Play: Types and functions in human development. In B. J. Ellis & D. F. Bjorklund (Eds.), *Origins of the social mind: Evolutionary psychology and child development* (pp. 271–291). New York: Guilford Press.

Smock, P. J. (2000). Annual Review of Sociology. Cited in Nagourney, E. (2000, February 15). Study finds families bypassing marriage. *The New York Times,* p. 8.

Smolka, E., & Eviatar, Z. (2006). Phonological and orthographic visual word recognition in the two cerebral hemispheres: Evidence from Hebrew. *Cognitive Neuropsychology, 23*(6), 972–989.

Smoll, F. L., & Schultz, R. W. (1990). Quantifying gender differences in physical performance: A developmental perspective. *Developmental Psychology, 26,* 360–369.

Snarey, J. R. (1994). Cross-cultural universality of social-moral development: A critical review of Kohlbergian research. In B. Puka (Ed.), *New research in moral development* (pp. 268–298). New York: Garland.

Snarey, J. R., & Bell, D. (2003). Distinguishing structural and functional models of human development. *Identity, 3*(3), 221–230.

Snedeker, J., Geren, J., & Shafto, C. L. (2007). Starting over: International adoption as a natural experiment in language development. *Psychological Science, 18*(1), 79–87.

Snegovskikh, V., Park, J. S., & Norwitz, E. R. (2006). Endocrinology of parturition. *Endocrinology and Metabolism Clinics of North America, 35*(1), 173–191.

Snow, C. (2006). Cross-cutting themes and future research directions. In D. August & T. Shanahan (Eds.), *Developing literacy in second-language learners: Report of the National Literacy Panel on Language-Minority Children and Youth* (pp. 631–651). Mahwah, NJ: Erlbaum.

Snyder, H. M., & Sickmund, M. (2006). *Juvenile offenders and victims: 2006 national report.* Washington, DC: U.S. Department of Justice, Office of Justice Programs, Office of Juvenile Justice and Delinquency Prevention.

Snyderman, M., & Rothman, S. (1990). *The IQ controversy.* New Brunswick, NJ: Transaction.

Society of Obstetricians and Gynaecologists of Canada. (2009a). Facts and statistics: Sexual health and Canadian youth—Teen pregnancy rates. Retrieved from http://www.sexuality-andu.ca/teachers/data-6.aspx

Society of Obstetricians and Gynaecologists of Canada. (2009b). Fact sheets: Sex facts in Canada 2006. Retrieved from http://www.sexualityandu.ca/media-room/fact-sheets-1.aspx

Solano, C. H., Batten, P. G., & Parish, E. A. (1982). Loneliness and patterns of self-disclosure. *Journal of Personality and Social Psychology, 43,* 524–531.

Soliz, J. (2007). Communicative predictors of a shared family identity: Comparison of grandchildren's perceptions of family-of-origin grandparents and stepgrandparents. *Journal of Family Communication, 7*(3), 177–194.

Solomon, C. G., & Dluhy, R. G. (2003). Rethinking postmenopausal hormone therapy. *New England Journal of Medicine, 348*(7), 579–580.

Sommerfeld, J. (2000, April 18). Lifting the curse: Should monthly periods be optional? MSNBC online.

Sommers, M. S. (2008). Age-related changes in spoken word recognition. In D. B. Pisoni, & R. E. Remez (Eds.), *The handbook of speech perception. Blackwell handbooks in linguistics* (pp. 469–493). Malden, MA: Blackwell Publishing.

Sonnentag, S. (2003). Recovery, work engagement, and proactive behavior. *Journal of Applied Psychology, 88,* 518–528.

Sontag, L. W., & Richards, T. W. (1938). *Studies in fetal behavior: Fetal heart rate as a behavioral indicator.* Child Development Monographs, 3(4).

Sorce, J., Emde, R. N., Campos, J. J., Klinnert, M. D. (2000). Maternal emotional signaling: Its effect on the visual cliff behavior of 1-year-olds. In D. Muir & A. Slater, (Eds.), *Infant development: The essential readings. Essential readings in developmental psychology* (pp. 282–292). Malden, MA: Blackwell.

Sousa, L., & Figueiredo, D. (2002). Dependence and independence among old persons. *Reviews in Clinical Gerontology, 12*(3), 269–273.

Soussignan, R., & Schaal, B. (2005). Emotional processes in human newborns: a functionalist perspective. In J. Nadel, & D. Muir (Eds.), *Emotional development: Recent research advances* (pp. 127–159). New York: Oxford University Press.

South, S. J., Haynie, D. L., & Bose, S. (2007). Student mobility and school dropout. *Social Science Research, 36*(1), 68–94.

Spelke, E. S., & Owsley, C. (1979). Inter-modal exploration and knowledge in infancy. *Infant Behavior and Development, 2,* 13–27.

Spieker, S. J., et al. (2003). Joint influence of child care and infant attachment security for cognitive and language outcomes of low-income toddlers. *Infant Behavior and Development, 26*(3), 326–344.

Spitz, R. A. (1965). *The first year of life: A psychoanalytic study of normal and deviant object relations.* New York: International Universities Press.

Spitzer, R. L., Gibbon, M., Skodol, A. E., Williams, J. B. W., & First, M. B. (2002). *DSM–IV–TR casebook.* Washington, D.C.: American Psychiatric Press.

Sprecher, S. (1998). Insiders' perspectives on reasons for attraction to a close other. *Social Psychology Quarterly, 61*(4), 287–300.

Sprecher, S., Sullivan, Q., & Hatfield, E., (1994). Mate Selection Preferences: Gender Differences Examined in a National Sample. *Journal of Personality and Social Psychology, 66*(6), 1074–1080.

Sroufe, L. A. (1998). Cited in S. Blakeslee (1998, August 4), Re-evaluating significance of baby's bond with mother, *New York Times,* pp. F1, F2.

Sroufe, L. A., Waters, E., & Matas, L. (1974). Contextual determinants of infant affectional response. In M. Lewis & L.

Rosenblum (Eds.), *The origins of fear.* New York: Wiley.

Staff, J., Mortimer, J. T., & Uggen, C. (2004). Work and leisure in adolescence. In R. Lerner & L. Steinberg, (Eds.), *Handbook of adolescent psychology* (2nd ed.) (pp. 429–450). Hoboken, NJ: Wiley.

Stagnitti, K., Unsworth, C., & Rodger, S. (2000). Development of an assessment to identify play behaviours that discriminate between the play of typical preschoolers and preschoolers with pre-academic problems. *Canadian Journal of Occupational Therapy, 67*(5), 291–303.

Stahmer, A. C., Ingersoll, B., & Koegel, R. L. (2004). Inclusive programming for toddlers autism spectrum disorders: Outcomes from the Children's Toddler School. *Journal of Positive Behavior Interventions, 6*(2), 67–82.

Stams, G. J. M., Juffer, F., & IJzendoorn, M. H. van (2002). Maternal sensitivity, infant attachment, and temperament in early childhood predict adjustment in middle childhood: The case of adopted children and their biologically unrelated parents. *Developmental Psychology, 38*(5), 806–821.

Stanford, J. N., & McCabe, M. P. (2005). Sociocultural influences on adolescent boys' body image and body change strategies. *Body Image, 2*(2), 105–113.

Stankoff, B., et al. (2006). Imaging of CNS myelin by positron-emission tomography. *Proceedings of the National Academy of Sciences of the United States of America, 103*(24), 9304–9309.

Stanley, M. A., & Beck, J. G. (2000). Anxiety disorders. *Clinical Psychology Review, 20*(6), 731–754.

Statistics Canada. (2005). Divorces. *The Daily.* Retrieved from http://www.statcan.gc.ca/daily-quotidien/050309/dq050309b-eng.htm

Statistics Canada. (2006). Life tables, Canada, provinces and territories. (Statistics Canada Catalogue no. 84-537-XIE.) Retrieved from http://www.heartandstroke.com/site/c.ikIQLcMWJtE/b.3483991/k.34A8/Statistics.htm

Statistics Canada, (2007a). Marriages, *The Daily.* Retrieved from http://www.statcan.gc.ca/daily-quotidien/070117/dq070117a-eng.htm

Statistics Canada. (2007b). 2006 census: Families, marital status, households and dwelling characteristics. *The Daily.* Retrieved from http://www.statcan.gc.ca/daily-quotidien/070912/dq070912a-eng.htm

Statistics Canada. (2008a). *Leading causes of death in Canada.* (Statistics Canada, Catalogue no. 84-215-X.) Retrieved from http://www.statcan.gc.ca/pub/84-215-x/2008000/hl-fs-eng.htm#3

Statistics Canada. (2008b). *National longitudinal study of children and youth (NLSCY).* Record no. 4450. Retrieved from http://www.statcan.gc.ca/cgi-bin/imdb/p2SV.pl?Function=getSurvey&SDDS=4450&lang=en&db=imdb&adm=8&dis=2

Statistics Canada. (2009a). Gay pride...by the numbers. Retrieved from http://www42.statcan.ca/smr08/smr08_118-eng.htm

Statistics Canada. (2009b). Ten leading causes of death by selected age groups, by sex, Canada—65 to 74 years. Retrieved from http://www.statcan.gc.ca/pub/84-215-x/2008000/tbl/t008-eng.htm

Statistics Canada. (2009c). *2006 Census: The evolving linguistic portrait, 2006 Census: Sharp increase in population with a mother tongue other than English or French.* Retrieved from http://www12.statcan.ca/census-recen-sement/2006/as-sa/97-555/p2-eng.cfm

Statistics Canada. (2010a). Infant mortality rates, by province and territory (Table 102-0504). Retrieved from http://www40.statcan.gc.ca/101/cst01/health21a-eng.htm

Statistics Canada. (2010b). Life expectancy, at birth and at age 65, by sex, Canada, provinces and territories, annual (years). (CANSIM, table 102-0512.) Retrieved from http://cansim2.statcan.gc.ca/cgi-win/cnsmcgi.exe?Lang=E&RootDir=CII/&Detail=1&ResultTemplate=CII/CII_&TbID-etail=1&C2SUB=HEALTH&Array_Pick=1&ArrayId=102-0512

Stauffacher, K., & DeHart, G. B. (2006). Crossing social contexts: Relational aggression between siblings and friends during early and middle childhood. *Journal of Applied Developmental Psychology, 27*(3), 228–240.

Stearns, V., Beebe, K. L., Iyengar, M., & Dube, E. (2003). Paroxetine controlled release in the treatment of menopausal hot flashes. *Journal of the American Medical Association, 289,* 2827–2834.

Steele, H. (2005a). Editorial. *Attachment & Human Development, 7*(4), 345.

Steele, H. (2005b). Editorial: Romance, marriage, adolescent motherhood, leaving for college, plus shyness and attachment in the preschool years. *Attachment & Human Development, 7*(2), 103–104.

Stein, D. J., Collins, M., Daniels, W., Noakes, T., & Zigmond, M. (2007). Mind and muscle: The cognitive–affective neuroscience of exercise. *CNS Spectrums, 12*(1), 19–22.

Steinberg, L. (1996). *Beyond the classroom: Why school reform has failed and what parents need to do.* New York: Simon & Schuster.

Stemberger, J. P. (2004). Phonological priming and irregular past. *Journal of Memory and Language, 50*(1), 82–95.

Sternberg, R. J. (2000). In search of the zippe-rump-a-zoo. *Psychologist, 13*(5), 250–255.

Sternberg, R. J. (2006a). A duplex theory of love. In R. J. Sternberg, & K. Weis (Eds.), *The new psychology of love* (pp. 184–199). New Haven, CT: Yale University Press.

Sternberg, R. J. (2006b). The nature of creativity. *Creativity Research Journal, 18*(1), 87–98.

Sternberg, R. J. (2007). A systems model of leadership: WICS. *American Psychologist, 62*(1), 34–42.

Sternberg, R. J., & Williams, W. M. (1997). Does the Graduate Record Examination predict meaningful success in the graduate training of psychologists? *American Psychologist, 52,* 630–641.

Stevenson, H. W., Chen, C., & Lee, S. (1993). Mathematics achievement of Chinese, Japanese, and American children: Ten years later. *Science, 259,* 53–58.

Stevenson, J. (1992). Evidence for a genetic etiology in hyperactivity in children. *Behavior Genetics, 22,* 337–344.

Stewart, A. J., Ostrove, J. M., & Helson, R. (2001). Middle aging in women: Patterns of personality change from the 30s to the 50s. *Journal of Adult Development, 8,* 23–37.

Stewart, J. Y., & Armet, E. (2000, April 3). Aging in America: Retirees reinvent the concept. *Los Angeles Times online.* Available at http://articles.latimes.com/2000/apr/03/news/mn-15453. Accessed October 5, 2008.

Stifter, C. A., & Wiggins, C. N. (2004). Assessment of disturbances in emotion regulation and temperament. In R. DelCarmen-Wiggins & A. Carter (Eds.), *Handbook of infant, toddler, and preschool mental health assessment* (pp. 79–103). New York: Oxford University Press.

Stipek, D., & Hakuta, K. (2007). Strategies to ensure that no child starts from behind. In J. L. Aber et al. (Eds.), *Child development and social policy: Knowledge for action, APA Decade of Behavior volumes* (pp. 129–145). Washington, DC: American Psychological Association.

Stipek, D., Recchia, S., & McClintic, S. (1992). *Self-evaluation in young children.* Monographs of the Society for Research in Child Development, 57(1, ser. 226).

Stoel-Gammon, C. (2002). Intervocalic consonants in the speech of typically developing children: Emergence and early use. *Clinical Linguistics and Phonetics, 16*(3), 155–168.

Storch, E. A., et al. (2007). Peer victimization, psychosocial adjustment, and physical activity in overweight and at-risk-for-overweight youth. *Journal of Pediatric Psychology, 32*(1), 80–89.

Stores, G., & Wiggs, L. (Eds.). (2001). *Sleep disturbance in children and adolescents with disorders of development: Its significance and management.* New York: Cambridge University Press.

Strassberg, D. S., & Holty, S. (2003). An experimental study of women's Internet personal ads. *Archives of Sexual Behavior, 32*(3), 253–260.

Stratton, T. D., et al. (2005). Does students' exposure to gender discrimination and sexual harassment in medical school affect specialty choice and residency program selection? *Academic Medicine, 80*(4), 400–408.

Strayer, J., & Roberts, W. (2004). Children's anger, emotional expressiveness, and empathy: Relations with parents' empathy, emotional expressiveness, and parenting practices. *Social Development, 13*(2), 229–254.

Streri, A. (2002). Hand preference in 4-month-old infants: Global or local processing of objects in the haptic mode. *Current Psychology Letters: Behaviour, Brain and Cognition, 7,* 39–50.

Striegel-Moore, R. H., et al. (2003). Eating disorders in White and Black women. *American Journal of Psychiatry, 160*(7), 1326–1331.

Stright, A. D., Neitzel, C., Sears, K. G., & Hoke-Sinex, L. (2001). Instruction begins in the home: Relations between parental instruction and children's self-regulation in the classroom. *Journal of Educational Psychology, 93*(3), 456–466.

Strock, M. (2004). *Autism spectrum disorders (pervasive developmental disorders).* NIH Publication NIH-04–5511. Bethesda, MD: National Institute of Mental Health, National Institutes of Health, U.S. Department of Health and Human Services. Available at http://www.nimh.nih.gov/publicat/autism.cfm.

Strohner, H., & Nelson, K. E. (1974). The young child's development of sentence comprehension: Influence of event probability, nonverbal context, syntactic form, and strategies. *Child Development, 45,* 567–576.

Strutt, G. F., Anderson, D. R., & Well, A. D. (1975). A developmental study of the effects of irrelevant information on speeded classification. *Journal of Experimental Child Psychology, 20,* 127–135.

Sukhodolsky, D. G., Golub, A., Stone, E. C., & Orban, L. (2005). Dismantling anger control training for children: A randomized pilot study of social problem-solving versus social skills training components. *Behavior Therapy, 36,* 15–23.

Sullivan, S. E., Martin, D. F., Carden, W. A., & Mainiero, L. A. (2003). The road less traveled. *Journal of Leadership & Organizational Studies, 10*(2), 34–42.

Sulloway, F. J. (2007). Birth order and intelligence. *Science, 316*(5832), 1711–1712.

Sun, S. S., et al. (2005). Is sexual maturity occurring earlier among U.S. children? *Journal of Adolescent Health, 37*(5), 345–355.

Suomi, S. J., Harlow, H. F., & McKinney, W. T. (1972). Monkey psychiatrists. *American Journal of Psychiatry, 128,* 927–932.

Supple, A. J., & Small, S. A. (2006). The influence of parental support, knowledge, and authoritative parenting on Hmong and European American adolescent development. *Journal of Family Issues, 27*(9), 1214–1232.

Sylva, K., et al. (2007). Curricular quality and day-to-day learning activities in pre-school. *International Journal of Early Years Education, 15*(1), 49–65.

Szaflarski, J. P., et al. (2006). A longitudinal functional magnetic resonance imaging study of language development in children 5 to 11 years old. *Annals of Neurology, 59*(5), 796–807.

Takahashi, M., & Sugiyama, M. (2003). Improvement and prevention of misbehavior in a junior high school student: An analysis of behavioral contingency and change of stimulus function in a social setting. *Japanese Journal of Counseling Science, 36*(2), 165–174.

Talbot, L. A., Morrell, C. H., Fleg, J., L., & Metter, E. J. (2007). Changes in leisure time physical activity and risk of all-cause mortality in men and women. *Preventive Medicine: An International Journal Devoted to Practice and Theory, 45*(2–3), 169–176.

Tallandini, M. A., & Valentini, P. (1991). Symbolic prototypes in children's drawings of schools. *Journal of Genetic Psychology, 152,* 179–190.

Tamis-LeMonda, C. S., Bornstein, M. H., & Baumwell, L. (2001). Maternal responsiveness and children's achievement of language milestones. *Child Development, 72*(3), 748–767.

Tamis-LeMonda, C. S., Cristofaro, T. N., Rodriguez, E. T., & Bornstein, M. H. (2006). Early language development: Social influences in the first years of life. In L. Balter & C. S. Tamis-LeMonda (Eds.), *Child psychology: A handbook of contemporary issues* (2nd ed.) (pp. 79–108). New York: Psychology Press.

Tan, R. S. (2002). Managing the andropause in aging men. *Clinical Geriatrics.* Available at http://www.mmhc.com/cg/articles/CG9907/Tan.html.

Tan, R. S., & Culberson, J. W. (2003). An integrative review on current evidence of testosterone replacement therapy for the andropause. *Maturitas, 45*(1), 15–27.

Tanner, J. L. (2006). Recentering during emerging adulthood: A critical turning point in life span human development. In J. J. Arnett & J. L. Tanner (Eds.), *Emerging adults in America: Coming of age in the 21st century* (pp. 21–55). Washington, DC: American Psychological Association.

Tanner, J. M. (1989). *Fetus into man: Physical growth from conception to maturity*. Cambridge, MA: Harvard University Press.

Tanner, J. M. (1991a). Adolescent growth spurt, I. In R. M. Lerner, A. C. Petersen, & J. Brooks-Gunn (Eds.), *Encyclopedia of adolescence*. New York: Garland.

Tanner, J. M. (1991b). Secular trend in age of menarche. In R. M. Lerner, A. C. Petersen, & J. Brooks-Gunn (Eds.), *Encyclopedia of adolescence*. New York: Garland.

Tapper, K., & Boulton, M. J. (2004). Sex differences in levels of physical, verbal, and indirect aggression amongst primary school children and their associations with beliefs about aggression. *Aggressive Behavior, 30*(2), 123–145.

Tashiro, T., Frazier, P., & Berman, M. (2006). Stress-related growth following divorce and relationship dissolution. In M. A. Fine & J. H. Harvey (Eds.), *Handbook of divorce and relationship dissolution* (pp. 361–384). Mahwah, NJ: Erlbaum.

Tassi, F., Schneider, B. H., & Richard, J. F. (2001). Competitive behavior at school in relation to social competence and incompetence in middle childhood. *Revue Internationale de Psychologie Sociale, 14*(2), 165–184.

Taylor, C. (2007). To the editor: Day care and a child's behavior. *New York Times online*.

Taylor, M. (1999). *Imaginary companions and the children who create them*. London: Oxford University Press.

Taylor, M. F., Clark, N., & Newton, E. (2008). Counselling Australian baby boomers. *British Journal of Guidance & Counselling, 36*(2), 189–204.

Tehrani, J. A., & Mednick, S. A. (2000). Genetic factors and criminal behavior. *Federal Probation, 64*(2), 24–27.

Terracciano, A., Costa Jr., P. T., & McCrae, R. R. (2006). Personality plasticity after age 30. *Personality and Social Psychology Bulletin, 32*(8), 999–1009.

Thapar, A., Langley, K., Asherson, P., & Gill, M. (2007). Gene-Environment interplay in attention-deficit hyperactivity disorder and the importance of a developmental perspective. *British Journal of Psychiatry, 190*(1), 1–3.

Thiele, D. M., & Whelan, T. A. (2006). The nature and dimensions of the grandparent role. *Marriage & Family Review, 40*(1), 93–108.

Thomas, A., & Chess, S. (1989). Temperament and personality. In G. A. Kohnstamm, J. E. Bates, & M. K. Rothbart (Eds.), *Temperament in childhood*. Chichester, England: Wiley.

Thompson, A. M., Baxter-Jones, A. D. G., Mirwald, R. L., & Bailey, D. A. (2003). Comparison of physical activity in male and female children: Does maturation matter? *Medicine and Science in Sports and Exercise. 35*(10), 1684–1690.

Thompson, J. K., & Tantleff, S. (1992). Female and male ratings of upper torso: Actual, ideal, and stereotypical conceptions. *Journal of Social Behavior and Personality, 7*, 345–354.

Thompson, I. M. et al. (2005). Erectile dysfunction and subsequent cardiovascular disease. *Journal of the American Medical Association, 294*(23). 2996–3002.

Thompson, M. P., Ho, C-H., & Kingree, J. B. (2007). Prospective associations between delinquency and suicidal behaviors in a nationally representative sample. *Journal of Adolescent Health, 40*(3), 232–237.

Thompson, R. A. (2006). The development of the person: Social understanding, relationships, conscience, self. In N. Eisenberg, W. Damon, & R. M. Lerner (Eds.), *Hand-book of child psychology* (6th ed.), Vol. 3, *Social, emotional, and personality development* (pp. 24–98). Hoboken, NJ: Wiley.

Thompson, R. A., Easterbrooks, M. A., & Padilla-Walker, L. M. (2003). Social and emotional development in infancy. In R. M. Lerner et al. (Eds.), *Handbook of psychology: Developmental psychology*. New York: Wiley.

Thompson, R. A., & Limber, S. P. (1990). "Social anxiety" in infancy: Stranger and separation reactions. In H. Leitenberg (Ed.), *Handbook of social and evaluation anxiety*. New York: Plenum.

Thompson, R. A., & Meyer, S. (2007). Socialization of emotion regulation in the family. In J. J. Gross (Ed.), *Handbook of emotion regulation* (pp. 249–268). New York: Guilford.

Thornton, L. M., Andersen, B. L., Crespin, T. R., & Carson, W. E. (2007). Individual trajectories in stress covary with immunity during recovery from cancer diagnosis and treatments. *Brain, Behavior, and Immunity, 21*(2), 185–194.

Thurstone, L. L. (1938). *Primary mental abilities*. Psychometric Monographs, 1.

Tiedemann, M., & Valiquet, D. (2008). *Euthanasia and assisted suicide in Canada*. (Current Issue Review, 91-9E.) Ottawa: Library of Parliament, Parliamentary Information and Research Service. Retrieved from http://www2.parl.gc.ca/content/lop/researchpublications/919-e.htm

Timmerman, L. M. (2006). Family care versus day care: Effects on children. In B. M. Gayle et al. (Eds.), *Classroom communication and instructional processes: Advances through meta-analysis* (pp. 245–260). Mahwah, NJ: Erlbaum.

Tjepkema, M. (2005). *Adult obesity in Canada: Measured height and weight* (Statistics Canada, Catalogue no. 82-620-MWE.) Retrieved from http://www.statcan.gc.ca/pub/82-620-m/2005001/article/adults-adultes/8060-eng.htm

Tobbell, J. (2003). Students' experiences of the transition from primary to secondary school. *Educational and Child Psychology, 20*(4), 4–14.

Togsverd, M., et al. (2008). Association of a dopamine beta-hydroxylase gene variant with depression in elderly women possibly reflecting noradrenergic dysfunction. *Journal of Affective Disorders, 106*(1-2), 169–172.

Tomaka, J., Thompson, S., & Palacios, R. (2006). The relation of social isolation, loneliness, and social support to disease outcomes among the elderly. *Journal of Aging and Health, 18*(3), 359–384.

Tomiyama, T., et al. (2008). A new amyloid ß variant favoring oligomerization in Alzheimer's-type dementia. *Annals of Neurology, 63*(3), 377–387.

Ton, M., & Hansen, J. C. (2001). Using a person-environment fit framework to predict satisfaction and motivation in work and marital roles. *Journal of Career Assessment, 9*, 315–331.

Towse, J. (2003). Lifespan development of human memory. *Quarterly Journal of Experimental Psychology: Human Experimental Psychology, 56A*(7), 1244–1246.

Towse, J., & Cowan, N. (2005). Working memory and its relevance for cognitive

development. In W. Schneider, R. Schumann-Hengsteler, & B. Sodian (Eds.), *Young children's cognitive development: Interrelationships among executive functioning, working memory, verbal ability, and theory of mind* (pp. 9–37). Mahwah, NJ: Erlbaum.

Trainor, L. J., & Desjardins, R. N. (2002). Pitch characteristics of infant-directed speech affect infants' ability to discriminate vowels. *Psychonomic Bulletin & Review, 9*(2), 335–340.

Trehub, S. E., & Hannon, E. E. (2006). Infant music perception: Domain-general or domain-specific mechanisms? *Cognition, 100*(1), 73–99.

Trevarthen, C. (2003). Conversations with a two-month-old. In J. Raphael-Leff (Ed.), *Parent–infant psychodynamics: Wild things, mirrors, and ghosts*. London: Whurr.

Trocmé, N., Fallon, B., MacLaurin, B., Daciuk, J., Felstiner, C., Black, T. et al. (2005). *Canadian incidence study of reported child abuse and neglect—2003: Major findings*. Ottawa: Minister of Public Works and Government Services.

Troxel, W. M., & Matthews, K. A. (2004). What are the costs of marital conflict and dissolution to children's physical health? *Clinical Child and Family Psychology Review, 7*(1), 29–57.

Trudel, G. A., Goldfarb, M. R., Preville, M., & Boyer, R. (2007). Relationship between psychological distress and marital functioning in the elderly. American Psychological Association, Conference abstract.

Tsuneishi, S., & Casaer, P. (2000). Effects of preterm extrauterine visual experience on the development of the human visual system: A flash VEP study. *Developmental Medicine and Child Neurology, 42*(10), 663–668.

Turkheimer, E. (1991). Individual and group differences in adoption studies of IQ. *Psychological Bulletin, 110*, 392–405.

Twist, M. (2005). Review of Relationship therapy with same-sex couples. *Journal of Marital & Family Therapy, 31*(4), 413–417.

U.S. Bureau of the Census. (2008). *Statistical abstract of the United States* (128th ed.). Washington, DC: U.S. Government Printing Office.

U.S. Census Bureau. (2004, March 22). International Programs Center, International Data Base. *Global Population Profile: 2002*, table A-12.

U.S. Department of Health and Human Services. (2004). *Child abuse and neglect fatalities: Statistics and interventions-Child maltreatment 2002*. Available at http://nccanch.acf.hhs.gov/pubs/factsheets/fatality.cfm

Umek, L. M., Podlesek, A., & Fekonja, U. (2005). Assessing the home literacy environment: Relationships to child language comprehension and expression. *European Journal of Psychological Assessment, 21*(4), 271–281.

UNAIDS. (2006). *Report on the global AIDS epidemic: Executive summary*. Joint United Nations Programme on HIV/AIDS (UNAIDS). UNAIDS. 20 Avenue Appia. CH-1211. Geneva 27 Switzerland.

UNICEF. (2006). *The state of the world's children: 2007*. New York: United Nations.

UNICEF. (2010). The Breastfeeding Initiative Exchange: Facts and figures. Retrieved from http://www.unicef.org/programme/breastfeeding/facts.htm

UNICEF Canada. (2009). *Canadian supplement to The State of the World's Children 2009:*

Aboriginal children's health: Leaving no child behind. Toronto: Author. Retrieved from http://www.unicef.ca/portal/Secure/ Community/502/WCM/HELP/take_action/ Advocacy/Leaving%20no%20child %20behind%2009.pdf

United Nations Statistics Division. (2004, March). *UNESCO: World and Regional Trends*, Table 8. Available at http://millenniumindicators. un.org/unsd/mi/mi_worldregn.asp.

USDA. (2005). *Adequate nutrients within calorie needs. Dietary guidelines for Americans.* U.S. Department of Agriculture. Available at http://www.health.gov/dietaryguidelines/ dga2005/document/html/chapter2.htm.

USDHHS. (2005, January 10). *Bone health and osteoporosis: A report of the Surgeon General.* http://www.surgeongeneral.gov/library/ bonehealth. Accessed October 5, 2008.

Uylings, H. B. M. (2006). Development of the human cortex and the concept of "critical" or "sensitive" periods. *Language Learning, 56*(Suppl. 1), 59–90.

Van Hiel, A., Mervielde, I., & De Fruyt, F. (2006). Stagnation and generativity: Structure, validity, and differential relationships with adaptive and maladaptive personality. *Journal of Personality, 74*(2), 543–574.

van IJzendoorn, M. H., & Hubbard, F. O. A. (2000). Are infant crying and maternal responsiveness during the first year related to infant–mother attachment at 15 months? *Attachment and Human Development, 2*(3), 371–391.

van IJzendoorn, M. H., & Juffer, F. (2006). The Emanuel Miller Memorial Lecture 2006: Adoption as intervention. Meta-analytic evidence for massive catch-up and plasticity in physical, socio-emotional, and cognitive development. *Journal of Child Psychology and Psychiatry, 47*(12), 1228–1245.

van IJzendoorn, M. H., Moran, G., Belsky, J., Pederson, D., Bakermans-Kranenburg, M. J., & Kneppers, K. (2000). The similarity of siblings' attachments to their mother. *Child Development, 71*(4), 1086–1098.

van Rijn, S., Swaab, H., Aleman, A., & Kahn, R. S. (2006). X chromosomal effects on social cognitive processing and emotion regulation: A study with Klinefelter men (47,XXY). *Schizophrenia Research, 84*(2–3), 194–203.

van Solinge, H., & Henkens, K. (2005). Couples' adjustment to retirement: A Multi-Actor Panel Study. *Journals of Gerontology: Series B: Psychological Sciences and Social Sciences, 60B*(1), S11–S20.

Vandello, J. A., & Cohen, D. (2003). Male honor and female fidelity: Implicit cultural scripts that perpetuate domestic violence. *Journal of Personality & Social Psychology, 84*(5), 997–1010.

Vander Ven, T., & Cullen, F. T. (2004). The impact of maternal employment on serious youth crime: Does the quality of working conditions matter? *Crime & Delinquency, 50*(2), 272–291.

Vares, T., Potts, A., Gavey, N., & Grace, V. M. (2007). Reconceptualizing cultural narratives of mature women's sexuality in the Viagra era. *Journal of Aging Studies, 21*(2), 153–164.

Vartanian, O., Martindale, C., & Kwiatkowski, J. (2003). Creativity and inductive reasoning: The relationship between divergent thinking and performance on Wason's 2-4-6 task. *Quarterly Journal of Experimental Psychology: Human Experimental Psychology. 56A*(4), 641–655.

Vastag, B. (2003). Many questions, few answers for testosterone replacement therapy. *Journal of the American Medical Association, 289,* 971–972.

Vellas, B., Gillette-Guyonnet, S., & Andrieu, S. (2008). Memory health clinics—A first step to prevention. *Alzheimer's & Dementia, 4*(1, Suppl 1), S144–S149.

Vellutino, F. R., Fletcher, J. M., Snowling, M. J., & Scanlon, D. M. (2004). Specific reading disability (dyslexia): What have we learned in the past four decades? *Journal of Child Psychology and Psychiatry, 45*(1), 2–40.

Veríssimo, M., & Salvaterra, F. (2006). Maternal secure-base scripts and children's attachment security in an adopted sample. *Attachment & Human Development, 8*(3), 261–273.

Villani, S. (2001). Impact of media on children and adolescents: A 10-year review of the research. *Journal of the American Academy of Child and Adolescent Psychiatry, 40*(4), 392–401.

Virji-Babul, N., Kerns, K., Zhou, E., Kapur, A., & Shiffrar, M. (2006). Perceptual-motor deficits in children with Down syndrome: Implications for intervention. *Down Syndrome: Research & Practice, 10*(2), 74–82.

Visscher, W. A., Feder, M., Burns, A. M., Brady, T. M., & Bray, R. M. (2003). The impact of smoking and other substance use by urban women on the birthweight of their infants. *Substance Use and Misuse, 38*(8), 1063–1093.

Vitiello, B. (Ed.). (2006). Guest editorial: Selective serotonin reuptake inhibitors (SSRIs) in children and adolescents. *Journal of Child and Adolescent Psychopharmacology, 16*(1–2), 7–9.

Volkova, A., Trehub, S. E., & Schellenberg, E. G. (2006). Infants' memory for musical performances. *Developmental Science, 9*(6), 583–589.

Volling, B. L. (2003). Sibling relationships. In M. H. Bornstein et al. (Eds.), *Well-being: Positive development across the life course* (pp. 205–220). Mahwah, NJ: Erlbaum.

Volterra, M. C., Caselli, O., Capirci, E., & Pizzuto, E. (2004). Gesture and the emergence and development of language. In M. Tomasello & D. I. Slobin (Eds.), *Beyond nature–nurture*. Mahwah, NJ. Erlbaum.

Volz, J. (2000). Successful aging: The second 50. *Monitor on Psychology; 31*(1), online.

von Gontard, A. (2007). Encopresis. *Praxis der Kinderpsychologie und Kinderpsychiatrie, 56*(6),492–510.

VonDras, D. D., Powless, D. R., Olson, A. K., Wheeler, D., & Snudden, A. L. (2005). Differential effects of everyday stress on the episodic memory test performances of young, mid-life, and older adults. *Aging & Mental Health, 9*(1), 60–70.

Vorauer, J. D., Cameron, J. J., Holmes, J. G., & Pearce, D. G. (2003). Invisible overtures: Fears of rejection and the signal amplification bias. *Journal of Personality & Social Psychology, 84*(4), 793–812.

Vukman, K. B. (2005). Developmental differences in metacognition and their connections with cognitive development in adulthood. *Journal of Adult Development, 12*(4), 211–221.

Vygotsky, L. S. (1962). *Thought and language*. Cambridge, MA: MIT Press.

Vygotsky, L. S. (1978). *Mind in society: The development of higher psychological processes*. Cambridge, MA: Harvard University Press.

Wachs, T. D. (2006). The nature, etiology, and consequences of individual differences in temperament. In L. Balter & C. S. Tamis-LeMonda (Eds.), *Child psychology: A handbook of contemporary issues* (2nd ed.) (pp. 27–52). New York: Psychology Press.

Wade, T. D., Bulik, C. M., Neale, M., & Kendler, K. S. (2000). Anorexia nervosa and major depression: Shared genetic and environmental risk factors. *American Journal of Psychiatry, 157,* 469–471.

Wahler, R. G., Herring, M., & Edwards, M. (2001). Coregulation of balance between children's prosocial approaches and acts of compliance: A pathway to mother–child cooperation? *Journal of Clinical Child Psychology, 30*(4), 473–478.

Wainright, J. L., Russell, S. T., & Patterson, C. J. (2004). Psychosocial adjustment, school outcomes, and romantic relationships of adolescents with same-sex parents. *Child Development, 75*(6), 1886–1898.

Wald, J., & Losen, D. J. (2007). Out of sight: The journey through the school-to-prison pipeline. In S. Books (Ed.), *Invisible children in the society and its schools* (3rd ed.) (pp. 23–37). Mahwah, NJ: Erlbaum.

Walitza, S., et al. 2006). Genetic and neuroimaging studies in attention deficit hyperactivity disorder. *Nervenheilkunde: Zeitschrift für interdisziplinaere Fortbildung, 25*(6), 421–429.

Walkup, J. T., et al. (2001). Fluvoxamine for the treatment of anxiety disorders in children and adolescents. *New England Journal of Medicine, 344*(17), 1279–1285.

Wall, A. (2007). Review of Integrating gender and culture in parenting. *The Family Journal, 15*(2), 196–197.

Wall, G., & Arnold, S. (2007). How involved is involved fathering? *Gender & Society, 21*(4), 508–527.

Wallerstein, J., Lewis, J., Blakeslee, S., Hetherington, E. M., & Kelly, J. (2005). Issue 17: Is divorce always detrimental to children? In R. P. Halgin (Ed.), *Taking sides: Clashing views on controversial issues in abnormal psychology* (3rd ed.) (pp. 298–321). New York: McGraw-Hill.

Walsh, B. T., et al. (2006). Fluoxetine after weight restoration in anorexia nervosa: A randomized controlled trial. *Journal of the American Medical Association, 295*(22), 2605–2612.

Walter, J. L., & LaFreniere, P. J. (2000). A naturalistic study of affective expression, social competence, and sociometric status in preschoolers. *Early Education and Development, 11*(1), 109–122.

Walther, F. J., Ouden, A. L. den, & Verloove-Vanhorick, S. P. (2000). Looking back in time: Outcome of a national cohort of very preterm infants born in The Netherlands in 1983. *Early Human Development, 59*(3), 175–191.

Wang, L. (2005). Correlations between self-esteem and life satisfaction in elementary school students. *Chinese Mental Health Journal, 19*(11), 745–749.

Wang, S.-H., Baillargeon, R., & Paterson, S. (2005). Detecting continuity violations in infancy: A new account and new evidence from covering and tube events. *Cognition, 95*(2), 129–173.

Washburn, D. A. (Ed,). (2007). *Primate perspectives on behavior and cognition*. Washington, DC: American Psychological Association.

Watson, J. B. (1924). *Behaviorism*. New York: Norton.

Waxman, S. R., & Lidz, J. L. (2006). Early word learning. In D. Kuhn, R. S. Siegler, W. Damon, & R. M. Lerner (Eds.), *Handbook of child psychology* (6th ed.), Vol. 2, *Cognition, perception, and language* (pp. 299–335). Hoboken, NJ: Wiley.

Wechsler, D. (1975). Intelligence defined and undefined: A relativistic appraisal. *American Psychologist, 30*, 135–139.

Weckerly, J., Wulfeck, B., & Reilly, J. (2004). The development of morphosyntactic ability in atypical populations: The acquisition of tag questions in children with early focal lesions and children with specific-language impairment. *Brain and Language, 88*(2), 190–201.

Weeks, C. (2009, March 30). Interracial relationships rise 30 per cent in five years. *Globe and Mail.* Retrieved from http://www.theglobeandmail.com/life/article677491.ece

Weems, C. F., Silverman, W. K., Saavedra, L. M., Pina, A. A., & Lumpkin, P. W. (1999). The discrimination of children's phobias using the Revised Fear Survey Schedule for Children. *Journal of Child Psychology and Psychiatry, 40*(6), 941–952.

Weinberg, R. A. (2004). The infant and the family in the twenty-first century. *Journal of the American Academy of Child and Adolescent Psychiatry, 43*(1), 115–116.

Weinshenker, M. N. (2006). Adolescents' expectations about mothers' employment: Life course patterns and parental influence. *Sex Roles, 54*(11–12), 845–857.

Weisler, R. H., & Sussman, N. (2007). Treatment of attention-deficit/hyperactivity disorder. *Primary Psychiatry, 14*(1), 39–42.

Weller, E. B., & Weller, R. A. (1991). Mood disorders. In M. Lewis (Ed.), *Child and adolescent psychiatry: A comprehensive textbook.* Baltimore: Williams & Wilkins.

Wellman, H. M., Cross, D., & Bartsch, K. (1986). *Infant search and object permanence: A meta-analysis of the A-not-B error.* Monographs of the Society for Research in Child Development, 5(3, ser. 214).

Wellman, H. M., Fang, F., Liu, D., Zhu, L., & Liu, G. (2006). Scaling of theory-of-mind understandings in Chinese children. *Psychological Science, 17*(12), 1075–1081.

Weng, X., Odouli, R., & Li, D-K. (2008, January 25). Maternal caffeine consumption during pregnancy and the risk of miscarriage: a prospective cohort study. *American Journal of Obstetrics and Gynecology, available online.*

Wenger, G. C., Dykstra, P. A., Melkas, T., & Knipscheer, K. C. P. M. (2007). Social embeddedness and late-life parenthood: Community activity, close ties, and support. *Journal of Family Issues, 28*(11), 1419–1456.

Wenger, G. C., & Jerrome, D. (1999). Change and stability in confidant relationships. *Journal of Aging Studies, 13*(3), 269–294.

Wennergren, A.-C., & Rönnerman, K. (2006). The relation between tools used in action research and the zone of proximal development. *Educational Action Research, 14*(4), 547–568.

Wentworth, N., Benson, J. B., & Haith, M. M. (2000). The development of infants' reaches for stationary and moving targets. *Child Development, 71*(3), 576–601.

Wentzel, K. R., Barry, C. M., & Caldwell, K. A. (2004). Friendships in middle school: Influences on motivation and school adjustment. *Journal of Educational Psychology, 96*(2), 195–203.

Werker, J. F. (1989). Becoming a native listener. *American Scientist, 77*, 54–59.

Werker, J. F., et al. (2007). Infant-directed speech supports phonetic category learning in English and Japanese. *Cognition, 103*(1), 147–162.

Werker, J. F., & Tees, R. C. (2005). Speech perception as a window for understanding plasticity and commitment in language systems of the brain. *Developmental Psychobiology, 46*(3), 233–234.

Werner, E. E. (1988). A cross-cultural perspective on infancy. *Journal of Cross-Cultural Psychology, 19*, 96–113.

Werner, L. A., & Bernstein, I. L. (2001). Development of the auditory, gustatory, olfactory, and somatosensory systems. In E. B. Goldstein (Ed.), *Blackwell handbook of perception., Handbook of experimental psychology series* (pp. 669–708). Boston: Blackwell.

Wethington, E., Kessler, R. C., & Pixley, J. E. (2004). Turning points in adulthood. In O. G. Brim, C. D. Ryff, & R. C. Kessler (Eds.), *How healthy are we?: A national study of well-being at midlife* (pp. 586–613). *The John D. and Catherine T. MacArthur foundation series on mental health and development. Studies on successful midlife development.* Chicago: University of Chicago Press.

Whitehead, B. D., & Popenoe, D. (2006) *The state of our unions: The social health of marriage in America.* New Brunswick, NJ: Rutgers University. Available at http://marriage.rutgers.edu/Publications/Print/PrintSOOU2006.htm.

Whitehouse, E. M. (2006). Poverty. In G. G. Bear & K. M. Minke (Eds.), *Children's needs III: Development, prevention, and intervention* (pp. 835–845). Washington, DC: National Association of School Psychologists.

Wickwire Jr., E. M., Roland, M. M. S., Elkin, T. D., & Schumacher, J. A. (2008). Sleep disorders. In M. Hersen & D. Michel (Eds.), *Handbook of psychological assessment, case conceptualization, and treatment. Vol 2: Children and adolescents* (pp. 622–651). Hoboken, NJ: Wiley.

Wierzalis, E. A., Barret, B., Pope, M., & Rankins, M. (2006). Gay men and aging: Sex and intimacy. In D. Kimmel, T. Rose, & S. David (Eds.), *Lesbian, gay, bisexual, and transgender aging: Research and clinical perspectives* (pp. 91–109). New York: Columbia University Press.

Willett, W. C. (2005). Diet and cancer. *JAMA: Journal of the American Medical Association, 293*, 233–234.

Willetts, M. C. (2006). Union quality comparisons between long-term heterosexual cohabitation and legal marriage. *Journal of Family Issues, 27*(1), 110–127.

Williams, M. S. (2004). The psychology of eating. *Psychology and Health, 19*(4), 541–542.

Willis, S. L., & Schaie, K. W. (2006). Cognitive functioning in the baby boomers: Longitudinal and cohort effects. In S. K. Whitbourne, & S. L. Willis (Eds.), *The baby boomers grow up: Contemporary perspectives on midlife* (pp. 205–234). Mahwah, NJ: Lawrence Erlbaum Associates Publishers.

Wilson, D. R., Langlois, S., & Johnson, J. (2007). Mid-trimester amniocentesis fetal loss rate: Committee opinion. *Journal of Obstetrics and Gynaecology Canada, 29*(7):586–590).

Retrieved from http://www.sogc.org/guidelines/documents/gui194CPG0707.pdf

Wilson, E. O. (2004). *On Human Nature.* Cambridge, MA: Harvard University Press.

Wilson, J. M. B., Tripp, D. A., & Boland, F. J. (2005). The relative contributions of waist-to-hip ratio and body mass to judgments of attractiveness. *Sexualities, Evolution & Gender, 7*(3), 245–267.

Wilson, P. (2004). A preliminary investigation of an early intervention program: Examining the intervention effectiveness of the Bracken Concept Development Program and the Bracken Basic Concept Scale–Revised with Head Start students. *Psychology in the Schools, 41*(3), 301–311.

Windsor, T. D., Anstey, K. J., Butterworth, P., & Rodgers, B. (2008). Behavioral approach and behavioral inhibition as moderators of the association between negative life events and perceived control in midlife. *Personality and Individual Differences, 44*(5), 1080–1092.

Winner, E. (2000). The origins and ends of giftedness. *American Psychologist, 55*, 159–169.

Winzelberg, A. J., et al. (2000). Effectiveness of an Internet-based program for reducing risk factors for eating disorders. *Journal of Consulting and Clinical Psychology, 68*, 346–350.

Witherington, D. C., Campos, J. J., Anderson, D. I., Lejeune, L., & Seah, E. (2005). Avoidance of heights on the visual cliff in newly walking infants. *Infancy, 7*(3), 285–298.

Witkowska, E., & Gådin, K. G. (2005). What female high school students regard as harassment. International Journal of *Adolescent Medicine and Health, 17*(4), 391–406.

Wocadlo, C., & Rieger, I. (2006). Educational and therapeutic resource dependency at early school-age in children who were born very preterm. *Early Human Development, 82*(1), 29–37.

Wodrich, D. L. (2006). Sex chromosome anomalies. In L. Phelps (Ed.), *Chronic health-related disorders in children: Collaborative medical and psychoeducational interventions* (pp. 253–270). Washington, DC: American Psychological Association.

Wojslawowicz Bowker, J. C., Rubin, K. H., Burgess, K. B., Booth-Laforce, C., & Rose-Krasnor, L. (2006). Behavioral characteristics associated with stable and fluid best friendship patterns in middle childhood. *Merrill-Palmer Quarterly, 52*(4), 671–693.

Wolfenden, L. E., & Holt, N. L. (2005). Talent development in elite junior tennis: Perceptions of players, parents, and coaches. *Journal of Applied Sport Psychology, 17*(2), 108–126.

Wong, S. S., Ang, R. P., & Huan, V. S. (2007). Externalizing problems, internalizing problems, and suicidal ideation in Singaporean adolescents: Sex differences. *Current Psychology: Developmental, Learning, Personality, Social, 25*(4), 231–244.

Woolfolk, A. (2008). *Educational psychology, Active learning edition* (10th ed.). Boston: Allyn & Bacon.

Worell, J., & Goodheart, C. D. (Eds.), (2006). *Handbook of girls' and women's psychological health: Gender and well-being across the lifespan.* New York: Oxford University Press.

Wozniak, J. R., & Lim, K. O. (2006). Advances in white matter imaging: A review of in vivo magnetic resonance methodologies and their applicability to the study of development and aging. *Neuroscience & Biobehavioral Reviews, 30*(6), 762–774.

Wright, C., & Birks, E. (2000). Risk factors for failure to thrive: A population-based survey. *Child: Care, Health, and Development, 26*(1), 5–16.

Wright, D. W., & Young, R. (1998). The effects of family structure and maternal employment on the development of gender-related attitudes among men and women. *Journal of Family Issues, 19*(3), 300–314.

Wulff, K., & Siegmund, R. (2001). Circadian and ultradian time patterns in human behaviour. Part 1: Activity monitoring of families from prepartum to postpartum. *Biological Rhythm Research, 31*(5), 581–602.

Xie, H. L., Yan, B., Signe M., Hutchins, B. C., & Cairns, B. D. (2006). What makes a girl (or a boy) popular (or unpopular)? African American Children's perceptions and developmental differences. *Developmental Psychology, 42*(4), 599–612.

Yaffe, K., Haan, M., Byers, A., Tangen, C., & Kuller, L. (2000). Estrogen use, APOE, and cognitive decline: Evidence of gene-environment interaction. *Neurology, 54*(10), 1949–1953.

Yamada, H., et al. (2000). A milestone for normal development of the infantile brain detected by functional MRI. *Neurology, 55*(2), 218–223.

Yarrow, L. J., & Goodwin, M. S. (1973). The immediate impact of separation: Reactions of infants to a change in mother figures. In L. J. Stone, H. T. Smith, & L. B. Murphy (Eds.), *The competent infant: Research and commentary.* New York: Basic Books.

Yarrow, L. J., Goodwin, M. S., Manheimer, H., & Milowe, I. D. (1971, March). *Infant experiences and cognitive and personality development at ten years.* Paper presented at the meeting of the American Orthopsychiatric Association, Washington, DC.

Yonelinas, A. P. (2002). The nature of recollection and familiarity: A review of 30 years of research. *Journal of Memory and Language, 46,* 441–517.

Yost, M. R., & Zurbriggen, E. L. (2006). Gender differences in the enactment of sociosexuality. *Journal of Sex Research, 43*(2), 163–173.

Youniss, J., & Haynie, D. L. (1992). Friendship in adolescence. *Developmental and Behavioral Pediatrics, 13,* 59–66.

Zacks, R. T., Hasher, L., & Li, K. Z. H. (2000). Human memory. In F. I. M. Craik & T. A. Salthouse (Eds.), *Age-related changes in memory: A cognitive neuroscience perspective. The handbook of aging and cognition* (2nd ed.) (pp. 293–357). Mahwah, NJ: Lawrence Erlbaum Associates Publishers.

Zaidi, A. U., & Shyraydi, M. (2002). Perceptions of arranged marriages by young Pakistani Muslim women living in a Western society. *Journal of Comparative Family Studies, 33*(4), 495–514.

Zajonc, R. B. (2001). The family dynamics of intellectual development. *American Psychologist, 56*(6/7), 490–496.

Zan, B., & Hildebrandt, C. (2003). First graders' interpersonal understanding during cooperative and competitive games. *Early Education and Development, 14*(4), 397–410.

Zarbatany, L., McDougall, P., & Hymel, S. (2000). Gender-differentiated experience in the peer culture: Links to intimacy in preadolescence. *Social Development, 9*(1), 62–79.

Zeifman, D. M. (2004). Acoustic features of infant crying related to intended caregiving intervention. *Infant and Child Development, 13*(2), 111–122.

Zeintl, M., Kliegel, M., & Hofer, S. M. (2007). The role of processing resources in age-related prospective and retrospective memory within old age. *Psychology and Aging, 22*(4), 826–834.

Zelazo, P. R. (1998). McGraw and the development of unaided walking. *Developmental Review, 18*(4), 449–471.

Zheng, S., & Colombo, J. (1989). Sibling configuration and gender differences in preschool social participation. *Journal of Genetic Psychology, 150,* 45–50.

Zimmerman, B. J. (2000). Self-efficacy: An essential motive to learn. *Contemporary Educational Psychology, 25*(1), 82–91.

Zimmermann, P., Maier, M. A., Winter, M., & Grossmann, K. E. (2001). Attachment and adolescents' emotion regulation during a joint problem-solving task with a friend. *International Journal of Behavioral Development, 25*(4), 331–343.

Zucker, A. N., Ostrove, J. M., & Stewart, A. J. (2002). College-educated women's personality development in adulthood: Perceptions and age differences. *Psychology and Aging, 17,* 236–244.

Zweigenhaft, R. L., & Von Ammon, J. (2000). Birth order and civil disobedience: A test of Sulloway's "born to rebel" hypothesis. *Journal of Social Psychology, 140*(5), 624–627.

Learning Outcomes

LO1 Relate the history of the study of human development

In centuries past, children often were viewed as innately evil and discipline was harsh. The philosopher John Locke focused on the role of experience in development. Jean-Jacques Rousseau argued that children are good by nature, and if allowed to express their natural impulses, will develop into moral people. Charles Darwin developed the modern theory of evolution and was an early keeper of a baby biography. G. Stanley Hall founded child development as an academic discipline. Alfred Binet developed the first standardized intelligence test. William Perry and Gisella Labouvie-Vief have studied the development of cognitive complexity from adolescence to late adulthood. K. Warner Schaie and others have studied trends in crystallized and fluid mental abilities throughout adulthood. All of these theories are integrated to form a definition of developmental psychology, which is the biological, psychological, and sociocultural study of development across the lifespan.

LO2 Compare and contrast theories of human development

Psychoanalytic theory focuses on the roles of internal conflict. Sigmund Freud believed that children undergo five stages of psychosexual development. Erik Erikson focused on social relationships and included adulthood by extending Freud's five developmental stages to eight.

Erikson's Stages

0–1 yr	Trust vs. Mistrust
1–3 yrs	Autonomy vs. Shame and Doubt
3–6 yrs	Initiative vs. Guilt
6 yr-adolescent	Industry vs. Inferiority
Adolescent	Identity vs. Identity Confusion
Young Adult	Intimacy vs. Isolation
Middle Adult	Generativity vs. Stagnation
Late Life	Integrity vs. Despair

Learning theorists focus on how learning influences behaviour. John B. Watson and B. F. Skinner stress classical and operant conditioning. Social cognitive theorists, such as Albert Bandura, argue that much learning occurs by observation and that we choose whether or not to engage in learned behaviour.

Jean Piaget's cognitive developmental theory hypothesizes that children's cognitive processes develop in an invariant series of stages, culminating with *formal operational* reasoning. Information-processing theory deals with the ways in we encode information, manipulate it, place it in memory, and retrieve it.

The biological perspective refers to genetics and developments such as conception, puberty, and peak performance and decline in adulthood. Ethology involves instinctive behaviour patterns.

Urie Bronfenbrenner's ecological theory explains development in terms of the *reciprocal interaction* between children and the settings in which development occurs. Lev Semenovich Vygotsky's sociocultural perspective has the key concepts of the *zone of proximal development (ZPD)* and *scaffolding*. The sociocultural perspective more broadly addresses the richness of diversity, as in the influences of ethnicity and gender on development. This perspective is of particular importance to Canadians, given the more than 200 cultures within our borders.

Key Terms

LO1
developmental psychology the biological, psychological, and sociocultural study of human change across the lifespan.

LO2
behaviourism Watson's view that science must study observable behaviour only and investigate relationships between stimuli and responses.

maturation the unfolding of genetically determined traits, structures, and functions.

psychosexual development the process by which libidinal energy is expressed through different erogenous zones during different stages of development.

stage theory a theory of development characterized by distinct periods of life.

psychosocial development Erikson's theory, which emphasizes the importance of social relationships and conscious choice throughout eight stages of development.

life crisis an internal conflict that attends each stage of psychosocial development.

identity crisis according to Erikson, a period of inner conflict during which one examines one's values and makes decisions about one's life roles.

classical conditioning a simple form of learning in which one stimulus comes to bring forth the response usually brought forth by a second stimulus by being paired repeatedly with the second stimulus.

operant conditioning a simple form of learning in which an organism learns to engage in behaviour that is reinforced.

reinforcement the process of providing stimuli following responses that increase the frequency of the responses.

positive reinforcer a reinforcer that, when applied, increases the frequency of a response.

negative reinforcer a reinforcer that, when removed, increases the frequency of a response.

extinction the cessation of a response that is performed in the absence of reinforcement.

punishments aversive events that suppress or decrease the frequency of the behaviour they follow

social cognitive theory a cognitively oriented learning theory that emphasizes observational learning.

cognitive-developmental theory the stage theory that holds that the child's abilities to mentally represent the world and solve problems unfold as a result of the interaction of experience and the maturation of neurological structures.

scheme an action pattern or mental structure that is involved in the acquisition and organization of knowledge.

adaptation the interaction between the organism and the environment, consisting of assimilation and accommodation.

assimilation the incorporation of new events or knowledge into existing schemes.

accommodation the modification of existing schemes to permit the incorporation of new events or knowledge.

equilibration the creation of an equilibrium, or balance, between assimilation and accommodation.

ethology the study of behaviours that are specific to a species.

fixed action pattern (FAP) a stereotyped pattern of behaviour that is evoked by a "releasing stimulus"; an instinct.

ecology the branch of biology that deals with the relationships between living organisms and their environment.

ecological systems theory the view that explains child development in terms of the reciprocal influences between children and environmental settings.

microsystem the immediate settings with which the child interacts, such as the home, the school, and peers.

mesosystem the interlocking settings that influence the child, such as the interaction of the school and the larger community.

exosystem community institutions and settings that indirectly influence the child, such as the school board and the parents' workplaces.

macrosystem the basic institutions and ideologies that influence the child.

chronosystem the environmental changes that occur over time and have an effect on the child.

zone of proximal development (ZPD) Vygotsky's term for the situation in which a child carries out tasks with the help of someone who is more skilled.

scaffolding Vygotsky's term for temporary cognitive structures or methods of solving problems that help the child as he or she learns to function independently.

LO3 **nature** the processes within an organism that guide it to develop according to its genetic code.

nurture environmental factors that influence development.

empirical based on observation and experimentation.

LO4 **case study** a carefully drawn biography of the life of an individual.

LO3 Enumerate key controversies in human development

There are three major debates in human growth and development:

Nature and Nurture	What aspects of behaviour are determined by our genetic programming (nature) and what aspects of behaviour can be traced to nutrition, cultural and family backgrounds, and learning opportunities (nurture)?
Continuity and Discontinuity	Maturational, psychoanalytic, and cognitive-developmental theorists see development as discontinuous (occurring in stages), whereas learning theorists see it as more continuous.
Active and Passive Roles	Some educators, such as John Locke, view children as passive, requiring external motivation to learn. Other educators, many of them more modern, view children as active, having a natural love of learning.

LO4 Describe ways in which researchers study human development

Development is studied through gathering sound information and conducting research. Naturalistic observation is conducted in "the field"—the settings in which people develop. The case study is a carefully drawn account or biography of behaviour. Correlational studies reveal relationships between variables but not cause and effect, as demonstrated in Figure 1.6. Experiments seek to determine cause and effect by exposing subjects to treatments and observing the results.

Researchers have devised different strategies for comparing children of one age with children or adults of other ages. Longitudinal research, such as Canada's National Longitudinal Survey of Children and Youth (NLSCY), studies the same people repeatedly over time. Cross-sectional research observes and compares people of different ages. A drawback to cross-sectional research is the cohort effect. Cross-sequential research combines the longitudinal and cross-sectional methods by breaking the span of the ideal longitudinal study down into convenient segments. Ethical standards outlined by the Canadian Psychiatric Association require that researchers not use treatments that harm participants.

standardized test a test that compares an individual's score to the scores of a group of similar individuals.

correlation coefficient a number ranging from +1.00 to −1.00 that expresses the direction (positive or negative) and strength of the relationship between two variables.

positive correlation a relationship between two variables in which one variable increases as the other increases.

negative correlation a relationship between two variables in which one variable increases as the other decreases.

experiment a method of scientific investigation that seeks to discover cause-and-effect relationships by introducing independent variables and observing their effects on dependent variables.

hypothesis a proposition to be tested.

independent variable a condition in a scientific study that is manipulated so that its effects can be observed.

dependent variable a measure of an assumed effect of an independent variable.

experimental group a group made up of subjects who receive a treatment in an experiment.

control group a group made up of subjects in an experiment who do not receive the treatment but for whom all other conditions are comparable to those of subjects in the experimental group.

longitudinal research the study of developmental processes by taking repeated measures of the same group of participants at various stages of development.

cross-sectional research the study of developmental processes by taking measures of participants of different age groups at the same time.

cohort effect similarities in behaviour among a group of peers that stem from the fact that group members are approximately of the same age.

cross-sequential research an approach that combines the longitudinal and cross-sectional methods by following individuals of different ages for abbreviated periods of time.

time lag the study of developmental processes by taking measures of participants of the same age group at different times.

Learning Outcomes

LO1 Describe the influences of heredity on development

Heredity is the biological transmission of traits from one generation to another. People normally have 46 strands of DNA called chromosomes, which are organized into 23 pairs (see Figure 2.3). Genes, which regulate the development of traits, are segments of chromosomes.

FIGURE 2.3

The 23 Pairs of Human Chromosomes

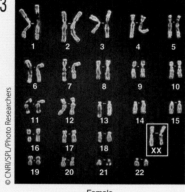 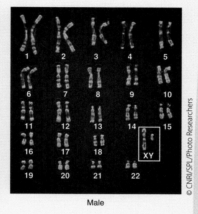

Female   Male

© CNRI/SPL/Photo Researchers

Sperm and ova are produced by meiosis and have 23 rather than 46 chromosomes. Monozygotic (MZ) or identical twins develop from a single fertilized ovum that splits in two. Dizygotic (DZ) or fraternal twins develop from two fertilized ova. Traits are determined by pairs of genes, either from "averaging" the genetic instructions, or by dominant genes. Carriers of a trait bear one dominant gene and one recessive gene for it.

Chromosomal abnormalities are more likely as parents age. Down's syndrome is caused by an extra chromosome on the 21st pair. Sex-linked disorders include XYY males and single-X girls. Genetic disorders include phenylketonuria (PKU), Huntington's disease, sickle-cell anemia, Tay-Sachs disease, cystic fibrosis, and hemophilia. Prenatal blood tests, ultrasound, and amniocentesis can determine the presence of various genetic and chromosomal abnormalities.

LO2 Describe the influences of the environment on development

Our genotypes are the sets of traits that we inherit. But environmental conditions can vary their expression, resulting in our phenotypes. Researchers can study the heritability of a trait by observing its expression among relatives who differ in genetic closeness. Parents and children have a 50 percent overlap in genes, as do siblings, with the exception of monozygotic (MZ) twins, who have 100 percent overlap. MZ twins resemble each other more closely than dizygotic (DZ) twins on physical and psychological traits, even when reared apart. Traits are likely to have a strong genetic basis if adopted children are closer to their natural parents than to their adoptive parents in their expression.

LO3 Explain what happens in the process of conception

Conception is the union of an ovum and a sperm cell and usually occurs in a fallopian tube (see Figure 2.8). More boys are conceived than girls, but they have a higher rate of miscarriage. Once a sperm cell has entered the ova, the chromosomes from the sperm cell line up across from

Key Terms

LO1
genetics the branch of biology that studies heredity.

chromosomes rod-shaped structures composed of genes that are found within the nuclei of cells.

gene the basic unit of heredity. Genes are composed of deoxyribonucleic acid (DNA).

polygenic resulting from many (poly) genes.

deoxyribonucleic acid (DNA) genetic material that takes the form of a double helix composed of phosphates, sugars, and bases.

mitosis the form of cell division in which each chromosome splits length-wise to double in number. Half of each chromosome combines with chemicals to retake its original form and then moves to the new cell.

mutation a sudden, or accidental, variation in a heritable characteristic that affects the composition of genes.

meiosis the form of cell division in which each pair of chromosomes splits so that one member of each pair moves to the new cell. As a result, each new cell has 23 chromosomes.

autosome a pair of chromosomes (with the exception of sex chromosomes).

sex chromosome a chromosome in the shape of a Y (male) or X (female) that determines the sex of the child.

monozygotic (MZ) twins twins that derive from a single zygote that has split into two; identical twins. Each MZ twin carries the same genetic code.

dizygotic (DZ) twins twins that derive from two separate zygotes; fraternal twins with separate genetic codes.

ovulation the releasing of an ovum from an ovary.

allele a member of a pair of genes.

homozygous having two identical alleles.

heterozygous having two different alleles.

dominant trait a trait that is expressed.

recessive trait a trait that is not expressed when the gene or genes involved have been paired with dominant genes.

carrier a person who carries and transmits characteristics but does not exhibit them.

multifactorial problems problems that stem from the interaction of heredity and environmental factors.

Down's syndrome a chromosomal abnormality characterized by mental retardation and caused by an extra chromosome in the 21st pair.

sex-linked chromosomal abnormalities abnormalities that are transmitted from generation to generation and carried by a sex chromosome.

Klinefelter syndrome a male chromosomal disorder that is caused by an extra X sex chromosome and that is characterized by infertility and mild mental retardation.

testosterone a male sex hormone produced mainly by the testes.

Turner syndrome a female chromosomal disorder that is caused by having a single X sex chromosome and is characterized by infertility.

estrogen a female sex hormone produced mainly by the ovaries.

phenylketonuria (PKU) a genetic abnormality in which phenylalanine builds up and causes mental retardation.

Huntington disease (HD) a fatal genetic neurologic disorder whose onset takes place is in middle age. It is a dominant trait, which is rare for a fatal genetic disorder.

sickle-cell anemia a genetic disorder that decreases the blood's capacity to carry oxygen.

Tay-Sachs disease a fatal genetic neurological disorder that causes degeneration and premature death.

cystic fibrosis a fatal genetic disorder in which mucus obstructs the lungs and pancreas.

hemophilia a genetic disorder in which blood does not clot properly.

sex-linked genetic abnormalities abnormalities resulting from genes that are found on the X sex chromosome. They are more likely to be shown by male offspring (who do not have an opposing gene from a second X chromosome) than by female offspring.

muscular dystrophy a chronic disease characterized by a progressive wasting away of the muscles.

prenatal before birth.

the corresponding chromosomes in the egg cell. They form 23 new pairs with a unique set of genetic instructions.

FIGURE 2.8

Female Reproductive Organs

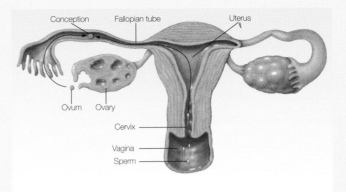

A couple is usually not considered to be infertile until they have failed to conceive on their own for 1 year. A low sperm count—or lack of sperm—is the most common infertility problem in men. The most common infertility problem in women is irregular ovulation or lack of ovulation; other reasons for infertility include infections such as PID, endometriosis, and obstructions. Fertility drugs regulate ovulation. Other ways of conceiving include artificial insemination and in vitro fertilization (IVF).

LO4 Recount the major events of prenatal development

During the germinal stage, the zygote divides repeatedly and travels through a fallopian tube to the uterus, where it implants. Before implantation, it is nourished by the yolk of the original egg cell. Once implanted in the uterine wall, it is nourished by the mother. The embryonic stage lasts from implantation until the eighth week of development, during which the major organ systems differentiate. Development follows cephalocaudal and proximodistal trends. The heart begins to beat during the fourth week. By the end of the second month, facial features are becoming distinct, teeth buds have formed, the kidneys are working, and the liver is producing red blood cells. Male sex hormones spur development of the male reproductive system. The embryo and fetus exchange nutrients and wastes with the mother through the placenta. Some disease organisms, such as those that cause syphilis and rubella, can pass through the placenta. Some drugs also pass through, including aspirin, narcotics, and alcohol.

FIGURE 2.11

A Human Embryo at 7 Weeks

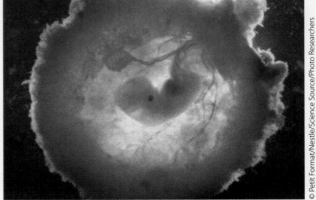

© Petit Format/Nestle/Science Source/Photo Researchers

Learning Outcomes

The fetal stage is characterized by maturation of organs and gains in size. It lasts from the end of the embryonic stage until birth. The fetus begins to turn at the ninth or tenth week. It responds to sound waves by the 13th week of pregnancy. By the end of the second trimester, the fetus opens and shuts its eyes, sucks its thumb, and alternates between wakefulness and sleep. During the third trimester, it becomes increasingly capable of sustaining independent life.

Maternal malnutrition is linked to low birth weight, prematurity, and cognitive and behavioural problems. Teratogens are most harmful during critical periods, when certain organs are developing. Women who contract rubella may bear children who suffer from deafness, mental retardation, heart disease, or cataracts. Syphilis can cause miscarriage or stillbirth. Toxemia is characterized by high blood pressure and is connected with preterm or small babies. In Rh incompatibility, the mother's antibodies cause brain damage or death. Environmental agents that can harm the embryo and fetus include thalidomide, tetracycline, DES, toxoplasmosis, high doses of vitamins A and D, narcotics, marijuana, cocaine, alcohol, cigarette smoke, heavy metals, PCBs, and radiation.

© George Steinmetz

Teenage mothers have a higher incidence of infant mortality and children with low birth weight. Older parents run an increasing risk of chromosomal abnormalities and stillborn or preterm babies.

The rapid pace of scientific technology has caused Canadians to closely examine medical ethics and to enact legislation to ensure that research in reproductive technology remains ethically sound.

Key Terms

amniocentesis a procedure for drawing and examining fetal cells sloughed off into amniotic fluid to determine the presence of various disorders.

chorionic villus sampling (CVS) a method for the prenatal detection of genetic abnormalities that samples the membrane enveloping the amniotic sac and fetus.

uterus the hollow organ within females in which the embryo and fetus develop.

ultrasound sound waves too high in pitch to be sensed by the human ear.

sonogram a procedure for using ultrasonic sound waves to create a picture of an embryo or fetus.

alpha-fetoprotein (AFP) assay a blood test that assesses the mother's blood level of alpha-fetoprotein, a substance that is linked with fetal neural tube defects.

 genotype the genetic form or constitution of a person as determined by heredity.

phenotype the actual form or constitution of a person as determined by heredity and environmental factors.

autism a developmental disorder characterized by failure to relate to others, communication problems, intolerance of change, and ritualistic behaviour.

LO3 conception the union of a sperm cell and an ovum that occurs when the chromosomes of each of these cells combine to form 23 new pairs.

endometrium the inner lining of the uterus.

spontaneous abortion unplanned, accidental abortion.

motility self-propulsion.

pelvic inflammatory disease (PID) an infection of the abdominal region that may have various causes and that may impair fertility.

endometriosis inflammation of endometrial tissue sloughed off into the abdominal cavity rather than out of the body during menstruation; the condition is characterized by abdominal pain and sometimes infertility.

artificial insemination injection of sperm into the uterus to fertilize an ovum.

in vitro fertilization (IVF) fertilization of an ovum in a laboratory dish.

donor IVF the transfer of a donor's ovum, fertilized in a laboratory dish, to the uterus of another woman.

LO4 germinal stage the period of development between conception and the implantation of the embryo.

blastocyst a stage within the germinal period of prenatal development in which the zygote has the form of a sphere of cells surrounding a cavity of fluid.

embryonic disk the platelike inner part of the blastocyst that differentiates into the ectoderm, mesoderm, and endoderm of the embryo.

trophoblast the outer part of the blastocyst from which the amniotic sac, placenta, and umbilical cord develop.

umbilical cord a tube that connects the fetus to the placenta.

placenta an organ connected to the uterine wall and to the fetus by the umbilical cord. The placenta serves as a relay station between mother and fetus for the exchange of nutrients and wastes.

embryonic stage the stage of prenatal development that lasts from implantation through the eighth week of pregnancy; it is characterized by the development of the major organ systems.

cephalocaudal from head to tail.

proximodistal from the inner part (or axis) of the body outward.

ectoderm the outermost cell layer of the newly formed embryo from which the skin and nervous system develop.

neural tube a hollowed-out area in the blastocyst from which the nervous system develops.

endoderm the inner layer of the embryo from which the lungs and digestive system develop.

mesoderm the central layer of the embryo from which the bones and muscles develop.

androgens male sex hormones.

amniotic sac the sac containing the fetus.

amniotic fluid fluid within the amniotic sac that suspends and protects the fetus.

fetal stage the stage of development that lasts from the beginning of the ninth week of pregnancy through birth; it is characterized by gains in size and weight and by maturation of the organ systems.

stillbirth the birth of a dead fetus.

teratogens environmental influences or agents that can damage the embryo or fetus.

critical period in this usage, a period during which an embryo is particularly vulnerable to a certain teratogen.

syphilis a sexually transmitted infection that, in advanced stages, can attack major organ systems.

congenital present at birth; resulting from the prenatal environment.

HIV/AIDS HIV stands for human immunodeficiency virus, which cripples the body's immune system. AIDS stands for acquired immunodeficiency syndrome, a condition in which the immune system is weakened such that it is vulnerable to diseases it would otherwise fight off.

rubella a viral infection that can cause retardation and heart disease in the embryo. Also called German measles.

toxemia a life-threatening disease that can afflict pregnant women; it is characterized by high blood pressure.

premature born before the full term of gestation. Also referred to as preterm.

Rh incompatibility a condition in which antibodies produced by the mother are transmitted to the child, possibly causing brain damage or death.

thalidomide a sedative used in the 1960s that has been linked to birth defects, especially deformed or absent limbs.

progestin a hormone used to maintain pregnancy that can cause masculinization of the fetus.

DES diethylstilbestrol, an estrogen that has been linked to cancer in the reproductive organs of children of women who used the hormone when pregnant.

fetal alcohol spectrum disorder (FASD) a cluster of symptoms shown by children of women who drank heavily during pregnancy, including characteristic facial features and mental retardation.

Learning Outcomes

LO1 Identify the stages of childbirth

The first uterine contractions are "Braxton-Hicks contractions," or false labour contractions. A day or so before labour begins, women may spot blood. About 1 woman in 10 has a rush of amniotic fluid. Maternal hormones stimulate contractions strong enough to expel the baby.

Childbirth begins with the onset of regular contractions of the uterus, which efface and dilate the cervix. The first stage may last from hours to more than a day. During transition, the head of the fetus moves into the birth canal. The second stage begins when the baby appears at the opening of the birth canal and ends with birth of the baby. Mucus is suctioned from the baby's mouth so that breathing is not obstructed. The umbilical cord is severed. During the third stage, the placenta is expelled.

LO2 Describe different methods of childbirth

General anesthesia and analgesics put the woman to sleep, but they decrease the strength of uterine contractions and lower the responsiveness of the neonate. Local anesthetics deaden pain in parts of the body. Prepared childbirth teaches women to dissociate uterine contractions from pain and fear by associating responses such as relaxation with contractions. A coach aids the mother. A cesarean section (C-section) delivers a baby surgically through the abdomen. C-sections are most likely when the baby is large or in distress. Herpes and HIV infections can be bypassed by C-section.

LO3 Discuss potential problems with childbirth

Prenatal oxygen deprivation can impair development of the nervous system and can be fatal. A baby is preterm when birth occurs at or before 37 weeks of gestation. A baby has a low birth weight when it weighs less than 2.5 kg (5.5 lb.). Risks of prematurity include infant mortality and delayed neurological and motor development. Preterm babies are relatively thin. Their sucking may be weak, and they may show respiratory distress. Preterm babies usually remain in the hospital in incubators, but they profit from early stimulation. Canadians want to ensure that all children have an equal opportunity to access health care services. The UNICEF Report, *Leaving No Child Behind,* looks at disparities between health statistics of Indigenous and non-Indigenous children in Canada.

LO4 Describe the key events of the postpartum period

Women may encounter the baby blues, postpartum depression, and postpartum psychosis. These problems probably reflect hormonal changes following birth, although stress can play a role.

Postpartum depression symptoms include:
- serious sadness
- feelings of hopelessness, helplessness, and worthlessness
- difficulty concentrating
- mood swings
- major changes in appetite (usually loss of appetite)
- abnormal sleep patterns (frequently insomnia)

Key Terms

term a set period of time, such as the typical period between the conception and birth of a baby.

Braxton-Hicks contractions the first, usually painless, contractions of childbirth.

prostaglandins hormones that stimulate uterine contractions.

oxytocin a hormone that stimulates labour contractions.

LO1
efface to become thin.

dilate to widen.

episiotomy a surgical incision between the birth canal and anus that widens the vaginal opening.

transition movement of the head of the fetus into the birth canal.

LO2
midwife an individual who helps women in childbirth.

anesthetics agents that lessen pain.

general anesthesia elimination of pain by putting a person to sleep.

local anesthetic reduction of pain in an area of the body.

natural childbirth childbirth without anesthesia.

Lamaze method a childbirth method in which women are educated about childbirth, breathe in patterns that reduce pain during birth, and have a coach present.

cesarean section delivery of a baby by abdominal surgery.

LO3
anoxia absence of oxygen.

hypoxia less oxygen than required.

breech (bottom-first) presentation buttocks-first childbirth.

preterm born prior to 37 weeks of gestation.

small for dates descriptive of neonates who are small for their age.

lanugo fine, downy hair on premature babies.

vernix oily white substance on the skin of premature babies.

respiratory distress syndrome weak and irregular breathing, typical of preterm babies.

incubator a heated, protective container for premature infants.

 postpartum period the period immediately following childbirth.

postpartum depression (PPD) serious maternal depression following delivery; characterized by sadness, apathy, and feelings of worthlessness.

bonding formation of parent–infant attachment.

LO5 Apgar scale a measure of a newborn's health that assesses appearance, pulse, grimace, activity level, and respiratory effort.

Brazelton Neonatal Behavioural Assessment Scale a measure of a newborn's motor behaviour, response to stress, adaptive behaviour, and control over physiological state.

reflex an unlearned response to a stimulus.

rooting reflex turning the mouth and head toward stroking of the cheek or the corner of the mouth.

Moro reflex arching the back, flinging out the arms and legs, and drawing them back to the chest in response to a sudden change in position.

grasping reflex grasping objects that touch the palms.

stepping reflex taking steps when held under the arms and leaned forward so the feet press the ground.

Babinski reflex fanning the toes when the soles of the feet are stroked.

tonic-neck reflex turning the head to one side, extending the arm and leg on that side, and flexing the limbs on the opposite side.

visual accommodation automatic adjustments of the lenses to focus on objects.

convergence inward movement of the eyes to focus on an object that is drawing nearer.

amplitude loudness (of sound waves).

pitch highness or lowness (of a sound), as determined by the frequency of sound waves.

rapid-eye-movement (REM) sleep a sleep period when dreams are likely, as suggested by rapid eye movements.

Early infant bonding has not been shown to be critical, despite oft-cited research suggesting that the first few hours after birth present a maternal-sensitive period during which hormone levels dispose the mother to bonding.

LO5 Describe the characteristics of the neonate

The neonate's health is usually evaluated by the Apgar scale, displayed below. The Brazelton Neonatal Behavioural Assessment Scale also screens for behavioural and neurological problems. The neonate's rooting and sucking reflexes are basic to survival. Other key reflexes include the startle reflex, the grasping reflex, the stepping reflex, the Babinski reflex, and the tonic-neck reflex. Most reflexes disappear or are replaced by voluntary behaviour within months. Neonates are nearsighted. They visually detect movement, and many track movement. Neonates are particularly responsive to the sounds and rhythms of speech. The nasal and taste preferences of neonates are similar to those of older children and adults. The sensations of skin against skin may contribute to attachment.

TABLE 3.1
The APGAR Scale

POINTS	0	1	2
Appearance: Colour	Blue, pale	Body pink, extremities blue	Entirely pink
Pulse: Heart Rate	Absent (not detectable)	Slow—below 100 beats/minute	Rapid—100–140 beats/minute
Grimace: Reflex Irritability	No response	Grimace	Crying, coughing, sneezing
Activity level: Muscle tone	Completely flaccid, limp	Weak, inactive	Flexed arms and legs; resists extension
Respiratory effort: Breathing	Absent (infant is apneic)	Shallow, irregular, slow	Regular breathing; lusty crying

Neonates are capable of classical and operant conditioning. Neonates spend two-thirds of their time in sleep, distributing sleep through naps. Neonates spend about half their time sleeping in REM sleep, but as time goes on, REM sleep accounts for less of their sleep. REM sleep may be related to brain development. Babies cry mainly because of pain and discomfort. Crying communicates hunger, anger, pain, and the presence of health problems.

SIDS is the most common cause of death in infants between the ages of 1 month and 1 year. SIDS is more common among babies who are put to sleep in the prone position, preterm and low-birth-weight infants, male infants, and infants whose mothers smoked during or after pregnancy. Shaken Baby Syndrome (SBS) is the impulsive act of an exhausted or frustrated caregiver. Harm to a child is preventable when caregivers seek help and the proper support systems are in place.

non-rapid-eye-movement (non-REM) sleep a sleep period when dreams are unlikely.

pacifier a device such as an artificial nipple or teething ring that soothes babies when sucked.

sudden infant death syndrome (SIDS) the death, while sleeping, of apparently healthy babies who stop breathing.

medulla a part of the brain stem that regulates vital and automatic functions such as breathing and the sleep–wake cycle.

Learning Outcomes

LO1 Describe trends in the physical development of the infant

Three key sequences of physical development are cephalocaudal development, proximodistal development, and differentiation. Infants usually double their birth weight in 5 months and triple it by their first birthday. Height increases by about half in the first year. Infants grow another 10 to 15 cm (4 to 6 in.) and gain another 1.8 to 3.2 kg (4 to 7 lb.) in their second year. The head diminishes in proportion to the rest of the body. Failure to thrive (FTT) impairs growth in infancy and early childhood. FTT can have organic causes or nonorganic causes, possibly including deficiencies in caregiver-child interaction.

Infants require breast milk or an iron-fortified formula. Introduction of solid foods is recommended at 4–6 months. Breast feeding is related to the mother's availability, knowledge of the advantages of breast feeding, support in caregiving, and availability of alternatives. Breast milk is tailored to human digestion, contains essential nutrients, contains the mothers' antibodies, helps protect against infant diarrhea, and is less likely than formula to lead to allergies.

LO2 Describe the physical development of the brain and the nervous system

Neurons receive and transmit messages in the form of neurotransmitters. As the child matures, axons grow in length, dendrites and axon terminals proliferate, and many neurons become wrapped in myelin, making them more efficient. The brain triples in weight by the first birthday, reaching nearly 70 percent of its adult weight. The brain has two major prenatal growth spurts: neurons proliferate during the first, and the second spurt is due mainly to the proliferation of dendrites and axon terminals. Sensory and motor areas of the brain begin to develop because of maturation, but sensory stimulation and motor activity spur development. Malnutrition is connected with a small brain, fewer neurons, and less myelination.

FIGURE 4.4

Structures of the Brain

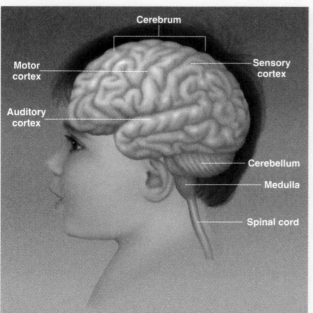

Key Terms

LO1

differentiation the processes by which behaviours and physical structures become specialized.

failure to thrive (FTT) a disorder of infancy and early childhood characterized by variable eating and inadequate gains in weight.

canalization the tendency of growth rates to return to normal after undergoing environmentally induced change.

LO2

nerves bundles of axons from many neurons.

neurons cells in the nervous system that transmit messages.

dendrites rootlike parts of neurons that receive impulses from other neurons.

axon a long, thin part of a neuron that transmits impulses to other neurons through branching structures called axon terminals.

neurotransmitter a chemical that transmits a neural impulse across a synapse from one neuron to another.

myelin sheath a fatty, whitish substance that encases and insulates axons.

myelination the coating of axons with myelin.

multiple sclerosis a disorder in which hard fibrous tissue replaces myelin, impeding neural transmission.

medulla an area of the hindbrain involved in heartbeat and respiration.

cerebellum the part of the hindbrain involved in coordination and balance.

cerebrum the part of the brain responsible for learning, thought, memory, and language.

LO3

ulnar grasp grasping objects between the fingers and the palm.

pincer grasp grasping objects between the fingers and the thumb.

locomotion movement from one place to another.

toddler a child who walks with short, uncertain steps.

LO4 **perceptual constancy** perceiving objects as maintaining their identity although sensations from them change as their positions change.

habituation becoming used to a stimulus and therefore paying less attention to it.

FIGURE 4.8

Eye Movements of 1- and 2-Month-Olds

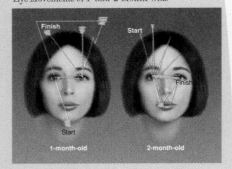

Source: Salapatek (1975).

LO3 Describe the key events in the motor development of the infant

Motor development is related to changes in posture, movement, and coordination. Children gain the ability to move their bodies through a sequence of activities that includes rolling over, sitting up, crawling, creeping, walking, and running. Although the sequence remains stable, some children skip a step. Both maturation (nature) and experience (nurture) play roles in motor development. Development of motor skills can be accelerated by training, but the effect is generally slight.

LO4 Describe patterns of sensory and perceptual development in infancy

Neonates are nearsighted and have poor peripheral vision. Acuity and peripheral vision approximate adult levels by the age of 6 months. Neonates look longer at stripes than at blobs, and by 8 to 12 weeks of age, they prefer curved lines to straight ones. Two-month-olds fixate longer on the human face than on other stimuli. Infants can discriminate their mother's face from a stranger's after about 8 hours of contact. Neonates direct their attention to the edges of objects, but 2-month-olds scan objects from the edges inward.

Researchers use the visual cliff apparatus to study depth perception. Most infants refuse to venture out over the cliff by the time they can crawl. Perhaps infants need some experience crawling before they develop fear of heights. Size constancy appears to be present by 2½ to 3 months of age; shape constancy develops by age 4 to 5 months. Neonates reflexively orient their heads toward a sound. Infants discriminate caregivers' voices by 3½ months of age. Early infants can perceive most of the speech sounds throughout the languages of the world, but by 10 to 12 months of age, this ability diminishes.

Neonates seem to be at the mercy of external stimuli, but later intentional action replaces "capture." Systematic search replaces unsystematic search, attention becomes selective, and irrelevant information gets ignored. Sensory changes are linked to maturation of the nervous system (nature), but experience (nurture) also plays a crucial role. Children have critical periods in their perceptual development when their sensory experience is required to optimize—or maintain—sensory capacities.

FIGURE 4.10

Declining Ability to Discriminate the Sounds of Foreign Languages

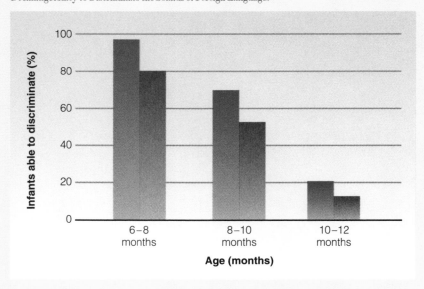

Source: Werker (1989).

Learning Outcomes

LO1 Examine Jean Piaget's studies of cognitive development

Piaget hypothesized that cognitive processes develop in an orderly sequence of stages: sensorimotor, preoperational, concrete operational, and formal operational. The sensorimotor stage refers to the first 2 years of cognitive development and involves the progression from responding to events with reflexes to displaying goal-oriented behaviour (see table below). A critical milestone in the sensorimotor stage is the appearance of early signs of object permanence, or the ability of an infant to appreciate that an object continues to exist physically even when out of view.

Researchers who question the validity of Piaget's claims argue the following:
- development is not tied to discrete stages
- adult and peer influences play a role in cognitive development
- infants are more competent than Piaget estimated.

STAGE	AGE	HALLMARKS
1. Simple reflexes	0–1 month	Assimilation of new objects into reflexive responses. Infants "look and see." Inborn reflexes can be modified by experience.
2. Primary circular reactions	1–4 months	Repetition of actions that may have initially occurred by chance but that have satisfying or interesting results. Infants "look in order to see." The focus is on the infant's body. Infants do not yet distinguish between themselves and the external world.
3. Secondary circular reactions	4–8 months	Repetition of schemes that have interesting effects on the environment. The focus shifts to external objects and events. There is initial cognitive awareness that schemes influence the external world.
4. Coordination of secondary schemes	8–12 months	Coordination of secondary schemes, such as looking and grasping to attain specific goals. There is the beginning of intentionality and means–end differentiation. We find imitation of actions not already in infants' repertoires.
5. Tertiary circular reactions	12–18 months	Purposeful adaptation of established schemes to specific situations. Behaviour takes on an experimental quality. There is overt trial and error in problem solving.
6. Invention of new means through mental combinations	18–24 months	Mental trial and error in problem solving. Infants take "mental detours" based on cognitive maps. Infants engage in deferred imitation and symbolic play. Infants' cognitive advances are made possible by mental representations of objects and events and the beginnings of symbolic thought.

Key Terms

LO1
primary circular reactions the repetition of actions that first occurred by chance and that focus on the infant's own body.

secondary circular reactions the repetition of actions that produce an effect on the environment.

tertiary circular reactions the purposeful adaptation of established schemes to new situations.

object permanence recognition that objects continue to exist when they are not in view.

deferred imitation the imitation of people and events that occurred in the past.

LO3
visual recognition memory the kind of memory shown in an infant's ability to discriminate previously seen objects from novel objects.

LO4
prelinguistic vocalizations made by the infant before the use of language.

cooing prelinguistic vowel-like sounds that reflect feelings of positive excitement.

babbling the child's first vocalizations that have the sounds of speech.

echolalia the automatic repetition of sounds or words.

intonation the use of pitches of varying levels to help communicate meaning.

receptive vocabulary the number of words one understands.

expressive vocabulary the number of words one can use in the production of language.

referential language style use of language primarily as a means for labeling objects.

expressive language style use of language primarily as a means for engaging in social interaction.

overextension use of words in situations in which their meanings become extended.

telegraphic speech type of speech in which only the essential words are used.

mean length of utterance (MLU) the average number of morphemes used in an utterance.

morpheme the smallest unit of meaning in a language.

holophrase a single word that is used to express complex meanings.

syntax the rules in a language for placing words in order to form sentences.

models in learning theory, those whose behaviours are imitated by others.

extinction decrease in frequency of a response due to absence of reinforcement.

shaping gradual building of complex behaviour through reinforcement of successive approximations to the target behaviour.

psycholinguistic theory the view that language learning involves an interaction between environmental influences and an inborn tendency to acquire language.

language acquisition device (LAD) neural "prewiring" that eases the child's learning of grammar.

surface structure the superficial grammatical construction of a sentence.

deep structure the underlying meaning of a sentence.

aphasia a disruption in the ability to understand or produce language.

Broca's aphasia an aphasia caused by damage to Broca's area and characterized by difficulty speaking.

Wernicke's aphasia an aphasia caused by damage to Wernicke's area and characterized by impaired comprehension of speech and difficulty producing the right word.

sensitive period the period from about 18 months to puberty when the brain is especially capable of learning language.

L◯2 Discuss the information-processing approach

The information-processing approach focuses on how children manipulate or process information from the environment or already stored in the mind. Two primary tools used in this processing are memory and imitation. Even neonates demonstrate memory to stimuli, and between 2 and 6 months of age, infants' memory develops dramatically. Infant memory can be improved if infants receive a reminder before given a memory test. Researchers disagree on how early nonreflexive imitation is exhibited in infants. Deferred imitation occurs as early as 6 months of age.

L◯3 Identify individual differences in intelligence among infants

The Bayley Scales of Infant Development are one of the most important tests of intellectual development among infants. A total of 287 scale items test for mental skills (verbal communication, perceptual skills, learning and memory, and problem-solving skills) and motor skills (gross and fine). Infant intelligence is tested to determine the presence of handicaps, and although the Bayley scales can identify gross lags in development and relative strengths and weaknesses, infant intelligence scores are generally poor predictors of intelligence scores taken more than a year later.

Assessing visual recognition memory is another way of studying infant intelligence. Longitudinal studies by Susan Rose and her colleagues showed that the capacity for visual recognition memory is stable and the trait shows predictive validity for broad cognitive abilities throughout childhood, including intelligence and language ability.

L◯4 Examine language development in children

Children develop language according to an invariant sequence of steps or stages. The first stage involves prelinguistic vocalizations, such as cooing, babbling, and echolalia. Once children can express themselves with words, they try to talk about more objects than they have words for. Just as first words are simple syllabic combinations, first sentences are often single words that express simple but complete ideas. Developing language skills are marked by changes in the mean length of utterance (MLU). In early language acquisition, children use telegraphic speech to communicate full ideas.

Theories on language development are divided into those emphasizing nurture and those emphasizing nature. Proponents of nurture theories build on the work of B. F. Skinner and cite the roles of imitation and reinforcement in language development. Proponents of the nativist view, like Noam Chomsky, argue that the ability to acquire language is innate and therefore biological. The work of Steven Pinker, among others, shows, however, that language acquisition results from an interaction of environmental and biological factors (or is a combination of nature and nurture). This notion is reinforced through the tragic story studied in *The Genie Project*, which allows us to see the impact of severe environmental conditions on language acquisition.

FIGURE 5.3
Mean Length of Utterance for Three Children

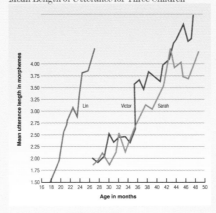

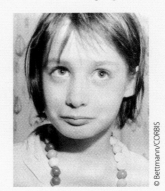

Genie's tragically unique experience provides support for *the sensitive period hypothesis* of language development.

Learning Outcomes

LO1 Describe the development of attachment in infancy and theoretical views of how it occurs

Most infants in Canada and the United States are securely attached. In the Strange Situation, secure infants mildly protest the mother's departure and are readily comforted by her. The two major types of insecure attachment are avoidant attachment and ambivalent/resistant attachment. Secure infants are happier, more sociable, and more competent. They use the mother as a secure base from which to explore the environment. Parents of securely attached infants are more likely to be affectionate and sensitive to their needs.

According to Ainsworth's studies of the development of attachment, the initial-preattachment phase lasts from birth to about 3 months and is characterized by indiscriminate attachment. The attachment-in-the-making phase occurs at about 3 or 4 months and is characterized by preference for familiar figures. The clear-cut-attachment phase occurs at 6 or 7 months and involves dependence on the primary caregiver.

FIGURE 6.2

Development of Attachment

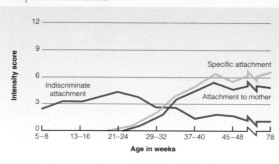

Cognitive theorists suggest that an infant must develop object permanence before specific attachment is possible. Behaviourists suggest that infants become attached to caregivers because caregivers meet their physical needs. Psychoanalysts suggest that the primary caregiver becomes a love object. The Harlows' experiments with monkeys suggest that contact comfort is a key to attachment. Ethologists view attachment as an instinct (fixed action pattern) that occurs during a critical period.

FIGURE 6.3

Contact Comfort

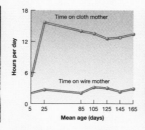

LO2 Discuss the effects of social deprivation, abuse and neglect, and autism spectrum disorders on attachment

The Harlows found that rhesus infants reared in isolation later avoided contact with other monkeys. Females who later had offspring tended to neglect or abuse them. Many institutionalized children who receive little social stimulation develop withdrawal and depression. Mistreated children are less intimate with peers and are more aggressive, angry, and noncompliant than other children. Child abuse tends to run in families, perhaps because abusive parents serve as role models. Some parents rationalize that they are hurting their children "for their own good" to discourage bad behaviour. The 2003 Canadian Incidence Study of Reported Child Abuse and Neglect (Trocmé et al., 2005) concluded there is no reliable way to track unreported incidents of child abuse, which experts believe is a significant number.

Key Terms

attachment an affectional bond characterized by seeking closeness with another and distress upon separation.

LO1 **separation anxiety** fear of separation from a target of attachment.

secure attachment a type of attachment characterized by mild distress at leave-takings and being readily soothed by reunion.

avoidant attachment a type of insecure attachment characterized by apparent indifference to leave-takings by and reunions with an attachment figure.

ambivalent/resistant attachment a type of insecure attachment characterized by severe distress at leave-takings by and ambivalent behaviour at reunions.

disorganized–disoriented attachment a type of insecure attachment characterized by dazed and contradictory behaviours toward an attachment figure.

indiscriminate attachment the display of attachment behaviours toward any person.

initial-preattachment phase the first phase in development of attachment, characterized by indiscriminate attachment.

attachment-in-the-making phase the second phase in development of attachment, characterized by preference for familiar figures.

clear-cut-attachment phase the third phase in development of attachment, characterized by intensified dependence on the primary caregiver.

contact comfort the pleasure derived from physical contact with another.

ethologist a scientist who studies the behaviour patterns characteristic of various species.

social smile a smile that occurs in response to a human voice or face.

critical period a period during which imprinting can occur.

imprinting the process by which waterfowl become attached to the first moving object they follow.

LO2 autism spectrum disorders (ASDs) developmental disorders characterized by impairment in communication and social skills, and by repetitive, stereotyped behaviour.

autism a disorder characterized by extreme aloneness, communication problems, preservation of sameness, and ritualistic behaviour.

mutism refusal to speak.

echolalia automatic repetition of sounds or words.

LO4 social referencing using another person's reaction to a situation to form one's own response.

emotional regulation techniques for controlling one's emotional states.

LO5 separation–individuation the process of becoming separate from and independent of the mother.

temperament individual difference in style of reaction that is present early in life.

goodness of fit agreement between the parents' expectations of a child and the child's temperament.

Autism spectrum disorders (ASDs) are characterized by impairment in communication skills and social interactions, and repetitive, stereotyped behaviour. The most striking feature of autism is the child's aloneness. Other features include communication problems, intolerance of change, and self-mutilation. Twin studies suggest that autism involves heredity, and neurological impairment is also suspected. Behaviour modification has been used to increase the child's attention to others and social play. The Autism Society of Canada reminds us that individuals should be valued for their differences and not viewed as person that should be changed.

LO3 Discuss the effects of day care

Day care was once see as a second alternative to home care but research shows many advantages. Infants with day-care experience are more independent, self-confident, outgoing, affectionate, and more cooperative with peers and adults than infants who are not in day care. Children in high-quality day care outperform children who remain in the home in terms of cognitive development. Children in day care are more aggressive than other children, but some aggression may indicate independence, not maladjustment.

LO4 Describe the emotional development of the infant

Researchers debate whether the emotional expression of newborns begins in an undifferentiated state of diffuse excitement or whether several emotions are present. Infants' initial emotional expressions appear to comprise either a positive attraction to pleasant stimulation or withdrawal from aversive stimulation. By the age of 2 to 3 months, social smiling has replaced reflexive smiling. Most infants develop fear of strangers at about 6 to 9 months.

Infants display social referencing as early as 6 months of age, when they use caregivers' facial expressions or tones of voice for information on how to respond in novel situations. Emotional regulation is emotional self-control. The children of secure mothers are more likely to regulate their emotions well.

LO5 Describe the personality development of the infant, focusing on the self-concept, temperament, and sex differences

Research using the mirror technique finds that the self-concept develops by about 18 months of age. Self-awareness enables the child to develop concepts of sharing and cooperation and emotions such as embarrassment, envy, empathy, pride, guilt, and shame.

Infants' temperament (see Table 6.2) involves their activity level, regularity, approach or withdrawal, adaptability, response threshold, response intensity, quality of mood, distractibility, attention span, and persistence. Thomas and Chess found that most infants can be classified as having easy, difficult, or slow-to-warm-up temperaments. Temperament remains moderately consistent from infancy through young adulthood.

Female infants sit, crawl, and walk earlier than boys do. By 12 to 18 months of age, girls prefer to play with dolls and similar toys, whereas boys prefer sports equipment and transportation toys.

TABLE 6.2

Types of Temperament

TEMPERAMENT CATEGORY	EASY	DIFFICULT	SLOW TO WARM UP
Regularity of biological functioning	Regular	Irregular	Somewhat irregular
Response to new stimuli	Positive approach	Negative withdrawal	Negative withdrawal
Adaptability to new situations	Adapts readily	Adapts slowly or not at all	Adapts slowly
Intensity of reaction	Mild or moderate	Intense	Mild
Quality of mood	Positive	Negative	Initially negative; gradually more positive

Sources: Chess & Thomas (1991) and Thomas & Chess (1989).

Learning Outcomes

LO1 Describe trends in physical development in early childhood

Children gain about 5 to 8 cm (2 to 3 in.) in height and 2 to 3 kg (4 to 6 lb.) in weight per year in early childhood. Boys are slightly larger than girls. The brain develops more quickly than any other organ in early childhood, in part because of myelination. The left hemisphere is relatively more involved in logical analysis, language, and computation. The right hemisphere is usually superior in visual-spatial functions, emotional responses, and creative mathematical reasoning. But the hemispheres work together. The brain shows plasticity in early childhood. Two factors involved in the brain's plasticity are the growth of new dendrites and the redundancy of neural connections.

LO2 Describe motor development in early childhood

Preschoolers make great strides in the development of gross motor skills. Girls tend to be better in balance and precision; boys have some advantage in throwing and kicking. Physically active parents are likely to have physically active children. Fine motor skills develop gradually. Kellogg identified 20 scribbles that she considers the building blocks of art. Handedness emerges by 6 months. Left-handedness may be connected with some language and health problems, yet a disproportionately large number of artists, musicians, and mathematicians are left-handed.

LO3 Describe nutritional needs in early childhood

Health Canada recommends that young children's diet should focus on food servings rather than caloric intake. During the second and third years, children's appetites typically wane and grow erratic. Many children eat too much sugar and salt.

LO4 Describe trends in health and illness in early childhood

The incidence of minor illnesses, such as colds, nausea and vomiting, and diarrhea, is high. In developing countries, diarrheal diseases are a leading cause of death and are almost completely related to unsafe drinking water and lack of adequate sanitation. Immunization and antibiotics reduce the incidence of disease. Air pollution contributes to respiratory infections. Lead poisoning causes neurological damage.

LO5 Describe sleep patterns in early childhood

Most 2- and 3-year-olds sleep about 10 hours at night and nap during the day. Sleep terrors are more severe than nightmares. Sleep terrors and sleep walking usually occur during deep sleep. Sleepwalkers' eyes are usually open; if awakened, they may show confusion but are unlikely to be violent.

LO6 Discuss the elimination disorders

Most Canadian children are toilet trained by age 2 or 3 but may continue to have "accidents." Enuresis is apparently connected with physical immaturity and stress. Encopresis can stem from constipation and stress.

Key Terms

LO1 corpus callosum the thick bundle of nerve fibres that connects the left and right hemispheres of the brain.

plasticity the tendency of new parts of the brain to take up the functions of injured parts.

LO2 gross motor skills skills employing the large muscles used in locomotion.

fine motor skills skills employing the small muscles used in manipulation, such as those in the fingers.

LO5 sleep terrors frightening dreamlike experiences that occur during the deepest stage of non-REM sleep, shortly after the child has gone to sleep.

somnambulism sleep walking.

LO6 enuresis failure to control the bladder (urination) once the normal age for control has been reached.

bed-wetting failure to control the bladder during the night.

encopresis failure to control the bowels once the normal age for bowel control has been reached. Also called soiling.

LO7 preoperational stage the second stage in Piaget's scheme, characterized by inflexible and irreversible mental manipulation of symbols.

symbolic play play in which children make believe that objects and toys are other than what they are. Also called pretend play.

egocentrism putting oneself at the centre of things such that one is unable to perceive the world from another person's point of view.

precausal a type of thought in which natural cause-and-effect relationships are attributed to will and other preoperational concepts.

transductive reasoning reasoning from the specific to the specific.

animism the attribution of life and intentionality to inanimate objects.

artificialism the belief that environmental features were made by people.

conservation in cognitive psychology, the principle that properties of substances such as weight and mass remain the same (are conserved) when superficial characteristics such as their shapes or arrangement are changed.

LO8 **scaffolding** Vygotsky's term for temporary cognitive structures or methods of solving problems that help the child as he or she learns to function independently.

zone of proximal development (ZPD) Vygotsky's term for the situation in which a child carries out tasks with the help of someone who is more skilled, frequently an adult who represents the culture in which the child develops.

LO9 **theory of mind** a commonsense understanding of how the mind works.

appearance–reality distinction the difference between real events on the one hand and mental events, fantasies, and misleading appearances on the other hand.

LO10 **autobiographical memory** the memory of specific episodes or events.

scripts abstract, generalized accounts of familiar repeated events.

rehearsal repetition.

LO11 **fast mapping** a process of quickly determining a word's meaning, which facilitates children's vocabulary development.

whole-object assumption the assumption that words refer to whole objects and not to their component parts or characteristics.

contrast assumption the assumption that objects have only one label.

overregularization the application of regular grammatical rules for forming inflections to irregular verbs and nouns.

pragmatics the practical aspects of communication, such as adaptation of language to fit the social situation.

inner speech Vygotsky's concept of the ultimate binding of language and thought. Inner speech originates in vocalizations that may regulate the child's behaviour and become internalized by age 6 or 7.

LO7 Describe Piaget's preoperational stage

Piaget's preoperational stage lasts from about age 2 to 7 and is characterized by the use of symbols. Preoperational thinking is characterized by pretend play, egocentrism, precausal thinking, confusion between mental and physical events, and ability to focus on only one dimension at a time. Conservation is lacking because it requires focusing on two aspects of a situation at once.

LO8 Discuss influences on cognitive development in early childhood

Vygotsky envisions scaffolding and the zone of proximal development as two factors in cognitive development. The "HOME" scale was developed to evaluate children's home environments. The scale includes six factors that influence child development, including parental emotional and verbal responsiveness, avoidance of restriction and punishment, organization of the physical environment, provision of appropriate play materials, parental involvement with the child, and opportunities for variety in daily stimulation. The children of parents who provide appropriate play materials and stimulating experiences show gains in social and language development. For example, First Nation Head Start programs enhance children's academic readiness and skills while instilling a sense of pride and an eagerness to learn. Television continues to be a primary focus in children's learning. Fortunately, some viewing (e.g., *Sesame Street*) shows mild to productive influences on cognitive development.

LO9 Explain how "theory of mind" affects cognitive development

Children come to understand the distinctions between external and mental events and between appearances and realities. By age 3, most children begin to realize that people gain knowledge through the senses, and by age 4, they understand which senses provide certain kinds of information.

LO10 Describe memory development in early childhood

Preschoolers recognize more items than they can recall. Autobiographical memory is linked to language skills. Factors affecting memory include what the child is asked to remember, interest level and motivation, the availability of retrieval cues, and the memory measure being used. Preschoolers engage in behaviour such as looking, pointing, and touching when trying to remember. Preschoolers can be taught to use memory strategies such as rehearsal and grouping of items.

LO11 Describe language development in early childhood

Preschoolers acquire about nine new words per day, some of which occur due to fast mapping. During the third year, children usually add articles, conjunctions, possessive adjectives, pronouns, and prepositions. Between the ages of 3 and 4, children combine phrases and clauses into complex sentences. Preschoolers overregularize irregular verbs and nouns as they learn grammar. Piaget believed that children learn words to describe classes they have created. Other theorists argue that children create classes to understand words. To Vygotsky, inner speech is the ultimate binding of language and thought.

Learning Outcomes

LO1 Describe the dimensions of child rearing and styles of parenting

Approaches to child rearing can be classified according to the dimensions of warmth–coldness and restrictiveness–permissiveness. Consistent control and firm enforcement of rules can have positive consequences for the child. Parents tend to use inductive methods, power assertion, and withdrawal of love to enforce rules. Inductive methods use "reasoning," or explaining why one sort of behaviour is good and another is not. Authoritative parents are restrictive but warm and tend to have the most competent and achievement-oriented children. Authoritarian parents are restrictive and cold. The sons of authoritarian parents tend to be hostile and defiant; daughters are low in independence. Children of neglectful parents show the least competence and maturity.

TABLE 8.1
Baumrind's Patterns of Parenting

	PARENTAL BEHAVIOUR PATTERNS	
PARENTAL STYLE	RESTRICTIVENESS AND CONTROL	WARMTH AND RESPONSIVENESS
Authoritative	↑	↑
Authoritarian	↑	↓
Permissive–Indulgent	↓	↑
Rejecting–neglecting	↓	↓

LO2 Explain how siblings, birth order, peers, and other factors affect social development during early childhood

Siblings provide caregiving, emotional support, advice, role models, social interaction, restrictions, and cognitive stimulation. However, they are also sources of conflict, control, and competition. Younger siblings usually imitate older siblings. Firstborn and only children are generally more highly motivated to achieve, more cooperative, more helpful, more adult-oriented, and less aggressive, but later-born children tend to have greater social skills with peers. Children learn social skills—such as sharing, taking turns, and coping with conflict—from peers. Peers also provide emotional support. Preschoolers' friendships are characterized by shared activities and feelings of attachment.

Play develops motor, social, and cognitive skills. Parten followed the development of six types of play among 2- to 5-year-olds: unoccupied play, solitary play, onlooker play, parallel play, associative play, and cooperative play. Children show preferences for gender-stereotyped toys by 15 to 30 months of age. Boys' toys commonly include transportation toys (cars and trucks) and weapons; girls' toys more often include dolls. Boys prefer vigorous outdoor activities and rough-and-tumble play. Girls are more likely to prefer arts and crafts. Preschool children generally prefer playmates of their own sex, partly because of shared interest in activities. Boys' play is more oriented toward dominance, aggression, and rough play. Prosocial behaviour begins

Key Terms

LO1

inductive characteristic of disciplinary methods, such as reasoning, that attempt to foster understanding of the principles behind parental demands.

authoritative a child-rearing style in which parents are restrictive and demanding yet communicative and warm.

authoritarian demanding submission and obedience.

permissive–indulgent a child-rearing style in which parents are warm and not restrictive.

rejecting–neglecting a child-rearing style in which parents are neither restrictive and controlling nor supportive and responsive.

LO2

regression a return to behaviour characteristic of earlier stages of development.

dramatic play play in which children enact social roles.

nonsocial play solitary forms of play.

social play play in which children interact with and are influenced by others.

disinhibit to stimulate a response that has been suppressed by showing a model engaging in that response.

LO3

categorical self definitions of the self that refer to external traits.

LO4

stereotype a fixed, conventional idea about a group.

gender role a cluster of traits and behaviours that are considered stereotypical of females and males.

hippocampus a brain structure that is involved in the formation of memories and the relay of incoming sensory information to other parts of the brain.

gender identity knowledge that one is female or male.

gender stability the concept that one's sex is unchanging.

gender constancy the concept that one's sex remains the same despite changes in appearance or behaviour.

gender-schema theory the view that one's knowledge of the gender schema in one's society guides one's assumption of gender-typed preferences and behaviour patterns.

psychological androgyny possession of both stereotypical feminine and masculine traits.

to develop in the first year, when children begin to share. Development of prosocial behaviour is linked to the development of empathy and perspective taking. Girls show more empathy than boys do. Preschool aggression is often instrumental. By age 6 or 7, aggression becomes hostile. Aggressive behaviour appears to be stable and to predict problems in adulthood. Genetic factors may be involved in aggressive behaviour, partly because of testosterone. Social cognitive theory suggests that children become aggressive as a result of frustration and observational learning. Aggressive children are often rejected by less aggressive peers. Children who are physically punished are more likely to behave aggressively. Observing aggressive behaviour teaches aggressive skills, disinhibits the child, and habituates children to violence.

FIGURE 8.1
Photos from Albert Bandura's Classic Experiment in the Imitation of Aggressive Models

Albert Bandura/Dept. of Psychology, Stanford University

LO3 **Discuss personality and emotional development during early childhood, focusing on the self, Erikson's views, and fears**

Children as young as age 3 can describe themselves in terms of behaviour and internal states. Secure attachment and competence contribute to self-esteem. Preschoolers are most likely to fear animals, imaginary creatures, and the dark. Girls report more fears than boys do.

LO4 **Discuss the development of gender roles and sex differences**

Females are stereotyped as dependent, gentle, and home-oriented. Males are stereotyped as aggressive, self-confident, and independent. Cultural expectations of females and males are called gender roles. Males tend to excel in math and spatial-relations skills, whereas girls tend to excel in verbal skills. Stereotypical gender preferences for toys and play activities are in evidence at an early age. Males are more aggressive and more interested in sex than females. Testosterone may specialize the hemispheres of the brain more in males than females, explaining why females excel in verbal skills that require some spatial organization, such as reading. Social cognitive theorists explain the development of gender-typed behaviour in terms of observational learning and socialization. According to Kohlberg's cognitive-developmental theory, gender-typing involves the emergence of gender identity, gender stability, and gender constancy. According to gender-schema theory, preschoolers attempt to conform to the cultural gender schema. Theorists differ as to whether it is beneficial to promote psychological androgyny.

Learning Outcomes

LO1 Describe trends in physical development in middle childhood

Children tend to gain a little over 5 cm (2 in.) in height and 2 to 3 kg (5 to 7 lb.) in weight per year during middle childhood. Boys are slightly heavier and taller than girls through ages 9 or 10, until girls begin the adolescent growth spurt. Overweight children usually do not outgrow baby fat. Heredity plays a role in weight. Sedentary habits also foster weight gain. Healthy food choices from the Canada Food Guide should be the rule.

LO2 Describe changes in motor development in middle childhood

Middle childhood is marked by increases in speed, strength, agility, and balance. Children improve in gross and fine motor skills as pathways that connect the cerebellum to the cortex become more myelinated. Reaction time decreases. Boys have slightly greater overall strength, whereas girls have better coordination and flexibility. Many Canadian children are not physically fit, in part because of the amount of time spent watching TV. Cuts to Canadian physical education programming have also hurt the health of our children.

LO3 Discuss ADHD and learning disabilities

Attention-deficit/hyperactivity disorder (ADHD) runs in families and may involve brain damage. Children with ADHD are often treated with stimulants, which trigger the cerebral cortex to inhibit more primitive areas of the brain. Dyslexia also runs in families and is commonly undiagnosed, according to the Canadian Dyslexic Centre. The double-deficit hypothesis suggests that dyslexic children have problems in phonological processing and naming speed. Some learning-disabled children profit from mainstream classrooms; others find them overwhelming.

LO4 Describe Piaget's concrete-operational stage

By the age of 11, many children begin to recognize ambiguities in grammar, and their thought processes become more logical and complex. Piaget characterized children during this period as entering the concrete-operational stage, in which children begin to think in logical terms but focus on tangible objects rather than abstract ideas. Concrete-operational children are less egocentric, engage in decentration, and understand concepts such as conservation, transitivity, seriation, and class inclusion.

LO5 Discuss Piaget's and Kohlberg's theories of moral development

Piaget and Kohlberg both presumed that moral reasoning in children was related to overall cognitive development. Piaget proposed that children's moral judgments develop in two overlapping stages, which he termed moral realism and autonomous morality. Kohlberg's theory emphasized the importance of being able to view a situation from multiple perspectives, and the reasons on which people base their judgments reflect their level of moral development. At a preconventional level, moral judgments are based on the positive or negative consequences of one's actions. At the conventional level, moral judgments are based on conformity to conventional standards. At a postconventional level, moral judgments are based on personal moral standards.

Key Terms

LO1
growth spurt a period during which growth advances at a dramatically rapid rate compared with other periods.

LO2
reaction time the amount of time required to respond to a stimulus.

LO3
attention-deficit/hyperactivity disorder (ADHD) a disorder characterized by excessive inattention, impulsiveness, and hyperactivity.

hyperactivity excessive restlessness and overactivity; a characteristic of ADHD.

stimulants drugs that increase the activity of the nervous system.

dyslexia a reading disorder characterized by letter reversals, mirror reading, slow reading, and reduced comprehension.

learning disabilities disorders characterized by inadequate development of specific academic, language, and speech skills.

mainstreaming placing children with disabilities in classrooms with children without disabilities.

LO4
concrete operations the third stage in Piaget's scheme, characterized by flexible, reversible thought concerning tangible objects and events.

decentration simultaneous focusing on more than one aspect or dimension of a problem or situation.

transitivity the principle that if A > B and B > C, then A > C.

seriation placing objects in an order or series according to a property or trait.

LO5
moral realism the judgment of acts as moral when they conform to authority or to the rules of the game.

objective morality the perception of morality as objective, that is, as existing outside the cognitive functioning of people.

immanent justice the view that retribution for wrongdoing is a direct consequence of the wrongdoing.

autonomous morality the second stage in Piaget's cognitive-developmental theory of moral development, in which children base moral judgments on the intentions of the wrongdoer and on the amount of damage done.

preconventional level according to Kohlberg, a period during which moral judgments are based largely on expectations of rewards or punishments.

conventional level according to Kohlberg, a period during which moral judgments largely reflect social rules and conventions.

postconventional level according to Kohlberg, a period during which moral judgments are derived from moral principles and people look to themselves to set moral standards.

LO6
sensory memory the structure of memory first encountered by sensory input. Information is maintained in sensory memory for only a fraction of a second.

sensory register another term for sensory memory.

working memory the structure of memory that can hold a sensory stimulus for up to 30 seconds after the trace decays.

encode to transform sensory input into a form that is more readily processed.

rehearse repeat.

long-term memory the memory structure capable of relatively permanent storage of information.

elaborative strategy a method for increasing retention of new information by relating it to well-known information.

metacognition awareness of and control of one's cognitive abilities.

metamemory knowledge of the functions and processes involved in one's storage and retrieval of information.

LO7
intelligence defined by Wechsler as the "capacity … to understand the world [and the] resourcefulness to cope with its challenges."

achievement that which is attained by one's efforts and presumed to be made possible by one's abilities.

intelligence quotient (IQ) (1) a ratio obtained by dividing a child's mental age on an intelligence test by his or her chronological age; (2) a score on an intelligence test.

mental age (MA) the months of credit that a person earns on the Stanford–Binet Intelligence Scale.

LO6 Describe developments in information processing in middle childhood

Key elements in children's information-processing capabilities include development in selective attention; development in the storage and retrieval of sensory, short-term, and long-term memory; development of recall memory; and development of metacognition and metamemory.

LO7 Describe intellectual development in middle childhood, focusing on theories of intelligence

Intelligence is usually perceived as a child's underlying competence or *learning ability,* whereas achievement involves a child's acquired competencies or *performance.* Factor theorists view intelligence as consisting of one or more major mental abilities. Sternberg proposed a three-part theory of intelligence (see Figure 9.7). Gardner theorized that intelligence reflected more than academic achievement, with nine different categories of intelligence, or "talents" (see Figure 9.8).

The Wechsler and SBIS scales have been developed to measure intelligence. Many psychologists and educational specialists have developed culture-free tests to avoid cultural biases they feel are present in the Wechsler and SBIS. About half of children score between 90 and 110 on IQ tests. Those who score below 70 are labelled "cognitively challenged" and those scoring above 130 are labelled "gifted." Most tests indicate only a moderate relationship between IQ scores and creativity. Intelligence tests usually rely on convergent thinking, and creativity is generally based on divergent thinking.

LO8 Describe language development in middle childhood, including reading and bilingualism

Children's language ability grows more sophisticated in middle childhood, when most children learn to read. Children learn to read as well. Bilingualism is of special interest in Canada, where more than 100 languages are spoken.

chronological age (CA) a person's age.

cultural bias a factor hypothesized to be present in intelligence tests that provides an advantage for test takers from certain cultural backgrounds.

culture-free descriptive of a test in which cultural biases have been removed.

cultural–familial retardation substandard intellectual performance stemming from lack of opportunity to acquire knowledge and skills.

creativity a trait characterized by flexibility, ingenuity, and originality.

convergent thinking a thought process that attempts to focus on the single best solution to a problem.

divergent thinking free and fluent association to the elements of a problem.

heritability the degree to which the variations in a trait from one person to another can be attributed to genetic factors.

LO8
word-recognition method a method for learning to read in which children come to recognize words through repeated exposure to them.

phonetic method a method for learning to read in which children decode the sounds of words based on their knowledge of the sounds of letters and letter combinations.

sight vocabulary words that are immediately recognized on the basis of familiarity with their overall shapes, rather than decoded.

bilingual using or capable of using two languages with nearly equal or equal facility.

Learning Outcomes

LO1 Explain theories of social and emotional development in middle childhood

Freud viewed middle childhood as the latency stage; Erikson saw it as the stage of industry versus inferiority. Social cognitive theorists note that children now depend less on external rewards and punishments and increasingly regulate their own behaviour. Cognitive-developmental theory notes that concrete operations enhance social development. In middle childhood, children become more capable of taking the role or perspective of another person. Selman theorizes that children move from egocentricity to seeing the world through the eyes of others in five stages.

In early childhood, children's self-concepts focus on external traits. In middle childhood, children begin to include abstract internal traits. Social relationships and group membership assume importance. In middle childhood, competence and social acceptance contribute to self-esteem, but self-esteem tends to decline because the self-concept becomes more realistic. Authoritative parenting fosters self-esteem. Children with "learned helplessness" tend not to persist in the face of failure.

LO2 Discuss the influences of the family on social development in middle childhood

In middle childhood, the family continues to play a key role in socialization. Parent–child interactions focus on school-related issues, chores, and peers. Parents do less monitoring of children; "coregulation" develops. Research does not indicate a difference in development when a child is raised by heterosexual or gay or lesbian parents. The sexual orientation of these children is generally heterosexual. Divorce disrupts children's lives and usually lowers the family's financial status. Children are likely to greet divorce with sadness, shock, and disbelief. Children of divorce fare better when parents cooperate on child rearing. Children appear to suffer as much from marital conflict as from divorce. Having both parents in the workforce may lead to lack of supervision, but there is little evidence that maternal employment harms children. Maternal employment fosters greater independence and flexibility in gender-role stereotypes.

LO3 Discuss the influences of peers on social development in middle childhood

Peers take on increasing importance in middle childhood and exert pressure to conform. Peers afford practice in social skills, sharing, relating to leaders, and coping with aggressive impulses. Popular children tend to be attractive and mature for their age. Early in middle childhood, friendships are based on proximity. Between the ages of 8 and 11, children become more aware of the value of friends as meeting each other's needs and having traits such as loyalty. At this age, peers tend to discourage contact with members of the other sex.

Key Terms

LO1

latency stage in psychoanalytic theory, the fourth stage of psychosexual development, characterized by repression of sexual impulses and development of skills.

industry versus inferiority the stage of psychosocial development in Erikson's theory occurring in middle childhood. Mastery of tasks leads to a sense of industry, whereas failure produces feelings of inferiority.

social cognition development of children's understanding of the relationship between the self and others.

learned helplessness an acquired (hence, learned) belief that one is unable to control one's environment.

LO2

co-regulation a gradual transferring of control from parent to child, beginning in middle childhood.

transsexual a person who would prefer to be a person of the other sex and who may undergo hormone treatments, cosmetic surgery, or both to achieve the appearance of being a member of the other sex.

LO4

Pygmalion effect a self-fulfilling prophecy; an expectation that is confirmed because of the behaviour of those who hold the expectation.

self-fulfilling prophecy an event that occurs because of the behaviour of those who expect it to occur.

sexism discrimination or bias against people on the basis of their sex.

sexual harassment unwelcome verbal or physical conduct of a sexual nature.

LO5

conduct disorders disorders marked by persistent breaking of the rules and violations of the rights of others.

attributional style the way in which one is disposed toward interpreting outcomes (successes or failures), as in tending to place blame or responsibility on oneself or on external factors.

serotonin a neurotransmitter that is involved in mood disorders such as depression.

TABLE 10.2
Stages in Children's Concepts of Friendship

STAGE	NAME	APPROXIMATE AGE (YEARS)	WHAT HAPPENS
0	Momentary physical interaction	3–6	Children remain egocentric. Their concept of a friend is one who likes to play with the same things and lives nearby.
1	One-way assistance	5–9[a]	Children are less egocentric but view a friend as someone who does what they want.
2	Fair-weather cooperation	7–12[a]	Friends are viewed as doing things for one another, but the focus remains on self-interest.
3	Intimate and mutual sharing	10–15[a]	The focus is on the relationship rather than on the individuals separately. Friendship is viewed as providing mutual support over a long period of time.
4	Autonomous interdependence	12 and above[a]	Children (adolescents, and adults) understand that friendships grow and change as people change and that they may need different friends to satisfy different needs.

Source: Selman (1980).
[a] Ages may overlap

generalized anxiety disorder (GAD) an anxiety disorder in which anxiety appears to be present continuously and is unrelated to the situation.

phobia an irrational, excessive fear that interferes with one's functioning.

separation anxiety disorder (SAD) an extreme form of otherwise normal separation anxiety that is characterized by anxiety about separating from parents; SAD often takes the form of refusal to go to school.

school phobia fear of attending school, marked by extreme anxiety at leaving parents.

LO4 Discuss the influence of the school on development in middle childhood

Schools make demands for mature behaviour and nurture positive physical, social, and cognitive development. Readiness for school is related to children's early life experiences, individual differences in development and learning, and the school's expectations. An effective school has an orderly atmosphere, empowers teachers and students, holds high expectations of children, and has solid academics. Teachers' expectations can become self-fulfilling prophecies. Many girls suffer from sexism and sexual harassment in school. Math and science are still often stereotyped as masculine, and language arts as feminine.

LO5 Discuss social and emotional problems that tend to develop in middle childhood

Conduct disorders may have a genetic component, but other contributing factors are sociopathic models in the family, deviant peers, and inconsistent discipline. Depressed children tend to complain of poor appetite, insomnia, lack of energy, and feelings of worthlessness. They blame themselves excessively for shortcomings. Psychotherapy focuses on cognitive errors; antidepressants are sometimes helpful but controversial. Separation anxiety disorder (SAD) is diagnosed when separation anxiety is persistent and excessive and interferes with daily life. Children with SAD tend to cling to parents and may refuse to attend school. Children may also refuse school because they find it to be unpleasant or hostile. The central aspect of treatment of school refusal is to insist that the child attend school.

Learning Outcomes

LO1 Describe the key events of puberty and their relationship to social development

G. Stanley Hall believed that adolescence is marked by "storm and stress." Current views challenge the idea that storm and stress are normal or beneficial. Puberty is a stage of physical development that is characterized by reaching sexual maturity. Sex hormones trigger the development of primary and secondary sex characteristics. Girls undergo a growth spurt earlier than boys do. Boys tend to spurt up to 10 cm (4 in.) per year, and girls, up to 7.5 cm (3 in.) per year. During their growth spurts, boys catch up with girls and grow taller and heavier. Boys' shoulders become broader, and girls develop broader and rounder hips. More of a male's body weight is made of muscle. Adolescents may look gawky because of asynchronous growth. Boys typically ejaculate by age 13 or 14. Female sex hormones regulate the menstrual cycle.

The effects of early maturation are generally positive for boys and often negative for girls. Early maturing boys tend to be more popular. Early maturing girls become conspicuous, often leading to sexual approaches, deviant behaviour, and a poor body image. Girls are generally more dissatisfied with their bodies than boys are. By age 18, dissatisfaction tends to decline.

LO2 Discuss health in adolescence, focusing on causes of death and eating disorders

Most adolescent health problems stem from their lifestyle. Unintentional injuries are the number one cause of death for Canadian adolescents. Car accidents are the most common cause of death, followed by suicide. To fuel the adolescent growth spurt, adolescents need to increase their food intake by making more healthy choices from the Canada Food Guide. Adolescents need high quantities of calcium, iron, zinc, magnesium, and nitrogen. Adolescents usually need more vitamins than they take in but less sugar, fat, protein, and sodium.

Eating disorders include anorexia nervosa and bulimia nervosa. Eating disorders mainly afflict females. Some psychoanalysts suggest that anorexia represents efforts to remain prepubescent. One risk factor for eating disorders in adolescent females is a history of child abuse. Eating disorders may develop because of fear of gaining weight resulting from cultural idealization of the slim female. Genetic factors may connect eating disorders with perfectionistic personality styles.

LO3 Discuss adolescent cognitive development and the key events of Piaget's stage of formal operations

In Western societies, formal operational thought begins at about the time of puberty. The major achievements of the stage involve classification, logical thought (deductive reasoning), and the ability to hypothesize. Adolescent egocentrism is shown in the concepts of the imaginary audience and the personal fable.

LO4 Discuss sex differences in cognitive abilities

The stage of formal operations is Piaget's final stage of development. Many children, but not all, reach this stage during adolescence. The formal operational stage is characterized

Key Terms

LO1
puberty the biological stage of development characterized by changes that lead to reproductive capacity.

feedback loop a system in which glands regulate each other's functioning through a series of hormonal messages.

primary sex characteristics the structures that make reproduction possible.

secondary sex characteristics physical indicators of sexual maturation—such as changes to the voice and growth of bodily hair—that do not directly involve reproductive structures.

asynchronous growth imbalanced growth, such as the growth that occurs during the early part of adolescence and causes many adolescents to appear gawky.

secular trend a historical trend toward increasing adult height and earlier puberty.

semen the fluid that contains sperm and substances that nourish and help transport sperm.

nocturnal emission emission of seminal fluid while asleep.

gynecomastia enlargement of breast tissue in males.

epiphyseal closure the process by which the cartilage that separates the long end of a bone from the main part of the bone turns to bone.

menarche the onset of menstruation.

LO2
osteoporosis a condition involving progressive loss of bone tissue.

anorexia nervosa an eating disorder characterized by irrational fear of weight gain, distorted body image, and severe weight loss.

bulimia nervosa an eating disorder characterized by cycles of binge eating and vomiting as a means of controlling weight gain.

LO3
formal operations the fourth stage in Piaget's cognitive-developmental theory, characterized by the capacity for flexible, reversible operations concerning abstract ideas and concepts, such as symbols, statements, and theories.

imaginary audience the belief that others around us are as concerned with our thoughts and behaviours as we are; one aspect of adolescent egocentrism.

personal fable the belief that our feelings and ideas are special and unique and that we are invulnerable; one aspect of adolescent egocentrism.

LO5 postconventional level according to Kohlberg, a period during which moral judgments are derived from moral principles and people look to themselves to set moral standards.

by the individual's increased ability to classify objects and ideas, engage in logical thought, hypothesize, and demonstrate a sophisticated use of symbols.

Adolescents show a new egocentrism in which they comprehend the ideas of other people, but have difficulty sorting out those things that concern other people from the things that concern themselves.

LO5 Discuss Kohlberg's theory of moral development in adolescence

Females tend to excel in verbal ability. Males tend to excel in visual-spatial ability. Females and males show equal ability in math. Boys are more likely than girls to have reading problems. Sex differences in cognitive abilities have been linked to biological factors and to gender stereotypes.

LO6 Discuss the roles of the school in adolescence, focusing on dropping out

In the postconventional level, according to Kohlberg, moral reasoning is based on the person's own moral standards. In Kohlberg's scheme, males reason at higher levels of moral development than females do, but Gilligan argues that this sex difference reflects patterns of socialization, with girls being encouraged to take a more "caring" orientation.

FIGURE 11.6
Age and Type of Moral Judgment

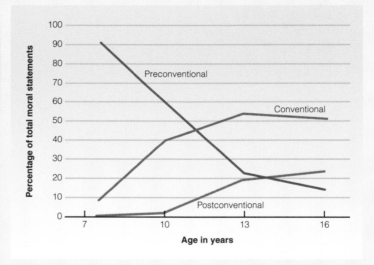

Source: Kohlberg (1963)

LO7 Discuss career development and work experience during adolescence

The transition to middle school, junior high, or high school generally involves a shift from a smaller neighbourhood elementary school to a larger, more impersonal setting. The transition is often accompanied by a decline in grades and a drop in self-esteem. High-school dropouts are more likely to be unemployed and earn lower salaries. Dropouts are more likely to show delinquent behaviours. Truancy and reading below grade level predict school dropout. Student employment can be a positive influence if working is kept to a reasonable amount (10 hours per week). If employment hours are greater than 10, or if the employment takes place late at night, working can be another barrier to completing high school.

Learning Outcomes

LO1 Discuss the formation of identity in adolescence

Erikson's adolescent stage of psychosocial development is identity versus identity diffusion. The primary task of this stage is for adolescents to develop a sense of who they are and what they stand for. Marcia's identity statuses represent the four combinations of the dimensions of exploration and commitment: identity diffusion, foreclosure, moratorium, and identity achievement. Development of identity is more complicated for adolescents who belong to ethnic minority groups. Minority adolescents are faced with two sets of cultural values and may need to reconcile and incorporate elements of both.

Researchers propose a three-stage model of the development of ethnic identity: unexamined ethnic identity, an ethnic identity search, and an achieved ethnic identity. As minority youth move through adolescence, they are increasingly likely to explore and achieve ethnic identity.

Erikson proposed that interpersonal relationships are more important to women's identity than occupational and ideological issues, bur research suggests that adolescent females and males are equally concerned about careers. Adolescents incorporate psychological traits and social relationships into their self-descriptions. Self-esteem tends to decline as the child progresses from middle childhood into early adolescence, perhaps because of increasing recognition of the disparity between the ideal self and the real self. Then self-esteem gradually improves.

LO2 Discuss relationships with parents and peers during adolescence

During adolescence, children spend much less time with parents than during childhood. Although adolescents become more independent of their parents, they generally continue to love and respect them. The role of peers increases markedly during the teen years. Adolescents are more likely than younger children to stress intimate self-disclosure and mutual understanding in friendships. The two major types of peer groups are cliques and crowds. Adolescent peer groups also include peers of the other sex. Romantic relationships begin to appear during early and middle adolescence. Dating is a source of fun, prestige, and experience in relationships. Dating is also a preparation for adult intimacy.

LO3 Discuss sexuality during adolescence, focusing on sexual identity and teenage pregnancy

Masturbation is the most common sexual outlet in adolescence. Some adolescents have a homosexual orientation. The process of "coming out" may be a long and painful struggle but as society becomes more inclusive, these adjustments will likely become a more positive experience. Early onset of puberty is connected with earlier sexual activity. Adolescents who have close relationships with parents are less likely to initiate sexual activity early. Peer pressure is a powerful contributor to sexual activity.

Many girls who become pregnant have received little advice about how to resist sexual advances. Many do not have access to contraception. Others misunderstand reproduction or miscalculate the odds of conception. Teenage mothers are more likely to have medical complications during pregnancy and birth, possibly because of inadequate medical care. Their babies are more likely to be premature and to have low birth weight. Teenage mothers, in general, have a lower standard of living and a greater need for public assistance. Their children are more likely than the children of older mothers to have academic and emotional problems.

Key Terms

LO1
ego identity according to Erikson, one's sense of who one is and what one stands for.

psychological moratorium a time-out period when adolescents experiment with different roles, values, beliefs, and relationships.

identity crisis a turning point in development during which one examines one's values and makes decisions about life roles.

identity diffusion an identity status that characterizes those who have no commitments and who are not in the process of exploring alternatives.

foreclosure an identity status that characterizes those who have made commitments without considering alternatives.

moratorium an identity status that characterizes those who are actively exploring alternatives in an attempt to form an identity.

identity achievement an identity status that characterizes those who have explored alternatives and have developed commitments.

ethnic identity a sense of belonging to an ethnic group.

unexamined ethnic identity the first stage of ethnic identity development; similar to the diffusion or foreclosure identity statuses.

ethnic identity search the second stage of ethnic identity development; similar to the moratorium identity status.

achieved ethnic identity the final stage of ethnic identity development; similar to the identity achievement status.

LO2
clique a group of five to ten individuals who hang around together and who share activities and confidences.

crowd a large, loosely organized group of people who may or may not spend much time together and who are identified by the activities of the group.

LO3
homosexual an erotic orientation toward members of one's own sex.

masturbation sexual self-stimulation.

LO4 **youth in conflict with the law** a child or adolescent whose behaviour is characterized by illegal activities.

Sexual Experience

Sexually Transmitted Infections (STIs)

© cisale/iStockphoto

Albert Ziganshin/Shutterstock

The Society of Obstetricians and Gynaecologists of Canada (SOGC)

LO4 **Discuss the statistics specific to youth in conflict with the law and measures that can reduce youth crime in Canada.**

Despite a decrease in Canada's national crime rates, youth crimes (assaults, drug-related crimes, and school-related offences) are on the rise. The important link between youth and crime seems to be socioeconomic deprivation, not race or ethnicity; however, more Canadian studies are needed.

Empowerment and community involvement are primary philosophies of the Youth Criminal Justice Act (2003), favouring community programs (such as those involving sports) over incarceration as a way to reduce these crime trends. Restorative justice focuses on community ownership and involvement, giving a voice to the victims, the offenders, the family and friends of both, and society as a whole.

© Jordan Chesbrough/iStockphoto

LO5 **Discuss risk factors in adolescent suicide**

Suicide is the second leading cause of death among Canadian adolescents. Most suicides among adolescents and adults are linked to stress, feelings of depression, identity problems, impulsivity, and social problems. Girls are more likely to attempt suicide, whereas boys are more likely to die, due to the methods of suicide boys typically choose.

Learning Outcomes

LO1 Discuss the (theoretical) stage of emerging adulthood

Emerging adulthood is a period of development, spanning the ages of 18 to 25, in which young people engage in extended role exploration. Emerging adulthood can occur in affluent societies that grant young people the luxury of developing their identities and their life plans.

LO2 Describe trends in physical development in early adulthood

Physical development peaks in early adulthood. Most people are at their height of sensory sharpness, strength, reaction time, and cardiovascular fitness in early adulthood. A higher percentage of men's body mass is made of muscle, and men are normally stronger than women. Peak fitness is followed by gradual declines in the cardiovascular, respiratory, and immune systems. Regular exercise helps maintain cardiovascular and respiratory capacity. As people age, the disease-fighting ability of the immune system declines. Fertility in both sexes declines as early adulthood progresses; after age 35, women are usually advised to have their fetuses checked for Down's syndrome and other abnormalities.

LO3 Discuss health in early adulthood, focusing on causes of death, diet, exercise, and substance abuse

Accidents are the leading cause of death in early adulthood. Most young adults do not eat the recommended five fruits and vegetables each day. About four in ten report insufficient exercise and being overweight. Sizeable minorities report smoking and binge drinking. Heredity affects a person's weight, and adaptive thermogenesis can sabotage dieting efforts. Substance abuse is use of a substance despite the social, occupational, psychological, or physical problems. Substance dependence is characterized by tolerance and withdrawal symptoms. Depressants such as alcohol, narcotics, and barbiturates are addictive substances that slow the activity of the nervous system. Alcohol also lowers inhibitions, relaxes, and intoxicates. Stimulants such as nicotine, cocaine, and amphetamines accelerate the heartbeat and other bodily functions but depress the appetite. Hallucinogenics such as marijuana and LSD give rise to perceptual distortions called hallucinations. About 45 percent of Canadians feel they do not have control over the stress in their lives.

LO4 Discuss sexuality in early adulthood, focusing on homosexuality, STIs, menstrual problems, and sexual coercion

Sexual activity with a partner tends to peak in the 20s. An international report found that Canadians are quite comfortable with their sexuality, reporting more partners and more time spent on sex than people in most other countries. From a learning theory point of view, early reinforcement of sexual behaviour influences sexual orientation. Researchers have found evidence for genetic and hormonal factors in sexual orientation. Sexually transmitted infections (STIs) include bacterial infections such as chlamydia, gonorrhea, and syphilis; viral infections such as HIV/AIDS, HPV, and genital herpes; and some others. Risk factors for contracting STIs include sexual activity with multiple partners and without condoms, and substance abuse. Fifty percent to 75 percent of women experience at least some discomfort prior to or during menstruation, including dysmenorrhea, menstrual migraines, amenorrhea, premenstrual syndrome (PMS), and premenstrual dysphoric disorder (PMDD). Sexual assault is significantly underreported in Canada, perhaps partly because victims usually know their attackers. Sexual assault obviously has sexual aspects, but it also relates to the male subjugation of women. Social attitudes such as the myth that "Women say no when they mean yes" support sexual assault, as does encouragement of young men to be aggressive.

Key Terms

LO1 emerging adulthood a theoretical period of development, spanning the ages of 18 to 25, in which young people in developed nations engage in extended role exploration.

LO3 adaptive thermogenesis the process by which the body converts food energy (calories) to heat at a lower rate when a person eats less, because of, for example, famine or dieting.

substance abuse a persistent pattern of use of a substance characterized by frequent intoxication and impairment of physical, social, or emotional well-being.

substance dependence a persistent pattern of use of a substance that is accompanied by physiological addiction.

tolerance habituation to a drug such that increasingly higher doses are needed to achieve similar effects.

abstinence syndrome a characteristic cluster of symptoms that results from a sudden decrease in the level of usage of a substance.

hallucinogenics drugs that give rise to hallucinations.

LO4 dysmenorrhea painful menstruation.

prostaglandins hormones that cause muscles in the uterine wall to contract, as during labour.

amenorrhea the absence of menstruation.

premenstrual syndrome (PMS) the discomforting symptoms that affect many women during the 4–6 day interval preceding their periods.

premenstrual dysphoric disorder (PMDD) a condition similar to but more severe than PMS.

sexual harassment deliberate or repeated unwanted comments, gestures, or physical contact.

LO5 crystallized intelligence one's intellectual attainments, as shown, for example, by vocabulary and accumulated knowledge.

fluid intelligence mental flexibility; the ability to process information rapidly.

epistemic cognition thought processes directed at considering how we arrive at our beliefs, facts, and ideas.

dualistic thinking dividing the cognitive world into opposites, such as good and bad, or us versus them.

relativistic thinking recognition that judgments are often not absolute but made from a certain belief system or cultural background.

pragmatic thought decision making characterized by willingness to accept reality and compromise.

cognitive–affective complexity a mature form of thinking that permits people to harbour positive and negative feelings about their career choices and other matters.

LO5 Discuss cognitive development in early adulthood, focusing on "postformal" developments and effects of college life

Schaie points out that the cognitive development of adults is strongly tied in to the societal developments of the day. Young adults can be said in some ways to engage in "postformal" thinking: Perry's theory of epistemic cognition concerns the ways in which we arrive at our beliefs, facts, and ideas; e.g., dualistic thinking may be replaced by relativistic thinking. Labouvie-Vief's theory of pragmatic thought notes that "cognitively healthy" adults are more willing than egocentric adolescents to compromise and deal within the world as it is, not as they would like it to be; they develop cognitive–affective complexity that enables them to harbor both positive and negative feelings about their choices. The diversity of college life can also broaden students.

LO6 Describe career choice and development during early adulthood

People work for extrinsic rewards, such as money and benefits, and for intrinsic rewards, such as self-identity and self-fulfillment. Stages of career development include a fantasy stage, a realistic-choice stage, a maintenance stage, perhaps job-changing or retraining stages, and a retirement stage. Developmental tasks when beginning a job include accepting subordinate status, learning to get along with co-workers and supervisors, finding a mentor, and showing progress.

FIGURE 13.1
Body Mass Index

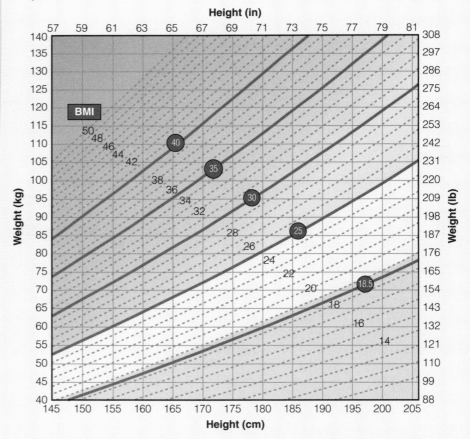

Source: Body Mass Index (BMI) Nomogram 2003. Health Canada. Reproduced with the permission of the Minister of Public Works and Government Services Canada 2010

You can find the Body Mass Index chart on page 244 of your text.

Learning Outcomes

LO1 Examine the issues involved in early adulthood separation

Havighurst's "tasks" for early adulthood include getting started in an occupation and courting a mate. Young adults who enter the job market out of high school may live at home for a while to save money. Other young adults may leave home to attend college or university or to enlist in the military. Traditional or insecure parents may find a child's—especially a daughter's—leaving for college or university stressful. Young adults need to become individuals by integrating their own values with those of their parents and society.

LO2 Describe the conflict between intimacy and isolation

Erikson's core conflict for early adulthood is intimacy versus isolation. Young adults who develop ego identity during adolescence are more ready to marry and develop friendships.

LO3 Discuss the stage of life for entry into adulthood

Levinson labels the ages of 17 to 33 the entry phase of adulthood for young men—when they leave home and strive for independence. Many young adults adopt "the dream," which serves as a tentative blueprint for life. Because women experience more social constraints, they may take longer to leave home. Young adults undergo an age-30 transition, when they commonly reassess their lives. Young adults often settle down during the later 30s.

LO4 Examine the emotional forces of attraction and love

Physical appearance is a key in selection of romantic partners. People tend to prefer slenderness in both sexes and tallness in males. Women are more likely to prefer socially dominant men, but many men are put off by assertive women. Women find physical attractiveness less important than men do, but they prefer steady workers. Some psychologists believe that sex differences in preferences for mates provide reproductive advantages. People prefer partners who are similar to them in attractiveness and attitudes. People tend to reciprocate feelings of attraction. Berscheid and Hatfield define romantic love in terms of arousal and cognitive appraisal of that arousal as love. Sternberg's "triangular theory" of love includes the building blocks of intimacy, passion, and commitment. Jealousy can lead to insecurity and loss of feelings of affection, but mild jealousy can show caring.

LO5 Explain why people get lonely and what they do in response

Loneliness is related to low self-confidence, depression, and physical health problems. Lonely people tend to lack social skills, interest in other people, and empathy. Many people remain lonely because of fear of rejection.

LO6 Discuss the lifestyle of being single

Being single is the most common Canadian lifestyle of people in their early 20s. Many people postpone marriage to pursue educational and career goals. Many cohabit. Some have not found

Key Terms

LO1
individuation the young adult's process of becoming an individual by means of integrating his or her own values and beliefs with those of his or her parents and society at large.

LO2
intimacy versus isolation according to Erik Erikson, the central conflict or life crisis of early adulthood, in which a person develops an intimate relationship with a significant other or risks heading down a path toward social isolation.

LO3
the dream according to Daniel Levinson and his colleagues, the drive to become someone, to leave one's mark on history, which serves as a tentative blueprint for the young adult.

LO4
attraction–similarity hypothesis the view that people tend to develop romantic relationships with people who are similar to themselves in physical attractiveness and other traits.

reciprocity the tendency to respond in kind when we feel admired and complimented.

romantic love a form of love fuelled by passion and feelings of intimacy.

intimacy the experience of warmth toward another person that arises from feelings of closeness and connectedness.

passion intense sexual desire for another person.

commitment the decision to devote oneself to a cause or another person.

LO6
serial monogamy a series of exclusive sexual relationships.

celibacy abstention from sexual activity, whether from choice or lack of opportunity.

LO7
cohabitation living together with a romantic partner without being married.

LO8
monogamy marriage between one man and one woman.

polygyny marriage between one man and more than one woman. (A form of *polygamy*, in which one partner has more than one partner of the other sex.)

polyandry marriage between one woman and more than one man. (A form of *polygamy*.)

gay marriage marriage between two gay males or between two lesbians.

homogamy the practice of people getting married to people who are similar to them.

the right partner. Some single people are lonely, but most are well adjusted. Many singles engage in serial monogamy.

LO7 Describe the practice of cohabitation

The number of people cohabiting has surged in the last two decades. In 2006, Statistics Canada recorded same-sex unions for the first time, as a result of Canada's legalization of same-sex marriages. Cohabitation rates vary internationally. Interestingly, the cohabitation rates of English-speaking Canadians are more similar to U.S. statistics, and Quebec's rates are more similar to those in Europe. Unions are much more likely to dissolve if cohabitation precedes marriage. Cohabitants tend to have less traditional views of marriage and gender roles.

LO8 Describe the practice of marriage

Families, for all of their different descriptions and labels, remain our most common form of Canadian lifestyle. Marriage legitimizes sexual relations, provides an institution for rearing children, and permits the orderly transmission of wealth from one generation to another. Types of marriage include monogamy, polygamy, polyandry, and arranged marriage. Gay marriage is legal in several countries and a couple of U.S. states. Similarity in physical attractiveness, attitudes, background, and interests plays a role in marital choices. Most marriages follow age homogamy. Intimacy and support of one's spouse are related to marital satisfaction. Gay and lesbian couples are more likely to distribute chores evenly.

FIGURE 14.2

Types of Households

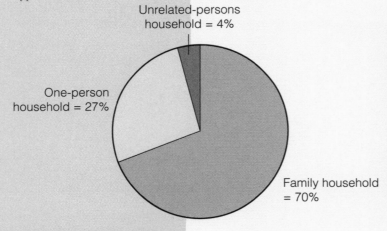

Unrelated-persons household = 4%

One-person household = 27%

Family household = 70%

Source: Statistics Canada. Family Portrait: Continuity and Change in Canadian Families and Households in 2006. 2006 Census. (Cat. No. 97-553-XWE2006001). Ottawa, 2007. found at http://www4.hrsdc.gc.ca/.3ndic.1t.4r@-eng.jsp?iid=37

TABLE 14.4

Happy Marriages

Percentage of Married Persons Age 18 and Older Who Said Their Marriages Were "Very Happy," by Period		
PERIOD	MEN	WOMEN
1973–1976	69.6	68.6
1977–1981	68.3	64.2
1982–1986	62.9	61.7
1987–1991	66.4	59.6
1993–1996	63.2	59.7
1998–2004	64.4	60.4

Source: The General Social Survey, conducted by the National Opinion Research Center of the University of Chicago. Reprinted from Whitehead & Popenoe, 2006, Figure 4.

LO9 Discuss the state of parenthood

Young Canadians are delaying parenthood into their later 20s. In developed nations, most couples say they choose to have children for personal happiness. In more traditional societies, people say children provide social security and social status, assist with labour, and secure property rights. Having a child is unlikely to save a troubled marriage. The mother is usually the primary caregiver and encounters more stress and role overload than fathers do when the mother is also in the workforce. Workplace tension affects home life, and vice versa. The mother usually cuts back on work when families want a parent in the home full-time.

LO10 Discuss divorce and its repercussions

In a survey of Canadian teenagers, 90 percent stated that when they marry it will be forever; yet the Canadian divorce rate is currently 38 percent. Changes in divorce laws and increased economic independence of women contribute to the divorce rate. Divorce hits women in the pocketbook harder than men, especially when women do not have careers. Divorced and separated people have the highest rates of physical and mental illness.

Learning Outcomes

LO1 Describe trends in physical development in middle adulthood

Hair begins to grey in middle adulthood, and hair loss accelerates. Ultraviolet rays worsen wrinkling. The skin loses elasticity. It becomes harder to focus on nearby objects or fine print. Reaction time increases. Breathing capacity declines. Fat replaces lean tissue and the basal metabolic rate declines. Strength decreases. Bone begins to lose density and strength. The cardiovascular system becomes less efficient. Sensitivity to insulin decreases, so the pancreas produces more; therefore, blood sugar levels rise, increasing the risk of adult-onset diabetes.

LO2 Discuss the major health concerns of middle adulthood, including cancer and heart disease

In middle adulthood, cancer and heart disease are the two leading causes of death in Canada. Cancer is a noncommunicable but malignant disease characterized by the uncontrolled growth of cells that invade and destroy surrounding tissue. Risk factors for cancer include heredity, problems in the immune system, hormonal factors, and carcinogens. Each week 300 Canadians die due to smoking-related causes. Men should begin screening for prostate cancer about age 50, women for breast cancer around age 40, and both sexes for cancer of the colon and rectum around age 50. African Canadian men are at greater risk for prostate cancer and are advised to start screening earlier. Family history, high blood pressure, high serum cholesterol, smoking, sedentary lifestyle, and arteriosclerosis are risk factors for heart disease.

TABLE 15.1
Leading Causes of Death in Middle Adulthood*

AGE GROUP	45–54	55–64
Cancer	119.0	333.4
Heart diseases	90.2	218.8
Accidents	40.7	33.2
Chronic liver diseases	18.0	22.6
Suicide	16.6	13.8
Strokes & other cerebrovascular diseases	14.9	34.3
Diabetes	13.4	37.1
Chronic respiratory diseases	8.4	40.4
Blood poisoning	5.4	12.9
Kidney diseases	5.0	13.6
Homicide	4.8	3.0
Influenza & pneumonia	4.6	10.8

*Annual deaths per 100,000 people.
Source: Arialdi M. Minino, Melanie P. Heron, Sherry L. Murphy, & Kenneth D. Kochanek. (2007, October 10). Deaths: Final data for 2004. *National vital statistics reports, 55*(19). Adapted from Table 9, pp. 27–29. http://www.cdc.gov/nchs/data/nvsr/nvsr55/nvsr55_19.pdf.

TABLE 15.2
Deaths Due to Cancer and Heart Disease in Middle Adulthood and Late Adulthood*

AGE GROUP	45–54	55–64	65–74	75–84	85 AND OVER
Cancer	119.0	333.4	755.1	1,280.4	1,653.3
Heart diseases	90.2	218.8	541.6	1,506.3	4,895.9

*Annual deaths per 100,000 people.
Source: Arialdi M. Minino, Melanie P. Heron, Sherry L. Murphy, & Kenneth D. Kochanek. (2007, October 10). Deaths: Final data for 2004. *National vital statistics reports, 55*(19). Adapted from Table 9, pp. 27–29. http://www.cdc.gov/nchs/data/nvsr/nvsr55/nvsr55_19.pdf.

Key Terms

LO1
interindividual variability the notion that people do not age in the same way or at the same rate.

presbyopia loss of elasticity in the lens that makes it harder to focus on nearby objects.

LO2
metastasis the transference of malignant or cancerous cells to other parts of the body.

arteriosclerosis hardening of the arteries.

atherosclerosis the buildup of fatty deposits (*plaque*) on the lining of arteries.

LO3
leukocyte white blood cell.

LO4
menopause the cessation of menstruation.

perimenopause the beginning of menopause, usually characterized by 3 to 11 months of amenorrhea or irregular periods.

climacteric the gradual decline in reproductive capacity of the ovaries, generally lasting about 15 years.

sexual dysfunction a persistent or recurrent problem in becoming sexually aroused or reaching orgasm.

LO5
multidirectionality in the context of cognitive development, the notion that some aspects of intellectual functioning may improve while others remain stable or decline.

plasticity the capability of intellectual abilities to be modified, as opposed to being absolutely fixed.

crystallized intelligence a cluster of knowledge and skills that depend on accumulated information and experience, awareness of social conventions, and good judgment.

fluid intelligence a person's skills at processing information.

LO3 Discuss the functioning of the immune system

The immune system combats disease by producing white blood cells (leukocytes), which engulf and kill pathogens. Leukocytes recognize foreign substances (antigens), deactivate them, and mark them for destruction. The immune system also causes inflammation, which rushes leukocytes to a damaged area. Stress suppresses the immune system. Stress hormones connected with anger can constrict the blood vessels to the heart, leading to a heart attack.

LO4 Discuss sexuality in middle adulthood, focusing on menopause and sexual dysfunctions

Most people in middle adulthood lead rich sex lives, but the frequency of sex tends to decline. Menopause is a normal process that lasts for about two years; perimenopause is usually characterized by months of amenorrhea or irregular periods. The climacteric generally lasts about 15 years and is caused by decline in estrogen production. Estrogen deficiency can cause night sweats, hot flashes, hot flushes—even dizziness, headaches, joint pain, tingling in the hands or feet, burning or itchy skin, heart palpitations, and brittleness and porosity of the bones (osteoporosis). Men show a more gradual decline in sex hormones and fertility. Sexual dysfunctions are quite common, beginning in middle adulthood. Women more often report painful sex, inability to reach orgasm, and lack of desire. Men often report erectile dysfunction.

LO5 Describe cognitive development in middle adulthood, distinguishing between crystallized and fluid intelligence

Intellectual development in adulthood shows multidirectionality, interindividual variability, and plasticity. Schaie's Seattle Longitudinal Study found that adults born more recently were superior to those born at earlier times in inductive reasoning, verbal meaning, spatial orientation, and word fluency. The earlier cohorts performed better in numeric ability. Horn distinguished between crystallized and fluid intelligence. Neurological factors apparently play a powerful role in fluid intelligence. Crystallized intelligence tends to increase with age through middle adulthood, but there is a decline in fluid intelligence. Perceptual speed, spatial orientation, and numeric ability are related to fluid intelligence and drop off. Verbal ability and reasoning mainly reflect crystallized intelligence; they increase through middle adulthood and hold up in late adulthood. Good health and staying intellectually active help stem cognitive decline in late adulthood.

LO6 Discuss opportunities for exercising creativity and continuing education in middle adulthood

The middle-aged decline in processing speed apparently reflects changes in the nervous system. Most researchers find that people in middle and late adulthood perform less well than young adults at memorizing lists. In later middle adulthood, we are less able both to learn by rote repetition and to screen out distractions. Elaborative rehearsal may suffer since we are less capable of rapid classification. Yet we tend to retain or expand our general knowledge. We can retain procedural memories for a lifetime. Middle-aged people have the verbal abilities of young adults, have lost little fluid intelligence, and have a greater store of expertise.

Mature learners in higher education are likely to be highly motivated and to find the subject matter interesting for its own sake. Ironically, women with the greatest family and work demands are most likely to return to school. Canada has the highest rate of postsecondary attainment in the world.

Learning . . .

The Perpetual Process

© Shauna Longmuir

Learning Outcomes

LO1 Discuss theories of development in middle adulthood

Havighurst's tasks for middle adulthood include helping our children establish themselves, adjusting to physical changes, and adjusting to caring for aging parents. Erikson believed that the major psychological challenge of the middle years is generativity versus stagnation. Van Hiel finds that generativity and stagnation are independent dimensions rather than opposites. Levinson characterizes the years of 40 to 45 as a midlife transition that is often accompanied by a midlife crisis, but many people are at the height of their productivity and resilience. Though it was once assumed that women without children in the home would undergo an "empty nest syndrome," this can be a positive event.

LO2 Discuss stability and change in social and emotional development in middle adulthood

Longitudinal research finds that the "big five" personality traits show a good deal of stability after age 30, but the traits of agreeableness and conscientiousness tend to increase and neuroticism declines.

TABLE 16.1
The "Big Five": The Five-Factor Model of Personality

FACTOR	NAME	TRAITS
I	Extraversion	Contrasts talkativeness, assertiveness, and activity with silence, passivity, and reserve
II	Agreeableness	Contrasts kindness, trust, and warmth with hostility, selfishness, and distrust
III	Conscientiousness	Contrasts organization, thoroughness, and reliability with carelessness, negligence, and unreliability
IV	Neuroticism	Contrasts nervousness, moodiness, and sensitivity to negative stimuli with coping ability
V	Openness to experience	Contrasts imagination, curiosity, and creativity with shallowness and lack of perceptiveness

Source: Zucker, A. N., Ostrove, J. M., & Stewart, A. J. (2002). College-educated women's personality development in adulthood: Perceptions and age differences. *Psychology and Aging, 17*, 236–244, Table 1.

Key Terms

LO1
generativity ability to generate or produce, as in bearing children or contributing to society.

stagnation the state of no longer developing, growing, or advancing.

midlife transition a psychological shift into middle adulthood that is theorized to occur between the ages of 40 and 45 as people begin to believe they have more to look back upon than forward to.

midlife crisis a time of dramatic self-doubt and anxiety during which people sense the passing of their youth and become concerned with their own aging and mortality.

empty nest syndrome a feeling of loneliness or loss of purpose that parents, and especially the mother, are theorized to experience when the youngest child leaves home.

LO2
"big five" personality traits basic personality traits derived from contemporary statistical methods: extraversion, agreeableness, conscientiousness, neuroticism (emotional instability), and openness to experience.

LO4
sandwich generation the term given middle-aged people who need to meet the demands of their own children and of aging parents.

Middle-aged college-educated women show greater identity certainty, confident power, and concern about aging than women in their 20s (see Figure 16.1 below).

FIGURE 16.1

Mean Scores of College-Educated Women of Different Ages According to Five Personality Themes

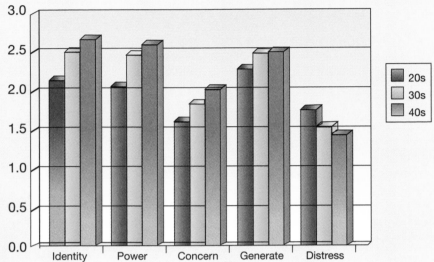

LO3 Discuss career developments typical of middle adulthood

A study of university employees found that job satisfaction increased through middle adulthood. Most career changes in midlife involve shifts into related fields. Unemployed middle-aged people show lower well-being than unemployed young adults.

LO4 Discuss trends in relationships in middle adulthood, focusing on grandparenting and being in the "sandwich generation"

When their children take partners or get married, middle-aged people need to adjust to having in-laws. Research generally finds that grandchildren are beneficial to grandparents socially and psychologically. Parents spend a higher proportion of their time with their children in child care, whereas grandparents spend relatively more time in recreational and educational activities. Grandchildren spend more time in activities with their grandmothers than with their grandfathers, and are relatively more involved with their mother's parents. In some cases, grandparents bear the primary responsibility for rearing grandchildren, and sometimes they are the sole caregivers. Such arrangements typically begin when the grandchild has a single parent. Acting as the parent again can be highly stressful for grandparents.

More than half of the middle-aged people in developed nations have at least one living parent, and most aging parents live near a child. When aging parents need help, the task usually falls to a middle-aged daughter, who then becomes "sandwiched" between caring for or helping her children (and grandchildren) at the same time she is caring for her parents. Most adult sibling relationships are close but can reflect the nature of sibling relationships in childhood. Sisters tend to have more intimate relationships than brothers. Sibling relationships that were antagonistic in childhood can grow closer in middle adulthood if the siblings cooperate in caring for parents. In middle adulthood, the number of friends tends to decline, and people tend to place more value on the friends they retain. The loss of a friend is felt more deeply. Men are less likely than women to have friends or other close social relationships.

After working for more than 15 years as a television and film actor, Clint Eastwood made his directorial debut with The Beguiled in 1971.

Learning Outcomes

LO1 Describe trends in physical development in late adulthood, focusing on life expectancy

One in eight North Americans is over the age of 65. The life span of a species depends on its genetic programming. Our life expectancy is the number of years we can actually expect to live. Disease prevention and treatment contribute to longevity. The average Canadian baby can expect to live about 80 years, but there are differences due to sex, race, geographic location, and behaviour. Men's life expectancy trails women's by about 4 years. Leading causes of death include cancer, heart disease, respiratory disease, brain disease, diabetes, and accidents. After we reach our physical peak in our 20s our biological functions gradually decline. Chemical changes of aging can lead to vision disorders such as cataracts and glaucoma. Presbycusis affects one senior citizen in three. Taste and smell become less acute. Osteoporotic hip fractures consume more hospital bed days in Canada than strokes or heart attacks. Insomnia and sleep apnea become more common in later adulthood.

Sexual daydreaming, sex drive, and sexual activity decline with age, but sexual satisfaction may remain high. Many of the physical changes in older women stem from a decline in estrogen production. Women's vaginal walls lose elasticity and they produce less lubrication so that sexual activity may become irritating. Men take longer to achieve erection, and erections become less firm. For both sexes, the contractions of orgasm become weaker and fewer. Sexual frequency declines with age.

LO2 Compare and contrast programmed and cellular theories of aging

Theories of aging have two main categories: (1) programmed theories such as cellular clock theory, hormonal stress theory, and immunological theory, and (2) cellular damage theories such as wear-and-tear theory, free-radical theory, and cross-linking theory.

LO3 Identify common health concerns associated with late adulthood

The three major causes of death of Canadians age 65 and older are cancer, heart disease, and respiratory disease. (see Table 17.2). Hypertension is a major risk factor for heart attacks and

TABLE 17.2
Ten Leading Causes of Death in Canada by Gender, 65 Years and Over

MEN	WOMEN
1. Cancer	1. Cancer
2. Heart disease	2. Heart disease
3. Respiratory disease	3. Respiratory disease
4. Brain disease	4. Brain disease
5. Diabetes	5. Diabetes
6. Accidents	6. Accidents
7. Liver disease	7. Pneumonia
8. Aneurysm	8. Alzheimer's disease
9. Pneumonia	9. Liver disease
10. Nephritis	10. Nephritis

Source: Statistics Canada. (2009b). Ten leading causes of death by selected age groups, by sex, Canada — 65 to 74 years. Retrieved from http://www.statcan.gc.ca/pub/84-215-x/2008000/tbl/t008-eng.htm

Key Terms

LO1
life span (longevity) the maximum amount of time a person can live under optimal conditions.

life expectancy the amount of time a person can actually be expected to live in a given setting.

ageism prejudice against people because of their age.

cataract a condition characterized by clouding of the lens of the eye.

glaucoma a condition involving abnormally high fluid pressure in the eye.

presbycusis loss of acuteness of hearing due to age-related degenerative changes in the ear.

osteoporosis a disorder in which bones become more porous, brittle, and subject to fracture, due to loss of calcium and other minerals.

sleep apnea temporary suspension of breathing while asleep.

LO2
cellular clock theory a theory of aging focusing on the limits of cell division

telomeres protective segments of DNA located at the tips of chromosomes.

hormonal stress theory a theory of aging that hypothesizes that stress hormones, left at elevated levels, make the body more vulnerable to chronic conditions.

immunological theory a theory of aging that holds that the immune system is preset to decline by an internal biological clock.

wear-and-tear theory a theory of aging that suggests that over time our bodies become less capable of repairing themselves.

free-radical theory a theory of aging that attributes aging to damage caused by the accumulation of unstable molecules called *free radicals*.

cross-linking theory a theory of aging that holds that the stiffening of body proteins eventually breaks down bodily processes, leading to aging.

LO3
arthritis inflammation of the joints.

osteoarthritis a painful, degenerative disease characterized by wear and tear on joints.

rheumatoid arthritis a painful, degenerative disease characterized by chronic inflammation of the membranes that line the joints.

dementia a condition characterized by deterioration of cognitive functioning.

Alzheimer's disease (AD) a severe form of dementia characterized by memory lapses, confusion, emotional instability, and progressive loss of cognitive functioning.

LO4 **implicit memory** automatic memories based on repetition and apparently not requiring any conscious effort to retrieve.

prospective memory memory of things one has planned for the future.

strokes. Arthritis becomes more common with advancing age and is more common in women. Many older adults are addicted to prescription drugs; many have adverse drug reactions. Older adults have a greater risk of accidents, especially falls. Dementia is not a normal result of aging, however, Alzheimer's disease (AD) is the leading cause of dementia. The risk of developing AD is greatest among people aged 75 to 84 (see Figure 17.3). Five hundred thousand Canadians currently show signs of dementia, and this number is expected more than double within the next generation. As AD progresses, people find it harder to manage daily tasks and may eventually no longer recognize family members. Memory loss may be caused by accumulation of plaque.

FIGURE 17.3

Rates of Alzheimer's Disease among Older Adults

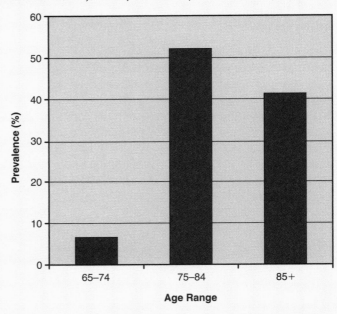

Source: Herbert, L. E., et al. (2003). Alzheimer's Disease in the U.S. Population: Prevalence Estimates Using the 2000 Census. *Archives of Neurology, 60*, 1119–1122.

LO4 **Discuss trends in cognitive development in late adulthood, focusing on memory, language development, problem solving, and wisdom**

Fluid intelligence is most vulnerable to decline in late adulthood. Crystallized intelligence can improve throughout much of late adulthood. Older adults have relatively more difficulty naming public figures than uncommon objects. The working memories of older adults hold less information than the working memories of young adults. The temporal memory of older adults may become confused. They may have trouble telling apart memories of actual events from illusory events. Older adults usually do as well as younger adults in tasks that measure implicit memory, such as memory of multiplication tables or the alphabet. Aging has a more detrimental effect on associative memory than on memory for single items, perhaps because of impairment in binding and in use of strategies for retrieval. Long-term memories are subject to distortion, bias, and even decay. Older people recall events from their teens and 20s in greatest detail and emotional intensity, perhaps because of the effects of sex hormones. Age-related declines in processing speed and working memory (fluid intelligence) impair retrospective memory. Distractibility also plays a role.

Knowledge of meanings of words can improve well into late adulthood, but a decline in reading comprehension is related to a decrease in working memory. Because of the decline in working memory and also because of impairments in hearing, many older adults find it more difficult both to understand the spoken language and to produce language. Older people are more likely to experience the "tip-of-the-tongue" phenomenon.

Problem solving requires executive functioning to select strategies, working memory to hold the elements of the problem in mind, and processing speed to accomplish the task while the elements remain in mind. All of these have fluid components that decline with age. Older adults tend to regulate their emotional responses when they experience conflict.

The greater distractibility of older adults may encourage them to take a broader view of situations, contributing to wisdom. People with wisdom tend to tolerate other people's views and to admit that life has its uncertainties and that we seek workable solutions in an imperfect world.

Learning Outcomes

LO1 Evaluate various theories of social and emotional development in late adulthood

Erikson's final stage is ego integrity versus despair; the challenge is to continue to see life as meaningful and worthwhile in the face of physical decline and the approach of death. Peck's three developmental tasks of late adulthood are ego differentiation versus work-role preoccupation, body transcendence versus body preoccupation, and ego transcendence versus ego preoccupation. Butler proposes that reminiscence, or life reviews, attempt to make life meaningful and accept the end of life. According to disengagement theory, older people and society mutually withdraw from one another, but well-being among older adults is generally predicted by pursuing goals rather than withdrawal. Activity theory argues that older adults are better adjusted when they are more active and involved. According to socioemotional selectivity theory, older people limit their social contacts to regulate their emotional lives.

LO2 Discuss psychological development in late adulthood, focusing on self-esteem and maintaining independence

Self-esteem is highest in childhood, dips sharply in middle childhood and into adolescence, rises gradually throughout middle adulthood, and declines again in late adulthood, as shown in Figure 18.2.

FIGURE 18.2

Mean Level of Self-Esteem as a Function of Age, for Total Sample, Males, and Females

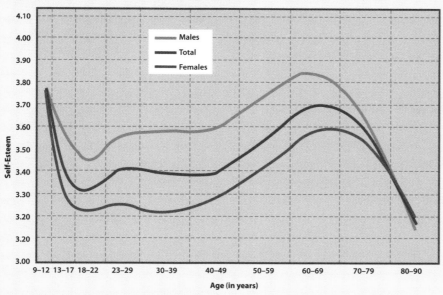

Source: Richard W. Robins, Kali H. Trzesniewski, Jessica L. Tracy, Samuel D. Gosling, & Jeff Potter. (2002). Global self-esteem across the lifespan. *Psychology and Aging, 17*(3), 423–434.

Life changes such as retirement, loss of a spouse or partner, and declining health may account for age differences in self-esteem. Older adults who are independent see themselves as normal, whereas adults who are dependent on others tend to worry more about physical disabilities and stress. Volunteerism in Canada increases with age, and those aged 65 and older contribute more volunteer hours to their communities than any other age group. Depression affects some 10 percent of older adults, and may be related to neuroticism, imbalances in norepinephrine, illness, loss of loved ones, and cognitive impairment. Depression can lead to suicide. The most common anxiety disorders among older adults are generalized anxiety disorder and phobic disorders.

Key Terms

LO1
ego integrity or despair Erikson's eighth life crisis, defined by maintenance of the belief that life is meaningful and worthwhile despite physical decline and the inevitability of death versus depression and hopelessness.

disengagement theory the view that older adults and society withdraw from one another as older adults approach death.

activity theory the view that older adults fare better when they engage in physical and social activities.

LO2
socioemotional selectivity theory the view that we place increasing emphasis on emotional experience as we age but limit our social contacts to regulate our emotions.

generalized anxiety disorder general feelings of dread and foreboding.

phobic disorder irrational, exaggerated fear of an object or situation.

panic disorder recurrent experiencing of attacks of extreme anxiety in the absence of external stimuli that usually evoke anxiety.

agoraphobia fear of open, crowded places.

LO5
selective optimization with compensation reshaping of one's life to concentrate on what one finds to be important and meaningful in the face of physical decline and possible cognitive impairment.

LO3 Discuss the social contexts in which people age, focusing on housing, religion, and family

Older Canadians prefer to remain in their homes as long as their physical and mental conditions permit. Older people with greater resources and community ties are more likely to remain in their homes. Older Canadians worry about crime, although they are less likely than younger people to be victimized. Older people who cannot live alone may hire visiting or live-in helpers, move in with adult children, or enter assisted-living residences or nursing homes. Relocation disrupts social networks. Religious involvement often provides social, educational, and charitable activities as well as the promise of an afterlife. Religious involvement in late adulthood is usually associated with less depression and more life satisfaction. A majority of Canadians will fulfill their marital commitment "until death do us part." A study of the Big Five personality factors and marital satisfaction found that similarity in conscientiousness and extraversion predicts marital satisfaction in the 60s. When couples reach their 60s, many midlife responsibilities such as childrearing and work have declined, and intimacy re-emerges as a central issue. As compared with couples in midlife, older couples are more affectionate when they discuss conflicts, and disagree less. Sharing power in the relationship and dividing household tasks contributes to satisfaction. Older adults are less likely than younger adults to seek divorce. As with heterosexuals, gay men and lesbians in long-term partnerships tend to enjoy higher self-esteem, less depression, fewer STIs, and less substance abuse. Losing one's spouse in late adulthood is a traumatic experience and leads to a decline in health. Widowed men are more likely to remarry. Single older adults without children are as likely as people with children to be socially active. Older sibling pairs tend to shore each other up emotionally. Older people often narrow their friendships to people who are most like them. Grandparents and their adult grandchildren often have very close relationships.

© Shauna Longmuir

LO4 Discuss factors that contribute to adjustment to retirement

Retirement planning is a key to successful retirement—e.g., putting money aside and investigating locales to which one might relocate. Couples in relationships often plan collaboratively. The best adjusted retirees are involved in a variety of activities. The most satisfied retirees maintain enjoyable leisure activities or replace work with more satisfying activities. Upscale professional workers appear to be well-adjusted as retirees.

© Bryan Sikora/iStockphoto

LO5 Discuss factors in "successful aging"

Definitions of successful aging often focus on physical activity, social contacts, the absence of cognitive impairment and depression, and health. Baltes and Carstensen focus on person–environment fit and see successful aging in terms of selective optimization with compensation, which is related to socioemotional selectivity theory. Successful agers also tend to be optimistic and to challenge themselves.

Learning Outcomes

LO1 Define death and dying, and evaluate views on stages of dying

Death is the end of life, but *dying* is a part of life. Medical authorities usually use brain death—absence of activity in the cerebral cortex—as the standard for determining whether a person has died. Whole brain death includes death of the brain stem. Kübler-Ross hypothesized five stages of dying: denial, anger, bargaining, depression, and final acceptance. But Kübler-Ross's view applies only to people who have been diagnosed with terminal illness, and other investigators find that dying does not necessarily follow a progression of stages.

LO2 Identify settings in which people die, distinguishing between hospitals and hospices

About 70 percent of all Canadians die in hospitals. Only a few—usually very old or terminally ill—die at home. Between 16 and 30 percent of Canadians who die have access to or receive hospice services. Hospices provide palliative care rather than curative care, and they help the whole family, not just the patient. People who are dying often want to focus on other things and may enjoy hearing about humorous events or a companion's life experiences.

LO3 Discuss various kinds of euthanasia and controversies about them

In active euthanasia, a lethal treatment is administered to cause a quick and painless death. Voluntary active euthanasia, or physician-assisted suicide, is illegal throughout Canada and most of the United States. American physicians have assisted some patients with terminal or incapacitating illnesses who wished to die, by providing lethal doses of drugs or sometimes administering them. Cases of involuntary euthanasia usually involve irreversibly comatose patients whose guardians believe they would not have wanted to remain alive. Terminal sedation is not intended to cause death. Highly religious physicians are more likely to object to physician-assisted suicide. Canadians, including those in the medical and legal communities, are deeply divided on this controversial end-of-life issue.

FIGURE 19.1

Percent of Physicians Who Object to Physician-Assisted Suicide or Terminal Sedation, According to Religiosity

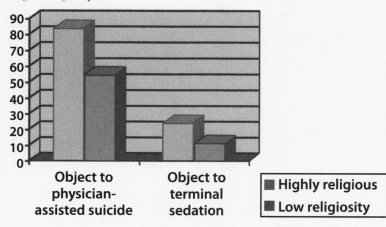

Object to physician-assisted suicide | Object to terminal sedation

■ Highly religious
■ Low religiosity

Key Terms

LO1
death the irreversible cessation of vital life functions.

dying the end-stage of life in which bodily processes decline, leading to death.

brain death cessation of activity of the cerebral cortex.

whole brain death cessation of activity of the cerebral cortex and brain stem.

LO2
hospice an organization that treats dying patients by focusing on palliative care rather than curative treatment.

palliative care treatment focused on the relief of pain and suffering rather than cure.

LO3
euthanasia the purposeful taking of life to relieve suffering.

active euthanasia the administration of a lethal treatment (usually a drug) to cause a quick and painless death.

voluntary active euthanasia the intentional administration of lethal drugs or other means of producing a painless death with the person's informed consent.

involuntary active euthanasia the intentional administration of lethal drugs or other means of producing a painless death without the person's informed consent.

passive euthanasia the withholding or withdrawal of life-sustaining treatment to hasten death.

living will a document prepared when a person is well, directing medical care providers to terminate life-sustaining treatment in the event of incapacitation or inability to speak.

LO5
bereavement the state of deprivation brought about by the death of a family member or close friend.

grief emotional suffering resulting from a death.

mourning customary methods of expressing grief.

Passive euthanasia is withholding or withdrawing life-support equipment or techniques when terminally ill people do not wish to be kept alive by such aggressive treatment but such acts remain illegal in Canada. The declaration of the wish to forego aggressive treatment can be in the form of a living will.

L○4 Discuss people's perspectives on death at various stages of development

Preschoolers may think that death is reversible or temporary, but they become progressively more realistic at the ages of 4, 5, and 6. Death of a parent is usually most difficult for a child to bear. It is normal for children to fear death. Adolescents know that when someone dies, life cannot be restored, but they may construct magical, spiritual, or pseudoscientific theories as to how some form of life or thought might survive. Most young adults in developed nations need not think too much about death. In middle adulthood, death comes more to the fore, often when screening for various deadly diseases is prescribed. Older people may come to fear disability almost as much as death. Some theorists suggest that ego transcendence enables some people to begin to face death with calmness.

L○5 Discuss coping with death, focusing on the funeral and possible stages of grieving

If you are present at someone's death, call the family doctor, the police, or 911. Funerals provide an organized response to death that is tied to religious and cultural traditions. Ritual allows people to grieve publicly and bid farewell to the deceased person and takes on many forms in multicultural Canada. Family may find it difficult to focus on financial and legal matters such as organ donation. A death can lead to bereavement and mourning. Grief can involve a variety of feelings—depression, loneliness, emptiness, numbness, fear, guilt, even anger. Bowlby proposed a stage theory of grief, and Maciejewski and his colleagues found some research evidence for five stages: disbelief, yearning, anger, depression, and acceptance. If you are grieving, allow yourself to feel the loss, accept offers of help, and give yourself time to let grieving run its course. Death is universal—a developmental event that we all encounter. Fittingly, those who have taken us by the hand in life—in death—often serve as our most insightful teachers. Death holds the gift of wisdom and teaches us that, through memories, loved ones live on forever.

FIGURE 19.3

Indicators of Grief among Bereaved People

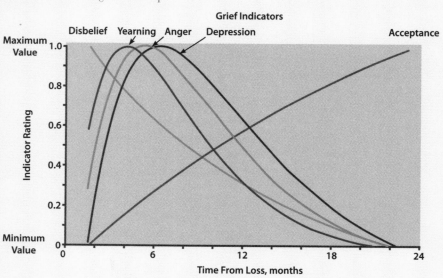

Source: Maciejewski, P. K., Zhang, B., Block, S. D., & Prigerson, H. G. (2007). An empirical examination of the stage theory of grief. *Journal of the American Medical Association, 297,* 716–723.